Encyclopedia of
MANAGEMENT
THEORY

Encyclopedia of
MANAGEMENT THEORY

VOLUME TWO

ERIC H. KESSLER EDITOR
Pace University

⑤SAGE reference

Los Angeles | London | New Delhi
Singapore | Washington DC

Los Angeles | London | New Delhi
Singapore | Washington DC

FOR INFORMATION:

SAGE Publications, Inc.
2455 Teller Road
Thousand Oaks, California 91320
E-mail: order@sagepub.com

SAGE Publications Ltd.
1 Oliver's Yard
55 City Road
London, EC1Y 1SP
United Kingdom

SAGE Publications India Pvt. Ltd.
B 1/I 1 Mohan Cooperative Industrial Area
Mathura Road, New Delhi 110 044
India

SAGE Publications Asia-Pacific Pte. Ltd.
3 Church Street
#10-04 Samsung Hub
Singapore 049483

Publisher: Rolf A. Janke
Acquisitions Editor: Jim Brace-Thompson
Developmental Editor: Sanford Robinson
Production Editor: David C. Felts
Reference Systems Manager: Leticia Gutierrez
Reference Systems Coordinator: Laura Notton,
    Anna Villaseñor
Copy Editors: Linda Gray, Patrice Sutton
Typesetter: Hurix Systems Pvt. Ltd.
Proofreaders: Jeff Bryant, Sue Irwin
Indexer: Wendy Allex
Cover Designer: Glenn Vogel
Marketing Manager: Carmel Schrire

Copyright © 2013 by SAGE Publications, Inc.

Printed in the United States of America.

Library of Congress Cataloging-in-Publication Data

Encyclopedia of management theory / edited by Eric H. Kessler, Pace University.

v. cm
Includes bibliographical references and index.

ISBN 978-1-4129-9782-9 (hbk.)

1. Management—Encyclopedias. I. Kessler, Eric H., editor of compilation

HD30.15.E493 2013
658.001—dc23   2012039568

SFI Certified Sourcing
www.sfiprogram.org
SFI-00453

13 14 15 16 17 10 9 8 7 6 5 4 3 2

Contents

Volume 2

List of Entries   *vii*

Entries

List of Entries

Editor's Note: Anchor entries are designated with an asterisk.

Narrative (Story) Theory

Storytelling theory is defined as the interplay of narrative past, living-story present, and *antenarrative futures*. The theory's central management insight is that linear narratives are in interplay with other forms of storytelling, such as living stories and antenarratives. Because humans are *homo narrens* (storytelling animals), storytelling is one of the preferred sensemaking currencies of management and organizations. Narrative is typically about the past, often has a linear plot about the past (i.e., a narrative arc) with a beginning, middle, and end, and, comprises only a few key events and characters in order to provide coherent meaning. Aristotle held that narrative had certain elements: plot, character, theme, dialogue, rhythm, and spectacle (in a hierarchic order). Narrative is also a way people and organizations craft their identities. Narratives negotiate order and change. Narrative phenomena occur at the individual, group, organization, community, regional, national, and global levels. Most authors make a distinction between narrative and living stories of the present and the future-oriented antenarratives.

Fundamentals

The theory of narrative has undergone many changes since its introduction in Aristotle's *Poetics*. In the 19th century, Karl Marx's historical materialism was a dialectic approach favoring social class and economic forces. Marx rejected philosopher G. W. F. Hegel's narrative of a dialectic of spirit-qua-perception/cognition. Later, United States and French structuralisms focused on form rather than elements or dialectics. Structuralists, such as Kenneth Burke, were critical of dialectical approaches and reduced Aristotle's six narrative elements to five elements (pentad) by combining dialogue and rhythm and changing the names of the elements: Plot became act, character became actor, theme became purpose, dialogue and rhythm were combined into agency, and spectacle became scene. In addition, scene took on a much more important role than in Aristotle's day, and the pentad was less hierarchical, allowing for combinations, such as act/scene and other ratios. Russian formalists began with a mechanistic split between narrative-plot (*sjuzhet*) and story (*fabula*). The mechanistic view was that narrative could change the plot sequence around, but story had to conform to chronology. Later Russian formalists looked at the poetic aspect as more important than the practical language of narrative and story. Critical-theory scholars, such as Mikhail Bakhtin, addressed more dialogical aspects of story (e.g., polyphonic manner of story) in their relationship to the more monologic manner of narrative. Jacques Derrida makes a similar differentiation. He looked at how different kinds of narratives (e.g., adventure) have different conceptions of time and space than more folkloric narratives, some of them emphasizing the more primordial. Post-structuralists (e.g., Derrida and Julia Kristeva) focused on text and intertextuality or emphasized discourse (Michel Foucault, Judith Butler, and many others). Hermeneutic approaches (particularly that of Paul Ricoeur) looked across iterative temporal events at how prenarrative (e.g., story), narrative (emplotment), and postnarrative discourse formed a hermeneutic circle (or *spiral*). Ricoeur also returns to a dialectic of difference and sameness in identity narratives. Social constructionism began with a focus on the relation of materiality to narrative (and discourse) constructions (e.g., Peter Berger and Thomas Luckmann). In recent years, social constructionism has been criticized for taking the linguistic turn too far and leaving out material conditions and materiality itself (see, e.g., Karen Barad, Bruno Latour).

There are several types of narrative (grand, counternarrative, antenarrative, etc.). The grand narrative is more macro in orientation, such as a grand narrative about Marxism or liberal democracy. There are counternarratives about a dominant narrative rendition of events, and accounts by other narrators. Narrative can also be more micro, such as the narrative of one's career. Narratives about the future or ones that are not as yet entirely coherent or stabilized are referred to as antenarratives. According to the theory of organizational narrative, it adapts slowly to circumstance, and it is what Barbara Czarniawska calls "petrified" in order to stabilize core values, rooted in the past. Dennis Mumby asserts that narratives can be quite political and hegemonic.

Narrative and Story

For those who distinguish between narrative and story, narrative often empties out or abbreviates story. The Italian approach is *microstoria*, a look at the stories and tellers who defy the grand narrative order of their community. This is often done with archival data. Yannis Gabriel, in his study *Storytelling in Organizations,* views story as something more than narrative such as something that is performative and has emotional carriage. People tell narratives of the past and living stories of their unfolding relationships (that may have neither identifiable beginnings nor foreseeable endings), as well as what some authors call antenarratives of the future. Such antenarratives are important to strategy, to leader visioning, and so forth. Living stories and antenarratives adapt and morph more readily. The three aspects of storytelling (narrative, story, and antenarrative) are in coadaptive relationships.

Narrative, story, and antenarrative are studied in their own right or used to substantiate other concepts such as efficacy, identity, agency, rhetoric,

ethics, motivation, politics, complexity, (explicit and tacit) knowledge, and learning. Work in narrative is focused on its relationship to discourse (i.e., narrative as a domain of discourse). Emotional contagion, intuition, and the unconscious are discussed in relation to narrative. Recent approaches are looking at moving from *homo narrens* to *species narrens,* or even *material narrens.* This is a more posthumanist perspective, where humans are not the only species doing the storytelling, and from a forensic or archaeological perspective, the materiality tells its own story. Actor-network theory and agential realism (Barad) looks at this later perspective.

In conclusion, the practical applications of storytelling theory are that an organization's storytelling needs to balance its past, present, and future. Modern managers can learn from this theory how a linear and petrified sensemaking narrative of the past can provide stability in stable equilibrium situations, but when the environment changes too far from equilibrium, there can be a need to look to nonlinear and noncyclical antenarrative paths of transformation to the future. The spiral-antenarratives of an organization can have upward ascents and downward plunges in its performance in its complexity and strategic flexibility. The storytelling can get out of sync with complex adaptive systems in more turbulent environments. We are just beginning to study and understand spiral- and assemblage-antenarratives because narrative (story) theory for the longest time has focused on the past, instead of the future.

David M. Boje

See also Actor-Network Theory; Appreciative Inquiry Model; Punctuated Equilibrium Model; Sensemaking; Strategic Flexibility; Tacit Knowledge

Further Readings

Bakhtin, M. M. (1981). *Dialogic imagination—Four essays.* Austin: University of Texas Press.

Boje, D. M. (2011). *The future of storytelling in organizations: An antenarrative handbook.* London, England: Routledge.

Czarniawska, B. (2004). *Narratives in social science research.* Thousand Oaks, CA: Sage.

Gabriel, Y. (2000). *Storytelling in organizations.* Oxford, England: Oxford University Press.

Latour, B. (2005). *Reassembling the social: An introduction to actor-network-theory.* Oxford, England: Oxford University Press.

Mumby, D. (1987). The political function of narrative in organizations. *Communication Monographs, 54,* 113–127.

Vaara, E., & Tienari, J. (2011). On the narrative construction of multinational corporations: An antenarrative analysis of legitimation and resistance in a cross-border merger. *Organization Science, 22*(2), 370–390.

NEEDS HIERARCHY

Central to theories of motivation in organizations, needs hierarchies suggest that organizational members are motivated by innate, universal human needs and that these needs can be arranged in a hierarchy. That is, some needs are more important in certain circumstances and thus serve as more motivating than others. For example, a hungry employee will be motivated to fulfill that need before others. Once the employee is no longer hungry, he or she can focus on "higher order," or more sophisticated, needs. The most enduring and well known of these theories is that of American behavioral psychologist Abraham Maslow. Developed in the 1940s, his hierarchy of needs has become ubiquitous, and it is rare to see a chapter on motivation in a business management textbook that doesn't include Maslow's hierarchy of needs, as depicted by the now famous pyramid. Not just an enduring management theory, Maslow's needs hierarchy can be found in a wide range of fields, including psychology, sociology, health care, and government policy. The following paragraphs explain Maslow's needs hierarchy, provide an overview of the critiques of the theory, and discuss the impact of Maslow's work on management theory and the practice of management.

Fundamentals

Needs-based theories of motivation suggest that if managers understand employees' needs, they can provide incentives that help meet these needs, thus, motivating the employees. These theories rest on the assumption that needs are motivators. Maslow's work supports this, and interpretations of his work contend that humans share basic categories of needs and that these needs can be arranged in a hierarchy. This hierarchy suggests a prepotency where the appearance of one level of need rests on the prior satisfaction of a more "prepotent" need.

Management textbooks suggest that Maslow's hierarchy of needs is best depicted by a pyramid with five levels. At the base of the pyramid lie our most basic needs—our physiological needs, which include the needs for food, air, water, and shelter. According to the theory, until these most basic needs are met, an individual will not be motivated by needs found at other levels. This suggests that these are the most prepotent of all the needs.

According to Maslow's theory, after physiological needs have been satisfied, the individual is most concerned with the next level of needs—the safety needs. This refers to the need for a safe, stable environment that is without pain or threats. Employees facing these needs might be best motivated by the promise of steady employment, a raise that affords them the ability to live in a safer neighborhood, or a benefit plan that includes medical and dental benefits.

Moving up the levels of the pyramid, the next category refers to belongingness needs. This category represents the need to be loved, the need for affection, and the need to form relationships with others. Managers familiar with Maslow's needs hierarchy might offer employees membership in elite teams or groups, social functions whereby employees can develop social relationships, or might promote an organizational culture that creates a sense of belonging.

The next level of needs refers to individuals' esteem needs—the need for personal and social achievement as signified by rewards, recognitions, and the trappings of success. Needs at this level can be categorized as internal or external esteem needs. *Internal esteem needs* refer to feelings of accomplishment and self-respect, whereas *external esteem needs* refer to external recognition of success and social status. In terms of organizations, this could mean a challenging assignment, a raise, a corner office, or a reserved parking space.

The final need category is self-actualization. This refers to self-fulfilment, reaching one's potential and "being all that one can be." According to Maslow, a painter must paint, and a writer must write. Until a person is doing what it is they are meant to do, they will be motivated by this unmet need. Proponents of Maslow's needs hierarchy contend that empowered employees who have some control over their own destiny and are maximizing their potential are self-actualized. According to modern interpretations of Maslow's work, this is the desired state, but it can be achieved only after all other needs have been met.

The first four levels of needs are considered to be deficiency needs. They are activated when they are not satisfied. For example, the individual who is hungry will be motivated to find food. Similarly, when an individual feels threatened, he or she will be motivated to remove the threat. After the deficiency needs are met, the individual can move on to self-actualization, which is considered a growth need. Unlike the other four levels, when self-actualization needs are met, the individual desires fulfillment of more of these needs and will stay at this level.

Despite what is most often published about Maslow, he was most interested in what happened after people reached the fifth stage and could focus on higher order needs. He actually created another hierarchy that describes higher order needs and exists above the five-stage hierarchy. These needs include the need for knowledge and the need for beauty. However, this additional hierarchy is rarely mentioned in management texts, and this focus on positive psychology is often lost in discussions of Maslow's work, which focus more on needs deficiencies.

Importance

Maslow's needs hierarchy is believed to have first appeared in a business textbook in North America in 1964. Since then, his work has served as the basis for many other management theories. For example, Clayton Alderfer's needs-based theory of motivation, Lyman W. Porter and Edward Emmet Lawler's expectancy theory, and several theories of organizational change management all appear to contain elements of Maslow's original theory of motivation. Use of Maslow's theory is widespread and applications are still plentiful in the fields of marketing, human resource management, and customer service.

Not only it is applied to organizational studies, but Maslow's theory continues to appear in health care, immigration policy, and the fields of psychology and sociology. The hierarchy of needs also makes frequent appearances in the popular media through newspaper articles, self-help books, and television and radio programs. Most, if not all, of these academic and popular press applications of the needs hierarchy focus on the five-stage pyramid, ignoring much of Maslow's other work and his desire to focus on what happens after self-actualization.

Despite this widespread acceptance and application of Maslow's needs hierarchy, the theory has received significant criticism. Arguably, the most serious of these criticisms brings into question the validity of the theory. Some argue that the theory is "untestable" and, therefore, not really science. In addition, very little scientific evidence exists to support several critical elements of Maslow's needs hierarchy, specifically, the prepotency of the needs categories and the universality of the hierarchy. Critiques emerged as early as 1973, as can be seen in Mahmoud Wahba and Lawrence G. Bridwell's presentation at the Academy of Management conference titled "Maslow Reconsidered: A Review of Research on the Need Hierarchy Theory" (published in 1976). Even Maslow himself questioned the validity of the needs hierarchy as early as 1979, as can be seen in his now published personal journals. In several entries, Maslow laments the fact that few, if any, researchers were attempting to replicate his work, and many were just accepting the theory as fact, without scientific support.

Other critiques contend that although humans share the same basic needs, some needs are more potent than others and this potency is not universal. Basically, more current theories suggest that need hierarchies vary from person to person. A common example held up as proof of this argument would be those artists who forgo lower order needs in order to pursue their craft. In essence, they forgo some physiological, safety, esteem, and belongingness needs in their quest for self-actualization. Other critiques suggest that individuals move up and down the hierarchy, depending on ever-changing circumstances, and that they may be motivated by more than one type of need simultaneously.

Maslow's hierarchy of needs has also been questioned in terms of its applicability in a modern-day, global society. Significant research suggests that culture of origin is a predictor of employee characteristics and motivations. For example, it is argued that more collectivist cultures would value relationships and group harmony over individual success and the display of wealth more often found in individualist cultures. These findings suggest that the hierarchy as depicted by Maslow cannot be universally applied.

More recently, the ubiquitous triangle has been criticized as being gendered—that it was developed by and for men and centers on masculine notions of success and self-actualization. As such, it does not represent all organizational members. Finally, studies of Maslow's diaries have revealed that the needs hierarchy, as it is most often presented, resembles little of what Maslow was actually attempting to accomplish. Maslow was concerned with the emancipation of humankind and saw the hierarchy as a means of helping individuals to achieve self-actualization and growth beyond the first hierarchy. He was also interested in other need categories, including dominance, sexuality, and knowledge and inquiry. Scholars argue that by presenting his work in this narrow fashion, his greatest contributions have been ignored.

Despite significant criticism, Maslow's work continues to inform teaching and research. Some suggest that the needs hierarchy has endured due to its intuitive nature and the simplicity of the pyramid. Others argue that it remains popular because it has been institutionalized as "truth" and, until recently, few have questioned its presence in management texts and academic writings. More recent discussions of the needs hierarchy in management texts acknowledge the criticisms but contend that Maslow's work is still valuable as it demonstrates that humans are motivated by more than money (contrary to early managerialist theories of motivation), that humans are motivated by different needs at different times in their lives and careers, and that some basic, universal, human needs do exist.

Maslow's needs hierarchy, owing to its widespread use and teaching, has been influential for managers. It suggests that employees are motivated by different rewards and that managers should identify which need category is most influential for each employee. For example, a new employee with student loans to repay may be motivated more by a pay raise than, perhaps, an employee who has been with the company for a long time and is seeking more challenging assignments, admittance to the executive cafeteria, or a national award. Similarly, the needs hierarchy provides insight into the behavior of people in organizations. If managers can understand what motivates behaviors, they may be better able to predict and influence those behaviors.

Kelly Dye

See also ERG Theory; Expectancy Theory; Leadership Practices; Role Theory; Theory X and Theory Y; Trait Theory of Leadership

Further Readings

Cooke, B., Mills, A. J., & Kelley, E. S. (2005). Situating Maslow in Cold War America: A recontextualization of management theory. *Group and Organization Management, 30*(2), 129–152.

Cullen, D. (1997). Maslow, monkeys and motivation theory. *Organization, 4*(3), 355–373.

Cullen, D., & Gotell, L. (2002). From orgasms to organizations: Maslow, women's sexuality and the gendered foundations of the needs hierarchy. *Gender, Work and Organization, 9*(5), 537–555.

Dye, K., Mills, A. J., & Weatherbee, T. (2005). Maslow: Man interrupted: Reading management theory in context. *Management Decision, 43*(10), 1375–1395.

Korman, A. K. (1974). *Psychology of motivation.* Englewood Hills, NJ: Prentice-Hall.

Maslow, A. H. (1943). A theory of human motivation. *Psychological Review, 50,* 370–396.

Maslow, A. H. (1954). *Motivation and personality.* New York, NY: Harper.

Wahba, M., & Bridwell, L. (1976). Maslow reconsidered: A review of research on the need hierarchy theory. *Organizational Behavior & Human Performance, 15*(2), 212–240.

Neo-Institutional Theory

Neo-institutional theory is a theoretical framework often used to explain the diffusion of practices and structural arrangements across organizations, one that emphasizes the effects of the environment, particularly external stakeholders' expectations and beliefs, on organizational decision making. Since the publication of key articles in this tradition in the mid-1970s, it has become one of the most prominent frameworks used by macro-organizational scholars to study and explain how and why the formal structure, or design, of organizations changes over time. Accumulated research supports key tenets of the framework, including the central thesis that such change is often driven by imitation of other organizations and normative pressures to have legitimate or "correct" formal structure. The entry begins by locating the development of neo-institutional theory in the context of early sociological research on formal organizational structure, with the aim of clarifying how it departed from existing work on this topic. Next is a summary of the major tenets of this theoretical perspective. While these focus primarily on macro-level change processes across organizations, they reflect assumptions about underlying micro-level processes within organizations; thus, we discuss the latter in the next section. The entry concludes with a consideration of some of the implications of this theoretical approach for practical decision making by managers, and some further readings are suggested.

Fundamentals

Understanding the sources and consequences of organizations' *formal structure* has been a central aim of organizational studies from the field's very beginning, driven by both theoretical and practical concerns. By formal structure, we refer to explicitly articulated rules, assignment of work tasks to particular groups or subunits, delegation of responsibility for decisions to particular positions, and so forth. (This is distinguished from informal structure, which usually refers to how things are actually done and who actually does them—that formal and informal structure may not be identical is axiomatic among organizational scholars.)

Virtually all of the early work on organizational structure, from the classic analysis of bureaucracy by Max Weber to contingency approaches often used in mid-20th-century organizational research, was characterized by a common assumption: Organizational decisions about formal structure are driven largely, if not entirely, by concerns with controlling and coordinating work activities. Because formal structure was understood to be critical to efficient production activity, studies of structure typically treated it as the result of decision-makers' calculations of how best to achieve this objective, calculations that took into account various task-related aspects of the organization (e.g., size) and its environment (e.g., speed of technological change).

Macro-Level Processes of Structural Change

The analysis laying the foundation for neo-institutional theory, proposed in a now-classic article published in 1977 by John Meyer and Brian Rowan, offered a radical departure from earlier thinking about both the purposes of formal structure and the nature of organizational decision making leading to variations in structure. One point of departure is reflected in the assertion that formal structure could serve symbolic functions, in addition to the practical ones of control and coordination. This implies that the adoption of a particular structure, such as a set of production processes advocated by prominent organizations (e.g., International Organization for Standardization—the ISO), or policies in line with those endorsed by agencies promoting social responsibility (e.g., the United Nations) may reflect efforts to communicate important information about the organization to individuals and groups outside it, rather than being a reflection of efforts to solve technical problems facing the organization. A second point of departure is that it assumes that organizational decision making is partly driven by attention to what other organizations are doing. Hence, this approach emphasized both the symbolic aspects of formal structure and the role of external social influences on organizational decision making.

Neo-institutional theory is characterized by three main tenets. The first is that components of formal structure (e.g., certain policies or positions) can, over time, come to be generally accepted as right and proper elements of well-managed organizations. This is referred to as the *institutionalization* of structures. A common focus of research in this tradition has been on identifying important sources of institutionalization processes, including governments or powerful organizations that have the ability to require other organizations to adopt structures (coercive); advocates who actively promote or endorse certain structures such as social movement groups or professional associations (normative); and other organizations that have adopted the structure and appear to be successful (mimetic). The term *institutional environment* is used to refer to the set of beliefs about appropriate organizational structures that exist at any given point in time, as well as to the various sources that promote such structures. Note that these beliefs and structures are not always consistent or compatible and that they are apt to shift over time. Scholars often talk about inconsistencies in the institutional environment as ones involving "competing logics." For example, open knowledge sharing has long been a defining characteristic of universities, but after a 1980 law (Bayh-Dole) allowed universities and researchers within them to patent and receive licensing revenue from federally funded discoveries, privatization of discoveries became a major goal of many universities. One structural consequence was the spread of technology transfer offices (TTOs) across many universities to promote development, disclosure, and patenting of university-based discoveries. Because of differing beliefs about the appropriateness of the private ownership of knowledge in universities, such offices have sometimes been sources of contention.

A second tenet is that, whatever the originating source of an institutionalization process, the process may ultimately take on a life of its own. That is, as a critical mass of adopters develops (and continues to increase), a bandwagon effect ensues, either because organizational decision makers become convinced by others' behavior that adoption will be beneficial for them as well, or, because they become concerned that others will evaluate their organization negatively for *not* adopting the structure, even if they are not actually convinced of the structure's benefits. Such pressures lead to *structural isomorphism,* or similarity among a set of organizations in terms of structural features, independent of particular characteristics of an adopting organization that would logically seem to affect its need for the structure. The production of structural isomorphism in response to external pressures is illustrated clearly by the spread of TTOs discussed above; most do not make enough licensing revenue to cover their operating costs.

A third tenet, underscored by Meyer and Rowan's theory, is that insofar as decision makers adopt structures primarily because of external pressures and are not convinced of their utility, the structures are apt to be *decoupled,* that is, not actually used on a regular basis or allowed to affect day-to-day activities in the organization. The idea that structures may be largely or entirely ceremonial emphasizes a distinction between adoption and implementation (and a potential gap between formal and informal structure). Most of the empirical research guided by an institutional theory framework has focused on adoption; relatively little is known about the conditions under which organizations that adopt institutionalized structures implement them or do not.

Micro-Level Processes and Decision Making

At the same time as early macro-level formulations of neo-institutional theory were being developed, Lynne Zucker was conducting research aimed at identifying micro-level mechanisms that drive both structural isomorphism and heterogeneity. Her experimental studies demonstrated that individuals' cognitive framing can be readily redefined when situations are highly ambiguous, that individuals are particularly susceptible to such reframing in organizational contexts, and that cognitive framings are more easily transmitted in organizations than in other contexts. This work provided the basic cognitive foundations for the claims of neo-institutional theory by linking psychological and perceptual processes involved in internal organizational decision making to environmental conditions (e.g., the increasing adoption of formal structures by competitors and other organizations).

This work also suggests an important connection between neo-institutional theory and classic sociopsychological research on conformity. The latter line of research, associated with work by Solomon Asch, Leon Festinger, and Stanley Milgram (among others), has provided compelling evidence that individuals are prone to adapt their behaviors to align with those of others, even when it is easy to see that those behaviors represent objectively poor choices. Such conformity can be attributed either to normative pressure (individuals go along with others because they want to be socially accepted) or to informational pressure (individuals use the behavior of others as data in efforts to make correct decisions). Although not typically acknowledged, neo-institutional theory's core tenets reflect assumptions about the operation of social influence processes documented in sociopsychological research. Institutional theorists extended this research to an organizational level of analysis, with other groups and organizations outside the boundary of a focal organization serving as sources of conformity pressure on organizational decision makers. Zucker's early work provides an explicit bridge between the sociopsychological literature and more macro-oriented work by neo-institutional researchers, one that is just beginning to be explored more fully in other studies.

Importance

Neo-institutional theory's central management insight is that managers need to be conscious of what are often strong social pressures to follow the lead of other organizations in adopting new structural arrangements and to gather as much systematic information as possible about conditions that affect the impact of such arrangements before making their own decisions about whether to adopt them or not. This implies that the search for "best practices," as sometimes advocated in the popular management literature, may be quixotic. That the effects of structural arrangements on organizational outcomes depend on particular characteristics of a given organization—its size, the composition of its workforce, the kinds of production technologies it uses, and so forth—is well documented by empirical studies.

Of course, observing what other organizations are doing can save managers much time and effort in terms of thinking about ways to solve problems that they may be confronting in their own organization (i.e., reduce search costs). If the observed organizations are sufficiently similar to a focal organization, organizations may receive notable benefits from imitation. Moreover, there is some evidence that conforming to social expectations about "correct" formal structure can have at least short-term positive consequences (e.g., increases in stock price).

However, neo-institutional theory alerts managers and administrators to the way in which observation of other organizations, and a lack of careful analysis of relevant contingencies, can create potential biases in decision-making processes and result in cycles of faddish and unproductive organizational change. Because changes in structure are far from costless, greater awareness among decision makers of the way in which institutional pressures may shape their choices can encourage more thoughtful weighing of the costs and benefits of such change.

Pamela S. Tolbert and Lynne G. Zucker

See also Contingency Theory; Decision-Making Styles; Environmental Uncertainty; Groupthink; Institutional Theory; Norms Theory

Further Readings

David, R., & Strang, D. (2006). When fashion is fleeting: Transitory collective beliefs and the dynamics of TQM consulting. *Academy of Management Journal, 49*(2), 215–253.

DiMaggio, P. J., & Powell, W. W. (1983). The iron cage revisited: Institutional isomorphism and collective rationality in organizational fields. *American Sociological Review, 48*, 147–160.

Meyer, J. W., & Rowan, B. (1977). Institutionalized organizations: Formal structure as myth and ceremony. *American Journal of Sociology, 83*, 340–363.

Scott, W. R. (2008). *Institutions and organizations: Ideas and interests.* Thousand Oaks, CA: Sage.

Sine, W. D., Haveman, H., Tolbert, P. S. (2005). Risky business? Entrepreneurship in the new independent-power sector. *Administrative Science Quarterly, 50*, 200–232.

Tolbert, P. S., & Zucker, L. G. (1983). Institutional sources of change in the formal structure of organizations: The diffusion of civil service reform, 1880–1935. *Administrative Science Quarterly, 28*, 22–39.

Tolbert, P. S., & Zucker, L. G. (1996). The institutionalization of institutional theory. In S. Clegg, C. Hardy, & W. R. Nord (Eds.), *Handbook of organizational studies* (pp. 175–189). Thousand Oaks, CA: Sage.

Zucker, L. G. 1977. The role of institutionalization in cultural persistence. *American Sociological Review, 42*, 726–743.

Zucker, L. G., Darby, M. R., Furner, J., Liu, R. C., & Ma, H. (2007). Minerva unbound: Knowledge stocks, knowledge flows and new knowledge production. *Research Policy, 36*, 850–863.

Norms Theory

We all look to others, either consciously or unconsciously, to make decisions about how to act in a particular context. Social norms—or group-based standards or rules regarding appropriate attitudes and behavior—play a crucial role in shaping how we interpret our social world and how we act, from the niceties of how much to tip in a restaurant to the critical decision of who to vote for in an election. Norms are also important in management contexts because for almost every workplace behavior, from which clothes to wear to whether to take a sick day when one is not ill, individuals will have an understanding of which behaviors are approved of by others and which behaviors others engage in themselves. Individuals' perceptions of the organizational norms, and the norms for their own teams within that organization, will guide and shape their own workplace behavior. That is, the attitudes and behaviors that are seen to be endorsed by one's colleagues and displayed by one's colleagues will define what is seen to be appropriate—or normal—behavior within the workplace context. And because individuals have a strong desire to display behavior that is accepted by others, employees' actions will reflect their perceptions of what is "normal" for their team or organization. In thinking about norms, it is important to first distinguish between two sources of norms—descriptive and injunctive norms—and understand their impact on behavior. Next, given that individuals often misperceive norms, it is of interest to consider how such misperceptions might influence behavior. Third, given that research has demonstrated that norms have a powerful impact on behavior, how can we harness the power of norms to change behavior? And, finally, how do norms impact upon organizational management?

Fundamentals

In thinking about social norms, prominent theorists such as Robert Cialdini have argued that it is important to distinguish between two sources of influence: descriptive norms and injunctive norms. *Descriptive norms* refer to what behavior is done commonly in a given context, and they motivate action by informing people about what behavior is likely to be effective or adaptive in that context. In contrast, *injunctive norms* refer to what behavior is approved or disapproved within a group, and they motivate action because of the social rewards and punishments associated with engaging (or not engaging) in the behavior. Thus, injunctive and descriptive norms are seen to represent separate sources of motivation and, hence, should have separate influences on behavior, a fact that has been demonstrated in a substantial body of field, laboratory, and survey research.

Although theorists may make a distinction between descriptive and injunctive norms, these two sources of norms are often confused or conflated by people. This is because although what is commonly approved of and what is commonly done within a group is often the same, this is not always the case. For example, although most people probably believe that employees should keep communal kitchen areas clean and tidy (injunctive norm), it may well be the case that many employees do not clean up after themselves (descriptive norm).

Given that there can be conflict between descriptive and injunctive norms, what determines which norm will prevail? One critical factor is the *salience* of the norm. That is, norms are seen to motivate and direct action to the extent that they have been activated in a particular situation. Returning to the example above, a messy and unclean communal kitchen area will make salient the descriptive norm that employees do not clean up after themselves, reducing the likelihood that a particular employee will clean up after him- or herself. In contrast, a large and prominent sign reminding employees that cleanliness and tidiness is approved of will make salient the relevant injunctive norm thereby increasing the likelihood of conformity with the injunctive norm.

One final point to consider is whether all norms are equal. That is, given that individuals are exposed to norms from multiple sources, such as family, friends, neighbors, and coworkers, and that these norms might be in conflict, which norms will individuals follow? Once again, salience is important. Put simply, coworker norms will be more important in determining workplace behavior while family norms will be more important in determining dinner-table behavior. However, over and above what might be considered to be contextual salience, some groups (and their norms) might be chronically salient, shaping and guiding behavior in multiple contexts. That is, an individual's gender identity might always be salient, such that gender norms influence the way she interacts at work, at home, or in the broader community.

Norm (Mis)Perceptions and Behavior

It is possible that the norms of a social group are objectively stated and clear to all members. However, because norms are rarely written down and explicit but are more informal and implicit, it is important to consider individuals' perceptions of the norms. But are people accurate in perceiving group norms? In fact, research has documented a consistent pattern of misperception about norms, particularly in relation to negative or harmful behavior. That is, when thinking about negative attitudes and behaviors, most people tend to incorrectly perceive the negative attitudes and behavior as the norm, despite the fact that such attitudes and behaviors are not typical. If people think that the negative behavior is more typical, they are then more likely to engage in that type of behavior because of the pressures that drive people to conform to norms. Indeed, Wesley Perkins argues that much, if not most, of the harm done by negative group influences occurs through one's misperceptions of group norms—a phenomenon that he labels a "reign of error." Applied to the management domain, such norm misperceptions could have negative organizational consequences. For example, if employees perceive that their coworkers are adopting a "go-slow" or a "work-to-contract" policy in their work, perhaps because of high-profile coworkers who espouse this policy, they may begin to work less productively themselves in order to fit in with the perceived group norm.

Norms and Behavior Change

If norms—and norm misperceptions—have such a powerful impact on behavior, is it possible to correct such misperceptions and use norms to promote more positive behavior, both in the workplace and in wider society? One approach to preventing problem behavior and promoting and reinforcing positive behavior is to correct misunderstandings that the problem behavior is typical and common. In taking a social norms approach, the first step is to gather credible data from the population of interest and identify the actual norms regarding the attitudes and behaviors of concern. Following this, a social norms intervention can communicate the true norms of the group in an effort to correct misperceptions and reduce engagement in the problem behavior. There is generally good support for the effectiveness of such an approach, with people responding to these initiatives with more realistic perceptions of peer behavior and reductions in the negative behaviors. Although this approach has been applied primarily in relation to health behaviors among young people (e.g., alcohol and tobacco consumption), it has also been used to tackle other negative behaviors, such as prejudice and discrimination and dishonesty in paying taxes.

Although a social norms approach is effective in tackling negative behaviors, there are some important caveats. For such campaigns to be successful, behavioral change agents must be aware of the distinction between injunctive and descriptive norms and focus their target audience only on the norm that is consistent with the desired behavior change. For example, there is an understandable tendency

of behavioral change agents to highlight the prevalence of the problem behavior in the hope that, once people are aware of the extent of the problem, they will change their behavior. For example, those who attempt to get adults to eat more fruits and vegetables often present data that "8 out of 10 adults do not eat enough fruits and vegetables each day." However, as noted by Cialdini, such messages draw attention to the negative descriptive norm, increasing its salience and its power to influence behavior. Thus, when faced with such a message, adults may ask, if no one else is bothering to eat healthily, why should they deviate from the norm? In other words, if used incorrectly, norms can be associated with backlash or boomerang effects.

In light of the potential for norm backlash effects, what advice can be given to behavior change agents. Well, according to Cialdini and his colleagues, injunctive norms may be more effective when negative behavior is common (i.e., one should focus on the disapproval for the negative behavior), but descriptive norms may be more effective when positive behavior is common. In addition, there is clear evidence that norms-based change attempts are most effective when the descriptive and injunctive norms are presented in alignment with one another. That is, when individuals are told that a particular behavior is both approved of and done commonly.

Importance

Norms are clearly an important determinant of behavior and can be used to change behavior. However, is there any evidence of their effectiveness in the management and organizational behavior domain? In fact, although there is recognition of the role of norms in organizational behavior, there have been few attempts to consider the distinction between descriptive and injunctive norms in organizations, or, to use norms to change employee behavior. This is surprising, given that some of the earliest work on employee behavior focused on the role of group norms. For example, Frederick Taylor's groundbreaking work on efficiency and productivity found that slow working groups of employees were more likely to corrupt a new productive worker than to be inspired and motivated by them. Similarly, in their Hawthorne studies, F. J. Roethlisberger and William Dickson found that some work groups displayed different forms of deviance in order to maintain and enforce a norm of productivity, bullying, and excluding more productive workers until they either conformed or left the group.

In recent years, however, there has been renewed interest in the role of descriptive and injunctive norms in organizational behavior. Interestingly, this interest has focused on understanding and explaining *negative* workplace behaviors, such as absenteeism, bullying, organizational deviance, and counterproductive workplace behavior, rather than on positive workplace behaviors, such as health and safety behaviors. The research has demonstrated that employees' deviant work behaviors are related to both the actual and perceived frequency with which coworkers engage in those behaviors (the descriptive norm) and approve of those behaviors (the injunctive norm). Moreover, norms are often better predictors of negative workplace behaviors than individual-level predictors, such as personality characteristics, level of stress, age, gender, or seniority.

Despite renewed interest in the role of norms in workplace behavior and the emerging evidence to support the role of norms in this context, research has yet to examine whether norms-based campaigns can be implemented to change, rather than just explain, workplace behavior. Nevertheless, it is critical that managers assess and understand the norms associated with different workplace behaviors, such as deviance or citizenship, before attempting to change these behaviors. Failure to consider the current normative climate may mean that organizational changes are less likely to succeed because employees resist change that is inconsistent with their perceptions of the appropriate and prevalent behaviors for their team. In order for change to be effective, managers need to survey employees' perceptions of norms and then communicate these back to employees in a way that corrects any misperceptions. For example, a manager interested in increasing the level of organizational citizenship behaviors within his or her team (e.g., mentoring and supporting new colleagues) could communicate that the majority of the team approves of such behaviors. Drawing on the injunctive norm in this way should increase the likelihood that team members will engage in this behavior in the future. On the other hand, given our understanding of the impact of norms on behavior, managers should clearly avoid messages that highlight unsupportive descriptive norms. That is, he or she should not try to rally engagement in mentoring and supporting newcomers by pointing out that this behavior is (regrettably) extremely uncommon within the team. Harnessing the power of norms to change and improve workplace behavior is an exciting and challenging avenue for future research and practice.

Joanne R. Smith and Deborah J. Terry

See also Compliance Theory; Influence Tactics; Organizational Culture Theory; Organizational Socialization; Social Identity Theory; Tacit Knowledge; Theory of Reasoned Action

Further Readings

Cialdini, R. B., Reno, R. R., & Kallgren, C. A. (1990). A focus theory of normative conduct: Recycling the concept of norms to reduce littering in public places. *Journal of Personality and Social Psychology, 58,* 1015–1026.

Goldstein, N. J., & Cialdini, R. B. (2010). Managing normative influences in organizations. In D. De Cremer, R. Van Dick, & J. K. Murnighan (Eds.), *Social psychology and organizations* (pp. 67–86). Hoboken, NJ: Routledge.

O'Boyle, E. H., Donelson, R. F., & O'Boyle, A. S. (2011). Bad apples or bad barrels: An examination of group and organizational-level effects in the study of counterproductive work behavior. *Group & Organization Management, 36,* 39–69.

Perkins, H. W., Haines, M. P., & Rice, R. M. (2005). Misperceiving the college drinking norm and related problems: A nationwide study of exposure to prevention information, perceived norms, and student alcohol misuse. *Journal of Studies on Alcohol, 66,* 470–478.

Taylor, F. W. (1971). *The principles of scientific management.* New York, NY: Harper & Row. (Original work published 1911)

Occupational Types, Model of

A model of occupational types is a framework with a system of key attributes of occupations or careers to enable individual evaluation. The concept is to analyze occupations or career paths down to the most important and common elements to provide insights into what this occupation requires from an individual. These analyses provide a framework to compare individual attributes to occupational attributes in an effort to improve fit (also referred to as congruence) between individuals and their occupations. Individual attributes could include personality, temperament, and preferences for types of tasks or environments. Occupational attributes could include skill sets, work environment, types of social interaction, or types of tasks to successfully complete the job. The fit evaluation can provide insights for the choice of a career or the recognition of change within a career across time. This model and its surrounding theory is used in management research as well as in the practice of career management and counseling, often occurring in human resource departments within organizations or in school settings, both high school and university. This entry describes this model and provides two key examples of this category of career models.

Fundamentals

Theoretically, a general set of attributes can be used to analyze all occupations; more practically, it has proven difficult to choose those attributes that provide sufficient distinction to sort occupations into enough groupings to provide insights without developing a system that is too complex to be practical. Over the past several decades, careers in general have become more unique by being both less bounded by formal organizational career ladders and more self-designed. Thus, while models of occupational types are useful for early career exploration and development, they have become less useful for career development or choice in later life or for issues beyond choice of general career directions.

While several such occupational type models exist, perhaps the most well-known and used model is John L. Holland's vocational codes (also called vocational personality) because he had a dual focus on both the attributes of the individual's preferences and the characteristics of occupations. Beginning with his early work published in 1959, Holland developed instruments to help an individual examine him or herself based on six characteristics and then also categorized occupations on the three important common attributes of the same six characteristics. The six characteristics are realistic, investigative, artistic, social, enterprising, and conventional. The simplicity of this six-trait system makes it fairly easy to apply and use, but documenting the effect of the person-occupation fit is very difficult because many occupations fit within the same code. Holland set up occupational codes as sets of the three most prevalent of these six characteristics within an occupation; thus, while there are hundreds of occupations, there are only 15 distinct sets of codes unless code order matters, and it is hard to distinguish between occupations based on code order. For example, how would an occupation differ if it was realistic, artistic, and social rather than realistic, social, and artistic?

Although some studies have shown increased positive outcomes for those individuals whose traits match the traits of their chosen occupation, there is little confirmation of what happens to less congruent people across time nor how enduring these congruence effects are over the course of a person's career. Further, especially in our diversified global economy, there is increasing variation of jobs within an occupational area. Also, it has become more common for people to develop boundaryless careers which cross traditional occupational delineations and blend aspects of two or more careers (e.g., a forensic chemist who combines chemistry with investigation with pathology). Holland's work has been particularly used for career counseling in terms of developing ideas for careers to explore among youths. One commonly used outgrowth of Holland's work is the Strong-Campbell Interest Inventory, which is often used in high school and college to help students identify their own traits and how they match with occupational groups and careers.

The second most commonly used model of occupational types is Schein's career anchors. Edgar H. Schein also focused on the idea of fit, but more broadly, in the sense that he looked at this model as being inherently variable but being anchored or rooted in enduring traits of both the individual and the occupation. The career anchors are technical/functional competence, managerial competence, autonomy/independence, security/stability, entrepreneurial creativity, service/dedication to a cause*, pure challenge*, and lifestyle* (asterisks denote anchors added in the second iteration of the model). Schein also developed an instrument (the Career Orientation Inventory) to help individuals understand their own anchors. Instead of developing the rigid codes to match for occupations, he suggested rather that understanding anchors could improve satisfaction if organizations tailored structures and rewards to their employee's anchors. Schein focused more on the idea of anchors being a theme for a person's life work and identity, rather than sorting mechanisms to match people to types of jobs. Thus, career anchors as model of occupational types focuses more on individual needs and then puts the burden on the organization to find ways to match

an individual's preferences, rather than as a tool for career counseling and development.

Barbara Ribbens

See also Career Stages and Anchors; Differentiation and the Division of Labor; Human Capital Theory; Job Characteristics Theory; Organizational Demography; Personal Engagement (at Work) Model; Self-Concept and the Theory of Self; Self-Determination Theory

Further Readings

Betz, N. E., Fitzgerald, L. F., & Hill, R. E. (1989). Trait-factor theories: Traditional cornerstone of career theory. In M. B. Arthur, D. T. Hall, & B. S. Lawrence (Eds.), *Handbook of career theory* (pp. 26–40). Cambridge, England: Cambridge University Press.

Holland, J. L. (1997). *Making vocational choices: A theory of vocational personalities and work environments* (2nd ed.). Odessa, FL: Psychological Assessment Resources.

Inkson, K. (2007). Careers as fit. In *Understanding careers: The metaphors of working lives* (Chap. 5, pp. 101–122). Thousand Oaks, CA: Sage.

Savickas, M. L. (2007). Occupational choice. In H. Gunz & M. Peiperl (Eds.), *Handbook of career studies* (Chap. 5, pp. 79–96). Thousand Oaks, CA: Sage.

Schein, E. H. (1993). *Career anchors: Discovering your real values* (Rev. ed.). London, England: Pfeiffer.

OPEN INNOVATION

Until the middle of the 20th century, corporate innovation was based on the assumption that full control of the entire new product development process will secure the long-term competitiveness of the company. Large companies invested heavily in corporate research and strongly competed for the best researchers. New findings were kept confidential to prevent outflow of knowledge and secure competitive advantage (closed innovation paradigm). At the beginning of the 1980s, many large corporations failed to appropriate the value generated by its corporate research institutions and were outperformed by new emerging companies investing significantly less resources in research and development (R & D) but relying on externally available resources. This anomaly founded the shift from a closed to an open innovation paradigm. Introduced by Henry William Chesbrough in 2003, *open innovation* is defined as the use of purposive inflows and outflows of knowledge to accelerate internal innovation and expand the markets for external use of innovation, respectively. The boundaries between a firm and its environment are permeable, allowing in- and outflow of knowledge. Within the last 10 years, open innovation has had a significant impact on management theory and has changed the way firms innovate. This entry provides an overview on the theory of open innovation and its implementation based on the three core modes of open innovation: outside-in innovation, inside-out innovation, and coupled innovation. The next section illustrates how existing implementations of open innovation differ in the motivation of interaction, in the direction of knowledge flow, in the type of involved external collaborator, and in the method of interaction used. The last section discusses managerial challenges and current business practices.

Fundamentals

Three core modes of open innovation, introduced by Ellen Enkel and Oliver Gassmann, provide a distinct typology of existing open innovation approaches and offer a categorization of various research fields under the roof of open innovation. The three core modes are subsequently described in further detail.

Outside-In Innovation

Externally available knowledge and ideas are integrated to leverage the innovativeness of the company. Outside-in flows of knowledge complement existing innovation resources with external resources from customers, suppliers, partners, and research institutions. However, though having access to a wide variety of peripheral resources, companies face difficulties in using and exploiting the external knowledge base. Employees proved to be reluctant to integrate outside ideas as they do not fully understand the external ideas or are unwilling to value them. This effect is known as the *not-invented-here syndrome* (see entry, this volume, on Transfer of Technology).

External collaborator.
A prominent stream of research in outside-in innovation is the integration of users in the innovation process. Being the only external actor that is actually using the product offerings, users are able to provide need- and solution-based information. Innovation speed, degree of innovation, and rate of market failure can be improved by early user integration (see the entry Lead Users). Due to the fact that only a selected number of users can be integrated in the innovation process, companies highly depend on the characteristics and attitudes of these users. As a downside, user integration may lead to a niche market orientation. Upstream on the value chain, the early integration of suppliers into the innovation process can significantly increase innovation performance and reduce technological risks in new product development. In recent years, the reduction of vertical integration and the increase of outsourcing intensified supplier integration of many original equipment manufacturers (OEMs).

Additionally, the integration of research institutes as technology suppliers offers the possibility to benefit from basic research without heavy infrastructural investments. Especially resource constrained small and medium sized enterprises (SMEs) can overcome the "liability of smallness" and profit from exchange with research institutions. Besides using external knowledge of their respective industries, companies look for existing solutions present at remote industries that may be transferred to their own context. Described as cross-industry innovation, the challenge is to systematically identify existing solutions for extant problems. The ability to abstract latent challenges and to use analogical thinking is crucial for cross-industry innovation.

Methods of interaction.
As a means to integrate externally available knowledge, numerous methods and approaches have emerged. In recent years, crowdsourcing has increasingly attracted attention of many scholars and practitioners. Crowdsourcing offers the possibility to publicly broadcast a problem via an open call. Tasks which were formerly carried out inside the company are outsourced to an undefined group of people. Crowdsourcing platforms—like InnoCentive, Nine Sigma, or Atizo—establish a virtual marketplace where companies can tender problems for remuneration. Solution seekers and problem solvers meet, exchange innovative ideas, and submit solutions. Predominantly, crowdsourcing is focused on solution-based information with the goal of exchanging technological know-how.

Since the emergence of the first virtual communities in the World Wide Web, their numbers have drastically increased. On the basis of community-based innovation, companies use blogs, forums, and social networks to discuss ideas with a mass of stakeholders. The goal is to absorb need-based information and to establish an open discussion on new products or services. The transfer of ethnographic studies to the World Wide Web (netnography) led to new forms of revealing innovative ideas that are freely accessible. Observation of the behavior of groups and their individual members in online communities are used to generate need and solution-based information for new product development. On the basis of graphical user interfaces, toolkits allow users to virtually create new products, adapt design, or add new features according to preferences. The entire exchange is based on digital artifacts. A central component of toolkits for open innovation is the iterative creation process—"learning by doing via trial and error." The immediate virtual feedback enables a cycle of lasting improvement until an ideal is found. The richness of the offered database within the toolkit's library determines complexity and innovation results. On the one hand, a large database allows the users to come up with more radical solutions. On the other hand, large databases may overstrain the users and limit innovation. The deployment of toolkits shortens development time and costs as the need to produce physical prototypes is reduced.

Inside-Out Innovation

Internally available knowledge is transferred outside the companies' boundaries. External roads for exploitation are advanced to bring ideas faster to market, to prevent conflicts with the existing business model, or to further multiply technologies and generate revenues. Similar to the not-invented-here syndrome, employees hesitate when it is about to bring internal ideas to the outside (not-sold-here syndrome). There is a tendency to hold on to internal ideas and knowledge, which ultimately prevents innovation.

Out-licensing and IP trade. According to Joseph Schumpeter, patents constitute the motivation for inventors and entrepreneurs to foster innovation as they secure temporary monopolistic profits. Patents are used as a means to ensure the company's freedom

to operate and prevent imitation. The open innovation paradigm has changed the role of intellectual property (IP) within the company's value creation process. The new paradigm gives IP a more active role. Companies can generate additional revenues through royalties by out-licensing or by selling. They can make IP available for third parties to establish formats or gain benefits through positive networking effects. The use of IP as a tradable good allows unfolding new business models in a secondary market. For example, Deutsche Bank and Credit Suisse founded a patent fund where both entities buy IP and leverage the value through professional management. The business model of so-called patent trolls is based on the enforcement of patents against infringers and the generation of revenues through lawsuit. It is to be expected that official markets for IP will be established in the upcoming years. This will enable new forms of IP trade and technology transfer.

Corporate venturing and spin-offs. The company's restriction toward its current business model may constrain the advancement of new business models. Corporate venturing and the creation of company spin-offs allow accelerating new business models, dislodged from current business. Fully owned by the mother company, internal corporate ventures benefit from corporate infrastructure but enjoy relatively high freedom. Spin-offs provide the possibility of getting other shareholders involved so as to benefit from their expertise and resources. Innovation clusters present fertile ground for technology spin-offs as large and small companies can exchange expertise based on common interests and goals.

Coupled Innovation

Coupled innovation can be described as long-term collaborative interaction of equal partners. Outside-in and the inside-out innovation is merged into one cocreation process, following shared goals of all involved partners. Complementarity of resources and capabilities are critical for the success of long-term collaborations.

R & D partnerships. Technological innovation is becoming more and more complex and interdisciplinary. Even large firms can hardly afford to develop new products on their own. Consequently, there is a strong trend toward R & D partnerships to share risk and development costs and to use synergies. Many large companies strive for being embedded in long-term vertical and horizontal alliances and cross-industry partnerships. These innovation networks are characterized by balanced in- and outflows of knowledge. Large corporations, such as Philips and International Business Machines (IBM) Corporation, have opened up innovation campuses to attract technology start-ups, build up long-term relationships, and create technology joint ventures.

Open source. The appearance of open-source initiatives not only drastically changed the software industry but also characterized a new division of labor. Based on self-selection, programming tasks are outsourced to everyone who wants to get involved. The community of programmers is self-organized. Its members decide to fragment self-contained tasks and put them back together. The appearance of thousands of open-source software initiatives generated under idealistic motives (e.g., Eric Raymond's famous 1999 essay "The Cathedral and the Bazaar") seemed to be often noncommercial. The business model will decide whether value can be not only created but also captured. In the case of Linux, many commercially successful service businesses have been developed around the open-source model.

Importance

Open innovation demonstrates a new era in innovation management research. In the last decade, several special issues in scientific journals on open innovation and open source underpinned a fundamental change in the perception of innovation and established open innovation as a distinct research field.

Open innovation enduringly impacted business models in a way where open innovation becomes an integral part of value creation. Following an open innovation strategy, large companies, such as Siemens and Proctor & Gamble (P&G) Company, created firm-specific programs to leverage their own innovation capacity and R & D budget by external resources. In some cases, dislodged units with defined roles were established for the management of open innovation. Within the last few years, numerous innovation intermediaries—companies that moderate open innovation activities between the collaborators—emerged.

For companies, the question is not whether but how to open the innovation processes. Based on business strategy, managers have to decide when and how to open the innovation processes as a means to best leverage internal resources. Nevertheless, being entirely open is not always beneficial. A more contingent approach is required. The three core process can help managers to choose the best way to collaborate with external partners and use external knowledge. Practice has shown that one of the most challenging aspects is to find the right partner. In recent years, distinct methods were developed to assist managers facing this challenge.

Oliver Gassmann and Bastian Widenmayer

See also Lead Users; Patterns of Innovation; Stages of Innovation

Further Readings

Chesbrough, H. W. (2003). *Open innovation: The new imperative for creating and profiting from technology.* Cambridge, MA: Harvard Business.

Enkel, E., Gassmann, O., & Chesbrough, H. W. (2009). Open R&D and open innovation: Exploring the phenomenon. *R&D Management, 39*(4), 311–316.

Gassmann, O. (2006). Opening up the innovation process: Towards an agenda. *R&D Management, 36*(3), 223–226.

Gassmann, O., Enkel, E., & Chesbrough, H. W. (2010). The future of open innovation. *R&D Management, 40*(3), 1–9.

Gassmann, O., Zeschky, M., Wolff, T., & Stahl, M. (2010). Crossing the industry-line: Breakthrough innovation through cross-industry alliances with "non-suppliers." *Long Range Planning, 43,* 639–654.

Keupp, M. M., & Gassmann, O. (2009). Determinants and archetype users of open innovation. *R&D Management, 39*(4), 331–341.

Laursen, K., & Salter, A. (2006). Open for innovation: The role of openness in explaining innovation performance among UK manufacturing firms. *Strategic Management Journal, 27*(2), 131–150.

Lichtenthaler, U., & Lichtenthaler, E. (2009). A capability-based framework for open innovation: Complementing absorptive capacity. *Journal of Management Studies, 46*(8), 1315–1338.

van de Vrande, V., Vanhaverbeke, W., & Gassmann, O. (2010). Broadening the scope of open innovation: Past research, current research and future directions.

International Journal of Technology Management,
52(3/4), 221–235.

von Hippel, E., & von Krogh, G. (2003). Open source
software development and the private-collective
innovation model: Issues for organization science.
Organization Science, 14(2), 208–223.

ORGANIC AND MECHANISTIC FORMS

Tom Burns and G. M. Stalker's distinction between mechanistic and organic forms emphasizes how particular organizational structures are appropriate for certain organizational environments. The theory's central management insights are that bureaucratic organizations operate best in stable environments, whereas decentralized organizations flourish in unstable environments. In other words, mechanistic management systems, which use bureaucratic practices to facilitate decision making, are better suited for stable, unchanging environments. Organic management systems, which apply more decentralized and fluid practices, are more appropriate for dynamic environments. Since unstable environments often pose novel problems and unfamiliar work processes that are difficult to address with mechanistic management practices, organizations need flexibility to tap and coordinate members' expertise. This distinction between two "poles" of management systems has shaped conceptions of how particular organizational forms dampen or enhance innovation. Rather than focusing solely upon the inner workings of organizations, as prior organizational theories had done, this theory identifies a relationship between environments and organizational structures. This entry first delves into the study that typologized mechanistic and organic forms. After explaining the relationship between these forms and environments, the entry outlines links with contemporaries' research, as well as affinities with more recent research and theories. Next, the entry summarizes the findings of research into mechanistic and organic forms, as well as related studies that examine contemporary examples of organic forms and their mixtures with mechanistic forms. Finally, the entry describes promising directions in future research.

Fundamentals

Identification of mechanistic and organic forms arose out of comparative studies of established firms engaged in new work and outputs. Burns and Stalker studied 16 Scottish and English firms during the post–World War II period, including engineering firms that were entering the then-new field of electronic equipment. They found that most of the studied firms attempted to replicate management practices that had worked in the past—namely, bureaucratic practices that worked well in stable environments—even though these did not match their organizations' current environments. Characteristics of this mechanistic management system include a division of labor, vertical hierarchy, centralized decision making, rules and regulations, and top-down communication of commands. Members are expected to demonstrate loyalty to superiors, and the organization's status system is based on specialist technical knowledge rather than general knowledge. To cope with the new tasks, organizations with a mechanistic management system reinforce existing bureaucratic practices by introducing more rules and bumping atypical decisions up the chain of command. However, these inflict undesired consequences, including overwhelming supervisors by the sheer volume of decision making. To coordinate this increased work and supervise line workers, organizations formed new departments and positions, as well as committees, thereby proliferating bureaucracy. In outlining these dysfunctions, Burns and Stalker emphasize that organizations are not just tools for reaching goals but also constituted by individuals whose aims may or may not coincide.

Few of the studied firms replaced their mechanistic form with the organic form, which Burns and Stalker claim better fosters innovation. The organic management system relies upon decision making by those who have the expertise at hand, rather than by those in a specified position, with fluid rules and responsibilities, flatter hierarchy, decentralized control and decision making, and communication of advice and information rather than directives. Members are committed to the organization by their shared beliefs in the advancement of the work itself rather than obedience to superiors to facilitate their career. Moreover, their status does not derive from their standing within the firm but instead from recognition across the field outside their organization.

Unlike the mechanistic management system, which segments members' efforts by a division of labor and departments, the organic management system encourages interdependency and cooperative effort. However, members may have difficulties understanding how their organic management system works. They thus may introduce bureaucracy as a means of decreasing uncertainty. This underscores the tension between members' desire for stability and predictability, as embodied in the mechanistic form, versus flexibility and responsiveness, as characterized by the organic form.

To some degree, this distinction between mechanistic and organic forms attempts to reconcile prior, seemingly exclusive, conceptions of organizations as (a) rational tools and (b) coalitions of members with multiple, conflicting interests. It does so by integrating and embedding these two perspectives in organizational environments. In the preface to the third edition of *The Management of Innovation*, Burns makes explicit links with several contemporaries who view organizations as decision-making tools that match their environment. For example, James G. March and Herbert A. Simon explain how organizations facilitate decision making, given individuals' bounded rationality and propensity to satisfice rather than maximize. Distinctions between types of decisions made and decision-making processes used correspond with the categories of mechanistic and organic forms, with the former expediting routine decisions and the latter dealing with untested situations. Joan Woodward's study of manufacturing firms in England uncovered similar differences in the management structures of routine, large-scale production and innovative, small-runs. In addition, Michel Crozier's study of cycles of conflict in the French governmental bureaucracy, Strauss and colleagues' study of the negotiated order in psychiatric hospitals, Richard M. Cyert and James G. March's study of organizational decision making each reveal the multivariegated and contested nature of organizations, in which decision-making goals and processes involve both contention and cooperation among members.

Although subsequent research and theories do not directly test Burns and Stalker's claims, they have affinities with mechanistic and organic forms. Typically, mechanistic and organic forms are grouped alongside contingency theory, which similarly posits that organizational structures should match their environments. Researchers have also identified several organizational forms that embody characteristics of the organic management system. For instance, William G. Ouchi elaborates how Japanese firms have operated as clan systems by using more diffuse, flexible practices to coordinate work and committing members via lifelong employment. Using worker cooperatives, communes, and other collectivities, Joyce Rothschild and J. Allen Whitt outline the characteristics of the collectivist organization, which secures members' commitment based on beliefs in the collective and relies upon rotating tasks, collective ownership, and decision making by consensus. Similarly, social movement research documents how organizations that pursue feminist, civil rights, or social change issues often use flexible forms to integrate rather than suppress members' multiple interests during organizing processes. Moreover, recent research has examined the increasing use of teamwork, which selectively applies characteristics of the organic form, such as coaching, rotating tasks, interdependency, and collective decision making, while retaining the vertical hierarchy of the mechanistic form.

Although Burns and Stalker outline ideal types of the mechanistic and organic forms, they do not suggest ways of measuring degrees of mechanistic and organic forms along a continuum. Thus, researchers have borrowed other survey instruments to operationalize variables.

Importance

Some research has examined whether the distinction between mechanistic and organic forms holds across other kinds of organizations and industries, with most supporting distinctions between the mechanistic and organic forms. For example, research that compares communication between management and workers at a self-managed and at a more conventionally bureaucratic plant shows that the former, organic form cultivated more consultative interactions whereas the latter, mechanistic form issued more commands via the vertical hierarchy.

Contemporary organizations increasingly incorporate selected characteristics of organic management systems. For instance, studies show that relative to mechanistic management systems, the organic management systems enable companies to mass customize products or that management's propensity to take risks, seek competitive advantage through innovation, and confront competitors is better suited for organic than mechanistic systems. The adoption of teamwork, also known as high performance workplace practices, quality circles, or total quality management (TQM), has offered additional opportunities to assess established firms' attempts to switch from mechanistic to organic management systems. As predicted by Burns and Stalker, managers and team members often reproduce bureaucratic practices, creating a more coercive and even dysfunctional organization that intensifies commitment and control. Although rank-and-file members have more responsibilities, managers are reluctant to share authority or rewards, underscoring how organizations involve relations of cooperation and contention.

However, fewer studies attempt to assess the relative effectiveness of mechanistic and organic forms and their environments, whether one form supports more innovation than the other, or how members fare under these two forms. More commonly, researchers propose or empirically document boundary conditions. Noting that Burns and Stalker's research examined established organizations, researchers of new Internet service ventures argue that nascent organizations in new, unsettled economic sectors benefit from the mechanistic rather than the organic form. Building upon Arthur L. Stinchcombe's liability of newness argument, such research argues that new ventures benefit from the mechanistic form's formalization, which decreases uncertainty and enhances members' abilities to carry out work via role formalization, specialization, and administration. Others hypothesize that organizations that are engaged in new product development under time constraints need both mechanistic and organic structures to gather and process information and coordinate collective action.

Mechanistic and organic forms' greatest impact has been in recommendations in how to design organizations. For several decades, researchers have anticipated the demise of mechanistic management systems in favor of organic ones. In particular, management articles contrast the mechanistic and organic poles to explain why organizations, including those involved with technology development or other complex outputs with unclear processes such as health care and education, should decentralize and flatten hierarchies for greater flexibility, creativity, and innovation. Indeed, the characteristics of the organic form have been widely adopted in collectivities, such as open-source projects and the annual Burning Man festival, which heavily rely upon volunteers to carry out creative outputs. The organic form is becoming more familiar through organizing experiences such as Wikipedia, occupy Wall Street movement, and participatory budgeting. As such organizational forms proliferate and organizational environments increase in instability, the organic form is more likely to become taken-for-granted.

Looking forward, future research is likely to shed additional insight into the applicability of mechanistic and organic forms. In particular, qualitative and comparative research is needed to understand how organizations actually operate. Promising avenues include researchers' renewed interest in the contested nature of relations within organizations under different management systems, an aspect of Burns and Stalker's concept that has received relatively little scholarly attention. In addition, research into how organizations manage relations with other organizations through, for example, overlapping members or shared endeavors may extend conceptions of mechanistic and organic forms.

Katherine K. Chen

See also Bounded Rationality and Satisficing (Behavioral Decision-Making Model); Bureaucratic Theory; Contingency Theory; Environmental Uncertainty; Stages of Innovation

Further Readings

Adler, P. S., & Borys, B. (1996). Two types of bureaucracy: Enabling and coercive. *Administrative Science Quarterly, 41*(1), 61–89.

Aiken, M., Bacharach, S. B., & French, J. L. (1980). Organizational structure, work process, and proposal making in administrative bureaucracies. *Academy of Management Journal, 23*(4), 631–652.

Burns, T., & Stalker, G. M. (1994). *The management of innovation* (3rd ed.). New York, NY: Oxford University Press. (Original work published 1961)

Chen, K. K. (2009). *Enabling creative chaos: The organization behind the Burning Man event.* Chicago, IL: University of Chicago Press.

Courtright, J. A., Fairhurst, G. T., & Rogers, L. E. (1989). Interaction patterns in organic and mechanistic systems. *Academy of Management Journal, 32*(4), 773–802.

Covin, J. G., & Slevin, D. P. (1988). The influence of organizational structure on the utility of an entrepreneurial top management structure. *Journal of Management Studies, 25*(3), 217–234.

Rothschild, J., & Whitt, J. A. (1986). *The cooperative workplace: Potentials and dilemmas of organizational democracy and participation.* New York, NY: Cambridge University Press.

Sheremata, W. A. (2000). Centrifugal and centripetal forces in radical new product development under time pressure. *Academy of Management Review, 25*(2), 389–408.

Sine, W., Mitsuhasi, H., & Kirsch, D. A. (2006). Revisiting Burns and Stalker: Formal structure and new venture performance in emerging economic sectors. *Academy of Management Journal, 49*(1), 121–132.

Vallas, S. P. (2006). Empowerment redux: Structure, agency, and the remaking of managerial authority. *American Journal of Sociology, 111*(6), 1677–1717.

ORGANIZATIONAL AND MANAGERIAL WISDOM

Management paradigms and their derivative theories have disproportionately focused, either explicitly or implicitly, on knowledge (resources) and information (processes). In comparison, a wisdom-based paradigm of management seeks to approximate the highest stage of human development and conduct to promote broad-based sustainable success. Despite its long and varied history, the pursuit of wisdom is elusive and difficult to incorporate in management theory and practice. Recent scientific attention has coalesced around three genres of inquiry: the integrative approach of Monika Ardelt, the developmental approach of Paul Baltes and colleagues, and the balanced approach of Robert J. Sternberg. In 2007, Eric Kessler and James Bailey published the *Handbook of Organizational and Managerial Wisdom* to further explore this perspective and facilitate its crystallization. They offer the following definition: Organizational and managerial wisdom (OMW) is the application to professional pursuits of a deep understanding and fundamental capacity for living well. This includes the visioning, integration, and implementation of multifarious dimensions (within logical, ethical, aesthetic, epistemological, and metaphysical domains) as well

as the development and enactment of interrelated elements (across individual, interpersonal, organizational, and strategic levels) to lead the good life and enable it for others. This entry reviews the essential elements of their OMW framework and traces its potential importance for advancing the field and profession.

Fundamentals

According to Kessler and Bailey, a model of organizational and managerial wisdom can be constructed both along analytical levels and content domains. First, wise management encapsulates individual, interpersonal, organizational, and strategic phenomena. Individuals are the fundamental unit of organizational analysis; their judgments create organizational logics, their morals create organizational ethics, their values create organizational designs, their interpretations create organizational knowledge, and their reflections create organizational realities. Interpersonal interactions are the fundamental connection between these individuals which may create process synergy or loss. The organizational environment provides the context for individual and interpersonal behavior, and its structure and systems have the potential to influence wise action. Strategic policies facilitate or impede wisdom through overarching visions and manifest policies.

Second, each of these levels of wisdom is engaged across fundamental philosophic (*philos-sophia,* or the "love of wisdom") issues of logic, ethics, aesthetics, epistemology, and metaphysics. *Logic* is concerned with the laws of valid reasoning, and its central property is soundness or fidelity. Thus, individual logic relates to sound judgment, interpersonal logic to sound dynamics, organizational logic to sound institutionalized context, and strategic logic to sound policy formulation and implementation. *Ethics* deals with problems of right conduct. Individual ethics relates to personal virtue, interpersonal ethics to negotiated interaction, organizational ethics to proper leadership, and strategic ethics to principled synthesis with embedded and overlapping systems. *Aesthetics* attempts to determine the nature of beauty and the character of tastes and preferences. Individual aesthetics relates to personal values and attitudes, interpersonal aesthetics to empathy and exchange, organizational aesthetics to change and development, and strategic aesthetics to human resource systems and practice. *Epistemology* investigates the nature of knowledge and the process of knowing. Individual epistemology relates to a person's sensemaking process, interpersonal epistemology to diversity and the synthesis of knowledge frameworks, organizational epistemology to processes of institutionalizing knowledge and learning, and strategic epistemology to innovation and the creation and application of new knowledge. *Metaphysics* inquires into the nature and ultimate significance of what exists as real. Individual metaphysics relates to personal reflection, interpersonal metaphysics to influence and power relationships, organizational metaphysics to international and intercultural mind-sets, and strategic metaphysics to pedagogy and education.

Thus, taken together, management can be more or less wise in multiple domains and across multiple levels.

Domains of OMW

By combining these content domains across these levels of analysis, the model of organizational and managerial wisdom takes shape:

Organizational and managerial logic is sound and balanced judgment (individual), integrated within a team framework that manages inherent tensions (interpersonal) and is institutionalized in a structure of checks and balances (organizational), which is used to leverage collective knowledge in order to maximize organizational and societal effectiveness (strategic). The essence then of organizational and managerial logic is that of a finely tuned machine.

Organizational and managerial ethics is prudent, moral behavior (individual), integrated within ethically negotiated relationships (interpersonal) and viability-enhancing leadership (organizational) that is used to discern the most appropriate action for achieving joint value in a multiplicity of complex stakeholder relationships and uncertain situations (strategic). The essence then of organizational and managerial ethics is that of a well-intentioned agent.

Organizational and managerial aesthetics is moderated facilitation of self-interests (individual), integrated within socially and emotionally intelligent interactions (interpersonal) and behaviorally grounded change processes (organizational), that are used to holistically seek a synergy between financial and personal well-being (strategic). The essence then of organizational and managerial aesthetics is that of a mutually reinforcing relationship.

Organizational and managerial epistemology is informed sensemaking and sensegiving (individual), integrated within multicultural contexts and views (interpersonal) and emergent in accepting, empathic, and congruent understanding (organizational) that is used to harmoniously facilitate and properly orient the creative transformation function (strategic). The essence then of organizational and managerial epistemology is that of an emergent common comprehension.

Organizational and managerial metaphysics is reflective and farsighted understanding (individual), integrated within intersubjectively created, collaboratively formed relationships (interpersonal) and a vision that inspires courage and hope to make a positive difference (organizational), used to marry knowing and doing (strategic). The essence then of organizational and managerial metaphysics is that of a meaningful journey.

Levels of OMW

Alternatively, one might view the model from the perspective of the relevant actor(s):

The wise *individual* is characterized by sound and balanced judgment (logical), prudent behavior (ethical), moderated facilitation of self-interests (aesthetic), informed sensemaking and sensegiving (epistemological), and reflective and farsighted understanding (metaphysical). The person who is the embodiment of individual wisdom within the domain of organization management is a complex and thoughtful contributor.

The wise *team* is characterized by managed tensions (logical), morally negotiated relationships (ethical), emotionally and socially intelligent interactions (aesthetic), multiculturally reconciled contexts and views (epistemological), and intersubjectively created, collaboratively formed relationships (metaphysical). The wise team, then, is the embodiment of interpersonal wisdom as a rich and supportive interaction.

The wise *organization* is characterized by an institutionalized structure of checks and balances (logical), viability-enhancing leadership (ethical), behaviorally grounded change processes (aesthetic), acceptingness, empathy, and congruent understanding (epistemological), and a vision that inspires courage and hope to make a positive difference (metaphysical). The embodiment then of organizational wisdom within the domain of organizational management is that of an enabling and synergistic context.

The wise *strategy* is characterized by leveraging collective knowledge in order to maximize organizational and societal effectiveness (logical), discerning the most appropriate action for achieving joint value in a multiplicity of complex stakeholder relationships and uncertain situations (ethical), seeking a balance between financial and personal well-being (aesthetic), improving and properly orienting the creative transformation function (epistemological), and the marriage of knowing and doing (metaphysical). The embodiment then of strategic wisdom within the domain of organization management is that of a productive and inclusive vision.

Importance

A framework of organizational and managerial wisdom elevates the academic dialog from commonly employed information-based and knowledge-based perspectives of management. Generally speaking, knowledge is necessary but not sufficient for wisdom. Scientific knowledge can tell us how to do things but not whether they ought to be done. Moreover, knowledge can be a double-edged sword with respect to wisdom insofar as it provides us not only with the raw materials from which to reflect but also may restrict perspectives, learning, and intensions. It is particularly ironic that the terminal degree in our field, doctor of philosophy (PhD), does not generally require even a precursory study of philosophy. It is thus little surprise that the academic literature is dominated by both narrowly defined inquiry and elaborate statistical manipulations, struggles so mightily with multilevel and cross-disciplinary research, and often fails to addresses the really "big" issues facing managers. We humans live in the information society and have witnessed the emergence of academic fields, such as management information systems; business departments, such as information technology (IT); advanced technologies and scientific capabilities; and corporate titles, such as chief information officer (CIO). We have also witnessed the popularity of knowledge management, knowledge workers, competitive advantage, resource-based views of the firm, and the chief knowledge officer (CKO). An OMW framework takes the next step toward wisdom-based discourse. Some encouraging trends include the broad, impressive array of management scholars contributing to the OMW

handbook as well as the emergence of areas such as sustainability, stakeholder theory, positive organizational scholarship, and triple-bottom-line metrics for assessing an expanded collection of performance metrics.

Moving forward, Kessler and Bailey propose several dimensions for modern managers to approximate wisdom and incorporate it into their organization. They are grouped into the following outcome categories: (a) *extraordinary intellectual prowess*—becoming a thinking manager/organization, (b) *extraordinary emotive capacity*—becoming a feeling manager/organization, (c) *extraordinary collective orientation*—becoming a synergistic manager/organization, (d) *extraordinary functional application*—becoming an engaged manager/organization, (e) *extraordinary introspective insight*—becoming a reflective manager/organization, and (f) *extraordinary principled objectives*—becoming an aspiring manager/organization. The model also discerns several best practices for managers to develop this wisdom by focusing on attitude, awareness, ability, application, and design interventions.

As the OMW approach to management matures, it will need to resolve several tensions from an intellectual as well as practical perspective. First, is there such a thing as a universal OMW? This requires that the global manager balance the realities of relativistic meanings in different contexts (e.g., cultures, industries) with the aspiration to common and collaborative ends. Therefore, the seeker and practitioner of OMW must simultaneously be a realist and idealist, demonstrating a resilient flexibility (to engage, as per Aristotle, multiple manifest wisdoms) while exhibiting a broad-mindedness and integrative, almost visionary quality (in pursuing, as per Plato, an overarching Wisdom). Second, is there a perennial OMW? This requires balancing the "state" of wisdom with the wisdom journey of perpetual development and growth. Therefore, to truly understand, practice, and develop OMW, managers must see it as both snapshot and cinema, as the fundamental interplay between acquiring and utilizing wisdom (and the virtual or vicious cycles that may result), and as the inseparable interaction of being and acting wise. As we face a world of increasing uncertainty and interconnectivity, complexity and uncertainty, and hence opportunity and peril, the need for wise management becomes that much more important.

Eric H. Kessler

See also Academic-Practitioner Collaboration and Knowledge Sharing; Authentic Leadership; Bad Theories; Corporate Social Responsibility; Double Loop Learning; Emotional and Social Intelligence; Engaged Scholarship Model; Knowledge-Based View of the Firm; Learning Organization; Moral Reasoning Maturity; Multilevel Research; Positive Organizational Scholarship; Principled Negotiation; Programmability of Decision Making; Sensemaking; Stakeholder Theory; Systems Theory of Organizations; Theory of the Interesting; Transnational Management; Triple Bottom Line

Further Readings

Ardelt, M. (2004). Wisdom as expert knowledge system: A critical review of a contemporary operationalization of an ancient concept. *Human Development, 47,* 257–285.

Baltes, P. B., & Staudinger, U. M. (2000). Wisdom: A metaheuristic (pragmatic) to orchestrate mind and virtue toward excellence. *American Psychologist, 55*(1), 122–136.

Birren, J. E., & Fisher, L. M. (1990). The elements of wisdom: An overview and integration. In R. J. Sternberg (Ed.), *Wisdom: Its nature, origins, and development* (Chap. 14, pp. 317–332). New York, NY: Cambridge University Press.

Burrell, G., & Morgan, G. (1979). *Sociological paradigms and organizational analysis.* London, England: Heinemann.

Kessler, E. H., & Bailey, J. R. (Eds.). (2007). *Handbook of organizational and managerial wisdom.* Thousand Oaks, CA: Sage.

Sternberg, R. J. (2003). WICS: A model of leadership in organizations. *Academy of Management Learning and Education, 2(4),* 386–401.

Sternberg, R. J., & Jordan, J. (Eds.). (2005). *A handbook of wisdom: Psychological perspectives.* New York, NY: Cambridge University Press.

Takahashi, M., & Bordia, P. (2000). The concept of wisdom: A cross-cultural comparison. *International Journal of Psychology, 35*(1), 1–9.

Weick, K. E. (1979). *The social psychology of organizing.* New York, NY: McGraw-Hill.

ORGANIZATIONAL ASSIMILATION THEORY

Organizational assimilation involves the processes by which individuals become integrated into an organization. Given that most individuals join numerous organizations throughout the course of their lifetime, organizational assimilation is a ubiquitous aspect of workers' lives. However, assimilating or integrating into an organization is neither simple nor guaranteed. Unsuccessful assimilation has been linked to premature turnover, costly to both organizations and newcomers. Therefore, facilitating and overseeing the assimilation of new workers is a significant function of management. This insight gives managers, members, and other stakeholders an ability to better anticipate and facilitate newcomers' successful assimilation. Several similar constructs are used in conjunction with or in lieu of assimilation. For example, some researchers do not use the term *organizational assimilation* and instead refer to similar processes as *organizational socialization.* However, most researchers use both terms, distinguishing socialization as the process by which newcomers learn about the organization role they will hold in it. Another increasingly used term is *membership negotiation.* Membership negotiation is employed to emphasize that members' integration into an organization is often achieved through negotiations between newcomers and old-timers. The entry begins by reviewing early theorizing about organizational assimilation through phase models. Next, it notes more recent assimilation research that explores processes involved in assimilation and factors commonly associated with member integration. Finally, it discusses four of the most commonly used theories to frame organizational assimilation research.

Fundamentals

Early research and theorizing about organizational assimilation involved segmenting the processes by time. Phase or stage models divide the assimilation process into three or four segments. The first phase, commonly referred to as *anticipatory,* is a precursor to organizational entry that includes introduction to the occupation through vocational socialization and introduction to a particular organization as an individual researches and gathers information prior to joining. The second phase is *encounter,* which commences when newcomers join an organization and entails the training and orientation newcomers receive soon after entry. The third is an *adjustment* phase. After their initial introduction to the job and the organization, individuals must adjust to the organization's requirements and norms. However, most persons also attempt to individualize, or adapt, the role to suit their own needs, and this also is part of this phase. Many phase models include a fourth phase, referred to as *stabilization*. Stabilization represents a period of time in which members are mostly assimilated into the organization, and although changes in the organization or within the members can alter their feelings of assimilation, they consider themselves—and others consider them—to be full members. Phase models have been criticized because they unrealistically present assimilation as a linear process with discrete phases, and they illustrate what happens during the phases rather than how it occurs. Nevertheless, most researchers regard phase models as useful heuristics.

Recent research indicates that seven processes are involved in organizational assimilation, including developing familiarity with supervisors, developing familiarity with coworkers, acculturating, becoming involved, feeling recognized as a contributing member, negotiating one's role, and developing task competency. These processes of assimilation are affected by several factors. First, elements of the organization can affect new members' assimilation including training offered by the organization and the organization's culture. Where some cultures are formal and members must adhere to strict rules of conduct, others are much less formal thus allowing members considerable leeway in how members behave and define their roles. Second, occupation has a strong influence on member assimilation. Individuals in many professions (e.g., physicians, professors, attorneys) undergo extensive training and develop strong identification with their occupation prior to entering careers causing them to be much more committed to their occupation than their organization. In occupations in which work is more a job rather than a career, individuals may be more committed to their organization than their occupation. This makes their organizational assimilation more personally important. Third, coworkers' interactions with newcomers influence assimilation through welcoming new members and acquainting them with others and the workplace. Finally, new members can influence their own assimilation. Some newcomers are more proactive in seeking out information to gain acceptance and reduce uncertainty.

Several theories have been used in the past and continue to frame assimilation research.

Uncertainty reduction theory is useful in examining how newcomers manage and reduce uncertainty associated with entering organizations, including meeting and developing productive relationships with others, developing task competency, and integrating into the organizational culture. *Sense-making theory* is a useful framing, enabling researchers to examine how newcomers make sense of events, behaviors, and relationships in new organizational contexts. *Social identity* is a less frequently used theoretical frame, but it is useful when researchers focus on how individual's social identity affects and is affected by assimilation into an organization. Recent research and theorizing also draws on elements of structuration theory. For example, studies have examined how organizational structures enable and constrain assimilation, and, how organizational discourse enforces and reinforces norms, policies, and ideologies associated with assimilation into organizations. Contemporary research in the area examines a variety of issues related to assimilation including mediating factors such as the effect of past organizational experiences and the effect of diversity.

Managers can use organizational assimilation theory in several ways. First, management can understand how socialization provided by the organization has a significant influence on whether newcomers successfully integrate or quickly turnover. Second, research in the area has identified newcomers' motivations to assimilate. In addition to attaining task competency, new members are motivated to make sense of early experiences, reduce or manage uncertainty, and to ascertain how their new role links to their social identity. Managers' awareness and anticipation of these motivations may therefore aid their roles in meeting those needs and in facilitating entry and retention. Third, newcomers assimilate in several ways including getting to know coworkers, learning about the culture of the organization, becoming involved, and being recognized as a contributing member. Management can play an important role by providing socialization experiences in each of these processes that help to ensure newcomers' assimilation success.

Karen K. Myers

See also Organizational Culture Theory; Organizational Identification; Organizational Socialization; Sensemaking; Social Identity Theory

Further Readings

Gailliard, B., Myers, K. K., & Seibold, D. R. (2010). Organizational assimilation: A multidimensional reconceptualization and measure. *Management Communication Quarterly, 24,* 552–578.

Jablin, F. (2001). Organizational entry, assimilation, and exit. In F. Jablin & L. Putnam (Eds.), *The new handbook of organizational communication* (pp. 732–818). Thousand Oaks, CA: Sage.

Louis, M. (1980). Surprise and sense-making: What newcomers experience when entering unfamiliar organizational settings. *Administrative Science Quarterly, 23,* 225–251.

McPhee, R. D., & Zaug, P. (2000). The communicative constitution of organizations: A framework for explanation. *Electronic Journal of Communication/ La Revue Electronique de Communication, 10*(1/2). Retrieved from http://www.cios.org/getfile/ MCPHEE_V10N1200

Miller, V., & Jablin, F. (1991). Information seeking during organizational entry: Influences, tactics, and a model of the process. *Academy of Management Review, 16,* 92–120.

Scott, C. W., & Myers, K. K. (2010). Toward an integrative theoretical perspective of membership negotiations: Socialization, assimilation, and the duality of structure. *Communication Theory, 20,* 79–105.

Waldeck, J., & Myers, K. K. (2007). Organizational assimilation theory, research, and implications for multiple divisions of the discipline: A state of the art review. In C. S. Beck (Ed.), *Communication yearbook 31,* (pp. 322–369). Mahwah, NJ: Erlbaum.

ORGANIZATIONAL COMMITMENT THEORY

Organizational commitment (OC) is, in general terms, an employee's sense of attachment and loyalty to the work organization with which the employee is associated. It is defined in terms of an employee's attitudes and intentions (understood as the precursors of behavior). Employees are said to be committed to the organization when their goals are congruent with those of the organization, when they are willing to exert effort on behalf of the organization, and when they desire to maintain their connection with the organization. Unsurprisingly, OC has been shown to be a key antecedent of other important attitudes and behaviors, including those related to performance and turnover. For instance, a large body of research suggests that organizations whose members have higher levels of commitment tend to get more out of those members, in terms of higher in-role and extra-role performance and lower levels of absenteeism and lateness. The study of organizational commitment has grown in popularity over recent years in the literature of management, industrial-organizational psychology, and organizational behavior. Indeed, OC is among the most studied of all the characteristics and attitudes that have drawn the attention of organizational scholars. Much of this interest is due to the fact that OC appears to predict some organizational outcomes, including extra-role performance and turnover, better than other work attitudes, such as job satisfaction. This entry reviews the dominant theories of organizational commitment from the 1960s to the present day and concludes with possible directions for the future development of this theory.

Fundamentals

Organizational scholars began seriously to conceptualize the notion of OC, and to delineate its antecedents and consequences, in the 1960s. Since then, the growing interest in OC has contributed to a conceptual richness in how we understand this construct. Over the years, there have been three main approaches to defining and measuring OC: the *calculative* approach, the *attitudinal* approach, and the *multidimensional* approach. These will now be described in turn.

The Calculative Approach

The calculative approach rests on the "side bet" theory of Howard Becker. Becker introduced this term in the 1960s to refer to the accumulation of investments valued by the individual that would be lost or deemed worthless if he or she were to leave the organization. In gambling, a side bet is a wager that is separate from the main bet or stakes in the game being played; for instance, two players in a card game might bet on whose hand holds the highest spade. Becker argued that over time, economic, social, and other investments—side bets—such as income, status, seniority, and friendships, even simply "knowing the ropes," tie people to a particular line of activity. The threat of losing these investments, along with a perceived lack of alternatives to replace or make up for them, commits the person to the organization. Measures reflecting this approach were developed in the late 1960s and the 1970s. These measures question respondents on the likelihood of their leaving the organization, given various levels of inducement in pay, status, responsibility, job freedom, and promotion opportunities.

The Attitudinal Approach

The second approach, also called the "organizational behavior" or "psychology" approach, sees commitment as affective or attitudinal. According to the attitudinal approach, employees feel committed to the organization because they identify with the organization's values and goals. More specifically, commitment under this approach has three dimensions: (a) a desire to maintain membership in the organization, (b) belief in and acceptance of the values and goals of the organization, and (c) willingness to exert effort on behalf of the organization. Commitment under the attitudinal approach has also been termed *affective commitment* and *value commitment*.

The attitudinal approach gave rise to one of the most important measures of OC, the Organizational Commitment Questionnaire (OCQ), which dominated the literature from the early 1970s to the mid-1980s. The OCQ consists of 15 items (a shortened version has nine positively phrased items) reflecting the three dimensions of commitment. Some studies noted that the relationships between this measure and some attitudinal variables, such as job satisfaction and job involvement, were too high for an acceptable level of discriminant validity. However, in separate examinations of the OCQ, other researchers supported the general conclusion that it contains good psychometric properties.

Because of the OCQ's dominance, most findings, conclusions, and proposals for a future research agenda on OC are based on this measure. But in the mid-1980s, new criticisms began to arise regarding this approach. The basic difficulty is that two of the dimensions of commitment in the OCQ, a strong desire to maintain membership in the organization and a willingness to exert considerable effort on behalf of the organization, overlap with intentions of outcome behaviors such as withdrawal and performance. The response to that criticism has

taken two directions. First, since the items in the full measure that deal with withdrawal and performance are among the six problematic items which are negatively phrased, researchers have tended to use the nine-item version of the OCQ more frequently than the full 15-item version. Second, a new trend has evolved in the definition and measurement of OC.

The Multidimensional Approach

Arguing that OC can be better understood as a multidimensional concept, two scholars—John P. Meyer and Natalie Jean Allen—proposed in 1984 a two-dimensional measure of OC. Conceptually, their distinction between the two dimensions paralleled that between the side-bet calculative approach of Becker and the attitudinal approach. The first dimension was termed *affective commitment* and was defined as positive feelings of identification with, attachment to, and involvement in, the work organization. The second was termed *continuance commitment* and was defined as the extent to which employees feel committed to their organizations by virtue of the costs that they feel are associated with leaving (e.g., investments or lack of attractive alternatives). Later, the scholars added a third dimension: *normative commitment,* defined as employees' feelings of obligation to remain with the organization.

The multidimensional approach is today the prevailing approach to OC. However, the theory remains in flux. For instance, some studies have found that continuance commitment is itself a two-dimensional construct, with one subdimension representing the sacrifices made by an employee in staying with the organization (this is termed *high-sacrifice continuance commitment*) and the other representing available employment alternatives (*low-alternatives continuance commitment*). For this reason, some scholars argue that commitment should be studied as a four-component model. In addition, the normative commitment scale is very highly correlated with the affective dimension of OC, raising concerns about the discriminant validity of the normative scale. In short, scholars have raised serious questions about the validity and reliability of two of the three dimensions advanced by the multidimensional approach, and much work still needs to be done before this approach can be used to draw firm conclusions.

Importance

Aside from these questions about the various approaches to the study of organizational commitment, researchers have raised more general concerns about the usefulness of OC as a predictive tool. The basic test of commitment—as for any other construct—is its predictive validity. OC has shown modest relationships with turnover and weak correlations with in-role performance. It does show relatively high correlations with organizational citizenship behavior (OCB), or extra-role behavior. This raise the question of whether the real power of OC is its ability to predict OCB, as opposed to in-role performance—a question that should be considered in future research.

Another promising direction for future research is the adoption of a multiple-commitment approach. Some scholars have begun to examine simultaneously several foci of commitment in the workplace, including not only the organization but also the workgroup, the job, the union, and the occupation. Several forces have advanced this approach. First, there is growing awareness that in the workplace, as in life generally, people can and do show commitment to more than one focus at the same time. For a real understanding of commitment in the workplace, it is therefore necessary to examine more than one object of commitment.

Second, changes in the work environment worldwide, particularly recent and continuing recessions in many economies, have led many organizations to reduce their workforces. Many have simply cut back, while others have turned to outsourcing—contracting jobs and tasks previously performed in-house to external providers. This has led, in turn, to a decline in the importance of the organization from the employees' point of view. The result is that in many occupations across many countries, organizations do not want to be tied to employees, and employees do not want to be tied to organizations. Long-term commitment is no longer seen as desirable, and organizations no longer put effort into creating a commitment culture.

There is some evidence that the move toward a multiple-commitment approach will increase the predictive validity of commitment. However, it is still too early to tell how fruitful this approach will prove. Do employees really distinguish among all the different possible foci of commitment at work, or are we researchers developing concepts that do not have strong meaning for employees? Concept redundancy and measurement problems may yet prove to bedevil the multiple-commitment approach. This is another important issue that needs to be examined in future research on commitment.

Better understanding of commitment theory has important practical implications for modern managers. First, by understanding what commitment entails for individual employees, managers may be better able to motivate them and increase their contribution to the organization. For instance, employees with higher levels of affective commitment may respond positively to work-sponsored social events, while employees with higher levels of calculative commitment might need more tangible incentives, such as the promise of pay raises. This may be particularly relevant for international managers, as commitment may have different meanings, antecedents, and implications in different cultures.

Second, an understanding of how commitment can extend to multiple foci might allow managers to characterize employees by commitment profiles. This can provide valuable practical information for employers. For example, which profile of commitment has the best fit to the organization in terms of employees' behavior in the workplace? Which profile of commitment is better from the viewpoint of the employee's well being? Commitment profiles can assist organizations in both selection and maintenance of human resource functions. If organizations know which profiles are more beneficial for them they can integrate some of this knowledge into their selection criteria. Also, they can include and increase the relevant commitments through their training programs. Commitment profiles can also be related to nonwork domains, potentially offering a means by which employers can help employees to better cope with the sometimes competing demands of work and nonwork. Career management, both through individual career planning and through household planning, may improve career commitment and, to a lesser degree, organizational commitment. Organizations, therefore, might benefit from programs intended to aid employees in planning their careers and managing household activities that might interfere with work-related commitments. Understanding these aspects can assist in finding positive ways to effect commitment forms.

Aaron Cohen

See also Affect Theory; Authentic Leadership; Management Roles; Organizational Culture Theory; Organizational Identity; Social Exchange Theory; Social Identity Theory; Trust

Further Readings

Becker, H. S. (1960). Notes on the concept of commitment. *American Journal of Sociology, 66,* 32–40.

Cohen, A. (1993). Organizational commitment and turnover: A meta-analysis. *Academy of Management Journal, 36,* 1140–1157.

Cohen, A. (2003). *Multiple commitments in the workplace: An integrative approach.* Mahwah, NJ: Lawrence Erlbaum.

Mathieu, J. E., & Zajac, D. M. (1990). A review and meta-analysis of the antecedents, correlates and consequences of organizational commitment. *Psychological Bulletin, 108,* 171–194.

Meyer, J. P., & Allen, N. J. (1997). *Commitment in the workplace: Theory, research, and application.* Thousand Oaks, CA: Sage.

Meyer, J. P., Stanley, J. D., Herscovitch, L., & Topolnytsky, L. (2002). Affective, continuance, and normative commitment to the organization: A meta-analysis of antecedents, correlates, and consequences. *Journal of Vocational Behavior, 61,* 20–52.

Morrow, P. C. (1983). Concept redundancy in organizational research: The case of work commitment. *Academy of Management Review, 8,* 486–500.

Morrow, P. C. (1993). *The theory and measurement of work commitment.* Greenwich, CT: Jai Press.

Mowday, R. T., Porter, L. M., & Steers, R. M. (1982). *Employee-organizational linkage.* New York, NY: Academic Press.

Reichers, A. E. (1985). A review and reconceptualization of organizational commitment. *Academy of Management Review, 10,* 465–476.

ORGANIZATIONAL CULTURE AND EFFECTIVENESS

Organizational culture encompasses the system of beliefs, assumptions, values, and norms held by the members of an organization. Over the past 30 years, scholars of management and organizational science have advanced a number of theoretical perspectives to explain how culture impacts organizational effectiveness. The purpose of this entry is to provide an overview of the major theories and what they contribute to our generalized understanding of the culture-effectiveness relationship. These theories can be broadly categorized into *process-oriented* and *resource-based* perspectives. The process-oriented perspective follows from an anthropological tradition (and more recently, organizational psychology) and considers how organizational cultures—as systems—evolve in response to environmental demands. The resource-based perspective is rooted in economics and describes the macro factors that allow culture to serve as a source of competitive advantage for the firm. The modern dimensionalized view of organizational culture is evident in both theoretical perspectives, providing the framework for comparing organizational cultures and studying the existence and nature of culture-effectiveness relationships. In light of growing evidence pointing to culture as an important antecedent of various organizational performance outcomes (for a recent overview of this literature, see Sonja Sackmann, 2011), these theories hold particular relevance for management scholars interested in human-social factors as drivers of organizational effectiveness.

Fundamentals

The process theory linking culture to effectiveness is perhaps best illustrated by Edgar Schein's work beginning in the early 1980s. Schein described culture as an adaptive feature of organizations with a recursive relationship with the organization's effectiveness. Founding leaders implant their personal values and assumptions within the organizations they create. As the group struggles to overcome competitive pressures and succeed together as an organization, the culture evolves and becomes deeply ingrained. As a consequence of this process unfolded over time, the organization's culture comes to reflect the collective learning of the group regarding what works and what doesn't (i.e., what is effective). Cultural elements and practices that inhibit the organization's effectiveness are eventually abandoned in favor of those that promote effectiveness and increase the likelihood that the organization will survive and flourish. If culture does not adapt to meet changing demands, the organization may face crisis or even perish.

Thus, culture shapes, and is shaped by, the organization's successes and failures. Yet two main questions remain for theories to address: What are the kinds of cultural values, norms, and work practices that promote success and deflect failure? And how do these elements of culture impact an organization's effectiveness? To address these questions, scholars have advanced dimensionalized models of culture and theories relating cultural dimensions to effectiveness outcomes. Dimensionalized models organize the total system of values, norms, and basic assumptions into cultural configurations that (a) reflect coherent categories or cultural themes (e.g., teams focus, risk orientation) and (b) help to prioritize the aspects of culture that are most likely to impact organizational effectiveness.

Daniel Denison's work in this area advances a theory of cultural effectiveness based on a dimensionalized model that was developed over a series of qualitative and quantitative studies. Together, these studies indicated that in general, the highest performing organizations find ways to empower and engage their people (*involvement*), facilitate coordinated actions and promote consistency of behaviors with core business values (*consistency*), translate the demands of the organizational environment into action (*adaptability*), and provide a clear sense of purpose and direction (*mission*). Underlying the cultural traits are "dynamic tensions" that reflect the inherent conflicts between maintaining an adaptive and externally focused culture versus stability and internal consistency (see also the entry Competing Values Framework in this encyclopedia). The theory proposes that organizations are most effective when they have higher levels of each cultural trait—that is, stronger cultural norms and values surrounding involvement, consistency, adaptability, and mission—thereby representing a more balanced cultural configuration.

Denison's theory is an example of a *direct effects* view of the culture-effectiveness relationship, proposing that higher intensity (or levels) of specific types of cultural values and norms cause higher effectiveness; hence, there is a direct relationship. Alternative views describe *mediated* and *moderated* culture-effectiveness relationships. Mediation implies an intervening causal factor. For example, culture shapes *human resource practices* which cause effectiveness. Moderation can take on several forms but in general describes how the culture-effectiveness relationship is dependent on certain boundary conditions.

Jay Barney's resource-based theory follows from a moderation view of the culture-effectiveness relationship. The theory complements process-oriented (micro) theories by describing the marketplace (macro) conditions required for organizational culture to causally impact firm profitability. First, the culture must be valuable to the firm, allowing it to operate in ways that achieve a higher degree of effectiveness than competitors—toward this end, the micro process-oriented theories are useful. Second, it must be rare. No advantage is conferred if the culture is common to many or most of the firm's competitors. Third, it must be imperfectly replicable, such that competitors cannot re-create the exact culture in their own organization. Taken together, the conditions specified by the theory address the *when* question: *When* is culture most likely to be a source of competitive advantage for the firm? In short, when the culture is valuable, rare, and not easily replicated by competitors.

Levi R. G. Nieminen and Daniel Denison

See also Cultural Values; High- and Low-Context Cultures; Meaning and Functions of Organizational Culture; Norms Theory; Organizational Culture Model; Resource-Based View of the Firm

Further Readings

Barney, J. B. (1986). Organizational culture: Can it be a source of sustained competitive advantage? *Academy of Management Review, 11,* 656–665.

Denison, D. R. (1984). Bringing corporate culture to the bottom line. *Organizational Dynamics, 13,* 4–22.

Denison, D. R. (1990). *Corporate culture and organizational effectiveness.* New York, NY: Wiley.

Denison, D. R., & Mishra, A. K. (1995). Toward a theory of organizational culture and effectiveness. *Organization Science, 6,* 204–223.

Sackmann, S. A. (2011). Culture and performance. In N. Ashkanasy, C. Wilderom, & M. Peterson (Eds.), *The handbook of organizational culture and climate* (2nd ed., pp. 188–224). Thousand Oaks, CA: Sage.

Schein, E. H. (1985). *Organizational culture and leadership.* San Francisco, CA: Jossey-Bass.

ORGANIZATIONAL CULTURE MODEL

This entry focuses on perhaps one of the best known conceptualizations of the abstract concept of organizational culture: Edgar H. Schein's organizational culture model. Organizational culture has been a prominent domain of inquiry in management and organizational theory for over three decades, yet culture continues to be a contested area of management research. Organizational analysts vary in their definitions and conceptions of culture and also disagree about how culture is observed and measured, how it is fostered and changed, the mechanisms through which it exerts its influence, and its effects on organizational performance. Some scholars claim that interest in the cultural perspective has waxed and waned. Schein's comprehensive and enduring model coupled with a surge of recent culture research belies this view. All signs suggest that organizational culture will continue to be a prominent explanatory construct in organization and management theory for years to come. Schein's model provides a useful template to ground our understanding. The following section explores aspects of Schein's culture model, with particular attention to his definition of culture and its key elements, content of culture, cultural dynamics, and theoretical tensions. Next, the entry considers the evolution of the organizational culture perspective more generally, and concludes with an assessment of the importance of the organizational culture model for management theory and practice.

Fundamentals

Schein defines culture as a pattern of shared basic assumptions, invented, discovered, or developed by a given group as it learns to cope with its problem of external adaptation and internal integration, in ways that have worked well enough to be considered suitable and, therefore, can be taught to new members as the correct way to perceive, think, and feel in relation to those problems. What Schein has spelled out in careful detail, many researchers and practitioners spell out more compactly: Culture consists of a system of shared taken-for-granted beliefs, values, and behavioral norms that shape how organizations and their members make sense of and cope with their worlds. Schein emphasizes the deeper manifestations of culture, its deep patterns of shared assumptions rather than its more superficial aspects such as overt behavior patterns. Behavioral regularities in the form of traditions, formal rituals, and customs certainly can reflect culture, but overt behaviors can also result from situational contingencies or other demand effects.

Structural Elements

Consistent with most other conceptualizations, Schein distinguishes three levels in which elements of culture are manifest. These elements are hierarchically ordered from deeper to more surface levels, with the deeper elements having a more profound influence on attitudes and behaviors. The analogy of an iceberg illustrates the visible and invisible structure of culture. Typically, only a small part of the iceberg is above water and the rest is hidden. We have only to think about the fate of the ship *Titanic* to get a sense of the enormity of the unseen part of the iceberg. Culture is similar. The surface-level elements, observable artifacts, include aspects of culture that are readily apparent to the outside observer. These include language, dress, policies and procedures, and statements of philosophy. Artifacts are easy to observe but hard to decipher without understanding how they connect to underlying assumptions. The intermediate-level elements of culture, espoused (and documented) beliefs, ideologies and philosophies, values, and norms, are less visible—manifest in myths and stories, public expressions during meetings or ceremonies, or written documents that outline the company and its strategy. These elements can be discerned through archival methods, questionnaires, or survey instruments as well as interviews. At its deepest level, culture consists of basic assumptions and beliefs about the organizational context and how things work. These deeper structures become taken-for-granted and unconscious over time because they have been successfully used as preferred solutions to past problems. These tacit, often unconscious, assumptions define what organizational members should pay attention to, signal what things mean, and shape how they should emotionally react and act in a variety of situations. Assumptions can be discerned through intensive observation, focused interviews and self-analysis. In any organization, the deeper-level elements will be expressed in a large variety of artifacts. This means that in any organization, one would observe only a few deeply held assumptions but many artifacts.

One point of disagreement between Schein and other culture researchers concerns whether the deeper structures that serve as guiding principles for meaning making and adapting represent shared basic assumptions or core values. Schein argues that these deeper structures reflect basic assumptions rather than values. People can agree or disagree about core values and generally are open to discussing them. In contrast, basic assumptions become so taken-for-granted that they are nonnegotiable and, often, not debatable or even confrontable. Questioning or challenging basic assumptions often provokes anxiety or defensiveness, and even reactance. This makes them sticky and very hard to change.

A second point of difference concerns the relationship between culture and organizational performance. Schein eschews the common notions that some cultures are better or worse or that good performance is the result of one right culture. The question of whether a particular culture is effective or ineffective depends on the nature of the relationship between the culture and the environment in which it exists.

To summarize, through the lens of Schein's conceptual model, when we talk about culture, we are talking about assumptions that preserve lessons learned from dealing with the outside and the inside; principles derived from these assumptions that prescribe how organizational members should perceive, think, and feel; artifacts or visible markers and activities that embody and give substance to the espoused principles and taken-for-granted assumptions.

Content of Culture

Cultural assumptions and manifestations cover all areas of organizational life. To understand an organization's culture requires an understanding of the content of the underlying assumptions. Management scholars have attempted to deal with the complexity of cultural analysis by creating typologies and organizing cultural manifestations into basic content categories. A well-known example is Geert Hofstede's bipolar categorization of work-related cultural assumptions into five categories that include high- versus low-power distance, strong versus weak uncertainty avoidance, individualism versus collectivism, masculinity versus femininity, long- versus short-term time orientation. Schein takes a more functionalist and evolutionary stance in his classification of content dimensions. He proposes, first and foremost, that cultural assumptions relate to the archetypical problems of (a) surviving and adapting to the external environment, and, (b) integrating internal processes to enable capabilities to survive and adapt. But there is more. Schein notes that all

organizations exist within the context of broader macrocultures, such as nations, ethnic and religious groups, and professions and occupations. Thus, an organization's cultural assumptions reflect many of the more abstract issues about which humans in any particular national and occupational macroculture (i.e., any society) need to agree. Schein proposes that in addition to external adaptation and internal integration, basic assumptions in all organizations relate to the nature of reality and truth, the nature of time and space, human nature, and the nature of human activity and human relationships. Schein further subdivides each of these basic dimensions. For example, assumptions about external adaptation include assumptions about the organization's core mission, goals and the means to achieve them, what criteria will be used to measure results, and remedial actions to be taken if goals are not met. Shared basic assumptions about internal integration include assumptions about common organizational language and concepts; group boundaries and criteria for inclusion and exclusion; criteria for allocating status, power, and authority as well as rewards and punishments; norms of trust, intimacy, and love; and concepts for explaining the unthinkable and uncontrollable.

Cultural Dynamics

The evolutionary perspective is central in Schein's conception of how organizational culture evolves, is perpetuated, and changes. The essence of culture is acquired through social learning and preserved through socialization processes. Cultural evolution can happen naturally or can be guided or managed. Natural and constant pressures for cultural adaptation and change come both from the multiple environments in which groups and organizations exist and also from the addition of new organizational members who import their own beliefs and assumptions. We noted earlier the tenacity of deeply held assumptions. They are not easily changed or relinquished even in the face of external events or new members that disconfirm them. Changes and adaptations can and do occur naturally from these processes. But leaders and leadership generally are critical to guiding and managing cultural evolution.

An organization's cultural assumptions often can be traced back to the beliefs and values of its founders or early leaders. Historical accounts often attribute a firm's culture to the charisma or vision of its leaders, but charisma per se is neither a common nor predictable explanatory factor. Rather as Schein shows, there are both primary and secondary theoretical mechanisms—things that leaders do and other factors that support and reinforce leaders' messages and actions—that influence the extent to which cultures are created and embedded. Primary embedding mechanisms include what leaders regularly attend to, measure, and control; how they react to critical events and organizational crises; how they allocate resources, rewards, and status; how they recruit, select, promote, and sanction employees; and the extent to which they deliberately act as a role model, teacher, and coach. Supportive secondary mechanisms include an organization's design and structure, systems and procedures, rites and rituals, physical space, buildings, myths and stories, and formal statements of organizational philosophy, such as mission statements, creeds, and charters.

Schein singles out three additional factors that affect the evolution of an organization's culture. These include the stability of the group, the length of time a group has existed, and the intensity of the group's shared experiences. Some organizations or groups within them may not have learning experiences that enable them to evolve and develop a pattern of shared assumptions. There must be enough of a stable membership and shared history for a culture to form.

A continuing theoretical tension identified by Linda Smircich in early culture research concerns whether culture is a state or static property of a given group or organization—something an organization has—or whether it is a human process of constructing shared meaning that goes on all the time—something an organization is. Managers favor the former functionalist view, whereas many management scholars favor the latter. Schein's model highlights the grain of truth in both assertions. Culture is perpetually evolving; it is something an organization has that eventually becomes something an organization is.

Subcultures

By definition, culture formation emphasizes the ideas of patterning, integration, and sharedness. Yet it is a gross oversimplification to talk about the monolith of an organizational culture. Organizational cultures may be composed of subcultures that are in alignment or at odds with the dominant culture. In fact, Schein and other culture scholars, such as Joann Martin, importantly acknowledge that there is wide variation in the extent to which organizational cultures are integrated. Cultures can be defined by assumptions that are harmonious and shared. But an organization's cultural landscape may be characterized by a set of differentiated subcultures whose assumptions are in bitter conflict or by a fragmented set of subcultures whose assumptions are contradictory, puzzling, and ambiguous.

Conflicts, differences, and contradictions in organizations often can be attributed to differing assumptions that derive not only from the macrocultures in which organizations operate (e.g., ethnic groups) but also from assumptions of functional microcultures. Schein proposes that three generic subcultures exist within all organizations. These include the operators, engineers, and executives. The operator subculture, also known as the line or technical core, is critical to actually running or producing things. The engineering and design subculture represents the group that designs products, processes, and structures to make the organization more effective. The executive subculture represents top managers who are concerned with the administrative and financial functions of the organization. These subcultures naturally share many assumptions of the total organization, but they also hold particular assumptions that reflect their occupations, unique experiences, and functions. These differences can be problematic if not resolved, as all three subcultures are necessary for organizational effectiveness. But, if harnessed, these differences can be an important and valuable organizational resource as they can provide a diversity of perspectives and interpretations of emerging problems.

Evolution

The study of organizational culture gained attention in the late 1970s and early 1980s as a way to characterize organizations and levels of stability in group and organizational behavior and to explain differences in organizational effectiveness, particularly among organizations within a society. Psychologists since the late 1930s had referred to the concepts of "group norms" and "climate," but the concept of organizational culture developed much later as the fields of organizational psychology and organizational behavior grew. In part, this reflected a move away from psychology and a focus on individuals toward a more systemic and integrated view based on social psychology, sociology, and anthropology. Two popular works on the topic of "corporate" culture published in 1982, *In Search of Excellence* by Tom Peters and Robert H. Waterman Jr. and *Corporate Cultures* by Terrence E. Deal and Allan A. Kennedy, were influential among practicing managers and fueled the growth of interest in the topic. Before that time, culture generally had referred to nationalities rather than organizations.

Research on organizational climate preceded research on organizational culture and consequently has a much longer history. Organizational climate is defined broadly as organizational members' socially shared perceptions of key characteristics of their organization. Climate perceptions can vary in terms of breadth and can range from narrow domain-specific perceptions such as a service, innovation, or safety climate perception, to a single, multidimensional global perception. Although climate initially was developed as an integrating concept to explain underlying organizational processes and events, Schein and other scholars generally agree that climate is an overt or superficial manifestation of culture. In other words, organizational culture is expressed through organizational climate.

Organizational climate research is rooted primarily in a sociopsychological framework, while organizational culture is rooted in anthropology. Each tradition naturally relies upon different research methods for the study of its research object. Climate researchers generally use more quantitative approaches, while most culture researchers use more qualitative techniques. In addition, culture research often is more focused on how dynamic processes at work within an organizational context continuously serve to create and reshape the culture.

Researchers have studied organizational culture using a variety of methods, including surveys and questionnaires; descriptive analyses of organizational symbols, stories, and language; rites and rituals; ethnography; and clinical or action research methods. Given the variety in organizational culture research approaches, it is not surprising to find variation and diversity in conceptualizations of culture and the frameworks and typologies for assessing it. Schein's organizational culture framework with its

hierarchically ordered three levels suggests a variety of methods that can be used to assess each of the levels. Yet Schein throughout his work has opined that progress in the field of organizational culture has been hampered because researchers too quickly privileged abstract methods, such as questionnaires and surveys, at the expense of deep observation. Schein questions whether surveys can get at the deeper levels of shared tacit assumptions. Thus, it is not surprising to find ethnographic methods—such as participant observation and content analysis of organizational artifacts, such as stories, myths, rituals and symbols, and action research, such as process consultation or organizational development methods—at the top of Schein's list of preferred methods.

Importance

Schein's conceptual model has been widely cited by scholars and practitioners alike, suggesting that it is both theoretically and practically important. The essence of culture, its tacit assumptions that operate below the surface, are extraordinarily powerful influences on individual and organizational behavior. Culture importantly helps to explain observed differences within organizations and organizational life, such as conflicts and contradictions between occupational and functional subcultures. It also can help to explain the differences between organizations, such as capabilities of some organizations within an industry to change, adapt, and survive.

Schein's model of culture isn't something to be "tested" in the traditional research sense. Rather, it is an explanatory concept and sensemaking tool for researchers who seek to understand culture relative to a particular research question. For example, culture figures prominently in the management and organizations literature on system safety and accident causation in high hazard industries and health care. The dynamics of culture (in particular how organizations can enable communication and understanding across cultural boundaries or how organizations can embed flexible learning cultures) are central, for example, in the literature on high-reliability organizations (HROs). This literature examines organizations that operate sufficiently complex technologies to be at risk for potentially catastrophic accidents, but which appear to operate reliably and safely for long periods under very trying conditions. The HRO paradigm does not necessarily examine or emphasize how accidents happen, but rather what organizations can do to promote and increase the likelihood of safe operations in complex systems. Schein's model helps to explain the challenges of embedding safety cultures in complex systems. For example, Schein's insights about multiple and competing professional and occupational cultures and subcultures (e.g., doctors, nurses, other occupations) is relevant to understanding why cultures of patient safety in health care are so elusive.

Schein's model also is important for leaders and others who have more pragmatic and practical concerns, such as a prospective employee who wants to understand what it would be like to work in a particular organization or a manager who wants to align her organization with a changing environment. Schein provides conceptual tools and methods for leaders and managers who want to assess culture's deeper levels so that they can be more effective in solving sticky organizational problems and guiding and managing change.

Kathleen M. Sutcliffe

See also Meaning and Functions of Organizational Culture; Norms Theory; Organizational Culture and Effectiveness; Organizational Culture Theory; Process Consultation; Process Theories of Change

Further Readings

Deal, T. E., & Kennedy, A. A. (1982). *Corporate cultures.* Reading, MA: Addison-Wesley.

Hofstede, G. (1991). *Cultures and organizations.* London, England: McGraw-Hill.

Martin, J. (2002). *Organizational culture: Mapping the terrain.* Thousand Oaks, CA: Sage.

Peters, T. J., & Waterman, R. H. Jr. (1982). *In search of excellence.* New York, NY: Harper & Row.

Schein, E. H. (2010). *Organizational culture and leadership* (4th ed.). San Francisco, CA: Wiley.

Smircich, L. (1983). Concepts of culture and organizational analysis. *Administrative Science Quarterly, 28,* 339–358.

Vogus, T. J., Sutcliffe, K. M., & Weick, K. E. (2010, November). Doing no harm: Enabling, enacting, and elaborating a culture of safety in health care. *Academy of Management Perspectives,* 60–77.

Zohar, D., & Hofmann, D. A. (in press). Organizational culture and climate. In S. W. J Kozlowski (Ed.), *Oxford handbook of industrial and organizational psychology.* Oxford, England: Oxford University Press.

ORGANIZATIONAL CULTURE THEORY

In order to understand how and why organizations function and how various kinds of employees experience their working lives, researchers have to go beyond such frequently studied variables as structure, size, technology, job descriptions, reporting of relationships, and so on to also study cultures in organizations. Culture researchers have shown how our scholarly understanding can be expanded by examining aspects of everyday life in organizations, including informal behavioral norms, rituals, stories and jokes people tell, organization-specific jargon that employees invent, and the physical arrangements of work, such as architecture and interior decor. Cultural researchers examine the interpretations that employees attach to these cultural manifestations. These interpretations differ because employees' situations differ; the patterns of interpretation that underlie these manifestations constitute culture and relate in direct and contradictory ways to more commonly studied variables such as organizational structure as well as formal policies and practices. This entry defines manifestations of culture, reviews the evidence supporting three empirically grounded theories of culture, offers a theoretical overview that integrates these complementary views, and concludes with several research questions that have not yet been satisfactorily addressed.

Fundamentals

It is tricky to define culture in a way that includes the full variety of cultural theories, because the results of cultural studies have been contradictory. When forced to define culture, cultural researchers usually define culture quickly, often in consensual terms as some aspect of "shared values." However, since values can be espoused but not enacted, most cultural researchers consider it essential to study a wide variety of cultural manifestations, not just espoused values. And although culture is often defined as that which is shared on an organization-wide basis, recent studies have found extensive evidence that organization-wide consensus is rare and often confined to highly abstract, platitudinous ideas that are interpreted in varying ways. A few studies define culture in terms of espoused values and organization-wide consensus, excluding as "not culture" any data that do not fit this narrow definition. For all these reasons, definitions of culture can be misleading and can become self-fulfilling prophecies that blind researchers to data suggesting alternative points of view.

It is important, therefore, to regard definitions of culture with skepticism and look, instead, at what cultural researchers actually study, when they claim to be studying culture—in other words, scholars need to distinguish implicit and explicit (enacted) definitions and theories of culture and figure out which implicit theory of culture has guided a particular piece of research. Only then can we begin to understand why the results of cultural research have been so contradictory. This is not an ideal situation, but the results of cultural studies are plentiful and fascinating and well worth the effort of working toward cultural theory in an inductive manner.

Manifestations of Culture

The building blocks of any implicit cultural theory are the manifestations that a researcher chooses to study. The most important manifestations are defined below.

- Formal policies and practices are generally available in written form and include job definitions, reporting relationships, pay levels, promotion and evaluation criteria, and so on.
- Informal behavioral practices are norms of behavior. They may, and often do, conflict with formal policies and practices. Behavioral norms often differ among individuals and across groups of employees. For example, is overt conflict frowned upon or is it seen as an avenue to better decisions?
- A ritual is a scripted minidrama. It consists of a carefully executed sequence of activities, carried out in a social context (audience) with well-demarcated beginnings and endings (like a play) with well-defined roles for participants (like a script).
- Organizational stories are not personal anecdotes. They star organizational employees other than the storyteller and are often passed on from old employees to new. Morals of stories are often tacit, multiple, and inconsistent.
- Organizational jargon is the organization-specific language that only cultural insiders comprehend. For example, in innovative technology

companies, employees speak of "idea hamsters" and "bleeding edge" products.
- Humor includes irony and sarcasm. Ironically, work-related humor is usually unfunny to cultural outsiders.
- Physical arrangements include dress norms for various types of jobs, architecture, and decor, including whether work takes place in a dirty and noisy shop floor, a cubicle-filled open room, or relatively luxurious offices with closed doors.

Implicit in this list of cultural manifestations is the argument that culture is not just ideational. It includes material aspects of work (physical arrangements, pay levels). Culture also includes formal practices and policies, which reflect the verticality of a hierarchy, the numbers of reporting relationships managers have, and overall, the structure of an organization. It includes not just values, cognitions, and feelings but also how people actually behave. This is a broader definition of cultural manifestations than some assume, but without studying the material and structural attributes of work, behaviors as well as meanings and interpretations, a researcher simply cannot begin to understand why people think and feel as they do. A purely ideational approach to the study of culture is too constricted to offer deep and context-specific interpretation of the patterns of meaning that constitute culture. The wider the range of manifestations studied (generalist rather than specialist studies), the more enriched and insightful the cultural portrait is likely to be.

The Complexity of Culture

Richer, more complete studies acknowledge the complexity of cultural phenomena. Such studies seek depth of understanding. They do not simply assume that cultural phenomena generate organization-wide consensus, are internally consistent, or are clear. Instead, these studies consider degree and content of consensus, consistency, and clarity to be empirical questions. Each of these issues is discussed in more detail below.

Depth of Interpretation

Edgar Schein has cogently argued that the study of manifestations, by themselves, is not enough. A cultural portrait must have depth of understanding to see the patterns that underlie interpretations of any manifestation. He distinguishes three levels of depth: artifacts (which are labeled manifestations above), and two kinds of unifying themes of interpretation: values (such as the importance of egalitarianism or concern with product quality) and fundamental assumptions (such as whether one has a short- or long-term perspective or how much weight one puts on concern for others' well-being).

The difficulty with searching for fundamental, underlying assumptions is that if a researcher goes deep enough, he or she may find fundamental assumptions that are common to most members of a regional, industrial, or even national culture. This implies that cultural borders are permeable so that an organization should be seen as a nexus, where elements of the surrounding cultures come together. Some cultural attributes that surface in organizations may be unique to that organization, or at least distinctive, while others will reflect cultural differences in the larger society. Claims of cultural uniqueness or distinctiveness should be treated as an empirical question, because attributes that someone may believe are unique or distinctive may in fact be familiar to experienced observers of a wide range of organizations.

Degree of Consensus

Claims about organizational consensus are often overstated. A relatively large and representative sample of cultural members must be studied, if a researcher is going to generalize about an entire organization. Limited samples (such as studies of managers and professionals only) are studies of, at best, a subculture, not an entire firm. Organizations contain overlapping, nested subcultures. The boundaries of these subcultures cannot be assumed, although levels of a hierarchy (such as top executives, middle managers, and hourly employees), functional specializations (such as engineering and marketing or accounting), and demographic groupings (such as Hispanic employees) sometimes evolve into subcultures. Subcultures can reinforce each other, conflict, or simply exist independently. Some themes generate varied interpretations (ambiguity) without coalescing into any recognizable organization-wide or subcultural consensus.

Degree of Consistency

Another way to see patterns of interpretation is to examine whether one theme is consistent with another. For example, a concern for fiscal responsibility may be seen as inconsistent, at least by engineers, with a commitment to product quality. Meanings associated with one kind of manifestation may be inconsistent with another. For example, a formal policy may conflict with informal behavioral norms, as when overtime records are regularly falsified or expense account rules are disregarded. The patterns of meaning in a culture will include both consistencies and inconsistencies, and some cultural elements will be ambiguously related—neither consistent nor inconsistent. To focus only on the consistent elements of culture would require excluding much of the complexity of organizational life.

Degree of Clarity

Aspects of a culture can vary in their clarity. Sometimes, meanings and interpretations are clear, as when a formal policy is spelled out in explicit detail or a contract is drawn up. In other instances, what seems clear to one person may seem unclear to another. An aspect of a culture, for example, a theme that is expressed in highly abstract terms (such as "we have a deep concern for employee well-being") is open to a wide range of interpretations. Irony, sarcasm, ambivalence, ignorance, and paradox all create and express a lack of clarity. Although researchers may be fond of clarity and seek to write about cultures clearly, it cannot be assumed that clarity is an attribute of culture; rather, degree of clarity varies.

Three Implicit Theories of Culture

Three implicit theories of culture dominate cultural research. Many cultural studies, particularly in the United States, work with an implicit cultural theory of *integration*: that cultures in organizations are characterized by organization-wide consensus, internal consistency, and clarity. If not, this is tacitly considered an undesirable shortfall that should be remedied.

In contrast, *differentiation* studies show how status, functional specialization, contact (through, for example, project teams), and demographic commonalities create subcultures. These subcultures are seen as coexisting in harmony, conflict, and emotionally neutral independence, without much evidence of organization-wide consensus. Clarity and consistency can be found in these studies but only within the boundaries of a subculture.

Fragmentation studies portray ambiguity as the heart of culture, with little evidence of organization-wide and subcultural consensus. Multiple meanings generate ambiguities in these studies, showing irreconcilable tensions, paradox, and ironies. These fragmentation studies are characterized by lack of consensus, lack of consistency, and lack of clarity. Fragmentation is not the absence of culture; it offers an exploration of the ambiguities and uncertainties that are inherent in organizational life.

Importance

Each of these three implicit theories (integration, differentiation, and fragmentation) has produced a large body of supporting empirical evidence. Martin, reviewing this body of conflicting evidence, argued that because all three, apparently contradictory, theories have strong empirical grounding, any organization should show evidence supporting all three theoretical perspectives. A variety of authors, working in various industries and nonprofit settings, and in a variety of countries, showed that in any organization studied, evidence supporting all three theoretical perspectives, simultaneously, can be found. In support of integration theory, some interpretations generated organization-wide consensus, consistency, and clarity. In support of differentiation theory, other interpretations coalesced within subcultural boundaries. Still other interpretations reflected fragmentation theory, focused on ambiguities, and showed no evidence of consensus, consistency, or clarity. Thus, when a study shows support for, or assumes the validity of only one of the three theoretical perspectives, support for the other two implicit cultural theories would have been forthcoming, if a three-perspective theory of culture were utilized.

Future Directions for Research

Three implicit cultural theories have dominated research to date. Crucially important questions and problem areas remain insufficiently explored.

- Is there a fourth or a fifth viewpoint that would add something new?
- We have too few studies of cultural change, and those we have seldom explore how all three perspectives coexist and change. Our conceptualizations of change have been too narrow. Majken Schultz and Mary Jo Hatch have argued that organizations and their members constantly switch from one implicit cultural theory to another, with ease. Others posit that cultural change is not planned or discrete but a state of constant flux. Cultural change, planned and unplanned, is perhaps the arena most in need of research.
- There are abundant studies that claim that a culture has been successfully created, managed, or altered, often by a single leader. Such claims are very difficult to substantiate in an empirically convincing manner, as are claims of a link between some kind of culture (usually integrationist) and organizational effectiveness or profitability. Until solid evidence of such comforting claims is forthcoming, which may be unlikely, such claims should be regarded as unproven.
- Studies that use quantitative measures of culture (usually seeking to compare cultures) generally rely on researcher-created measures that may not reflect cultural attributes or interpretations considered important by cultural members.
- Many researchers have begun to explore overlaps between cultural and other theories, such as organizational identity, institutional theory, organizational ecology, and positive emotions in organizations. What other theoretical traditions might inform and be informed by cultural studies? Where else might the three perspectives of integration, differentiation, and fragmentation be applied?

Applications of Cultural Research

As suggested by the list of unresolved problems above, management should be very careful about moving, in any easy way, from theory to application in the cultural arena. In spite of the claims of many integrationist studies, cultures in organizations are seldom dominantly characterized by internally consistent, organizational-wide consensus around clear meanings and shared values, however attractive such ideas may be to executives who would like employees to share their viewpoints. The idea that a leader can create a culture, cast in his or her own image, is seductive but misleading—a potentially expensive way to approach planned change. Attempts to control or impose culture from the top down are not likely to succeed and may well generate a boomerang effect—resistance and skepticism. Claims of any link between particular kinds of culture and productivity or financial performance should be regarded as unproven, although obviously specific corporate goals or organizational strategies can have beneficial effects.

What, then, should managers do about culture? It is more effective to consider culture a lens for understanding the views and experiences of employees as they make sense of their surroundings in varying ways, depending on their place in the organization and the events and interpretations that emerge in their immediate contexts. Asking employees directly what their values and interpretations are is not useful; direct questions can elicit misleading answers that reflect job satisfaction, the social desirability of certain values, impression of management efforts, or general morale. Instead, an indirect approach (for example, asking employees to recount and interpret the meanings of organizational stories they have heard) can give a fuller and more honest cultural account. Because of the central importance of culture in organizational functioning, it is an expensive and time consuming, potentially dangerous strategy to accept and try to apply easy answers about what culture is and how it can be changed. The complexity of the evidence, and hence the theories of culture, need to be taken seriously.

Joanne Martin

See also Competing Values Framework; Cultural Intelligence; Managing Diversity; Organizational Assimilation Theory; Organizational Culture Model; Organizational Identity; Organizational Learning; Organizational Socialization

Further Readings

Frost, P. J., Moore, L. F., Louis, M. R., Lundberg, C. C., & Martin, J. (Eds.). (1991). *Reframing organizational culture.* Newbury Park, CA: Sage.

Martin, J. (2002). *Organizational culture: Mapping the terrain.* Thousand Oaks, CA: Sage.

Meyerson, D. (1994). Interpretations of stress in organizations: The cultural production of ambiguity and burnout. *Administrative Science Quarterly, 39,* 628–653.

Schein, E. (1985). *Organizational culture and leadership.* San Francisco, CA: Jossey-Bass.

Schultz, M., & Hatch, M. J. (1996). Living with multiple paradigms: The case of paradigm interplay in organizational culture studies. *Academy of Management Review, 21,* 529–557.

Van Maanen, J., & Barley, S. (1984). Occupational communities: Culture and control in organizations. In B. Staw & L. Cummings (Eds.), *Research in organizational behavior* (Vol. 6, pp. 287–366). Greenwich, CT: JAI.

Van Maanen, J., & Kunda, G. (1989). "Real feelings": Emotional expression and organizational culture. In B. Staw & L. Cummings (Eds.), *Research in organizational behavior* (Vol. 6, pp. 43–103). Greenwich, CT: JAI.

ORGANIZATIONAL DEMOGRAPHY

Organizational demography theory maintains that while it may be somewhat overstated to argue that demography is destiny, many organizational processes are profoundly affected by the distribution of demographic characteristics in the workforce. Therefore, it is incumbent on managers to understand demographic effects and focus on managing demography as one lever to effect organizational functioning. As one example, demographic diversity, for instance, in age or organizational tenure, can lead to intercohort conflict and, as a result, problems with communication and integration among employees and increased turnover. As another example, the age distribution of the workforce has important implications for medical costs, pension costs, and the need to recruit replacements for retiring workers, illustrating the important effect of demography on personnel planning. Women's career processes depend, in part, on the proportion of women in the company. Rosabeth Moss Kanter described the problems confronting women who were so few in number as to be tokens, while other research has shown the effects of the proportion of women on salaries (other things being equal, higher proportions of women lead to lower pay) and on the likelihood of women reaching senior executive ranks (greater numbers of women, particularly in management, lead to enhanced promotion chances for women). By focusing attention on manageable, observable, distributional characteristics of the work force, organizational demography emphasizes the effect of "facts on the ground" properties on organizational management. This entry explores the definition and measurement of organizational demography, some of its substantive predictions, and considers its importance and place in management research and practice.

Fundamentals

Organizational demography borrowed its essential insight—that demographic distributions could shed light on important social processes—from analyses that had typically occurred at the level of societies or other geographic units. For instance, it is well known that people's spending and saving patterns vary with their age, a fact that has implications for a country's asset prices—when the percentage of the population at an age to begin liquidating savings for living expenses rises, there will be a downward push on asset values—as well as levels and patterns of consumption, because people in their childbearing and rearing years spend money differently from those either younger or older. Political attitudes are somewhat age dependent, so the conservatism or liberalism of an area depends in part on the age distribution of its population. A recent example of cohort effects on political decisions is attitudes toward gay marriage. In part because of their greater familiarity with acknowledged gays, younger people are much more likely than older ones, at least in the United States, to favor the legalization of gay marriage and other laws that provide equal rights. This fact has led to a steady increase in the legalization of gay marriage as older voters die off and are replaced by younger ones and also to the observation that the legalization of marriage among gays is only a matter of time, as each new cohort exhibits higher support for this policy than the one before it. As another example of societal-level demographic effects, the rate of intermarriage across racial or religious groups depends on the relative size of the groups—other things being equal, those in a relatively small group are more likely to marry outsiders because the odds of meeting someone from one's own group is smaller simply as a function of relative group size.

But perhaps the most fundamental theoretical insight from demography relevant to understanding organizational processes is the importance of cohort effects. Groups of people who share a similar, and potent, experience at a formative time in their lives will tend to have similar views and, as a consequence of the shared experience and attitudinal similarity, will bond together more than they will with others that have not had the same life course similarities.

One can observe cohort effects on societies: People who went through the Great Depression have different attitudes toward debt, saving, and consumption than those that never experienced that financial trauma. Cohort effects also occur in companies: People present at an organization's founding are bound together in ways that later entrants are not.

Organizational demography proceeds from the well-established principle that similarity is a fundamentally important basis of interpersonal attraction and that many organizational processes and interpersonal processes within organizations reflect a preference for homogeneity. Similarity is defined not just by homogeneity in attitudes and values but also by similarity in age, organizational tenure, educational and occupational background, race, and gender. Because of the preference for similarity, organizations are more homogeneous than the workforce as a whole. A related perspective, upper-echelons theory, argues that educational and functional background imprints executives with a perspective on the world, including the information to which they pay the most attention, that affects their strategic choices. The fundamental presumption is, then, that organizational decisions and processes can be predicted, at least to some extent, by the demographic characteristics of the relevant groups.

Because similarity is such a fundamental concept in organizational demography, the measurement and operationalization of similarity is crucial. Various measures have been employed, including the Gini index and the coefficient of variation, both of which measure the degree of inequality and variation, and a measure of Euclidean distance between a given person and others in the group. One important hypothesis is that groups that are more dissimilar, that have greater heterogeneity or distance among members, will experience (a) more difficulties in communication, (b) less social integration and cohesion, (c) more conflict, and, as a consequence, (d) higher levels of turnover. This is a group-level prediction about turnover rates and also about a number of intermediate processes including communication frequency and conflict that affect turnover. A related hypothesis holds that the greater the diversity at the level of the work unit, the lower the level of psychological attachment exhibited by group members. At the individual level of analysis, the hypothesis is that it is those individuals who are most dissimilar to and socially distant from the others in their work unit who are the most likely to leave and to be the least committed to their work unit.

The effects of demographic similarity also play out at the dyadic level. The hypothesis is that to the extent that superiors and subordinates are more similar along demographic characteristics, such as race, age, education, and so forth, the higher the performance ratings subordinates will receive, the less role ambiguity they will experience, and the greater liking there will be in the superior-subordinate pairs.

A second line of argument hypothesizes that the relative size of demographic groups determines their power. One hypothesis consistent with this line of reasoning is that the higher the proportion of women in more senior leadership ranks, the greater the likelihood that—controlling for other things such as years of experience, education, and performance—women will be promoted and receive raises. Another hypothesis consistent with such reasoning would be that the higher the proportion of people with low (or high) number-of-years-of-service in a unit, the greater their power, as assessed by representation on important committees and task forces, influence on decisions, and formal governance arrangements that provide them more or less control over decisions.

The third set of hypotheses proceeds from arguments about the effects of demographic backgrounds on strategic decision making. For instance, in one study, researchers argued and found that top management groups with lower average age, shorter organizational tenures, more education, and more heterogeneity in educational specialization were more likely to lead organizations that undertook greater strategic change. Another study examined the effect of top management team demography on innovation, also finding that educational heterogeneity was associated with banks being more innovative.

Importance

The publication of the first theoretical arguments about organizational demography in the early 1980s stimulated quite a bit of empirical research. As already noted, upper-echelons theory, which also argued for the importance of demographic characteristics of the top team, appeared at approximately the same time. Research in the organizational demography tradition generally supported the predictions. This is not surprising, as similarity is such a fundamental basis of interpersonal relationships and such an important factor in understanding the working of many organizational processes ranging from recruiting through social networks to appraisals of others' job performance.

Concepts related to organizational demography continue to appear in both the research and the popular literatures. For instance, the fact of the baby boom following the end of World War II means that the coming years will see many exits from the workforce as people from that generation retire or die. In some industries that have not grown over the years, including parts of the public sector, the oil and gas industry and the nuclear power industry, replacing the knowledge and skills of those about to leave their organizations is a subject of discussion in personnel planning efforts. There has been much discussion, and many books and articles have been written, about cohort effects on job preferences, work values, and, when cohorts with important differences have to coexist, intercohort conflicts. Discussion of the millennials, generation X, and so forth implicitly acknowledge the importance of cohorts and cohort effects as well as the possibility of intercohort conflict and resulting organizational stresses and strains.

Nonetheless, it seems fair to state that not much empirical work currently proceeds from organizational demography ideas. After about 15 years of great empirical attention, the research focus in management has moved on to other topics. But as the examples of replacement and work values that vary across cohorts illustrate, demography remains a substantively important way of understanding organizational processes.

At the same time, it should be acknowledged that particularly the original work on organizational demography was not without its critics. Demographic processes presumably work *through* various mechanisms such as the tendency to communicate with similar others, to share an orientation to the world with those of your same cohort, and so forth. Much, although certainly not all, of the research on organizational demography explored demographic effects on outcomes such as turnover or individual-level organizational attachment without measuring the intervening processes and mechanisms that presumably produced those effects. As originally proposed, that shortcut was one advantage of organizational demography: Demographic information was generally accessible and did not require the collection of communication, attitudinal, or other data in order to predict and explain a number of important organizational-level outcomes. But that shortcut also left much demographic work showing somewhat impoverished, as researchers did not always go on to answer the question of *why* demographic effects actually occurred.

Because of the importance of demographic processes and because the mechanisms through which such processes have yet to be fully empirically explored, organizational demography remains a substantively important and fertile area for management research as well as a crucial focus for human resource and other management professionals.

Jeffrey Pfeffer

See also Attraction-Selection-Attrition Model; Decision-Making Styles; High-Performing Teams; Managing Diversity; Multicultural Work Teams; Upper-Echelons Theory

Further Readings

Bantel, K. A., & Jackson, S. E. (1989). Top management and innovations in banking: Does the composition of the top team make a difference? *Strategic Management Journal, 10,* 107–124.

Blau, P. M. (1977). *Inequality and heterogeneity.* New York, NY: Free Press.

Gruenfeld, D. H., & Tiedens, L. Z. (2010). Organizational preferences and their consequences. In S. T. Fiske, D. T. Gilbert, & G. Lindzey (Eds.), *Handbook of social psychology* (Vol. 2, 5th ed., pp. 1252–1287). New York, NY: Wiley.

Hambrick, D. C., & Mason, P. (1984). Upper echelons: The organization as a reflection of its top managers. *Academy of Management Review, 9,* 193–206.

Kanter, R. M. (1977). *Men and women of the corporation.* New York, NY: Basic Books.

O'Reilly, C. A., Caldwell, D. F., & Barnett, W. P. (1989). Work group demography, social integration, and turnover. *Administrative Science Quarterly, 34,* 21–37.

Pfeffer, J. (1983). Organizational demography. In L. L. Cummings & B. M. Staw (Eds.), *Research in organizational behavior* (Vol. 5, pp. 299–357). Greenwich, CT: JAI Press.

Tsui, A. S., & O'Reilly, C. A., III (1989). Beyond simple demographic effects: The importance of relational demography in superior-subordinate dyads. *Academy of Management Journal, 32,* 402–423.

Wagner, W. G., Pfeffer, J., & O'Reilly, C. A., III (1984). Organizational demography and turnover in top-management groups. *Administrative Science Quarterly, 29,* 74–92.

Wiersema, M. F., & Bantel, K. A. (1993). Top management team demography and corporate strategic change. *Academy of Management Journal, 36,* 996–1025.

ORGANIZATIONAL DEVELOPMENT

Organizational development (OD) is a process of planned change in an organization that is (a) systemwide, (b) based on open system theory and the application of behavioral science knowledge, (c) involving organizational members in the process, (d) long-range (months if not years), (e) grounded in humanistic values, (f) aimed toward modification of the organization's culture, and (g) intended to improve an organization's capacity for managing change and development in the future. Even though this definition of OD is rather elaborate, it does not capture the essence of what this field is all about. What follows in the next section, Fundamentals, therefore, is coverage of the theory, conceptual frameworks, and practice that compose the field of OD. Fundamentals is then followed by a section on education and professional development; in other words, how does one learn about OD? In the next section, on the evolution of OD, the entry answers the question, Where did OD come from? And then in the final section, the question of OD's importance is addressed. References that are primary to this coverage of OD are provided at the end.

Fundamentals

The content and substance of OD may be considered in three categories: *theory, conceptual frameworks,* and *practice.*

Theory

There is no all-encompassing, singular theory of OD. Although not a theory of OD or organizational change as such, most OD practitioners think nevertheless in terms of open system theory, that is, an organization has *input* from its external environment and translates that input into *throughput* within the organization; thus, throughput is producing a service and/or product, which in turn becomes *output* to the consumer, and the output—performance, sales, profit, consumer satisfaction, and so on—becomes feedback for the organization in the form of input and the cycle continues. For most OD practitioners, the metaphor of choice is an organism. An organization can be considered as a living, breathing organism that for survival is dependent on its external environment. Thus, astute practitioners start with external forces in the organization's environment— for example, the marketplace, competitors, changing technology, or workforce talent. This metaphor, organism, goes hand-in-hand with open systems theory, which comes from cell biology. Comparisons between a living cell and an organization help to explain and understand certain concepts associated with change—chaos, disequilibrium, self-organizing, and the like.

Although there is no all-encompassing theory of OD, there are a number of minitheories that underlie the field. *Mini* in this case means that the theory relates to some aspect of OD but not to its entirety. Together and across three organizational levels, these minitheories provide a foundation. From an *individual* perspective, theories of motivation are relevant as is research on job satisfaction and reward systems. From a *group* perspective, Kurt Lewin's work on norms and values, the work of Chris Argyris on interpersonal competence and organizational learning, and Wilfrid Bion's theory on the collective unconscious undergird OD practice. And from a *total system* perspective, Rensis Likert's focus on consensus and participative management, the work of Paul Lawrence and Jay Lorsch on contingency theory regarding organizational structure, and Edgar Schein's contribution on organizational culture provide additional theoretical foundation for the field of OD.

Conceptual Frameworks

Experienced OD practitioners follow a framework for their work that is based on a concept that is known as *action research*. This means that OD practice is data based. Data are collected from the organization and the action that follows—a change intervention—is derived from the data that were collected in the first place. These data can be summaries of interviews, survey results, archival information, observations, or combinations of these methods. The practice of OD therefore follows Kurt Lewin's dictum: "No action without research and no research without action."

OD practitioners also rely on organizational models, conceptual frameworks that depict and help to simplify a large, complex organizational system. Four such models are the most common ones: Marvin Weisbord's six-box model, perhaps the most popular one in OD practice, consists of (a) purposes, (b) structure, (c) rewards, (d) helpful mechanisms, (e) and relationships, all surrounding (f) leadership, the coordinating function, in the center of a circle. David A. Nadler and M. L. Tushman's congruence model incorporates many of Weisbord's "boxes" and adds more complexity as does Noel Tichy's organizational model which emphasizes levers (boxes) for change. The fourth and more recent model is by Burke and George H. Litwin, which relies, like the other three, on open systems theory. Burke and Litwin propose that organizational performance and change should be viewed as either transformational or transactional so that appropriate action can be taken based on the scope of the change effort.

Conceptual frameworks for how planned organizational change should occur also exist. John Kotter has developed an eight-stage process, including such components as creating a sense of urgency, developing a vision and strategy, and so on. Jerry Porras and Robert Silver's in their framework suggest that cognitive change precedes behavioral change, whereas Burke, relying on the James-Lange theory, takes the opposite view that behavior change should precede attitude and changes in one's mental set. The debate about which comes first can be summarized: Organizational change should begin with an attempt to change people's thinking—their beliefs and attitudes—then behavioral change will follow versus an attempt to change organizational members' behavior initially, and subsequently, their attitudes will shift.

Practice

Most practitioners in OD ground their consultation in Kurt Lewin's three-phase model. The initial phase, *unfreezing*, consists of activities that (a) test the organization's readiness and motivation for change and (b) attempt to confront the organization, particularly executives and managers, with relevant forces in the external environment (changes in technology, consumer unrest, competition, and the like) that need to be considered and dealt with for long-term survival and effectiveness. This latter point, in short, can be referred to as "creating a sense of urgency." The second phase, *changing,* refers to movement in the organization toward change goals, that is, planned interventions in the system that facilitate this action (movement) toward the change goal(s) such as team building, creating or revising the organization's mission and strategy, inter-unit conflict resolution, survey feedback, structural modifications, and so on. The third and final phase, *refreezing,* is a matter of integrating the changes into daily operations and management of the organization. Integrating mechanisms can be a new reward and incentive system linked to new directions, a new strategy for dealing with consumer dissatisfaction, revised information technology system, launching a six-sigma initiative to improve quality, and so forth.

Others such as Edgar Schein have elaborated on Lewin's three-phase model by explaining the importance of providing psychological safety for organizational members during the unfreezing phase. Other phased models have been developed as well, such as the one by Richard Beckhard and Reuben T. Harris on transitions, that is, defining the *present state* of the organization, then moving toward the change goal—that is, the *transition state*—and establishing the change objectives which lead to the *future state.* William Bridges developed another transition model which describes the importance of *endings* (leaving the present state), moving through a *neutral zone,* and then adopting *new beginnings.* Bridges explains the behavior required for each of these three phases for ultimate realization of the change both at an individual as well as organizational level. The term *phase* is deliberate, that is, these steps are not discrete but blend into each other.

From the standpoint of what specific steps and actions the OD practitioner takes, a sequencing process has also been described. Although there are some language differences, most frameworks follow a sequence of *entry*—establishing contract and rapport with the client, that is, the person(s) in the organization responsible for the change initiative (the actual change agent)—*contracting*—an agreement, usually in writing, on what both the OD practitioner and the client are going to do, including what the outcomes are expected to be. Next is *data gathering*—collecting data from and about the organization—then *diagnosis*—analyzing the data and providing some interpretation and *feedback*—reporting to the client a summary of the data, organized and analyzed. *Intervention* follows—taking action steps that are based on the diagnosis. *Evaluation* questions include, did the intervention(s) result in the intended outcome? *Separation* concludes the consultation on the part of the OD practitioner in a satisfactory manner for both parties, the practitioner and the client.

A satisfactory conclusion will probably mean that the interventions conducted in the organization met the three criteria for effectiveness specified by Chris Argyris. He stated that to be effective an intervention must (a) provide valid and useful information—valid meaning the client agrees that the data underlying the action accurately reflect the state of the organization at the time and that independent diagnoses lead to the same intervention; (b) be one of free choice—the client makes the decision regarding the action to be taken; and (c) lead to internal commitment—the client has a sense of ownership of the choice(s) made and feels responsible for implementation.

Examples of OD interventions by organizational level include the following: *individual*—coaching, job/work redesign, and training and development; *teams and groups*—process consultation, role negotiation, appreciative inquiry, responsibility charting, team building, and virtual teams; *intergroup relations*—intergroup conflict resolution and cross-functional task forces; and *total organization*—large group interventions, survey feedback, strategic planning, and implementation.

Before ending this section, a final note of clarification regarding OD practice is required. The planning of OD work is a linear process—Phase 1 followed by Phase 2, and so on, but the implementation of organizational development and change is anything but linear. Organization change rarely goes according to plan. The process is usually messy, chaotic, and frustrating. People simply don't behave according to plan. Keeping the change goal(s) clearly in mind, practitioners must (a) assume that unanticipated reactions to and unintended consequences of change interventions are to be expected and (b) immediately attend to these reactions and consequences by correcting mistakes, reordering priorities, paying more attention to the political processes, and reminding organizational members about what aspects of the organization will *not* be changing as well as those that will be affected. Not attending to these unintended consequences and unexpected reactions to the change initiatives causes a slowdown if not reversal to the plans, and momentum is lost.

Evolution

Evolution rather than "birth" is a better characterization of the beginnings of OD; in other words, where did OD come from? Three precursors were extremely important to the evolution of OD: sensitivity training, sociotechnical systems, and survey feedback.

Sensitivity Training

Two versions of this educational process of group dynamics emerged around the same time, circa 1946, on either side of the Atlantic. On the American side, it was the T-group (T for training in laboratory training) and developed by the National Training Laboratories, at that time a department within the Adult Education Division of the National Education Association. On the British side, it was the *human reactions* conference, a major arm of the Tavistock Institute in London. The theoretical father and founder of the T-group was Lewin, whereas the *human relations* conference's theoretical father and founder was Bion. Both versions emphasize individual change and are composed of eight to twelve people in a group who consider the primary source of learning the behavior of the group members themselves. A major difference between the two versions is that the T-group focus is on interpersonal relations and individual feedback whereas the human relations conference emphasis is on issues of authority, roles, and boundaries.

Some 15 years after the emergence of the T-group, this form of education and training began to be used as a lever for change in organizations. Sensitivity training with members of the same organization was composed of a cross section of the organization so that individuals would not be in a group with their work-unit colleagues. The assumption was that if a critical mass of organizational members were trained, then the organization itself would change. Such interventions in the 1950s were conducted in Union Carbide with Douglas McGregor in the lead and at Esso (now Exxon-Mobil) and at the Naval Ordnance Test Station, China Lake, California.

This kind of training later became known as team building.

Also during the 1950s decade, McGregor and Beckhard, consulting with the General Mills company, introduced teamwork activities in various plants. They referred to their work as "bottom-up" management but eventually did not like the term and instead chose "organization development." Others (Herbert Shepard, Henry Kolb, and Robert R. Blake) were doing similar work at Esso. They eventually also adopted the label of organization development to describe their change work.

Sociotechnical Systems

Also during the 50s decade, creative work regarding change in organizations was emerging. Eric Trist and Ken Bamforth of the Tavistock Institute were consulting with a coal mining company in northern England. The company had installed a new method of mining that was supposed to increase productivity, but the opposite had occurred. Trist and Bamforth found that the new technology had affected the way the miners had worked together—from a team effort to a more individualistic mode of mining the coal. The company had installed new machinery but paid little attention to the impact this change would have on the way the miners worked together. Teamwork was very important to them. Trist and Bamforth suggested to the company executives that they rearrange the operations so that a form of teamwork could be installed again: in other words, to pay equal attention to the social implications of the change not just the technological intervention. Following the consultants advice the executives experienced a significant increase in productivity coupled with a significant decrease of absenteeism among the miners. From the standpoint of organizational change, what emerged as a consequence of the consulting effort of Trist and Bamforth was the concept of sociotechnical systems and that an organization is simultaneously a social and a technical system. The early bias of OD was toward the social system, but by the 1960s, it was clear that both subsystems and their interactions must be considered for effective organizational change to occur.

Survey Feedback

The subdisciplines of psychology that have helped to shape OD are industrial-organizational psychology and social psychology. Survey feedback emerged from both of these subdisciplines. Again, around 1946, at the University of Michigan, Likert founded the Survey Research Center. And with the premature death of Lewin at that time, his Center for Group Dynamics at Massachusetts Institute of Technology (MIT) was moved to the University of Michigan, also under the direction of Likert. These two centers became the basis for the establishment of the Institute for Social Research at Michigan with Likert as its first director. Survey feedback therefore emerged from the combined expertise of the two centers—survey work and group dynamics. Within a year of the institute's beginnings, questionnaires (surveys) were in use to assess for organizations' employee morale and attitudes. A member of the institute and colleague of Likert was Floyd Mann. He had noted that when surveys were conducted in organizations and data were summarized and analyzed little was done with the information. Unless managers discussed the survey results with their subordinates nothing happened, no improvement in the workplace occurred. Moreover, without discussion and action taken, matters would often become worse, that is, for example, frustration on the part of employees would arise with their having taken the time to answer the survey and then never hearing anything about the findings. Mann developed a systematic way of dealing with this problem. First, a survey would be conducted with all employees in the organization, including management. Second, a reporting of the survey results in summary form would be provided for all those who had answered the survey, in other words, "feedback." The feedback occurred in phases, beginning with the top executives and then passed downward via the formal hierarchy and within units or work teams. Mann referred to this cascading process as the "interlocking chain of conferences." Each work unit received two sets of feedback—a summary of the overall organizational results and a summary of its unit's results. And each manager would participate in this process twice—as the manager of his or her work unit and as a member of his boss's work unit, that is, the interlocking chain to use Mann's words. Third, once the feedback was discussed, analyzed, and understood, the manager with his or her work unit members would then plan action steps for improvement based on the data from the survey.

These three precursors—sensitivity training, sociotechnical systems, and survey feedback—were central to the emergence of OD. While sensitivity training, as such, is no longer a commonly used intervention in OD, its roots are in the form of team building today. Sociotechnical systems and survey feedback as originally conceptualized and applied remain much the same today as when they both originated.

Finally, it should be noted that there are other precursors to OD such as the research that was conducted at the Hawthorne Works of Western Electric in the late 1920s and early 30s and the even earlier works of Frederick W. Taylor, but the three summarized in this section were the ones that had the greatest impact on the formation of OD.

Importance

When OD emerged in the late 1950s and into the following decade, there was excitement and enthusiasm about this burgeoning field. And much of the promise associated with OD has been realized. Research regarding the effectiveness of OD as a mode of change has been more positive than negative, OD practitioner groups and networks are plentiful, the field is more global today, the literature on OD continues to flourish, there are numerous academic programs on OD in colleges and universities, and the Organization Development and Change Division of the Academy of Management is very much alive and well.

Occasionally, a course on OD may be taught at the undergraduate level in a college or university but more typically is at the graduate level. There are at least three options for aspiring OD practitioners. One option is simply to take a course, say, an elective in a graduate program at the master's level (MBA, MPA, for example). A second option is to enroll in a graduate program, either master's or doctoral, such as organizational psychology, organizational behavior, or industrial-organizational psychology and concentrate on OD-related courses, such as organizational change, group dynamics, conflict management and resolution, coaching and counseling, and organizational dynamics and theory. Some universities offer a degree program, master's or doctorate devoted to OD, which is a third option.

Programs that provide a certificate but not a degree are plentiful in the United States. Colleges and universities offer such programs as well as organizations, profit and nonprofit, that are in the business of some form of training and development. Also, these kinds of organizations and institutes often provide conferences of 2 or 3 days devoted to OD, and some offer professional-development workshops just prior to the larger conference that focus on OD or some aspect of OD, such as team building, conflict management, coaching, and so on. Because OD is a field of study and practice and not a profession, choosing an educational route or professional development option is not all that obvious. It is therefore wise for an aspiring OD practitioner to seek advice from more experienced practitioners about such choices. In any case, attending a 1-or-2-day workshop on OD to see if this is a field that one would want to pursue is usually a good idea.

Yet if we examine the definition of OD provided in the opening paragraph of this entry, particularly parts that refer to systemwide, long-term, cultural modification and to increasing capacity for managing change, involving all organizational members, we would have to conclude that very few OD efforts conform to and realize these objectives. Most OD practitioners use the processes and techniques that the field comprises, such as team building, conflict management, survey feedback, appreciative inquiry, and multirater feedback systems, but in the end, they do not practice OD strictly according to certain aspects of the definition of the field—systemwide change and especially those aspects concerning culture change. Moreover, recent evidence has shown that organizational change efforts whether planned or not rarely succeed. The failure rate approaches 70%, and for mergers and acquisitions, it is even higher, approximately 75%.

The promise of OD yet to be realized is that the practice does not adequately match the need. How can OD better match this need? By paying much more attention to six areas that have been neglected, according to Larry Greiner and Thomas Cummings; these are: top management decision making, strategy formulation, mergers and acquisitions, globalization, alliance and virtual organizations, and corporate governance and personal integrity. The practice of OD has much to offer in each of these six areas. And involvement in these areas would help to ensure OD's relevance for the future.

W. Warner Burke

See also Action Research; Force Field Analysis and Model of Planned Change; Large Group Interventions; Learning Organization; Process Consultation; Punctuated Equilibrium Model; Strategies for Change; Systems Theory of Organizations

Further Readings

Bradford, D. L., & Burke, W. W. (Eds.). (2005). *Reinventing organization development: New approaches to change in organizations.* San Francisco, CA: Pfeiffer/ Wiley.

Burke, W. W. (1994). *Organization development: A process of learning and changing* (2nd ed.). Reading, MA: Addison-Wesley.

Burke, W. W. (2011). *Organization change: Theory and practice* (3rd ed.). Thousand Oaks, CA: Sage.

Cummings, T. G. (Ed.). (2008). *Handbook of organization development.* Thousand Oaks, CA: Sage.

Greiner, L. E., & Cummings, T. G. (2004). OD: Wanted more alive than dead. *Journal of Applied Behavioral Science, 40*(4), 374–391.

Lewin, K. (1951). *Field theory in social science.* New York, NY: Harper.

Marrow, A. J. (1969). *The practical theorist: The life and work of Kurt Lewin.* New York, NY: Basic Books.

Porras, J. I., & Robertson, P. J. (1992). Organizational development: Theory, practice and research. In M. D. Dunnelte & L. M. Hough (Eds.), *Handbook of industrial and organizational psychology* (2nd ed., Vol. 3, pp. 719–822). Palo Alto, CA: Consulting Psychologists Press.

Rioch, M. (1970). The work of Wilford Bion on groups. *Psychiatry, 33,* 56–66.

Schein, E. H. (1988). *Process consultation: Its role in organization development* (Vol. 1). Reading, MA: Addison-Wesley.

ORGANIZATIONAL ECOLOGY

Organizational ecology is a research paradigm in organizational sociology that provides a theoretical framework for analyzing the evolutionary dynamics of organizations. Organizational ecology builds on a core sociological premise that concerns the duality of actor and position—the behavior of social actors is shaped by their position in social structure but, *collectively,* the behavior of actors *over time* also spawns and effectively constitutes the parameters of social structure. The collective nature of the process requires that all relevant social actors are observed at once as members of a certain population—a mandate which calls for an ecological approach. And to make the dynamic nature of the process analytically tractable requires the use of evolutionary theories. Organizational ecology originated with Michael T. Hannan and John Freeman's 1977 programmatic paper and has since grown to comprise multiple theories that study how the evolving interdependence among organizations both shapes and is shaped by the features of social structure. The three central theoretical lenses of the field are discussed below along with their evolution and contemporary relevance.

Fundamentals

Density-Dependent Legitimation and Competition

Density-dependence theory posits that the evolution of new organizational populations is driven by two processes (legitimation and competition) that are hard to observe directly but are both driven by the proliferation of organizations that belong to the population. The two processes operate concurrently but with different strength. In the formative years of a population, increases at low-level density drive legitimacy more than competition, while the opposite occurs when density increases at high levels.

Legitimation is a process by which an organizational form becomes institutionalized in the sense that it attains a taken-for-granted social standing. This process entails the formation of social and cultural rules that define the form's identity until the form itself becomes an institutionalized blueprint for organizing and conducting social action. Unlike legalization, which has specific bureaucratic-legal implications explicitly stated in a regulatory framework, legitimation is a broader social phenomenon that takes time to develop. Its dynamics are hard to observe directly. In ecological theory, the diffusion process by which the social audience learns about and becomes accustomed to a new type of organization is driven by that type's proliferation (organizational population density); hence, constitutive legitimation is known as density-dependent legitimation. The competitive process measured by

population density captures the diffuse competition among organizations. Similar organizations exhibit resource homogeneity and thus seek to acquire the same resources. Even if these organizations are unaware of each other's existence or do not view each other as direct competitors, their resource homogeneity means that they compete indirectly or diffusely. The greater the number of organizations with homogeneous resource dependence, the more intense the competition for resources among them becomes. Formally, the theory predicts that density increases legitimation at a decreasing rate (until a form becomes taken-for-granted and the ceiling effect of legitimacy is reached) and competition at an increasing rate. The empirical predictions based on these relationships with respect to organizational foundings and failures predict a U-shape between density and mortality and an inverted U-shape between density and foundings. In other words, low-level increases in population density improve survival chances and stimulate new foundings (legitimation), but high-level increases in density elevate failure hazards and depress new organization building (competition).

Niche Width and Resource Partitioning Theory

As Hannan and Freeman originally explained, the *niche width* of an organization refers to the variance in its pattern of resource utilization. In terms of this concept, organizations pursuing strategies based on performance over a wide range of environmental resources possess a wide niche and are classified as generalists. Organizations following strategies based on performance within a tight band of resources are considered specialists—their niches are narrow. Organizational ecology contains two major theory fragments based on niche width, the original theory of Hannan and Freeman, and Glenn R. Carroll's 1985 theory of resource partitioning. It is confusing that the two theories use the generalist-specialist concept in somewhat different but related ways. Each reflects an intuition about resource utilization but makes different assumptions about how resources are distributed and related. This distinction is clarified below.

The original theory of organizational niche width addresses what Freeman and Hannan call the "Jack-of-all-trades" problem; namely, how does an organization cope with the demands of many different (or changing) environmental conditions when only one is confronted at any particular point in time. According to a 1983 article by Freeman and Hannan, niche width reflects "tradeoffs between tolerance of widely varying conditions and capacity for high performance in any particular situation. Specialist populations follow the strategy of betting all their fitness chips on specific outcomes; generalists hedge their bets" (p. 1119).

The original theory builds on the observation that a specialist organization designed well for a particular environmental state will always outperform a generalist in that same state. This is so because the generalist organization must carry extra capacity—appearing as slack at any point—that allows it to perform adequately in other environmental states. To quote Hannan and Freeman's seminal 1977 article, the specialist "maximizes its exploitation of the environment and accepts the risk of having that environment change," while the generalist "accepts a lower level of exploitation in return for greater security" (p. 948). This theory of niche width predicts that specialists do better in environments that are stable or certain and in environments where change is *fine grained* (short durations in environmental states). However, when environmental variation is high and *coarse* (long durations in states), specialists have trouble outlasting the long unfavorable periods, and the generalist strategy conveys advantage. The original niche width theory assumes that environmental resources and conditions are disjointed or highly dissimilar. Because of this assumed dissimilarity, generalist organizations that straddle two different resource pockets, or conditions, pay a price in terms of overhead or excess capacity.

Resource-partitioning theory uses a different assumption about environmental resources. It holds that the different pockets, or conditions, are not so dissimilar. This shift is important because when environments are not so dissimilar, generalists may not be burdened by the straddle (as they are in original niche width theory). In fact, they may actually benefit from it because participation in more than one environmental state may entail advantageous economies—activities common to participation in both states can be conducted on a larger scale. Scale differences may also arise because some environmental states are blessed with higher resource levels (original niche width theory implicitly assumes a balanced distribution across

states), again yielding economies to the larger firms. Moreover, these economies of scale and scope might be so strong that they outweigh any overhead costs or the like, thus, giving the overall advantage to the generalist organization. This seems especially likely when the different environmental states do not alternate across time, as in original niche theory, but instead can be experienced simultaneously. Carroll's resource-partitioning theory uses insights about economies of scale to make different predictions about niche width based on this second type of generalism. Research in this direction shows that smaller organizations sometimes find ways to avoid the severe pressures of direct scale competition by identifying and exploiting market segments or product-space locations that are too obscure and small to be exploited profitably by very large organizations.

The theoretical imagery of resource partitioning relies on notions of crowding among organizations in a market characterized as a finite set of heterogeneous resources. Organizations initially attempt to find a viable position within this market by targeting their products to various resource segments. Specialist organizations choose narrow homogenous targets, while generalist organizations choose targets composed of heterogeneous segments. It is essential to the theory that environmental resources are distributed in a particular way. It is also essential that some aspect of product delivery in the market possesses a scale advantage; this is typically envisioned as a strong economy of scale in production, marketing, or distribution. Resource-partitioning theory assumes that environmental resources are distributed across multiple dimensions. Each dimension consists of states or a smooth gradient of states, a combination of which are experienced simultaneously by organizations. That is, every firm is located within a particular region of multidimensional environmental space. The theory assumes that environmental resources are unevenly distributed within each dimension, with a unimodal peak. The distribution of resources along each dimension is assumed to be roughly symmetric around that peak. In the joint distribution of all relevant dimensions, a unimodal peak is also assumed; it represents what is called "the market center." This distribution means that some environmental areas are much more bountiful or lucrative than others, providing potential scale advantages to those located there.

When scale advantages are strong and the resource distribution is unimodal, the center of the market will be populated mainly with generalists. In the competition among these generalists, relative size becomes increasingly important. Competition among generalist organizations consists of an escalating war for resources based on scale, with larger generalists eventually outcompeting smaller ones. When the smaller generalists fail, their target markets become free resources. Generalists occupying adjacent regions hold the best positions for securing these newly available areas, and they typically do so. The surviving generalist thus becomes larger and more general, occupying the market center.

The main device for explaining the rise of specialist firms in resource-partitioning theory involves the resource space that lies outside the generalist target areas. It is here, away from the intense competitive pressure of the dominant large generalists, that specialist organizations can find viable locations. And because resources tend to be thin in these regions, the specialists located here also tend to be small. Small highly specialized locations are also less likely to be invaded by the ever-encroaching generalists than are broader locations; they also tend to be more defensible if they are. When these resources are sufficient to sustain a specialist segment, the market is "partitioned" as it appears that generalist and specialist organizations do not compete; they depend on different parts of the resource base.

The original insight of resource-partitioning theory comes from comparing the amount of resource space available for specialists when overall market concentration rises. Because market concentration derives from generalist consolidation, this comparison can be made by measuring the total area outside generalist targets under different stages of the generalist competition scenario. When the total space does not decline, this area (space outside generalist targets) is larger when concentration is higher (fewer and larger generalists). So, as market concentration rises, the total amount of resource space open to specialist organizations expands. As the resource space open to specialists expands, the founding rates of specialist organizations rise and the mortality rates of specialist organizations fall.

Structural Inertia

The key mechanism behind predictions about the likelihood and outcome of organizational change in ecological theory relates to the evolution of structural inertia in organizations, as theorized by Hannan and Freeman in 1984. Inertia is relative, meaning that it constrains organizations from keeping pace with exogenous change. Distinguishing between the content (the properties of the origin and destination states in a transition) and process (the time it takes to transition between the two states) of change is important: The theory of structural inertia is about the impediments endemic in the process of change. Organizational inertia develops as a by-product of structural reproducibility, which emerges in response to demands for the reliability and accountability with which an organization can perform certain actions. Reliability and accountability, in turn, are engendered as the organization gains experience and becomes better at the tasks it performs. In short, and in contrast to many managerial intuitions, inertia is not necessarily a pathology but a by-product of success—a firm cannot do well and gain a selection advantage unless it functions as a reliable and accountable social actor. This notion directly contradicts virtually all contemporary organization theories which make avowedly adaptationist claims. Much prior research on organizational change has aimed to reconcile these conflicting predictions.

Selection and adaptation models of organizational change can be studied in terms of the different consequences brought about by change in the organizational core and periphery. Because reliability and accountability emerge from the reproducibility of core structures, inertial forces (along with the selection advantage derived from reliability and accountability) emanate from core features of organizations. Many studies find that core structural change is a precarious process; it leads to an elevated probability of organizational failure, even if the desired end state is on target. Changes affecting the noncore or periphery structure do not produce the same outcome; they might even lead to a lower risk of mortality.

Hannan and Freeman's original definition of the organizational core gave a hierarchical list of four core features, including organization's mission, its authority structure, its technology, and its marketing strategy. Empirical applications of the inertia theory using this definition of organizational core are not unequivocal in their interpretations of core structures, though most do find support for the prediction that core change elevates mortality.

Recent elaboration of the inertia story claims that the deleterious process effects result from the length of time necessary to replace structural and cultural codes governing blueprints for conducting transactions. The time to complete such replacements depends on the location of change within the organization—specifically, on the centrality of units subjected to transformation attempts.

Most studies of inertia resolve the location-of-change issue by applying the core-periphery framework for analyzing structural change in organizations. A typical research design of this sort usually begins by defining what organizational features constitute the core and then formulates predictions about transformations in those features. So the *coreness* of any structural element is based on analysts' assumptions about a specific class of organizations. Partly, the problem pertains to excess generality in conceptualizing the core-periphery distinction: What constitutes a core organizational feature in one organization can be a peripheral structure in another. These discrepancies appear not only with comparisons of organizations with different forms and identities but also to firms within the same population.

Evolution

The original density-dependence theory has undergone several important subsequent modifications, two of which are discussed next. First, important modification of the traditional density-dependent specification builds on the idea that legitimation and competition are better represented as time-variant functions of density. That is, the evolution of an organizational population alters the dependence of these two processes on variation in density. For example, as an organizational population matures, the form's legitimacy may become enforced by the form's sheer persistence (rather than numbers) in the organizational landscape, as well as by the emergence of tangible networks between members of the population and other social actors, such as regulators, supporting industries, and the like. Similarly, as the population matures, simple diffuse competition for resources may be supplanted by competitive relationships based on dimensions such as status and product scope specialization that lead to the evolution of population structure. To deal with the decreasing dependence of legitimacy and competition on density, in 1997 Hannan proposed a model where the effects of legitimation and competition

as driven by density are allowed to decline with population age. The second improvement of original density-dependence theory specifies cognitive and institutional processes as operating at a broader social level than competition, which is tied to material inputs and thus is more localized. In the context of the European automobile industry, Hannan and colleagues demonstrated the advantage of this multilevel specification and estimated legitimation effects as a function of total European density while competitive as a function of the density of each national population. The substantive argument is that ideas and images diffuse across national borders, while resource rivalry unfolds primarily among local competitors.

Original resource-partitioning theory places primary emphasis on an organization's location in resource space, especially relative to other types of organizations. This logic serves as the primary predictions for the specialist phenomenon. In some industries, however, other factors often take on greater importance than sheer location of products in resource space. Recent studies have proposed three alternative mechanisms to location: (a) customization, (b) anti-mass-production cultural sentiment, and (c) conspicuous status consumption. The first of these features the role of dynamic organizational capabilities, while the second two highlight identity.

Adding to original theorizing regarding structural inertia, a recently developed more intuitive way of conceptualizing core features and change in the organizational core stems from the insight that the adverse impact of transformation arises from its unintended effects. Because the unanticipated consequences of organizational change are a direct function of the extensiveness of the change, core transformation is defined in terms of the additional subsequent unplanned changes that need to be implemented as a result of the initial change attempt. That is, intended change in centrally located units triggers unintended change in units to which they are connected in the overall organizational structure. It is such cascades of change throughout the organization that largely account for the indirect and opportunity costs associated with the transition between two states.

In addition to density-dependence theory, niche width, and resource-partitioning theory, and structural inertia theory, there are several other research streams in organizational ecology that merit serious discussion. Liability of newness and adolescence theories focus on the mechanisms (e.g., lack of established track record or initial resource endowments) that shape patterns of age dependence in organizational failure rates. Density-delay theory posits that competitive pressures and legitimacy vacuum at the time of founding imprint in nascent organizations' structures and continuously affect their life chances even after competitive and institutional configurations at the time of founding have shifted. The Red-Queen theory of learning and competition views the competitive strength of an organization as a function of both its own competitive history and the competitive profile of its rivals. The size-localized competition model predicts that within populations, organizational size distributions tend to resolve themselves toward a bimodal pattern, with organizations occupying the middle of the size gradient eventually falling out due to crowding pressures from specialized small firms on one end and larger scale competitors on the other. The theory of scale-based competition predicts that among large (generalist) rivals within an organizational population, the greater the aggregate distance of a firm from each of its larger competitors, the higher its mortality hazard. Legitimacy transfer theory argues that the early evolution of a new form may be either aided or retarded by its overlap in identity space with other taken-for-granted organizational forms, depending on the extent of the overlap, leading either to *de alio* legitimation or violation by comparison.

Importance

One feature that sets organizational ecology apart from other research programs is the continuous effort at cumulativeness and integration among ecological studies and theories. Recent efforts at formalizing the original theoretical segments have come a long way in crafting a coherent paradigm with clear directions for future research. The combination of logically formalized predictions, substantive mechanisms explaining these predictions, and the intense empirical scrutiny to which they are subjected makes organizational ecology perhaps the most "scientific" framework in contemporary organization and management theory.

Contrary to an unthinking misconception that organizational ecology is "antimanagerial," the paradigm's theories can be a source of sound insights for contemporary managers. For example,

understanding the sources of inertia in organizations as endemic to its structure rather than driven by pure incompetence or behavioral mismanagement can help to avoid costly resource commitments. The implications of niche theory for diversification and its relationship to competition suggest that managerial incentives ought to be structured in a way that encourage maintaining a focused firm scope. Resource-partitioning theory may help entrepreneurs identify the market timing and location of new opportunities, and notions of constitutive legitimacy can guard against underestimating the potential cost of a first mover or a monopolist position. Overall, for any practitioner who understands that good ideas can sometimes lead to bad outcomes, organizational ecology has much to offer.

Stanislav Dobrev

See also First-Mover Advantages and Disadvantages; Neo-Institutional Theory; Organizational Demography; Organizational Identity; Organizational Learning; Organizational Structure and Design; Social Movements; Strategies for Change

Further Readings

Barnett, W. P., & Carroll, G. R. (1995). Modeling internal organizational change. *Annual Review of Sociology, 21,* 217–236.

Carroll, G. R. (1985). Concentration and specialization: Dynamics of niche width in populations of organizations. *American Journal of Sociology, 90,* 1262–1283.

Carroll, G. R., & Hannan, M. T. (2000). *The demography of corporations and industries.* Princeton, NJ: Princeton University Press.

Dobrev, S. D., & Carroll, G. R. (2003). Size (and competition) among organizations: Modeling scale-based selection among automobile producers in four major countries, 1885–1981. *Strategic Management Journal, 24,* 541–558.

Dobrev, S. D., Kim, T.-Y., & Carroll, G. R. (2003). Shifting gears, shifting niches: Organizational inertia and change in the evolution of the U.S. automobile industry, 1885–1981. *Organization Science, 14,* 264–282.

Dobrev, S. D., Kim, T.-Y., & Hannan, M. T. (2001). Dynamics of niche width and resource partitioning. *American Journal of Sociology, 106,* 1299–1337.

Freeman, J., & Hannan, M. T. (1983). Niche width and the dynamics of organizational populations. *American Journal of Sociology, 88,* 1116–1145.

Hannan, M. T., & Freeman, J. (1977). The population ecology of organizations. *American Journal of Sociology, 82*, 929–964.

Hannan, M. T., & Freeman, J. (1984). Structural inertia and organizational change. *American Sociological Review, 49*, 149–164.

Hannan, M. T., & Freeman, J. (1989). *Organizational ecology.* Cambridge, MA: Harvard University Press.

Hannan, M., Pólos, L., & Carroll, G. (2007). *Logics of organization theory: Audiences, codes, and ecologies.* Princeton, NJ: Princeton University Press.

ORGANIZATIONAL EFFECTIVENESS

A central insight associated with the theory of organizational effectiveness is that there is no one single theory of effectiveness. Rather, there are multiple models, each of which has a legitimate claim to being the key approach for defining and determining the effectiveness of an organization. This entry is a review of the most important of these frameworks, how they developed, and their application in both research and management practice. An integrative framework of effectiveness models is also reviewed.

Fundamentals

The earliest models of organizational effectiveness emphasized "ideal types," that is, forms of organization that maximized certain attributes. Max Weber's characterization of bureaucracies is the most obvious and well-known example. This "rational-legal" form of organization was based on rules, equal treatment of all employees, separation of position from person, staffing and promotion based on skills and expertise, specific work standards, and documented work performance. These principles were translated into dimensions of bureaucracy, including formalization of procedures, specialization of work, standardized practices, and centralization of decision making. Early applications of the bureaucratic model to the topic of effectiveness proposed that efficiency was the appropriate measure of performance—that is, avoidance of uncoordinated, wasteful, ambiguous activities. Thus, the more nearly an organization approached the ideal bureaucratic characteristics, the more effective (i.e., efficient) it was. The more specialized, formalized, standardized, and centralized, the better.

Subsequent scholars challenged the assumptions of ideal-type advocates, however, suggesting that the most effective organizations are actually nonbureaucratic. Chester Barnard for example, argued that organizations are cooperative systems at their core. An effective organization, therefore, channels and directs cooperative processes to accomplish productive outcomes, primarily through institutionalized goals and decision-making processes. Barnard's work led to three additional ideal-type approaches to organization—Philip Selznick's institutional school, Herbert Simon's decision-making school, and Roethlisberger and Dickson's human relations school. Each of these schools of thought represents an ideal to which organizations should aspire—such as shared goals and values, systematic decision processes, collaborative practices, or profitability. Whereas devotees disagreed over what the ideal benchmark must be for judging effectiveness, all agreed that effectiveness should be measured against an ideal standard represented by the criteria.

Mounting frustration over the conflicting claims of ideal-type advocates gave rise, however, to a "contingency model" of organizational effectiveness. This perspective argued that effectiveness is not a function of the extent to which an organization reflects qualities of an ideal profile but, instead, depends on the match between an organization's attributes and its environmental conditions. The differentiation between organic and mechanistic organizational types represents an early bridge from ideal type to contingency models. Contingency theorists argued that mechanistic organizations (e.g., those reflecting Weber's bureaucratic dimensions) are best suited to highly stable and relatively simple environments. In contrast, organic organizations (e.g., those reflecting Barnard's cooperative dimensions) are better suited to rapidly changing, highly complex situations. Complex and changing environments give rise to different appropriate effectiveness criteria than do stable and undemanding environments.

A third shift occurred in the conception of organizations as economists and organizational theorists became interested in accounting for transactions across organizational boundaries and their interactions with multiple constituencies. This emphasis highlighted the relevance of multiple stakeholders in accounting for an organization's performance. Effective organizations were viewed as those which had accurate information about the demands and expectations of strategically critical stakeholders and, as a result, adapted internal organizational activities, goals, and strategies to match those demands and expectations. This viewpoint held that organizations are elastic entities operating in a dynamic force field which pulls the organization's shape and practices in different directions—that is, molding the organization to the demands of powerful interest groups, including stockholders, unions, regulators, competitors, customers, and so forth. Effectiveness, therefore, is a function of qualities such as learning, adaptability, strategic intent, competitive positioning, and responsiveness.

Models of Organizational Effectiveness

From these various viewpoints about the nature of organizations, their relevant features and dimensions, and their key effectiveness criteria, multiple models of organizational effectiveness naturally arose. Debates about which approach was best, which model was most predictive, and which criteria were most appropriate to measure were typical of the organizational studies literature from the 1970s to the 1990s.

Six models, in particular, became representative of the best known and most widely used in scientific investigations. Michael Jenson, Larry Mohr, Jim Price, and Alan Bluedorn, for example, are among those who argued that the *goal model* is the most appropriate model of choice—that is, organizations are effective to the extent to which they accomplish their stated goals. In Jenson's terms, the fundamental indicator of effectiveness is enhancing shareholder value. This single goal dominates all others, and all other considerations are secondary and subservient to this goal. In Mohr's and Bluedorn's terms, multiple goals (not just one) exist in organizations, and the reason for organizing at all is because goals cannot be achieved by an individual. Hence, organizational effectiveness is inherently linked to the extent to which both formal and information goals are accomplished.

Stan Seashore and Ephraim Yuchtman, Frank Friedlander and Hal Pickle, and Jeff Pfeffer and Gerry Salancik represent those that argued for a *resource dependence model*—that is, organizations are effective to the extent to which they acquire needed resources. In order for organizations to maintain viability and to grow, sustaining resources must be captured from the external environment. Effectiveness depends, therefore, on the extent to which organizations manage the environment such that scarce and valued resources are obtained.

David Nadler and Michael Tushman, Tom Mahoney and Bill Weitzel, and David Doty, Bill Glick, and George Huber, are among the advocates of an *internal congruence model* of effectiveness. That is, organizations are effective to the extent to which their internal functioning is consistent, efficiently organized, and functions with minimal strain. Aligning functional, structural, and strategic elements of an organization produces both short and long-term advantages, predictable outcomes, minimal waste, and hence, organizational effectiveness. Karlene Roberts illustrates an extreme case of internal congruence in describing high reliability, error-free, near-perfectly performing organizations.

Somewhat related is the *human relations model* championed by a large number of human relations advocates. Among the best known are Rensis Likert, Raymond Miles, and Chris Argyris who argued that organizations are effective to the extent to which they are healthy systems for the individuals who work in them. The emphasis is on engaging members, developing human resources, and providing a collaborative climate. Likert, for example, argued that almost any organization considered to be highly effective would possess "system 4" attributes—focused on supportive relationships, trust, participation, and peer group loyalty. The well-being of organizational members is of central concern.

Terry Connolly, Ed Conlon, and S. J. Deutsch, Ray Zammuto, and Anne Tsui represent scholars who maintained that a *multiple constituencies model* is most accurate in defining effectiveness. That is, organizations have many groups or constituencies with whom they interact—for example, suppliers, customers, providers of capital, employees, managers, regulators, and so forth. Organizations are effective to the extent to which they satisfy their dominant stakeholders or their strategic constituencies—the constituencies that have the most impact on or power relative to the organization.

Several other less well-known models have appeared periodically as well (e.g., legitimacy models, fault-driven models), but the above are the five most recognized models of organizational effectiveness available during this period of time.

Competing Values Model

A sixth framework, which attempted to integrate these other five models of effectiveness, is the *competing values framework* or *paradox model*. This framework was developed empirically after Robert Quinn and John Rohrbaugh submitted a comprehensive list of criteria used in assessments of organizational effectiveness to a multidimensional scaling procedure. These effectiveness criteria clustered together into four groupings, divided by a vertical dimension and a horizontal dimension. These clusters of criteria indicated that some organizations are effective if they demonstrate flexibility, change, and adaptability. Other organizations are effective if they demonstrate stability, order, and control. This vertical dimension is anchored on one end by effectiveness criteria emphasizing predictability, steadiness, and mechanistic processes and on the other end by criteria emphasizing dynamism, adjustment, and organic processes. In addition, some organizations are effective if they maintain efficient internal processes and congruence, whereas others are effective if they maintain competitive external positioning and success in managing outside stakeholders. This horizontal dimension is anchored on one end by criteria emphasizing internal maintenance and on the other end by criteria emphasizing external positioning. The competing or conflicting emphases represented by each end of the two dimensions constitute the rudiments of the competing values framework.

The resulting four quadrants into which the criteria clustered represent opposite or competing models of effectiveness, but they also tend to encompass the previously proposed models. Specifically, the key effectiveness criteria in diagonal quadrants are opposite to one another or paradoxical in their orientation. The upper left quadrant, for example, is consistent with the *human relations model*—emphasizing cohesion, harmony, collaboration, and coordination criteria. The lower right quadrant, on the other hand, is consistent with both the *goal achievement* and *external constituencies models*—emphasizing the management of the external environment, aggressive goal attainment, competitive positioning, and profitability. The upper left quadrant emphasizes human-centered criteria, similar to those advocated by Elton Mayo, Raymond Miles, Rensis Likert, and Chris Argyris, whereas the lower

right quadrant emphasizes goal achievement and competitive criteria with an emphasis on dominant stakeholders as advocated by the goal and multiple constituencies models.

Similarly, the upper right quadrant is consistent with the acquisition of new resources (the *system resource model),* which emphasizes growth, innovation, and change criteria, whereas the lower left quadrant emphasizes the *internal congruence, or efficiency model,* with an emphasis on error reduction, standardized processes, measurement, and cost control criteria. The upper right quadrant focuses on growth, change, innovation, and new resources, whereas the lower left quadrant emphasizes efficiency, quality control, and high reliability.

These competing or opposite criteria in each quadrant give rise to one of the most important features of the competing values model and, by implication, the literature on organizational effectiveness—the presence and necessity of paradox. A variety of writers, including Kim Cameron, Karl Weick, Tom Peters and Bob Waterman, Kathleen Eisenhart and Bill Wescott, and Marshall Meyer and Vipin Guptz, are among the writers who argued that effectiveness is inherently paradoxical. Effective organizations simultaneously operate in competing quadrants and manifest paradoxical characteristics. Thus, whereas discussions in the academic literature have often focused on which model of effectiveness is most appropriate or most useful, the point of view introduced by the paradox model suggests that all these models have an important role in defining and determining effectiveness. No single model is adequate alone.

Importance

Organizational effectiveness is usually considered to be the ultimate dependent variable in organizational studies. It is the end to which organizations strive. Its definition, however, depends a great deal on the assumptions made and the framework used to determine what an organization exists to accomplish. In pursuing organizational effectiveness, scholars and managers will want to keep in mind the following seven propositions, which summarize the state of the organizational effectiveness literature. (a) Despite the ambiguity and confusion surrounding it, the construct of organizational effectiveness is central to the organizational sciences and cannot be ignored in theory and research. (b) Because no conceptualization of an organization is comprehensive, no conceptualization of an effective organization is comprehensive. As the metaphor describing an organization changes, so does the definition or appropriate model of organizational effectiveness. (c) Consensus regarding the best, or sufficient, set of indicators of effectiveness is impossible to obtain. Criteria are based on the values and preferences of different constituencies, and no specifiable construct boundaries exist. Criteria change as dominant constituencies change. (d) Different models of effectiveness are useful for research (and practice) in different circumstances. Their usefulness depends on the purposes and constraints placed on the organizational effectiveness investigation and application. (e) Organizational effectiveness is mainly a problem-driven construct rather than a theory-driven construct. The challenge is to make appropriate choices regarding suitable criteria. (f) In pursuing organizational effectiveness, managers will want to consider the core purpose for which the organization exists, which constituency's values and preferences take priority, and the contradictory trade-offs inherent in the pursuit of the organization's preferred outcomes.

Kim Cameron

See also Bureaucratic Theory; Competing Values Framework; Excellence Characteristics; High-Performance Work Systems; Organic and Mechanistic Forms; Organizational Culture and Effectiveness; Resource Dependence Theory; Resource-Based View of the Firm

Further Readings

Bluedorn, A. C. (1980). Cutting the Gordian knot: A critique of the effectiveness tradition in organizational research. *Sociology and Social Research, 64,* 477–496.

Cameron, K. S. (1986a). A study of organizational effectiveness and its predictors. *Management Science, 32,* 87–112.

Cameron, K. S. (1986b). Effectiveness as paradox: Consensus and conflict in conceptions of organizational effectiveness. *Management Science, 32,* 539–553.

Cameron, K. S. (2010). Organizational effectiveness. Northampton, MA: Edward Elgar.

Cameron, K. S., & Whetten, D. A. (1983). *Organizational effectiveness: A comparison of multiple models.* New York, NY: Academic Press.

Connolly, T., Conlon, E. J., & Deutsch, S. J. (1980). Organizational effectiveness: A multiple-constituency approach. *Academy of Management Review, 5,* 211–217.

Goodman, P. S., & Pennings, J. M. (1977). *New perspectives on organizational effectiveness.* San Francisco, CA: Jossey Bass.

Pfeffer, J., & Salancik, G. R. (1978). *The external control of organizations.* New York, NY: Harper & Row.

Quinn, R. E., & Rohrbaugh, J. (1983). A competing values approach to organizational effectiveness. *Public Productivity Review, 5,* 122–140.

Zammuto, R. F. (1984). A comparison of multiple constituencies models of organizational effectiveness. *Academy of Management Review, 5,* 211–217.

ORGANIZATIONAL IDENTIFICATION

Organizational identification relates to the sense of collective self (a sense of "us-ness") that individuals derive from their membership in an organization or organizational unit. Organizational identification has been shown to differ from related concepts such as organizational commitment or job involvement, and it has a range of consequences for work-related behavior that are distinct from those associated with individual-level self-definition. The entry begins as an outline of the theoretical basis of organizational identification and then shows how it differs from the related construct of organizational commitment. Next, research findings are summarized that demonstrate the importance of organizational identification for organizational functioning, and finally, factors are discussed that help to create and maintain organizational identification among employees.

Fundamentals

In the late 1970s, Henri Tajfel and John Turner developed social identity theory to help understand intergroup competition and hostility. The starting point for this was so-called minimal group studies in which individuals were randomly assigned to essentially arbitrary categories (e.g., according to their alleged preferences for one or the other of the painters Klee or Kandinsky, respectively) and asked to allocate rewards (points signifying money) to members of their own group and another. In the studies, Tajfel and his colleagues found that individuals systematically favored members of their own group (i.e., the in-group) over those in the other (the out-group). The key point that Tajfel and Turner drew from these studies was that such behavior was possible only because participants internalized their group membership—as part of their social identity—so that this became a basis for their thoughts, feelings, and actions.

Later, these ideas were refined and extended by Turner and colleagues within self-categorization theory. This argues that all group behavior is mediated by the capacity to define the self in terms of social identity and that this can be differentiated from self-definition in terms of personal identity (one's personality, individual skills, strengths, etc.). The theory argues that all self-definition arises from a process of self-categorization and that whether (and which) social identity becomes salient (so as to determine behavior in any given context) depends on principles of category salience. More specifically, the salience of particular identities is seen to vary as an interactive function of *accessibility* and *fit*, such that people are more likely to define themselves in terms of a particular group membership (e.g., as a psychologist, a Canadian, or an employee of Company X) to the extent that they have a prior history of self-definition in these terms, and this self-definition makes sense in the context at hand. For example, a female psychologist is more likely to define herself as a psychologist (rather than as a woman or as an individual) if this group is meaningful to her (e.g., if she is a member of a national psychological association) and if she is at a psychology conference where she is discussing psychology with colleagues.

Blake Ashforth and Fred Mael were the first to apply social identity theorizing to the organizational domain in a systematic way. They emphasized the cognitive, self-definitional aspect of identification with organizations (or organizational subunits, such as teams, departments, etc.) and defined organizational identification as the individual's feeling of oneness with his or her organization. In this way, organizational identification—as a special form of social identification—describes the perceived overlap between the individual and his or her organization's goals, values, and norms and involves experiencing the organization's failures and successes as one's own. Typical measures of organizational identification thus include statements such as "When I talk about this organization, I usually say

'we' rather than 'they,'" or "I identify with other members of this organization."

Those who perceive themselves as sharing the common organizational identity see themselves as relatively interchangeable members of the same organization (or unit) and, as specified by self-categorization theory, this is a basis for mutual influence and the coordination of behavior with reference to in-group norms (e.g., those that define the group as positively distinct from other groups) as well as collaborative endeavor aimed at advancing the interests of the group as a whole. Indeed, it follows from this theory not only that organizational identity is a central feature of organizational psychology but also that it is this that makes organizational behavior (i.e., the coordinated, collective goal-oriented activity of employees) possible.

The Difference Between Identification and Commitment

It is the self-definitional aspect of identification that distinguishes it from its close relative, organizational commitment. Organizational commitment can be thought of as a positive attitude toward the organization that develops out of consideration of the costs and benefits that organizational membership affords. Dominant conceptualizations of organizational commitment focus on three dimensions: affective commitment, normative commitment, and continuance commitment. Affective commitment sees liking for the organization and its members as the basis for employees' attachment, normative commitment relates to employees' sense that it is appropriate to be committed and hence their sense of obligation, and continuance commitment reflects a desire to remain with the organization primarily in the absence of a better alternative. In studies that have investigated the correlations between these constructs, organizational identification is found to be quite closely associated with affective commitment (but not with normative or continuance commitment). Nevertheless, it is also clear that these constructs tap into distinct states such that each is predictive of rather different things. In particular, while organizational identification is a good predictor of organizational citizenship (e.g., an individual employee's willingness to do more than asked of them), this is less true of all forms of commitment. This indeed is what self-categorization theory would predict: since identification (and the behavior it leads to) reflects a sense that the organization and its members are part of self, whereas this is not necessarily the case for commitment.

Antecedents of Organizational Identification

All employees are members of organizations. But why do they identify with some organizational units rather than others? And why do some of them identify strongly and others only loosely or not at all? One important antecedent for strong employee organizational identification is a strong and distinctive organizational identity—that is, a clear understanding of the organization's characteristics that are enduring and which distinguish it from its competitors. Among other things, this is predicted by social identity theory's assertion that individuals can enhance their self-esteem by seeing their in-groups (in this case their own organization) as different from and better than other comparison out-groups (other organizations). Providing they are credible, the more organizations satisfy this by presenting positive external and internal images, the more employees will tend to identify with them.

Importance

Numerous studies and meta-analyses have found that organizational identification relates to a range of positive job-related attitudes and behaviors, such as job satisfaction and employees' intention to remain with their organizations. As we have noted, the stronger their organizational identification, the more likely employees are to work collaboratively to live up to their group's norms and achieve its goals. Typically, in organizations, the norm is to be productive and effective. Accordingly, a number of studies have shown positive associations between identification and employees' motivation to perform well and to "go the extra mile." For example, in research and development departments (where the norm is to be innovative), identification has to be found to relate positively to employee creativity, and in service settings (where there is a norm to be friendly toward customers), identification has been found to encourage higher employee customer orientation. There is also evidence for a positive effect of identification on bottom-line parameters such as financial turnover and customer satisfaction. Finally, strong identification can activate group members' social support for each other which, partly because it helps them

cope with stress, engenders greater satisfaction and enhanced well-being. At the same time, a sense of shared identity tends to ensure that communication between organizational members is trusted and taken at face value rather than being met with skepticism or paranoia.

Despite these generally positive effects for individual and organization, a few caveats should also be outlined. First, as highly identified employees consider the organization's successes and failures their own, these employees suffer more than others when the organization is not doing well (e.g., as in times of economic downturn). Second, highly identified employees may provide support to other strongly identified colleagues, but if other members of the organization are seen as not fitting into the group, these members may become targets for bullying or harassment by those colleagues. Third, strong identification may hinder organizational change if that change is seen as threatening for the organizational identity in question. Accordingly, if they are to win those employees over, change leaders have to work to ensure that strongly identified employees retain a sense of identity continuity throughout the change process. For a range of reasons, this may not always be possible, and this is one case where the majority of attempts to produce organizational change actually fail.

So what can managers do to promote a sense of shared identity among employees? In particular, how is this possible given the strong subgroupings in organizations that are often associated with the siloing effect, or lack of motivation and communication in organizations? First, managers can foster short-term identity relatively easily by, for instance, encouraging comparisons with a competitor. Other activities (e.g., corporate newsletters) that highlight successes of the organization can promote employee identification. Again, though, these activities have to be legitimate and credible, otherwise they can easily backfire. At the level of different subunits, team-building or other related training programs can also foster a sense of unity and stimulate identification. These measures will all have positive effects on situated identity and may help employees to overcome short-term problems. Alongside these short-term strategies, though, it is important to focus on the underpinnings of long-term identification. Managers should see identity-creation not as a one-off activity but as a continuous process that demands continuous attention. In this regard too, the creation of shared identity is not a silver bullet, or an organizational cure-all, that is unrelated to what managers do and the example they set through their own actions. Most particularly, managers have to be fair and respectful of group members, their actions have to be authentic, and they have to act as models for the form of identity that they want to cultivate. Managers who represent their organizations well and who serve as prototypes for relevant organizational identities are more likely to be supported by their employees and will also tend to have greater leeway when it comes to challenging established practice and taking the group in new directions.

Since the 1970s, social identity theory has provided an important framework for understanding intergroup phenomena and to improving intergroup relations. However, over the past two decades, the strong theoretical framework that it and self-categorization theory provide has also become increasingly influential in the area of management. Here, a substantial and growing body of research provides managers with a better understanding of the dynamics of human resource management and tools with which this can be enhanced. In the last few years, these ideas have also started to take hold in the field of economics. There, it has been suggested that the creation of shared identity offers a much more viable pathway to organizational success than the traditional managerial control and monitoring approach, and, that the social identity approach might also be a much more useful framework for understanding and improving employer-employee relations.

Rolf van Dick and Alex Haslam

See also Organizational Commitment Theory; Organizational Identity; Organizationally Based Self-Esteem; Self-Concept and the Theory of Self; Social Identity Theory

Further Readings

Akerlof, G., & Kranton, R. (2010). *Identity economics: How our identities affect our work, wages, and well-being.* Princeton, NJ: Princeton University Press.

Ashforth, B. E., & Mael, F. (1989). Social identity theory and the organization. *Academy of Management Review, 14,* 20–39.

Cornelissen, J. P., Haslam, S. A., & Balmer, J. M. T. (2007). Social identity, organizational identity and corporate identity: Towards an integrated understanding of processes, patternings and products [Special issue]. *British Journal of Management, 18,* 1–16.

Haslam, S. A. (2004). *Psychology in organizations: The social identity approach.* London, England: Sage.

Haslam, S. A., & Ellemers, N. (2005). Social identity in industrial and organizational psychology: Concepts, controversies and contributions. In G. P. Hodgkinson & J. K. Ford (Eds.), International *review of industrial and organizational psych*ology (Vol. 20, pp. 39–118). Chichester, England: Wiley.

Haslam, S. A., Postmes, T., & Ellemers, N. (2003). More than a metaphor: Organizational identity makes organizational life possible. *British Journal of Management, 14,* 357–369.

Riketta, M. (2005). Organizational identification: A meta-analysis. *Journal of Vocational Behavior, 66,* 358–384.

Tajfel, H., & Turner, J. C. (1979). An integrative theory of intergroup conflict. In W. G. Austin & S. Worchel (Eds.), *The social psychology of intergroup relations* (pp. 33–47). Monterey, CA: Brooks/Cole.

Turner, J. C., Hogg, M. A., Oakes, P. J., Reicher, S. D., & Wetherell, M. S. (1987). *Rediscovering the social group.* Oxford, England: Blackwell.

van Dick, R., Grojean, M. W., Christ, O., & Wieseke, J. (2006). Identity and the extra-mile: Relationships between organizational identification and organizational citizenship behavior. *British Journal of Management, 17,* 283–301.

ORGANIZATIONAL IDENTITY

The term *organizational identity* was originally proposed by Stewart Albert and David Whetten to mean the elements of an organization that are widely believed to be (a) central, (b) enduring, and (c) distinctive. Since its introduction in 1985, various interpretations of this definition and the relative weighting of each element—especially "enduring"—have taken root. Diversity of thought and breadth of application have become hallmarks of this literature. Moreover, the concept has been applied at multiple levels of analysis—spanning populations, organizations, and individuals. This entry outlines the history of organizational identity, followed by examples of how it has been applied within organizational studies.

Fundamentals

Organizational identity builds on decades of scholarship devoted to the study of individual identity in psychology, sociology, and philosophy, broadly characterized as each individual's answer to the existential question, Who am I? It is often equated with a person's self-concept, self-definition, or self-view, and thus the basis for "self-directed behavior." A person's identity is said to be encoded as a distinctive pattern of similarities and differences, encompassing both social comparisons (self-other) and temporal comparisons (self-self). Salient components of an individual's identity might include family name, personality traits, gender, acquired skills, roles, or social status. These self-identifiers specify to whom an individual is similar and how the individual is different from those similar others. Similarity and difference can thus be thought of as dimensions of the identity concept. The posited need for "optimal distinctiveness" set forth in this literature highlights an inherent tension between these dimensions.

Conceptualizing organizational properties as analogous to individual properties is a controversial practice within organizational studies. Among scholars studying organizational identity, this controversy is reflected in how they interpret the "we" in the so-called organizational identity question, Who are we? On one hand, scholars adopting a "social constructionist" view of organizations associate this plural pronoun with the current organizational membership. On the other hand, their colleagues who view organizations as "social actors" interpret it to mean the organization itself, as a social entity. While recent efforts to formulate complementary, even integrated, conceptions of organizational identity are encouraging, it is useful for readers of this literature to be aware of these two distinct applications of the concept.

Organizational identity scholars who employ the *social constructionist* approach emphasize the "believed to be" portion of Albert and Whetten's organizational identity definition referenced earlier. Consistent with a psychological orientation, proponents argue that inasmuch as individuals alone are capable of self-reflection and self-governance, organizations are best viewed as collections of individual actors gathered together to accomplish shared objectives. This view of organizational identity treats members' shared answers to the Who are we? question as the product of collective "sensemaking"—that is, a shared representation satisfying a shared need to make sense of shared experiences. This bottom-up conception of organizational identity is similar to what psychologists refer to as *collective identity* (e.g., the identity of a demographic social category).

Understanding how shared representations of organizational identity emerge within organizations and how they are subsequently sustained and inevitably changed, are key topics addressed within this body of organizational identity scholarship. The focus here is on understanding an organization from the perspective of its members, including members' interpretations of what's central, distinctive, and enduring about their organization. Scholars adopting this perspective have examined how changing environmental circumstances necessitate changes in an organization's identity, including the meanings associated with a particular identity (e.g., high quality). They also consider how an organization's strategic response to shifting external expectations might be driven by organizational leaders envisioning and encouraging new conceptualizations of the organization. Recalling the two dimensions of identity, this branch of organizational identity scholarship has mostly focused on the "difference" dimension (e.g., the unique elements of an organization's culture).

On the other hand, the *social actor* perspective on organizational identity emphasizes the actor-like social role of organizations as functionally analogous to that of individuals. This more sociological view is based on the supposition that among the myriad types of social entities within modern society, only "corporate" organizations (exemplified by, but not limited to, business corporations) are granted roughly the same rights and responsibilities as individuals. According to this perspective, compared with other collectives (e.g., affinity groups, communities, social movements), organizations-as-social-actors are expected to behave as if they were individual social actors. Hence, it is posited that a shared understanding among members about who we are, *as a particular organization* at any point in time is a prerequisite for coherent internal collective action and sustainable external social exchange.

Scholars within this perspective point out that the attributes comprising an organization's identity are adopted from culture-specific "menus" of self-defining social categories, ranging from widely shared population-level differences to individuating organizational differences. For example, an organization's identifying features (identity "claims") might include its industry, product category, type of ownership, competencies, and values. These features are expressed formally as credos, policies, and procedures and informally as taken-for-granted practices and other elements of the organization's culture. This "top-down" view of organizing focuses on the "sensegiving" properties of an organization's identity, delineating the zone of appropriate behavior for members when they represent an organization as its agents, in word or deed. Scholarship adopting this view of organizational identity is likely to focus on widely shared organizational identifiers (e.g., type of organization, such as agricultural co-op, hospital, community college, bank) and the use of an organization's identity to inform consequential organizational activities, including strategic decisions (e.g., acquisition, merger) that might be perceived as inconsistent with the organization's historical identity.

These two perspectives generally espouse different interpretations of Albert and Whetten's tripartite definition of organizational identity, especially the enduring aspect. Social constructionists view the elements of an organization's identity as quite malleable, given that they are the products of members' emergent beliefs about shared experiences. In contrast, inasmuch as scholars adopting the social actor perspective treat an organization's identifying features as keys to predictable, sustainable inter- and intraorganizational activity, they focus on enduring organizational attributes that predate and transcend (thus shaping and guiding) the experience of current members.

Importance

One of the reasons why identity has found a welcome home in organizational studies is its potential for application across different levels of analysis. At the supraorganizational (sometimes referred to as the institutional) level, an organization's identity is typically equated with the membership requirements associated with particular groups or social categories (e.g., commercial banks, community colleges, zoos). Scholars interested in this level of analysis are interested in how a shared understanding of these requirements allows various audiences (e.g., customers,

regulators, employees) to recognize different kinds of organizations, interact appropriately with them, and apply suitable evaluation criteria.

It is worth noting, especially at this level of analysis, that the similarity-difference "dimensions" of organizational identity span the central questions posed by organizational sociologists and organizational economists. An organizational sociology perspective focuses on between-group (e.g., population, social category) differences, arguing that the need for social legitimacy pressures organizations claiming a particular group membership to behave like the *prototypical* group members (i.e., appear and act like similar others; see also Institutional Theory, this volume). On the other hand, an organizational economics perspective focuses on within-group differentiation, proposing that the need for competition pressures otherwise similar organizations to emulate the *ideal*, if only mythical, group member (e.g., trustworthy, employee-friendly). The effectiveness of these efforts is reflected in the strength of an organization's reputation. Organizational identity (who we are) is thus sometimes portrayed as the base of a conceptual triangle, connecting organizational legitimacy (we're the same as [and thus as good as]—) and organizational reputation (we're better than—).

Utilizing a narrower field of vision, the majority of organizational-identity empirical research has focused on the organizational level of analysis. To date, this genre has produced numerous in-depth, qualitative case studies. These studies typically examine the origins of an organization's identity, subsequent changes in that identity, and/or how a particular identity has influenced other organizational features and activities. Those interested in identity origins have explored both the internal and external "roots" of a particular organization's identity, as well as the actual identity-formation process. Studies of identity change have examined the impact of shifting environmental conditions, often focusing on how leaders used a crisis to imprint the organization with their values. Scholars focusing on identity consequences have examined how an existing organizational identity is utilized to guide organizational responses to competitive challenges, including the formulation of new strategic plans.

Narrowing the focus of organizational identity scholarship even further, the concept of identity is increasingly invoked by scholars studying individuals within organizations. A few studies have examined how the identity of a single member can impact an organization's identity, as exemplified by the legacy of influential organizational founders. To shift perspectives, a related concept, *organizational identification,* is defined as the perceived congruence between an individual member's personal identity and the organization's identity. A high level of identification with an organization suggests that a member has internalized key elements of the organization's identity (who we are → who I am). As one might expect, high levels of organizational identification have been shown to predict organizational satisfaction and organizational commitment. It has also been shown that prospective members gravitate to organizations whose core values (identities) are consistent with their own.

It is worth noting that a sizable number of studies, spanning the institutional, organizational, and individual levels of analysis, have focused on the distinctive characteristics of "hybrid" identity organizations. These are organizations that deliberately chose to operate according to the requirements associated with seemingly incompatible social categories (organizing logics or scripts)—such as family businesses, professional orchestras, and church-affiliated universities. Said differently, a distinguishing, central, and enduring feature of organizational identity hybrids is that they are *both* an X- and a Y-type organization. The obvious challenge facing hybrids is that rather than a shared understanding of who we are as an organization being the final arbiter of internal conflicts over strategic direction, any major decision that seemingly requires leaders to choose between the incompatible components of the organization's identity risks provoking a civil war.

This brief overview of organizational identity suggests several "orienting questions" for readers seeking to gain a more-than-casual understanding of the organizational identity literature.

1. Which broader, paradigmatic approach to organizational scholarship is being adopted (social constructionist, social actor)?

2. Which level of analysis is addressed (institutional, organizational, individual)?

3. What is being compared (different views of an organization's identity, the identities of multiple organizations)?

4. Is organizational identity distinguished from related concepts (image, reputation, legitimacy)?

5. Whose perspective is being examined (internal and/or external points of view)?

Readers seeking practical implications for management practice will be especially interested in several of the following related topics. A growing literature on corporate identity, including corporate branding strategy, extends the concept of brand identity in marketing to the organizational level of analysis. The notion of a sustainable organizational story, from the field of organizational communications, is also relevant. Closer to home, some organizational studies researchers have examined ways in which organizations project a "positive image." And possibly of greatest relevance, the literature on organizational culture—a concept that is often confused with organizational identity—is brimming with practical implications.

David A. Whetten

See also Core Competence; Institutional Theory of Multinational Corporations; Organizational Culture and Effectiveness; Organizational Identification; Organizationally Based Self-Esteem; Self-Concept and the Theory of Self; Social Construction Theory; Social Identity Theory; Typology of Organizational Culture

Further Readings

Albert, S., & Whetten, D. A. (1985). Organizational identity. *Research in Organizational Behavior, 7,* 263–295.

Corley, K. G., Harquail, C. V., Pratt, M. G., Glynn, M. A., Fiol, C. M., & Hatch, M. J. (2006). Guiding organizational identity through aged adolescence. *Journal of Management Inquiry, 15*(2), 85–99.

Dutton, J. E., & Dukerich, J. M. (1991). Keeping an eye on the mirror: Image and identity in organizational adaptation. *Academy of Management Journal, 34,* 517–554.

Gioia, D. A., Price, K. N., Hamilton, A. L., & Thomas, J. B. (2010) Forging an identity: An insider-outsider study of processes involved in the formation of organizational identity. *Administrative Science Quarterly, 55,* 1–46.

Hatch, M. J., & Schultz, M. (2000). Scaling the Tower of Babel: Relational differences between identity, image, and culture in organizations. In M. Schultz, M. J. Hatch, & M. H. Larsen (Eds.), *The expressive organization: Linking identity, reputation, and the corporate brand* (pp. 11–35). Oxford, England: Oxford University Press.

Hsu, G., & Hannan, M. T. (2005). Identities, genres, and organizational forms. *Organization Science, 16*(5), 474–490.

Pratt, M. G., & Foreman, P. O. (2000). Classifying managerial responses to multiple organizational identities. *Academy of Management Review, 25,* 18–42.

Ravasi, D., & Schultz, M. (2006). Responding to organizational identity threats: Exploring the role of organizational culture. *Academy of Management Journal, 49*(3), 433–458.

Whetten, D. A. (2006). Albert and Whetten revisited: Strengthening the concept of organizational identity. *Journal of Management Inquiry, 15,* 219.

ORGANIZATIONAL LEARNING

The idea of organizational learning can be traced to a seminal book titled *A Behavioral Theory of the Firm*, published in 1963. In contrast to rational conceptions of organizations as entities solving maximization problems, this behavioral view depicts organizational learning as a function of experience and an organization's success and failure in meeting performance targets. In the decades since, the topic of organizational learning has generated volumes of subsequent work, spanning disciplines, levels of analysis, and theoretical perspectives. It is not possible to review the entire field in this entry. Instead, the entry focuses on theoretical models of organizational learning which have built on the original behavioral theory of the firm.

Fundamentals

As James G. March points out in his 2007 reflective essay on the behavioral theory of the firm,

> [T]he idea that organizations adapt over time to local search and feedback on the relation between performance and aspiration was a welcome one for many, but the implications for traveling on a rugged domain, for superstitious learning, for competency traps, and for risk avoidance were not equally compelling to all. (p. 540)

Subsequent work has elaborated on several implications of the behavioral theory of the firm, which will be discussed here: (a) implications for risk taking, (b) implications for traveling on a rugged domain, (c) implications for organizations as interpersonal networks, and (d) implications for organizational learning curves.

First, a set of models have elaborated on the original idea by studying the impact of experiential learning on organizational risk taking. One stream argues that risk-taking tendencies are not constant or fixed but are responsive to changing fortune creating psychological responses to danger, slack, aspirations, and perception as well as self-confidence. In the aspiration reference point model, risk is seen as a function of the ratio of aspiration to the wealth level of the organizations. Risk preference is thus positively related to the aspiration level and negatively related to wealth levels. Given this simple assumption, the model shows that those who accumulate losses become risk prone whereas those who accumulate gains become risk averse.

Aspiration can also be socially determined by other firms in the same population. The dual reference point model further refines the aspiration point model, by introducing risk taking as a function of survival in addition to aspirations. Both models produce behaviors that approximate observed empirical regularities. A second stream of work argues that risk taking and the selection among alternatives are not a calculated, consequential process but are a response learned from experience. Individuals learn how to respond to situations involving risks the same way they learn other things, by experiencing the apparent consequences of their behavior and modifying their rules of behavior as a result of cumulated experience. The main finding is that learning in the domain of gains (where expected returns of alternatives are positive) leads to behavior that is decidedly more risk averse than does learning in the domain of losses. Thus, risk preferences are interpreted as a learned response, rather than as an inexplicable personal trait. In addition, such learning involves a process of sequential sampling. Because humans learn from experience by reducing the probability of sampling alternatives with poor past outcomes, the reproduction of successful actions inherent in adaptive processes results in a bias against alternatives that initially may appear to be worse than they actually are. Adaptive search, rather than fixed or variable risk preferences, may explain the empirical association between performance and organizational risk taking. These models of learning from experience and selected samples provide alternative theories of risk aversion and risk taking.

Second, organizations learn by responding to local feedback, which may or may not be indicative of true consequences. This complication is especially severe when choices are interdependent both cross-sectionally and intertemporally. First, when choices influence each other, the resulting payoff surface is characterized by many local peaks rather than a single peak (in the case of no or little interaction among choices). The presence of a local peak means that incremental changes from it are unlikely to lead to performance increases as the corresponding solution to the peak has higher associated payoffs than its immediate neighbors. As such, organizations following local feedback may be guided toward a local peak and get stuck there if no radical adaptations are made. A series of models has elaborated on the consequences of varying interdependency on a variety of outcomes ranging from imitation to competition to organizational structure. Second, organizations also face choices that are dependent intertemporally. Local feedback may be biased, ambiguous, or simply not available because a sequence of decisions needs to be made before the outcome is revealed. For instance, many organizational decisions are sequentially interdependent: Upstream decisions need to be made well before downstream consequences are clear. This absence of immediate outcome feedback is also known as the credit assignment problem in artificial intelligence. It implies that learning based solely on reinforcement or local feedback (also known as hill-climbing) would not prove effective. Instead, organizations need to develop cognitive models of the environment by bootstrapping from their repeated experience.

Third, while there is a long tradition in organizational learning that uses individual models of learning to understand collective organizational activities, there has been more focus on the idea that organizations learn in the context of many individuals. Rather than modeling organizations as unitary actors, this emergent stream of work explicitly models how organizations learn as individual members interact with each other, combining and recombining their fragmentary knowledge into coherent routines

and patterns of behavior. In particular, recent work models interpersonal learning as a network process, building on March's model of exploration and exploitation. Although March models learning between an organizational code and many noninteracting individual members, this stream of work has begun to introduce direct interpersonal learning among members. Individuals look to those with whom they share a connection in the interpersonal networks of the organization. Organizations are represented by a variety of interpersonal networks ranging from a two-dimensional cellular automata to small world networks. Thus, structural network characteristics of the interpersonal networks influence the learning outcomes. For instance, interpersonal networks that have a moderate degree of cross-group links tend to produce highest performance. The explanation is that too many cross-group links quickly drive out deviant ideas and eliminate requisite variety, while too few links prevent good ideas from being efficiently conveyed across the entire organization. Thus, the amount of cross-group links serves as a lever to fine-tune the productive balance between exploration and exploitation. In this sense, incorporating an interpersonal networks model does not change the fundamental insights from the March model. This body of work also contributes to the literature on organizational structure. Both formal and informal structures have long been seen as a vehicle for organizational learning. By systematically exploring the locus of interpersonal learning at dyadic and network levels, this stream of work enriches researchers understanding of learning as it unfolds in interpersonal networks of the organizations. What distinguishes this work from models in economics and physics is a common focus on outcomes of interest to organizational scholars: performance, innovation, and learning in addition to diffusion.

Lastly, a set of models has tried to theoretically explain robust empirical observations pertaining to the learning curves. These empirical regularities are that (a) organizational performance improves with experience at a decreasing rate across a variety of settings, (b) rates of learning vary, and (c) organizations typically suffer from negative transfer of learning as they adapt to a new environment. Several streams of learning models have tried to provide a theoretical underpinning for organizational learning curves. One stream has modeled learning as a trial-and-error search process of all possible configurations and combinations of the activities. A second stream of work estimates parameters associated with the models directly from production data. However, the first two streams are often criticized as being unable to account for all three regularities, and it is often not clear whether the specific mechanisms in the models correspond to the actual processes by which learning occurs in organizations. A more recent stream of work models organizational learning curves as a result of the formation of novel interaction routines. This line of work explicitly models the emergence of connections or relationships among component activities. This differs from the first stream which views the entire configuration of activities as the unit of analysis. It views organizational learning as resulting from the formation of routines that connect individual actions into patterned behavior. Modeling organizational learning as routine formation seems to produce the best fit with empirical observations.

Importance

Future extensions of these existing ideas may follow two directions. First, more studies should explore organizational learning as the explicit outcome of interacting individuals. There are two challenges involved in modeling organizational learning as learning individuals interacting with one another. First, we need a good understanding of how individuals learn. Second, we would need to specify detailed mechanisms of aggregation. For instance, a majority voting rule may be needed to aggregate individual preferences into a coherent set of organizational preferences. Ideally, both need to take place before the field can have a well-grounded theory of organizational learning. If individual behavior is not well understood, then aggregation yields little additional insight as the microfoundations may be shaky. One way to potentially overcome such dual difficulties is to empirically validate existing models of learning based on individuals, and use them as building blocks to provide a solid baseline model.

Introducing models that incorporate more realistic organizational features (such as aggregation rules) opens an old debate between the simplicity of models and the realism they entail. While clean, simple models make intuitions transparent and easy to follow, they are often seen as inadequate guides for actions because of the limited range of factors considered. Thus, a second potentially fruitful future extension is the empirical testing of the ideas generated by the existing models to explore their external validity and to increase their empirical relevance. For instance, models of risk taking have attracted a sizable following among empirical researchers who are motivated to verify organizational risk-taking tendencies in a variety of empirical contexts ranging from shipbuilding to investment banks. The resulting evidence, while perhaps not conclusive enough to prompt a revision of the theoretical models, certainly represents an important dialogue between models and data. At the very least, it provides a useful reminder that the test of models eventually has to be their ability to produce and explain real-world behavior. In contrast, the body of work surrounding the rugged terrains, due to its recency, has remained mostly theoretical. With the availability of novel sources of data (e.g., patents, online communities), large-scale empirical testing may be more feasible and may readily yield further insights.

In a nutshell, theoretical models of organizational learning have been an area of active and fruitful research within the *A Behavioral Theory of the Firm* tradition. In the past decades, our understanding of how organizations learn has been greatly enriched by formal work in this area. Future work will continue to explore, refine, and validate these ideas both theoretically and empirically.

To conclude, the central management implication is that modern managers need to first recognize the many complications brought by the experiential nature of organizational learning. First, managers may obtain a more systematic understanding of their risk-taking behavior by exploring underlying determinants, such as the performance aspiration discrepancy. Second, as modern decisions often involve many interdependent parts, managers need to caution against prematurely converging upon an inferior set of solutions. The idea that learning is experiential also implies that the way an organization is structured also may impact the knowledge flow and subsequently learning and performance outcomes within a firm. In structuring the interpersonal networks of a firm, managers need to consciously balance two dual objectives: information diffusion and the preservation of heterogeneous ideas. Lastly, managers may improve learning within their firms by paying attention to key variables underlying the organizational learning curves.

Christina Fang

See also Action Learning; Behavioral Theory of the Firm; Complexity Theory and Organizations; Double Loop Learning; Learning Organization

Further Readings

Argote, L., & Greve, H. (2007). A behavioral theory of the firm—40 years and counting: Introduction and impact. *Organization Science, 18,* 337–349.

Cyert, R. M., & March, J. G. (1963). *A behavioral theory of the firm.* Oxford, England: Blackwell.

Denrell, J. (2005). Why most people disapprove of me: Experience sampling in impression formation. *Psychological Review, 112,* 4, 951–978.

Denrell, J., Fang, C., & Levinthal, D. A. (2004). From T-mazes to labyrinths: Learning from model-based feedback. *Management Science, 50,* 1366–1378.

Fang, C. (in press/2012). Organizational learning as credit assignment: A model and two experiments. *Organization Science,* Forthcoming.

Fang, C., Lee, J., & Schilling, M. A. (2010). Balancing exploration and exploitation through structural design: The isolation of subgroups and organizational learning. *Organization Science, 21*(3), 625–642.

Levinthal, D.A. (1997). Adaptation on rugged landscapes. *Management Science, 43,* 934–950.

March, J. G. (1991). Exploration and exploitation in organizational learning. *Organization Science, 2,* 71–87.

March, J. G. (1996). Learning to be risk averse. *Psychological Review, 103,* 309–319.

March, J. G. (2007). Scholarship, scholarly institutions, and scholarly communities. *Organization Studies, 18,* 537–542.

March, J. G., & Shapira, Z. (1992). Variable risk preferences and the focus of attention. *Psychological Review, 99,* 172–183.

ORGANIZATIONAL SOCIALIZATION

Organizational socialization refers primarily to the process by which an organization integrates new members, but it can also include a focus on influencing existing members. Key elements of this process include a demonstration of the organization's principal values and expectations, an introduction to role-specific technical details, and insights into the political landscape within the organization, which are often conveyed informally by current organizational members, or "insiders." More than anything else, however, socialization represents a transformation whereby an individual learns critical information about the organization that she has joined and either modifies her relevant behaviors and attitudes accordingly in order to attain congruence with the expectations of organizational colleagues or, finding herself ultimately incompatible with the organization, elects to depart—albeit sometimes after a protracted period of dissatisfaction. While socialization is most acutely felt—and therefore most commonly considered—at the time that an individual joins an organization, socialization also occurs on an ongoing basis during her tenure and is made more salient when she is promoted, transfers to a different work group, or when her organization merges with another organization. This entry discusses the two primary approaches to socialization, antecedents of successful socialization, and the outcomes of effective socialization for both employees and organizations.

Fundamentals

An organizational member is considered socialized when he has attained a sustainable equilibrium between his own goals and beliefs and those of his organization. "Successful" socialization, in and of itself, is not always positive, however. Instead, socialization simply reflects the degree to which an individual has attained congruence with an organization or organizational work group. Consider an early investigation of socialization that focused on an urban police department. Research indicated that newly minted officers started out their careers with high levels of motivation. Their motivation rapidly declined, however, as they were socialized into a culture that emphasized "not rocking the boat." Thus, officers that were rapidly and successfully socialized became demotivated and prone to a routinized, uninspired, and by-the-book approach to their daily responsibilities.

Approaches to Socialization

Organizations employ drastically different approaches to socialization, depending on their goals, operating environment, and the ideal end state for organizational members. For example, the U.S. Army expects its soldiers to exhibit discipline, teamwork, and physical excellence. Thus, military socialization—commonly known as "boot camp"—requires individuals to follow orders, dress identically, and exercise rigorously. At the other end of the spectrum, one can envision the archetypical Silicon Valley start-up firm, in which individuals routinely question the decisions of their superiors, dress casually, and work for numerous hours in front of a computer screen.

These two archetypical organizations would be well advised to approach the socialization of new members differently, in accordance with their divergent goals, operating environments, and organizational cultures. A military organization is more likely to employ "institutionalized" socialization tactics, whereas a start-up firm is more likely to employ "individualized" socialization tactics. Under the former, new entrants undergo formal and standardized socialization processes as a group, often at remove from current organizational insiders. New entrants are made aware of the progression they will undergo, its timetable and fixed end point, and the critical checkpoints along the way. Such institutionalized socialization processes tend to be favored by new entrants over the alternative, due to their comprehensible structure and corresponding uncertainty-reducing properties. When organizations use individualized socialization, by contrast, individuals are treated distinctly (instead of as part of a collective), often following different schedules and interacting with current organizational insiders along the way. It is worth noting that effectively distinguishing between individualized socialization programs and the absence of a socialization program has been a challenge to academic researchers, as individualized socialization can often resemble no socialization at all due to an inherent lack of formality or standardization.

Not surprisingly, these two approaches to socialization are associated with radically different outcomes. Individuals who undergo institutionalized socialization tend to exhibit higher organizational commitment, job satisfaction, task mastery, intention to remain with the organization, and less overall anxiety about their place in the organization. However, some studies have found that institutionalized socialization tactics are negatively associated with performance as compared with individualized tactics, particularly concerning innovation. This could be due to the fact that institutionalized socialization provides a cognitive framework

for what is expected, allowing a person to become comfortable in their role so long as they stay within that framework. Such a situation may ultimately prove constraining for individuals and organizations, especially in terms of innovation. In contrast, by "throwing" individuals into their new roles with little in the way of coaching or guidance, individualized socialization may produce employees who are better able to think creatively, challenge the status quo, and otherwise perform innovatively. Significant risks attend this approach, however, as employees may be less certain for a longer time about how to conduct themselves in the organization, which could ultimately hamper mastery of their job.

The Role of Insiders

It is important to note that institutionalized socialization, despite its more formalized nature, need not refer solely to officially sanctioned presentations, exhaustive details pertaining to human resources (HR) policies, and reminders about the organization's particular code of ethics. In fact, one could argue that such "pure play" training programs hardly represent effective socialization at all. Instead, some of the most critical socialization occurs between newcomers and proximal insiders or those more senior colleagues with whom they will be working closely. Continuing with the example of a military organization, a new recruit is likely to learn far more about what is actually expected of him from veteran comrades than from a training manual.

Such insiders can provide new entrants with relevant advice, social and moral support, access to intraorganizational networks, and regular feedback on their performance and potential. Their participation in socialization processes represents a significant tradeoff for organizations, however. While new entrants tend to learn the most relevant information for effective socialization from proximal insiders, ceding aspects of the socialization process to them may necessitate abdicating control over the messages which are being relayed to new entrants, thus, potentially enabling the transmission of unsanctioned or even erroneous information. On the other hand, research has shown a more nuanced benefit of this approach: Assigning insiders the task of socializing newcomers actually enhances insiders' own organizational commitment.

Selection as "Anticipatory Socialization"

What types of people are more likely to be successfully socialized? One notable dispositional predictor of successful socialization is proactivity. Proactive newcomers will make an effort to find out—often through informal discussions with coworkers—what kind of behavior and beliefs are expected of them and will subsequently make an effort to fit in. A second important consideration is an individual's self-efficacy, or the degree to which new organizational members view themselves as capable of performing well in certain settings; highly self-efficacious individuals tend to demonstrate a greater propensity for successful socialization. Finally, a person's tendency to regularly seek feedback has been shown to predict socialization success, because seeking feedback leads them to recalibrate their perceived performance and standing within the organization as they attain new information.

In addition to such dispositional attributes, organizations can increase their chances of successfully socializing newcomers by focusing on person-organization fit, or the degree to which the values, beliefs, and skills of a prospective hire match what is required and expected by the organization. Newcomers who join an organization whose values they already internalize will be more open to the organization's influence. However, while some consider such selection approaches an effective substitute for socialization programs, research has shown that socialization is significantly more critical to establishing person-organization fit.

Importance

While this entry focuses on socialization within professional settings, it is important to note that socialization is a prevalent and potent force across all facets of modern life. As individuals, we maintain a deep and abiding need to be accepted by and connected to proximal others, an imperative which often requires one to behave according to others' expectations. Teenagers in search of social acceptance rigorously emulate the fashion choices of popular peers; adults often undergo religious conversions at the behest of friends and family; and, at the extreme end of the spectrum, suicide cults, such as Heaven's Gate or the Jonestown Peoples' Temple, tragically demonstrate the degree to which socialization can induce individuals to harm themselves

in the pursuit of social approval. Therefore, leaders who recognize the universality of the psychological drive for social approval will be well positioned to construct effective socialization programs contingent on their organization's culture, operating environment, and strategic goals.

Organizational Benefits

Organizations can benefit substantially from a swift and successful socialization process, for a variety of reasons. First, the faster an individual is socialized, in terms of learning to work effectively in an organization and conduct that work according to the organization's true strategic priorities, the faster they will be able to contribute to accomplishing their organization's goals. Second, the experiences that a new organizational entrant processes during the earliest days of their tenure have a stronger and more enduring influence than experiences which are processed later on. This is due to the fact that in such a situation, new members face the maximum amount of ambiguity about their standing, and many respond to this condition by rigorously internalizing every bit of information that they come across about their organization's norms and their own role within it. Additionally, because people are most open to influence when they are new to an organization, socializing members at later stages is typically less effective and may require far greater expenditures of time and resources to successfully influence their attitudes and behaviors. Third, socialization processes are an integral part of ensuring the continuity of organizational culture. Corporate cultures are sustained, even in the face of regular employee departures and critical changes, such as restructuring, mergers, and growth, by imparting to new hires the standards, norms, and lore that characterize an organization.

Failing to socialize newcomers can result in a variety of adverse organizational outcomes. The most extreme example is turnover, which is usually costly for an organization and can ultimately become disruptive and adversely affect morale if it is extensive enough. Socialization failures can, however, also negatively influence employees who elect to remain. In the absence of successful socialization, organizational members are likely to exhibit lower levels of organizational commitment, job satisfaction, clarity about their role, and intention to remain. It may be simplistic to state that a happy worker is a productive worker, but it is certainly true that organizational members are less likely to perform well when they are unclear about relevant expectations and displeased with the manner in which they have been treated, particularly in the early stages of their organizational tenure.

Individual Benefits

Socialization can also be highly beneficial for individuals. Consider the ambiguous environment which confronts a new organizational entrant. There is a new role to learn, new colleagues to become acquainted with, a new organizational culture to assess and adhere to, and ultimately, a fundamental and overriding question to grapple with: Will I be successful at this new job? In other words, new organizational members can easily become overwhelmed by the uncertainty that they face. As decades of psychological research amply demonstrate, uncertainty is an unpleasant cognitive state for individuals, who will almost universally seek to reduce it as quickly and completely as possible. Therefore, individuals have a natural incentive to make their environment more predictable and understandable, and they look to both formal and informal socialization processes as a means to accomplish this end. In addition to uncertainty reduction, however, individuals benefit from successful socialization as it often offers them a window into the political landscape of their organization—the understanding of which has been shown to effectively predict future professional success within the organization, as well as a gratifying sense of person-organization fit.

Overall, individuals derive a substantial component of their identity from their professional affiliations and accomplishments. Organizations that recognize this—and that have a clear understanding of their own culture, operating environment, and corresponding socialization techniques—are capable of responsibly leveraging their members' innate desire for acceptance to better achieve strategic organizational ends. Leaders would therefore do well to be cognizant of the power and potency of socialization processes within their own organizations and beyond.

Eliot L. Sherman and Jennifer A. Chatman

See also Attraction-Selection-Attrition Model; Groupthink; Organizational Assimilation Theory; Organizational Identification; Social Identity Theory

Further Readings

Allen, N. J., & Meyer, J. P. (1990). Organizational socialization tactics: Longitudinal analysis of links to newcomers' commitment and role orientation. *Academy of Management Journal, 33,* 847–858.

Ashford, S. J., & Black, J. S. (1996). Proactivity during organizational entry: Antecedents, tactics, and outcomes. *Journal of Applied Psychology, 81,* 199–214.

Ashforth, B. E., & Saks, A. M. (1996). Socialization tactics: Longitudinal effects on newcomer adjustment. *Academy of Management Journal, 39,* 149–178.

Bauer, T. N., Bodner, T., Erdogan, B., Truxillo, D. M., & Tucker, J. S. (2007). Newcomer adjustment during organizational socialization: A meta-analytic review of antecedents, outcomes, and methods. *Journal of Applied Psychology, 92,* 707–721.

Chao, G. T., O'Leary-Kelly, A. M., Wolf, S., Klein, H. J., & Gardner, P. D. (1994). Organizational socialization: Its content and consequences. *Journal of Applied Psychology, 79,* 730–743.

Chatman, J. A. (1991). Matching people and organizations: Selection and socialization in public accounting firms. *Administrative Science Quarterly, 36,* 459–484.

Kim, T.-Y., Cable, D. M., & Kim, S.-P. (2005). Socialization tactics, employee proactivity, and person-organization fit. *Journal of Applied Psychology, 90,* 232–241.

Morrison, E. W. (2002). Newcomers' relationships: The role of social network ties during socialization. *Academy of Management Journal, 45,* 1149–1160.

Van Maanen, J., & Schein, E. H. (1979). Toward a theory of organizational socialization. In B. M. Staw (Ed.), *Research in organizational behavior* (Vol. 1, pp. 209–264). Greenwich, CT: JAI Press.

Wanous, J. P. (1992). *Organizational entry: Recruitment, selection, orientation, and socialization.* Reading, MA: Addison-Wesley.

Organizational Structure and Design

Organizational structure and design is a major part of management theory. Organizational structure refers both to the official, formal relationships between organizational members and to the informal relationships between them that arise more spontaneously. Some typical examples of formal structure are hierarchy, rules, and the organizational chart. Some examples of informal organizational structure are members choosing to take their lunch break in each other's company or acting corruptly. Organizational design is the conscious molding of the organizational structure so that it attains ends that are valued, such as efficiency or profit. The main contemporary theory of organizational structure and design is contingency theory. It says that for a structure to produce a beneficial outcome, such as high organizational performance, it must fit certain factors, called *contingencies*. Some major contingencies are strategy, size, and innovation. Contingency theory is widely used as the main framework about organizational design in business schools and in textbooks on organizational design. In any organization, its managers are faced by needing to organize the members so that their collaborative efforts will attain the goals of the organization, be they sales growth, profit, quality products, quality services, safety, or whatever. This in turn raises questions such as how work is to be specialized and distributed among members, whether work is to be governed by rules or direct personal supervision, and so on. Because organizational design provides guidance on how to structure any organization, it is a valuable part of the manager's toolbox. However, it is not the case that one single design is right for all organizations. The right structure varies across organizations, and the correct design for an organization must fit its circumstances, which is to say, its contingencies. The following sections describe the main structures and the main contingencies, followed by the structures that fit the contingency variables. The entry then outlines the evolution of structural contingency theory before closing with a discussion of its importance.

Fundamentals

Core Dimensions of Organizational Structure

Every organizational structure comprises several core dimensions:

Differentiation. Differentiation refers to how far an organization is broken into numerous pieces and how much these pieces differ from each other. An organization may be differentiated horizontally and/or vertically. Horizontal differentiation includes the number of divisions, departments, sections, and job specialities. Two departments might differ in whether they have few rules (e.g., research) or many (e.g., production). Vertical differentiation includes the number of levels in the hierarchy of the organization. The head office may differ from an operational department in the degree of conformity to rules.

Integration. Integration refers to how well the farthest parts of an organization are coordinated with each other. Some organizations such as a business unit need to have high integration, because their parts depend upon each other (e.g., sales sells what production makes), whereas other organizations such as a diversified corporation need only low integration, because any one of its divisions operates separately from the other divisions. Integration is provided by integrating individuals (e.g., project managers), hierarchy, planning, and rules.

Centralization. Centralization refers to how far up the organizational hierarchy a decision is made. In a centralized structure, many decisions are made by upper level managers, whereas in a decentralized structure many decisions are made by middle or junior managers.

Formalization. Formalization refers to the extent to which the activity in the organization is governed by rules and standard procedures, often existing in writing.

Contingency Factors Driving Organizational Structure

Every organization needs to fit the core dimensions of organizational structure to five contingency factors of uncertainty, innovation, interdependence, strategy, and size.

Uncertainty. The tasks in organizations vary from those low in uncertainty (predictable tasks) to those high in uncertainty (unpredictable tasks). Tasks low in uncertainty can be governed by rules and standard operating procedures. Tasks high in uncertainty cannot, so they require one-off decisions made by managers and/or discussions between employees. A major source of task uncertainty is the environment that surrounds the organization (e.g., competitor actions).

Innovation. Producing the same product or service repeatedly can be governed by standard operating procedures supplemented by direct supervision; such an organizational structure is seen as mechanistic.

But creating and producing new products or services requires solving novel problems and dealing with uncertainty. Experts have to be recruited and encouraged to use their initiative, freed from close supervision and organizational rules. This organizational structure is often called organic. Organizations routinely producing products or services can centrally plan the flow of activities between functional departments and out to the customer, whereas organizations creating and producing new products or services must foster spontaneous interactions between specialist functions, facilitated by cross-functional project teams that bridge between functional departments. The subcultures of these departments are necessarily different, reflecting differences in time horizons (e.g., short for production versus long for research) and so on.

Interdependence. Tasks vary in their interdependence between pooled, sequential, and reciprocal. In *pooled interdependence,* organizational subunits are only indirectly interdependent on each other, in that they all draw on a common pool, such as "branches" drawing on shared resources from the head office. The simplest and cheapest coordination mechanism suffices, such as rules. In *sequential interdependence,* each organizational subunit is linked to the others in a chain, so that a subunit takes in input from one subunit and gives its output to another. This requires coordination by planning, which is more complex and costly than coordination by rules. In *reciprocal interdependence,* organizational subunits interact back and forth with each other, so they must mutually adjust to each other, the most demanding and costly form of coordination mechanism. (For these coordination mechanisms to be appropriate, the sequence of pooled-sequential-reciprocal interdependencies needs to be a series marked by increasing uncertainty.)

Strategy. For organizational design, key aspects of organizational strategy are diversification and vertical integration. *Diversification* refers to the degree of difference among the products or services produced by an organization. It is useful to distinguish between undiversified organizations, that is, organizations producing a single product or service; medium diversified organizations, that is, organizations producing multiple but *related* products or services, and highly diversified organizations, that is, organizations

producing multiple but *unrelated* products or services. Undiversified organizations are best fitted by a functional organizational structure, in which the managers who directly report to the CEO are each specialized by a function, such as marketing or manufacturing. Having organizational members specialized by function facilitates their expertise in that activity and fosters economies of scale, leading to superior efficiencies and lower costs. The functions are highly dependent on each other, in that marketing sells what manufacturing makes. Functional organizations are relatively centralized, in that the CEO is involved in some of the coordination of the functions and may make some of the operational decisions, such as what priority in production and delivery to give to key customers.

In contrast, for highly diversified organizations, their unrelated product-markets are diverse, so managers and organizational subunits specialized by each are required. Such organizations are best fitted by a multidivisional organizational structure, in which the managers who directly report to the CEO are each in charge of a division, that is, a business that focuses on a particular product or service or customer. Each division has a range of operating functions, such as manufacturing and marketing. Their emphasis is upon devising and delivering products or services that suit their market. The divisions have a lot of autonomy on operational matters because they have that expertise, whereas the head office lacks it. Thus, the organization is decentralized in much of its decision making. The corporate head office needs only contain specialists in finance, legal, and other administrative functions.

In between, medium diversified organizations are also best fitted by a multidivisional organizational structure. But because their products and services are related, there are synergies to be extracted; hence, specialists, such as in procurement and corporate marketing, are needed in the corporate head office, alongside the administrative specialists. The divisions have to be more coordinated in their actions so that the medium diversified organization is decentralized only to a medium level in its decision making.

In vertically integrated organizations, there is a strong connection between its products, such as mined aluminum, refined aluminum, and goods fabricated from that aluminum (e.g., window frames). Therefore, on the one hand, the mines, refineries, and factories are each a division and need some autonomy to run their operations. On the other hand, the flow of material between the divisions requires coordination, so there are production planning and transport functions in the head office, which limit the autonomy of the divisions. Thus, there is some centralization of decision making in vertically integrated organizations.

Strategies with a dual focus, such as being diversified on both product and area, tend to be fitted by a matrix in which a manager reports to two bosses, for instance, both to the heads of the product and of the area.

Size. For organizational structure, the key aspect of organizational size is the number of members, such as the number of employees of a business firm. Increasing size leads to structural differentiation and bureaucracy. Larger organizations are of course more structurally differentiated than smaller organizations, with more departments, more sections, more job titles, and a greater number of levels in the organizational hierarchy that runs from the CEO to the bottom-level worker. Larger organizations are also more bureaucratic than smaller organizations. Bureaucracy here means formalization: rules, standard operating procedures, written job descriptions, and the like. Bureaucratic organizations also tend to be decentralized in their decision making. As organizational size increases, top managers are less able to control things by directly supervising people and making the decisions themselves. They are forced to delegate decision-making authority down to middle-level managers, but they compensate by creating rules and procedures (i.e., formalization) that indirectly control lower level members.

Putting the size and innovation contingencies together, scholars can say that as organizations grow in size, they increase their formalization and decentralization, but if they are innovative, they also reduce their formalization to a degree and increase their decentralization to a degree. This is accomplished by having research and development (R & D) departments and cross-functional project teams that work free from rules and enjoy autonomy, alongside manufacturing departments that are more bound by rules and are more centralized in their decision making. This is also known as being an ambidextrous organization.

The domain of the foregoing organizational structure and design theory is wide. It generalizes to organizations in many industries such as electronics and insurance, and, many types such as manufacturing and service. The main exception is that, as they grow in size, some organizations do not decentralize as much as business firms decentralize. These organizations are governmental and public-sector organizations, and labor unions. Whereas business organizations are prepared to grant some discretion to managers as to how they produce their results (e.g., sales growth), in these other types of organizations, their governing boards wish to exert more control over how their managers do things.

Evolution

The classic pioneers of management theory, for example, Edward F. L. Brech, expressed views about organizational structural design and its relevance for managers across many organizations. Their principles of management included the idea of organizational hierarchy as necessary and functional for effective operations. Specialization of workers, and indeed of foremen, was seen as enhancing productivity. The whole idea of studying management questions scientifically and coming up with valid guidelines for managerial practice promotes the notion of consciously designing and redesigning organizations. However, such knowledge was to be restricted to managers and their advisers and was to be oriented toward discovering a universal one best way for all organizations. And the image of the worker and of the effective production system tended to be very impersonal. This was echoed in early organizational sociological concepts from Max Weber of rational organization and bureaucracy.

Partly in response, the human relations movement, with roots in social psychology, stressed the emotional side of workers and the dynamics of groups, as well as propounding the benefits of communications and participation by members from lower organizational levels, as espoused, for example, by Rensis Likert.

Subsequently, structural contingency theory reconciled these two divergent views, proposing that the classical management view, the mechanistic organization model, was valid for tasks low on uncertainty, while the human relations view, the organic organization model, was valid for tasks high on uncertainty.

Tom Burns and George McPherson Stalker proposed that the mechanistic structure fits organizations that are low on the rate of technological and market change (e.g., firms in the textile industry), whereas organizations that are high on the rate of technological and market change (e.g., firms in the electronics industry) do fit the organic structure. In similar vein, Jerald Hage proposed that efficiency and low rates of program change in organizations are suited by highly formalized (e.g., many rules) and highly centralized structures, whereas high rates of program change in organizations are suited by less formalized (e.g., few rules) and decentralized structures.

Also, Paul R. Lawrence and Jay W. Lorsch proposed that organizations facing predictable environments had low amounts of differentiation between their functional departments and so required only relatively weak integration to match, whereas organizations facing unpredictable environments had high amounts of differentiation between their functional departments and so required relatively strong integration. Thus, the level of differentiation must be matched by the level of integration for high performance to result. However, this held only for undiversified organizations whose major subunits are functional departments (e.g., sales, production, and research) and therefore are highly interdependent. In a subsequent study of diversified corporations, there was no relation between the match of differentiation-integration and performance. J. D. Thompson had proposed that organizations vary in the interdependence of their subunits. Therefore, subsequently, Lorsch and colleagues proposed that differentiation and integration need to match only in an organization whose subunits are interdependent. However, for an organization whose subunits are not interdependent, differentiation and integration need not match. Lawrence and Lorsch described their approach as a contingency theory. There had already been a contingency theory of leadership, but theirs was the first application of this term to organizational structure. This became known as structural contingency theory.

At about the same time as Burns and Stalker, Alfred D. Chandler conducted histories of the strategy and structure of some large U.S. corporations and concluded that their adoption of the multidivisional structure was necessary to match their diversification. This was assimilated into structural contingency theory as the fit between organizational structure and organizational strategy.

Likewise, the relationship between organizational size and structural differentiation was an empirical discovery by Peter Michael Blau and Richard A. Schoenherr that Blau turned into an axiomatic theory. Similarly, the relationship between organizational size and bureaucracy was an empirical discovery that was then given a theoretical interpretation by John Child.

Importance

There has been a considerable body of empirical research into organizational structure and design. Much of it supports structural contingency theory. For instance, following the lead of Chandler, studies using large numbers of observations have shown that his "strategy leads to structure" and that the relationship holds in a range of countries such as Australia, France, Germany, Italy, Japan, and New Zealand. And studies using statistical methods have shown that the fit of structure to strategy has a positive effect on performance. A rival theory is that *divisionalization is a fit* to organizational size, but this relationship has not been so strongly supported empirically. Divisionalization is the change from the major subunits of an organization being differentiated typically by function to being differentiated by product or service or customer or area. Divisionalization, though creating autonomous divisions, is a means of decentralization.

Similarly, the relationship between size and structural differentiation has been well supported in many different types of organizations (e.g., governmental and retail businesses) and some different countries. Contingency theory tends to interpret the relationship between size and structure differentiation as due to the level of structural differentiation needing to fit size. However, researchers in structural differentiation tended not to see size as being a contingency of structural differentiation. Instead they saw structural differentiation as having a direct positive effect on performance. Neither this, nor the contingency fit effect on performance, has received much empirical study.

Moreover, the relationship between size and various aspects of bureaucratic structure has been extensively empirically researched and received much support, generalizing across types of organization and countries. The relationship between fit of bureaucracy (e.g., formalization) to the size contingency has also been studied empirically and gives support to structural contingency theory. Some of these aspects of bureaucracy, such as specialization, could also be regarded as aspects of structural differentiation and so provide support for a contingency theory interpretation of the relationship between size and structural differentiation.

Furthermore, the relationship between uncertainty, unpredictability and innovation, on the one hand, and the organic (i.e., low on both formalization and centralization), as opposed to mechanistic (i.e., high on both formalization and centralization), structure, on the other hand, has been extensively studied and well supported. The relationship between different types of interdependence and the various coordination mechanisms has been tested in only a few intensive case studies and some surveys but is generally supported. The relationship between innovation and the Lawrence and Lorsch integration mechanisms, such as cross-functional project teams, has been examined in a few studies and received some support.

Overall, the structural contingency theory provides a logical theory of the various organizational structures and why they exist: namely, because they are needed to fit all the combinations of the various contingency variables. Much of the empirical research finds associations between the contingencies and the structural variables. Thus, some managers have been able to choose fitting structures without guidance from the theory, which often arose after the initial empirical discoveries of those associations. This might seem to make structural contingency theory of limited practical value. However, empirical studies almost invariably find that a substantial number of organizations studied are in misfit and therefore losing performance through having suboptimal structures. For instance, a study of multinational corporations found that many of them had a structure that misfits the contingencies. Moreover, even where the correct structure has been chosen—for example, the multidivisional structure—some of its component parts may be missing, rendering it suboptimal.

Therefore, there is a role for formally educating managers in organizational design based on the contingency approach, to improve their structural choices. Consistent with this, many courses for managers, such as master of business administration (MBA) or executive programs, present some variant of the structural contingency theory model given here—though they may not be called that. Instead, they may be called organizational design, strategic organization, or organization for innovation, or some such. On the basis of his experience teaching in business schools, Lex Donaldson says most students and managers find the structural contingency theory model of organizations to be informative and reasonable. While the model features a number of contingencies and structural aspects, it is only of moderate complexity. Today, there is a computer program, the OrgCon, by Richard Burton and Børge Obel, which generates the optimal organizational design, given the scores on the contingency variables.

Lex Donaldson

See also Bureaucratic Theory; Contingency Theory; Differentiation and the Division of Labor; Environmental Uncertainty; Matrix Structure; Organic and Mechanistic Forms; Strategy and Structure

Further Readings

Blau, P. M. (1972). Interdependence and hierarchy in organizations. *Social Science Research, 1*(1), 1–24.

Brech, E. F. L. (1957). *Organisation: The framework of management.* London, England: Longmans.

Burns, T., & Stalker, G. M. (1961). *The management of innovation.* London, England: Tavistock.

Burton, R. M., & Obel, B. (2004). *Strategic organizational diagnosis and design: The dynamics of fit.* Boston, MA: Kluwer Academic.

Chandler, A. D., Jr. (1962). *Strategy and structure: Chapters in the history of the industrial enterprise.* Cambridge, MA: MIT Press.

Child, J. (1975). Managerial and organizational factors associated with company performance, Part 2: A contingency analysis. *Journal of Management Studies, 12*(1), 12–27.

Donaldson, L. (2001). *The contingency theory of organizations.* Thousand Oaks, CA: Sage.

Likert, R. (1961). *New patterns of management.* New York, NY: McGraw-Hill.

Thompson, J. D. (1967). *Organizations in action.* New York, NY: McGraw-Hill.

Woodward, J. 1965. *Industrial organisation: Theory and practice.* Oxford, England: Oxford University Press.

ORGANIZATIONALLY BASED SELF-ESTEEM

Self-esteem, one of the most researched constructs in the behavioral sciences, pertains to an individual's overall evaluation of his or her competencies. The construct's central management insight is that an individual's self-esteem can be shaped by the work setting, affecting the individual's view of how capable and valuable he or she is as a member of the organization. Self-esteem is viewed as a hierarchical phenomenon that operates at different levels of specificity, each one articulated around a different facet of the self (physical, social, psychological, etc). This self-evaluation includes a cognitive component (being competent and adequate) as well as an affective one (liking or disliking oneself). Organizationally based self-esteem (OBSE), a term first coined by J. L. Pierce and colleagues in 1989, focuses on self-esteem within the context of work, consequently reflecting individuals' self-perceptions of worth as organizational members acting in an organizational context. This entry discusses the factors that influence OBSE, as well as how it is related to other facets of self-esteem. Next, it delineates some of the characteristics of OBSE, presents the most relevant findings regarding the consequences of OBSE, and analyzes the role of OBSE as an important moderator for various organizational dynamics. The entry is concluded with a discussion of some of the practical implications of OBSE.

Fundamentals

OBSE is influenced by three different factors. First, it is affected by signals from environmental structures, such as control systems that carry assumptions about the individual ability to self-regulate. In fact, job complexity, autonomy, and perceived supervisor support have all been found to be related to OBSE. Second, it is shaped by messages sent from significant others that reinforce an individual's sense of self-worth. Following this rationale, coworker social support, for example, has been found to contribute to OBSE. Finally, OBSE also develops from an individual's direct and personal experiences, most notably successes and failures. As a dimension embedded within the higher order self-esteem construct, OBSE is intimately linked to other facets of self-esteem such as global (general, overall self-esteem) self-esteem and task-related self-esteem. Because global self-esteem is already developed upon organizational entry, organizational newcomers' level of OBSE is mostly driven by global self-esteem. With work experience however, OBSE develops and becomes better integrated with global self-esteem. Not surprisingly, much research on OBSE pertains to its development in organizational newcomers.

Although OBSE can fluctuate over time, it is generally stable when the work environment is stable as well. Moreover, self-consistency theory suggests that individuals seek to maintain a consistent level of self-esteem and, as a result, will respond to work stimulus in a manner that coincides with their level of self-esteem. Thus, someone with high OBSE is more likely to develop positive work attitudes and perform effectively at their work. The self-reinforcing cycle purported by self-consistency theory has been supported empirically.

Consequences of OBSE include motivation, attitudes, and work behaviors. For example, much research supports the relationship between OBSE and different facets of satisfaction and commitment, such as general satisfaction, organizational satisfaction, and organizational commitment. The reasoning behind these findings is that individuals with high OBSE will perceive themselves as valuable members of the organization, which in turn will increase their satisfaction at work and commitment to the organization. With regard to behaviors, empirical findings support a link between OBSE and turnover, job performance, citizenship behavior, and other high-level career elements. The literature argues that an individual who exhibits high levels of OBSE will have fewer intentions to leave the organization and will perform at higher levels than individuals with lower OBSE.

A vast literature focuses on the role of OBSE as a moderator of the relationships between work stimulus and behavior. For example, it has been noted that OBSE moderates the relationship between specific types of challenges (which include job transitions, task-related challenges, and obstacles) and development in organizations. OBSE has also been found to moderate the relationship between organizational uncertainty perception (job insecurity and anticipation of organizational changes) and intrinsic motivation, organizational commitment, and absenteeism.

Another example of OBSE as a moderator can be found in the relationship between role conditions (role ambiguity, role conflict, role overload, work environmental support, and supervisory support) and response (achievement satisfaction and role performance). Most of the work on OBSE has relied on the instrument developed by J. L. Pierce and colleagues. The 10-item measure requires the respondent to think about his or her relationship with his or her organization and is composed of statements such as "I count around here" and "I am trusted around here." Empirical evidence supports the validity of this instrument in North American and also in international contexts.

There are several practical implications of OBSE for managers and practitioners. OBSE can serve as an important and fundamental indicator for organizations. Organizational practices that provide opportunities for the worker to develop self-direction and self-control may boost OBSE and its positive consequences. Any signal that the organization can give employees to make them feel worthy members of the organization will not only positively impact OBSE, but also it may have an effect on employee satisfaction and commitment to the organization. The organization may also want to decrease adverse work conditions that negatively impact OBSE, such as role ambiguity, job insecurity, discrimination, and harassment in the workplace.

Stéphane Brutus and
Maria Carolina Saffie Robertson

See also Job Characteristics Theory; Leadership Practices; Organizational Commitment Theory; Organizational Identification; Self-Concept and the Theory of Self; Theory of Self-Esteem

Further Readings

Brockner, J. (1988). *Self-esteem at work: Research, theory and practice.* Lexington, MA: D. C. Heath & Co.

McAllister, D. J., & Bigley, G.A. (2002). Work context and the definition of self: How organizational care influences organization-based self-esteem. *Academy of Management Journal, 45*(5), 894–904.

Pierce, J. L., & Gardner, D. G. (2004). Self-esteem within the work and organizational context: A review of the organization-based self-esteem literature. *Journal of Management, 30*(5), 591–622.

Pierce, J. L., Gardner, D. G., Cummings, L. L., & Dunham, R. B. (1989). Organization-based self-esteem: Construct definition, measurement and validation. *Academy of Management Journal, 32*(3), 622.

Participative Model of Decision Making

A participative model of decision making takes into consideration that various situational forces influence, to some degree, the type of participatory approach managers should select during decision-making efforts. To this end, this entry first presents the seminal framework of Victor Vroom, Philip Yetton, and Arthur Jago, which offers a normative decision model (NDM)—or "decision tree"—to guide managers in systematically examining the structure of a decision context, assessing a defined set of criteria and relevant contingencies, and subsequently adopting the appropriate degree of participation in their decision-making style. Second, the entry presents Laurie K. Lewis and Travis L. Russ's model focusing on participation during planned change efforts. The model incorporates dimensions that may influence managers' choices as well as different approaches for facilitating varying degrees of stakeholder participation. Implications for contemporary management practices are discussed.

Fundamentals

Following the tradition of preceding situational leadership models, NDM can help leaders choose the most appropriate approaches for facilitating decision-making processes. The central premise of NDM is that the best approach for making organizational decisions is contingent on a number of situational factors, including quality, commitment of group or organization members, and time restrictions. NDM also argues that different decision-making situations require different leadership styles. NDM highlights five potential leadership styles and arranges them along a continuum, ranging from autocratic to consultative to group. Advancing a decision tree-type framework, NDM provides a systematic formula for identifying the most appropriate style that leaders can use when determining the degree to which they should involve subordinates in decision-making processes.

Yes or No Questions

NDM advances a series of seven questions to help leaders determine to what degree they might involve subordinates in decision-making processes. These questions are designed to be answered with either "yes" or "no" responses, creating a decision tree-type framework for determining the most appropriate decision-making style for a particular situation. The following highlights the eight assessment questions:

1. Is it absolutely critical that the "right" (or high-quality) decision is made? In other words, are the consequences of a "wrong" (or low-quality) decision significant?

2. Is it critical that subordinates are committed to the decision?

3. Do you (the leader) possess adequate information to make a high-quality decision on your own?

4. Is the problem structured in a way that the key issues and potential solutions are clear?

5. If you (the leader) made the decision independently, is it likely that your subordinates would be committed to the decision?

6. Do subordinates share the organizational goals to be obtained vis-à-vis the decision-making process?

7. Is it probable that conflict will emerge among subordinates when identifying the right decision?

8. Do subordinates possess adequate information to make a high-quality decision?

Decision-Making Styles

NDM advances a systematic decision tree-type framework for using the answers to the preceding yes or no questions to determine which style leaders should use in specific decision-making situations. NDM distinguishes five types of decision-making approaches organized into three styles, ranging from autocratic to consultative to group. Generally, an autocratic decision-making style is most appropriate when the leader possesses greater expertise about the problem than others, acting alone is not expected to cause any adverse consequences, subordinates will likely embrace the proposed solution, and there is little time to make a decision. Conversely, a consultative or collaborative style is generally appropriate when additional information is needed to make a decision, the structure of the problem is unclear, subordinate commitment is vital, and the leader has time to facilitate a participative decision-making process. The following describes NDM's decision-making styles in more detail.

Autocratic style. This style involves the leader independently making the decision and then informing others about it in an autocratic fashion. There are two types of autocratic decision making.

- *Autocratic Type 1.* This approach involves the leader's using information that is readily available to him or her and independently making a decision.
- *Autocratic Type 2.* This approach concerns a leader's collecting the requisite information from others and then independently making a decision. The leader may or may not inform others about why the information is needed and/or the final decision.

Consultative style. This style describes the act of a leader soliciting input and/or information from others and then making a decision. There are two types of consultative decision making.

- *Consultative Type 1.* This approach involves a leader's soliciting input about a decision from select individuals one at a time (versus as a group). The leader makes the ultimate decision.
- *Consultative Type 2.* This approach involves a leader's soliciting input from selected stakeholders who, as a group, discuss the problem and possible solutions. The ultimate decision is made by the leader and may or may not be influenced by external input.

Collaborative style. The leader and stakeholders collaboratively discuss the problem and possible solutions. The leader facilitates the discussion, but the ultimate decision is made by the group. The goal is shared consensus around the best course of action.

Participative Decision Making During Organizational Change

Lewis and Russ advanced a model illustrating how individuals solicit and use input during organizational change. They argue that during organizational change, managers' choices of participatory approaches are influenced by two dimensions in particular: (1) fidelity goals and (2) degree of emphasis on resource orientation. The following describes these forces.

Fidelity goals. Fidelity is the degree of alignment between managers' preconceived goals and actual outcomes of the decision-making process. In some contexts, it may be desirable for employees to abandon the original decision and explore new and innovative alternatives. In other cases, managers may treat "fidelity" as a hallmark of success, desiring very specific a priori outcomes.

Resource orientation. Managers with a high resource orientation actively solicit and use input. These managers involve diverse stakeholders, asking for and acting on those ideas, suggestions, objections, and contributions that enhance decision-making processes. Managers with a low resource orientation take no real action on others' feedback and treat soliciting others' input as a symbolic exercise.

When combined, the two dimensions presented above—fidelity goals and resource orientation–produce four general approaches for soliciting and using input during decision-making processes. The following describes each approach.

Open. This approach is used when managers have a low resource orientation and a low-to-moderate value for fidelity. In using this approach, managers seek input in a passive manner (e.g., a suggestion box) and use a flexible litmus test for evaluating "useful" input. This approach is used when managers do not have a strong "stake" in the decision-making process and/or do not face tremendous pressure to achieve specific, predetermined outcomes.

Restricted. This approach is used when managers have a low resource orientation and a high value for fidelity. In using this approach, managers solicit input from a narrow pool of stakeholders who are directly impacted by the decision-making outcomes and/or predicted to provide low to no resistance and/or minimal disruption to the decision-making process. Upon receiving input, managers apply strict litmus tests to find reasons for rejecting suggestions or critiques.

Political. This approach is used when managers have a moderate resource orientation and a low-to-moderate value of fidelity. Using this approach, managers grant more opportunities for participation in the decision-making process to those stakeholders with high perceived levels of perceived political power.

Advisory. This approach is used when managers have a moderate resource orientation and a high value for fidelity. Using this approach, managers solicit input from stakeholders, including advisers and opinion leaders who can provide advice for implementing the original vision as well as individuals who can persuade others to become supportive.

Importance

The NDM makes several valuable contributions to the landscape of literature on participative decision making. First, this model advances a systematic road map that can help leaders determine the most appropriate approach for making organizational decisions, ranging from autocratic to consultative to collaborative. In this sense, the NDM is very objective focused, providing leaders with a helpful decision-making tree that matches the goals and needs of the situation with the most appropriate decision-making style and approach. While valuable, NDM does possess some limitations. The greatest limitation may be that the NDM could be perceived as a one-size-fits-all framework and appear too rigid, mechanical, and limiting. For example, the assessment questions proposed by the NDM may be too general and lack specific contextualization. The NDM does not take into account the unique nature of the target problem nor does the NDM consider subordinates' experiences, emotions, or interpersonal relationships. For this reason, the NDM may not be adaptable and/or useful to unique decision-making situations and diverse organizational populations.

The participative model of decision making (PMDM) makes several valuable contributions to the landscape of literature on participative change approaches. First, this model recognizes that different forces likely influence managers' decisions about the type of participatory approach they use in change situations. Indeed, such patterns of input solicitation and use may be prevalent across contexts and types of organizations and change contexts. Second, the PMDM provides a language for talking about and classifying different types of participatory change approaches. The framework names the theoretical strategies that can be helpful when describing implementers' common practices in soliciting and using stakeholders' input during change. Third, the PMDM provides a predictive framework for anticipating when managers might use each change approach. Considering fidelity goals (i.e., the degree of variation desired) and resource-orientation goals (i.e., focusing on stakeholders' input as a means to discover errors and information that might enhance the decision-making process) helps us understand why, how, when, and with whom managers use different participatory approaches during change efforts.

Travis L. Russ

See also Contingency Theory of Leadership; Decision-Making Styles; Leadership Continuum Theory; Situational Theory of Leadership; Strategic Decision Making; Theory X and Theory Y

Further Readings

Lewis, L. K. (2011). Organizational change: Creating change through strategic communication. Chichester, England: Wiley-Blackwell.

Lewis, L. K., Richardson, B. K., & Hamel, S. A. (2003). When the stakes are communicative: The lamb's and the lion's share during nonprofit planned change. *Human Communication Research, 29,* 400–430.

Lewis, L. K., & Russ, T. L. (2012). Soliciting and using input during organizational change initiatives: What are practitioners doing? *Management Communication Quarterly, 26,* 268–295.

Lewis, L. K., Schmisseur, A., Stephens, K., & Weir, K. (2006). Advice on communicating during organizational change: The content of popular press books. *Journal of Business Communication, 43,* 113–137.

Lewis, L. K., & Seibold, D. R. (1993). Innovation modification during intraorganizational adoption. *Academy of Management Review, 18,* 322–354.

Russ, T. L. (2008). Communicating change: A review and critical analysis of programmatic and participatory implementation approaches. *Journal of Change Management, 8,* 199–211.

Russ, T. L. (2011). Theory X/Y assumptions as predictors of managers' propensity for participative decision making. *Management Decision, 49,* 823–836.

Vroom, V. H., & Jago, A. G. (1988). *The new leadership: Managing participation in organizations.* Englewood Cliffs, NJ: Prentice Hall.

Vroom, V. H., & Sternberg, R. J. (2002). Theoretical letters: The person versus the situation in leadership. *Leadership Quarterly, 13,* 301–323.

Vroom, V. H., & Yetton, P. W. (1973). *Leadership and decision-making.* Pittsburgh, PA: University of Pittsburgh Press.

PATH-GOAL THEORY OF LEADERSHIP

The path-goal theory of leadership considers the effectiveness of alternative leader behaviors in different situations. The idea that there are no universally effective leadership behaviors and that situational factors determine optimal leadership behavior, path-goal theory is in a category of leadership theories termed "situational theories of leadership." Simply stated, situational leadership theories such as path-goal theory emerged out of the realization that characteristics of the situational context in which leaders find themselves must play a critical determining role in how a leader should behave to maximize important employee outcomes such as satisfaction, motivation, and work performance. As one of a number of situational leadership theories, path-goal theory has found a prominent and enduring place among leadership theories within the field of management. More than 40 years have passed since the theory was first articulated by Robert House in 1971, yet the theory continues to be a mainstay entry in chapters on leadership and in most organizational behavior textbooks. As such, inclusion of the theory in this encyclopedia is clearly warranted. This entry reviews the theory, considers how it was developed and has evolved over time, and concludes by discussing the importance of the theory for leadership theory and research.

Fundamentals

According to path-goal theory, the principal function of leadership is to engage in behaviors that facilitate employees in the pursuit of their goals. Thus, the theory proposes that leaders should help remove obstacles and clear the path for employees so that they may enact whatever work-related behaviors are requisite to obtaining valued outcomes (e.g., pay, promotion, performance, status, etc.). Importantly, the theory is concerned with dyadic relationships between leaders and their employees: Therefore, the theory does not consider, for example, leadership processes in larger work units or groups. In sum, the theory focuses on leader behaviors directed toward or relating to individual employees.

According to path-goal theory, there are four major categories of leadership behavior: (a) directive behaviors, (b) supportive behaviors, (c) achievement-oriented behaviors, and (d) participative behaviors. Directive behaviors include a constellation of leadership behaviors designed to provide employees with structure and vital information required for them to clearly see the path to their individual goals. Examples of these behaviors include clarifying employee roles and expectations, providing technical guidance and assistance, and coordinating and scheduling work. Not included in this category are punitive or otherwise sanction-based actions that do not support employees as they strive for valued outcomes.

Supportive behaviors represent leadership behaviors aimed at creating a supportive work environment while serving to boost employee confidence and lowering perceived stress at the same time. Examples of supportive leadership behaviors include seeking out employees to hear and potentially address their concerns, displaying warmth and an openness to meet with employees as required, and creating a friendly work atmosphere.

Achievement-oriented behaviors consist of those leadership behaviors directed toward attempts to maximize employee performance. Examples of this category of leadership behaviors include setting difficult yet attainable employee work goals, encouraging employees to strive for performance excellence, and boosting employee confidence so that they can achieve a high level of performance.

Participative behaviors consist of leadership behaviors designed to involve employees in decision making by giving them an opportunity to provide input into work-relevant decisions. For example, leaders may engage employees by soliciting their opinions, empowering employees to make their own decisions concerning certain aspects of their work activities, and collaborating with employees while setting work goals.

Given that there are four major categories of leadership behaviors with a number of distinct behaviors embedded within each category, the theory provides some guidance concerning which behaviors leaders may use when clarifying path-goal relationships and helping employees achieve valued outcomes. Specifically, the theory posits that situational factors, including both employee characteristics (e.g., employee skills) and environmental factors (e.g., difficulty of work tasks), must be considered when leaders decide on specific actions. Based on an analysis of the situational context, leaders then choose to engage in certain behaviors from one or more of the major categories. This allows them to assist individual employees as they navigate the path toward valued goals.

For example, if an employee is highly skilled and knowledgeable, a leader may be more inclined to choose participative and/or achievement-oriented behaviors and concomitantly less inclined to choose directive behaviors. However, in a highly uncertain and unstable environment, even a highly accomplished and skilled employee may require more directive behavior from a leader. As another example, a stressful and demanding job may necessitate a leadership style that balances supportive behaviors (to address the stress component) with achievement-oriented behaviors designed to reinforce the employee's confidence reflecting performance requirements that are both realistic and achievable. It should be noted that the theory does not map out all possible situational contingencies and their interactions to predict specific optimal leadership behaviors. Rather, the theory acknowledges that effective leadership requires leaders to choose their actions in accord with their perceptions of situational factors. According to Robert House, critical to path-goal theory are the consequences of effective leadership behavior for employee motivation. Although widely considered a leadership theory, path-goal theory is equally concerned with employee motivation. As discussed below, a number of specific theories of work motivation are embedded within path-goal theory.

The theory of motivation most clearly and directly part of the foundation of path-goal theory is Victor Vroom's expectancy theory of work motivation—one of a number of similar theories that emerged in the 1960s. The conceptual importance of expectancy theory was acknowledged by Robert House in his formulation of path-goal theory. Here, we will describe only elements of expectancy theory directly related to path-goal theory. Because the topic of expectancy theory is covered separately in this encyclopedia, this entry will describe only key aspects of the theory in general terms as they relate to path-goal theory.

Specifically, path-goal theory predicts that effective leadership has a direct effect on employee cognition. According to expectancy theory, employees are motivated to engage in certain behaviors when (a) they expect that exerting effort will enhance their performance and (b) they believe that high performance will lead to valued outcomes. How does leader behavior affect employee cognition in this regard? First, an assumption is that an effective leader determines precisely which outcomes are most valued by an individual employee. These outcomes may be tangible, such as enhanced pay, or more intrinsic, such as enhanced self-esteem or a sense of achievement. The leader must also ensure that an employee perceives himself or herself as capable of achieving the level of performance necessary for attaining valued outcomes. For example, a leader can remove obstacles to performance and boost the employee's confidence. The leader must also clarify linkages between performance and outcomes for the employee. Thus, if an employee erroneously believes that valued rewards are forthcoming regardless of his or her performance level, the leader must clarify and help the employee understand that a high level of performance is instrumental for attaining rewards. In essence, a fundamental assumption of path-goal theory is that a leader's role is to help employees cognitively navigate through decisions and motivate them to engage in behavior that will lead to valued outcomes.

Assuming that the leader is successful in clarifying the various path-goal linkages and motivating an employee to attain high levels of performance, both leader satisfaction and employee satisfaction will be enhanced. A rational cognitive process is assumed to underlie decisions to exert increased work effort toward personal goal attainment. However, Robert House acknowledged that the utility of his theory for predicting employee attitudes and behavior hinges on the assumption that the employee is a rational actor who engages in rational decision-making processes concerning effort exertion. He suggested that there may be situations where the tenability of this assumption is challenged (e.g., when employees are under severe work stress and cannot think rationally)—and this may create a boundary condition on the validity of path-goal theory for understanding the link between leader behavior and employee motivation.

Relationship With Other Theories

Beyond expectancy theory, path-goal theory incorporates other theoretical perspectives on work motivation. As such, motivational theories commonly construed as need theories of motivation (e.g., Abraham Maslow's hierarchy of needs theory) have a conceptual link to path-goal theory, insofar as the leader is assumed to assist employees in meeting their most important needs. In addition, Edwin Locke and Gary Latham's goal-setting theory of motivation finds a conceptual home within the larger path-goal framework. A key tenet of goal-setting theory is that difficult goals will be more motivating than easier goals, conditional upon employee goal acceptance. Path-goal theory incorporates these ideas, with the inclusion of achievement-oriented leader behaviors directed toward enhancing goal difficulty and participative behaviors concerned with fostering goal acceptance.

To the extent that path-goal theory consolidates various motivational theories under a single conceptual umbrella, it may best be characterized as a metatheory—a theory that integrates or consolidates more than one theoretical perspective. However, unlike metatheories of motivation (e.g., Howard Klein's control theory of motivation comes to mind here) specifically focused on the topic of motivation, path-goal theory is considered a theory of leadership—and was not developed with the goal of conceptual integration of diverse motivational perspectives. The fact that organizational behavior textbooks commonly place path-goal theory in chapters on leadership (and not in motivation chapters) underscores this point. Clearly, Robert House developed the theory as a leadership theory, while acknowledging the critical role of motivational processes as a subcomponent of the theory.

Path-goal theory also shares elements with other theories of leadership. For example, a series of studies emanating from Ohio State University in the late 1940s uncovered two broad leadership styles: initiating structure and consideration. This led to the development of measures intended to assess the extent to which leaders engage in each of these behavioral styles (e.g., Leader Behavior Description Questionnaire) and considerable research examining the correlates (e.g., job satisfaction) of these alternative styles. Conceptually, initiating structure is similar to the path-goal category of directive leadership, while consideration is similar to the category of supportive leadership. Similarly, research from the University of Michigan (conducted around the same time as the Ohio State studies) uncovered two dimensions that parallel directive and supportive behavior categories, respectively: production-oriented leaders and employee-oriented leaders.

Path-goal theory also shares elements with other situational theories of leadership. For instance, Fred Fiedler's contingency model and Paul Hersey and Ken Blanchard's situational leadership theory share commonalities with path-goal theory insofar as all three theories suggest that effective leadership depends on the degree of fit between the leader's behavior and various factors in the particular situation.

Evolution

The genesis of path-goal theory can be traced to research conducted by Martin Evans from the University of Toronto in the late 1960s. Robert House was intrigued by Evans's incorporation of expectancy theory as a mechanism for understanding the effects of either initiating structure or consideration leadership styles (see description above) on employee behavior. Moreover, he was intrigued that the same leader behaviors proved to be effective or ineffective, depending on the organization in question. This led him to theorize that contextual factors play a role in determining whether and to what extent specific leader behaviors are effective. The theory evolved, and Robert House and Terrence Mitchell published a paper in 1974 introducing the directive and supportive leadership behavior categories—effectively replacing the initiating structure and consideration categories, which were included in the earliest instantiation of path-goal theory published by Robert House in 1971. In addition, to better and more fully capture the ways in which leader behavior may influence employee motivational processes, the achievement-oriented and participative leadership categories were added to the theory in 1974.

In a subsequent paper published in 1996, House reviewed the original theory and presented additional insights and suggested modifications in light of existing empirical evidence and further conceptual analysis. First, the theory was relabeled as "the path-goal theory of work unit leadership," owing to the fact that the theory was broadened to consider both the performance of individuals as well as larger work units. Second, House presented a variety of conceptual propositions around an expanded set of eight leadership behavior categories—building on and extending the original set of four categories.

Notably, one of the new categories is value-based leadership. This category is conceptually similar to a leadership theory that has gained prominence in the literature: transformational leadership theory. In the updated theory, House offered a number of propositions concerning value-based leadership. For example, he conjectured that a value-based leadership strategy would be most effective when a leader refrains from linking performance to extrinsic rewards. This proposition has been tested in recent research, although it has received only minimal support to date. The incorporation of value-based leadership in the updated theory represents yet another example of the conceptual linkages of path-goal theory with other prominent leadership theories as delineated above.

Along with an expanded set of leadership categories, the updated theory considers a variety of situational variables that suggest particular choices of leadership behavior designed to assist employees in meeting their goals. Much like the original theory, the updated theory is employee focused, suggesting that the role of leadership is to assist employees in overcoming personal and/or environmental deficiencies that provide roadblocks on the path to meeting personal goals. Accordingly, leadership is considered necessary only when employees need path-goal clarifications. Therefore, the updated theory also allows for substitutes and neutralizers for leadership. That is, in some situations leaders are irrelevant and certain situational factors can act as substitutes for leadership or neutralize the leader's ability to influence his or her employees. For example, the training or experience of employees can replace the need for a leader's support or ability to create structure.

Importance

Given that the pre-1996 conceptualization of the path-goal theory has been the subject of most scientific scrutiny, our discussion will be focused on this version of the theory. Overall, the theory has received mixed support, especially when using work performance as the outcome. As House and others have noted, however, there have been deficiencies in prior testing that call into question whether the theory has been properly tested at all.

On this, Martin Evans suggested that the theory has not been properly tested in that researchers typically correlate leadership behavior with employee outcomes, without due consideration and examination of cognitive-motivational processes fundamental to the theory. House has raised myriad concerns, including the fact that poor measures have been used to assess leadership behavior and that the contribution of the theory in predicting employee performance and job satisfaction beyond other variables (e.g., organizational commitment) has not been considered. In addition, self-report measures were commonly used in prior research to test various components of path-goal theory (e.g., moderator and outcome variables), and this could have led to research participant biases influencing study results. Also, John Jermier pointed out that the complexity of the theory has not been well served by relatively simplistic research approaches typically used to test the theory components.

Notwithstanding mixed research findings and interpretational difficulties arising from various study weaknesses, path-goal theory has had a significant and lasting impact on leadership theory and research. House noted that the theory's assumption that leaders serve to trigger a motivational process became a conceptual starting point for the development of his charismatic leadership theory. In addition, path-goal theory may have played a role in the development of substitutes for leadership theory. Specifically, substitutes for leadership theory considers the idea that given certain situational factors, employees may be able to self-lead. The idea that the nature and extent of leadership behavior will hinge on the situational context can be traced directly back to path-goal theory.

Jermier stated that the lasting impact of path-goal theory may be better appreciated when it is realized that it was the first leadership theory to (a) consider a variety of leadership behaviors, (b) focus on leadership as a dyadic process, (c) map out some of the complexities inherent in the situational context that influence leaders, and (d) consider leadership as a function serving the needs of subordinates and a function that may be undertaken by nonleaders in certain situations.

The focus on the needs of followers implies that path-goal theory is focused on followership, a hot topic in leadership theory today. With well over 300 citations and continued exposure in management textbooks, it is clear that the path-goal theory remains relevant and represents far more than a historical footnote in the field of leadership. Hopefully, future research will consider the important link between leadership and motivation as explicated in the theory, thereby furthering our knowledge concerning the importance of leadership for employee motivation.

Modern managers can benefit by understanding the theory and the implications it provides for leadership practice. Explicitly, the theory provides managers with a contingency-based strategy for aligning leader behaviors with the needs and desires of followers. A key take-away message of the theory is that there is no "one size fits all" when it comes to leadership. Rather, by properly diagnosing the situational context, leaders may choose those behaviors that best serve to motivate followers in helping them achieve work-related goals. By achieving these goals, this should serve to both enhance employee performance as well as job satisfaction.

*Heather MacDonald and
Mary Sully de Luque*

See also Charismatic Theory of Leadership; Expectancy Theory; Leadership Practices; Situational Theory of Leadership; Substitutes for Leadership

Further Readings

Evans, M. G. (1996). R. J. House's "A Path-Goal Theory of Leader Effectiveness." *Leadership Quarterly, 7,* 305–309.

House, R. J. (1996). Path-goal theory of leadership: Lessons, legacy, and a reformulated theory. *Leadership Quarterly, 7,* 323–352.

House, R. J., & Mitchell, T. R. (1974, Autumn). Path-goal theory of leadership. *Journal of Contemporary Business,* pp. 81–97.

Jermier, J. M. (1996). The path-goal theory of leadership: A subtextual analysis. *Leadership Quarterly, 7,* 311–316.

McLaurin, J. (2006). The role of the situation in the leadership process: A review and application. *Academy of Strategic Management Journal, 5,* 97–114.

Podsakoff, P. M., MacKenzie, S. B., Ahearne, M., & Bommer, W. H. (1995). Searching for a needle in a haystack: Trying to identify the illusive moderators of leadership behaviors. *Journal of Management, 21,* 422–470.

Schriesheim, C. A., Castro, S. L., Xiaohua T. Z., & DeChurch, L. A. (2006). An investigation of path-goal and transformational leadership theory predictions at the individual level of analysis. *Leadership Quarterly, 17,* 21–38.

Schriesheim, C. A., & Neider, L (1996). Path-goal leadership theory: The long and winding road. *Leadership Quarterly, 7,* 317–321.

Vecchio, R. P., Justin, J. E., & Pearce, C. L. (2008). The utility of transactional and transformational leadership for predicting performance and satisfaction within a path-goal theory framework. *Journal of Occupational and Organizational Psychology, 8,* 71–82.

Wofford, J. C., & Liska, L. Z. (1993). Path-goal theories of leadership: A meta-analysis. *Journal of Management, 19,* 857–876.

PATTERNS OF INNOVATION

While the phrase *patterns of innovation* can refer to any research program attempting to explain modes, models, and typologies of innovation, it is most typically used to refer to research spawned by two seminal works by James M. Utterback and William J. Abernathy. Abernathy and Utterback used the phrase to refer to cycles of product and process innovation that make up industry life cycles and to describe three stages—fluid, transitional, and specific—that co-align characteristics of productive units and the innovation types they produce. Utterback and Abernathy developed their strategic framework for patterns of innovation in two papers that present a new model for understanding a business unit's capacity for and methods of innovation based on its stage of evolution. This entry presents the central themes in these two articles, distinguishes the life cycle stages that Abernathy and Utterback identify, and discusses their importance.

Fundamentals

Utterback and Abernathy introduced the term *productive unit* to refer to a product line and its associated production process collectively and argued this was the appropriate unit of analysis from which to study patterns of innovation. In "Patterns of Industrial Innovation" Abernathy and Utterback link the evolution of a productive unit to the kinds of innovations it is most likely to produce, and in "A Dynamic Model of Process and Product innovation," they describe a corresponding industry life cycle pattern. Generally, they argued that early in an industry's development, the product space is somewhat ambiguous, and functional improvement is the overriding focus of productive units' innovative efforts. Small, flexible productive units tend to focus on radical innovations, and are internally fluid organizations, capable of responding quickly to shifts in the demand for their products. Later, larger, mature productive units focus on operating tight and highly structured organizations and develop incremental innovations. Demand for their product has stabilized, enabling these productive units to focus on creating the most efficient and effective modes of delivering products with specific properties.

The Dynamic Model of Product and Process Innovation

In their 1975 publication, Utterback and Abernathy hypothesized a systematic relationship between the stage of development of a firm's productive processes and the character of its innovations, strategy and competitive focus. They proposed a coherent pattern, linking market and technology triggers for innovation to innovation types (product and process) and to barriers to innovation. As industries mature, the competitive space becomes standardized, rigid, and stable, and flexible processes are exchanged for low cost and consistency.

The process stages. In the *uncoordinated* stage, Utterback and Abernathy argue that market expansion and redefinition result in high rates of product and process change and in competitive diversity. The greatest variety of processes exists in the uncoordinated stage because everyone is using manual operations and/or general-purpose equipment, and all producers use processes that have "unsettled" relationship between process elements. High-process slack is adaptive and organic but inefficient. In the *segmental* stage, they argue, price competition intensifies, tasks become more specialized, and the production system becomes integrated through automation and process control of subprocesses. They stress the segmented quality of the process since it is mainly subprocesses that are special purpose. The impetus for this development is higher sales volume and a few stable product designs. In the *systemic* stage, selective improvement of process elements becomes increasingly difficult. The process becomes highly integrated, making change costly. Incentive to change these processes is either a new technology or shifts in the requirements of the market. If changes are resisted by existing producers because of cost pressure, the window for *revolutionary* instead of *evolutionary change* opens.

The product stages. Performance-maximizing product innovation is typical in the uncoordinated stage. The rate of innovation is high and profit margins are large. Firms competing in this space will tend to rely on external sources of information, and diverse sources of information, to spur innovations. The industry will be made up of relatively few firms and either small, new firms or older firms attempting to take advantage of their technological strengths. Production will tend to take place in affluent markets where a wide variety of inputs are accessible. The organization that is intimately familiar with customers and their needs will innovate best. Sales-maximizing strategies become more common as the industry ages and experience reduces market uncertainty. Innovations geared toward improving product performance tend to decline, unless customers can easily compare and evaluate performance improvements. Varieties of products are offered that best fit certain user needs so that both the market and the process are segmented. Cost-minimizing strategies become dominant in the mature industry, and product diversity declines. The industry moves toward oligopoly, capital investments are very high, and production is relocated to achieve the lowest possible costs. Major innovations are scant because they cannot justify the necessary costs of adjusting production.

Evolution of stages. Abernathy and Utterback are quick to point out that the progression of stages is not obvious nor is it necessarily linearly advancing. Sometimes industrial competition may halt or reverse stages of development. As a consequence, the model cannot be viewed as a strictly sequential model, and it becomes difficult to predict, using the model alone, what strategies are ideal for any particular firm competing in the space. Firms that rush toward cost minimizing may find themselves eliminated by the innovativeness of some firms still maximizing sales. On the other hand, firms that do not recognize powerful cost pressures may also be eliminated from the competitive space because they cannot survive against price pressure. In essence, this is a dynamic model determined by uncertainties in technological development and customer needs, which change over time. However, at a snapshot, one should be able to identify the overall fit of the model to reality. Finally, they stress that the locus of innovation shifts across stages, the type of innovation likely to succeed is stage dependent, and the total array of barriers to an innovation are associated with stages.

Productive Unit Characteristics and Innovation

In their 1978 article, Abernathy and Utterback defined the productive unit as their unit of analysis and distinguished its life cycle stages in greater detail. They also developed the concept of a dominant design—a set of attributes shared by most product offerings, whose emergence marks a turning point in an industry's competitive and innovative focus. Productive units come into being with a particular novel product in mind and develop fluidly as the firm experiments and learns about the market's reaction to it. As productive units move to a transitional stage, they begin to focus on process innovation. Later on, the same mature productive unit commits to certain key elements of product design. This, in turn, enables the production process to be standardized, to gain economies of scale, and to realize general cost advantages from efficiency and effectiveness within its productive niche. Product innovation occurs at a slower rate and becomes largely incremental. To further distinguish the three stages of a productive unit's life cycle, Abernathy and Utterback identified nine dimensions, ranging from innovation focus and product line characteristics to organizational governance mode, that characterize each stage.

Fluid pattern. New productive units come into being in response to specific user needs. In the *fluid* state, the performance requirements for new products and market needs are not well defined, and the pace of technological innovation is rapid. As firms work to understand and address these nascent needs and to deliver a sufficient level of functional product performance, a diverse product line is created. Experimentation produces major changes to product design and includes customizing designs to respond to particular users. The production process for these products is flexible and inefficient, and changes are easily accommodated. They exploit materials and equipment that are generally available and rely on highly skilled labor. Often, small-scale plants located near the user or the source of technology are used. Organizational control is informal and entrepreneurial.

Transitional pattern. As firms come to understand user needs and match technical capabilities to those demands, they begin to specialize product design and associated production processes to improve reliability and work toward gaining some cost efficiencies. The focus during the *transitional* phase is on leveraging core product advantages through variations, expanding market reach, and leveraging opportunities created by expanding internal technical capabilities. Productive units also struggle with the need to make major changes in processes to increase volume. Usually, this means they must focus and commit to one product design, which is stable enough to have sufficient production volumes and allow for some parts of the production process to be standardized and automated. While the trend is for them to become more rigid, there is still the possibility for big changes to occur in major production steps. Specialized materials may be demanded from some suppliers, and the general-purpose plant may be specialized in certain sections. Organizational control occurs through relationships, projects, and task groups.

Specific pattern. The product is now a commodity product, and the basis of competition shifts from performance to price and cost considerations. Innovation is less rapid and more incremental in nature. In the *specific* state, the organizational structure and control are more formal, with technology planning and forecasting being formally delegated tasks; control occurs through structure, goals, and rules. Productive units focus on driving margins through cost reductions and improving productivity and quality; production processes are rigid and capital intensive, so the cost of change is high. Specialized equipment and materials are employed, and production processes are mostly automated, requiring labor primarily for monitoring and control. If specialized materials are not available, vertical integration will be extensive.

Importance

Abernathy and Utterback's core observations have found empirical support in a wide range of industries and have become central tenets in subsequent research. For instance, the progression from fluid to rigid product designs and associated production processes is a core theme in research on dominant design and cycles of technological change. Other industry life cycle theories also posit a progression from product or quality innovation to a focus on cost reduction. However, the theory's boundary conditions have been questioned, and alternate cycles of innovation have also been predicted and empirically supported.

The premise that competitive/innovative foci in industries shift with the emergence of widely accepted product features established the concept of a dominant design. The tight link between product and productive unit, and the rigidities associated with standardizing these, implied that new and entrenched firms would have particular innovative advantages and foreshadowed work on architectural and modular innovation and the mirroring hypothesis.

The Abernathy and Utterback model alerts managers to the trade-offs associated with design standardization and tight coupling with productive units. It has helped sensitize managers to the tendency of competitive forces and innovation patterns to move in cycles. It has encouraged them to not only match organizational processes with these cyclical demands but also to keep an eye out for discontinuous innovation, which could unleash a new cycle of innovation that destroys the advantages of established productive units.

The Abernathy and Utterback model encourages managers to attend to the patterns of innovation that characterize their industry and to understand the underlying structural drivers. As fundamental uncertainties about market demand and technology capabilities are resolved, firms' strategic choices change. For example, process research and development and outsourcing may appear more attractive at one stage than in another. Because the specific cycles and their structural precursors differ across industries, managers will need to devise their own metrics to assess which stage their industry is in. Regardless of industry context, managers ought to appreciate core rigidities that accompany their efforts to attain greater operational efficiency and anticipate the kinds of product and process innovations that could undo their firm's competitive advantages.

Susan Cohen, Robert Ryan,
and Sean Tsuhsiang Hsu

See also Architectural Innovation; Continuous and Routinized Change; Core Competence; Punctuated Equilibrium Model; Quantum Change; Technological Discontinuities; Technology S-Curve

Further Readings

Abernathy, W. J., & Utterback, J. M. (1978). Patterns of industrial innovation. *Technology Review, 80*(7), 40–47.

Adner, R., & Levinthal, D. (2001). Demand heterogeneity and technology evolution: Implications for product and process innovation. *Management Science, 47*(5), 611–628.

Agarwal, R., Sarkar, M. B., & Echambadi, R. (2002). The conditioning effect of time on firm survival: An industry life cycle approach. *Academy of Management Journal, 45*(5), 971–994.

Anderson, P., & Tushman, M. L. (1990). Technological discontinuities and dominant designs: A cyclical model of technological change. *Administrative Science Quarterly, 35*(4), 604–633.

Henderson, R. M., & Clark, K. B. (1990). Architectural innovation: The reconfiguration of existing product technologies and the failure of established firms. *Administrative Science Quarterly, 35*, 9–30.

Levinthal, D. A. (1998). The slow pace of rapid technological change: Gradualism and punctuation in technological change. *Industrial and Corporate Change, 7*(2), 217–247.

Malerba, F. (2006). Innovation and the evolution of industries. *Journal of Evolutionary Economics, 16*, 3–23.

Murmann, J. P., & Frenken, K. (2006). Toward a systematic framework for research on dominant designs, technological innovations, and industrial change. *Research Policy, 35*, 925–952.

Suarez, F. F., & Utterback, J. M. (1995). Dominant designs and the survival of firms. *Strategic Management Journal, 16*, 415–430.

Utterback, J. M., & Abernathy, W. J. (1975). A dynamic model of product and process innovation. *Omega, 3*(6), 639–656.

Patterns of Political Behavior

Although contemporary management theory has a rich diversity befitting an interdisciplinary endeavor, the beginnings of the field were dominated by a constellation of rational approaches. Early on, theories of bureaucracy, scientific management, administrative management, and rational decision making established the primary concerns of management theory. An understanding of political behavior supplements such rational approaches and provides insights into many key aspects of life in organizations. Recognition of the importance played by politics and power in organizations can certainly be traced to some of the classical organizational writings of Max Weber, Karl Marx, Robert Michels, and others. A major rediscovery of politics in organizations began during the late 1970s and the 1980s. Since then, a rich literature on political behavior in organizations has developed. A variety of definitions of political behavior have been proposed in this body of work, in some cases reflecting different levels of analysis that focus on the individual, subgroups, the organization as a whole, or interorganizational networks. Perhaps the most frequent definition of political behavior views it as those discretionary actions undertaken by members of the organization to promote group and self-interest. Thus, the nonorganizationally sanctioned behavior of individuals may shape the distribution of advantages and disadvantages within an organization. The many forms that political behavior in organizations can take have provided numerous opportunities for empirical work, although the difficulties in measuring political behavior have also resulted in a good deal of work that looks at perceptions of political behavior rather than direct measures. In addition, some types of political behavior have received a great deal of attention in empirical studies, whereas other types have been largely neglected. This entry identifies the range of political behavior in organizations and reports key empirical trends. Knowledge of political behavior helps explain anomalous behaviors in routine management matters as well as extreme behaviors such as whistle-blowing.

Fundamentals

Political behavior in organizations varies along a number of dimensions. One major distinction is between political behaviors that are viewed as either legitimate or illegitimate within the organization. Even though political behavior is nonsanctioned behavior, some forms such as symbolic protests or forming coalitions may be accepted within the culture of an organization as everyday behavior, whereas other behaviors such as threats or open rebellion are viewed as going beyond acceptable behavior. A second major distinction is between political behaviors that are internal or focused within the organization such as obstructionism or reprisals and external behaviors that go outside the boundaries of the organization in an attempt to gain new resources as in contacting the media or a regulatory agency. Hierarchy is a central feature of organizations, and a third important distinction is between vertical political behaviors that involve influence processes between superiors and subordinates, such as bypassing the chain of command and mentor-protégé relationships and lateral behaviors among peers such as exchanging favors.

Over the past three decades, empirical research on political behavior in organizations has examined a wide range of organizational decision making, some unexpected. Information technology projects, often known for their delays and cost overruns, can be effectively managed through the use of non-threatening and nonpossessive political behaviors. Organizational strategic planning is coming to be understood as an area where competing objectives, preferences, and priorities are natural and legitimate. Hiring and selection interviews have also proven to be a fruitful area for inquiries into how political behavior can either improve or reduce the effectiveness of hiring decisions. Pay and promotion decisions have been studied and have led to recommendations for human resource professionals to take political behaviors into account. The role played by political behavior in the implementation of information technology has been studied. Even studies of accounting, that presumably most rational business specialty, have shown the impact of political behavior in setting accounting standards. Disputes as to what is good accounting may be settled by political processes when technical and theoretical foundations are exhausted.

In general, researchers have focused more attention on antecedents of political behavior in organizations than on the consequences of these acts. When consequences have been examined, greater attention has been paid to the impacts on the individuals who engaged in political behavior than to the consequences for the organization. This is especially true of the extensive literature on one form of political behavior, whistle-blowing. There are examples of research that has looked at the impacts of whistle-blowing on organizational policies and procedures for handling dissent, techniques for resolving disputes, management turnover, stock values, and other effects. One international study found that whistle-blowing can deter collusion and cartel formation. A much more extensive literature exists, however, on how whistle-blowers were sanctioned, often very severely, by their organizations and what impacts there were for their subsequent careers. The growth of whistleblower protections laws and the emergence of incentives for whistle-blowers have shaped scholarship both on motivations of whistle-blowers and consequences for those who blow the whistle.

Those writing about whistle-blowing range from those who see it as altruistic and prosocial to those who view it as self-serving and destructive. Such divergent views call for those who write about political behavior to be transparent about the values and ethical positions that may shape their work. It appears that, with the exception of whistle-blowing, greater attention has been paid in the scholarly literature on political behavior in organizations to legitimate rather than illegitimate forms of political behavior. Although both internal and external forms of political behavior have received a good deal of attention, lateral forms of political behavior have not received the attention paid to vertical forms. This may reflect the traditional attention paid to hierarchy in organizations, or it may reflect the consequences of research methods such as those relying on reports from supervisors.

Management is a multidisciplinary science. Managers need to understand that to be effective they must employ skills drawn from sociology and political science in addition to economics and decision sciences. Effective organizations must manage a range of political behaviors even though they may fall outside the formal organizational structure. A full understanding of management includes the recognition that many member actions are political behaviors that are often critical in determining the direction and success of the organization.

Dan Farrell and James C. Petersen

See also Conflict Handling Styles; Influence Tactics; Organizational Demography; Resource Dependence Theory; Social Exchange Theory

Further Readings

Bradshaw-Camball, P., & Murray, V. (1991). Illusions and other games: A trifocal view of organizational politics. *Organization Science, 2,* 379–398.

Farrell, D., & Petersen, J. C. (1982). Patterns of political behavior in organizations. *Academy of Management Review, 7,* 403–412.

Ferris, G. R., Harrell-Cook, G., & Dulebohn, J. H. (2000). Organizational politics: The nature of the relationship between political perceptions and political behavior. *Research in the Sociology of Organizations, 17,* 89–130.

Miceli, M., Near, J., & Dworkin, T. M. (2008). *Whistle-blowing in organizations.* New York, NY: Routledge.

Zani, A., & O'Neill, R. M. (2001). Sanctioned versus non-sanctioned political tactics. *Journal of Managerial Issues, 13,* 245–262.

PERSONAL ENGAGEMENT (AT WORK) MODEL

The concept of personal engagement was developed to explain what traditional studies of work motivation overlooked—namely, that employees offer up different degrees and dimensions of their selves according to some internal calculus that they consciously and unconsciously make. Traditional motivation studies implicitly assume that workers are either "on" or they are "off"; that is, based on external rewards and intrinsic factors, they are either motivated to work or not, and that this is a relatively steady state that they inhabit. The engagement concept is framed on the premise that workers are more complicated. Like actors, they make choices about how much of their real selves they would bring into and use to inform their role performances. They might truly express themselves, to the extent the role allowed, or they might not, with degrees in between. Rather than label workers as motivated or unmotivated, these personal movements into or out of role performances change a great deal as various conditions shift. The concept of personal engagement at work captures that process. This entry defines personal engagement and its contributing psychological conditions.

Fundamentals

Personal engagement is the harnessing of organization members' selves to their work roles. Personally engaged workers employ and express their selves physically, cognitively, and emotionally during role performances. The combination of employing and expressing one's preferred self yields behaviors that bring alive the relation of self-in-role. To personally engage is to keep one's self within the role, without sacrificing one for the other. Self and role exist in some dynamic, negotiable relation in which the person both drives personal energies into role behaviors (self-employment) and displays the self within the role (self-expression). In contrast, *personal disengagement* involves the uncoupling of people's selves from their work role performances; people withdraw and defend their selves during role performances. People thus remove their own, internal energies from physical, cognitive, and emotional labors. Their behaviors display an evacuation or suppression of their expressive and energetic selves in discharging role obligations. Role demands guide task behaviors, without an interplay between internal thoughts and feelings and external requirements. Tasks are performed at some distance from people's preferred selves, which remain split off and hidden. People thus become physically uninvolved in tasks, cognitively automatic or unvigilant, and emotionally disconnected from others in ways that hide what they think and feel, their creativity, their beliefs and values, and their personal connections to others.

Three psychological conditions influence how much people personally engage at any moment in time. These conditions are powerful enough to survive the gamut of individual differences. They are momentary rather than static conditions of people's experiences that shape behaviors. Like conditions in contracts, if they are met to some acceptable degree, people will personally engage in moments of task behaviors; if they are not met, people will personally disengage.

The three psychological conditions are *meaningfulness, safety,* and *availability.* Together, the three conditions shape how people inhabit their roles. It is as if organization members ask themselves (though not consciously) three questions in each situation and personally engage or disengage depending on the answers: (1) How meaningful is it for me to bring myself into this performance? (2) How safe is it to do so? (3) How available am I to do so? The answers to these questions are shaped by particular factors.

Psychological meaningfulness is feeling a return on investments of one's self made in the currencies of physical, cognitive, or emotional energies. People experience such meaningfulness when they feel worthwhile, useful, and valuable—as though they make a difference and are not taken for granted. They feel able to give themselves to others and to their work. The lack of meaningfulness is connected to feeling that little is asked or expected of one's self, and that there is little room to give or to receive in work role performances. Psychological meaningfulness is correlated with work that is challenging, allows variety and creativity, is clearly delineated, and allows for autonomy. It is also shaped by the extent to which people are able to wield influence, occupy valuable positions in their systems, and gain desirable status. Meaningfulness is also higher when task performances involve interpersonal interactions with co-workers or clients that promote dignity, self-appreciation, and a sense of worthwhileness.

Psychological safety is feeling able to show and employ one's self without fear of negative consequences to self-image, status or career. Psychological safety is heightened by relationships that are supportive and trusting, marked by the absence of threat that enable people to try and to fail without fearing the consequences. Group dynamics also shape the extent to which organizational members take on "characters" in groups associated with relative degrees of respect and authority. Psychological safety is heightened by leaders that are supportive and resilient, allowing people to try and to fail without fearing the consequences—which in turn create systemic norms that encourage or discourage self-disclosure.

Psychological availability occurs when people have the physical, emotional, or psychological resources to personally engage at particular points in time. It is a readiness statistic of how available people are amidst distractions. People are more or less available to place their selves fully into role performances: personal engagement requires physical, cognitive and emotional resources that may or may not be scarce, given the competing demands of other aspects of people's work and nonwork lives. These psychological conditions shape the extent to which workers are able and willing to personally engage—and thus become psychologically present—in performing specific tasks and roles.

The theory of personal engagement offers managers a diagnostic tool by which to analyze workers' efforts, energies and involvements in their roles. Rather than make certain assumptions about workers' personality dimensions, managers can use the theory to identify the conditions that influence workers' engagements. Through informal conversations, surveys, performance reviews, and other opportunities for dialogue and assessment, managers can assess the extent to which workers' role engagements are affected by influences on how meaningful they find those roles, how safe they feel in expressing themselves in role performances, and how available they are to fully engage in those performances. Effective managers look carefully for such influences and use their own influence and authority to enhance the conditions necessary for their workers' engagements.

William A. Kahn

See also Job Characteristics Theory; Leadership Practices; Role Theory; Self-Concept and Theory of the Self; Social Identity Theory

Further Readings

Albrecht, S. (2010). *Handbook of employee engagement: Perspectives, issues, research and practice.* Northampton, MA: Edward Elgar.

Beugré, C. (2010). Organizational conditions fostering employee engagement: The role of "voice." In S. Albrecht (Ed.), *Handbook of employee engagement: Perspectives, issues, research and practice* (pp. 174–181). Northampton, MA: Edward Elgar.

Kahn, W. A. (1990). Psychological conditions of personal engagement and disengagement at work. *Academy of Management Journal, 33*(4), 692–724.

Kahn, W. A. (1992). To be fully there: Psychological presence at work. *Human Relations, 45*(4), 321–349.

Kahn, W. A. (2010). The essence of engagement: Lessons from the field. In S. Albrecht (Ed.), *Handbook of employee engagement: Perspectives, issues, research and practice* (pp. 20–30). Northampton, MA: Edward Elgar.

Macey, W. H., & Schneider, B. (2008). The meaning of employee engagement. *Industrial and Organizational Psychology, 1,* 3–30.

Nakamura, J., & Csikszentmihalyi, M. (2003). The construction of meaning through vital engagement. In C. L. M Keyes & J. Haidt (Eds.), *Flourishing: Positive psychology and the life well-lived* (pp. 83–104). Washington, DC: American Psychological Association.

Pratt, M. G., & Ashforth, B. E. (2003). Fostering meaningfulness in working and at work. In K. S. Cameron, J. E. Dutton, & R. E. Quinn (Eds.), *Positive organizational scholarship: Foundations of a new discipline* (pp. 309–327). San Francisco, CA: Berrett-Koehler.

Rothbard, N. P. (2001). Enriching or depleting? The dynamics of engagement in work and family roles. *Administrative Science Quarterly, 46,* 655–684.

Wrzesniewski, A. (2003). Finding positive meaning in work. In K. S. Cameron, J. E. Dutton, & R. E. Quinn (Eds.), *Positive organizational scholarship: Foundations of a new discipline* (pp. 296–308). San Francisco, CA: Berrett-Koehler.

POSITIVE ORGANIZATIONAL SCHOLARSHIP

In 2003, Kim Cameron, Jane Dutton, and Bob Quinn published an edited volume titled *Positive*

Organizational Scholarship. The volume helped introduce positive organizational scholarship (POS) as a lens for understanding the conditions and processes that explain flourishing in organizational contexts. Since then, a POS lens has enriched organizational studies by expanding the range of topics and constructs seen as valuable and legitimate within organizational behavior and organizational theory. POS helps us see new possibilities for organizational studies; it helps move constructs and ideas that are often in the background, or even invisible, to the foreground. This entry articulates what POS is, what topics fall within the domain of POS, and why management scholars should care about POS.

Fundamentals

POS is just one of several "cousin" movements in the social sciences. Alongside POS, positive psychologists (led by Martin Seligman) have advocated that psychology needs to move beyond treating mental illness to also focus on the conditions that enable people to flourish in their lives. In addition, positive organizational behavior (POB; led by Fred Luthans) has applied positive psychology to the workplace, focusing on the application of positively oriented human resource strengths and psychological capacities for performance improvement at work. Finally, in the field of organizational development, appreciative inquiry (developed by David Cooperrider) focused on what is working in any system rather than what is not working as a core method for positive change.

The *O* in POS refers to investigating positive processes and states that occur in association with *organizational* contexts. It examines positive phenomena within organizations and among organizations, as well as positive organizational contexts. This extends beyond the largely individual focus of positive psychology and even POB. The *S* in POS emphasizes pursuing rigorous, systematic, and theory-based foundations for positive phenomena. POS requires careful definitions of terms, a rationale for prescriptions and recommendations, consistency with scientific procedures in drawing conclusions, a theoretical rationale, and grounding in previous scholarly work. The *P* in POS refers to at least four different facets of *positive*, as articulated in the *Oxford Handbook of Positive Organizational Scholarship:*

- *A unique lens or an alternative perspective.* Challenges and obstacles are reinterpreted as opportunities and strength-building experiences rather than tragedies or problems. While adopting a POS lens means that adversities and difficulties reside as much in the domain of POS as do successes, a positive lens focuses attention on the good that can come from difficult situations.
- *A focus on extraordinarily positive outcomes or positively deviant performance.* POS focused on outcomes that dramatically exceed common or expected performance. This definition of positive focuses on identifying and explaining spectacular results, surprising outcomes, and extraordinary achievements that inspire people and organizations to aim higher.
- *An affirmative bias that fosters resourcefulness.* Positivity can involve unlocking latent resources in individuals, groups, and organizations so that capabilities are broadened and capacity is built and strengthened. This resourcefulness means that individuals and organizations generate, grow, and discover new resources in the doing of work.
- *The examination of virtuousness or the best of the human condition.* POS assumes that individuals are attracted to the highest aspirations of humankind. All societies and cultures possess catalogs of traits that they deem virtuous, that represent what is morally good, and that define the highest aspirations of human beings. POS seeks to understand the how virtues play out in organizational life.

These four facets of positive articulate the blossoming of different approaches and perspectives that flourish within the domain of POS. The next section describes the substantive core of the domain of POS.

What Falls Within the Domain of POS?

As described earlier, POS is a lens for understanding the conditions and processes that explain flourishing in organizational contexts. To provide a flavor of the kinds of topics and constructs that fit within the domain of POS, we draw on the key categories and topics covered in the *Oxford Handbook of Positive Organizational Scholarship*. While these do not cover the entire conceptual landscape of POS, they represent a good sampling of significant subjects in this field of study. They cut across different levels of analysis—from individual-level topics to organization- and societal-level topics. The nine categories and their embedded topics include the following:

- *Positive individual attributes.* These include psychological capital, prosocial motivation, calling at work, work engagement, positive identity, proactivity, creativity, curiosity, and positive traits.
- *Positive emotions.* Topics addressed include positive energy, subjective well-being, passion, and socioemotional intelligence.
- *Strengths and virtues.* A wide variety of virtues have been proposed as being universal and include, among others, forgiveness, humility, compassion, hope, courage, justice, and integrity.
- *Positive relationships.* Addressing relationships in both temporary encounters and long-term relationships between people, these topics include high-quality connections, relational coordination, reciprocity, intimacy, civility, trust, humor, and psychological safety.
- *Positive human resource practices.* These topics are most pertinent to the effective workings of organizations and include career development, mentoring, socialization, diversity, communication, conflict resolution, negotiating, and work-family dynamics.
- *Positive organizational processes.* These organizational features and dynamics include the design of work, mindful organizing, ambivalence, organizational identity, and innovation.
- *Positive leadership and change.* The topics include organizational development, appreciative inquiry, positive change attributes, authentic leadership, leadership development, and strategic change.
- *A positive lens for seeing the good that can come from problems and challenges.* POS also includes the positive dynamics that can arise from negative phenomena, including healing after trauma, responding to crisis, resilience under adversity, and posttraumatic growth.

These topics reflect but a sampling of the core topics and themes that constitute the core of POS. In the next section, the entry lays out some of the mechanisms that explain how and why POS matters.

What Theoretical Mechanisms Explain POS?

POS seeks to be driven by strong theoretical foundations. To this end, POS articulates a variety of generative mechanisms to explain the how and why of how "positive" organizational constructs produce key outcomes. *Generative* captures the mechanisms in particular that are life building, capability enhancing, and capacity creating. As articulated in the POS handbook, POS scholars tend to draw on five sets of mechanisms to set a secure foundation for their conceptual ideas. *Cognitive* mechanisms such as meaning making, identity, learning, and sensemaking operate through changes in how people become aware, know, think, learn, and judge. *Affective* mechanisms such as the broaden-and-build theory operate through changes that evoke or elicit individual or collective feelings. Relational mechanisms such as relational coordination, laterality, and mindful organizing operate through changes in the connections among people and groups. *Agentic* mechanisms such as proactivity, endogenous resourcefulness, and participation operate through changes in how people interpret their relationship with their environment in terms of what they can do. Finally, *structural* mechanisms such as institutionalized practices, systems, and structures operate through routines and leadership. These theoretical mechanisms are important because they flesh out the theoretical underpinnings of POS.

Importance

POS research has been conducted using diverse methods, including rich, descriptive qualitative research as well as rigorous, large-sample quantitative research. POS theories draw from related disciplines, including psychology, sociology, social work, and medicine. As evidenced in the *Oxford Handbook of Positive Organizational Scholarship.,* POS constructs and dynamics have been empirically linked to a variety of outcomes relevant to management research. One cluster of outcomes is *individual flourishing and well-being.* These kinds of outcomes capture what psychologist Martin Seligman refers to as the "pleasant life"—a life that successfully pursues positive emotions about the present, past, and future. A second cluster of outcomes is inherent to what Seligman refers to as the "meaningful life"—*personal fulfillment* through a life worth living. Here, research focuses on how individuals take actions to "craft" more meaning into their work life and also how organizations can provide opportunities for individuals to find their purpose and to make a contribution. A third cluster of outcomes focuses on *exemplary performance,* whether at the individual, team, or organizational level. A fourth cluster of outcomes deals with *adaptation and learning.* Here, researchers are interested in how organizations build their agility/flexibility for more innovation, creativity, resilience, and personal growth. Finally, a fifth cluster of outcomes focus on the long-term *sustainability of people, organizations, society, and the environment.* Sustainability can be defined as ensuring that our ecosystem supports life over time; it includes efforts to preserve, conserve, renew, and generate resources to support life. So POS not only explains more traditional outcomes, such as well-being and performance, but also outcomes that indicate longer term impact, such as adaptation and sustainability over time. In this way, a POS lens helps address a broad array of outcomes.

POS has also been embraced in the world of practice by those seeking to create more positive workplaces, units, and organizations. Practitioners have found that their organizations can improve only so much through a problem-solving lens that seeks to move the organization to address its deficit and gaps. In contrast, a POS approach seeks to inspire change by creating resourcefulness that creates, unlocks, and multiplies latent resource to build new possibilities. A POS approach creates positive spirals and buffers against countervailing forces to propel the organization in a more positive direction. These ideas are at the core of practice-based interventions such as appreciative inquiry. Practitioners and coaches using a POS lens have transformed organizations and individuals in health care, financial services, and retail industries—all realms where human capital is particularly critical to organizational success.

POS has also been embraced by teachers at undergraduate, graduate, and executive levels. Syllabi for POS courses and modules are available at the POS website. And teaching tools, including videos and cases as well as assessments (such as the Reflected Best Self) and exercises (such as the Job Crafting exercise) have been used by management teachers around the world. These help students, managers, and executives better understand how to leverage their unique strengths (rather than just their developmental opportunities), how to stay resilient in

the face of crisis or challenges, and how to develop high-quality relationships even with those who initially seem difficult.

Gretchen Spreitzer

See also High-Performance Work Systems; Humanistic Management; Personal Engagement (at Work) Model; Servant Leadership

Further Readings

Cameron, K. (2008). *Positive leadership: Strategies for extraordinary performance.* San Francisco, CA: Berrett-Koehler.

Cameron, K., Dutton, J., & Quinn, R. (2003). *Positive organizational scholarship.* San Francisco, CA: Berrett Koehler.

Cameron, K., & Spreitzer, G. (2012). *Oxford handbook of positive organizational scholarship.* New York, NY: Oxford University Press.

Dutton, J., & Ragins, B. (2006). *Exploring positive relationships at work.* New York, NY: Routledge.

James, E. H., & Wooten, L.P. (2010). *Leading under pressure: From surviving to thriving before, during, and after a crisis.* New York, NY: Routledge.

Quinn, R., & Quinn, R. (2010). *Lift: Becoming a positive force in any change.* San Francisco, CA: Berrett Koehler.

Seligman, M. E. P. & Csikszentmihalyi, M. 2000. Positive psychology: An introduction. *American Psychologist,* 55(1), 5–14.

PRACTICE OF MANAGEMENT, THE

Peter Drucker's 1954 book *The Practice of Management* was a landmark achievement. It codified into a discipline the practice of management so that it could be taught and learned systematically by executives and students. Building on existing knowledge in the scientific method of management in manufacturing, industrial psychology and sociology, human relations and worker motivation, organization and administration, and managerial economics, Drucker added concepts relating to the structure of top management, organizational decentralization, management by objectives, and business policy and created an integrated configuration focusing on the work of the manager. *The Practice of Management* was written soon after Drucker's 18-month study, during 1944 and 1945, of the structure and policies of the General Motors Corporation, published in 1946 as *Concept of the Corporation*. The remainder of this entry clarifies these contributions and shows their relevance to Drucker's life's project and to the central role of the practice of management.

Fundamentals

In response to a request from the then-dean of the Peter F. Drucker Graduate School of Management at Claremont Graduate University, Drucker provided a carefully worded document: "What do I consider my most important contribution?" This document is reproduced below exactly as written by Peter Drucker on January 18, 1999, at the age of 89.

- That I early on—almost sixty years ago—realized that MANAGEMENT has become the constitutive organ and function of the Society of Organizations;
- That MANAGEMENT is not "Business Management"—though it first attained attention in business—but the governing organ of ALL institutions of Modern Society;
- That I established the study of MANAGEMENT as a DISCIPLINE in its own right; and
- That I focused this discipline on People and Power; on Values, Structure and Constitution; AND ABOVE ALL ON THE RESPONSIBILITIES—that is focused the Discipline of Management on Management as a truly LIBERAL ART.

The Practice of Management

The Practice of Management contains what Drucker called "the constitutionalist approach" to governance in the 1990 reissue of Alfred P. Sloan's 1963 book, *My Years With General Motors,* as opposed to the "character and moral principles of the leader," the approach Drucker called "the education of the prince." Managing a business was first and foremost a task of satisfying the customer—the customer was the business for Drucker. And for this purpose he fashioned the theory of the business, first in *The Practice of Management* and then more fully in his September-October 1994 *Harvard Business Review* article.

Drucker, in "The Theory of the Business," always asks the same three questions: What is our business? Who is our customer? And what does the customer consider value? He asks them in different ways with multiple extensions, but he is trying always to get at the same thing. He asks these questions both for profit and nonprofit businesses and for personal and work situations. To answer these questions, one needs a good deal of information about the specific market environment, including information on demographics, technology, government, the economy, and competition. And a theory of the business is merely a hypothesis about the way an organization intends to create value for its customers. It has to be tested against reality; if it does not produce expected results, it must be altered. So there is always the innovation question, "What should our theory of the business be?"

Innovation and entrepreneurship. Drucker's master project was to help executives manage discontinuities using the dual processes of continuity and change. He fully adopted Joseph Schumpeter's view of the entrepreneur as the economic agent in capitalism, who seeks profit or economic rent through the process of innovation. And profit in turn becomes the means whereby the entrepreneur is able to continue his or her innovative activity. Because of the discontinuities caused by innovation, which Schumpeter called the process of "creative destruction," profit became to Drucker a moral force for stimulating innovation and for maintaining continuity in society. But to eliminate the discontinuities caused by major innovations, Drucker proposed in his 1985 seminal book, *Innovation and Entrepreneurship,* seven windows or sources of potential innovation opportunities whereby each organization in society may engage in systematic, continuous innovation to eliminate or minimize the disruptive effects of the process of creative destruction. He also put forth policies and strategies that should be followed to institutionalize innovation within the management structure of all organizations.

Social impacts and social responsibilities. Drucker's purpose was to create a society of functioning organizations so there would be no temptation to succumb to the appeals of dictators who promise to solve society's problems only to subsequently make citizens live in bondage, misery, and fear. To create a society of functioning organizations, a nation needs a cadre of professional managers, especially those who care about the negative impacts their actions could create on society. While the business sector is the first sector in the sense that it must create the wealth for all other sectors to grow and prosper, for the society to be a healthy one, its businesses must seek as objectives the elimination of any negative impacts. In addition, after meeting its primary mission, executives should support public efforts to build society through volunteerism and financial support.

The spirit of performance. The primary objective of Drucker's model is to create an organization with a high spirit of performance, and this can be done only in what Drucker calls the "moral realm." Why? Because it requires that an organization overcome natural entropic forces that human organizations display toward deterioration and decay. Thus, in *The Practice of Management*, he states:

> The purpose of an organization is to "make common men do uncommon things." . . . it is the test of an organization that it make ordinary human beings perform better than they are capable of, that it bring out whatever strength there is in its members and use it to make all other members perform better and better. It is the test of an organization that it neutralize the weaknesses of its members. (pp. 144–145)

An organization high in spirit of performance is one that is led by executives who are committed to doing the right thing (efficiency) and to getting the right things done (effectiveness). These executives possess integrity of character, have a vision for the purpose of their organization, focus on opportunities, are change leaders, and follow essential tasks, responsibilities, and practices of management.

System for the Practice of Management

Each element of Drucker's system for the practice of management is presented in context in Figure 1 below. We observe from Figure 1 that the practice of management has many centers and the elements are interrelated. One could say that the practice of management is a polycentric configuration of related elements that should be viewed as a whole to appreciate the role and function of each part.

Evolution

Born in Vienna, Austria, on November 19, 1909, Peter Drucker was educated at the University of Frankfurt where in 1932 he earned his JD in international and public law. The prestigious publishing house, J. C. B. Mohr in Tübingen, Germany, published his first monograph, *Frederick Julius Stahl: His Conservative Theory of the State* in April 1933. Stahl was a German legal philosopher at the University of Berlin and a parliamentarian. Stahl studied and wrote about governmental institutions and sought to describe and promote a society of institutions able to achieve a balance between continuity and change. This balance between continuity and change, as a remedy for radical discontinuity in turbulent times, became a recurring theme in Drucker's work, and the practice of management was the vehicle Drucker codified and elaborated to minimize disruptions during turbulent times for the benefit of society. The Nazis banned Drucker's monograph immediately upon its publication. The monograph was translated much later into English by Martin M. Chemers and published in 2002. Foreseeing the future of Germany under Hitler from this and other events, Drucker left for London in 1933 where he worked as a journalist and investment-banking analyst. He married Doris Schmitz in London in 1937, whom he first met in Frankfurt. They moved to the United States in that same year.

In 1939, Drucker published his first major book, *The End of Economic Man,* an exposition of the failure of "'Economic Man" as the basis for organizing society's institutions and as an explanation for the masses turning to the dictators of totalitarian Europe—Hitler in Germany, Stalin in Russia, and Mussolini in Italy—to relieve them of their despair when Economic Man failed to deliver on its promises. Winston Churchill thought enough of the book to review it for *The London Times Literary Supplement* and to make it required reading for his officers. Churchill was very much like Drucker in "seeing the future that had already happened." He saw that the appeasement of Adolf Hitler by British Prime Minister Neville Chamberlain in the Munich agreement of 1938 would never produce peace and warned of the imminence of war with Germany. In his review of the book, published in *The London Times Literary Supplement* on May 27, 1939, Churchill said,

> Mr. Drucker is one of those writers to whom almost anything can be forgiven because he not only has a mind of his own, but has the gift of starting other

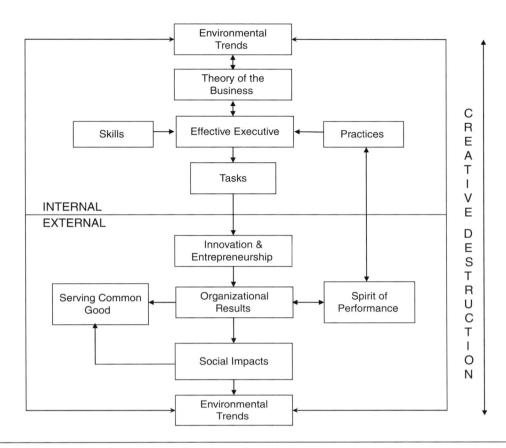

Figure 1   Peter F. Drucker on the Practice of Management

Source: Peter F. Drucker on Executive Leadership and Effectiveness, by Joseph A. Maciariello, Leader of the Future 2, Jossey-Bass, San Francisco, p. 4. Copyright © 2006, Leader to Leader Institute. Reprinted with permission of the author.

minds along a stimulating line of thought. . . . [He has written] a book that successfully links the dictatorships which are outstanding in contemporary life with that absence of a working philosophy which is equally outstanding in contemporary thought. (p. 306)

The Ultimate Case Study

For 18 months beginning in January 1943, Drucker had an opportunity that made an important impact on his thinking about industrial society, organizations, and individuals. Donaldson Brown, then an assistant to General Motors chairman Alfred Sloan, invited him to study the structure and policies of the company. Donaldson Brown's invitation came as a result of his reading Drucker's second major book, *The Future of Industrial Man,* published in 1942, in which Drucker describes the requirements of a functioning society in general with particular application to the emerging industrial societies.

The General Motors project eventually led to Drucker's first major management book, *The Concept of the Corporation,* published in 1946 and reissued in 1990. Drucker believed the book was "the first study of management as a discipline, the first study of a big corporation from within, of its constitutional principles, of its structure, its basic relationships, its strategies and policies" (p. v). In this book, Drucker saw that a relatively new institution—the modern corporation—was going to have a major impact on society. Writing from the vantage point of society, a premise of the book is "what is good for America must be made good for General Motors." And while Sloan and the executives of General Motors thought Drucker's advice too radical, the book had a major influence on other industrial organizations throughout the world.

Sloan, a genuinely warm human being, was known as a brilliant and effective executive and organizational architect. He served as a mentor to Drucker. During Drucker's study period at GM, Sloan invited him to many management meetings in both Detroit and New York. After each one, Drucker debriefed himself as to why Sloan did what he did. Drucker analyzed the new decentralized management structure of General Motors using concepts that were influential in creating the Constitution of the United States, especially federalism with its emphasis on states' rights, a strong chief executive, and checks and balances on power and authority. General Motors was formed as a union of separate companies—Chevrolet, Pontiac, Buick, Cadillac, and so on—that had to be brought together, just as the 13 original U.S. colonies were brought together by the U.S. Constitution. Sloan chose decentralization as the organizational principle and granted autonomy to each company (division) while maintaining central control. Drucker saw that this resembled the concepts contained in the *Federalist Papers*, 85 essays written by Alexander Hamilton, James Madison, and John Jay in 1787 and 1788 promoting the ratification of the U.S. Constitution and supporting the design of national and state governments, including an executive, legislative, and judicial function. Drucker labeled the organization structure designed by Sloan as "federal decentralization" because of its attempt to balance decentralized operations (each company or division) with central control (the office of the chief executive). Each company managed itself autonomously, although certain policies and decisions were reserved for top management (central control). GM was thus a study in "structure and constitution," dealing with the pervasive issues in organizations of the distribution of power and authority.

Ultimately, when Drucker's book was ready to be published, the company didn't know what to make of it. Among his recommendations was that GM should go even further in decentralization. In a letter to Sloan transmitting the book, he called for GM to break up its largest division—Chevrolet—so that both Chevrolet and the General Motors Corporation could compete with each other, forcing each other to improve and innovate, while solving General Motors' antitrust problem that came about because of its control of over 50% of the automobile market in the United States. Drucker's analysis proved completely correct in hindsight. However, the company did not adopt his ideas.

Nevertheless, it was evident that Drucker was well on his way to defining the study of the practice of management. He perceived in the "corporation" a new and major institution of society that was developing rapidly and was worthy of study. The corporation simply could not be ignored because of its impact on the lives of people and society. And this new social institution needed to be integrated with the interests of the individual on the one hand and the state on the other to promote a functioning society of organizations.

In the early 1950s, Drucker worked extensively with the General Electric Company and its vice president, Harold Smiddy, and CEO, Ralph Cordiner. At the end of the Korean War, GE anticipated that the move from wartime to peacetime would set off explosive growth in consumer demand. The question was how could GE best take advantage of that growth? The answer was through the federal decentralization that Drucker explored at General Motors—implementing it across GE's departments. That's what GE did, and GE grew. Almost every GE CEO since Cordiner had some contact with Peter Drucker, including Jack Welch.

Drucker's classic 1954 book *The Practice of Management* grew out of his work with the General Electric Company. Drucker even called Harold Smiddy the godfather of the book in the preface of the original hardcover volume. This is the book where Drucker codifies the nuts and bolts of the discipline and practice of management.

Importance

At the time of his death, the contributions of Peter Drucker's ideas to the practice of management were extolled worldwide across multiple media, including by John Byrne in a 2005 *Business Week* article. Here, management titans commented on his impact: Jack Welch—"The world knows he was the greatest management thinker of the last century"; Tom Peters—"He was the creator and inventor of modern management"; Andrew Grove—"Statements from him have influenced untold numbers of daily actions; they did mine over decades." Byrne adds to this that "What John Maynard Keynes is to economics or W. Edwards Deming to quality, Drucker is to management," citing contributions to areas such as decentralization, human resources, social responsibility, knowledge workers, the corporation as a human community, leadership practices, and the importance of a customer focus.

Drucker considered the practice of management to be among the most significant innovations of the 20th century in the United States, Germany, and Japan. In his final public interview, on December 8, 2004, with Tom Ashbrook of *National Public Radio,* Drucker commented,

> Management is a new social function that has made possible a society of organizations. And while business management was the first one to emerge, it is not the most important one. The most important ones are the management of non-businesses, which made possible a developed society—hospitals, universities, churches. They are also the more interesting ones because they have to define what they mean by results. In a business, profit and loss determines what is meant by results. You asked me, how do you define results of that large church I am working with which has grown from 500 to 6,000 members? What are results of Claremont Graduate University? These are questions that are much more important and much more difficult and much more interesting. (http://onpoint.wbur.org/2004/12/08/management-guru-peter-drucker)

In summary, management as a theoretical discipline and specifically management as a practice is one of the fundamental social innovations of modern times because it has made possible a society of functioning organizations. Peter Drucker, as its innovator and chief expounder, is therefore not only one of its most important contributors but one of the most important innovators of the 20th century.

Joseph A. Maciariello

See also Core Competence; Corporate Social Responsibility; Knowledge Workers; Management (Education) as Practice; Management by Objectives; Organizational Structure and Design; Stages of Innovation; Technological Discontinuities; "Unstructured" Decision Making

Further Readings

Byrne, J. A. (2005, November 28). The man who invented management: Why Peter Drucker's ideas still matter. *Business Week,* 96–106.

Drucker, P. F. (1954). *The practice of management.* New York, NY: Harper & Row.

Drucker, P. F. (1974). *Management: Tasks, responsibilities, practices.* New York, NY: Harper & Row.

Drucker, P. F. (1985). *Innovation and entrepreneurship.* New York, NY: Harper & Row.

Drucker P. F. (1990). Introduction: Why *My Years With General Motors* is must reading. In A. P. Sloan, *My years with General Motors* (pp. v–xii. New York, NY: Doubleday.

Drucker, P. F. (1994, September/October). The theory of the business. *Harvard Business Review,* 94–104.

Drucker, P. F. (1999). *Management challenges for the 21st century.* New York, NY: HarperCollins.

Drucker, P. F. (with Maciariello, J. A.) (2004). *The Daily Drucker.* New York, NY: HarperCollins.

Drucker, P. F. (with Maciariello, J. A.) (2008). *Management* (Rev. ed.). New York, NY: HarperCollins.

Maciariello, J. A., & Linkletter, K. E. (2011). *Drucker's lost art of management: Peter Drucker's timeless vision for building effective organizations.* New York, NY: McGraw-Hill.

Sloan, A. P. (1963). *My years with General Motors.* New York, NY: Doubleday.

PRINCIPLED NEGOTIATION

Principled negotiation, a term originally proposed by Roger Fisher and William Ury, generally applies to the process that negotiators employ to achieve win-win or value-creating agreements. Principled negotiation, however, is not a term common to the general parlance among those who conduct academic research on negotiation. Those authors might use other terms to describe the principled approach, such as *integrative negotiation* or *problem-solving negotiation.* And an entry on "principled" negotiation suggests that there is such a thing as "unprincipled" negotiation, which implies an approach in which negotiators do not subscribe to commonly accepted standards of fair treatment, respect for the other parties, honorable conduct, and willingness to stand by agreements and commitments made during negotiation. In the research literature on negotiation, this process has more typically been called *distributive bargaining, competitive bargaining,* or *win-lose bargaining.*

When applied to negotiation, the term *principled* refers to an underlying ethical orientation in one's approach. But the distinction between principled and unprincipled negotiation may not be as clean and transparent as the reader might wish. It may not be that some negotiators are unprincipled but instead that they subscribe to a different set of principles! Advocates of the more unprincipled views most likely subscribe to a *teleological* view of ethics; this view generally holds that the moral worth of a behavior is best judged by its consequences. The more extreme view of the teleological view is called *egoism,* in which acceptable behavior is judged based on its consequences for the self, while less extreme views are defined as *utilitarianism,* in which acceptable behavior is judged based on the best consequences for the greatest number. These are further explained in the writings of philosophers John Stuart Mill and Jeremy Bentham. In contrast, principled negotiators tend to subscribe to different sets of ethical principles, generally called *deontology,* which advocates that there are clear standards of right and wrong and that all individuals deserve minimal standards of respect, or *virtue ethics,* which stresses adherence to a clear set of moral virtues on how one should treat others, such as standards of truthfulness, honesty, and fairness. These are further explained in the writings of philosophers Immanuel Kant and Jean-Jacques Rousseau. Thus, it is not that some negotiators are unprincipled; instead, they most likely subscribe to ethical principles that advocate self-gratification and the acceptability of pursuing those outcomes regardless of the costs and consequences. Principled negotiation is certainly a topic that is central to the practice of management. Managers negotiate all the time—with coworkers, subordinates, bosses, salesmen, purchasing agents, labor unions, financial institutions, and others. While the early theory on negotiation was generally restricted to labor relations and purchasing, the last two to three decades has seen a strong emergence— in research and teaching—of negotiation as a critical skill, part of a larger portfolio of skills related to managing organizational conflict and maintaining productive interpersonal and intergroup relations with others. This entry describes the fundamental nature of principled negotiation and the principled negotiation process. It discusses the relevant theory and research that support this process as well as the nature of the strategy and tactics used to execute a principled negotiation. In doing so, comparisons will inevitably be drawn to the more competitive, distributive negotiation strategy and tactics. Next, the entry shows how the theory has evolved and how some of the tactics often associated with unprincipled negotiation can become entangled in the principled negotiation process. Finally, the entry suggests some ways that a principled negotiator can convert his or her competitive opponent to a more principled process.

Fundamentals

The essence of principled negotiation, as it distinguishes itself from "unprincipled" negotiation, is inherent in the very nature and dynamics of negotiation itself. Assume a common definition of negotiation proposed by negotiation researcher Dean Pruitt in 1981: "a form of decision making in which two or more parties talk with one another in an effort to resolve their opposing interests" (p. xi). For each party to maximize what he or she receives in that decision-making conversation, each attempts to persuade the other to "see it my way." Persuasion processes involve the sharing and positioning of information to convince the other, and negotiators are likely to use and present that information in a way that puts their interests, desires, and needs in the best possible light. Positioning this information may often lead negotiators to exaggerate their perspective of their own needs and desires, inflate the strengths of their own position, mislead the other through the selective inclusion or exclusion of critical facts, all while not being fully honest and transparent about the weaknesses of their own position. In fact, since each negotiator expects a series of exchanges in which the parties will attempt to resolve their conflicting interests, all negotiators must implicitly resolve two fundamental dilemmas: how honest to be for the amount for which they are willing to settle (which is likely to be less than their original requests) and how much to believe or trust what the other is telling them. On the first dilemma, negotiators realize that if they are fully honest and transparent about their minimum needs, the other party may go no further than to meet those minimum needs (or even attempt a resolution below that minimum), but if they exaggerate and inflate too much, achieving resolution of those conflicting interests may be impossible. Similarly, if a negotiator trusts the other completely, he or she may be caught up in the other's exaggerations and inflations, but not to trust the other may also preclude achieving an effective resolution. Thus, achieving a fully principled negotiation requires parties to not only share a compatible ethical ideology but also to successfully navigate the dilemmas of trust and honesty that lead them to a productive agreement.

Working from the context of negotiation in international relations and the law, Fisher and Ury first introduced the term *principled negotiation* in the early 1980s. The work was originally not considered to be a contribution to management theory because it was not visibly grounded in microeconomic or psychological theory, contained no citations or footnotes, and was far more prescriptive since it was directed toward negotiation practitioners. The authors proposed an antithesis to the problems and dangers of "hard" (positional or distributive) bargaining: They stressed that the solution was not "soft" negotiation (where parties often sacrificed gains to protect a good relationship with the other party) but instead principled negotiation. Principled negotiation, they argued, had five major components:

1. Pursue the goal of a wise outcome that is reached efficiently and amicably with the other party.

2. Separate the people from the problem (be nice to the people but still be tough on finding an acceptable solution to the bargaining problem).

3. Focus on interests, not positions—move beyond positions to the underlying needs and motives.

4. Invent options for mutual gain—arrive at multiple possible settlements and choose later.

5. Insist on using objective criteria to choose among alternatives, based on what is fair, reasonable, and right.

Fisher and Ury also introduced the term *BATNA*—best alternative to a negotiated agreement—suggesting that deals should be evaluated less on arbitrary walkaway points and more on how the proposed deal compares to other deals the negotiator could strike. They also suggested ways for principled negotiators to deal with more traditional distributive bargainers, advice that again was pioneering relative to available research support. While some researchers began to recognize the important grounding and application of these principles for research on negotiation, it took almost two decades for Fisher and Ury's fundamental model to be tested in rigorous research and

for the theory to be interwoven with the more traditional integrative approach described by Robert McKersie, Richard Walton, Pruitt, and others. Since that time, a wealth of research has examined the strategic, tactical, and contextual elements that serve to promote or inhibit principled negotiation processes.

Evolution

In its infancy, the study of negotiation focused on outcomes and not processes, and thus ethical principles were not a central consideration of the exchange. Early writing on negotiation was dominantly in the context of understanding labor relations or international diplomacy. These works approached negotiation as a process heavily shaped by the contexts in which it occurred. During the 1960s, the focus fundamentally changed to an increased attention on negotiation processes across contexts through the contributions of economics, game theory, psychology, and social psychology. For example, the distinction between intrapersonal and interpersonal systems in negotiation was raised by Howard Raiffa. Intrapersonal systems focused on a negotiator's behavior as it relates to his or her own perceptions and experiences, while interpersonal systems focused on a negotiator's behavior and how it may change in the presence of others. Raiffa and colleagues also translated principles of microeconomics and decision making to the dynamics of behavior in conflict. Walton and McKersie shifted the platform of labor relations from cases and grounded descriptions to the now-classic distinction between distributive and integrative negotiation. Finally, Morton Deutsch combined the tools of game theory with the understanding of human behavior in conflict into the research laboratory, and Jeffrey Rubin and Bert Brown integrated the extensive social psychological research on two-person bargaining behavior.

The fundamental foundation of principled negotiation rests in groundwork laid by Walton and McKersie and Pruitt. Through their observations of the processes being used in multiple labor negotiations but using the language of psychology and microeconomics, Walton and McKersie identified four types of negotiation: distributive bargaining, integrative bargaining, attitudinal restructuring, and intraorganizational bargaining. The authors addressed the fundamental strategy and tactics of each and also discussed the dilemmas of each approach. The first two—distributive and integrative bargaining—gained the most immediate attention in the emerging negotiation literature. Distributive bargaining was described as the dynamics of two or more parties working inside some defined settlement range, characterized by opening bids (what the parties initially proposed), target points (where the parties hoped to settle), and resistance points (the negotiator's minimally acceptable deal). Behavior was characterized by negotiators evaluating the utility of each possible settlement point compared to alternative settlements, and the discussion of tactics focused on the use of threats, commitments, and credibility. Some allusion was made to the appropriateness of these tactics, but not to the propriety. In contrast, integrative negotiation was described as a more classical problem-solving process. Parties were described as identifying the problem, searching for alternative solutions, and selecting the optimal solution from viable alternatives. Dilemmas were identified in terms of (a) processes for finding the optimal solution and (b) dynamics that occurred when one party wanted to approach a problem distributively and the other integratively. In the early 1980s, Pruitt elaborated on Walton and McKersie's integrative bargaining approach, tying it back more strongly to choice-optimizing behavior rather than a problem-solving model and expanding our understanding of the range of tactics available to integrative negotiators. After Pruitt's work, Fisher and Ury introduced principled negotiation, building from the characteristics of integrative bargaining.

Importance

By and large the strategy and tactics of the principled negotiation approach has been supported by the research, both descriptively and prescriptively. Writing in the preface to the 2011 third edition of *Getting to Yes*, authors Fisher, Ury, and Patton note the dramatic revolution in both negotiation research and in informed practice over the 30 years since the first edition was published. The approach also spawned a major research and teaching initiative among the professional schools at Harvard University and other university-based dispute resolution centers. Principled negotiation is a core component of negotiation courses taught to business, law, government, public administration, and other professional school students in universities around the world. Executive education programs for managers at all levels traditionally feature training in the principled negotiation approach. But in spite of the incredibly powerful and thorough dissemination of this approach, it is clear that much work remains. Negotiators in a variety of venues and contexts—including sales, purchasing, and labor relations—still negotiate distributively. Negotiators and their institutions continue to embrace competitive motives that favor maximizing self-interest and the associated distributive strategy and tactics that accompany these motives. While distributive bargaining has its time and place, negotiators must weigh the expense of destroying their trustworthiness and credibility over the long term.

For a principled negotiation to be effective, certain conditions must exist prior to the start of the negotiation. First, the parties must be motivated and willing to work together to achieve some common goal. In his work, Pruitt explained that there are four different strategies negotiators can adopt: they can problem solve, contend, yield, or take no action. Whereas contending (i.e., a competitive orientation) may be too tough a negotiating style for integrative negotiation and yielding (accommodating to the other) may be too weak, joint problem solving requires both parties to take an active role in working toward a solution. Second, as introduced by Roger Mayer, James Davis, and F. David Schoorman in 1995, there must be some degree of trust between the parties regarding the trustee's abilities, benevolence, and integrity. That is, the parties must believe that their opponent (a) is competent in executing the techniques of negotiation, (b) does not have the intention of harming the other, and (c) adheres to some set of basic ethical guidelines. Speaking to competence specifically, when negotiators have been trained in and understand integrative negotiation, they are more likely to reach higher joint outcomes. But it is the second and third aspects of trust that can differ the most between distributive and integrative negotiation. In a distributive negotiation, the parties are far less likely to trust one another—either because they believe that the other will not act benevolently or because the negotiator himself or herself intends to use whatever tactics may be appropriate to gain advantage and be successful. Furthermore, although each negotiator may have integrity and adhere to a standard of ethics outside a negotiation, the negotiation context alters the framework by which ethical actions are judged. But in a principled negotiation, parties must be sensitive to the possible destructive nature of negotiation and still maintain a personal level of integrity.

The key to a principled negotiation is that both parties can achieve their goals simultaneously; that is, the parties' goals are not mutually exclusive. With this in mind, it is imperative that negotiators signal their principled intentions to the other party, affirm the intentions of the other party, and pay attention to managing not only the process of the negotiation but also the context in which it occurs. By doing this, value can be created in the negotiation so that when the distributive mind-set of claiming value becomes necessary, the increased value can work to satisfy both parties' goals.

Fisher and Ury emphasize that focusing on interests, not positions, is crucial to the process of a principled negotiation and ultimately a win-win outcome. Furthermore, recognizing the types of interests at play is important. David Lax and James Sebenius specified the different types of interests seen in negotiations substantive interests, or interests about the central issues of the negotiation; process interests, or interests regarding how to go about negotiating; relationship interests, or interests concerning the importance of the association after the negotiation; or interests in principle, or interests pertaining to the ethicality of negotiation. These different types of interests exist simultaneously, and some may be more important to one negotiator than the other. Thus, protecting one's own interests while working to understand another's interests, all while watching for changing interests, requires both alertness and sensitivity.

Part of "expanding the pie" in principled negotiation requires the invention or generation of solutions. The first step here is to gather information to see what is possible, which may require an action as simple as brainstorming or a more lengthy survey collection. Once data have been gathered, solutions to the problem(s) can be generated or the problem can be redefined to fit possible solutions. "Logrolling" is a popular method of capitalizing on differences to reach a satisfying solution. As long as the parties can put multiple issues on the table and have different orders of priorities, then issues can be traded, so to speak, until a desired outcome is reached. At the time of the current writing, one has to look only as far as the polarization of national politics and the incapacitation of national and state legislative bodies or the behavior of major financial institutions in the wake of the mortgage banking debacle of 2008 to see how the motives and perceptions of the distributive approach persist. In the end, principled negotiation requires a *mutual* commitment by the parties to focus on the problem, define interests, invent options for mutual gain, and make decisions according to standards of fairness and reasonableness. When one or more parties in a negotiation choose to maximize self-interest over mutual interest, principled negotiation can be one of the early casualties. Much has been learned from research, but much needs to be done in education and intervention to improve a more widespread embrace of principled negotiation.

Roy J. Lewicki and Beth Polin

See also Bounded Rationality and Satisficing (Behavioral Decision-Making Model); Conflict Handling Styles; Ethical Decision Making, Interactionist Model of; Participative Model of Decision Making; Trust

Further Readings

Fisher, R., Ury, W., & Patton, B. (2011). *Getting to yes* (3rd ed.). New York, NY: Penguin.

Latz, M. E. (2004). *Gaining the edge*. New York, NY: St. Martin's Press.

Lewicki, R. J. (2006). The wise negotiator. In E. H. Kessler & J. R. Bailey (Eds.), *Handbook of organizational and managerial wisdom* (pp. 109–132). Thousand Oaks, CA: Sage.

Lewicki, R. J., Barry, B., & Saunders, D. M. (2010). *Negotiation* (6th ed.). Burr Ridge, IL: McGraw-Hill Irwin.

Malhotra, D., & Bazerman, M. H. (2007). *Negotiation genius*. New York, NY: Bantam.

Pruitt, D. G. (1981). *Negotiation behavior*. New York, NY: Academic Press.

Shell, G. R. (2006). *Bargaining for advantage: Negotiation strategies for reasonable people*. New York, NY: Penguin.

Principles of Administration and Management Functions

Henri Fayol (1841–1925) was a French industrialist, consultant, and writer who first published what would later be referred to as a management theory.

As a person, Fayol is often ignored, even forgotten, but his management principles and methods still constitute what most people think of as management. Management students are told to put the interests of their organization first and to plan, organize, command, coordinate, and control in order to contribute to productivity and organizational success. Management education is now popular all over the world. More often than not it is based on a Fayolist notion of general management. This entry summarizes Fayol's view of a company and the management principles that Fayol found most important. It describes the five basic management activities (i.e., planning, organizing, commanding, coordinating, and controlling) that Fayol identified and his interest in management generally. As indicated below, Fayol asked for the establishment of management education, as well as management theory. Fayol's enormous impact on contemporary management thinking is summarized at the end of the entry.

Fundamentals

According to Fayol, the same six *important functions* are to be found in all companies, regardless of their size and production: These are the technical, commercial, financial, security, accounting, and management functions. Because the first five functions were well known, Fayol did not discuss them in any detail, but concentrated instead on the management function.

Fayol compared management to the nervous system of an animal. It should be present in all kinds of organizations (though Fayol referred mostly to companies) and at all organizational levels, transmitting information from one level to another. Management is not only a question for managers, Fayol maintained, but for all employees, including the workers. Everyone must possess some management knowledge. The relative importance of this knowledge varies, however, depending on the size of the organization and the position of the employee. It is more important the larger the organization and the higher the position of the employee.

For a large company, Fayol estimated the relative importance of management knowledge to five for workers, 15 for foremen, and 35 for heads of technical departments. For a CEO of a small company, the corresponding number was 25, for a CEO of a large company 40, and for the CEO of a very large company 50. These numbers were based on Fayol's personal judgment and are open for discussion, however. Fayol emphasized that the meaning of management depends on the specific production of the company and the position of the manager.

Management Is People Oriented

In contrast to the other functions of a company, where raw materials and machines form an important part, the management function is made up of a group of people, expected to accomplish certain tasks together. Consequently, many of Fayol's management principles and methods concern the personality of the individual manager. Most important, managers should be intelligent, have integrity and understand "the art of handling people." Fayol's moral advice to future engineers focuses on relationships—with workers and foremen in particular—and includes advice to seek out a worthy spouse. The number of management principles is unlimited, said Fayol. Rules and initiatives are situation specific and must change as the conditions of work change. Based on his own experience, Fayol identified 14 important management principles:

- **Division of work:** The objective of division of work is to increase productivity. It is an acknowledged fact that increased specialization leads to more knowledgeable employees. The degree of specialization cannot be taken too far but must be carefully considered.
- **Authority and responsibility:** Authority means the right to give orders and the power to demand that the orders be followed. A manager needs a combination of formal authority, which comes with the position, and personal authority, including knowledge, experience, and a knack for getting things done. With authority comes responsibility as well as sanctions. The fact that many like to have authority (power) but shun responsibility makes the integrity of the individual manager all the more important.
- **Discipline:** The discipline within the company depends on its managers. Industry, obedience, persistence, and good behavior should be encouraged, as should compliance with the agreements between employer and employees.
- **Unity of command:** Problems arise as soon as an employee receives instructions from more than one manager. This is true of all kinds of

organizations: the military, the industry, the family, or the state. In each management situation, authority and responsibility should be clearly defined.

- **Unity of direction:** Unity of direction is a prerequisite for the unity-of-command principle, but it is about organizing and planning work so that related tasks are duly coordinated.
- **A subordination of private interests:** The interests of the organization, whether those of a company, the family, or the state, should always be given priority.
- **Fair wages:** There is no one solution to the problem of deciding on wages that are at the same time fair and reasonable from the company's point of view. Wages should motivate the employees to do a good job but must also reflect external circumstances, such as the supply of labor or the competitive situation of the company.
- **Centralization:** To what extent work should be centralized or decentralized depends on the manager's judgment, his or her own work capacity, and the situation. As situations change, the balance between centralization and decentralization should be changed accordingly.
- **Hierarchy:** The purpose of hierarchy is to regulate and facilitate communication. But shortcuts are often necessary. The employees should inform their superiors of their nonhierarchical contacts when possible. In urgent situations, they should have the courage to decide for themselves which action to take. The interests of the organization should guide behavior at all times.
- **Order:** Two kinds of order should prevail: material order (a place for everything and everything in its place) and social order (a place for everyone and everyone in his or her place). Organization and the successful recruitment of personnel are prerequisites for social order.
- **Fairness and impartiality:** Managers must not only be just; they must also treat their subordinates with respect and friendliness. Judgment, experience, and good nature should rule their behavior.
- **Stable employment:** A high turnover of employees has proved detrimental to companies, because of the time it takes to learn the job. This is particularly true when it comes to managers: It is expensive to employ managers as apprentices. The appropriate time of employment depends on the specific situation, however.
- **Initiatives:** All employees should be encouraged to present new ideas, while respecting the authority of their manager. Managers must learn to combine discipline with freedom for the employees to suggest and implement changes.
- **A team spirit:** Employees who work in a coordinated manner and with a strong sense of loyalty are an important asset to a company. Managers should encourage cooperation and should strive to make use of the skills of all their subordinates. Further, they should solve problems by means of oral communication when possible. Letters are a waste of time and will often lead to misunderstandings.

According to Fayol, principles function like a lighthouse: They guide those who already know their way to the port. Certain methods—management activities—are necessary to guarantee that the management principles are observed.

Management Is Future Oriented

Management is undertaken in the interests of the organization; as a result, management activities concern its future. To Fayol *planning, organizing, coordinating,* and *controlling* were obvious management activities. Whether or not a definition of management should also include *commanding* might be debated, however. Commanding might as well be regarded as an activity in its own right, Fayol argued. His decision to include commanding in his definition of management was based on the view that commanding is closely related to the other management activities. Further, people should understand that management is as important as the technical function, or even more important.

Planning. The general purpose of planning is to allocate the company's resources in the best possible way. Planning includes evaluating and preparing for the future: to plan is to act. Although a plan may be a composite of a number of functional plans—for the technical, marketing, finance, and other functions—it is important that the company rely on one plan only. In its comprehensive plan, the company should estimate available resources, the value of its ongoing work, and the technical, commercial, financial, and other changes that it expects will take place. A plan should be unique, connect to other plans, and be flexible and exact. As a rule, large companies plan for 1 year at a time. But they often make additional plans of shorter and longer duration. Such plans should connect to the 1-year plan. The first year of a 10-year plan is then identical to the 1-year plan. The second year will have to be adjusted as the plan for the following year is compiled and so on. In the end, so many changes take place that a new 10-year plan must be constructed. Normally, that will happen about every 5 years. Successful planning is highly dependent on the qualifications of the managers. Fayol was quite critical of the predominantly short-term national planning procedures, which he blamed on the rapid turnover of ministers. The ministers did not stay in office long enough to understand the importance of management, nor did they feel financially responsible. Fayol suggested that their time in office be prolonged.

Organizing. To organize is to provide the company with all necessary resources: raw materials, machines and equipment, capital and personnel. All organizations consist of two parts: one material part and one social part. Further, all kinds of organizations are organized in a manner similar to that of an industrial company. Companies whose work is similar are organized in more or less identical ways, and even companies whose production differs organize in strikingly similar ways. But depending on their employees, similarly organized organizations may be either well functioning or malfunctioning. One of the most important duties for a managing director is to continuously introduce new methods to increase productivity. His or her work is facilitated by the use of organizational charts. When regularly updated, such charts provide managers with a comprehensive overview over the entire organization. Managers may then easily detect overlapping or absent activities. In practice, many directors are preoccupied with running the company on a daily basis. This is why they may need the support of a staff. A staff should add to the capacity of the managing director and assist in finding areas for improvement. Staff members may work on a full-time or part-time basis or be called on when specialist knowledge is required. It is important that the staff does not simultaneously work for another department, but other than that, the organization of the staff should depend on the situation and the capacity of the managing director.

Commanding. Fayol defined the character and behavior of good managers by means of eight rules, which should also facilitate their work. Thus, good managers are well acquainted with their subordinates, are ready to dismiss employees who do not meet the standards of work, take pains to comply with the formal agreements that exist between the company and its employees, set themselves as good examples, evaluate their organization regularly, make arrangements so that they have timely information about what is going on within the company, are careful not to interfere in the detailed work of their subordinates, and encourage their subordinates to be active by giving them as much freedom as their position and competence permits.

Coordinating. The purpose of coordination is to give the right proportions to different aspects of the company's work, adjust expenses to available financial resources, understand the relationships between the company's different functions, and give priority to urgent issues. Fayol saw regular, preferably weekly, meetings, of the heads of different departments as the most effective coordinating mechanism. At such meetings, questions of common interest might be analyzed from different perspectives and problems solved. Moreover, spontaneous cooperation between different departments is stimulated, as the different managers became familiar with each other's work.

Controlling. The purpose of control is to make sure that work is carried out in accordance with a plan, the instructions of the managers, and generally accepted principles. Every department should be responsible for controlling its own operations. Especially appointed inspectors are required only when this is too extensive or complicated. Such inspectors must have a strong sense of duty and good judgment. They should be independent of those to be inspected and have no responsibility for amending the deficiencies that they find. Should the principle of unity of command be violated, the company might be seriously harmed.

Evolution

Henri Fayol derived his management recommendations from his own long experience as chief executive of a large industrial company. Having graduated as a mining engineer in 1860, at the age of nineteen, Fayol was hired into the coalmine at Commentry in central France, later to be reorganized as the Commentry-Fourchambault, or Comambault, Company and one of the largest iron and steel companies in France at the time. He was promoted as manager of a group of mines in 1866 and became managing director in 1888, when the company was on the verge of bankruptcy. Prosperity was restored, however, a fact that Fayol attributed to his own capacity as manager. Fayol worked for the same company for 58 years, until his retirement at the age of 77. He remained on the company's board of directors until his death.

As a young mining engineer and line manager Fayol published papers on underground fires, buried mine shafts, and the geology of coal formations in the Commentry district. For these he was awarded the prestigious Delesse Prize by the French Academy of Science.

At the end of his career, when he was 75 years old, Fayol summarized his experience as a manager. In *Administration industrielle et générale*, first published in the bulletin of the Societé de l'Industrie Minerale in 1916, he systematized his management recommendations into principles and methods for good, orderly management. His book was translated into English in 1929, but published in the United States only in 1949 as *General and Industrial Management*.

To promote his management principles, Fayol then founded the Center of Administrative Studies (*Centre d'Études Administratives*). Situated in Paris, the center functioned from around 1917 until 1925 (or 1926). It held meetings for representatives of a variety of professions, published articles and lectures on management, and responded to commentaries on this subject.

Importance

The ubiquity of management in all kinds of organizations led Fayol to recognize management as a topic for education, theory, and practice.

Fayol Asked for Management Education

Because everyone must possess some management knowledge a management education should start with the family and continue through elementary school to universities, special schools, and the individual workplaces. In particular, the higher technical schools should include management in their syllabi.

The higher technical schools did not prepare their students for their future positions as managers, Fayol argued. These schools concentrated on training professional engineers and neglected the fact that many, if not all, of these engineers would need management knowledge. To rely solely on learning from experience was a mistake, Fayol maintained. Like other company functions, management should be taught, and a management education was of urgent importance. In particular, Fayol questioned the time-consuming teaching of advanced mathematics when, in effect, the simple rule of three would suffice.

Fayol Asked for Management Theory

Fayol referred the absence of management education to the fact that there was no management theory. He defined *theory* as a collection of principles, rules, methods, and procedures that were tested and verified by experience. True, an abundance of principles and methods already existed, but they were put together and employed in a haphazard manner; there were principles that were not accompanied by methods and methods that might as well prove detrimental.

In contrast to religious or moral principles, which regulate the behavior of individuals, or theological issues, management principles should benefit organizations and promote their economic interests.

It would not be difficult, Fayol believed, to find principles that experienced managers had found valuable. A dozen or so well-founded and generally accepted principles would suffice. Unfortunately, CEOs were often too busy, even uninterested, in contributing to management theory. But Fayol was optimistic: Even minor observations might add up, first to a general discussion and then to a theory. The purpose of *Administration industrielle et générale* was to initiate and stimulate such a discussion. Hopefully, with time, a management theory would emerge.

Fayol's Notion of Management Is Now Common Knowledge

Over the years, many asked for a management theory. But no such generally accepted theory was presented. Instead, Fayol's management principles and methods have made a lasting impact on how management is perceived and taught, to the extent that most managers are in effect Fayolists, although perhaps unawares.

Fayol's general management principles and methods have often been mistaken for those of his contemporary, the U.S. engineer and consultant Frederick Winslow Taylor (1856–1915), and seen as a European version of scientific management. But Fayol's management principles stand in sharp contrast to those of Taylor in a number of respects. Where Taylor focused on standardizing the work of the individual worker, Fayol's perspective is clearly top-down. In effect, and as stated in his book, Fayol recalled and systematized his own experience as head of a large industrial company. Polemicizing with Taylor, Fayol explicitly dismissed Taylor's functional organization and defended instead the principle of unity of command.

Taylor and his scientific management principles are well known, much discussed, and often criticized, but Fayol fared differently. Neither his principles nor Fayol as a person have received much attention. One reason for this partial oblivion may be his enormous impact: Fayol was so influential that his management principles and methods are taken for granted, even apprehended as "natural."

After 100 years, Fayol's book is still highly modern. His management principles and methods are repeated over and over again in ever-new editions of management control and management accounting textbooks. Students are still instructed to memorize the acronym POSDCORB (planning, organizing, staffing, directing, coordinating, reporting, budgeting) in order to remember what they are expected to do as managers.

In retrospect, Fayol's ambition to initiate a discussion on management principles and methods seems too modest. In fact, his principles and methods came to constitute the very management theory that he asked for.

Karin Holmblad Brunsson

See also Bureaucratic Theory; Management Control Systems; Management Roles; Neo-Institutional Theory; Organizational Effectiveness; Organizational Structure and Design; Process Theories of Change

Further Readings

Fayol, H. (1916/1949). *General and industrial management* (with a foreword by Lyndall Urwick). London, England: Pitman.

Holmblad Brunsson, K. (2007). *The notion of general management.* Malmö, Sweden: Liber/Copenhagen Business School Press.

Holmblad Brunsson, K. (2008). Some effects of Fayolism. *International Studies of Management & Organization,* 38(1), 30–47.

Parker, L. D., & Ritson, P. (2005). Fads, stereotypes and management gurus: Fayol and Follett today. *Management Decision,* 43(10), 1335–1357.

Pryor, M. G., & Taneja, S. (2010). Henri Fayol, practitioner and theoretician—Revered and reviled. *Journal of Management History,* 16(4), 489–503.

Wren, D. A. (2005). *The history of management thought.* Hoboken, NJ: Wiley.

PROCESS CONSULTATION

Process consultation is a term developed by Edgar Schein in the late 1960s as a contribution to organization development theory and practice. While his intention was to articulate an approach to consultation, he found that it was being used by managers as much as by consultants. The term *process consultation* has become established in the field of organization development and management theory as an approach to being helpful to think out and work through problems. This entry describes process consultation with regard to more expert-based approaches and discusses how it also serves as the foundation of clinical inquiry/research.

Fundamentals

Schein describes and contrasts three helping models: the doctor-patient model, the purchase model, and process consultation. The doctor-patient model of helping is grounded in the familiar process of a client experiencing a problem and going to an expert, who performs an assessment and prescribes a solution that the client implements. This approach to receiving help is both prevalent and most useful as the knowledge of experts is an important contribution to addressing problems. However, as Schein points out, certain elements need to be in play for this approach to be effective. The client needs to have identified the problem area correctly and reveal the necessary information for an accurate assessment by the expert. The expert needs to have the necessary expertise for effective assessment and prescription. The client has to accept the assessment, implement the prescription, and have the problem solved after withdrawal of the expert. In the purchase model, the client purchases the skills of the expert, who implements them on behalf of the client. This approach also depends on the client's performing a correct assessment and so identifying the relevant expert and the client's accepting what the expert has done; similarly, the problem is solved after the expert has withdrawn. Organizations draw on the doctor-patient model when external experts are brought in to perform an analysis and to write a report with recommendations for organizational action. They draw on the purchase model when they employ external expert skills, for example, to design and install technology or other systems.

The third model, process consultation, is defined by Schein as the creation of a relationship with the client that permits the client to perceive, understand, and act on process events that occur in the client's internal and external environment to improve the situation as defined by the client. From this definition, it can be seen that core elements of process consultation are building a collaborative relationship between consultant and client so that the client sees what is going on, develops some understanding, and builds a plan to act. Process consultation is based on the underlying assumptions that managers often do not know what precisely is wrong in an organization and so need a special kind of help to understand what their problems actually are. They may think only of the doctor-patient model and therefore have a limited knowledge of the different kinds of help consultants can give and so may benefit from help in knowing what kind of help to seek. More important, they may want to solve the problems themselves and not hand over to an expert who provides a prescription, but at the same time they need help in deciding what to do. In this manner, it may be understood how process consultation is an organizational equivalent of what occurs in therapy, where the therapist helps clients solve their own problems.

Assessment and Intervention

In the expert-based models described above, assessment or diagnosis is undertaken by the expert as an antecedent to intervention. In process consultation, assessment and intervention are simultaneous processes as the process consultant engages with the client in trying to understand what is going on and why. Process consultants ask questions and make comments that aim to be helpful in structuring the client's thinking further and in revealing information about what is really going, thereby teaching the client to be able to look at his or her own information and analyze it. Their interventions must seem normal and not be mysterious so that clients themselves may learn the skills of attending to their experience, testing their insights, and taking actions based on their understanding. Hence, through the interaction between the process consultant and the client, the client performs the assessment. A key tacit process is that process consultants are communicating to the client that they are willing to help but not take the problem onto their own shoulders.

Schein frames a typology of interventions through which the client is enabled to think through the problem and develop an action plan for addressing it. In *pure inquiry*, process consultants listen carefully and neutrally and prompt the elicitation and exploration of the story of what is taking place, thereby demonstrating the client's ownership of the issues and the facilitative role of the process consultant. The second type of inquiry is what Schein calls *diagnostic inquiry*, in which process consultants begin to manage the process of how the content is understood by the client by exploring (1) reasoning processes, (2), emotional processes, and (3) actions. The third type of inquiry is what Schein calls *confrontive inquiry*. This is where the process consultants, by sharing their own ideas, challenge the client to think from a new perspective. These ideas may refer to (1) process and (2) content and focus on possible decisions and actions.

Process Consultation and Clinical Inquiry/Research

There are ongoing debates about the philosophy and methodologies of organizational and management research and their relevance to management practice. In this context, Schein argues that the knowledge obtained by traditional research models frequently do not reflect what "things are really like" in organizations and so are inadequate for studying organizational processes. Accordingly, he describes clinical inquiry/research as synonymous with process consultation.

Clinical inquiry/research is based on three basic assumptions. These assumptions are grounded in the notion of a clinician as a professional who can diagnose a problem in terms of a deviation from "health" and work with a client to return to health.

- Clinical researchers are hired to help. The research agenda comes from the needs of the client system, not from the interests of the researchers. In this regard, clinical inquiry and research may be distinguished from traditional action research that typically begins from the researcher's initiative and where the organization accommodates the researcher's needs. In clinical inquiry/research the researcher is hired, and is being paid, to help, which means that the researcher may be afforded richer access to organizations that might not be shared readily with outsiders.
- Clinical researchers work from models of health and therefore are trained to recognize pathological deviations from health. Clinical researchers, therefore, need to be trained in organizational dynamics and have models of organizational health so that they know what to notice in organizations.
- Clinical researchers are not only concerned with diagnosis but have a primary focus on treatment. Accordingly, they need to be skilled in providing help in the manner of process consultation, which as described above is focused on being helpful.

There are several working principles underpinning the practice of clinical inquiry/research. The issues that clinical researchers work on are important for the organization because they have been hired to help. They accept the assumption that unless they attempt to change the system, they cannot really understand it. The primary sources to organizational data are not what is "out there" in the system but are in the effects of and responses to intervention. Through being present in a helping role, clinical inquiry/researchers are noticing how data are continuously being generated as the change process proceeds. Clinical researchers engage in observing incidents of learning and change, studying the effects of interventions, focusing on puzzles and anomalies that are difficult to explain, and thereby working to build theory and empirical knowledge through developing concepts that capture the real dynamics of the organization and focusing on the characteristic of systems and systemic dynamics. In this way, clinical researchers'

data is "real-time," generated in the act of managing change, not data created especially for the research project.

At the heart of process consultation and clinical inquiry/research is the relationship with the client and the mode of collaborative inquiry. Clinical inquiry/research is a complete form of collaborative research because the knowledge is produced in collaboration with clients in a manner that serves both the practical needs of the clients and knowledge for the academic community. Working to be helpful is the central theme of process consultation and clinical inquiry/research. It is the key starting point and a constant focus of attention. It is the client who owns the problem and the solution, and clinical researchers must constantly be aware that the interactions in the here and now continually provide diagnostic information about what is going on, how the client is responding, and the relationship between clinical researcher and client. As assessment and intervention are parallel and simultaneous, rather than sequential, clinical researchers are always intervening. Everything is data. Accordingly, clinical researchers need to think out the consequences of their actions.

What is central, therefore, to the theory and practice of process consultation and clinical inquiry/research is the focus on and skill of learning how to be helpful. For the process consultant, this involves recognizing the limitations of expertise-based models and attending to how to be helpful to the client. It is not that the process consultant has no expertise. Process consultants' expertise is in establishing a helping relationship, knowing what to look for in organizations, and intervening in such a way that organizational process are improved. So there may be occasions that a particular expertise is needed by the client, and the process consultant may offer that expertise. Schein's advice is always to begin in the process consultation mode—that is, with a spirit of inquiry. When one begins as the expert, it is difficult to step out of that role, whereas beginning in the process consultation mode and remaining firmly in it allows the process consultant to step into an expert role when the occasion demands and then step out of it.

Importance

Process consultation is a foundational element of organization development; it articulates a core philosophical value on being helpful. The focus of much scholarship is on content knowledge and expertise, with little attention paid to the scholarship of practice. The scholarly and educational implications of process consultation are that scholars and researchers would benefit from learning to be helpful. Schein suggests that as part of their education, business, and organization studies, students spend time in organizations, hanging around, learning the skills of how to be helpful.

The professional implications of process consultation for modern managers are that as expertise becomes more narrowly defined, the role of the general managers increasingly becomes one of enabling professionals to do their own jobs well. As Schein himself experienced, what was articulated initially as a form of consultation became adopted by managers in working with their own staff. He also found that process consultation skills are useful for parents, professionals in all fields, and for the informal exchanges between colleagues and friends. Process consultation also gives managers more choice in relation to using consultants, and so they can avail of the different forms of help that consultants can provide.

David Coghlan

See also Academic-Practitioner Collaboration and Knowledge Sharing; Action Research; Double Loop Learning; Engaged Scholarship Model; Force Field Analysis and Model of Planned Change; Management Roles; Organizational Development; Theory X and Theory Y

Further Readings

Coghlan, D. (2009). Toward a philosophy of clinical inquiry/research. *Journal of Applied Behavioral Science, 45*(1), 106–121.

Schein, E. H. (1969). *Process consultation: Its role in organization development*. Reading, MA: Addison-Wesley.

Schein, E. H. (1995). Process consultation, action research and clinical inquiry: Are they the same? *Journal of Managerial Psychology, 10*(6), 14–19.

Schein, E. H. (1999). *Process consultation revisited: Building the helping relationship*. Reading, MA: Addison-Wesley.

Schein, E. H. (2008). Clinical inquiry/research. In P. Reason & H. Bradbury (Eds.), *Handbook of action research* (2nd ed., pp. 266–279). London, England: Sage.

Schein, E. H. (2009). *Helping*. San Francisco, CA: Berrett-Kohler.

PROCESS THEORIES OF CHANGE

Organizational change is defined as a difference in form, quality, or state over time in an organizational entity. The entity may be an individual's job, a work group, an organizational subunit, the overall organization, or its relationships with other organizations. Change can be determined by measuring the same entity over two or more points in time on a set of characteristics and then observing the differences over time in these characteristics. If the difference is noticeable, we can say that the organizational entity has changed. Much of the voluminous literature on organizational change focuses on two questions about this difference: (1) How and what produced it? (2) How might the change process be managed in constructive directions over time? The first question focuses on process theories that explain how organization change unfolds over time. The second question focuses on the processes of implementing theories of change. Based on an extensive literature on processes of organization change and implementation, this entry addresses these two questions.

Fundamentals

On the basis of an extensive review of the social science literature, Andrew Van de Ven and Marshall Scott Poole found four basic process models of organizational change and development: teleology (planned change), life cycle (regulatory change), dialectics (conflictive change), and evolution (competitive change). As the figure indicates, these process models differ in terms of whether they apply to single or multiple organizational entities and if the change process follows a prescribed sequence or is constructed (emerges) as the process unfolds. The cells in Figure 1 illustrate how each theory views the process of development as unfolding in a fundamentally different progression of change events and being governed by a different generative mechanism or motor.

Understanding these four process models of change, and interactions among them, provides a rich repertoire of models for explaining change processes in organizations. In addition, an appreciation of the different breakdowns and remedies in implementing each of the four models of change provides a useful framework for diagnosing implementation processes. As discussed in the conclusion, this

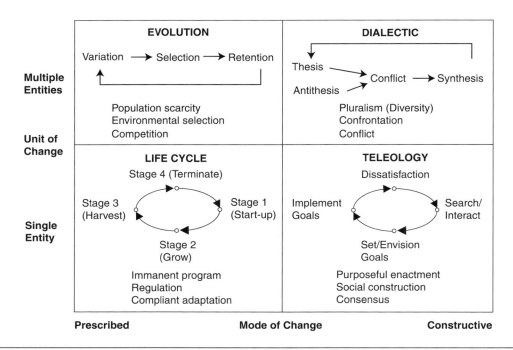

Figure 1   Process Models of Organization Change

Source: Van de Ven and Poole (1995), p. 520. Copyright © 1995 by Academy of Management Review. Reproduced by permission.

Note: Arrows on lines represent likely sequences among events, not causation between events.

diagnosis becomes complex when change agents use different models to manage multiple change initiatives ongoing in organizations.

Teleological Process Theory (Planned Change)

A *teleology* or *planned change* model views development as a repetitive sequence of goal formulation, implementation, evaluation, and modification of an envisioned end state based on what was learned or intended by the people involved. This sequence emerges through the purposeful social construction among individuals within the organizational entity undergoing change. Teleological processes of planned change break down either because participants do not recognize the need for change, they make erroneous decisions, or they do not reach agreement on goals or actions.

Models of planned change assume that people initiate efforts to change when their attention is triggered by significant opportunities, problems, or threats. Teleological processes often fail because only a minority of participants recognize the need for change. Dissatisfaction with existing conditions stimulates people to search for improved conditions, and people stop searching when a satisfactory result is found. A satisfactory result is a function of a person's aspiration level—a product of past successes and failures that people have experienced. When the difference between perceptions of current situations and aspiration levels is not significant, the need for change is hardly recognized. Direct personal experiences with opportunities or problems are more likely to trigger individuals' attention than are reports or exhortations about the need for change.

Teleological change processes also break down when there is a lack of consensus on plans or goals among organizational participants. Socialization activities provide a way of building consensus because team building, training sessions, and social gatherings, for example, facilitate frequent interactions that in turn lead to shared understandings, common norms, and cooperative attitudes. However, even when consensus for change is apparent initially, it may not last when divergent cultures in a loosely coupled organizational system lock in on maintaining their cultural traditions. Repeated conversations among relevant stakeholders throughout the change process are typically needed for consensus to evolve on a change initiative.

Finally, a teleological process may also fail because of faulty plans or goals because of biases in individual or group judgments—errors in critical thinking and decision making. Studies show that human beings lack the capability and inclination to deal with complexity. For example, "self-justification" is one of the major reasons for escalating commitments to failing projects. Individuals who are responsible for an initial decision tend to become more committed to a failing course of action than individuals not involved in the initial decision. Common strategies for reducing cognitive biases include engaging other informants in focus groups or brainstorming processes to provide information and interpretations of the issue being considered.

Life Cycle Process Theory (Regulated Change)

A *life cycle* model depicts the process of change in an entity as progressing through a prescribed sequence of stages and activities over time. Activities in a life cycle model are prescribed and regulated by natural, logical, or institutional routines. In most organizational applications of a life cycle model, the rules prescribing the change process are based on routines learned in the past for managing recurrent changes in efficient and effective ways, or they may be externally induced; that is, they come from sources outside of the organizational entity undergoing change. Life cycle theory is not simply a model of passive compliance to mandated change by an entity; it also considers how proactive individuals adapt to their environments and make use of rules to accomplish their purposes.

In deviating from prescribed change routines, local adaptations are typically viewed as breakdowns by those who design and mandate a change routine. Prescriptions for change are perceived differently by "planners," who design a change program, and "doers," who implement it but did not participate in its development. Breakdowns happen when planners are separated from doers, because learning fails when events are caused and consequences are felt by different people. Consistent with the "not-invented-here" syndrome, people are more likely to implement and comply with changes in which they have a part in planning and adapting to fit to their local situations. Studies have found that local

adaptation of a regulated change to fit a particular applied setting facilitates implementing change programs. Local adaptation is fundamentally a learning process triggered by the inevitable setbacks and mistakes people encounter as they attempt to implement a change program. This requires some local autonomy to adapt and modify mandated changes to local situations.

Managers of regulated changes tend to dichotomize employee responses into those who support and those who resist the proposed change and to view the latter as being disobedient. Recent studies examine a number of reasons why employees resist a prescribed change, including constructive intentions to correct errors that may prevent implementation. The ambivalence that employees feel toward an organizational change initiative does not necessarily represent opposition as disobedience; instead, it may reflect the complexity of most organizational changes as having both positive and negative characteristics.

Dialectical Process Theory (Conflictive Change)

Dialectical theories explain stability and change in terms of the relative balance of power between opposing entities. Stability is produced through struggles and accommodations that maintain the status quo between oppositions. Change occurs when challengers gain sufficient power to confront and engage incumbents. Change is generated through the resolution of conflict between the current thesis (A) and an antithesis (Not-A), which results in a synthesis (Not Not-A). Conflict is the core generating mechanism of dialectical change. Dysfunctional methods of conflict resolution tend to impede dialectical change processes and may lead to undesirable win-lose outcomes.

To be a constructive force, conflict has to be resolved effectively. Studies at individual and group levels suggest that problem solving and open confrontation of conflicts are more likely to lead to expressions and debates of different opinions, which in turn facilitates the resolution of differences and conflicts. A collaborative conflict culture can foster adaptation to change, given that there is an emphasis on active listening to others' points of view and seeking the best solutions for all parties involved. In contrast, organizations with avoidant conflict cultures are likely to be less adaptive to change because norms against open discussion and the lack of information sharing can prevent effective solutions to disagreements.

Power is another concept that is central to a dialectical model of change. A necessary condition for conflict to be expressed is that the opposing parties have sufficient power to confront each other and engage in struggle. Conflict tends to remain latent or to be squelched by dominant actors until challengers can mobilize sufficient power to confront opposing parties.

Evolutionary Process Theory (Competitive Change)

Evolutionary change unfolds as a recurrent and probabilistic progression of variation, selection, and retention activities. Variations, the creation of novel forms, are often viewed as emerging by blind or random chance. Selection occurs principally through competition among forms, and customers in the environment or higher-level decision makers select those forms best suited for the resource base of an environmental niche. Retention involves the forces and routines that perpetuate and maintain certain organizational forms.

Evolutionary processes, at the organization and industry levels, are subject to two common types of breakdowns: (1) a small number of homogeneous variations and selection criteria and (2) lack of competition for scarce resources. An evolutionary model of change emphasizes the need for a heterogeneous pool of variations and competition for scarce resources.

Variations provide the raw materials from which selection can be made. A greater number of diverse variations are more likely to produce innovations than a process that generates a small number of homogenous variations. A lack of diverse variations may result from the success of existing routines and of obtaining short-run rewards from them. Organizational experiments represent remedies to generate diverse variations by investing more resources in research and development, supporting innovation "champion" and "entrepreneurial" roles, and creating parallel projects in which several teams compete on the same general problem. Selection processes, such as setting goals without methods to reach them, establishing broad values, and setting project screening and selection criteria are also important ways to facilitate evolutionary

change. Finally, retention processes are influenced by the application of consistent controls, formalized routines, and organization culture and values.

A key characteristic of variation is its "blindness" with respect to its ability to improve an organization's fitness. When variations are not "blind," evolutionary selection processes tend to be biased in directions that may not promote adaptation and fitness. One source for this lack of blindness is the existence of powerful incentives that lead decision makers to favor variations believed to produce good outcomes. Finally, evolutionary theory only works under conditions of competition for scarce resources; they break down when resources are munificent and competition is low because in these situations both efficient and inefficient variations tend to survive and grow.

Evolution

Since their 1995 introduction, the four process models of change have received extensive study and attention by management scholars and practitioners. Useful variations of these four basic process models have also been proposed. Central to the evolution of this recent research is appreciating that organizational change and implementation processes often appear more complex than the four process models suggest. This may be due to several reasons.

First, errors or omissions in implementing one model of change may trigger the start-up of another change model. For example, a failure to reach consensus among leaders of a planned change may bifurcate the leaders into two opposing factions who then engage in dialectical conflict and struggle. So also, age and size may lead to inertia in the life cycles of organizational products, processes, and routines and make them less responsive to environmental changes. Adaptation failures in these life cycles may trigger an evolutionary process of the environment selecting out the misfit. There are many possible ways that the four process models may trigger, compensate, and complement each other.

A second reason why organizational change is often complex is that positive and negative interactions among several models of change can move an organization toward (1) equilibrium, (2) oscillation, and (3) chaos. Organizational equilibrium results when its routines, goals, or values are sufficiently dominant to suppress opposing minority positions and thereby produce incremental adaptations flowing toward equilibrium. For example, an existing organizational culture, structure, or system can remain intact by undertaking incremental adaptations that appease or diffuse opposing minority positions. Organizational business cycles, fads, or pendulum swings occur when opposing interest groups, business regimes, or political parties alternate in power and push the organization somewhat farther from a stable equilibrium. Such cycles explain recurrent periods of organizational feast and famine, partisan mutual adjustment among political parties, and alternating organizational priorities on efficiency and innovation. Third, seemingly random organizational behaviors are produced when strong oscillations or shifts occur between opposing forces that push the organization out of a single periodic equilibrium orbit and produce multiple equilibria and bifurcations. Currently, there is growing interest in recent advances in chaos theory and nonlinear dynamic models to explain such seemingly random behavior in organizations. Thus, different patterns of interaction between change motors can push an organization to flow toward equilibrium, to oscillate in cycles between opposites, or to bifurcate far from equilibrium and spontaneously create revolutionary changes.

As these complexities and implementation errors imply, it is important to caution that existing theories of organizational change are explanatory but not predictive. Statistically, we should expect most incremental, convergent, and continuous changes to be explained by either life cycle or evolutionary theories and most radical, divergent, and discontinuous changes to be explained by teleological or dialectical theories. But these actuarial relationships may not be causal. For example, the infrequent statistical occurrence of a discontinuous and radical mutation may be caused by a glitch in the operation of a life cycle model of change. So also, the scale-up of a teleological process to create a planned strategic reorientation for a company may fizzle, resulting only in incremental change.

Importance

The mental model one uses to manage organization change is a strategic choice, and making this choice implies knowing alternative models from which to choose. We reviewed Van de Ven and Poole's four process models of organization change and development and proposed that each model applies in the different situations. Useful variations of these four basic process models have been introduced since 1995. The important point of these models is that they encourage managers and scholars to expand their repertoire of models for managing organizational change. This enables us to think beyond a single change model—such as the dominant model of planned change—and to identify situations when each process theory of organization change applies. Current and future research is underway that examines the different situations when teleology, life cycle, dialectical, and evolutionary models—and their interactions—reflect the change processes unfolding organizations.

When change processes occurring in organizations do not unfold in a manner suggested by our mental model, they tend to trigger two kinds of strategies. Typically, the first strategy is to take actions intended to correct the people or processes in the organization that prevent the change model from running as expected. A second strategy for dealing with breakdowns is to reflect on and revise the mental model in use to one that better fits the process of change unfolding in the organization. This strategy represents the scientific method of testing and rejecting a theory if data do not support it and then revising or adapting a theory that fits the observed data. This second strategy appears prudent only after reasonable attempts are made but fail to implement the first strategy. Correcting or replacing one's conceptual model of change to fit the people and organization undergoing change has received very little research attention and presumes a multidimensional change agent who can mentally shift between different conceptual models of organizational change. This second strategy requires developing an appreciation of the interdependencies and interactions among various models of change and their associated breakdowns.

Andrew H. Van de Ven

See also Compliance Theory; Conflict Handling Styles; Path-Goal Theory of Leadership; Stages of Innovation; Strategies for Change

Further Readings

Burke, W. W., Lake, D. G., & Paine, J. W. (Eds.). (2009). *Organization change: A comprehensive reader*. San Francisco, CA: Jossey-Bass.

Huber, G. P., & Glick, W. H. (1993). Organizational change and redesign: Ideas and insights for improving performance. New York, NY: Oxford University Press.

Meyer, A. D., Brooks, G. R., & Goes, J. B. (1990, Summer). Environmental jolts and industry revolutions: Organizational responses to discontinuous change. *Strategic Management Journal, 11,* 93–110.

Poole, M. S., & Van de Ven, A. H. (2004). *Handbook of organizational change and innovation.* New York, NY: Oxford University Press.

Poole, M. S., Van de Ven, A. H., Dooley, K., & Holmes, M. E. (2000). *Organizational change and innovation processes: Theory and methods for research.* New York, NY: Oxford University Press.

Van de Ven, A. H., & Poole, M. S. (1995). Explaining development and change in organizations. *Academy of Management Review, 20,* 510–540.

Van de Ven, A. H., & Sun, K. (2011). Breakdowns in implementing models of organization change. *Academy of Management Perspectives, 25*(3), 58–74.

Weick, K. E., & Quinn, R. E. (1999). Organizational change and development. *Annual Review of Psychology, 50,* 361–386.

PRODUCT CHAMPIONS

The theory of product champions is based on the political mediation needed to implement any major change in an organization. This role is important for management of complex organizations. New products or processes, whether they are technical, administrative, social, or economic, involve many steps and involve many people for successful implementation. In other words, they involve innovation and some changes in many domains. Depending on the complexity and the scope of the impact of the innovation, it requires one or more committed individuals to steer the innovation through the many hurdles it must cross. In management theory, this type of individual has been defined as a champion. The following entry will review the characteristics, roles, behaviors, and impact of product champions.

Fundamentals

Donald Schon explained that the champion is one who identifies with an innovation and valiantly pushes it with some personal risks. The primary barriers to innovation are (a) organizational inertia, (b) fear of criticism, (c) feeling of futility in pursuing the innovation, and (d) the lack of attention given to an idea that is in its early stages. Stephen Markham

has shown that a champion helps in the innovation process by (a) developing a personal commitment to the innovation, (b) helping develop the idea, and (c) navigating the idea through organizational bureaucracy at his or her own personal risk. In this context James Quinn and James Muller provided an apt analogy with the development of a child. A child needs a loving and nurturing mother, a father to provide the resources and support and a pediatrician to heal the problems that the parents can't solve. Similarly, an innovation or a new idea needs committed nurturing, resources to support it, and expert knowledge to solve technical problems.

Personality Characteristics of Champions

Research has shown that product champions have distinct personality type, occupy a distinct role, and do so in a distinct way. Alok Chakrabarti identified several personality characteristics and skills that champions often have: (a) drive and aggressiveness, (b) political astuteness, (c) knowledge about the organization, (d) knowledge about the market, and (e) technical competence. A successful champion has to understand the reality of his or her environment, both internal and external, and have the capacity to deal with the multiple stakeholders in the organization.

Jane Howell and Christopher Higgins found that champions have a high need for achievement, a personality trait of entrepreneurs. They also observed that the champions share some of the personality traits of transformational leaders, such as persuasiveness, persistence, risk taking, and innovativeness. Like transformational leaders, successful champions are able to inspire and provide intellectual stimulation to others in the organization for nurturing the innovation.

Multidimensional Nature of Champion Role

Alok Chakrabarti and Juergen Hauschildt classified the different roles of individuals involved in different phases in the innovation process. In the initial phase of idea development, there are the *idea stimulator,* the *initiator,* and the *catalyst.* They work on the fuzzy front end of the innovation process. The next phase is technical development of the idea to establish its technical viability. The role incumbents in this phase are termed *information specialists, technologists,* and *solution givers.* When the idea passes the technical feasibility tests, other organizational units get involved in the implementation process. The role of champion becomes important in managing the process. The role incumbents have been termed *orchestrator, facilitator,* and *process helper.* Executive decisions are needed to keep the innovation moving forward toward implementation and commercialization. That is why one needs *legitimizers* or *decision makers.* At the implementation or commercialization phase, one needs an *executor* or *realizator.*

Another way to distinguish among various types of champions is on the dimension of power base of the incumbents. People with expert power are termed *inventors, technical innovators,* and *technologists.* The role incumbent with the hierarchical base of power is *executive champion, chief executive,* or *machtpromotor* (in German). Champions with access to resources are *sponsors, business innovators,* and *investors.* Those who work with their organizational knowledge and communication skills are termed *product champions, project champions,* and *entrepreneurs.*

Hans Georg Gemuenden and his colleagues in Germany strongly recommend that the earlier model of champion being an all-encompassing role to promote an innovation needs to be expanded to recognize the roles of multiple specialists. Since there is no suitable German equivalent of the word *champion,* German scholars have used the word *promoter.* According to them, there are five types of promoters: power promoter, expert promoter, process promoter, technology promoter, and marketing promoter. The *power promoter* supports the project through his or her hierarchical power. The *expert promoter* uses his or her technical knowledge to overcome the barriers. The *process promoter,* through his or her knowledge of the organizational processes, helps the project to progress without any undue hitch. *Technology and marketing promoters* are viewed as boundary spanners for importing knowledge and information from external sources in an open innovation environment.

Champion Behavior

Jane Howell and her associates proposed a division of the behavior of champions into three categories: (a) expression of enthusiasm and confidence (b) persistence in adversity, and (c) getting the right people involved. The champion's enthusiasm goes beyond what is organizationally required; it is a personal commitment similar to a parental affection for the innovation. The behavior of effective champions in the different stages of the innovation process can be summarized as follows: (a) They rely on their personal networks to explore new ideas from different sources. (b) They use their wide general knowledge and breadth of experience for dealing with technical and marketing problems. (c) They use both formal and informal channels of communication to "sell" the idea to different stakeholders. (d) They monitor themselves and anticipate the pockets of resistance to new ideas so as to be prepared to respond. (e) They "sell" their idea as an opportunity in the context of the organization's strategy.

Champions use many strategies to influence their adversaries and people not convinced about the innovation. *Reasoning* is the rational strategy where one uses facts and data in developing a logical argument for the innovation. Forming a *coalition* of like-minded colleagues is an effective strategy to influence others. Sometimes a champion may deploy *ingratiation* as a strategy. *Bargaining* is also another influence strategy where one exchanges favors or benefits. *Assertiveness* is another strategy where one takes a forceful approach. Appealing to *higher authority* is also a strategy used by champions. If the champion has authority, then *sanctions* are used to coerce. Effective champions use a variety of influence strategies.

Champions don't guarantee the success of an innovation. They often invoke antagonists. When an organization has an open culture, the antagonists may play the role of loyal opposition and actually be constructive in the innovation process. When the climate is repressive, then opposition may become hidden. Hidden opposition is more dangerous. Opposition can take place in any the following ways: (a) challenging the credibility of the experts, (b) coalescing the pockets of opposition to form a sizeable block, (c) doubting the economic viability of the idea, (d) doubting the technical feasibility, (e) pointing out the inadequacy of the organizational infrastructure to support the idea, and (6) explaining the incongruity of the innovation and the organizational culture and tradition. Champions need to overcome these objections to get the innovation to proceed.

Importance

The importance of champions has been emphasized in any innovation process that involves multiple organizations as sources and users. Ulrich Lichtenthaler and Holger Ernst found that champions contribute positively in external knowledge acquisition. They help overcome potential negative attitudes and establish contacts with sources of external technology. However, champions need a favorable organizational climate to emerge and be successful.

Edward Sim and his colleagues found that the importance of the role of champion differs in different contingency conditions of technical uncertainty and marketing uncertainty. *Innovators* are most important in radical innovation where both the technical and market uncertainties are high. *Champions* are important in market innovation with a high level of market uncertainty but a low level of technical uncertainty. *Inventors* are important in technological innovation with high technical uncertainty. *Implementers* are important in incremental innovation with a low level of uncertainty in both technical and marketing domains. Incumbents in these four roles have different skills. For example, innovators must have technical expertise, market expertise, and political acumen. The biggest asset of a champion is political acumen, while technical and marketing expertise are of secondary importance. Inventors have technical expertise as their core skill. Implementers must be good at process implementation. Other dimensions in which these people can be differentiated are as follows:

1. *Motivation:* Inventors focus on technology, champions focus on financial success and reputation, implementers are concerned with a good living, and innovators are concerned with developing solutions for their customers.

2. *Openness:* Inventors are strongly introverted, champions are strongly extroverted, implementers are extroverts, and innovators can be either introverts or extroverts.

3. *Organizational politics:* Inventors use avoidance, champions use an embracing attitude, implementers use rational arguments, and innovators use positive influence tactics.

4. *Orientation:* Inventors have task orientation, champions are communication oriented, implementers have task and people orientation, and innovators have multiple orientation.

The implications for managers involve recognizing people who can effectively fulfill the role of a champion and recruiting them accordingly. Empowering them is also important; a champion needs a sponsor. Champions will be confronted with opposition from different persons in the organizations for various reasons. The champion may resolve some of these conflicts as long as there is clear recognition of top management support.

Cultural Implications

Scott Shane and his colleagues have found that the effectiveness of the influence strategies of champions are related to culture. One cannot use the same behavior that makes one successful in a Western country in a country that has a different culture. Shane used three dimensions of culture to differentiate countries. These are *power distance, uncertainty avoidance,* and *individualism.* Power distance is an indicator of social acceptability of an unequal distribution of power. Uncertainty avoidance represents the tolerance for ambiguity in a society. Individualism represents the preference for one's immediate family first over social group and organization.

A society with high power distance prefers champions who work with a budget and approval in a closely monitored situation. This is contrary to what has been observed in the United States and Europe where champions are more empowered to work in a flexible environment with more autonomy to take initiatives. The effective championing strategy in societies with high uncertainty avoidance is to work within organizational rules, norms, and procedures. In societies with a high level of individualism, people prefer that champions don't use their personal appeal to gather cross-functional support.

These findings show that much of we have learned about innovation process and champion behavior in the West may not be applicable in Asia and elsewhere in emerging economies.

Managerial Implications

To understand the managerial implications in terms of fostering champions and motivating them, one needs to understand what champions like and don't like. Jane Howell has made the following points about champions: They like to work in organizations that provide opportunities for innovation, they want to work in a flexible work environment, they like challenges, they like to be networked, and they want to be recognized for their contributions. Managers should therefore provide opportunities to innovate. Imposing rigid bureaucratic rules stifle the would-be champion. Also, managers should provide opportunities for networking and thus increase the social capital of these individuals.

Since the role of champions is self-selected, managers should resist the temptation to appoint somebody to champion an innovation. Because innovation involves uncertainty, managers ought to consider any failure as an opportunity for learning instead of finding a scapegoat to blame. There should be a proper mechanism for recognizing the contributions of the champion. Monetary and other instruments of reward may be used to reward and motivate the champion behavior. Most important, champions need both emotional and organizational support from their managers when they face intense opposition.

Alok Chakrabarti

See also Innovation Speed; Patterns of Innovation; Patterns of Political Behavior; Process Theories of Change

Further Readings

Chakrabarti, A. K. (1974). The role of champion in product innovation. *California Management Review, 17*(2), 58–62.

Chakrabarti, A. K. (1989). The division of labor in innovation management. *R&D Management, 19*(2), 161–171.

Gemuenden, H. G., Salomo, S., & Holzle, K. (2007). Role models for radical innovations in times of open innovation. *Creativity and Innovation Management, 16*(4), 408–421.

Howell, J. M. (2005). The right stuff: Identifying and developing effective champions of innovation. *Academy of Management Executive, 12*(2), 108–119.

Howell, J. M., & Higgins, C. A. (1990). Champions of technological innovation. *Administrative Science Quarterly, 35*, 317–341.

Lichtenthaler, U., & Ernst, H. (2009). The role of champions in the external commercialization of knowledge. *Journal of Product Innovation Management, 26*, 371–387.

Markham, S. K. (2000). Corporate championing and antagonism as forms of political behavior: An R&D perspective, *Organization Science, 11*(4), 429–447.

Markham, S. K., & Aiman-Smith, L. (2001). Product champions: Truths, myths and management. *Research Technology Management, 44*(3), 44–50.

Schon, D. A. (1963). Champions for radical new inventions. *Harvard Business Review, 41*, 77–86.

Sim, E. W., Griffin, A., Price R. L., & Vojak, B. A. (2007). Exploring differences between inventors, champions, implementers and innovators in creating and developing new products in large, mature firms. *Creativity and Innovation Management, 16*(4), 422–436.

PRODUCT-MARKET DIFFERENTIATION MODEL

Igor Ansoff's *product-market differentiation model* is a strategic planning tool that relates a firm's product-market engagements and marketing strategy with its general strategic direction. It was a result of his work when he undertook a diversification study for Lockheed Aircraft Corporation. The foundation of the Ansoff "matrix" was placed in a 1957 article in *Harvard Business Review* and later published in Ansoff's seminal book of 1965. It was a critical contribution in the history of management since it provided managers with a tool to move beyond operational work and basic planning into a new domain. Moreover, it provided a mechanism for managers to begin to think about allocation of resources in a more deliberate approach. The premise of the basic matrix provided a simple methodology for firms to *diversify*. Moreover, it provided a launchpad for resource-based theories, since managers had to actively allocate resources for diversification. Ansoff's interests were always with practicing management, and the creation of the matrix continues to be a major foundational framework of the modern approach of strategic management. This entry provides an overview of his framework and its influence on management education and practice.

Fundamentals

Ansoff's product-market differentiation model, often depicted as a matrix, analyzes differentiation options along two dimensions—products (new, existing) and markets (new, existing). As such, it presents managers with four growth strategies: (1) *market penetration:* pushing existing products and services to existing markets; (2) *market development:* developing new markets for existing products; (3) *product development:* developing new products for existing markets; and (4) *diversification:* developing new products for new markets.

Growth Strategies

Market penetration. Growth was defined as market penetration for existing products and services into existing markets. It is the least risky since it leverages existing resources and capabilities. In a growing market, simply maintaining market share will result in growth, and there may exist opportunities to increase market share if competitors reach capacity limits. However, market penetration has limits, and once the market approaches saturation, another strategy must be pursued if the firm is to continue to grow. Market penetration pursues realization of the following: (1) Preserve or increase the market share of current products; this can be accomplished by a combination of competitive pricing strategies and existing functional management. (2) Protect and dominate growth markets. (3) Reorganize a mature market by driving out competitors. (4) Increase usage by existing customers.

Market development. Market development is also a growth strategy, but the goal is to enter new markets with existing products and services, including new geographical regions. The development of new markets for the product may be a good strategy if the firm's core competencies are related more to the specific product than to its experience with a specific market segment. Because the firm is expanding into a new market, a market development strategy typically has more risk than a market penetration strategy. There are many possible ways of approaching this strategy, including (1) new geographical markets, (2) new product dimensions or packaging, (3) new distribution channels, and (4) different pricing policies to draw different customers or create new market segments.

Product development. Product development aims to introduce new products and services into existing markets. This approach may require the development of new capabilities. A product development strategy may be appropriate if the firm's strengths are related to its specific customers rather than to the specific product itself. In this situation, it can leverage its strengths by developing a new product targeted to its existing customers. Similar to the case of new market development, new product development carries more risk than simply attempting to increase market share. Considering the product life cycle elements, this approach was aimed to have new products available in the existing markets before the product life cycle of previous products expired. Such an approach will keep the customers returning while the revenue stream remains constant.

Diversification. Diversification aims at new markets with new products and services. This is fundamentally a more risky strategy because the business is moving into markets in which it has little or no experience. For a business to espouse a diversification strategy, therefore, it must have a clear idea about what it expects to gain from the strategy and a candid assessment of the risks. Diversification pursues an increase in profitability through greater sales volume obtained from new products and new markets. Diversification can transpire either at the business unit level or at the corporate level. At the business unit level, it is most likely to grow into a new segment of an industry that the business is already in. At the corporate level, it attempts to enter an area where the firm has no previous knowledge and experience. Ansoff pointed out that a diversification strategy stands apart from the other three strategies. The first three strategies are usually pursued with the same technical, financial, and merchandising resources used for the original product line, whereas diversification usually requires a company to acquire new skills, new techniques, and new facilities.

How to Choose Between These Methods?

Managers should be able to scan the environment and determine the degree of the organization's turbulence. Some relatively low-intensity environments provide the manager with time to change. Therefore, the *market penetration* and *market development* are ideal. The organization has time to incrementally identify familiar geographical areas, new usages of product or service, innovations in pricing and distributing, and different marketing approaches. This approach also allows the organization to use existing managerial capability as well as existing managerial behavior. However, when the intensity of the external environment increases, then managers must be ready to respond quickly. In this instance, *product development* and *new markets* are appropriate response mechanisms. This high-turbulence environment requires that managers have the budget to engage in developing new products and new markets. For example, expanding from a region of one country to the next with an existing product normally requires incremental changes in skills and behavior. However, when an organization is attempting to introduce a new product into a foreign market, this may require capabilities and behavioral approaches that the organization may not have. Therefore, this is a more risky approach considering the resources required. Such environments require a diversification approach.

Importance

To this date, management and marketing textbooks are still using the Ansoff matrix to describe the relationship between products and markets. For over 50 years the Ansoff matrix has given generations of marketers and small-business leaders a quick and simple way to develop a strategic approach to growth. Hence, Ansoff's work continues to provide simplicity for marketing choices. Although the initial thrust for Ansoff was to provide a new thinking of diversification, the matrix proved to have a lasting effect on academics as a clear and concise approach to diversification. At the time the matrix was developed, diversification was an emerging strategic approach for managements.

In addition, the Ansoff matrix became a consulting foundation for future tools still being used today. The Boston Consulting Group (BCG) used the matrix approach to develop a new approach to describe relative market share versus market growth rates. The GE/McKinsey matrix was developed around the same time as the BCG to provide a relationship between a business unit's strengths and industry attractiveness. In addition, Ansoff may have provided a framework for Michael E. Porter to develop his approach to generic matrix and strategy approaches. Ansoff provided the framework for diversification (how to move into a new market), and Porter provided a tool to position the products-services into this new market. So the Ansoff matrix provided a launchpad to the consulting world to "translate" complex tasks into simple managerial approaches. Moreover, it provided a tool to facilitate

management thinking into translating qualitative information into quantitative data.

According to Ansoff, simultaneous pursuit of market penetration, market development, and product development is usually a sign of a progressive, well-run business and may be essential to survival in the face of economic competition. Such elements are fundamentally accepted today as well. However, the diversification strategy stands apart from the other three, particularly when considering the time it was created. While the first three strategies are usually followed with the same technical, financial, and marketing resources used for the original product line, diversification generally requires new skills, new techniques, and new facilities. As a result, it almost always leads to physical and organizational changes in the structure of the business that represent a distinct break with past business experience. Hence, the Ansoff matrix forces firms to separate operational and strategic work; it provides them with a domain to think beyond their endogenous planning cycles and begin to explore external dynamics. Moreover, it remains a useful tool to teach students and practicing managers how to evaluate and select between basic product-market choices.

Robert Moussetis

See also BCG Growth-Share Matrix; Competitive Advantage; Core Competence; Diversification Strategy; Firm Growth; Modes of Strategy: Planned and Emergent; Resource-Based View of the Firm; Strategy and Structure; SWOT Analysis Framework

Further Readings

Ansoff, I. (1965). *Corporate strategy.* New York, NY: McGraw-Hill.

Chandler, A. D. (1962). Strategy and structure: Chapters in the history of the American industrial enterprise. Cambridge, MA: MIT Press.

Emery, F. E., & Trist, E. L. (1965). The casual texture of organizational environments. *Human Relations, 18,* 21–32.

Guru: Igor Ansoff. (2008, July 18). *Economist.* Retrieved from http://www.economist.com/node/11701586

Hofer, C., & Schendel, D. (1978). *Strategy formulation: Analytical concepts.* St. Paul, MN: West.

March, J. G., & Simon, H. A. (1958). *Organizations.* New York, NY: Wiley.

Moussetis, R. (2011). Ansoff revisited: How Ansoff interfaces with both the planning and learning schools of thought in strategy. *Journal of Management History*, *17*(1), 102–125.

Porter, M. E. (1980). *Competitive strategy: Techniques for analyzing industries and competitors*. New York, NY: Free Press.

Prahald, C. K., & Hamel, G. (1994, Summer). Strategy as a field of study: Why search for a new paradigm? *Strategic Management Journal, 15*, 5–16.

Selznick, P. (1957). *Leadership in Administration: A sociological Interpretation*. Evanston, IL: Row, Peterson.

Profiting From Innovation

Innovators—firms that are the first to commercialize a new product or process in the market—do not always profit the most from their innovation. Sometimes a fast second entrant or even a slow third will outperform the innovator. The technology behind the computerized axial tomography (CAT) scanner, now a standard medical diagnostic tool, was developed in the late 1960s by a senior engineer at EMI Ltd., a diversified U.K.-headquartered entertainment and electronics conglomerate. Although EMI brought the technology to market fairly quickly, introducing a commercial model in the United States in 1973, 8 years later it had dropped out of the scanner business, leaving the market to later entrants. The EMI story is far from unique. The earliest vendors of microcomputers for home use (R2E, CTC, MITS, Commodore) are all but forgotten today. Xerox (in its PARC laboratory) and Apple invented the graphical user interface, but Microsoft Windows dominates the PC market with its follow-on version. Apple's iPod was not the first portable digital music player, but it has a commanding position in the category today. Merck was a pioneer in cholesterol-lowering drugs (Zocor), but Pfizer, a late entrant, secured a superior market position with Lipitor. At first glance, it is tempting to say that these examples reflect the result of creative destruction as described by Joseph Schumpeter. But creative destruction results from challenges by disruptive technology, while the cases cited above involved mostly incremental/imitative entrants building on the efforts of the pioneer. This is not to say that there is no such thing as a first-mover advantage. Genentech was a pioneer in using biotechnology to discover and develop drugs, and

30 years later was the second largest biotechnology firm, right up to its acquisition by Hoffmann-La Roche in 2009. Intel co-invented the microprocessor and still has a leading market position 40 years later. Dell pioneered a new distribution system for personal computers and, despite recent challenges and many would-be imitators, remains one of the world's leading PC vendors. Toyota's much studied production system has provided the automaker a source of competitive advantage for decades, contributing to the company's becoming the world's biggest car manufacturer in 2008. The profiting from innovation (PFI) framework, introduced in a highly cited 1986 article by David J. Teece, provides deep insight into cases where industry pioneers thrived and those where they vanished. This entry explains the fundamental concepts of the theory and how they combine to provide insight for innovators formulating competitive strategies to commercialize their innovations.

Fundamentals

In its original formulation, the PFI framework integrated three concepts: appropriability, industry evolution, and complementarity. Additional concepts, such as system integration and industry structure, have subsequently been introduced to increase the framework's explanatory power.

Appropriability

Appropriability means the extent to which the innovator can capture the profits generated by the innovation. The degree of capture is impacted by characteristics of the technology and the legal environment and by the ownership of complementary assets needed to bring the innovation to market. These characteristics determine the strength of the innovation's appropriability regime—that is, how difficult it will be to imitate the innovation and undermine the innovator's profitability.

An appropriability regime is "weak" when innovations are difficult to protect, as when they can be easily codified and legal protection of intellectual property is ineffective. Appropriability can be "strong" when innovations are easy to protect because knowledge about them is tacit and/or they are well protected legally. Regimes differ across fields of endeavor, not just across industries and countries.

Appropriability regimes change over time, and the regime applicable to a given innovation may be malleable to the innovator's strategy. For example, a firm with a strong position in downstream complementary assets might decide it is in its interest to weaken the upstream appropriability regime, as in the case of IBM making its server operating system available as a nonproprietary product to gain advantage in the sale of related hardware, applications, and services.

It is vital for firms to recognize that patents, which may have strategic value beyond the direct profit goals discussed here, rarely confer strong appropriability, outside of special cases such as new drugs, chemical products, and rather simple mechanical inventions. Many patents can be "invented around" at modest cost. Moreover, the legal and financial requirements for upholding a patent's validity, or for proving its infringement, are high. Validity is never firmly established until a patent has been upheld in court.

In some industries, particularly where the innovation is embedded in processes, trade secrets are a viable alternative to patents, which are especially ineffective at protecting process innovation. Trade secret protection is possible in cases where a firm can put its product before the public and still keep the underlying technology secret. Many industrial processes, including semiconductor fabrication, are of this kind.

Industry Evolution

In the early stages of an industry's development, product design is often the basis for competition. After considerable trial and error in the marketplace, one design or a narrow class of designs begins to emerge. As this happens, late entrants may be able to modify the pioneering innovator's product (or process) and make one of these follow-on designs the industry standard, placing the pioneer at a disadvantage.

The establishment of standards is a critical stage in the evolution of an industry. An innovating firm can solidify the demand for its technology when standard setting bodies adopt standards that "read on" (that is, incorporate) their patents. Ownership of key patents, whether used in a standard or not, can have other benefits. Patents can be used to help generate licensing revenue, gain privileged access to new technologies, and steer evolution of technology.

Many of the newer growth industries that rely on the Internet or on telecommunications networks bring an important caveat to this view of industry evolution. Most network-based industries are characterized by mechanisms of positive feedback—including positive adoption externalities, increasing returns to scale, and switching costs—that provide a built-in advantage for early entrants. Nevertheless, later entrants, such as Google, in the case of search engines, can still become the category leader.

Complementary Assets

Successful commercialization of an innovation almost always requires that technical knowledge be used in conjunction with assets or capabilities such as marketing, manufacturing, after-sale service, distribution, and software. Necessary complements may also include a host of intangible assets, such as a viable business model, customer relationships, reputations, and organizational culture. If an innovator is slow to realize the importance of these assets/capabilities, does not have them, or cannot easily contract to access them, it is likely to lose out to an imitator that is strong in these areas.

EMI's CAT scanner, for example, was a sophisticated machine that required a high level of customer training, support, and servicing. EMI had none of these capabilities, could not easily contract for them, and was slow to realize its strategic vulnerability. Competitors like GE with more experience manufacturing and selling complex health care equipment (along with the important complements of a sales and marketing organization and a good reputation) were in large measure able to work around EMI's intellectual property and get into the market quickly with improved versions. EMI's situation, in which the appropriability regime for its innovation had weaknesses and whose missing specialized assets left it compromised, is a common one. In these circumstances, the innovator must decide whether to contract for the supply of a critical capability (potentially creating a rival), build the capability internally (thus sacrificing flexibility), or find a joint venture partner to share the risk and rewards.

Business model design (in this instance, the choice of which inputs to source internally) is therefore one of the most critical steps for determining the innovator's profitability. The innovator must correctly assess the firm's existing capabilities and/or its ability to develop new ones in a timely, cost-effective manner. Bureaucratic and human resource issues also come into play when reshaping the activities of the enterprise.

In certain cases, internal supply (i.e., [vertical] integration) may be worth pursuing even if it looks unattractive from a cost or time-to-market perspective. One such strategic reason is that the complement is co-specialized with the innovation (or, worse, the innovation is specialized to the complement but not the reverse). The dependence creates a potential holdup problem that could allow an external supplier to extract a large share of profits. An example of an external supplier advantage is Intel's ability to sustain high prices (and profits) for its microprocessors from the computer companies that depend on it. If, during the initial development of its PC, IBM had asked its internal chip division to develop a microprocessor, then it would have been later entering the market but would probably still have dominated based on its reputation with business customers and its marketing muscle while denying its imitators access to a key input. More important, it would have captured much of the profit that it unwittingly delivered to Intel.

Another situation in which building internal supply capabilities makes sense is when the innovation creates a new industry and no existing suppliers/complementors have the required capabilities in place. In such cases, strategic or time-to-market considerations, the risks involved, and the deep codependencies that arise could make it counterproductive to spend time convincing a potential supplier of the value of making the necessary investments. This was, for example, the logic behind the emergence of large, vertically integrated industrial firms that emerged in the late 19th century. Companies exploiting new products (like sewing machines) or processes (like meat packing) often chose to integrate upstream into materials or other inputs and downstream into marketing and distribution.

Contracting for components or complements has obvious benefits but also contains strategic hazards. One of these is the risk of technology leakage (unintentional or otherwise) to competitors who are not part of the contract. A subtler hazard in such a relationship is the inability to pace or direct the evolution of a supplier's proprietary technology. Microsoft, for example, develops certain applications that run on its Windows operating system,

competing in some cases with independent software vendors who must rely on Windows for their development environment. Microsoft's ability to pace its upstream operating system technology and its ability to use its intimate knowledge of that technology in its applications software helped it become one of the dominant players in applications.

Even when an innovator and its strategic allies collaborate with good incentive alignment, they may find it difficult to accomplish the coordination of their activities across multiple generations of technology. Delays are frequent and need not result from strategic manipulation; they may simply flow from uncertainty, asymmetric capabilities, and divergent goals among the allies.

In the presence of these hazards, shaping the path of learning and innovation sometimes requires vertical integration. When this is not possible because of time-to-market or other considerations, other strategies for (re)shaping the industry's architecture must be pursued through, for example, corporate venture investments in the supply base to build a competitive market for key complements.

System Integration

Since the PFI framework was introduced, many intermediate goods and services that were once hard to access in numerous industries are now available "off the shelf." The global transfer of technological know-how and capabilities through the investment and trading activities of multinational firms has helped spread know-how and capabilities across the globe. As a result, creative purchasing and partnering arrangements with offshore enterprises have become everyday occurrences.

In this altered landscape, the "system integration" function, those capabilities required for business enterprises to orchestrate global resources, remains in scarce supply. With innovation happening in different parts of the supply chain, the innovator must decide which technologies/features to incorporate into its products and then make those elements work together in a product that is useful and attractive to customers.

Boeing's recent experience with its new 787 Dreamliner provides an instructive negative example. Boeing, against the advice of some of its engineers, decided to rely far more than ever before on a global array of suppliers to develop parts for its new plane.

This was seen as a cost- and risk-sharing measure; but Boeing reportedly failed to build sufficient internal monitoring capacity to verify progress. Because some suppliers lacked the capabilities to develop parts of the necessary quality, the entire project experienced years of (very costly) delay. In the end, Boeing had to step back in and help its suppliers develop the subsystems they were supposed to design and build for Boeing.

Importance

The PFI framework provides the basis of an explanation for how managerial decisions, intellectual property protection, and the asset structure of the firm impact the business enterprise's ability to capture value from its innovation. It is both a normative theory of strategy and a predictive theory of how the benefits from a focal innovation are likely to be distributed between the innovator, customers, imitators, suppliers, and the owners of complementary assets.

The PFI theory is testable. It leads to unambiguous predictions about how the private gains from innovation will be shared. The framework also provides a valuable template for guiding strategy formation by innovators. Each element of the framework—the stage of industry evolution, the appropriability regime, the necessary complementary assets—requires careful analysis and reflection by itself. The framework, as elaborated in the initial 1986 article and elsewhere, also provides guidance for understanding the interactions of these elements. For example, complementary assets (and hence the firm's internal investments and external contracting relationships) play a more important role in industries where a dominant design has already emerged. The PFI framework can help structure the numerous and seemingly unconnected strategic decisions that arise when planning to commercialize an innovation in any industry.

David J. Teece

See also Competitive Advantage; First-Mover Advantages and Disadvantages; Resource Orchestration Management; Strategic Alliances; Value Chain

Further Readings

Chandler, A. D. (1992). Organizational capabilities and the economic history of the industrial enterprise. *Journal of Economic Perspectives, 6*, 79–100.

Chesbrough, H., & Rosenbloom, R. S. (2002). The role of the business model in capturing value from innovation: Evidence from Xerox corporation's technology spin-off companies. *Industrial and Corporate Change, 11*, 529–555.

Chesbrough, H., & Teece, D. J. (1996). When is virtual virtuous? Organizing for innovation. *Harvard Business Review, 74*(1), 65–73.

Figueiredo, J. M. de, & Teece, D. J. (1996). Mitigating procurement hazards in the context of innovation. *Industrial and Corporate Change, 5*, 537–559.

Henderson, R. M., & Clark, K. B. (1990). Architectural innovation: The reconfiguration of existing product technologies and the failure of established firms. *Administrative Science Quarterly, 35*, 9–30.

Pisano, G. P., & Teece, D. J. (2007). How to capture value from innovation: Shaping intellectual property and industry architecture. *California Management Review, 50*, 278–296.

Prencipe, A., Davies, A., & Hobday, M. (Eds.). (2003). *The business of systems integration.* Oxford, England: Oxford University Press.

Teece, D. J. (1986). Profiting from technological innovation. *Research Policy, 15*, 285–305.

Teece, D. J. (2006). Reflections on profiting from innovation. *Research Policy, 35*, 1131–1146.

Tushman, M. L., & O'Reilly, C. A. (1997). *Winning through innovation: A practical guide to leading organizational change and renewal.* Cambridge, MA: Harvard University Press.

PROGRAMMABILITY OF DECISION MAKING

A usual reference in studies and textbooks related to decision making, the *programmability* of a decision problem, also referred to as the *structure* of a decision problem, is concerned with the extent to which managers facing decisions have a complete understanding of the factors that have a bearing on the situations they faced. The concept is associated with Herbert Simon, a leading writer in management science and 1978 Nobel laureate in economics for his pioneering research into the decision-making process within economic organizations. It was Simon who first reflected on the degree of structure of decision situations. As Simon's thoughts gradually turned toward the power of computers and the potential of artificial intelligence (a field that he contributed to establishing), he introduced the oft-quoted distinction between programmed decision and nonprogrammed decision. Simon's reflection was guided by the idea that organizations, like computers, are systems designed for "complex information processing." Thus, programmed decisions can be coded in computer programs or other programs that are computerizable, while nonprogrammed decisions must be treated as "problem solving" and therefore are not amenable to processing by computer systems to any extent. This entry considers the richness of the concept of programmability of decisions and its implications for research and practice in a number of areas.

Fundamentals

Simon's basic scientific progress must be viewed in terms of his attempt to study the manager as a decision maker. In seeking to theorize about managerial decision making, Simon initially discussed the difference between facts and values. Facts can be verified or falsified, whereas values are the objectives of the decision maker and, beyond this, his or her actual wishes. This is important for both research and practice because it indicates that decisions made by managers can be evaluated properly only when the objectives of the decision maker are known. Thus, to evaluate the quality of a decision, researchers must know the utility of the decision maker and understand his or her preferences and expectations in terms of the probabilities of future events. These factors are directly related to the degree to which a decision problem can or cannot be programmed.

Simon also observed that the problems that managers faced and that are found to trigger decision-making processes are not facts but constructs: They do not present themselves "carefully wrapped in bundles." There are basic uncertainties relating to the cause-and-effect relationship between the key factors in the analysis of these problems as well as in their solution. Second, Simon observed that decision "is a matter of compromise"; that is, all decision makers have several more or less contradictory objectives in mind.

James D. Thompson and A. Tuden have formalized this issue in their influential model that classified uncertainty in decision making based on how well managers understand how the world

works on the one hand and on whether managers agree among themselves about the objectives they pursue on the other hand. They presented their model as a two-by-two matrix, where both above dimensions—ambiguity of objectives and uncertainty of cause and effect—can be either high or low, thereby distinguishing between decisions by computation (most certain), decisions by judgment, decisions by compromise, and decisions by inspiration (least certain).

As technology and in particular, computing technology developed, Simon started to consider the potential impact of computational devices on decision making. It was then, in his seminal 1977 book *The New Science of Management Decisions* that he proposed the distinction between programmed and nonprogrammed decisions:

> Decisions are programmed to the extent that they are repetitive and routine, to the extent that a definite procedure has been worked out for handling them so that they don't have to be treated from scratch each time they occur. (p. 46)

On the other hand, decisions are nonprogrammed "to the extent that they are novel, unstructured and unusually consequential" (p. 46). Organizations, like computers, are systems designed for "complex information processing," and information processing by human operators, organizations or computers is a fundamental aspect of management. Programmed decisions obey computer programs or other programs that are computerizable, while nonprogrammed decisions come under the heading of problem solving.

Importance

In addition to Simon's framework, alternative theories have been proposed to model managers' understanding of the problems they face and the extent to which it may be possible to model them in a decision support application. Among these, the representation-level model proposed in 1989 by Patrick Humphreys is a top-down process whereby the structuration of the concepts manipulated by managers is refined from one level to the next over time, as a function of which additional information is available or as a function of definitive choices having been made in terms of manager's and organizations' preferences (as in Thompson and Tuden). As such, the Humphreys framework constitutes an alternative to Simon's conception of programmability.

Humphreys proposes to represent the extent to which managers understand the problems they face in terms of (a) the degree of abstraction in the representation managers have about the problems to be tackled and (b) the degree of formalization in the representations of proposed solutions and models to be applied to finding solutions.

Level 1: At the highest level, representations are mainly cultural and psychological; managers are more or less aware of what a problem involves, but its expression is mostly beyond language. It is at this level that the problem is shaped, and one can wonder whether representations at this level are beyond any modeling endeavor and therefore whether they are way beyond decision support.

Level 2: At this level, the representations become explicit, and the problem can be broken down into a number of subproblems, some of which can be formalized. The structuration of the problems is still partial rather than detailed, and managers refer to "the marketing function" or "the marketing process" without being able to formalize processes in greater detail. Data mining may be used at this level as a way to help formalize ideas to a greater extent and to test hypotheses. Some premodels maybe developed in broad terms by managers, but it is still difficult for them to discuss these with analysts.

Level 3: At this level, decision makers are able to define the structure of the problems they must solve. They are able to put forward models that can be used for the investigation of the alternatives they will pursue and discuss these with analysts; these discussions can then be used to develop small applications leveraging online analytical processing (OLAP) tools or multidimensional tools.

Level 4: At this level, decision makers are able to perform sensitivity analysis with the models they have defined in the previous stage so as to determine which input values are the most suitable; saved searches and saved views created using scrutinizing tools can become increasingly formalized over time and progress toward increased specification from Level 3 to Level 4.

Level 5: Finally, at the lowest level, managers can decide on the most suitable values, and the representation of the problem they must solve is stable and fully operational. At that stage, report templates can be created, based on which regular or ad hoc reports will be made available to managers with minimum effort or time required.

Notwithstanding, one key dimension of the application of the concept of programmability is how it must take into account that the programmability of a decision problem is not universal. On the one hand, organizations can learn about the problems they face and may therefore be able to resolve the uncertainty inherent in them to some degree, giving rise to the notion of a semi-programmable or semi-structured problem. On the other hand, depending on market conditions and competitive position of the firm, certain categories of problems may be more or less programmable for different managers in different firms. It is therefore important, in applying the concept of programmability, to understand where, when, and how the uncertainty arises that makes problems complex to solve.

Over time, through organizational learning, it is expected that problems should travel from the unstructured toward the structured as managers learn how to solve them. Ultimately, whether problems become programmable or not, the quality and speed of the organization's response will improve as routines emerge and then become institutionalized in the organization. At the core of these routines, decision support systems (DSS) or business intelligence (BI) tools may be developed to provide managers with the information they need to make rapid and robust decisions.

There is, however, one potential danger if firms push the routinization of their decision-making practices to an excessive degree. It has been noted that any form of modeling involves the simplification of some of the factors inherent in the decision. For instance, some element of prediction/forecast may be introduced, and it is critical that managers remember that the predictions or assumptions built into the models they are using (for instance, in the form of a DSS application—even a spreadsheet) are only assumptions about the future that may not come to pass. Thus, rationalizing decisions is a good thing when it makes the firm quicker and more responsive to its environment, but it becomes a bad thing when it is used to mask the uncertainties in the firm's environment. Sidney G. Winter has made such observations about what he terms *mechanistic decision making,* and Michael J. Earl and Anthony G. Hopwood have commented on the need for the decision support systems used by managers to be fit for the purpose and therefore to help managers find answers rather than provide ready-made solutions when they may not be applicable. Winter shows that organizations can speed up their decision making when they reach a certain level of mechanistic or automatic decision making—in other words, are able to reenact previous decisions in tackling new ones, because their managers understand how different or similar the new decisions are in comparison to the older ones. However, it is easy to see how changes in the environment of the firm that would go unnoticed could result in the routines of the organizations becoming out of touch with the reality facing managers, a case when problems thought to have become programmable have shifted in their nature and have gone back to be semi-programmable or unprogrammable. Managers need to stay alert to such changes. Winter concludes that there should be a conscious choice by managers in the selection of which matters to treat mechanistically and which to treat with some deliberation.

Frédéric Adam

See also Bounded Rationality and Satisficing (Behavioral Decision-Making Model); Decision Support Systems; Garbage Can Model of Decision Making; Intuitive Decision Making; Organizational Learning; Sensemaking; Strategic Decision Making; Tacit Knowledge; "Unstructured" Decision Making

Further Readings

Earl, M. J., & Hopwood, A. G. (1980). From management information to information management. In H. Lucas, F. Land, T. Lincoln, & K. Supper (Eds.), *The information systems environment* (pp. 133–143). Amsterdam, Netherlands: North-Holland.

Humphreys, P. (1989). Intelligence in decision making—A process model. In G. Doukidis, F. Land, & E. Miller (Eds.), *Knowledge-based management support systems* (pp. 22–51). Chichester, England: HellisHovwood.

March, J., & Simon, H. (1993). *Organisations* (2nd ed.). Cambridge, MA: Blackwell.

Pomerol, J. C., & Adam, F. (2006). On the legacy of Herbert Simon and his contribution to decision making support systems and artificial intelligence. In J. Gupta, G. A. Forgionne, & M. Mora (Eds.), *Intelligent decision-making support systems: Foundations,*
applications and challenges (pp. 25–43). London, England: Springer-Verlag.

Simon H. (1977). *The new science of management decisions.* Englewood Cliffs, NJ: Prentice-Hall.

Thompson, J., & Tuden, A. (1959). Strategies structures and processes of organisational decision. In J. D. Thompson, P. B. Hammond, R. W. Hawkes, B. H. Junker, & A. Tuden (Eds.), *Comparative studies in administration* (pp. 195–216). Pittsburgh, PA: University Pittsburgh Press.

Winter, S. G. (1985). The case for "mechanistic" decision making. In J. M. Pennings & associates (Eds.), *Organisational strategy and change* (pp. 99–113). London, England: Jossey-Bass.

Prospect Theory

In the last half of the 20th century, a plethora of papers demonstrated that the expected utility model did not adequately explain the choices of experimental subjects facing risky choices. In a typical study, a subject chooses between a prospect (alternative involving more than one potential outcome) offering a 0.5 chance of gaining $10 and a 0.5 chance of losing $5, and a prospect offering a certain $3. In 1979, Daniel Kahneman and Amos Tversky proposed a general model, termed *prospect theory,* that captures the main features of the experimental results. Prospect theory predicts individuals' choices when faced with well-defined prospects that include uncertain outcomes. The theory encompasses the results of a number of experiments in which individuals made such choices. Management papers have used prospect theory to explain a wide variety of managerial and organizational decisions. This entry examines the principles, extensions, and applications of prospect theory. A detailed description of the theory is followed by a section describing the roots of the theory and a later version of it, termed *cumulative prospect theory.* The entry concludes with a discussion of the application of prospect theory to strategic decision making.

Fundamentals

Prospect theory predicts individual decision making under risk. It originally applied to relatively simple problems with monetary outcomes, stated probabilities, and two prospects. Prospect theory conceptualizes choice using two phases. In the first, "editing" phase, the subject simplifies the prospects or prospects facing the decision maker. Then in the "evaluation" phase, the decision maker chooses between the prospects. As with many theories, we should view this theory as saying people act as if they operate according to these stages, not that they actually calculate in such stages.

The Editing Phase

The simplification of prospects in the editing phase occurs through four major operations: coding, combination, segregation, and cancellation. In *coding*, the subject subtracts a reference point from the gamble's potential outcomes, making them into a series of gains or losses with respect to the reference point. The wording of the problem and the decision maker's expectations can influence the reference point and, consequently, the coding of outcomes as gains or losses. *Combination* refers to the simplification of prospects by combining the probabilities associated with identical outcomes. *Segregation* refers to the simplification of prospects by separating out a riskless component from a risky component. While coding, combination, and segregation apply to each prospect separately, the final operation, cancellation, applies to a set of two or more prospects. *Cancellation* occurs when decision makers ignore components common to the prospects, discard common outcome probability pairs, round up probabilities or outcomes, or discard extremely unlikely or dominated outcomes.

While the editing phase simplifies the choice problem for the decision maker, it can also result in inconsistent preferences. For example, differences in presentation of the problem that do not influence the actual gambles can influence coding. Experiments often do this by changing the reference point without changing the probabilities or potential outcomes.

The Evaluation Phase

The evaluation phase begins with the decision maker implicitly assigning subjective values to the edited prospects ($\upsilon(x)$ and $\upsilon(y)$), and transforming the prospect's probabilities (p and q) into decision weights ($\pi(p)$). The subject multiplies the values of the prospects by the associated decision weights and sums over then-potential outcomes associated with a given prospect. The subject chooses the prospect with the highest sum (total Value, denoted by V).

For a prospect with one positive and one negative potential outcome (x with probability p and y with probability q), the value thus is this:

$$V(x, p; y, q) = \pi(p)\upsilon(x) + \pi(q)\upsilon(y)$$

where the value of a zero outcome is zero, the probability weight for a prospect with zero probability is 0 ($\pi(0) = 0$), and the probability weight for a certainty (probability of 1) is 1 ($\pi(1) = 1$).

This equation resembles its precursor, expected utility theory. Like expected utility theory, the value (utility) of a prospect equals a sum of the weighted values (utilities) of the different potential outcomes of the alternative. However, the model differs from expected utility in several ways. Unlike expected utility theory, the probability weights depend on, but in general are not equal to, the probabilities associated with the different outcomes. In addition, while expected utility theory assumes that value attaches to the final states of the decision maker (which includes his or her previous wealth or assets), prospect theory assumes that value is associated with changes from the decision maker's reference point. The value function has a different curvature for outcomes above the reference point than for outcomes below the reference point. In practical terms, this means that decision makers dislike losses more than they like gains.

In addition to regular prospects, prospect theory can apply to strictly positive (all potential outcomes positive) or strictly negative (all potential outcomes negative) prospects. The equation for these prospects is slightly different. For these prospects, in the editing phase, decision makers recode the prospects into a riskless component (the minimum gain or loss that will accrue for sure) and a risky component (the additional gain or loss, over and above the minimum gain or loss, that could accrue). Similar to a regular prospect, the value of a strictly positive or strictly negative prospect is the weighted sum of the values of their components.

We now examine the two components that determine the value of the prospect—namely, the value function and the weighting function, in more detail.

The Value Function

Kahneman and Tversky proposed that the value function is (1) defined on deviations from the reference point; (2) generally concave for gains and convex for losses, reflecting risk aversion for potential outcomes above the reference point and risk seeking below; and (3) steeper for losses than for gains, reflecting the finding that people dislike losing money more than gaining an equivalent sum. They proposed a hypothetical S-shaped value function that fits these three properties and takes the following general form:

The Weighting Function

The decision weights in the equation for prospect theory are not the same as the probabilities that the outcomes associated with a prospect will occur. Rather, they measure the impact of the uncertainty of events on the desirability of prospects. In other words, $\pi\ (p)$ does not necessarily equal p; a gamble with a 0.50 probability of winning a certain amount of money will likely be given a smaller weight than 0.50. In addition, an impossible outcome is ignored, and a certain outcome is given a weight of 1.

Kahneman and Tversky proposed a hypothetical weighting function that has several noteworthy properties. Away from the endpoints, the weighting function is relatively linear but the weights generally are less than the probabilities. Close to the end points, however, the function is curved. For extremely low probabilities, the weight may exceed the probability until the subject reaches a probability at which the outcome is coded as probability zero.

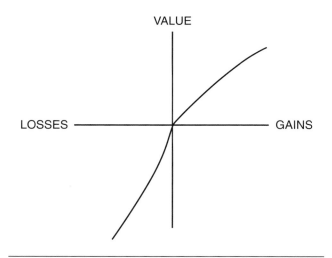

Figure 1   Hypothetical Value Function

Source: Kahneman, D., & Tversky, A. (1979). Prospect theory: An analysis of decision under risk. *Econometrica, 47,* 263–291.

This is consistent with findings that indicate that highly unlikely events are either ignored or overweighted and that individuals tend to either neglect or overemphasize the difference between high probability and certain events.

Evolution

Prospect theory is best viewed against the backdrop of expected utility theory. Specifically, expected utility theory states the following:

a. The overall utility of a prospect equals the utility of its potential outcomes weighted by their probabilities. Returning to our subject choosing between one alternative offering a 0.5 chance of gaining $10 and a 0.5 chance of losing $5 and an alternative offering a certain $3, in expected utility, the subject chooses the course of action with the highest expected utility where the utility of the certain $3 is U($3) and the utility of the prospect is (U($10) * 0.5) + (U(−$5) * 0.5).

b. Utility depends on the final outcome of a series of gambles. For example, in the gamble above, if the experimenter said the subject would receive $5 and then face the choice, the outcomes considered would be the utilities of $8 ($3 + $5), $15 ($10 + 5) and $0 (i.e.,−$5 + $5).

c. While the theory allows for individual variation in curvature of utility functions, most applications of expected utility theory assume concave utility functions. A concave utility function means people are risk averse, preferring a certain prospect to a risky prospect with the same expected value as the certain prospect.

In 1979, Kahneman and Tversky cited research demonstrating that individuals' choices in the experiments deviated from expected utility theory predictions in four specific ways.

The isolation effect: In contrast to the assumptions of expected utility theory, perceived value depends on changes in wealth rather than final asset states. This is termed the *isolation effect.* People disregard shared components among alternatives (e.g., the decision makers' preexisting wealth or money given to the subject before the choice), focusing instead on their distinguishing characteristics. This can lead to inconsistent preferences because subjects may decompose a prospect into shared and unique components in different ways; differences in decomposition can lead to difference in choices. In our gamble above, a subject given $5 before the gamble would ignore the $5 and code the gamble as having a positive and a negative potential outcome, whereas faced with the substantively identical gamble that added $5 to each potential outcome, the subject would code all the outcomes as positive.

The certainty effect: Contrary to the expected utility theory formulation that individuals weight individual outcomes by their probabilities to calculate the overall utility of an outcome, people systematically underweight risky outcomes relative to certain ones.

The reflection effect: Subjects are generally risk seeking for gambles with strictly positive outcomes and risk avoiding for gambles with strictly negative outcomes. In the model, this occurs because the function assigning values to outcomes (termed a *value function* to distinguish it from the utility function in expected utility theory) is not always concave; that is, people are not always risk averse or always risk seeking.

Cumulative Prospect Theory

In 1992, Tversky and Kahneman proposed a new version of prospect theory called *cumulative prospect theory.* Unlike prospect theory, which applies only to two-outcome prospects, cumulative prospect theory applies to prospects with any number of outcomes and allows different weighting functions for gains and for losses. Cumulative prospect theory also uses cumulative instead of separable decision weights for outcomes.

In 2010, Philip Bromiley plotted a value function based on Tversky and Kahneman's formulation, with their exact parameter values. His plot suggests two critical features of the value function. First, the value function has a substantial kink or curvature at zero (where the value of the gamble equals the reference point); this kink at zero represents substantial risk aversion. For prospects with both positive and negative outcomes, the value function predicts extreme risk aversion. Philip Bromiley also found that prospect theory is consistent with a wide variety of risk preference patterns, depending on the values

of the parameters and the part of the x-axis examined. For the most part, to derive predictions of risk preferences from prospect theory requires full specification of the parameters and potential outcomes.

Importance

Scholars from a variety of disciplines, including management, operations, behavioral economics, decision theory, and psychology, have used and extended prospect theory in an attempt to understand individual choices under uncertainty. Studies range from those that develop better measures of loss aversion to those that examine the context in which prospect theory is valid. For example, in a 1996 study, Eric Kessler and colleagues found that decision objects' valence (i.e., intrinsic attractiveness or unattractiveness) moderates the relationship between frame of reference and risk preferences. Individuals are risk averse when faced with value-increasing contingencies and risk seeking when faced with value-decreasing contingencies.

In 2011, R. Michael Holmes and colleagues reviewed a number of studies that apply prospect theory to managerial issues. They classify these studies into two groups: studies that use prospect theory to predict decisions and behaviors of individual managers and studies that apply prospect theory to explain organizational level variables. Studies in the first group cover managerial decisions in a wide variety of contexts, including compensation, negotiations, motivation, and human resource management issues. Studies in the second group use prospect theory to predict, among other things, relations between firm risk and return, firm investments in innovation, and firm acquisitions and divestitures.

The usefulness of prospect theory to managerial decision making lies perhaps not so much in its formal statement as in its key insights relating to risk taking under conditions of uncertainty. As a number of studies demonstrate, prospect theory (sometimes in combination with other organizational theories) can provide a reasonable explanation for a wide variety of organizational decisions such as those related to new product investments, divestment, exploitation and exploration. At the same time, some scholars have critiqued the use of prospect theory in the latter group of studies, given that prospect theory was not originally developed to explain individual decisions and risk preferences and not organizational decisions. In addition, Philip

Bromiley demonstrates that most strategic management studies consider only the value function's impact, ignoring the probability weighting function, and test predictions that apply only to choices with either all positive or all negative outcomes, whereas most strategic decisions would qualify as mixed gambles (having positive and negative potential outcomes).

However, these academic debates should not obfuscate the potential value of prospect theory's general arguments for practicing managers. Prospect theory, and a substantial experimental literature in psychology, suggests that individuals are far more likely to take risks when they perceive a future that lies below some reference point. Vice versa, individuals perceiving that the future is above the reference point generally take fewer risks.

These arguments have immediate implications for the design of incentive systems. Depending on the details of the system, and the actual outcomes on which the system bases incentives, managers could find themselves facing incentive systems that they view as largely offering gains or different levels of loss. As Robert Wiseman and Luis Gomez-Mejia argue, such framing should strongly influence managerial reactions to incentive systems.

These framing issues could also come into play at the corporate level. Top managements that see largely negative future outcomes probably tend to take riskier actions than top managements that perceive positive future outcomes. When a project or acquisition has gone poorly, managers may see most of the potential outcomes as negative, which may encourage further, often unwise, risk taking in the form of additional investment.

The use of prospect theory in organizational contexts raises a number of questions regarding the determination of the reference point, measurement of risk, and the distinctiveness of the predictions of the theory—especially as compared with other theories of organizational choice such as the behavioral theory of the firm. These are promising avenues for future research in this area.

Philip Bromiley and Devaki Rau

See also Behavioral Theory of the Firm; Bounded Rationality and Satisficing (Behavioral Decision-Making Model); Escalation of Commitment; Managerial Decision Biases; Strategic Decision Making; "Unstructured" Decision Making

Further Readings

Bromiley, P. (2010). Looking at prospect theory. *Strategic Management Journal, 31*, 1357–1370.

Holmes, R. M., Jr., Bromiley, P., Devers, C. E., Holcomb, T. R., & McGuire, J. B. (2011). Management theory applications of prospect theory: Accomplishments, challenges, and opportunities. *Journal of Management, 37*, 1069–1107.

Kahneman, D., & Tversky, A. (1979). Prospect theory: An analysis of decision under risk. *Econometrica, 47*, 263–291.

Kessler, E. H., Ford, C. M., & Bailey, J. R. (1996). Object valence as a moderator of the framing effect on risk preference. *Journal of Economic Behavior and Organization, 30*(2), 241–256.

Tversky, A., & Kahneman, D. (1992). Advances in prospect theory: Cumulative representation of uncertainty. *Journal of Risk and Uncertainty, 5*, 297–323.

Wiseman, R. M., & Gomez-Mejia, L. R. (1998). A behavioral agency model of managerial risk taking. *Academy of Management Review, 23*(1), 133–153.

PROTEAN AND BOUNDARYLESS CAREERS

The protean and boundaryless career conceptualizations of careers are used to inform the trend in self-management of the career. Earlier career theories focused on adult development and linear advancement in organizations. Donald Super and Daniel Levinson, for example, presented models describing career and life stage models of development that were seen as applicable across genders and work contexts. The combination of factors such as a more diverse workforce that includes career-focused women in much greater numbers and the new global economic environment has brought greater attention to individual management of the career. Earlier career theories have fallen short in capturing the mobility and psychological dynamics of career management in the contemporary work environment where lifetime employment in one organization, or even one industry, is becoming rare. Individuals are often not afforded the opportunity of career development or career management from organizations. This entry provides an overview of the protean and boundaryless models and discusses how they provide overlapping and complementary views of the self-managed career.

Fundamentals

Original conceptualizations of protean and boundaryless careers took different perspectives on careers. The protean career concept focuses on the individual's motives and abilities to adapt to a changing environment. The notion of a boundaryless career takes a slightly different view by focusing on the aspects of the environment that are defining the career.

The metaphor of the Greek god Proteus who could change shape at will underlies the concept of the protean career. Douglas Hall characterized the protean career as one in which the individual can adapt to a changing work environment by repackaging or developing new knowledge, skills, and abilities. The protean careerist maintains marketability by being flexible and having a career management attitude focused on personal values and self-direction. This person is seen as less likely to be bound by organizational structures or direction and more likely to design a personal career trajectory. In short, an individual with a protean career orientation takes responsibility for navigating his or her career.

Observing the changing nature of careers, Michael Arthur and Denise Rousseau presented an emerging model of career experiences that they called a *boundaryless career*. According to Arthur and Rousseau, a boundaryless career can differ from the traditional organizational career in six ways that characterize independence from rather than dependence on traditional organizational career arrangements: (1) career experiences across employers, (2) validation and marketability from outside the organization (e.g., academics or carpenters). (3) external networks or information sustain the career (e.g., a real estate agent), (4) traditional organizational career boundaries such as hierarchical and advancement principles are broken, (5) rejection of career opportunities for personal or family reasons, and (6) perception of a boundaryless future regardless of structural constraints. As articulated, the boundaryless career is seen as different from traditional organizational careers in physical mobility both across and within organizations. Boundaryless careers also differ from traditional organizational careers in the nature of employment relationships and role management. A reconceptualization of the boundaryless career by Sherry Sullivan and Michael Arthur portrays the boundaryless career as defined by mobility along the two continua of physical career mobility and psychological career mobility.

Both the protean and boundaryless career concepts are used to explore the changing nature of careers, career management, and related individual and organizational outcomes. Simply, the boundaryless career provides a framework for investigating how careers are changing and the resulting effects on performance, satisfaction, and other outcomes. The protean career offers a framework for examining how and why an individual adapts to the changing environment and the implications of an individual's protean career orientation on career success and/or satisfaction.

Currently, two scales for measuring an individual's protean career orientation have been developed through validation studies. Jon Briscoe and Douglas Hall developed a 14-item scale of the protean career orientation that measures the two dimensions of value-driven and self-directed career management. Yehuda Baruch developed a 7-item scale to measure the protean career orientation more generally. Earlier measures of the boundaryless career focused on whether or not the boundaryless career exists based on the original conceptualization of Arthur and Rousseau. The reconceptualization of the boundaryless career by Sherry Sullivan and Michael Arthur extended the boundaryless career concept to include what is referred to as a *boundaryless career mind-set*, the degree to which the person desires physical career mobility and/or psychological career mobility. This has facilitated the development of a scaled measurement of the boundaryless career. Jon Briscoe and Douglas Hall developed a 13-item scale to measure these two dimensions of the boundaryless career mind-set.

A series of three studies to explore the distinctiveness of the protean career orientation and the boundaryless career mind-set were conducted by Jon Briscoe, Douglas Hall, and Rachel Frautschy DeMuth. They found that the protean and boundaryless careers as measured by attitudes, not behavior, were distinct but related. These two models of careers are still developing as concepts and in the way they are measured and combined to study careers.

Practical Applications

The protean and boundaryless career theories offer practical applications for both individuals and organizations. Individuals are cautioned not to rely on others for direction and development. Rather, these theories suggest that a career can be and, more often, should be self-managed. Workers are advised to develop a mind-set and attitudes toward work and career that makes one more adaptable. The more one becomes adaptable, the more career paths and career opportunities will be available.

Managers charged with succession planning, training, or work policies find wise advice from these theories. Foremost, more options for how work is done is advised. Some will still prefer the linear career, but given the challenges of non-work-related commitments facing an increasing number of valued workers, flexible work arrangements such as part-time work and working from home should be a staple offering of organizations when possible. Managers should listen to the desires and needs of employees to generate creative career paths and jobs that will be more fulfilling for workers and better for the organization because fulfilled workers tend to be more committed and productive. Finally, managers are cautioned not to label employees. An individual's concept of career may change with time so career development opportunities should evaluated frequently.

Susan M. Adams

See also Career Stages and Anchors; Individual Values; Psychological Contract Theory; Role Theory; Self-Concept and the Theory of Self; Self-Determination Theory

Further Readings

Arthur, M. B., & Rousseau, D. M. (1996). *The boundaryless career.* New York, NY: Oxford University Press.

Briscoe, J. P., & Hall, D. T. (2006). The interplay of boundaryless and protean careers: Combinations and implications. *Journal of Vocational Behavior, 69,* 4–18.

Briscoe, J. P., Hall, D. T., & Frautschy DeMuth, R. L. (2006). Protean and boundaryless careers: An empirical exploration. *Journal of Vocational Behavior, 69,* 30–47.

Hall, D. T. (1996). The career is dead—Long live the career: A relational approach to careers. San Francisco. CA: Jossey-Bass.

Hall, D. T. (2002). *Careers in and out of organizations.* Thousand Oaks, CA: Sage.

Sullivan, S. (1999). The changing nature of careers: A review and research agenda. *Journal of Management, 25*(3), 457–484.

Sullivan, S. E., & Arthur, M. B. (2006). The evolution of the boundaryless career concept: Examining physical and psychological mobility. *Journal of Vocational Behavior, 69,* 19–29.

Sullivan, S. E., & Baruch, Y. (2009). Advances in career theory and research: A critical review and agenda for future exploration. *Journal of Management, 35*(6), 1542–1571.

Psychological Contract Theory

According to psychological contract theory (PCT), psychological contracts are individual-level cognitive structures that reflect how people think about their exchange relationships. More specifically, a psychological contract is individuals' systems of beliefs regarding the obligations that exist between themselves and exchange partners. Such obligations motivate current judgment and behavior through anticipation of the exchange's future. Psychological contracts are important to management scholars and practitioners because they influence how individuals think, feel, and behave in organizations, thus providing the basis for coordination and cooperation among employees, managers, executives, and business owners. This entry begins with a description of the fundamental tenets of PCT and is followed by a discussion of the historical roots and later significant contributions that led to current-day understanding. Empirical support for the theoretical propositions of PCT is then reviewed, and the practical implications of psychological contracts for management are discussed.

Fundamentals

Generally, a psychological contract represents any exchange relationship wherein two parties trade things of value. Applications of PCT exist in online marketing, distributor-supplier relations, information systems outsourcing, law, marital relations, and doctor-patient relations. The greatest theoretical and empirical attention has been directed at the employment relationship, particularly from the employee's perspective, the focus of this entry.

Several theoretical domains influence PCT, including cognitive, social, and organizational psychology, law, and economics. In organizational research, PCT is positioned between broad theories such as social exchange and social information processing and more discrete theorizing regarding constructs such as perceived organizational support (an employer's contribution) and organizational commitment (an employee's contribution). PCT is thus a midrange theory addressing how individuals' beliefs influence their judgments, affect, and behavior in exchange arrangements.

PCT is related to, but distinct from, theorizing on general employee expectations. Although psychological contract beliefs can be influenced by pre-employment expectations, the psychological contract reflects a wider array of obligation-based beliefs, including perceived promises. As such, reactions to *psychological contract breach* (failure to fulfill psychological contract obligations) are theorized to be much stronger than are reactions to unmet expectations, an effect meta-analytic findings support. Breach (and its positive counterpart, psychological contract fulfillment) has stronger effects than do unmet expectations on job satisfaction, turnover intentions, and performance.

Underlying Rationale of Psychological Contract Theory

The qualities and dynamics of psychological contracts are rooted in psychological principles. Psychological contracts are developed through an individual's social and organizational experiences. At the same time, their cognitive architecture is shaped by limitations in human cognitive capacity (i.e., bounded rationality). For instance, people can pay attention to only a portion of the information in their environments. They do so selectively, attending to highly salient or easily accessible information (e.g., employees tend to believe that their immediate manager speaks for the organization). They also tend to interpret events in a manner confirming their existing beliefs, thereby interpreting the exchange through the lens of their psychological contract. This makes the psychological contract a means of ensuring continuity and predictability in the employment relationship.

Psychological contracts are dynamic. Once formed, they tend to be relatively stable, operating at a high-order, subconscious level. Nevertheless, psychological contracts are subject to more systematic

cognitive processes and revision as circumstances change. On-the-job experiences such as unexpected events (e.g., a surprise promotion or demotion) and observations (e.g., coworker experiences) can lead to new beliefs being integrated into an individual's psychological contract to influence subsequent judgments and behavior. People must actively alter the way they think about the exchange in order to revise the psychological contract.

Content and Dynamics of the Theory

Psychological contract beliefs. Employees tend to join organizations with preconceived notions about their obligations (e.g., loyalty, operate in best interest of the company) and their employer's obligations in return (e.g., skill development opportunities, a competitive wage). Perceived employer promises from recruiters and others impact the initial structure of the psychological contract. However, neither worker nor employer can spell out all the details of what might be an indefinite employment arrangement. As a result, psychological contracts tend to evolve over time as a function of new salient information. Recruiting practices generally have less impact on employees' psychological contracts than do their postentry experiences. As such, employees' psychological contract beliefs can be influenced by various sources over the course of employment, including recruiters, supervisors, formal policy, human resource practices, and coworker experiences within the organization.

Whatever the source, fundamental to PCT is that psychological contract beliefs reflect perceived reciprocal *obligations* between the employee and the organization. In turn, these perceived obligations affect the parties' feelings, attitudes, and behaviors toward each other. Types of psychological contract obligations can vary considerably across workers, firms, and even cultures. They can be limited to wholly economic terms as in a *transactional* psychological contract (e.g., an hourly wage for a temporary worker who ships packages over the holidays) or be as complex and broad as personal support and developmental investment as in a *relational* psychological contract (e.g., characteristic of high-involvement work by research and development scientists). Commonly, psychological contracts contain elements of each.

Regardless of content type, ideally, the psychological contract should be perceived as high in mutuality (the parties hold common beliefs regarding contract obligations), reciprocity (the parties report commensurate obligations), and alignment (the psychological contract reflects balanced reciprocity between employee and employer obligations). These characteristics are associated with positive evaluations of psychological contract fulfillment and positive employee reactions. They can be cultivated through open communication and trust between the parties and by ensuring that contract-relevant signals are consistent. Creating and sustaining such psychological contracts remains an enduring organizational challenge.

Psychological contract evaluation. Emotional and attention-grabbing events trigger systematic, effortful cognitive processing. In particular, direct experiences with supervisors and managers are salient, providing contract-relevant information, from the enjoyment of promised recognition to the frustration experienced when promises go unfulfilled. Because psychological contracts unfold over repeated cycles of exchange, as a general principle, how exchange experiences are evaluated impacts the parties' perceived future obligations. An employee who believes that the employer has fulfilled prior commitments is more likely to view his or her employment as having a relational focus (e.g., open-ended, socioemotional obligations), making him or her more likely to react positively to requests or opportunities to contribute to the employer in new ways. On the other hand, lower past fulfillment is likely to diminish subsequent feelings of obligation toward the other party, prompting revision of certain beliefs. Failure to meet one's obligations typically increases the other's suspicions and monitoring and as such, leads to a decline in the perceived value of the employment arrangement.

Evaluations of psychological contract fulfillment impact various employee attitudes, affect, and behaviors beyond its impact on future obligations. Generally speaking, psychological contract fulfillment is associated with positive outcomes, whereas psychological contract breach is related to negative outcomes for both employees and the firm. A psychological contract breach refers to the judgment that a party has failed to fulfill its obligations (e.g., an employer who fails to promote a high-performing worker after agreeing to do so). In itself, the experience of breach is not rare, as psychological contracts can be evaluated as having been unfulfilled

in varying degrees. PCT distinguishes breach, the judgment of low contract fulfillment, from an act of "violation—that is, the willful failure to honor one's commitments. Violation is associated with negative emotional reactions (e.g., anger, outrage, disappointment, frustration), collectively referred to as *feelings of violation.* Feelings of violation and breach, though interrelated, are distinct. The extent to which psychological contract breach results in feelings of violation depends on how individuals interpret the breach. When deemed under the control of the organization, breaches will be associated with strong feelings of violation.

Several factors influence perceptions of and reactions to psychological contract breach. First, breach tends to be more prevalent in employment arrangements with limited interactions between employee and organizational agents (as in a lack of socialization or mentoring activities). When left to learn about the organization from their peers more informally, incidences of breach tend to be greater. Second, breaches that engender emotions are more likely to be noticed, an effect associated with certain personality traits. Individuals higher in neuroticism or an external (rather than internal) locus of control tend to perceive higher levels of breach. Personality also plays a role in the severity of postbreach reactions. Individuals higher in equity sensitivity or internal locus of control tend to respond with stronger feelings of violation. Finally, certain factors within the control of the organization can mitigate reactions to breach. Cultivating high-quality socioemotional relationships, offering retribution in the form of idiosyncratic deals (e.g., special perks for that particular employee), and providing "social accounts" such as explanations justified by resource constraints, can all help reduce negative employee reactions to breach.

Evolution

Although ideas consistent with PCT can be traced back to the early 1900s (e.g., equilibrium theory, the contribution-inducements model), the first formal application of the psychological contract construct to organizational settings is credited to Chris Argyris in 1960. He used the term *psychological work contract* to describe an implicit agreement between employees and their foremen that, when honored by the foremen, ensured continued employee effort and performance. Harry Levinson and colleagues subsequently defined the psychological contract as a series of mutual expectations, often implicit in nature, that governed relationships. Both Argyris and Levinson emphasized human needs as the primary driver of psychological contract processes and on maintaining positive well-being. Building on earlier work, Ed Schein offered predictions about the effects of a correspondence between employee and employer's expectations (later empirically supported by John Kotter) and called attention to the employer's perspective regarding the employment arrangement. Despite these initial developments, active research regarding the psychological contract did not commence until the construct was reconceptualized by Denise Rousseau in 1989.

Rousseau's seminal article marks a transition in the development of the psychological contract construct and PCT. She defined the psychological contract as people's beliefs regarding the terms and conditions of a reciprocal exchange agreement between themselves and another. Setting this conceptualization apart from earlier ones was her claim that psychological contract obligations were promissory in nature and that the exchange of these promises between employees and employers (not employee needs) was the driver for the development and maintenance of the psychological contract. Rousseau also cast psychological contracts as an individual-level phenomenon (making the construct more readily testable) and introduced the notion of psychological contract violation. Her 1995 book developed PCT more fully. This work coincided with significant change in employment reflecting the rise in global competition, economic deregulation, and a trend toward organizational restructuring and downsizing. The need to understand and manage such changes, coupled with Rousseau's work on PCT, stimulated a flurry of empirical research and further theory building.

Much subsequent work on PCT has been survey based, predominantly from the employee perspective, and focused on contract content or the outcomes of breach. There remains inconsistency regarding the types of beliefs that constitute the psychological contract, particularly with regard to its operationalization in research. Some scholars have focused on promises, whereas others focus on non-promissory-based expectations or fail to distinguish clearly among promises, obligations, and

expectations. Regardless, the distinction between relational and transactional contracts has garnered theoretical and empirical attention over the years. Researchers have examined theoretical predictions, often but not always supported, that relational contracts lead to more favorable outcomes than do transactional contracts. The transactional-relational distinction and its effect on important employee behaviors have been extended beyond North America to cultures such as China, Japan, and Singapore. Additionally, there has been widespread testing of Elizabeth Wolfe Morrison and Sandra Robinson's 1997 model of psychological contract violation wherein the constructs of unmet expectations, psychological contract breach, and feelings of violation were distinguished. Propositions related to the mediating and moderating mechanisms put forth in their model have guided empirical work that culminated in a meta-analysis by Hao Zhao and colleagues, demonstrating the strong negative effects that breach of relational contracts have on employee affect, attitudes, and behaviors.

Other advances to PCT have occurred over the years. For instance, basic principles of social exchange theory (e.g., norm of reciprocity) and employment relationships in general have been integrated into psychological contract research. In a published exchange, David Guest and Denise Rousseau argued critically regarding tenets of PCT, pushing scholars to question and empirically test and thereby clarify its underlying assumptions. Violet Ho along with her colleagues expanded understanding of the key players of the psychological contract to include people other than the employee and employer. Specifically, a social network perspective has been found to inform how employees evaluate their psychological contract. J. Stuart Bunderson and Jeffrey Thompson expanded the relational versus transactional content focus of modern-day psychological contracts to include ideology, a dimension reflecting the obligation to act in accordance with core values (e.g., professionalism or socially responsible causes).

Neil Conway and Rob Briner undertook a critical review of the psychological contract literature. They questioned whether the beliefs making up the psychological contract are purely promissory, or whether they might also include expectations based on sources other than promises made by the employer. Expanding on Rousseau's original work, research by Mark Roehling and by Samantha

Montes and David Zweig suggest that the beliefs that constitute the psychological contract may not be limited to perceived promises. Conway and Briner also called for research to begin examining psychological contracts as a process of reciprocal exchange. Researchers have begun examining changes in psychological contracts over time. As such, PCT is slated for further development as it incorporates new research findings.

Importance

Psychological contract research has largely supported PCT's main propositions. Traditionally, it has relied on a narrow range of methods—that is, cross-sectional and survey-based. Concern exists regarding its conflicting measures of breach, use of difference scores versus direct measures of breach, and the confounded effects of promises and delivered inducements. Stronger methods are being introduced to the study of psychological contracts. Conway and Briner introduced the use of diary methods. Lisa Lambert has demonstrated the advantages of examining the separate and joint effects of promised and delivered inducements using sophisticated statistical methods. Researchers also have begun employing longitudinal designs to capture causal relations and changes in psychological contracts over time, and others have begun using experimental designs to test basic assumptions of PCT. Use of these advanced methodologies continues to improve the theoretical insights reported findings yield.

Once thought of as a useful heuristic to describe implicit employment agreements, the psychological contract and the theory it has spawned represent an evolving theoretical map to establishing and maintaining positive employee-employer relationships—and to identifying and overcoming dysfunctions in employment. The impact of PCT has been far-reaching in management training and practice in North America, Europe, and beyond. Textbooks in organizational behavior, marketing, and human resource management typically include sections devoted to the psychological contract to help management professionals understand the dynamics of exchange relationships and how employment relationships affect attitudes and behaviors within organizations. Educators and administrators use the construct of the psychological contract to describe and manage relationships among faculty, students, and staff within universities.

Perhaps because of professional education, increasing numbers of managers actively apply PCT to the workplace to establish clarity, manage expectations, foster positive relationships, and maintain positive attitudes and productive behaviors among employees. David E. Guest and Conway report that 36% of 1,300 human resources managers surveyed in the U.K. use the psychological contract as a tool in managing their employment relationships, and a full 90% agreed that it is a useful tool. PCT has helped managers understand that there is more to maintaining a positive relationship with employees than sheer economic exchange. Indeed, in times of economic crisis and belt-tightening, shifting promissory obligations from the more transactional to the more relational sort can help retain committed, high-performing employees while incurring lower overall costs. PCT also helps managers understand the impact of implied promises and the implications of failing to fulfill such promises. Concurrently, generational and societal changes are introducing new facets to the psychological contract of employment, building on worker concerns with life balance and the social consequences of their employer's business strategy and actions.

Denise M. Rousseau, Maria Tomprou,
and Samantha D. Montes

See also Human Resource Management Strategies; Leader–Member Exchange Theory; Organizational Socialization; Social Exchange Theory; Trust

Further Readings

Conway, N., & Briner, R. (2005). Understanding psychological contracts at work: A critical evaluation of theory and research. New York, NY: Oxford University Press.

Guest, D. E., & Conway, N. (2002). Communicating the psychological contract: An employer perspective. *Human Resource Management Journal, 12*, 22–39.

Lambert, L. S. (2011). Promised and delivered inducements and contributions: An integrative view of psychological contract appraisal. *Journal of Applied Psychology, 96*, 695–712.

Montes, S. D., & Zweig, D. (2009). Do promises matter? An exploration of the role of promises in psychological contract breach. *Journal of Applied Psychology, 94*, 1243–1260.

Morrison, E. W., & Robinson, S. L. (1997). When employees feel betrayed: A model of how psychological contract violation develops. *Academy of Management Review, 22,* 226–256.

Roehling, M. V. (1997). The origins and early development of the psychological contract construct. *Journal of Management History, 3,* 204–217.

Rousseau, D. M. (1989). Psychological and implied contracts in organizations. *Employee Responsibilities and Rights Journal, 2,* 121–138.

Rousseau, D. M. (1995). Psychological contracts in organizations: Understanding written and unwritten agreements. Thousand Oaks, CA: Sage.

Rousseau, D. M. (2011). The individual-organization relationship: The psychological contract. In S. Zedeck (Ed.), *Handbook of industrial and organizational psychology* (Vol. 3, pp. 191–220). Washington, DC: American Psychological Association.

Zhao, H., Wayne, S. J., Glibkowski, B. C., & Bravo, J. (2007). The impact of psychological contract breach on work-related outcomes: A meta-analysis. *Personnel Psychology, 60,* 647–680.

Psychological Type and Problem-Solving Styles

Psychological type in its Myers Briggs Type Indicator (MBTI) sense is the most widely used applied personality theory and has been for many years. Over 2 million copies of the MBTI are completed each year, and it has been translated into over 30 languages, including Chinese. Among its many important management applications are leadership development and team-building programs. This entry is in two main sections. First, the central concepts of preference and type are defined and discussed, and second, the strong evidence for the validity of the preferences is touched on, with reference to five-factor or "Big Five" theory; the strengths and weaknesses of the preferences in problem solving are outlined; and a four-stage model of problem solving is presented and discussed.

Fundamentals

The Concept of Preference

Preference can be defined as "feeling most natural, energized, and comfortable with particular ways of behaving and experiencing." At a general level, there is a strong relationship between preference and Alex Linley's revival of the concept of strengths.

However, there are many strengths and, in classical type theory, eight preferences. Like strengths, the preferences are predispositions and, in a good-enough environment, they are expressed more and thus develop more. Type theory is optimistic in this respect: It assumes that most people's early lives encourage, or at least do not unduly discourage, development of their preferences.

Psychological type theory suggests eight preferences, organized in pairs. With a brief indication of their meanings, the preferences are for the following:

- Extraversion—more outgoing and active—versus Introversion—more reflective and reserved
- Sensing—more practical and interested in facts and details—versus Intuition—more interested in possibilities and an overview
- Thinking—more logical and reasoned—versus Feeling—more agreeable and appreciative
- Judging—more planning and coming to conclusions—versus Perceiving—more flexible and easy-going.

Self-assessment from these or longer descriptions will be tempting for many but should be done very provisionally. Accurate assessment can be straightforward, but it is best done with expert feedback or in experiential training in which groups of people with different preferences take part in exercises that illustrate type in action.

People generally behave in ways consistent with their preferences but can and do behave in the opposite way, though usually with more effort. If you prefer Extraversion to Introversion for example, then reading quietly and reflectively is likely to take more effort than being sociable, but most extraverts can reflect and most introverts can be sociable. Type theory assumes that people who do not express their preferences most of the time are less fulfilled and less effective than they would be as their real selves.

The positive tone of the descriptions of the preferences is radically different from that of five-factor theory. For example, the preferences for Judging and Perceiving are broadly parallel to the factor of conscientiousness. Scoring high on conscientiousness is generally regarded as positive, with terms such as *organized* and *decisive* being used as they are for the preference for Judging. In contrast, scoring low on conscientiousness is generally regarded as negative, with terms such as *aimless* and *weak-willed* being used. Perceiving, as indicated above, is described as flexible and easygoing, which has a radically different tone, but could be describing the same behavior as the Big Five terms.

A controversial issue in psychological type theory is whether there are two further preferences. This possibility arises from a comparison with Big Five theory: four of the five factors map well onto the eight preferences. The fifth factor is called *emotionally stable* versus anxious or neurotic, and it has recently been reconceptualized, for example, by Daniel Nettle, in a way that allows it to be treated as a preference. This involves using more positive or at least neutral terms because the five factors each have a negative end and the preferences are all described positively. Accordingly, the factor of neuroticism can be renamed as a preference for Calm versus a preference for Worrying. Calm is in part about being bold and taking risks; Worrying about considering the worst possibilities and effects of an action.

The Concept of Psychological Type

In classical psychological type theory, there are 16 types—the 16 combinations of the four pairs of preferences. There is also a further level of the theory called *type dynamics,* which proposes a personality structure for each of the types. Specifically, it states that one of the four preferences for Sensing, Intuition, Thinking, and Feeling is like the managing director of the personality, another is like a personal assistant, and the opposite preference to the dominant managing director one is called the "inferior." This level of the theory is alluring and widely used. It is generally regarded as sophisticated and as explaining behavior that is out of character as well as some mysterious and problematic interactions between people. However, it is also a second controversial issue. First the term *type* is a problem because it sounds like stereotyping and gives a (misleading) impression of rigid "boxes." More important, the validity of type dynamics is much less well supported empirically than the validity of the preferences.

The Ten Preferences and Problem-Solving Styles

Each preference can make a positive contribution to problem solving or has a distinctive approach to it that should be valued, as follows:

1. *Extraversion* by talking about problem, with or without others listening, in effect thinking (speculating) aloud

2. *Introversion* by reflecting privately and then sharing the considered results

3. *Sensing* by gathering facts, details, and evidence and a realistic, pragmatic perspective

4. *Intuition* by brainstorming alternative interpretations and possible solutions and bringing a more imaginative and optimistic perspective

5. *Thinking* by analyzing the consequences of solutions logically and objectively

6. *Feeling* by focusing on how the people affected by each solution are likely to react to it

7. *Judging* by deciding on the best solution and implementing it

8. *Perceiving* by exploring a variety of solutions and keeping the options open

9. *Worrying* by being cautious and suggesting the worst possible outcomes (these will probably seem unlikely and even absurd to people who prefer Calm).

10. *Calm* by being optimistic and suggesting risky strategies

Several of the preferences have weaknesses that are the opposite of their strengths or the result of lack of balance with the opposing preference. Thus, if Sensing is ignored or underused, there may not really be a problem to solve or the wrong problem may be tackled; if Intuition is underused, good options may be missed; if Thinking, Feeling, or Worrying are underused, or Calm overused, negative consequences are more likely; if Judging is overused, decisions and actions are more likely to be premature; and if Perceiving is overused, decisions and actions are more likely to be unduly delayed.

Importance

The validity of preference theory (but not type dynamics) is strongly supported by most of the research on five-factor theory. This research is extensive, of high quality (it has dominated the leading personality journals for many years), and shows significant relationships between personality and important outcomes in the real world, such as work performance and health. The effects are large in practical terms, comparable to those for cognitive ability. Where preference theory and five-factor theory differ is in tone (as touched on earlier), versatility, and experience of application. In each respect, preference theory is currently stronger.

A Four-Stage Model of Problem Solving

The four-stage model is a simpler, applied version of the 10-preferences approach to problem solving. A perfect manager would be skilled at all of them. However, perfection in this sense is rare and most of us are more energized and at ease with one or more of the stages than the others. The model is as follows:

Stage 1: Define the problem (Sensing). What are the facts? (have they been double-checked, particularly by someone with well-developed Sensing?) Is there really a problem? What has actually happened? If similar problems have occurred before, what solutions were tried? What resources are realistically available?

Stage 2: Interpret the problem (Intuition). In this stage, nothing is ruled out, however absurd it may seem. What ways of looking at this problem are there? What solutions are there? What theories or models might be relevant?

Stage 3: Analyze the possible solutions (Thinking). What are the arguments for and against each solution, short and long term?

Stage 4: Assess the personal impact (Feeling). What are the likely effects of each solution on the people affected by it (e.g., demoralizing or engaging)? How consistent is each solution with the organization's values and philosophy?

For example, a car manufacturer was faced with a design fault in one its models: When it was struck by another car from behind there was a small risk of its gasoline tank exploding. Thus the problem was clear enough and various solutions were explored. The cost of recalling all the cars was very high, much higher than settling claims with the few owners whose cars exploded. The company decided not to recall the cars, a rational decision based on short-term cost and ignoring broader ethical concerns as well as customers' and potential customers' feelings about the brand. Other companies faced with a similar problem have swiftly and expensively recalled their products, enhancing their reputations for integrity and customer care as a result.

In theory, good solutions therefore rest on (1) a realistic assessment of (and sometimes search for) the facts, (2) being open to a range of possible interpretations and solutions, (3) analyzing them incisively and (4) taking the impact on those people who are or may be affected into account. Each stage is vital. For example, the members of the management team in the example above may all have preferred Sensing and Thinking, and thus their approach to solving the problem was to gather the facts, analyze them, and make a logical decision. None of the team had developed their Stage 4 skills enough to influence the decision. They would have solved the problem better if one or more of them had developed Feeling enough or if they had consulted someone who had and respected their contribution—in other words, a training or selection issue or both.

Preferences and nonpreferences develop through practice, although with the proviso, central to type theory, that each person's preferences have a higher potential or ceiling that with a normal upbringing, their preferences will develop more than their nonpreferences. In addition, some people develop their nonpreferences more than others develop their preferences. That is why it is unethical to state in an advertisement, as happened for an organizational psychologist post, that "ESTJs and people who do not know what that means need not apply." ESTJ is shorthand for prefers Extraversion, Sensing, Thinking, and Judging and if the job required, say, skills associated with Intuition, then a particular ESTJ might have developed those skills more than any of the other candidates, including those who actually have a preference for Intuition. Asking for knowledge of psychological type theory is a much more defensible job criterion.

Generally, both preferences and nonpreferences develop through life experience, but deliberate attempts can be made to develop them too. For example, Sensing can be developed through practicing observation (including mindfulness techniques), Intuition through brainstorming and writing overviews, Thinking through designing flowcharts and doing cost-benefit analyses, and Feeling through clarifying values and practicing being empathic. However, accurate feedback is also needed, and the practice needs to be sustained and energizing to achieve a high level of expertise with any skill. This is a defining quality of strengths and preferences and implies that any one person cannot be and do everything, that achieving the best solutions to problems involves recognizing and valuing all the preferences and resulting styles.

Rowan Bayne

See also Big-Five Personality Dimensions; Decision-Making Styles; Emotional and Social Intelligence; High-Performing Teams; Humanistic Management; Intuitive Decision Making; Participative Model of Decision Making; Trust

Further Readings

Bayne, R. (2004). Psychological types at work: An MBTI perspective. London, England: Thomson.

Bayne, R. (in press). The counsellor's guide to personality: Preferences, motives and life stories. Basingstoke, England: Palgrave Macmillan.

Hirsh, S. K., & Kummerow, J. M. (2000). *Introduction to type in organizations* (3rd ed.). Palo Alto, CA: Consulting Psychologists Press.

Linley, A. (2008). Average to A+: Realising strengths in yourself and others. Coventry, England: CAPP Press.

Myers, I. B. (1998). *Introduction to type* (6th ed.). Palo Alto, CA: Consulting Psychologists Press.

Nettle, D. (2007). *Personality*. Oxford, England: Oxford University Press.

Reynierse, J. H. (2009). The case against type dynamics. *Journal of Psychological Type, 69*(1), 1–29.

Reynierse, J. H. (2012). Toward an empirically sound and radically revised type theory. *Journal of Psychological Type, 72*(1), 1–25.

PUNCTUATED EQUILIBRIUM MODEL

Change is ubiquitous and pervasive, often threatening the survival of organizations as well as entire industries. There are two primary competing theoretical perspectives outlining how organizations adapt to change. The first, based on the Darwinian model of evolution, argues that systems adapt gradually through a steady, cumulative incremental process. The alternate perspective, the "punctuated equilibrium model" (PEM) counters this claim of cumulative, consistent change and argues that the adaptation process is marked by long periods of incremental or evolutionary change "punctuated" by sudden bursts of radical or revolutionary change.

In both cases, organizations compete for scarce resources from the environment, but the Darwinian model argues that the environment selects out organizations that do not adapt, whereas the PEM makes the case that organizations that make revolutionary or radical changes are better able to cope with the environmental changes. This entry will examine the unique characteristics of the PEM, contrast it with the Darwinian theory of evolution, and finally analyze how some industries, organizations, and groups develop mechanisms that enable them to cope with revolutionary changes and adapt to the environment.

Fundamentals

The term *punctuated equilibrium,* coined by biologists Niles Eldridge and Stephen Gould, has three basic concepts: stasis, punctuation, and dominant relative frequency. *Stasis* refers to a long period of relatively unchanged form, *punctuation* is a radical change over a short duration, and *dominant relative frequency* is the rate these events occur in a particular situation. Michael Tushman and Elaine Romanelli (at the macro level) along with Connie Gersick (at the micro level) propose that the main constructs that define the PEM are deep structures, equilibrium periods, and revolutionary periods.

Systems with a deep structure share two characteristics: (1) They have differentiated parts, and (2) the units that make up the system "work" by exchanging resources with the environment to maintain it. The deep structures are stable because the current choices and structures of the system are constrained by past actions, and the overall activity patterns reinforce the system as a whole through feedback loops. If the deep structure is synonymous with the game design and rules of play, the equilibrium period is similar to "a game in play." Systems in equilibrium make incremental changes to compensate for internal and external perturbations without changing their deep structures.

There are three barriers to radical change that encourage systems to maintain their equilibrium position—cognition, motivation, and obligation. First, current frameworks cognitively limit the awareness of alternatives and consequently constrain behavior. Second, the uncertainty, fear of failure, and apprehension of change in the status quo prevents systems from adopting significant change.

Finally, systems are embedded in interdependent networks with resource relationships and obligations to current stakeholders that also inhibit their ability to change. These barriers prevent many large incumbent players from adapting when the dominant design or the industry standard for a technology changes. The last construct in the PEM is the revolutionary period. The difference between equilibrium and the revolutionary periods is that during the former, the deep structure is intact, and during the latter, the underlying structure is dismantled, changing the basic rules of play. For example, a change in the dominant design often creates disorganization and displaces many existing players and starts a revolutionary period. This dismantling destroys the existing system, resulting in the emergence of a new configuration with parts of the old system and some new pieces. The new configurations often emerge from new entrants from outside the industry who supplant the industry leaders.

What are some of the precursors to the revolutionary period? One is performance pressures, anticipated or actual, that can emerge from internal or external sources. The internal trigger is below-par financial performance over an extended period; the external triggers are competitive action and emergence of new technologies in the focal or neighboring industries or changes in the regulatory environment. A second precursor is when organizational systems recognize they need to change the inertia of equilibrium by initiating radical change. Theorists propose that events themselves do not cause the change, but the timing of when an event occurs influences changes in the deep structure of a system.

The prevalence of the PEM has been demonstrated at multiple levels. At the industry level, deregulation and emergence of new technologies are some factors that fundamentally alter the deep structure of industries. Regulatory punctuations alter both technical and institutional features of industries by raising or lowering barriers to entry. For example, the deregulation of airlines in the 1970s and of telecommunications and financial services in the 1980s caused revolutionary periods that dismantled the deep structure of the industry. In each of these industries, the industry shakeout postderegulation was followed by a period when the surviving members within the industry adjusted to a period of relative stability. At the firm level, revolutionary periods occur when the strategy, structure, and culture of the company become misaligned. Some firms then revamp their approach by realigning strategy through revolutionary changes and adapting their structure and culture to the new competitive dynamics thereby leading to periods of relative stability. For example, if one examines Apple's 32-year history, several periods of evolutionary change have been punctuated by discontinuous or revolutionary change. At the group level, the deep structure is defined by an integrated web of performance strategies, interaction patterns, and general assumptions toward its task and outside context. The PEM argues that work groups progress through two main phases separated by a transition period. Within each phase, groups approach their work using stable frameworks of assumptions. The transition period provides a limited opportunity for radical progress and quantum change.

The PEM attributes greater power to managers when compared to the Darwinian model, which is theoretically closer to population ecology or natural selection. The natural selection model claims that some organizational forms get selected out through a process of variation, selection, and retention. Selection occurs because the environment selects those entities that fit the resource base of the environmental niche, and retention involves the forces that perpetuate certain organizational forms. In this model, organizations are inert and destined to fail in the face of environmental change. The PEM views organizations as learning systems that can adapt to changing environmental contexts, making the case for managerial action. In groups, managers can also use formal control systems as levers to consistently manage evolutionary and revolutionary change. The control processes can act as agents for both intended change and autonomous emergent change.

The PEM emphasizes that organizations need to develop ambidexterity, which is the ability to simultaneously handle incremental, sustaining changes and radical, revolutionary changes. This creates a learning paradox for the organization that involves building on as well destroying the past to create the future. The executive leadership within the organization has to cultivate the capability to "manage organizational attention" so that it is not cognitively constrained and when radical changes are encountered in the environment, they can be made sense of and responded to adequately.

The insights from the PEM can/should be used by modern managers to help cultivate capabilities that involve managing the stasis during which time the cultivation of efficiency and the ability to institutionalize practices is key and managing revolutions where radical innovation and adaptive capabilities are the skills to be developed.

Shanthi Gopalakrishnan

See also Adaptive Structuration Theory; Continuous and Routinized Change; Group Punctuated Equilibrium Model; Organizational Ecology; Organizational Learning; Patterns of Innovation; Technological Discontinuities; Technology S-Curve

Further Readings

Eldredge, N., & Gould, S. (1972). Punctuated equilibria: An alternative to phyletic gradualism. In T. J. Schopf (Ed.), *Models in paleobiology* (pp. 82–115). San Francisco, CA: Freeman, Cooper.

Gersick, C. J. G. (1988). Time and transition in work teams: Toward a new model of development. *Academy of Management Journal, 32,* 274–309.

Gersick, C. J. G. (1991). Revolutionary change theories: A multilevel exploration of the punctuated equilibrium paradigm. *Academy of Management Review, 16*(1), 10–36.

O'Reilly, C.A. III, & Tushman, M. (2008). Ambidexterity as a dynamic capability: Resolving the innovator's dilemma. *Research in Organizational Behavior, 28,* 185–206.

Romanelli, E., & Tushman, M. T. (1994). Organizational transformation as punctuated equilibrium: An empirical test. *Academy of Management Journal, 37,* 1141–1166.

Tushman, M., & Romanelli, E. (1985). Organizational evolution: A metamorphosis model of convergence and reorientation. In L. L. Cummings & B. M. Staw (Eds.), *Research in organizational behavior* (Vol. 7, pp. 171–222). Greenwich, CT: JAI Press.

Van de Ven, A. H., & Poole, M. S. (1995). Explaining development and change in organizations. *Academy of Management Review, 20*(3), 510–540.

QUALITY CIRCLES

The systematic use of quality circles (QCs) began in Japan approximately 50 years ago. Since then, the method has been taken up in most of the world with varying results. The original purpose of the quality circles was that they should constitute training groups through which the participants could learn to use basic statistical tools. Nonetheless, in time, the activities more and more came to be aimed at improving the organizations' processes, and they have been found to be particularly useful for this purpose. In this entry, the fundamentals of quality circles and the different member roles are described. Subsequently, their development in Japan and the West along with their connection to teamwork are discussed.

Fundamentals

In general, the Japanese scholar Kaoru Ishikawa is regarded as the father of quality circles. The term he used for them was *quality control circles*. He emphasized the following characteristics:

- The circle is a small group of people who perform quality control activities.
- The members participate on a voluntary basis.
- The members are recruited from the same workshop.
- The activities of the circle carry on continuously.
- The activities of the circle constitute an integrated part of the company-wide quality control activities.

- The activities include self-development, mutual development, control, and improvement within the workshop.
- Quality control techniques are used.
- All members participate actively.

The overall purpose of the quality circles is the improvement and development of the enterprise as a part of the company-wide quality control activities. Nevertheless, Ishikawa also held that the circles should respect humanity and build a happy, bright work environment that is worthwhile to participate in. Moreover, he argued that they should exercise human capabilities fully and eventually draw out infinite possibilities.

The main points that have been retained from Ishikawa's work are that the participation should be voluntary and active and that the activities should continue for a fairly long time. In addition, the group should use improvement tools such as *Ishikawa's seven basic tools for quality* and *the seven new tools for improvement*. The members of the quality circle are assigned different roles. Usually, the following roles are defined as follows:

The members. In the original quality circles the members were factory workers in industrial manufacturing. Since then, many different organizations from various sectors have started to use quality circles. This means that today the members can be employees with very different backgrounds and daily tasks. Furthermore, the original quality circles were always constituted of members from the same department. Lately, the use of interdepartmental quality circles has become more and more common because problems in organizations are often complex and involve more than one department.

The moderator. This is the person leading the activities of the group. Usually, a manager of the participants is chosen as moderator. Nevertheless, trying other options is definitely worthwhile, in particular for interdepartmental quality circles. If the mission of the quality circle is to handle a specific problem, choosing someone who is especially knowledgeable regarding this problem area is normally suitable. However, the most important criteria regard the personality of the person in question. She or he should be a good leader with a high level of empathy and an ability to promote the effectiveness of the activities as well as the well-being of the participants.

The coordinator. This person is supposed to constitute the connecting link between the different quality circles as well as between them and management. Her or his responsibilities also include training of moderators, ensuring that the quality circles have sufficient resources, and providing general support. Consequently, the coordinator is a very important person since the most usual reason for lacking success in quality circle activities is that they tend to live a life of their own with limited influence on the overall performance of the organization. With a skilled coordinator who is supported by top management, this can be avoided.

The steering group. This is the unit that makes the overall decisions regarding the organization and running of the company-wide quality circle activities. The group should consist of representatives from top management.

In Japan, quality circles have been used continuously since the early 1960s. In the Western world, quality circles suddenly became very popular in the mid-1980s when Western industry tried hard to learn Japanese quality management methods to counter the competition from Japanese industry. However, the initial quality circles in Western industry showed mediocre results, and in many companies, they were abandoned. The reasons for this was that Western industry tended to use quality circles as a method in isolation while Japanese industry used them as an integrated part of a holistic quality management system also involving other techniques and models based on quality management values. When they were used in isolation quality circles received inadequate resources and limited authority. In addition, their missions were restricted and the interest from top management was small or nonexistent. In fact, support from top management has since been shown to be a key factor for the successful use of quality circles.

Over time, a number of Western organizations have realized the importance of using quality circles as a part of an integrated quality management system. This has led to an increase in usage in industry as well as in other sectors such as health care. If they are used in this way, quality circles are powerful tools for achieving profound quality improvements.

In addition to quality circles becoming more common, their principles are often taken up in other connections. Teams and teamwork have become increasingly common in all industries as well as in the public sector. Even when the term is not used, *teamwork* is often inspired by the principles of quality circles.

Stefan Lagrosen

See also Multicultural Work Teams; Quality Trilogy; Total Quality Management

Further Readings

Boaden, R. J., & Dale, B. G. (1992). Teamwork in services: Quality circles by another name? *International Journal of Service Industry Management, 4*(1), 5–24.

Hill, S. (1991). Why quality circles failed but total quality management might succeed. *British Journal of Industrial Relations, 29*(4), 541–568.

Ishikawa, K. (1985). *What is total quality control, the Japanese Way?* Eaglewood Cliffs, NJ: Prentice Hall.

Ishikawa, K. (1990). *Introduction to quality control.* London, England: Chapman & Hall.

Salaheldin, S. I. (2009). Problems, success factors and benefits of QCs implementation: A case of QASCO. *TQM Journal, 21*(1), 87–100.

QUALITY TRILOGY

Quality does not happen by accident. Rather, it is achieved through quality planning, quality control, and quality improvement. This concept is known as the *quality trilogy* and was introduced by one of the leading gurus of quality management—Joseph M. Juran. According to Juran, quality planning establishes a capable system development plan to meet quality standards, quality control provides a monitoring process to take corrective actions when necessary, and quality improvement aims at finding better and more efficient ways of doing things. The research on quality trilogy is still evolving. The applications of quality trilogy on the evolving field of quality management and sustainability management are also explored in this entry.

Fundamentals

Competition is the order of the day in the corporate world today. Although businesses compete on several fronts, the essential features of management have always centered on customer needs and requirements. In a knowledge-based economy, customers expect firms to introduce better and cheaper products, offer higher service levels, reduce wastes, and provide job opportunities. The mission statements of business enterprises today often emphasize the need to create quality and value for the customer. In practice, a three-step quality management process that represents the quality trilogy is normally adopted in realizing such a goal:

- Planning for quality
- Identifying control activities and taking corrective actions in ensuring the performance of the system in question
- Introducing continuous improvement initiatives to create and maintain a more capable system.

The objective of planning for quality is to outline ways to "do the right things correctly" so that the cost of poor quality can be minimized. To ensure a stable system performance, executable control actions need to be taken based on the principles of quality assurance. The main function of continuous improvement is to find opportunities for enhancing system capabilities and subsequently achieving a better system performance. This practical engagement, known as *quality trilogy,* is one of Juran's methods to tackle quality problems. The ultimate aim of this process is to achieve quality.

To many organizations, quality is conformance to specifications. To others, quality is in the eyes of the beholders. Quality means different things to different people. The most commonly stated quality definitions for tangible products are presented by James Robert Evans and W. M. Lindsay. They define product quality as a function of a specific, measurable variable that reflects differences in quantity of some product attributes such as the life span of a laptop battery. A somewhat different view of quality is *process centric.* A typical operations system today, as stated by Christian Madu and Chuhua Kuei, involves a variety of processes: customer engagement, manufacturing, and sourcing. With respect to each process, a unique set of attributes can contribute to what a customer perceives as quality. For example, as per Leonard Berry and A. Parasuraman, customer engagement quality consists of five dimensions: reliability, responsiveness, assurance, empathy, and tangibles. Gravin's model can be adopted to represent dimensions of manufacturing quality. We can also use the 2009 model presented by Lars-Eric Gadde and Kajsa Hulthén to evaluate sourcing quality.

With this goal (product and/or process quality) in mind, businesses need to find proven paths to help find ways to structure, bundle, and leverage their resources and produce high-quality outputs and outcomes. It is apparent from Juran's teachings that quality trilogy can maximize the likelihood of business success since it is a learning framework based on three critical steps: planning, controlling, and improving. Thus, the call for quality trilogy is not only good for maintaining a stable operation but is also good in finding new opportunities and improving the long-term capabilities of the operational system.

Evolution

Building a total quality system to deliver quality products and/or processes requires business vision and institutional expertise. The role of quality trilogy is critical in linking vision and institutional expertise. In other words, through quality planning efforts, quality control activities, and continuous improvement initiatives, it is possible that business vision and company mission can be conceptualized and institutional expertise can be monitored, developed, and improved over time. Major stages are reviewed as follows:

At the *planning* stage, policy and decision makers focus on the effects of quality planning and organizing. They identify causes of poor quality and may use a variety of tools to analyze the causes. Standards and guidelines are then established on how to detect quality problems.

At the *control* stage, policy and decision makers pay attention to routine functions, control activities, and take corrective actions to ensure stable capabilities and to maintain a desired level of quality. The aim here is to ensure that the process is behaving as expected or what could be said to be under statistical quality or process control. Thus, the process is in conformance and will meet the expectations for precision and accuracy. Deviations observed from the process behavior may be due to chance or random occurrences.

At the *improvement* stage, policy and decision makers focus on innovative initiatives that would help to further improve on the process. Before continuous improvement can be initiated, the process must first be under statistical control. Thus, when the available feedback shows that the process is behaving as expected, it is then time to think about the smaller and incremental changes that would help to further improve the performance of the process. All these stages that make up the quality trilogy rely on the applications of proven methods. Such methods could be managerial or statistical in form.

In a similar fashion, perhaps the other best known mechanism is plan-do-study-act (PDSA). Oftentimes, the *study* is replaced with *check*. This method was introduced by Walter Shewhart but was made popular in 1993 by Edward Deming. The PDSA orchestrates the stages in planning for quality. The plan stage involves problem identification, brainstorming sessions, and use of tools such as flow charts to understand the process. The process is then implemented on a smaller scale rather than a large scale to avoid potential failures and associated consequences. The study part helps understand the process, addresses "what if" questions, learns from mistakes and errors observed, and uses the information to further improve on the product or process before embarking on a large-scale implementation. Once the large-scale process is implemented, frequent monitoring and collection of feedback is necessary to ensure that the process is still adequate and meeting expectations. At this stage, continuous improvement can be applied. However, when it is

clear that the process is no longer able to meet expectations, breakthrough thinking or reengineering may become necessary. At this stage, continuous improvement will be a wasteful effort since it cannot revive a process that no longer meets the demands of the time.

Importance

The following sections apply the concepts of quality management and sustainability management to the concept of the quality trilogy.

Quality Management

Quality management involves providing enabling conditions and also mobilizing human resources to achieve quality. Organizational structure is important in achieving quality. For more than three decades, business professionals have been challenged to increase their focus on quality planning. Thus, how an organization is designed and the processes within the organization are associated with the level of quality that is attained. Process decisions often involve how tasks are performed, how work is done, policies and procedures that guide work, and all the steps to create value to satisfy the organization's goals and needs. Processes must be managed effectively because they involve the operational procedures to create goods and services. Effective analysis of processes would help identify the causes of problems with the process and how process problems can be resolved. This phase of effective process diagnosis, cause-and-effect analysis, and problem identification and solution is known as *quality planning*.

Quality management aligns internal value chain activities with the purpose of achieving quality. Porter identified primary value chain activities to include inbound logistics, operations, outbound logistics, marketing and sales, and service. To enhance multitier, multilevel, and cross-functional performance quality, quality management scholars such as Deming and Juran contend that higher process control in an integrated format should be a norm, not an exception. The needs and wants of the customer may be understood by exploring the internal value chain activities. These activities could be used to set process goals with established standards and expectations. A control mechanism is then set up once standards are established and meaningful results are obtainable.

Quality management relies on continuous improvement efforts to achieve incremental improvements on a process that is relatively stable and performing as expected. The right things are done, and they are done right the first time. Thus, quality management encourages efficiency and effectiveness. Doing the right things requires effective leadership, policy deployment, process development, and practical engagement. Quality management thus serves as an input factor, and quality is the result. Although the creation of quality and value requires a set of appropriate and effective actions in the first place, one needs to follow a continuous improvement approach that is never ending. Effective quality management ensures that actions will be followed through to achieve the intended results.

Sustainability Management

Sustainability management (SM) is a competitive tool that companies employ today. Businesses need to differentiate their products and services from those of their competitors by offering considerable sustainability value. As a result, businesses today need to create an infrastructure of resource use (e.g., materials and energy) that meets the objectives of the triple bottom line by considering uncertainties in the natural system (e.g., ecological balance), social systems (e.g., social equity), and competitive forces. According to Jianguo Wu and Tong Wu, managers and business leaders in this era of sustainability are beginning to ask series questions at the *planning* stage based on the Bellagio principles of sustainable development. These questions include the following:

- What is my organization's vision for sustainability?
- What are the guiding principles from a holistic perspective; that is, what are our beliefs with respect to the triple bottom line?
- Are we certain that our scope, statement of purpose, and analysis, from work contents to expected outcomes, are adequate?
- Can we clearly define our sustainability indicators and assessment criteria?
- Can we make our methods and data more accessible?
- Have we created an effective communication plan?
- Does the board participate in the transformation process?

- Do we have ongoing assessment plans on sustainability?
- De we have institutional capacities and expertise to match the context outlined by the triple bottom line?

Planning for sustainability enables conditions and structures, leverages resources, and produces actionable plans through which organizations can develop their capabilities and sustainability at every stage—strategic, tactical, and operational.

At the *control* stage, policy and decision makers ascertain that a desired level of sustainability is achieved at all times. A performance framework with a specific set of sustainability indicators is therefore needed to guide the routine functions to achieve such a goal. Control is then possible through feedbacks on operations characteristics based on a predetermined performance-driven framework. Wu and Wu report that there are five such frameworks: (1) driving force-state-response (DSR), (2) theme-based, (3) capital-based, (4) integrated accounting, and (5) Bossel's systems-based orientor theory. The DSR framework, used to guide the selection of sustainability indicators, was published in 1996 by the UN Commission on Sustainable Development (UNCSD). The theme-based framework offers indicators in four areas: social, environmental, economic, and institutional. The general areas of a capital-based framework may be divided into four main subareas: manufacturing capital, natural capital, human capital, and social capital. These four constituents of capital represent the wealth of an entity. A change in one form of capital might lead to a positive or negative change in others. The challenge from a control perspective is to find balance among these four forms of capital. Integrated accounting frameworks, such as the system of integrated environmental and economic accounting (SEEA), are used to develop data systems for measuring the interrelationship between the economic and environmental data. The emphasis is on both economic and environmental statistics and data analyses. If discrepancies are found when assessing the level and cost of emissions and other wastes along the product life cycle, for example, the control team can advise on the remedial actions to ensure that the standards are met. Bossel's "orientor" framework suggests that seven basic factors must be satisfied to meet the challenges of any ecological and socioeconomic systems: (1) existence (i.e., the compatibility between built systems and the normal environmental state), (2) effectiveness (i.e., doing the right things correctly given the scarce resources), (3) freedom of action (i.e., the system's ability to find paths to deal with environmental uncertainties), (4) security (i.e., the system capability to cope with effects of environmental variability in a robust manner), (5) adaptability (i.e., the system's ability to learn, adapt, and generate response strategies in the unpredictable and ever-changing "wants" of the stakeholders), (6) coexistence (i.e., the coexistence of all subsystems in their natural or social environments), and (7) psychological needs. There is a need to explore the implications of performance-driven frameworks and derive sustainability indicators from them. The objective of control activities based on a specific performance framework is to have in place a formal, structured approach that continuously surveys and monitors the capabilities of the firm in ensuring a desired level of sustainability. As a result, the primary deliverable here is a data system.

At the *improvement* stage, as a result of this recognition, policy and decision makers need to adjust and leverage the resources to the requirements of SM. Most important, they need to acknowledge the need to undergo a transformation from the traditional management approach to SM. The data system established at the *control* stage is central to this operation. The transformation in fact is driven by both the vision of the firm and the integrated sustainable development data analyses and reports from the control stage. Three areas will normally be impacted by the exercise of transformation: a system transformation process, working with suppliers, and a cultural transformation process. The unique feature of this continuous improvement effort is the cultural transformation process. It involves leadership, employee fulfillment, conflict management, individual learning, whole systems learning, and cultural acceptance. The incorporation of this "soft" component of continuous improvement and relevant interventions distinguishes this part from the control perspective. The changes, based on the essence of the transformation model, may lead to a new organization with new competencies for sustainability.

Christian N. Madu and Chuhua Kuei

See also Action Learning; Business Process
  Reengineering; Process Theories of Change; Quality
  Circles; Six Sigma

Further Readings

Berry, L. L., & Parasuraman, A. (1991). *Marketing services—Competing through quality.* New York, NY: Free Press.

Deming, W. E. (1993). *The new economics for industry, government, education.* Cambridge, MA: MIT Press.

Evans, J. R., & Lindsay, W. M. (2005). *The management and control of quality.* Mason, OH: South-Western.

Gadde, L., & Hulthén, K. (2009). Improving logistics outsourcing through increasing buyer-provider interaction. *Industrial Marketing Management, 38,* 633–640.

Garvin, D. A. (1991). Competing on the eight dimensions of quality. In *Unconditional quality* (pp. 43–51). Boston, MA: Harvard Business School.

Juran, J. M. (1992). *Juran on quality by design.* Old Tappan, NJ: Free Press.

Kuei, C., Madu, C. N., & Lin, C. (2011). Developing global supply chain quality management systems. *International Journal of Production Research, 49*(15), 4457—4481.

Madu, C. N., & Kuei, C. (2004). *ERP and supply chain management.* Fairfield, CT: Chi.

Porter, M. E. (1996, November–December). What is strategy? *Harvard Business Review,* 61–78.

Wu, J., & Wu, T. (2012). Sustainability indicators and indices: An overview. In C. N. Madu & C. Kuei (Eds.), *Handbook of sustainability management* (pp. 65–86). Singapore: World Scientific Publishing.

QUANTUM CHANGE

Discussions of quantum change have been featured in the discourses of several theoretical disciplines, including, among others, biology, chemistry, and psychology. While the term has different emphases in each of these, it generally concerns some form of transformative event. In organizational studies, a quantum view of change is predominantly concerned with the relationship among an organization's structure, strategy, and environment. It is grounded on the premise that organizational success will be achieved through the balancing of stability and change. An organization, under this scenario, is described as existing in a stable configuration of elements underpinned by a set of values that gives rise to a particular set of behaviors. These periods of stability are interrupted occasionally by some process of transformation—a quantum leap to another configuration. Quantum change, therefore, is typically described as consisting of change to many elements of the organization very quickly or even simultaneously, in contrast to incremental change in which one element is altered at a time. Because a theory of quantum change is concerned with the problem of structural change, research has often focused on uncovering those structural elements or variables that experience change as the environment alters. Furthermore, because of the interdependency among these elements, some work has explored the links between the pace and sequence that change should follow to be successfully implemented. Given the globalized, hypercompetitive, and uncertain nature of the environment within which organizations operate, this theory is particularly relevant for change leaders as organizations are pressured to respond to fluctuations in their internal and external environments. Further, while change leaders may be reluctant to initiate quantum change because of the many difficulties inherent in introducing and implementing large-scale change, an organization's survival is often predicated on its ability to negotiate some form of radical transformation. Indeed, while organizations tend to favor incremental change, the alteration of only some elements may destroy those complementarities associated with a specific configuration, which, in turn, will result in substantive operational difficulties. Thus, the theory of quantum change offers a useful lens through which change leaders can conceptualize and implement large-scale changes. First, with its approach of organizations as configurations, it provides a comprehensive framework for understanding how change unfolds, bringing together the cognitive school of change (how strategists think), the entrepreneurial school (how they act), and the cultural school (what they believe in). Further, it encourages change leaders to engage in a thorough analysis of internal and external environments so as to better evaluate the costs and benefits of engaging in quantum or incremental change. In the next section, we offer an examination of the major factors influencing quantum change and explicate the relationships between these factors. We further highlight related psychological and social dynamics and discuss some of the contextual and situational conditions that have been found to be key in either hindering or facilitating quantum change. We conclude with some implications and applications of our discussion.

Fundamentals

As we note above, a quantum view of change is primarily concerned with the relationship between an organization's structure, strategy, and environment. From the classic Aston studies of the late 1960s to more contemporary work in the 2000s, organizational structure has been predominantly considered to involve the interrelationship among centralization, standardization/formalization, and specialization. Of particular interest has been how these elements position the organization to operate differently in different environments, often depending on imperatives such as technology or environmental uncertainty. In the early 1960s, Tom Burns and George MacPherson Stalker argued that organizations should be more mechanistic or organic, depending on the degree of environmental fluctuation. This early theorizing was built on the idea that organizations are composed of elements arranged in specific configurations. A configuration is not only expected to fit the organization's environment, but it will also have major implications for the strategies available to it. However, because of the uncertain nature of the organization's environment, changes in the environment will force the organization into considering the need to restructure in order to maintain fit. Such a restructuring can be carried out in one of two ways, either through quantum change where most elements of the structure will be altered in a concerted way, or incrementally, where only some elements will be changed at a time.

Danny Miller and Peter H. Friesen warn change managers against an incremental type of restructuring, indicating that such a process generates increased costs, disruptions, and risks. Their theorizing has two major elements of immediate relevance here. First, organizational coherence, or the patterning of component elements, is to be understood as forming an organization's design. Understanding the parts of an organization can be gained only by examining how they interact together as a coherent whole. Second, the notion of configuration points to the highly interdependent nature of those elements and encourages a view of change whereby an alteration of one element of the structure will impact others that are mutually supportive. For Miller and Friesen, understanding which configuration an organization is in is crucial for understanding structural change and its difficulties. Indeed, the coherence of a configuration is not accidental; it represents the appropriate design for adequate performance. Thus, according to this line of thought, when organizations respond to environmental fluctuations by selecting an incremental approach, they take the risk of destroying those complementarities.

Work on configurations led to the development of the concept of organizational archetypes, most influentially through the work of Bob Hinings and John L. Greenwood. Here, an important addition to the work on configurations was bringing in the central role of values, often articulated as an interpretive scheme, in underpinning structural design. The inclusion of values in the specification of organizational form pointed to a major reason why quantum change, articulated by Hinings and Greenwood as a shift from one archetype to another, is so difficult. The elements in an organization are not neutral or value free—they encapsulate preferences, embedded interests, and power arrangements that organization members will often strive hard to protect.

The work on configurations and archetypes suggests that long periods of relatively stable operation involving only incremental adjustments, interspersed by infrequent but revolutionary periods of quantum change, may be the most viable strategy for accomplishing large-scale change. Known as the *punctuated equilibrium theory,* this points to how overreliance on piecemeal change is likely to result in transforming an organization's configuration in such a way that coherence will be lost. Change leaders will then have the option of either making other structural modifications to regain coherence or reverting back to the former structure. In both cases, costs and disruption are likely to be high. However, while change managers may be reluctant to select a quantum approach, the move from one configuration to another may be less likely to generate an incoherent design.

Others scholars have emphasized the importance of examining the pacing and sequencing of change processes and suggested that fast-paced change to key parts of the organization may be most important in the initial stages of a change program to generate early momentum. Following this, slower paced change that allows the development of trust and understanding among organization members may be more effective than trying to force through widespread changes quickly.

While this theoretical approach is very similar to the punctuated equilibrium approach of change, where organizations undergo occasional dramatic revolutions to overcome their tendency toward inertia, it departs from somewhat similar views of change such as organizational adaptation or contingency theory. Indeed, where organizational adaptation presents firms adjusting gradually and incrementally to changes in the environment, the quantum view, with its simultaneous focus on structure, strategy, and environment, concludes that certain environments might encourage revolutionary strategies, whereas others will call for evolutionary change. Similarly, a quantum theory of change, though it too embraces the ideal of environmental fit, breaks from the dominant contingency view by proffering a viewpoint that change should encompass all organizational elements, not simply those limited few on which performance is viewed to be contingent.

The quantum theory of change has provided unique insights into organizational change. However, Henry Mintzberg argues that the quantum theory of change is most applicable to large, established, mass-production organizations. Because they are so reliant on highly standardized procedures, they tend to be most resistant to large-scale change and are thus most amenable to long periods of relative stability punctuated by short bouts of large-scale transformation. Mintzberg further suggests that this approach is particularly well suited for organizations that are regularly challenged by their interaction with competitors and clients. However, other scholars have demonstrated that quantum change has relevance for public sector and other types of private sector organization beyond large manufacturing firms.

Importance

The quantum theory of change paved the way to classifying change processes on the basis of their provision of a shift to greater organizational coherence or departure from one archetype to another. Furthermore, while the previously dominant views of organizational change, largely centered on the contingency model, were guided by a rational paradigmatic approach that favored a view that changes in inputs produce linear, predictable changes in outputs, in contrast, a quantum view takes a nonlinear approach to change. As such, it perhaps offers a more realistic understanding of how change takes place. Indeed, the complexity of the change process and the interconnectedness of structural elements suggest that it is unlikely that change can be approached in a linear fashion whereby change in one element can neatly precede change in another.

In sum, the quantum view of change has encouraged management scholars and practitioners to adopt a holistic view of organization, one that focuses on organizational coherence. As such, it has provided important insights into how and when organizational change leaders should focus on incremental change versus how and when organizations should engage in quantum change. For instance, Miller suggested that organizations make substantial changes only when it is absolutely necessary or extremely advantageous for them to do so because of the disruption and risks associated with it. In other words, since change is disruptive, organizations will tend to cluster changes temporally to minimize or shorten the disruption, a pattern that has been found in several empirical studies. Thus, while much remains to be understood about the pace and sequence of quantum change, the theory offers a comprehensive view of change efforts, one that accounts simultaneously for the content (structural elements), context (internal and external environments), and the process through which quantum change should be carried out. Similarly, it has encouraged change managers to approach change in terms of costs versus benefits in their selection of a particular type of change.

Rachida Aïssaoui and John M. Amis

See also Contingency Theory; Logical Incrementalism; Organizational Structure and Design; Punctuated Equilibrium Model

Further Readings

Amis, J., Slack, T., & Hinings, C. R. (2004). The pace, sequence, and linearity of radical change. *Academy of Management Journal, 47*(1), 15–39.

Greenwood, R., & Hinings, C. R. (1988). Organizational design types, tracks and the dynamics of strategic change. *Organization Studies, 9*(3), 293–316.

Greenwood, R., & Hinings, C. R. (1993). Understanding strategic change: The contribution of archetypes. *Academy of Management Journal, 36*(5), 1052–1081.

Miller, D. (1982). Evolution and revolution: A quantum view of structural change in organizations. *Journal of Management Studies, 19*(2), 131–151.

Miller, D., & Friesen, P. H. (1984). *Organizations: A quantum view.* Englewood Cliffs, NJ: Prentice Hall.

Mintzberg, H. (1979). *The structuring of organizations.* Englewood Cliffs, NJ: Prentice-Hall.

Pettigrew, A. (1987). Context and action in the transformation of the firm. *Journal of Management Studies, 24*, 649–670.

Plowman, D. A., Baker, L. T., Beck, T. E., Kulkarni, M., Solansky, S. T., & Travis, D. V. (2007). Radical change accidentally: The emergence and amplification of small change. *Academy of Management Journal, 50*, 515–543.

Romanelli, E., & Tushman, M. L. (1994). Organizational transformation as punctuated equilibrium: An empirical test. *Academy of Management Journal, 37*, 1141–1166.

REINFORCEMENT THEORY

Reinforcement theory is a learning theory that provides the foundation for behaviorist theories of motivation. It is based on the central tenet that a relatively permanent change in behavior is achieved from reinforced practice or experience. Reinforcement theory is often referred to as *operant learning* or *operant conditioning,* and it serves as the basis for the organizational behavior modification (OB Mod) movement. This entry, highlights the fundamentals of the theory, discusses various types of reinforcement (e.g., positive or negative) as well as schedules of reinforcement (e.g., continuous or intermittent), reviews the evolution of the theory, and addresses application for today's organizations.

Fundamentals

At its most basic premise, reinforcement theory asserts that the causal agents of human action are found in the relationship between antecedents, behavior, and consequences (A-B-C). Antecedents are the environmental conditions upon which desired behavior occurs, and consequences act as reinforcers after the behavior is performed. The overarching principle is that behavior increases in strength and/or probability when followed by a reinforcer. Behavior with positive consequences tends to be repeated, whereas behavior with negative consequences tends to *not* be repeated. For example, managers often reward employees for good behavior and successful performance through the use of both social rewards

(e.g., praise, recognition) and monetary rewards (e.g., salary, bonuses). Employees who engage in behavior that is not productive for the organization will not be rewarded or may potentially lose their jobs. Employee behavior is therefore a function of contingent consequences, or stimuli. There are four different approaches to applying stimuli: Two are used to strengthen the desired (or positive) behavior, and two are used to weaken undesired (or negative) behavior. B. F. Skinner's research on operant conditioning in the early 20th century provided the foundation for understanding the various types and schedule of reinforcement.

Positive reinforcement. According to Skinner, a positive reinforcer is a stimulus which, when added to a situation, strengthens the probability of an operant response. Positive reinforcers are generally used to increase positive behavior. In a work setting, these may include praise and recognition, a promotion, or money. It should be noted, however, that positive reinforcers are not universal. What acts as a positive motivator for one person may not do so for another. In addition, the desired behavior must be achievable so that employees can meet their goals and objectives. Reinforcement cannot occur if the desired behavior does not happen. Skinner therefore described the importance of shaping behavior, or training, through a process of reinforcing positive behavior in graduated steps.

Avoidance learning. A second way to promote desired behavior is to remove unpleasant consequences when the behavior occurs. This may happen by either preventing the onset of a negative consequence or by removing an unpleasant stimulus that already exists. An example of a negative stimulus in the workplace is supervisor criticism. A boss may berate his employee until the desired behavior is achieved. Most reinforcement theory advocates, however, prefer the use of positive reinforcement over avoidance learning.

Extinction. Extinction occurs when a positive reinforcer that has been used before is withheld or removed in order to weaken adverse behavior. The undesirable activity may continue for a while, but eventually the behavior should diminish and eventually stop if the positive reinforcer is withheld. Extinction may be most effective when undesirable behavior has been rewarded in the past. It is important for organizations to recognize that reinforcers often maintain the dysfunctional behavior of employees if reward systems are not designed with organizational goals in mind.

Punishment. Punishment is the application of an unpleasant consequence to stop or change undesirable behavior. It is often viewed as the harshest approach for behavior modification, but it can be effective in some situations. A waiter who provides bad service may not receive a tip from his customers, which is a punishment that may induce him to provide better service next time. At its most extreme, an employee could be suspended or terminated for dishonest behavior, such as stealing from the company.

The timing of reinforcement schedules may vary and as such can affect the desired outcome. Continuous reinforcement occurs when you apply the stimulus (whether positive or negative) each time the behavior is achieved. This approach promotes rapid learning and is often used during the initial stages of learning. While it may be an effective means to toilet train a child, it is generally not practical in an organizational setting where managers supervise many employees. Intermittent or partial reinforcement schedules are more common, where reinforcers are applied at some fixed or variable rate. This may lead to behavior that is less resistant to extinction.

In a fixed interval schedule, the behavior is rewarded after a specified amount of time has elapsed, and in a variable interval schedule, the behavior is rewarded after an unpredictable amount of time has passed. An example of a fixed interval schedule is an employee who gets paid on the same day every week, or every other week. This results in average or irregular performance. For example, performance may improve just before pay day. An example of a variable interval schedule is a bartender who relies on tips. Some customers will come in for a few quick drinks and leave a tip, whereas others may order the same number of drinks but linger over conversation before leaving a tip, or, leave no tip at all. The bartender is therefore incentivized to provide steady, consistent service.

Ratio schedules depend on the number of responses or occurrences of the behavior. With a fixed ratio schedule, the behavior is rewarded after a specified number of responses occur. For example, an employee who sells gym memberships may receive a bonus every time they sign up 10 customers. This may result in a slight dip in performance once the reward is received, but after a short time, the employee generally bounces back to a steady rate of response. When the employee is close to signing up that 10th customer, his performance may rise sharply. With a variable ratio schedule, the behavior is rewarded after a random number of responses occur. An example of the variable ratio schedule is a sales person who works on commission. Some clients may require only two or three calls before a sale is made, whereas other customers may require 10 calls.

There are some general rules regarding reinforcement techniques in the workplace. First, it is important to differentiate rewards, or positive reinforcers, based on a performance standard. Ideally, the best performers should receive the greatest rewards. Rewards can and should come in different sizes and be contingent upon employee behavior. The most common type of reinforcer in the workplace is financial, which includes cash payments in the form of wages, salary or bonuses, prizes, time off, or paid vacation. In contrast, performance feedback is a nonfinancial reinforcer. To be most effective, feedback should be immediate, graphic, specific, and positively conveyed. Social reinforcement is one-on-one communication from boss to subordinate, consisting of compliments, praise, and recognition. Organizations often use a combination of these reinforcers.

Feedback is an essential part of the reinforcement process. Employees need to know what they are doing well and being rewarded for, as well as what they are doing wrong. Nonaction or neglecting to respond to behavior may also have reinforcing consequences. These should be recognized and adjusted if necessary. Finally, if punishment must be used as a method of reinforcement, make sure the consequences are in balance with the behavior. For example, a factory employee who misses several shifts without excuse may be docked wages, but not necessarily fired. Also, never punish in front of others as there may be undesirable side effects.

Evolution

Reinforcement theory has roots in the early 1900s with the classic conditioning experiments of Ivan Pavlov and Edward Thorndike's law of effect. The law of effect focuses on how the consequences of certain behavior will affect that behavior in the future. Behavior that results in a pleasant outcome is likely to be repeated, whereas behavior that results in an unpleasant outcome will likely not be repeated. In the 1940s, B. F. Skinner developed the operant conditioning theory largely based on the law of effect. He conducted extensive experiments using animals and his "Skinner box." Within the box, Skinner could manipulate positive stimuli to act as reinforcers of good behavior, or, negative stimuli to act as punishers for bad or undesired behavior. For example, positive reinforcers might be a pellet of food, whereas a negative reinforcer, or punisher, might be a mild shock from the electrified floor. The process of changing the animal's behavior through reinforcement is called *operant conditioning*. Skinner's studies in operant conditioning laid the foundation for the types of reinforcers and schedules of reinforcement.

In the 1970s and 1980s, management scholars took reinforcement theory out of the laboratory and began to apply behavior modification techniques to the workplace. Drawing also from Albert Bandura's social learning theory, Fred Luthans and Robert Kreitner developed the organizational behavior modification (OB Mod) model. They wrote that the underlying assumption of OB Mod, like reinforcement theory, is that behavior is a function of its contingent consequences. OB Mod consists of a systematic, analytical, and action-oriented approach to assess and modify employee behavior for performance improvement. The process can be summarized in five one-word steps: identify, measure, analyze, intervene, and evaluate.

A classic study at Emery Air Freight in the early 1970s illustrates the OB Mod process. First, managers must identify behaviors that can be changed. These should be observable, measurable, task related, and critical to the task. At Emery Air Freight, management wanted to encourage packers to use freight containers for grouping shipments together, which provided a significant cost savings to the organization. Second, the behaviors should be measured to find a baseline by which to assess improvement. This can be done with direct observation, a time-sampling technique, or by using archival data. At Emery, employees were asked how often they used containers and reported 90% of the time. Usage based on actual reports, however, was 45%. This provided a baseline upon which to improve.

Next, managers must analyze the behavioral antecedents and contingent consequences of the behavior. These need to be indentified in order to ascertain what factors cue the behavior in the workplace and also to assess what the current reinforcing consequences are, in case these need to be changed. At Emery Air Freight, it was more time consuming to group shipments together in one container rather than ship them separately. An intervention is then applied to try and change the behavior, whether attempting to increase desirable behavior or decrease dysfunctional behavior. It is recommended that positive reinforcers be used to either increase functional behavior or extinguish dysfunctional behavior. Punishment should be used as a last resort. Management at Emery was able to change the dysfunctional behavior through a process of feedback and positive reinforcement with praise and recognition. Finally, the effectiveness of the intervention needs to be tested by evaluating the performance improvement in observable and measurable terms. Emery packers were required to keep a daily checklist of packings and compute the container utilization rate. Almost overnight, the rate jumped up to over 90%, and it held at that rate with the use of continued positive reinforcement.

Since the 1970s, OB Mod programs have been implemented in a wide range of manufacturing, service and not-for-profit organizations throughout the world. Research has shown the approach to positively affect manufacturing productivity, sales performance, customer service, absenteeism, tardiness, and safety. Alex Stajkovic and Fred Luthans conducted a meta-analysis of all the empirical findings of studies conducted from 1975 to 1995 and found an average 17% improvement in performance across all organizations. This varied based on the type of organization and type of reinforcement intervention implemented. For example, the percentage of performance improvement among manufacturing organizations was 33% but only 13% for service organizations. Although monetary reinforcers provided the largest effect for manufacturing organizations, a combination of monetary and performance feedback was more effective in service organizations. Stajkovic and Luthans conducted a second meta-analysis to examine whether the combined reinforcement effects of money, feedback, and social recognition on task performance are additive, redundant, or synergistic (e.g., combined effects are greater than the sum of individual effects). They found that each reinforcer had a significant impact on task performance, but when all three were used in combination, they produced the strongest effects.

OB Mod is not without its critics, however. Edward Lawler and Steven Kerr have noted that process and design problems may limit the effectiveness of different reinforcers. For example, reinforcers may be aimed at the wrong behavior, and this can have inadvertent and even detrimental consequences. Steven Kerr's widely read article, "On the Folly of Rewarding A, While Hoping for B," illustrates this surprisingly common problem, providing examples from the world of politics, medicine, rehabilitations centers, universities, businesses, and even war. For example, he notes that universities hope professors will not neglect their teaching responsibilities but oftentimes reward tenure based on research and publications which take considerable time away from teaching. In addition, Kerr addresses the importance of distributing rewards based on meaningful differences in performance. A 1% variance in a wage increase between high performers and average performers will hardly incentivize employees to go the extra mile. Furthermore, organizations that focus solely on the highly visible or objective behaviors of employees may overlook more subtle indicators of excellent performance which may be difficult to measure, such as creativity or team building.

Other detractors contest the pure behaviorist stance of the theory, suggesting that there are cognitive processes related to thinking and feeling that affect our behavior as well. Reinforcement theory assumes that behavior is based solely on the antecedents and consequences of our actions, and our thoughts and feelings are irrelevant. While this may be plausible for laboratory rats, many critics argue that the behavior of human beings involves a more complex cognitive process.

Importance

Reinforcement theory has been studied for over half a century and supported by the aforementioned work of Skinner, Bandura, Luthans, Kreitner, and many other management scholars who have used it as the foundation of the OB Mod model. Despite Kerr's words of caution, a large body of research has proven that reinforcement theory is an effective way to modify employee behavior. Fortunately, 40 years of research has also provided today's organizations with some general guidelines for proper implementation.

First, managers should only reward, or reinforce, desired behavior and do so as soon as possible after the behavior appears. If rewards are not received right away, then they will not be linked to the behavior, and OB Mod will not be effective. Rewards come in many shapes and sizes and can be both extrinsic (e.g., salary, bonuses, paid vacation) and intrinsic (e.g., recognition, praise). Extrinsic rewards are tangible and can be powerful motivators used to satisfy physical or psychological needs, but they do not provide much information concerning performance. Thus, employees may not know what to do to improve subsequent task performance. Intrinsic rewards, in contrast, do provide more task-specific information that can be used to improve performance. Feedback is an important reinforcer as it provides employees with specific cues as to what was done well and what needs to be done in the future to improve performance. Likewise, social recognition has been increasingly used as a behavioral management intervention in organizations with great success. Research has shown that feedback and social rewards can be just as powerful reinforcers as money, particularly when used in some combination.

Employees need to understand exactly what is expected of them, which is why providing clear goals and objectives is a critical component of the process. Feedback through a review system is essential and should be provided on a timely basis. Objective performance standards that can be measured are advisable, but they should not be used to the detriment of less objective criteria (e.g., finding innovative solutions). Feedback can act as a positive reinforcer in the form of praise, or, as punishment if the employee is reprimanded for not following procedures. Punishment should only be used sparingly, if at all. Punishment should be only for undesirable behavior and done immediately after the offending action, preferably in private. Employees should know exactly why they are receiving disciplinary action.

Finally, it is important to recognize that there are individual differences among employees, and what acts as a positive reinforcer for one employee may not do so for another. Many factors should be considered when selecting rewards, including profession, job level, culture, and employee needs.

Reinforcement theory, at its core, is based on the premise that behavior increases in strength and/or probability when followed by a reinforcer. Luthans and Stajkovic take great care to emphasize that a reinforcer is not the same as a reward. A reward may or may not increase desired behavior, but a reinforcer will always increase the strength and frequency of the functional and performance-related behavior. While many organizations adopt the pay-for-performance approach, proponents of reinforcement theory would advise to *reinforce* for performance to achieve the best results.

Katherine M. Richardson

See also Expectancy Theory; Experiential Learning Theory and Learning Styles; Goal-Setting Theory; Organizational Learning

Further Readings

Cherrington, D. J., Reitz, H. J., & Scott, W. E. (1973). At Emery Air Freight: Positive reinforcement boosts performance. *Organizational Dynamics, 1*(3), 41–50.

Kerr, S. (1975). On the folly of rewarding A, while hoping for B. *Academy of Management Journal, 18*(4), 769–783.

Luthans, F., & Kreitner. R. (1985). *Organizational behavior modification and beyond.* Glenview, IL: Scott, Foresman.

Luthans, F., & Stajkovic, A. D. (1999). Reinforce for performance: The need to go beyond pay and even rewards. *Academy of Management Executive, 13*(2), 49–57.

Miner, J. B. (2002). *Organization behavior: Foundations, theories and analyses.* New York, NY: Oxford University Press.

Rubin, R. S., Bommer, W. H., & Bachrach, D. G. (2010). Operant leadership and employee citizenship: A question of trust? *Leadership Quarterly, 21,* 400–408.

Stajkovic, A. D., & Luthans, F. (1997). A meta-analysis of the effects of organizational behavior modification on task performance, 1975–1995. *Academy of Management Journal, 40*(5), 1122–1149.

Stajkovic, A. D., & Luthans, F. (2003). Behavioral management and task performance in organizations: Conceptual background, meta-analysis, and test of alternative models. *Personnel Psychology, 56,* 155–194.

RESOURCE DEPENDENCE THEORY

Resource dependence theory argues that organizations, as open systems, necessarily transact with other organizations in their environment to obtain the resources necessary for their survival. Such resources include social legitimacy, financing including debt and equity capital, the inputs necessary to produce the products and services offered, and the funds received from the provision of the organization's output to others. These transactions inevitably create power-dependence relationships among the entities because only in very rare cases will the dependence of the focal organization on its transaction partners be identical to their dependence on it. These power-dependence relations subject the focal organization to potential influence and constraint by those that hold power over it because of that dependence. Thus, the argument from resource dependence theory maintains that understanding organizational actions requires examining the pattern of constraints and the preferences of other important actors in the organization's environment—that management behavior can be understood in part as a response to the resource dependencies leaders confront.

The second argument from resource dependence theory holds that organizational leaders seek to create as much autonomy as possible, given the system of interdependent relationships they confront. This autonomy can free them from constraints on their decision making, increase profits, and help ensure the organization's survival. To manage external interdependencies, organizations engage in strategies such as co-opting others onto their boards of directors, merging in an effort to absorb interdependence and gain competitive leverage, forming joint ventures as a strategy of partial cooptation and absorption, and engaging in various forms of political activity, such as lobbying and organizing campaign contributions. Because these actions are presumably designed to mitigate resource dependence and the resulting constraint, patterns of mergers, joint ventures, and co-optive board relationships can be predicted and explained by the pattern of resource dependence a given organization or set of organizations faces.

A third strand of resource dependence theory links the *internal* organizational power of people and subunits to the *external* power-dependence relations that the focal organization faces. The theory argues that those units (and people) that can best cope with the most critical external resource dependencies come to have relatively more power because of that capacity to deal with external threats and constraints. The increased internal power is manifested, for instance, in the proportion of senior leaders with backgrounds from the more powerful units, representation on the board of directors and critical committees, the salaries leaders and frontline employees of the most important units earn, as well as other manifestations of relative status. Therefore, internal organizational power dynamics reflect the external constraints and contingencies organizations confront. This entry shows the arguments and empirical support for the theory, its evolution and relationship to other perspectives on organization-environment interaction, and the critiques and challenges to its approach to organizational analysis.

Fundamentals

The most fundamental idea in resource dependence theory is the organization's dependence on a particular resource. That has typically been measured by the proportion of inputs accounted for by some resource. Because such data are not always available for individual companies, input-output tables, which assess transaction patterns across industry sectors, have typically been employed and analyses of the effects of resource dependence are then conducted at the industry level. Of course a resource can be used a great deal but be less critical, so criticality is a second important dimension, albeit one that is much more difficult to assess and therefore seldom considered in empirical research. And a related but distinct construct is the concentration of control over resources, typically measured by the concentration ratio of the industry from which a given resource comes. The idea is that a given proportion of resources that come from highly concentrated sectors are more problematic in terms of their supply because there are fewer alternative sources.

One hypothesis is that organizations are more attentive to the demands of those in their environment to the extent they provide a higher proportion of resources. For instance, companies are more compliant with governmental preferences—for instance, to invest in economic development areas in Israel or to comply with nondiscriminatory hiring policies in the United States—to the extent that they do a higher percentage of their business with the government.

A second hypothesis is that activities designed to manage resource dependence follow transaction patterns. Thus, interindustry merger frequencies are significantly related to interindustry transaction relationships, with the higher the percentage of transactions occurring with a given other industry, the higher the percentage of mergers that take place with that industry, even after other factors such as profitability and industry concentration are statistically controlled. Similarly, board of director composition tends to follow resource dependencies. Representatives from agricultural organizations are more likely to sit on public utility or hospital boards, as one example, to the extent that agriculture is a more important industry in the relevant local environment. Companies with more leveraged financial structures are more likely to have people from financial organizations on their boards. And on their boards of directors, companies are more likely to have representatives from industries that they engage in a higher proportion of transactions with. Publicly regulated companies, with greater dependence on public support, are hypothesized to have larger boards than companies not publicly regulated, because of the greater need to co-opt important external sources of support.

Third, organizations face competitive interdependence as well as commensal, or buyer-seller, interdependence. At very low levels of industrial concentration, there are too many competitors to absorb or potentially coordinate with. At very high levels of industrial concentration, with only a handful of major industry players, tacit coordination is possible. Thus, it is at intermediate levels of concentration where there is both a greater need for managing competitive interdependence coupled with the possibility of successfully accomplishing this task. Therefore, the hypothesis is that activities such as mergers that are designed to manage competitive interdependence will be higher at intermediate levels of industrial concentration.

The fourth hypothesis relates internal power to external resource dependence and holds that those units that bring in the most external resources possess the most internal power. One interesting manifestation of this effect occurs in universities. In public universities, the overhead associated with grants and contracts are a relatively more important source of money. Those departments, often in the hard sciences, that bring in the most outside research funding with the associated overhead hold more power inside public universities. In private universities, donations are a comparatively larger source of outside funding. Not surprisingly, in private universities, professional schools, such as business, law, and medicine, with their comparatively well-off alumni, have relatively more power compared to other departments than they do in public universities. Or, to take another example, as the strategic dynamics in book publishing have changed and the industry has become more competitive and economically challenged, power has shifted away from those with editorial backgrounds, useful in acquiring books, to people with backgrounds in business, more useful in dealing with the emergent resource dependencies.

Evolution

Resource dependence theory emerged as a natural outgrowth of the increasing interest in the 1960s about the important connections between organizations and their environments. For instance, the structural contingency theory of organizations maintained that whether firms would have more or less bureaucratic arrangements and also have the effectiveness of various structural choices depended on the amount of uncertainty and change in the environment. More uncertain and unstable environments tended to be associated with organizations having less bureaucratic structures, while stable and certain environments were conducive to more formalized, hierarchical and bureaucratic structures. Furthermore, more formalized and hierarchical arrangements were comparatively more effective when the environment was more stable and more certain while less bureaucratic structures performed better in less stable and certain contexts.

Around the same time that structural contingency theory developed, discussions of organizational effectiveness increasingly acknowledged the reality that many and varied external actors impinged on organizations and that these external entities often had inconsistent criteria by which they evaluated the effectiveness of organizational actions. Thus, organizations were linked to their environments, and those environments comprised multiple actors with differing preferences.

A third influence on the development of resource dependence theory was James Thompson's important treatment of organizations. Thompson argued that effective organizational performance virtually required that managers buffer the organization's technical core as much as possible from outside influences. Without such buffering, the pursuit of technical rationality would be diminished as internal organizational decisions would face disruptions and demands that interfered with technically rational choices.

These three ideas—of environmental contingency, the need for buffering, and the incompatible demands of important external actors—constitute the theoretical underpinnings of what became resource dependence theory. The theory also developed partly as a reaction to the emphasis in the leadership literature on the importance of leaders for organizational performance and the explanatory value of leaders' values and personal psychology in understanding organizational decisions. Resource dependence challenged the idea that leaders mattered a great deal in determining what organizations did or in affecting company performance. Instead, the theory argued that organizations were constrained by the preferences and demands of external actors whose importance for organizational survival required that they be taken seriously, rendering internal leader preferences less important as an explanation for organizational decisions and causing performance to reflect primarily the conditions of the environment in which the organization operated. So, for instance, Ronald Burt found that patterns of constraint emanating from conditions of resource dependence predicted profit margins.

The original formulation of resource dependence theory used a relatively crude measure of dependence, namely, the proportion of transactions that occurred with a given other industry. Burt noted that dependence would reflect not just the relative importance of another industry with which the focal organization transacted but also the structural conditions of that industry and, in particular, its degree of economic concentration. If a firm engaged in a lot of transactions with some given other industry, but that industry was relatively unconcentrated, the firm would have many transaction options and would be less dependent on any given firm in that other industry compared to a situation of great industrial concentration such that there would be few other options for the focal firm to use. Burt's use of network methods to better operationalize many of the insights of resource dependence theory marked an important step in the evolution of the theoretical arguments of resource dependence and their operationalization and measurement.

Importance

Resource dependence is considered a "foundational" macro-organizational theory and is among the most cited of all organizational theories. With its focus on mergers, joint ventures, and strategic choice, resource dependence has influenced some elements of strategic management. The emphasis on power dynamics, both internal and external to the focal organization, distinguishes resource dependence from other theories of organization-environment interaction and comports well with observations of the role of power in organizational life. The focus on the importance of the environment as an explanation for behavior is compatible with situational explanations in other social sciences, such as social psychology. And the theory's broad scope in terms of the dependent variables it can and has considered also has added to its appeal.

Several challenges and critiques, however, are important to consider. The population ecology perspective on organizations agrees with resource dependence theory that environmental conditions are important for understanding organizations, but it suggests that organizational forms and arrangements emerge much more through birth and death processes than through strategic managerial choice. Population ecology argues that the degree of managerial discretion implied by resource dependence theory's predictions about managing the environment may hold for some larger organizations but

that most organizations are fairly small, with very limited ability to strategically influence their environments. This challenge implicitly raises the issue of the relative importance of large organizations in the economy—as employers and creators of new jobs and as economic actors—which is itself a subject of considerable debate. On the one hand, there have been significant mergers in industries such as airlines, oil and gas, steel, telecommunications, financial services, and retailing that have clearly resulted in a more concentrated market characterized by large companies possessing seeming strategic discretion. It was, after all, the risky decisions about leverage and loans, made possible by the absence of effective regulation that came from companies' ability to influence the political system, that led to the failures of large financial services organizations and that triggered the deep economic collapse of 2008 and 2009. On the other hand, the proliferation of new organizations in both the profit and nonprofit spheres, the fact that most organizations are small, the importance of entrepreneurial activity for the development of new technologies and even new industries, the fact that large organizations often cut jobs as part of cost-cutting initiatives so that new job creation mostly comes from small businesses, and the fact that incumbent organizations infrequently create or even participate in the next generation of innovative products even in their own industries, means that smaller organizations, with inherently less power, are prominent in the aggregate as economic actors.

A second challenge comes from the argument that even large, economically significant private sector organizations increasingly lack the managerial discretion to do anything other than what the financial markets demand thereby making a core proposition of resource dependence—the idea of managerial strategic choice—increasingly problematic. Gerald Davis has forcefully argued that resource dependence theory developed at a time when predominantly larger private sector organizations enjoyed a degree of managerial autonomy that no longer exists. As such, he maintains the theory was once suited for and a good explanation of the world but that world has fundamentally changed. Financial markets have become increasingly important; companies that do not adhere to the dictates of what analysts and investors want them to do suffer declines in stock price that then make them attractive takeover targets. Takeovers and arbitrage activities know almost no bounds in terms of size, because of the development of the leveraged buyout and private equity industries and the ready availability of debt and equity capital to finance enormous transactions. Consequently, there is no protection for inefficient companies and limits exist on managerial discretion regardless of organizational size. In this view, managerial succession is as much about the ability to please Wall Street as it is about internal power dynamics. Thus, firms are constrained in ways that make responding to resource dependence constraints or achieving autonomy through mergers, joint ventures, or co-optation, using boards of directors, almost impossible.

However, a study by Sydney Finkelstein of one aspect of resource dependence, its predictions about patterns of merger activity, found no evidence that the predictive power of the theory had declined over time. Although one could argue that the growing influence of financial institutions on organizational decision making is just a different manifestation of resource dependence, the problem with this reasoning is that capital seems to be abundantly available. Therefore, resource dependence would maintain that the ability of suppliers of capital to constrain organizational decision making should be diminished, not increased.

A third challenge to resource dependence theory comes from its emphasis on power relations, both externally and internally, as consequential for understanding managerial behavior. Economics emphasizes the importance of efficiency, broadly conceived, as the prevailing logic that explains organizational actions, where efficiency constraints emerge as a consequence of competitive pressures. Actions or structures that do not serve efficiency should, over time, disappear through a process of competitive natural selection. Or, as economist Oliver Williamson has argued, over sufficiently long time horizons, efficiency drives out power as an explanation for behavior. The problem with this critique is that it posits an equilibrium condition and is largely uninterested in departures from the long-run optimal state of affairs, even though apparently irrational behavior (from an efficiency perspective) can and does persist for substantial periods of time. As one example, although studies from both consulting firms and academics consistently report that most mergers fail to achieve economic benefits for the acquiring firm and instead destroy

value, merger activity continues apace. This and similar examples, such as persistent underinvestment in high performance work practices, do call into question whether the economic value-destroying quality of decisions will necessarily curtail their frequency in the presence of strong economic incentives—fees and the fact that executive compensation depends importantly on organizational size—as well as ego and self-enhancement motives to persist in the inefficient behavior.

A fourth challenge to resource dependence comes from its focus on organizations as being central to understanding social life. Donald Palmer and other theorists with a more political, social class perspective argued that rather than being important in their own right, corporations and, for that matter, non-profits were mostly arenas where people of a certain social class came together to develop shared understandings of the world and determine what decisions to make. Instead of emphasizing an imperative for organizational survival and managing dependence, as resource dependence theory does, this alternative perspective emphasizes social class-based dynamics as explanations for organizational behavior. For instance, studies of organizational interlocks noted the effect of shared geography on board composition, arguing that the personal ties among elites was at least as important as organizational dependencies in affecting board structure.

And a fifth challenge to resource dependence theory derives from its very success as a metaphor accounting for much of organizational life. After some initial flurry of activity, empirical research on resource dependence almost disappeared until quite recently. This absence of empirical work has limited further refinement and development of theory after its initial statement. And the failure to pursue a large empirical agenda also has meant that the theory's scope conditions—when it would and, would not, hold—remain largely unexamined. For instance, although as already noted, there is an argument that suggests that resource dependence is particularly relevant in a particular time period, with one exception of a study examining the ability of resource dependence to predict patterns of merger behavior, that argument about the time-dependent character of resource dependence has not been empirically examined.

The absence of empirical work exploring the challenges to resource dependence theory, for instance, studies that investigate its predictive power over time and research that pits resource dependence predictions against alternatives, means that there are many research opportunities that remain.

Jeffrey Pfeffer

See also Business Policy and Corporate Strategy; Contingency Theory; Environmental Uncertainty; Institutional Theory; Stakeholder Theory; Systems Theory of Organizations

Further Readings

Burt, R. S. (1983). *Corporate profits and cooptation,* New York, NY: Academic Press.

Child, J. (1972). Organizational structure, environment and performance: The role of strategic choice. *Sociology, 6,* 1–22.

Davis, G. F. (2009). *Managed by the markets: How finance re-shaped America.* Oxford, England: Oxford University Press.

Finkelstein, S. (1997). Interindustry merger patterns and resource dependence: A replication and extension of Pfeffer (1972). *Strategic Management Journal, 18,* 787–810.

Lieberson, S., & O'Connor, J. F. (1972). Leadership and organizational performance: A study of large corporations. *American Sociological Review, 37,* 117–130.

Palmer, D. (1983). Broken ties: Interlocking directorates and intercorporate coordination. *Administrative Science Quarterly, 28,* 40–55.

Pfeffer, J., & Salancik, G. R. (2003). *The external control of organizations: A resource dependence perspective* (Classic ed.). Stanford, CA: Stanford University Press.

Thornton, P. H., & Ocasio, W. (1999). Institutional logics and the historical contingency of power in organizations: Executive succession in the higher education publishing industry, 1958–1990. *American Journal of Sociology, 105,* 801–843.

RESOURCE ORCHESTRATION MANAGEMENT

Evidence demonstrates that a firm's portfolio of resources, which includes tangible and intangible assets, such as financial, physical, human, and social capital, strongly affects competitive advantage, organizational growth, and performance. However, such portfolios do not simply materialize nor are they self-directing. Resource orchestration describes and examines the roles of managerial actions in the structuring, bundling, and leveraging of the firm's resource portfolio. By synthesizing and extending previous models—David G. Sirmon and colleagues' resource management and Constance E. Helfat and colleagues' asset orchestration—resource orchestration provides a comprehensive treatment of managerial roles, and the synchronization of these actions, in the realization of resource-based competitive advantage and resulting performance outcomes. Moreover, the related empirical results strongly support this logic. This entry explains the fundamentals of resource orchestration by briefly describing its development from previous literatures, current empirical evidence, and directions of future research.

Fundamentals

Resource management focuses on the three major components of managerial action and their attendant subprocesses. The first action, structuring the resource portfolio, provides the "working material" in the resource orchestration model. Specifically, managers either (a) acquire existing resources for various markets or (b) accumulate resources via internal development activities, such as research and development (R & D) investment or training activities. Third, divesting resources is also useful as it may provide cost benefits and, more importantly, may assist the firm in deviating from path-dependent strategies. Bundling resources into capabilities is the second major action in resource orchestration. Managers can bundle resources in three ways. First, they may stabilize existing capabilities with slight improvements in the component resources. Second, they can enrich existing capabilities with more substantial alterations. Or third, they can pioneer new capabilities for the firm. The last major action is leveraging. Here managers mobilize, coordinate, and deploy sets of capabilities for specific market opportunities. Leveraging is where value is finally realized. It is important to note that resource management argues, and evidence supports the logic, that synchronizing a set of actions is more important than the specific choice of subprocesses to engage.

Developed concurrently, the asset orchestration model complemented the resource management model. While asset orchestration did not specify bundling actions, this work suggests that structuring actions should also contain choices related to organizational governance and design, and leveraging should address a concern for innovation. Similarly to resource management, asset orchestration emphasizes that the internal fit or synchronization among processes is vital for positive outcomes. As an integration of these two complementary models, resource orchestration provides a comprehensive framework to guide a growing number of empirical investigations of managerial roles in developing and exploiting a resource-based advantage.

The empirical record of resource orchestration is quite strong. For example, evidence shows that (a) managerial actions mediate the resource and performance relationship; (b) when managers attend to both capability strengths and weaknesses, performance is optimized; (c) resource bundling choices drive important strategic and performance outcomes, especially when considering human capital; (d) managers are able to realize greater value from their resources when they make context-specific resource bundling choices; (e) managerial actions increase in importance as rivals' resource portfolios drive toward parity; (f) managers differ in the quality of their resource orchestration abilities; and (g) synchronization of various subprocesses of resource orchestration leads to successful outcomes, while the lack of synchronization leads to negative results regardless of which action and subprocesses are selected.

Current work aims to extend the scope of resource orchestration. Specifically, ongoing work is focused on understanding resource orchestration across the breadth of business activities, depth of managerial roles within an organization, and across all organizational life cycle stages. In terms of resource orchestration, the breadth of a firm's activities highlights how various corporate- and business-level strategies require and utilize different resources and capabilities. Thus, to implement organizational strategies, such as product diversification, international diversification, differentiation, and cost leadership strategies, resource orchestration actions must provide the appropriate resources. Attempts to engage such strategies with an inappropriate resource portfolio and synchronization of bundling and leveraging will result in ineffective implementation. Beyond the structuring of a portfolio, managers must also integrate across diverse business divisions and locations to promote efficient resource utilization and even find valuable synergy. The duplication of resource sets across strategies provides the basis of cost disadvantages. Moreover, incentives to develop cooperation can help facilitate enriching and pioneering bundling activities, which allow the firm to explore new product and geographic markets.

Resource orchestration actions necessary to develop and implement corporate and business level strategies occur throughout a hierarchy of management. This makes the synchronizing of resource orchestration actions more complicated. Understanding the proper incentives to align managers across levels to promote synchronization is nascent. However, it is argued that achieving synchronization across managerial levels is somewhat dependent on the locus of the initiative (top-down or bottom-up). Regardless of the locus, middle management bears the brunt for achieving resource orchestration synchronization. For example, top-down mandates require middle managers to interpret and direct implementation by overseeing the accumulation and bundling of resources that operational managers utilize. Conversely, in bottom-up flows of variation, middle managers champion effective resource orchestration actions to top managers in order to support their replication across the firm. Fundamentally, synchronizing resource orchestration actions requires middle managers to deeply understand, and be empowered to correct, bidirectional information flows.

Finally, the life cycle stage of a firm affects the relative importance of different resource orchestration actions. Focused on viability in the start-up stage, managers concentrate on structuring a portfolio of resources, which provides relevance and a source of uniqueness relative to rivals. During the growth stage, managers increase their attention on bundling enriched capabilities. Also, managers' skills in developing and maintaining relationships with suppliers, investors, creditors, and others are instrumental to fostering future growth, which in turn require skills in mobilizing and deploying firm resources. The mature stage of a firm's life cycle is characterized by a balance between innovation and efficiency. The bureaucratic structures developed to enable efficient firm growth can limit innovation; therefore, managers actively pursue innovation through pioneering resource bundling. Finally, in a decline stage, managerial attention is paid to both restructuring the firm's portfolios through the investing in new resources and divesting of resource weaknesses and in new leveraging actions to extend the markets of the firm.

David G. Sirmon and
Christina L. Matz

See also Competitive Advantage; Dynamic Capabilities; Environmental Uncertainty; Firm Growth; Management Roles; Resource-Based View of the Firm; Strategic Entrepreneurship

Further Readings

Adner, R., & Helfat, C. E. (2003). Corporate effects and dynamic managerial capabilities. *Strategic Management Journal, 24,* 1011–1025.

Helfat, C. E., Finkelstein, S., Mitchell, W., Peteraf, M., Singh, H., Teece, D., & Winter, S. G. (2007). *Dynamic capabilities: Understanding strategic change in organizations.* Malden, MA: Blackwell.

Holcomb, T. R., Holmes, R. M., & Connelly, B. L. (2009). Making the most of what you have: Managerial ability as a source of resource value creation. *Strategic Management Journal, 30,* 457–485.

Morrow, J. L., Sirmon, D. G., Hitt, M. A., & Holcomb, T. R. (2007). Creating value in the face of declining performance: Firm strategies and organizational recovery. *Strategic Management Journal, 28*(3), 271–283.

Ndofor, H. A., Sirmon, D. G., & He, X. (2011). Firm resources, competitive actions and performance: Investigating a mediated model with evidence from the in-vitro diagnostics industry. *Strategic Management Journal, 32*(6), 640–657.

Sirmon, D. G., Gove, S., & Hitt, M. A. (2008). Resource management in dyadic competitive rivalry: The effects of resource bundling and deployment. *Academy of Management Journal, 51*(5), 919–935.

Sirmon, D. G., & Hitt, M. A. (2009). Contingencies within dynamic managerial capabilities: Interdependent effects of resource investment and deployment on firm performance. *Strategic Management Journal, 30*(13), 1375–1394.

Sirmon, D. G., Hitt, M. A., Arregle, J.-L., & Campbell, J. T. (2010). The dynamic interplay of capability strengths and weaknesses: Investigating the bases of temporary competitive advantage. *Strategic Management Journal, 31*(13), 1386–1409.

Sirmon, D. G., Hitt, M. A., & Ireland, R. D. (2007). Managing firm resources in dynamic environments to create value: Looking inside the black box. *Academy of Management Review, 32*(1), 273–292.

Sirmon, D. G., Hitt, M. A., Ireland, R. D., & Gilbert, B. A. (2011). Resource orchestration to create competitive advantage: Breadth, depth and life cycle effects. *Journal of Management, 37*(5), 1390–1412.

RESOURCE-BASED VIEW OF THE FIRM

According to the resource-based view of the firm (RBV), resources and capabilities are the fundamental sources of firm-level value creation from which firms can create competitive advantages, which may in turn improve their overall performance. Given that predicting and explaining performance differentials among firms is a core objective of strategists, it is perhaps no surprise that the RBV, which provides an intuitively pleasing framework for understanding this outcome, has become one of the most widely accepted theoretical perspectives in the strategic management field, spawning many variants (e.g., knowledge-based view, natural resource-based view) in the process. As such, the RBV is the focus of a long and growing stream of academic studies and is featured prominently in most major strategy textbooks. Notwithstanding the RBV's prominence, it is not without its critics. Due to certain limitations in its articulation and a debatable level of empirical support, many question the RBV's usefulness and validity. In light of this condition, this entry explores the logic, evolution, criticisms, and implications of the RBV.

Fundamentals

The RBV is a theoretical framework for understanding firm-level competitive advantage. The RBV views resources and capabilities as the fundamental sources of value creation and rests on two fundamental assumptions: that resources and capabilities are heterogeneously distributed among firms and that they are imperfectly mobile. These assumptions allow for differences in firm resource endowments to both exist and persist over time.

Given these assumptions, RBV scholars maintain that firms that control (i.e., possess and/or have access to) resources and capabilities that are both valuable and rare can attain a competitive advantage in the short term. RBV scholars also contend that in order to sustain these advantages over time, these resources and capabilities must also be inimitable and non-substitutable. As the mere control over resources and capabilities does not necessarily imply their exploitation, the RBV further specifies that the firm must not only be organized in such a way as to encourage, promote, and facilitate their effective utilization, but also it must possess the capabilities to utilize them in intended ways. Due to the shifting nature of the industries in which all firms compete, the RBV also maintains that firms seeking a sustained competitive advantage (or a series of short-term competitive advantages, which is generally argued to be a more viable strategy) must develop the ability to reconfigure their resource bases in ways that match the extant opportunities and threats in their environments.

Finally, it is important to note that the attainment of a competitive advantage (temporary or sustained) may not always manifest in improved performance as appropriating the resulting economic value at a cost lower than that required to create it may not always be tenable. Thus, while the performance of firms that are able to create resource-based advantages is likely to be greater than the performance of firms that are unable to do so, competitive advantage and performance should not be assumed to be equivalent constructs.

Due to the fact that the RBV was developed as a defiant response to deterministic, environmental models of firm performance, the RBV is largely unconstrained by contextual limitations. In response, most empirical research in the RBV has sought to either control for industry effects or examine firms from a single industry setting. As a result, the RBV has become a widely accepted framework for the identification of *ex post* sources of competitive advantage amid a given context.

Evolution

In order to best understand the central arguments of the RBV, it is helpful to examine the history of the strategic management field. The 1960s saw the origin of the field, then known as business policy. During this decade and into the 1970s, scholars began searching for the sources of competitive advantage. The resulting paradigm, known as

strengths-weaknesses-opportunities-threats (SWOT), suggested that firms that successfully matched their internal strengths with external opportunities while neutralizing external threats and minimizing internal weaknesses would outperform their competitors.

During the 1980s, a fundamental shift occurred in the field. Due to the infiltration of economics, the SWOT framework was replaced by models developed by industrial organization (IO) economists. Scholars such as Michael Porter believed that firms were defenseless against the opportunities and threats that existed in their industry and that their behavior (and performance) were dictated by the structure of the industry. In what became known as the structure-conduct-performance (SCP) framework, IO economists argued that competitive advantage was unsustainable in a perfectly competitive, equilibrium economy where performance differences among competing firms could easily be competed away. Thus, the best a firm could hope for was to achieve competitive parity in the highest performing industry or strategic group.

This line of reasoning did not sit well with those who believed that certain factors internal to the firm were capable of generating different performance levels which could be sustained. Thus, during the latter part of the 1980s, a new group of scholars responded to these deterministic, industry-based models by developing an alternative model of competitive advantage. This theoretical paradigm, which has become known as the RBV, largely ignores the external forces that exist in the economy and instead stresses the importance of internal strengths in determining firm-level competitive advantage.

Although the RBV's assumptions and theoretical relationships were not formally articulated until 1991, the RBV's genesis can be found in the writing of Edith Penrose, who was one of the first scholars to recognize the importance of resources to a firm's competitive position. In 1959, Penrose maintained that a firm consists of a bundle of resources that may contribute to its competitive position (signaled primarily by its growth) if they are exploited in such a manner that their potentially valuable services are made available. Aside from Penrose, Paul Rubin is one of the few scholars to conceptualize firms as resource bundles prior to the formal origins of the RBV. Like Penrose, Rubin recognized that resources were not of much use by themselves; rather, firms must process them in order to access their utility.

Building on the inroads made by Penrose and Rubin, Birger Wernerfelt, in the first attempt at formalizing the RBV, argued that while a firm's performance is driven directly by its ability to sell products and services, it is driven indirectly (and ultimately) by the resources from which they are produced. Given this logic, Wernerfelt proposed that firms may earn profits above that earned by the average competitor by acquiring resources that are critical to the development of demanded products. Because of the novel and abstract nature of Wernerfelt's work, it did not immediately gain support from academics. As such, widespread appreciation for the RBV did not begin to accumulate until several years later with the publication of two seminal papers.

The first was published by C. K. Prahalad and Gary Hamel in 1990. In this paper, Prahalad and Hamel argued that the critical task of management was to create radical new products, which was enabled by the exploitative nature of the firm's core competences. Much like Penrose and Rubin before them, Prahalad and Hamel focused not only on static resources but also on the firm's inimitable skills, technologies, knowledge, and so on, with which they are deployed. Despite the merits of their argument, coupled with the fact that they presented no testable propositions, it was largely ignored at the time by academics.

The second influential paper was published by Jay Barney in 1991. This paper is widely regarded as the first formalization of the then-fragmented resource-based literature into a comprehensive (and thus empirically testable) theoretical framework. Drawing on arguments by Penrose, Wernerfelt, and others, Barney argued that resources (i.e., assets, capabilities, processes, attributes, information, knowledge, etc.) were the fundamental units of value creation within firms. In addition, Barney specified two critical assumptions. First, Barney assumed that resources are heterogeneously distributed among firms, which allowed for the existence of differences in the resource controlled by individual firms. Second, Barney assumed that resources are imperfectly mobile, which allowed for these differences in resource endowments to persist over time.

With these assumptions in place, Barney argued that firms that possess and exploit resources that are simultaneously valuable (i.e., they enable the firm to exploit an opportunity or neutralize a threat in its environment) and rare (i.e., the resource is controlled by a small number of firms) will attain a competitive advantage (i.e., the implementation of a strategy not currently being implemented by other firms that facilitates the exploitation of opportunities and/or the neutralization of competitive threats). While the importance that resources must be valuable may seem rather obvious, that they must also be rare may not be. For Barney, rareness was important given that widely available resources, no matter how valuable, should afford all firms the opportunity to implement identical value-creating strategies and, thus, could only lead to competitive parity.

In addition to the conditions necessary for a firm to achieve a competitive advantage, Barney also articulated the conditions necessary for the firm to maintain an advantage over time. In order to achieve a sustained competitive advantage (i.e., the implementation of a value-creating strategy that current or potential competitors are unable to duplicate), the resources on which the competitive advantage is based must be both inimitable (i.e., firms that do not control the resource face a considerable cost disadvantage in obtaining or developing it) and non-substitutable (i.e., firms that do not control the resource cannot obtain similar benefits from other resources), since otherwise the advantage could easily be competed away. In other words, if valuable, rare resources are not protected from imitation or if other resources can yield equivalent value, the benefits those resources provide to the firm will not remain rare for long.

One of the primary criticisms of Barney's paper was his all-inclusive definition of resources. In response, scholars began to emphasize the difference between tangible and intangible assets (i.e., resources) on the one hand and the processes by which they are exploited (i.e., capabilities) on the other. Another critique of Barney's articulation of the RBV was that it was rather static. Many argued that the process by which resources generate competitive advantage remains in a "black box." In response to this missing link between resource possession and resource exploitation, many scholars have since emphasized that the best performing firms are not merely those who possess better resources but, more importantly, that they use those resources better than competing firms. Subsequently, a great deal of theoretical work began to emerge regarding the types of processes to which resources must be subjected in order to exploit their latent value.

This rediscovered attention to process led to the emergence of three important theoretical approaches within the RBV. The first was Barney's value-rarity-imitability-organization (VRIO) framework. As a follow-up to his 1991 paper, Barney argued that in addition to simply possessing valuable, rare, inimitable (which by then included non-substitutable) resources, a firm also needed to be organized in such a manner (via such mechanisms as structure, control systems, and compensation policies) that it could exploit the full potential of those resources if it were to attain a competitive advantage. In this view, the organization of a firm was considered to be a firm-level orientation, strategy, or context that encouraged a general and unified approach to the utilization of its resources.

Concurrent with the publication of Barney's VRIO framework was a second and radically new theoretical approach that more specifically defined the types of processes by which firms could exploit resources. In their influential 1997 paper, David Teece, Gary Pisano, and Amy Shuen proposed that it was not the resources themselves but rather the firm's ability to integrate, build, and reconfigure resources in response to changes in the firm's environment that enabled firms to outperform competitors. Building on this "dynamic capabilities" framework, Kathleen Eisenhardt and Jeffrey Martin added specificity to the discussion in 2001 by emphasizing that effective execution of a dynamic capability requires knowing both the "ingredients" (the specific components that must be executed) *and* the "recipe" (the manner in which they must be executed).

Most recently, attention has been given to detailing the specific processes by which resources and capabilities are best utilized by managers. In a paper published in 2007, David Sirmon, Michael Hitt, and Duane Ireland argued that managers seeking resource-based advantages must effectively bundle resources and capabilities together via three practices. *Stabilizing practices* enable a firm to maintain the strength of the resources and capabilities in existing bundles. *Enriching practices* enable a firm to add complementary resources and capabilities to existing bundles and/or extend the use of existing bundles into new areas. *Pioneering practices* enable a firm to acquire new resources and capabilities in order to create entirely new bundles.

As is obvious from the above discussion, the RBV has evolved considerably over time. Interestingly, what began as a dynamic understanding of the firm as articulated by Penrose, Rubin, and Prahalad and Hamel, became rather static with the initial formalization of the framework by Barney (no doubt due to the challenge of articulating such a complex set of relationships). Nevertheless, the dynamism that once characterized the RBV has reemerged with the VRIO, dynamic capabilities, and resource management perspectives. While it is now understood that it is necessary for a firm to possess valuable, rare, inimitable, non-substitutable resources and capabilities, it is also understood that such a condition is insufficient. In addition to possessing these ingredients, a firm seeking a competitive advantage must effectively exploit the resources and capabilities it possesses with an eye on continually upgrading them in ways that match the shifting opportunities and threats in the environments in which it competes.

Importance

The RBV has become a dominant theoretical framework upon which thousands of academic journal articles have been grounded and which is prominently featured in virtually all textbooks on strategy. Thus, much of what academics study, write about, and teach managers of today's organizations has been greatly influenced by the RBV. Given this level of acceptance, one might assume that the RBV has received overwhelming support for its central tenets in empirical research. Surprisingly, such is not the case. In fact, of the three scholarly reviews of the results of this research to date, all utilize different methods and draw different conclusions.

In the first assessment of RBV research in 2001, Barney and Asli Arikan conclude that virtually all of the RBV studies with which they were familiar provide results that are consistent with RBV logic. However, Barney and Arikan counted articles as supportive of the RBV if they reported *any* findings consistent with its hypotheses; in so doing, they ignored nonfindings (such as insignificant regression coefficients). Given that most empirical articles fail to find support for *all* hypotheses tested (i.e., some portion of tests will yield insignificant results), Barney and Arikan's study cannot be used (nor was it intended to be used) to assess the actual level of support for the RBV.

In order to more precisely assess support for the RBV, in 2007, Scott L. Newbert analyzed a random sample of RBV studies from which he found that roughly half (53%) of all empirical tests conducted stand in support of the RBV. More importantly, he found that this support varied considerably based on the theoretical approach tested, with tests relying on early incarnations of the RBV receiving far less support than its more recent extensions. Based on these findings, he concluded that a firm's organizing context and its capabilities (dynamic and otherwise) have a far greater effect on its competitive position than its static resources and that, as a consequence, these areas ought to be the focus of future empirical inquiry.

In response to these findings, Russell Crook, David Ketchen, James Combs, and Samuel Todd conducted a meta-analysis of the literature in 2008 and concluded robust support for the RBV. However, because these authors assessed only the relationship between resources and performance, and not the many other relationships that fall under the RBV umbrella as discussed above, their conclusion of support for the RBV as a whole is tenuous.

Ultimately, the RBV is an important and widely regarded theoretical framework that can be used to understand the sources of a firm's competitive position. For managers, this means that the success (or failure) of their firms is largely in their control. Rather than rely on external structural forces to provide opportunities for profit as IO economists would suggest, the RBV allows for the attainment of a competitive advantage on the basis of internal factors. As such, managers who can gain access to valuable, rare, inimitable, and non-substitutable resources and capabilities and organize their organizations in such ways so as to facilitate their exploitation are likely to outperform rivals who are unable to do so. While implementing the prescriptions of the RBV is no small task, it nevertheless provides managers with a framework by which they may exact more control over the performance of their firms as compared to other theories of competitive advantage.

Notwithstanding the promise of the RBV for theory and practice, research on the more recent extensions of the RBV, which seem to hold the most promise for understanding this real-world phenomenon, is still in its infancy. With increased empirical inquiry into these theoretical advances, we will no doubt improve the precision with which this important theoretical perspective is tested and in turn enhance our understanding of how and to what degree resources and capabilities facilitate the attainment and sustainability of firm-level competitive advantage.

Scott L. Newbert

See also Competitive Advantage; Dynamic Capabilities; Knowledge-Based View of the Firm; Strategic Groups; SWOT Analysis Framework

Further Readings

Barney, J. B. (1991). Firm resources and sustained competitive advantage. *Journal of Management, 17,* 99–120.

Eisenhardt, K. M., & Martin, J. A. (2000). Dynamic capabilities: What are they? *Strategic Management Journal, 21,* 1105–1121.

Newbert, S. L. (2007). Empirical research on the resource-based view of the firm: An assessment and suggestions for future research. *Strategic Management Journal, 28,* 121–146.

Penrose, E. T. (1959). *The growth of the firm.* New York, NY: Wiley.

Prahalad, C. K., & Hamel, G. (1990). The core competence of the corporation. *Harvard Business Review, 68,* 79–91.

Priem, R. L., & Butler, J. E. (2001). Is the resource-based "view" a useful perspective for strategic management research? *Academy of Management Review, 26,* 22–40.

Rubin, P. H. (1973). The expansion of firms. *Journal of Political Economy, 84,* 936–949.

Sirmon, D. G., Hitt, M. A., & Ireland, R. D. (2007). Managing firm resources in dynamic environments to create value: Looking inside the black box. *Academy of Management Review, 32,* 273–292.

Teece, D. J, Pisano, G., & Shuen, A. (1997). Dynamic capabilities and strategic management. *Strategic Management Journal, 18,* 509–533.

Wernerfelt, B. (1984). A resource-based view of the firm. *Strategic Management Journal, 5,* 171–180.

ROLE THEORY

Role theory is based on the concept that individual behavior in social settings is governed by perceptions of role, a socially constructed position, or category, such as "spouse" or "manager." Connecting theories of social structure and individual behavior, role theory explains how actors translate perceived societal norms and expectations into scripts for action in a given context. Role theory extends to all realms of social life, including family, religion, and political settings, and it is of no less importance for the management of organizations. The concept of role is necessary in any system, from small groups to global economies, predicated upon a division of labor across constituents. It is also essential to the persistence of organizations over time; individuals may join or depart, but roles endure and establish continuity. This entry will explore the key features of role theory and their relation to organizational functioning, outline the development of different perspectives on roles, and specify how an appreciation for the elements of role theory can benefit managers seeking to build high-performing work teams and organizations.

Fundamentals

A *role* is a position constructed within a larger social system. It is constructed in the sense that normative expectations specify a range of obligatory, acceptable, and prohibited conduct on the part of individuals inhabiting the role, otherwise known as *actors*. Actors' perceptions and interpretations of others' expectations lead them to generate scripts for action in a situation, which they follow as they play or perform their role. These expectations govern interaction with other members of the social system, as actors attempt to conform to expectations, in order to garner rewards for doing so or to avoid sanctions for unacceptable behavior. An actor may occupy several roles simultaneously, although one role will be dominant in providing the scripts for a performance; for example, parents do not cease to be mothers or fathers while at the workplace, yet their professional roles will be of greater importance in directing behavior at the weekly staff meeting. Thus, role theory explains why different individuals behave similarly in a social context (when they occupy the same role), as well as why the same individual may behave very differently across contexts (in playing different roles).

Role theory is relevant in various ways to the functioning of organizations. First, a role does not exist in isolation; it is only meaningful when situated within a network of connected roles. The collection of positions in the network that both influence and depend upon a role is referred to as the *role set*. The ability of actors to understand their place in a role set is essential to achieving organizational objectives; consider the futility of an auto assembly line where all workers individually attempt to construct a vehicle from scratch. Successful performances require an actor to engage in *role-taking*, seeing his or her role as it is seen by others and responding accordingly. Feedback from role set members can lead actors to revise their scripts to ensure more acceptable performances in the future. These scripts guide role performances even as actors perform by themselves: Actors learn to conduct themselves as though engaging with a generalized other, a composite of the expectations of their organizational community. From drafting a memo for a companywide audience to editing a report, much of the performance of a role takes place with the generalized other in mind.

A key distinction in role theory exists between *positional roles* created and formally recognized by the organization and *functional roles* that arise from group interaction. Positional roles are captured in job titles and reporting relationships diagrammed on organizational charts. Tasks and obligations associated with these roles are cataloged in performance objectives and used to evaluate role occupants. Such measures heighten consensus in regard to the expectations of multiple actors concerning the same role. Actors thus play roles with greater certainty in expected behaviors, as members of the role set coordinate performances on the basis of shared expectations. Positional roles enable continuity in the organization; as personnel change, new actors conform to existing roles and produce performances acceptable to role set members. Role continuity provides stability, although this may become problematic under conditions of rapid change and uncertainty. If patterns of rewards and sanctions for roles do not reflect changes in the environment, actors may adhere to codified expectations regardless of the impact on organizational performance.

Functional roles, in contrast, result from social interactions that are not formally specified by the organization but are no less necessary for its operation. Work teams may include positions, such as supervisor, business analyst, and data entry specialist, but these roles do not provide scripts for responding to every operational contingency. In pursuit of a specific objective, individuals may take on functional roles of project leader, subject matter expert, or external liaison. These roles may be isolated to a single initiative, but to the degree that they are affirmed in repeated interactions, they can come to exert a more powerful influence on subsequent performances than the formal positions that actors occupy, especially when the titles or responsibilities of those positions are largely symbolic. Thus, the everyday performance of roles in organizations is as much about *role-making* as traditional notions of *role-playing,* if not more so. To this end, actors take part in an ongoing negotiation with members of a shifting role set, learning standards of acceptable performance within a community while also defining opportunities for personal variation. This approach can be seen in the practice of job crafting, where role occupants fulfill the basic expectations of a role while adding new features that provide enhanced personal meaning.

The potential for role-making highlights another important consideration in role theory, namely, the presence of functional and symbolic aspects of a role, both for the actor and the organization. Thus far, the discussion has emphasized the functional performances necessary for the organization to achieve its stated operational goals; from the actor's perspective, functional rewards for conformity are usually conceived of in instrumental terms, in the form of financial rewards, job promotions, and hierarchical status. However, organizations also need actors to fill representational roles that satisfy expectations for symbolic value. Consider the founder of a cutting-edge technology start-up: Depending on whether the organization succeeds or fails, he may be cast into the role of visionary leader or irresponsible crackpot, respectively. Either way, the role provides meaningful symbolism demanded by the organization's stakeholders. The symbolism offers targets upon which those inside and outside the organization can express positive or negative reactions to the organization and its activities.

The symbolic function of roles is important for actors as well as for the organization and its stakeholders. Because of the importance accorded to work in modern society, occupational roles play a critical part in the formation of identity. Positional roles that are held in high regard (e.g., physician, CEO) confer status on the occupant, and the successful performance of any role is associated with increased esteem from an actor's peers or other role set members. Even in roles that lack prestige, individuals may join with actors occupying similar roles

to develop identities that accord positive meaning to their work. This practice has been observed in occupations such as sanitation worker or gravedigger, roles that are often symbolically stigmatized as "dirty" by the rest of society. Unable to create a positive identity in such roles, actors may conform to expectations, not to earn approval but to accumulate goodwill in the form of idiosyncrasy credits, enabling them to engage in a certain amount of deviant behavior and express other desired identities within a role without sanction from their role set.

Playing a role may present challenges for actors even when the role is associated with desirable identities and a high level of consensus exists. *Role strain* occurs when various sets of expectations associated with the role interfere with one another. Frontline supervisors, for example, may be expected to perform large amounts of analytical work in addition to their managerial duties. Those managerial tasks may also contain contradictions, requiring supervisors to serve as mentor, coach, and disciplinarian. Strain can arise in balancing representational and functional aspects of the role as well. Managers may welcome the opportunity to perform as leaders, inspiring and motivating employees to exceptional levels of performance, yet they still must fulfill the routine administrative functions expected of their role. Role strain can be relieved to a degree through increased differentiation, creating more roles with constrained expectations. However, this creates extra work for role set members who must coordinate performances with additional actors, as well as for role occupants further up the organizational hierarchy as they become responsible for integrating the functions of a greater number of subordinates.

While role strain represents competing expectations within a role, *role conflict* is a case where expectations associated with multiple roles are incompatible. Conflicts may arise between roles within an organization, for instance, a positional role as full-time human resources (HR) representative that must be performed alongside a functional role as leader of an ad hoc committee to overhaul the organization's payroll system. Often, conflicts exist when expectations linked to occupational roles and family roles (e.g., spousal or parental roles) are at odds. Actors may be forced into undesirable choices between the demands of the two salient, but distinct, role sets. At the same time, if roles are seen as complementary, such that the financial benefits of employment allow an actor to fulfill a provider role in the family, the possibility for role enrichment exists. The effects of occupational roles on nonwork roles, and the corresponding potential for both role conflict and role enrichment, have been the subject of considerable interest in the area of work-life balance.

Evolution

Ideas that figure prominently in the theory of roles, such as the division of labor or bureaucratic systems that separate office from officeholder, can be traced back to the political philosophy of Adam Smith in the 18th century and to 19th-century sociologists Émile Durkheim and Max Weber. It was not until the early 20th century, however, that social scientists would come to establish theories primarily concerned with the concept of role.

Interactionist role theory originated in the writings of George Herbert Mead, who saw roles in terms of the negotiated relationships of actors creating and refining their social world. The metaphors of "role" and "actor" were taken to their greatest extension by sociologist Erving Goffman, who characterized all social life as theatre, with actors dependent upon one another to execute performances faithfully so that the production could continue with minimal disruption. While few modern theorists adhere to such an extreme position, an interactionist view persists in theories that describe roles emerging from repeated patterns of interaction and persists in recent work on role-making, job crafting, and the enactment of identities through role performances.

At midcentury, Talcott Parsons and other sociologists expanded on earlier work by anthropologist Ralph Linton, articulating functionalist theories based on roles as positions within a stable social system and performance as conformity to the expectations of society in general and to role sets in particular. This perspective influenced organizational researchers focused on how actors managed role strain and role conflict to achieve desirable outcomes for their organization and for themselves. Functionalist theories of role can be seen in research on management and job design that emphasize the formal specification of responsibilities and expectations for acceptable role performance.

Role theory was explicitly grounded in organizational behavior through the work of Daniel Katz and Robert Kahn. They defined roles in terms of patterns of behavior, developed from specific task requirements, which are associated with positions in an organizational system. Roles thereby provide the avenue through which organizational members participate in daily activities or work. From this perspective, role behavior consists of the recurring actions of individuals, interrelated with the repetitive activities of others in the service of predictable outcomes. Roles thus serve as the building blocks of organizations. They are regulated by norms, the general expectations for role occupants. Through collective awareness of norms, organizational members develop shared expectations for themselves and others that guide predictable routines. These seminal ideas form the foundation for organizational role theory.

Scholars of recent work in role theory have attempted to reconcile views of role as either dynamically constituted (and reconstituted) through interpersonal interaction or imposed through societal structure and demands for conformity. Theorists such as Ralph Turner and Bruce Biddle have described the reciprocal process whereby relevant others provide information regarding expectations, which actors perceive with varying degrees of accuracy, interpret in light of other roles and associated expectations, and subsequently incorporate into their scripts and performances. Feedback from role set members begins the process all over again. This view has strong connections to cognitive theories of social behavior that detail processes of learning and development based on observation of social referents and the incorporation of iterative feedback into modified behavior. Research in this vein focuses on individual perceptions and interpretations of social expectations, as well as on the degree of ambiguity and consensus in those expectations.

Importance

Role theory provides the underpinnings for some of the most important work in management theory. For example, theories of job design emphasize the need to clearly define tasks and responsibilities associated with work roles, in addition to specifying performance expectations. These directives are supported by research on role ambiguity and its negative effects on performance and job satisfaction. Leaders are directed to ensure that team members are aware not only of their inclusion in a team but also of the roles that they have been selected to fill on the basis of their skills and knowledge. As teams undertake their performances, leaders facilitate integration with the role set, helping to both identify stakeholder expectations and communicate performance feedback to the team.

From an interactionist perspective, role theory is linked to research in the areas of identity and engagement. Actors will engage in a role to the extent that it allows them to express preferred identities through their performances. Absent these opportunities, actors will satisfy basic expectations but are unlikely to fully engage. In some cases, actors will not be satisfied with the expressive potential of their role as specified by the organization and will undertake job crafting to fashion positive identities, either by changing the tasks associated with the role, the manner in which they are performed, or, at the very least, reconceptualizing the meaning of those performances. These findings have implications for job design as well, namely, that managers hoping to elicit full employee engagement must provide opportunities to enact desirable identities through role performances. This approach goes beyond traditional concepts of recognition and prestige and can involve helping actors perceive the significance of their performance outside the immediate role set or leaving room within formal specifications for individual variation in performance. Managers willing to provide this latitude may discover the capacity for positive deviance, as actors augment their roles with additional tasks and prosocial behaviors.

Finally, role theory is at the heart of recent inquiries into work-family balance and how organizations can develop policies that help actors balance the expectations of professional and family roles. Managers should not assume that these roles are necessarily in conflict as evidence suggests that successful performance and positive feedback in family roles may enrich the performances of work roles, and vice versa, provided that expectations concerning acceptable performances can be conceptualized as complementary. Research indicates, however, that this is more easily accomplished for men, who reconcile roles as professionals and as providers, than for women, who seek to balance roles as careerists and caretakers. While work in this area continues, the message to managers is that one-size-fits-all policy approaches are likely to be flawed, and that actors should be involved in developing programs and setting expectations regarding work-family balance.

Role theory provides a valuable perspective on the reciprocal influence of social structure and individual behavior in organizations, as actors translate expectations into scripts for performance, while modifying those expectations and the definition of their roles through subsequent performances. The insights generated by role theory demonstrate the need for managers to account for the structural design of role expectations and relationships, as well as the ongoing change and construction that help actors respond to the situational demands of role performance and craft desirable identities within roles.

Steven Fellows and William A. Kahn

See also Management Roles; Norms Theory; Personal Engagement (at Work) Model; Social Exchange Theory; Systems Theory of Organizations

Further Readings

Ashforth, B. E., & Kreiner, G. E. (1999). "How can you do it?": Dirty work and the challenge of constructing a positive identity. *Academy of Management Review, 24,* 413–434.

Biddle, B. J. (1986). Recent developments in role theory. *Annual Review of Sociology, 12,* 67–92.

Goffman, E. (1959). *The presentation of self in everyday life.* New York, NY: Doubleday Anchor.

Kahn, W. A. (1990). Psychological conditions of personal engagement and disengagement at work. *Academy of Management Journal, 33,* 692–724.

Katz, D., & Kahn, R. L. (1978). *The social psychology of organizations* (2nd ed.). New York, NY: Wiley.

Mead, G. H. (1934). *Mind, self, and society.* Chicago, IL: University of Chicago Press.

Rothbard, N. P. (2001). The dynamics of engagement in work and family roles. *Administrative Science Quarterly, 46,* 655–684.

Sveningsson, S. F., & Alvesson, M. (2003). Managing managerial identities: Organizational fragmentation, discourse, and identity struggle. *Human Relations, 56,* 1163–1193.

Turner, R. H. (2002). Role theory. In J. H. Turner (Ed.), *Handbook of sociological theory* (pp. 233–254). New York, NY: Kluwer Academic/Plenum.

Wrzesniewski, A., & Dutton, J. E. (2001). Crafting a job: Revisioning employees as active crafters of their work. *Academy of Management Review, 26,* 179–201.

S

SCHEMAS THEORY

Schemas (also schemata or schema) theory can be defined as a set of ideas related to the cognitive structures that help individuals order, present, evaluate, and apply human knowledge and skills by dividing available information into meaningful units. This constructivist approach is important in many areas of modern life, including management, as it organizes past experiences in order to understand new situations and to make novel positions and environments more familiar—for example, by reducing ambiguity and enhancing comprehension. This entry approaches the complexities of schemas theory and its application in management by presenting the basic notions of schemas, together with the history of schema foundation and its relation to other theories and various types of schemas, paying special attention to the schemas related to business and organizational studies.

Fundamentals

The origins of schemas theory can be traced back to the 18th century, to the writings of Immanuel Kant, who discussed the allocation of experience into the concepts of higher order. Although philosophy provided the foundations for schemas theory, it is psychology that is most strongly correlated with schemas. The traces of schemas theory can be observed in the works of the first Gestalt psychologists, who researched the role of context in interpretation. Another area of study that has contributed to many research points in schemas theory is cognitive psychology—for example, in the investigation of the application of already-possessed knowledge to deduce and categorize new information. The 20th century was prolific in the writings of psychologists whose findings are used in schema theory, such as the work of Jean Piaget on infants or in the study by Frederic Bartlett on memory. Apart from psychology that simultaneously supplies knowledge to schema theory and benefits from its tenets, schema approaches are applicable in various fields of study, including sociology, linguistics, and law. Since schemas are created and stored in the brain, researchers engaged in neuroscience are also interested in using this approach to discuss mental functions, for example. As far as management is concerned, most organizational studies on schema theories are centered on the role of information and knowledge in the life of organizations. Among others, one field of organizational study that makes use of schema theory is public relations, with the application of schema approach to observe the reaction of stakeholders to media coverage and its implication for organizational communication. Advertising also benefits from schemas, which are used to persuade customers to buy certain products or services, by inducing certain moods, attitudes, and needs. Moreover, schemas are also used in intercultural communication, branding, and marketing to study the cultural differences of workers and stakeholders and their implications for the performance of organizations. Looking at schemas from the individual perspective of workers, schemas serve at least two functions for employees since they allow them to comprehend organizational events and they provide information on required organizational behavior.

Types of Schemas

According to many classifications of schemas, they can be divided into person schemas, group schemas, self-schemas, role schemas, event schemas, and content-free schemas. *Person schemas* provide information on various types of individuals and facilitate the understanding of people's behavior. *Group schemas* (stereotypes) are related to group affiliations, including information, among others, on the race, ethnicity, and religion of constituting members. *Self-schemas* concern individual self-knowledge that makes a person behave consistently with one's opinions and beliefs. *Role schemas* are connected with information on social roles and concern mostly occupational duties or functions in various groups, teams, classes, or clubs. *Event schemas* (also called scripts or event sequences) provide the user with data on the order of actions in daily activities and some special or official situations, such as weddings, funerals, or job interviews. As far as the elements of event sequences are concerned, the scripts contain the theme, typical roles, entry conditions, and the order of actions. *Content-free schemas* deal with some information about the links between entities and elements, but not the content itself. What they stress are the relations among people and things and how these relationships and dependencies determine systems.

Organizational Schemas

In-organization schemas include self-in-organization schemas, person-in-organization schemas, organization schemas, object/concept-in-organization schemas, and event-in-organization schemas. *Self-in-organization schemas* are connected with how individuals view themselves in organizational environments, including aspects such as personality, values, roles, and behavior. These schemas help individuals react to organizational impulses by taking into account one's personal opinion on his or her position within the organization. *Person-in-organization schemas* are the memories, opinions, and expectations on some individuals or groups of people. These schemas help individuals understand organizational reality by assigning people to various organizational schemas—for example, regarding their position in a hierarchy. *Organization schemas* mirror how organizational culture is present in employees' or stakeholders' cognition by referring to the image or identity of organizations perceived by individuals. *Object/concept-in-organization schemas* concern organizational knowledge from the individual perspective that may vary among employees and stakeholders. *Event-in-organization schemas* are connected with one's knowledge on organizational social meetings. They may entail events such as organizational anniversaries or national holidays.

Since individual and social factors determine the schemas of particular organizations, the strength of schemas depends on their internal features as well as external environmental factors. When taking into account the personal sphere of organizational schemas, factors such as an individual's attention or motivation, past experience and future expectations, and upbringing, education, and social/professional situation can be enumerated. When analyzing meso-factors, issues such as types of organizations, their performance and goals, can be taken under closer scrutiny. In the case of a macro level, environmental factors such as the social, cultural, or political situation on the national or international level determine the characteristics of organizational schemas. Taking into account the strength of knowledge schemas (or scripts), they can be divided into weak and strong scripts. *Weak scripts* provide information on the behavioral events that are likely to happen, whereas *strong scripts* additionally help predict the future sequence of activities. As far as script usage is concerned, knowledge schemas can be used unconsciously (*automatic script processing*) and consciously (*controlled script processing*).

Schemas theory can be used by modern managers to be more effective at both the individual and organizational level since cognitive knowledge allows them to understand and shape their own performance as well as comprehend, predict, and facilitate various organizational behaviors.

Magdalena Bielenia-Grajewska

See also Actor-Network Theory; Behavioral Theory of the Firm; Critical Management Studies; Cultural Values; Meaning and Functions of Organizational Culture; Role Theory; Social Cognitive Theory

Further Readings

Brewer, W. F., & Nakamura, G. V. (1984). *The nature and functions of schemas*. Washington, DC: National Institute of Education.

Bridges, J. A., & Nelson, R. A. (2000). Issues management: A relational approach. In J. A. Ledingham & S. D. Bruning (Eds.), *Public relations as relationship management: A relational approach to the study and practice of public relations* (pp. 95–115). Mahwah, NJ: Lawrence Erlbaum.

Delamater, J. D., & D. J. Myers. (2007). *Social psychology*. Belmont, CA: Wadsworth Cengage Learning.

Fiske, S. T., & Morling, B. A. (2004). Schemas/schemata. In A. S. R. Manstead & M. Hewstone (Eds.), *The Blackwell encyclopedia of social psychology* (pp. 489–494). Malden, MA: Blackwell.

Gioia, D. A., & Poole, P. P. (1984). Scripts in organizational behavior. *Academy of Management Review, 9*(3), 449–459.

Goldstone, R., & Gureckis, T. (2010). Schema. In P. C. Hogan (Ed.), *The Cambridge encyclopedia of the language sciences* (pp. 725–726). New York, NY: Cambridge University Press.

Harris, S. G. (1994). Organizational culture and individual sensemaking: A schema-based perspective. *Organization Science, 5*(3), 308–321.

Kellogg, R. T. (2003). *Cognitive psychology*. Thousand Oaks, CA: Sage.

Nishida, H. (1999). A cognitive approach to intercultural communication based on schema theory. *International Journal of Intercultural Relations, 23*(5), 753–777.

Velasco Sacristán, M. S., & Cortes de Los Rios, M. E. (2009). Persuasive nature of image schematic devices in advertising: Their use for introducing sexism. *Revista Alicantina de Estudios Ingleses, 22*, 239–270.

SCIENTIFIC MANAGEMENT

The theory of scientific management (or "Taylorism") is most closely associated with Fredrick W. Taylor (1856–1815), who is generally considered the founding father not only of scientific management (as he called it) but also of management studies. Scientific management theory examines how to hierarchically structure factory organization and how to design job functions for factory workers, clerical employees, and operational, factory managers, the latter being conceptualized by Taylor as "functional foreman." The ultimate purpose of the theory is to resolve, through proper incentives, potential conflict in interactions between employees and managers / employers. A key proposition of scientific management is to precisely set out job structures by defining in great detail job content, job accomplishment targets, work tools, time allowed to complete a job, and so on. Taylor conducted in this respect many "scientific" experiments in the factory to specify these job elements—for instance, through his famous/infamous stop-watch experiments. This led to widespread criticism of Taylor as mechanizing and dehumanizing work performance and entertaining a rather dark, mechanistic image of human nature. This was also a key issue of investigation when Taylor was summoned by the U.S. Congress to testify on the nature and program of scientific management. Scientific management theory has withstood the test of time with a very consistent body of ongoing research connecting to it, evaluating it, adopting it, and critiquing it, in fields as varied as organization theory (organizational economics, organization sociology, organization psychology, organizational anthropology, etc.), human resource management theory, business history research, the engineering sciences, and many others. In general, for many discussions of management theory, Taylor's scientific management provides a starting point, a key reference point for critique and criticism or a point of comparison for developing agreeing or contrasting approaches to management studies. The subsequent discussion first analyzes the key theoretical features of scientific management. A second section deals with the historical evolution of scientific management and contemporary applications of this theory. A third section argues for the continued importance and relevance of scientific management, for the need to understand its key ideas and key premises but also to clarify certain misunderstandings that Taylor may have had when formulating and proposing his theory. This is important for both the further development of management theory and the understanding of and application of (elements of) scientific management in contemporary management practice.

Fundamentals

Taylor's works are viewed by many as the origin and starting point of modern management theory. Scientific management theory emerged in force in the last decades of the 19th century and the early decades of the 20th century in the United States. The typical corporate organizations Taylor encountered were companies that nowadays would be considered small-sized factories in the manufacturing sector, such as the steel industry. This type of small-scale factory organization began to replace in Taylor's time very loosely coordinated structures, which only linked together a very small number of workers, mainly independent entrepreneurs.

A key starting premise of Taylor's research was that workers tried to avoid and minimize work contributions in the factory. He spoke of *soldiering* in this respect, and broke down this idea into two elements: *natural soldiering* and *systematic soldiering*. By natural soldiering he meant work-avoiding behaviors that were "inborn" to humans, a natural inclination to laziness. Systematic soldiering, on the other hand, reflected a systemic problem of factory organization and management practice. He argued in this connection that ill-designed organization and management structures, which left workers to conceive their own jobs while rewards were fixed at the same time, were to blame for work performance problems on the side of employees.

Taylor's concept of natural soldiering has led to widespread criticism that scientific management entertained a rather negative image of human nature, the worker being portrayed as lazy, opportunistic, and work avoiding. Early on, Elton Mayo led the human relations school in developing this criticism. Many later publications in fields such as organization psychology, organization sociology, industrial relations, and a significant amount of research in postmodern and critical management theory have advanced this position, too. If Taylor's writings are taken at face value, this criticism has to be accepted. However, one can argue that Taylor fell for a self-misunderstanding when he introduced the idea of natural soldiering. Various points support this critical line of argumentation.

First, Taylor entertained in his theory the idea of systematic soldiering, which directed management research and management intervention toward a systemic problem (of ill-designed organization and management structures) but not at the human condition; only the latter would conceptualize workers as "naturally lazy." From his conception and intervention strategies with management practice, as spelled out below regarding training systems, job structures,

organizational hierarchy, and incentive systems, it is rather obvious that his theory was concerned with the systemic side of management, or the "logic of the situation," to use a key phrase of Taylor's. The idea of natural soldiering represents in this reading an unnecessary conceptual disconnect and distraction in his theory.

Second, the argument that Taylor fell for a self-misunderstanding regarding the idea of natural soldiering receives further support from an economic reconstruction of scientific management. Economics, conventionally understood, applies ideas such as self-interest or even opportunism and predation behavior, to follow the writings of Oliver Williamson and James Buchanan, in order to develop conceptual proposals, in *systemic* perspective (with regard to "economic institutions"): The purpose is to prevent self-interest, opportunism, or predation to derail cooperation among interacting parties. In organizational economics, the idea of self-interest constitutes a merely pre-empirical, heuristic method for analyzing potential cooperation problems, but not an empirical statement about human nature as such. This type of methodological argument can be transferred to Taylor's concept of soldiering. Seen from this perspective, it becomes clear that all Taylor was after by invoking the idea of soldiering, even in its version as natural soldiering, was to develop *systemic* analysis and proposals to prevent any such problems (but not to interfere with the human condition in workplace organization, for instance, through sociopsychological strategies or other behavioral approaches).

Training Systems, Job Structures, and Organizational Hierarchy

For factory workers, clerical employees, and operational factory managers ("functional foremen"), scientific management set out in great detail how job structures were to be improved and specified; how job structures were to be hierarchically governed through the system of functional foremanship, which saw functionally specialized foremen interacting with and supervising workers; and how training and skills management was to be systematically provided to organization members (factory workers, clerical employees, the functional foremen).

The skills formation problem encountered by Taylor in the factory of the late 19th and early 20th centuries was of a comparatively simple nature. The typical employee who entered the Taylorite factory then basically came with no industrial skills. Taylor's key methods to raise skills levels focused on job conception and the standardization of work procedures, tool usage, support processes to job execution, and so forth, as well as an increase in the functional specialization of skills. Through various, detailed individual case studies, Taylor outlined how individuals who had entered the factory with no or very low skills could be trained to do jobs at a considerably higher level of skills formation and skills application. The same approach applies, in principle, to what Taylor said about clerical employees and the functional foremen, although a considerable amount of his research and writings focused on factory workers.

A deskilling and degrading thesis has been prominently associated with scientific management, explicitly so by Harry Braverman from the 1970s onward, but indirectly already by the human relations school, and possibly as early as by the U.S. congressional committee that questioned Taylor in 1911/1912. Critical comments apply. The typical employees who entered the Taylorite factory were not craftsmen but unskilled immigrants, former slaves, or former farm workers. In addition, and as outlined, Taylor had a very distinctive program for skills development. This admittedly was of a comparatively simple nature, but it reflected the historic societal and business context in which industrial and management organization took root.

Incentive Systems

Scientific management proposed a distinctive system of incentives management, including a premium wage system, but also nonfinancial rewards, such as the reduction of work time, the provision of educational and recreational facilities, housing facilities, and other benefits. Taylor's key argumentation was in this respect that these incentives should *not* be uniformly provided to employees but in strict relation to work contributions and skills development. In this way, the "employee condition" or what Taylor otherwise termed *soldiering* should be systemically resolved.

Taylor's approach to handling and theorizing about incentive systems and how they were to be used in systemic perspective—to reduce problems arising from lack of skills in the factory, and the potential condition of soldiering—compares well to modern institutional and constitutional economic literature on the principal-agent problem. Some key writers in this tradition are James Buchanan and Oliver Williamson. Taylor explicitly spoke of potentially antagonistic (self-)interests of workers and employers, which caused conflict in the factory, and his key solution to this problem was to propose organization systems that incentivized work contributions with rewards so that the interests of employees and employers became aligned. Modern institutional economics uses in this connection the concept of *incentive-compatible* economic institutions, to apply a term of Williamson's. As a result, cooperation and mutual gains (win-win outcomes) materialize for the parties involved. What Taylor called the employee condition is then resolved in economic, systemic terms. Scientific management reflects in this respect a mutual gains model with a pluralistic understanding of industrial democracy. As such, its association with a so-called unitary ideology, as it has been promoted by some in the industrial relations literature can be called into question.

An institutional economic reconstruction of scientific management easily succeeds in this manner, demonstrating that Taylor anticipated many ideas of modern institutional economic theory and even some of its pitfalls, especially regarding the concept of natural soldiering, which can be found, in different albeit comparable terminology in some modern economic research on empirically (mis-)claimed, lazy, opportunistic "human nature."

The Managerial Condition: Hearty Cooperation

Taylor had a clear understanding that deep conflicts of interest existed between employees and managers/employers. He was very much aware that cooperation in an organization could be derailed (through soldiering) not only by workers/employees but also by the top company managers/employers. For instance, Taylor argued that incentives allocated to workers for sustained and high-skills contributions needed to be permanent, and it should not be feasible that raised rewards be taken back by management ad hoc. In distinction from the employee condition, however, Taylor targeted the managerial condition nearly exclusively in empirical behavioral, sociopsychological terms but not in economic ones.

He proposed the concept of *hearty cooperation,* to be achieved through the "great mental revolution of managerial attitudes." In this manner, he aimed to resolve the managerial condition. No systemic, economic proposals were put forward to handle this conflict problem and to prevent managers/employers already on grounds of self-interest to renege on incentive promises that had been made to employees.

As indicated above, Taylor did not clearly understand the need and purpose of differentiating natural soldiering from systemic soldiering. When conceptualizing the employee condition, this lack of understanding in relation to empirical, behavioral concepts did not derail his theory since he basically applied the concept of soldiering in economic terms (as "systematic soldiering") and thus could successfully deal with the problem of employee opportunism, as outlined above. Regarding the managerial condition, however, his lacking understanding of how to conceptually handle soldiering had graver consequences since he erred on the side of sociopsychological and sociological proposals in order to conceptually handle this issue. As laudable as behavioral proposals may be in themselves, they are noneconomic and do not resolve basic problems of underlying (interest) conflicts that relate to the guarantee of incentives and the systemic economic resolution of conflicting interests between employees and managers.

In terms of practical problems, Taylor realized with hindsight that the real implementation problems and cooperation conflicts that management encountered in his time were caused by management, not by workers. The key problem was that in many instances, managers and employers had reduced incentives—for example, cut wages or taken-away fringe benefits—and as a result, strikes against scientific management had happened. This subsequently led to Taylor's summoning by the U.S. Congress. The chairman of the inquiring congressional committee pointed out this problem when reminding Taylor that managers and employers should not have been modeled as intrinsically "hearty" cooperative parties, with revolutionized mental attitudes, but as "lions." Modern institutional economics can conceptually deepen this proposal by projecting the idea of lions to opportunistic and predatory behavior, as it reflects models of (extreme) self-interest. Such models are widely applied (in heuristic, nonempirical, methodical terms) in institutional and constitutional economics.

Evolution

As noted, a fundamental conceptual asymmetry existed in the scientific management approach, as it was initially proposed by Taylor: For employees, self-interested, even opportunistic behavior was explicitly acknowledged *and* systemically handled; for managers, such behavior was aimed to be behaviorally resolved. This led to significant implementation problems for scientific management in Taylor's time; to strikes against scientific management because of uncooperative, opportunistic managerial behavior ("managerialism"); and ultimately to Taylor's being summoned by the U.S. Congress. Only after Taylor's death did his followers begin in force to revise scientific management with regard to managerial opportunism. One important change was that unions were brought into work organization to strengthen employee rights and control manager opportunism. Union involvement in tasks such as negotiating and setting wage levels and other rewards for organization members removed such tasks from the sole sphere of influence and control of managers/employers.

By the 1920s, this moved scientific management, in its revised version, closer to being considered a rather "complete," generic theory, especially when read as an institutional economic organization theory. Modern institutional economic research (e.g., that of Oliver Williamson), explains the emergence of unions in a similar manner, as a constraining influence of management opportunism, although the economic reconstruction of scientific management has generally not been picked up by this research tradition.

Nevertheless, a considerable amount of management theory has not appraised scientific management in its revised version. Rather, in many instances, fragments and selected elements of the original scientific management approach were picked up when connecting to Taylor's research. The efficiency-oriented works of Frank and Lillian Gilbreth or of Henry Gantt are exemplary in this respect, as is Fordism, which focused on division of labor and work standardization techniques.

Similarly, in the further course of the 20th century, managers in many countries have drawn on some of Taylor's proposals and his suggestions on work standardization to reorganize organization structures. A substantial body of empirical research documents this. Also, Taylor's suggestions have been explicitly or implicitly connected to many modern approaches to work organization, albeit often in a rather selective, eclectic manner that does not do justice to the conceptual framework Taylor set out. Certain concepts of management by objective (MBO), total quality management (TQM), business process reengineering (BPR), or just-in-time (JIT) management are exemplary and can easily be classified as neo-Taylorism. The McDonaldization literature and the management practice it critiques at least implicitly targets Taylorite ideas on work organization too, but again, both the management practice concerned and its conceptual critique tend to reflect a fragmentary understanding of Taylorism (already with regard to its original version and the more so regarding its revised version from the 1920s).

Importance

For various reasons, scientific management theory is still of high, continued relevance and significance to management theory and practice. First, since the initial publication of concepts of scientific management around the turn of the 19th to the 20th century, management theory and practice has continually critiqued and reassessed scientific management. Yet hardly any textbook in management and organization studies has been published with some kind of deeper evaluation of scientific management. For this reason, scholars, researchers, and consultants who engage with management practice, as well as managers and students of management, need to be aware of what scientific management stands for.

Second, from early on, criticism of scientific management as a mechanistic, dehumanizing management concept has not abated. Most recently, some writings in postmodern and critical organization theory have (re-)advanced such claims, especially so since certain modern technology concepts, such as advanced manufacturing systems, computer-based information systems for structuring work organization, and MBO, BPR, TQM, and JIT techniques seem to connect to work standardization techniques reminiscent of Taylorism. Criticism of scientific management as dehumanizing work had to be accepted if one interpreted scientific management and neo-Taylorism as a behavioral, sociopsychological or sociological theory of management. However, the important question in this connection is whether this does justice to what Taylor was really after when setting out his management concepts.

Institutional economic reassessments of scientific management warn in this connection that scientific management is much closer to organizational economics than to any other research program on management. Seen from this perspective, the upskilling of labor in the factory through structural reorganization, which scientific management envisaged, and the rising rewards allocated to organization members in relation hereto allow for a positive image of human nature evaluations for scientific management. Such images of human nature assessments are the more feasible when put into perspective with regard to the historic, socioeconomic context in which scientific management emerged, with largely unskilled and ethnically diverse labor entering the company in Taylor's time, both at the worker level and the management level.

Third, scientific management is an excellent case study of a partly incomplete, partly inconsistent management theory, Taylor being caught up between organizational economics and behavioral organization research. The conceptual asymmetry regarding his theorizing on the employee condition and the managerial condition reflected this. Such inconsistency may be hardly surprising considering the early days of management theorizing when scientific management emerged. Concepts of modern institutional economics, as they were abstractly developed in force by James Buchanan and Oliver Williamson from the 1960s and 1970s onward, most fruitfully help to understand and clarify such misunderstandings in the scientific management approach, and they illuminate why Taylor's followers modified the scientific management approach with regard to unionism after his death in 1915.

Modern management is well advised not to simplistically reduce scientific management to a program of work standardization techniques. The theory is much more complex, centrally aiming at the resolution of cooperation conflict between managers/employers and employees. Despite being more than a century old, Taylor's theory has a lot to say on this issue, especially so when assessed from an institutional economic perspective and when corrected for certain (self-) misunderstandings Taylor may have had when dealing with the problem of managerial opportunism in the organization.

Sigmund Wagner-Tsukamoto

See also Agency Theory; Business Process Reengineering; Critical Management Studies; Equity Theory; Humanistic Management; Management by Objectives; Managerialism; Organizational Structure and Design

Further Readings

Merkle, J. A. (1980). *Management and ideology: The legacy of the international scientific management movement.* Berkeley: University of California Press.

Pruijt, H. D. (1997). *Job design and technology: Taylorism vs. anti-Taylorism.* London, England: Routledge.

Roper, M. (1999). Killing off the father: Social science and the memory of Frederick Taylor in management studies, 1950–1975. *Contemporary British History, 13*(3), 39–58.

Taylor, F. W. (1919). *Two papers on scientific management.* London, England: Routledge & Sons.

Taylor, F. W. (1964). *Scientific management: Shop management. The principles of scientific management. Taylor's testimony before the Special House Committee.* London, England: Harper & Row.

Wagner-Tsukamoto, S. A. (2003). *Human nature and organization theory.* Cheltenham, England: Edward Elgar.

Wagner-Tsukamoto, S. A. (2007). An institutional economic reconstruction of scientific management: On the lost theoretical logic of Taylorism. *Academy of Management Review, 32,* 105–117.

Wagner-Tsukamoto, S. A. (2008). Scientific management revisited: Did Taylorism fail because of a too positive image of human nature? *Journal of Management History, 14,* 348–372.

Wood, S., & Kelly, J. (1982). Taylorism: Responsible autonomy and management strategy. In S. Wood (Ed.), *The degradation of work* (pp. 74–89). London, England: Hutchinson.

Wrege, C. D., & Greenwood, R. G. (1991). *Fredrick W. Taylor: The father of scientific management: Myth and reality.* Burr Ridge, IL: Irwin.

SELF-CONCEPT AND THE THEORY OF SELF

As a psychological construct, the *self* has long occupied a preeminent place in both psychological and management theories regarding human behavior. In fact, the self is among the most widely studied concepts in the social sciences. The substantial attention afforded the self as a topic of research is hardly surprising given that it has been viewed as a primary locus of human motivation and agency, as well as judgment and decision making. This entry first describes some of the prominent definitions and conceptions of the self and summarizes some of the major constructs associated with it. The next section then elaborates on why the self—and theory about the self—is so important to organizational theory and management practice. The concluding section outlines some of the most recent and important developments in the conception of the self and its role in organizational life.

Fundamentals

What precisely do we mean by the self as a psychological entity? Defining what we mean by the self or, more precisely, an individual's *self-concept*, has proven a daunting task and one that has preoccupied psychologists of every generation since the discipline's inception. As a result, there exists today a bewildering proliferation of definitions, theoretical frameworks, and empirical evidence regarding the self's nature and origins and the consequences of its actions.

In laying a foundation for how best to think about the self, social psychologist and leading self theorist Mark Leary has proposed the notion of *selfhood* to connote the aggregate thoughts, feelings, and behaviors that arise from people's awareness of themselves as possessing a self that operates as both subject and agent. The *self-as-object* represents the agentic actor that we experience when we actively engage the world and interact with other people. The *self-as-subject*, in contrast, encompasses the more phenomenological dimensions of selfhood, including the experiencing, knowing, and reflective dimensions of selfhood that people associate with their self-awareness.

An important contribution to our understanding of the self as a psychological entity came from early work on *self-schemata*. Self-schemata are defined as the basic cognitive structures regarding the self that function to organize and shape how people process self-relevant information. Research by Hazel Markus and others has demonstrated substantial individual differences, as well as cross-cultural variations, in the way the self is conceptualized or construed. Among the most important distinctions has been the idea of independent self-construals versus interdependent self-construals. *Independent self-construals* are defined in terms of individuals' distinctive attributes and traits and have been associated largely with individuals from Western cultures, with their characteristic emphasis on individual reasoning and choice. *Interdependent self-construals,* in contrast, have been conceptualized in terms of individuals' relational connections to others and are widely associated with Eastern cultures, which tend to focus on more collectivistic modes of thinking and behavior. Researchers have also recognized, however, that considerable individual differences exist with respect to both the content of our self-schemata and self-construals, even within a given culture or point in time. Moreover, people's self-construals have been shown to be highly dependent on social contextual factors.

Multidimensional Nature of the Self: The Self as Kaleidoscope

A large body of theory and research over the past several decades has demonstrated the fundamentally multidimensional nature of the self. Marilynn Brewer's work, along with that of other social identity theorists, has shown that the psychological self includes an individual-level self-concept, an interpersonal or relational self-concept, and a collective self-concept. The *individual-level self-concept* refers to all the personal and distinctive attributes we associate with ourselves as unique individuals. The *relational self-concept* reflects our dyadic relationships with others. Finally, the *collective self-concept* encompasses and reflects our larger social group memberships. Based on these theoretical distinctions, numerous laboratory experiments have demonstrated that even subtle variations in language can "cue" the activation of these different senses of self, resulting in significant changes in psychological and behavioral consequences. For example, experiments on choice behavior in social dilemma situations (i.e., situations where a conflict exists between individual interests or well-being and a group's interests or well-being) have shown that cuing or making the individual self more salient results in relatively "selfish" choices in such situations, whereas activating the collective self results in more group-oriented, cooperative behavior.

On the basis of such evidence, as well as the results of many other studies, social psychologist Kay Deaux has gone so far as to characterize the psychological self as fundamentally *kaleidoscopic*. This metaphor, she proposes, succinctly captures the shifting, varied, and multifaceted experiencing of the self and its many manifestations across differing contexts and under differing motivational orientations or needs. As a consequence, she argues, there is considerable plasticity in the way the self is experienced and construed.

Along similar lines, motivational theories regarding the self highlight the role that individuals' psychological needs and goals play in self-expression and behavior. Among the most important motivational constructs is *self-efficacy*. Self-efficacy refers to people's beliefs regarding their capacity to achieve their desired goals and objectives. The complex and varied effects of such motivational processes on self-assessment is also evident in competing ideas or images regarding the ultimate goals underlying our self-related cognitions and behaviors.

Motivational conceptions grounded in *self-esteem* maintenance, for instance, posit that individuals will think and act in the service of protecting or maintaining their sense of self-worth. *Self-enhancement theories,* in contrast, posit that individuals are motivated to distort judgment in the direction of overly positive self-appraisals. Finally, *self-verification theories* argue, provocatively, that individuals are motivated to confirm self-images, even when those images have negative implications for self-esteem or self-enhancement. Research on *self-affirmation* provides another cogent example of how motivational processes can drive self-assessment and the content of self-perceptions. Claude Steele and others have shown that when one part of a person's sense of self is threatened, people can invoke other positive or untarnished aspects of self in an almost compensatory, restorative fashion.

Importance

Much of the psychological theory and research on the self has highlighted the largely functional roles that our construal and understanding of self plays in human behavior. This functional perspective is evident in organizational perspectives on the self as well.

Adaptive Nature of the Self

Among the most important functional capacities of the self are self-awareness, self-regulation, and self-reflection. *Self-awareness* refers to our capacity to develop a conscious awareness of the self as both a subject and object capable of engaging the world in particular ways. *Self-regulation* refers to our capacity to think and act in the service of goal pursuit and other important motives and also to inhibit counterproductive thoughts and behaviors. Finally, *self-reflection* reflects people's capacity to observe their actions and their consequences, to change their self-concepts in the face of their cumulative experiences, and to better regulate their future thoughts, feelings, and behaviors. In concert, these three functional capacities contribute to the ability of the self to navigate effectively in the world. Understanding and effectively engaging these three capacities is particularly useful for managers insofar as one of the vital jobs of the manager is to influence the attitudes and behaviors of those individuals under his or her management. By harnessing individuals' self-awareness, self-regulatory capacities, and self-reflective strengths, managers can more fully use the human capital under their management.

Self-Relevant Processes and Their Organizational Implications

A number of self-relevant functional psychological processes have proven particularly important to organizational theory and management practice. The first of these pertains to *self-evaluation processes.* Self-evaluation processes reflect those factors that influence people's assessments of themselves, including their capabilities and their experiences in organizations. These evaluative processes include individuals' judgments regarding their abilities, their expectations about their performance, their sense of entitlement, and whether they are being treated fairly in their exchanges within an organization.

Psychologists have extensively studied *self-esteem* as one major psychological dimension along which people evaluate their individual abilities. Although some psychologists treat self-esteem as a personality variable, others have noted the important role that situational factors can play in the development and maintenance of low or high self-esteem. *Self-categorization* represents another major psychological process that helps people locate themselves in the social order of an organization and define themselves relative to other people in that organization. People can self-categorize in terms of many different dimensions, but research suggests they do so most

often and readily in terms of the prominent and salient social categories to which they belong and with which they identify. The major, and also widely studied, social categories pertain to individuals' race and gender. These social category memberships also play a pivotal role in how people evaluate others via the process of social stereotyping. Although less widely studied, age-related self-categorizations and stereotyping have been recognized increasingly as important social categorization processes as workforces around the world age.

Social comparison can also be used to help individuals assess themselves across a variety of important organizational dimensions, including their comparative abilities and performance. The particular type of social comparison individuals engage in, however, can be affected by their motives for comparing. For example, individuals can use *downward social comparisons* (i.e., compare their performance against others who are less capable or doing less well) to bolster their perceptions of ability or enhance their feelings of self-worth. On the other hand, they can employ *upward social comparisons* (i.e., compare their performance with others who are more accomplished or expert) to learn how to perform better. Individuals can also use *nonsocial comparisons* to assess their progress or regress on some dimension (e.g., compare their own performance or skill level when they were first hired by an organization to their current performance or skill level).

Bias and Distortions in Self-Awareness and Self-Appraisal: How and Why the Self Gets in Trouble

Given the adaptive value of the self-schemata and accurate self-knowledge, as embodied most famously in the Greek admonition to "know thyself," one might presuppose that people's self-concepts progress toward increasingly veridical or accurate self-conceptions. Yet research has shown instead that, however desirable and adaptive such accurate self-knowledge might seem, it nonetheless is not easily attained. In this regard, Shelley Taylor and others have convincingly demonstrated that people suffer from a variety of self-enhancing illusions and other self-related distortions. Psychologist David Dunning has elaborated on this perspective, documenting and organizing our understanding of the substantial and robust barriers to self-insight that such positive illusions foster.

Although much of the psychological literature on the self highlights the functional and adaptive properties of people's self-concepts, other work has highlighted the stresses of selfhood and the sundry barriers to its attainment. For example, social psychologist Roy Baumeister's research highlights the myriad creative ways individuals find to escape the "burdens" of selfhood. Such work has contributed to our understanding of the origins and dynamics of paradoxical forms of self-denigration, including masochism and other seemingly paradoxical forms of self-destructive behavior. Similarly, research on self-defeating behavior and self-handicapping illustrates the complex and perversely ingenious ways in which individuals can sabotage themselves when pursuing seemingly important goals. Choking under pressure provides one example of such self-sabotage or undermining.

Research on *self-presentation* or impression management might lead one to conclude that an individual's publicly presented self is, at best, an ephemeral, fickle, and self-consciously "strategic entity," ever responsive to changing goals, audiences, and/or concerns about conforming to cultural norms and social conventions. In short, individuals are motivated to put their "best face" forward and adapt that best face to suit the circumstances of the moment. Yet a more positive framing of this literature highlights the responsive, adaptive nature of people's skillful self-presentations. Psychologists have increasingly recognized the inherent sociality of human beings: We are motivated to fit in and get along. Thus, individuals do care about their status and standing in the social groups to which they belong and attach psychological importance. As social identity theorists have shown, this so-called social self is inherently relational and, by implication, responsive to the presence of others.

The Cutting Edge and the Future of Self Theory and Research

Psychological and organizational research on the self progresses at an impressive pace today. Although research continues in all the areas identified above, several additional streams of research have recently had an impact on our understanding of the self.

One major area of current research attempts to approach our understanding of the self from the perspective of evolutionary theory. Evolutionary psychologists have proposed, for instance, that it is more useful to think of the evolved psychological self as *modular* rather than conceiving the self as a single,

coherent psychological entity. These psychologists note that the human brain itself evolved in a modular fashion, with newer parts of the brain literally being superimposed or "added onto" older parts. From this perspective, these theorists argue, it is not at all surprising that self-conflicts, competing motives, internal dissonance, and other manifestations of our multiple selves lead to competition for attention, the pursuit of incompatible goals, and other seeming inconsistencies in attitude, affect, and behavior.

Neuroscientific theories and methods represent another exciting direction of research that is rapidly advancing knowledge regarding the self. For example, brain-imaging studies are illuminating our understanding of the organization of the self in the human brain and how and where self-relevant information is stored and processed. Finally, cross-cultural theory and research on the self is emerging as increasingly important to management scholars, given the globalization of business and the increasingly multinational character of large, complex organizations.

As this brief entry is intended to make clear, research on the self remains one of the most active areas of psychological research in contemporary management theory. Among the most useful implications of this research for managers is recognition that the adequacy of their knowledge regarding the psychological complexity of the self will directly impact their ability to effectively motivate and influence others' organizational behavior. Second, their ability to regulate their own behavior, especially in leadership contexts, will depend on the complexity of their own self-representations and level of self-awareness. In a very real sense, therefore, managers' self-knowledge constitutes a foundation on which their leadership effectiveness ultimately depends.

Roderick M. Kramer

See also Self-Determination Theory; Self-Fulfilling Prophecy; Sensemaking; Social Cognitive Theory; Social Identity Theory; Theory of Self-Esteem

Further Readings

Baumeister, R. F. (Ed.). (1993). *Self-esteem*. New York, NY: Plenum.

Baumeister, R. F. (Ed.). (1999). *The self in social psychology*. New York, NY: Psychology Press.

Brewer, M. B., & Hewstone, M. (Eds.). (2004). *Self and social identity*. New York, NY: Blackwell.

Brown, J. (1998). *The self*. New York, NY: Routledge.

Dunning, D. (2005). *Self-insight: Roadblocks and detours on the path to knowing thyself*. New York, NY: Psychology Press.

Gergen, K. J. (1991). *The saturated self: Dilemmas of identity in contemporary life*. New York, NY: Basic Books.

Hoyle, R. H., Kernis, M. H., Leary, M. R., & Baldwin, M. W. (Eds.). (1999). *Selfhood: Identity, esteem, and regulation*. Boulder, CO: Westview Press.

Kramer, R. M., Tyler, T., & Oliver J. (Eds.). (1999). *Psychology of the social self*. Mahwah, NJ: Lawrence Erlbaum.

Kurzban, R. (2010). *Why everyone else is a hypocrite: Evolution and the modular mind*. Princeton, NJ: Princeton University Press.

Leary, M. R., & Tangney, J. P. (Eds.). (2003). *Handbook of self and identity*. New York, NY: Guilford Press.

SELF-DETERMINATION THEORY

Self-determination theory (SDT) is an empirically based theory of human motivation, optimal functioning, and wellness. SDT assumes that people have an inherent growth tendency, which is referred to as the *organismic integration process*. Through this process, development occurs both by the unfolding of intrinsic motivation and interests and by the process of internalizing practices and values from the external world. Accompanying people's development and ongoing functioning are subjective human experiences of autonomy, competence, and relatedness, or what in SDT are called people's *basic psychological needs*. That is, SDT relies on human experiences related to these three basic needs as the central inputs to development and functioning and also as an important focus for testing hypotheses empirically. Experiences related to these needs are assessed through subjective reports as well as a variety of supplementary methods from brain imaging to implicit measurements and priming of nonconscious motivational processes. Although SDT is a complex theory that will only be partially reviewed herein, at its core it proposes a multidimensional motivational model that is unified by the concept of autonomy. SDT then deals with how to promote the most functional types of motivation—that is, the types associated with optimal functioning and growth.

SDT also specifies individual differences, called *general causality orientations*, that represent the type of motivation a person most typically embraces, and it also differentiates the nature and consequences of people's life goals or aspirations, which shape both proximal behaviors and individuals' overall wellness trajectories. Each of these fundamental issues is addressed in the next sections; the final section discusses empirical evidence specific to the field of management.

Fundamentals

Self-determination theory proposes two overarching types of motivation: autonomous motivation and controlled motivation. When people are autonomous, they act with a full sense of volition, choice, and congruence. When controlled, they act with a sense of pressure, tension, and demand. To understand more fully the meaning of autonomous and controlled motivation, it is helpful to begin with the distinction between intrinsic motivation and extrinsic motivation.

Intrinsic motivation is defined as doing an activity out of interest and enjoyment—that is, for its own sake. A child playing with toys, or with the packages they came in, is a beautiful example of intrinsic motivation. But intrinsic motivation is not limited to children's play—it is evident in sport, learning, gaming, and other challenge-seeking activities throughout the life span. It is important in adults' learning of new information and gaining new skills and competencies, and thus it is important in both work and play environments. Intrinsic motivation is the prototype of autonomous motivation, for when acting out of interest and enjoyment, people feel a full sense of willingness and endorsement of what they are doing.

Extrinsic motivation is defined as doing something for an instrumental reason, to obtain separate consequences, such as gaining rewards or approval, avoiding punishments or criticism, boosting self-esteem, or living up to deeply held values. These various reasons, while all instrumental, are quite different and have been found to lead to different performance and affective outcomes. Therefore, SDT has specified different types of extrinsic motivation that vary in terms of the degree to which they are autonomous.

The most controlled, or least autonomous, form of extrinsic motivation is called *external regulation*.

Such behaviors are perceived as being controlled by concrete rewards and threatened punishments. It involves rewards (e.g., monetary rewards, plaques, approval, or promotions) or punishments (e.g., pay cuts, sanctions, ostracism, or job loss) that are either tangible or social. Although external regulation can powerfully motivate behavior in the short term, it is often poorly maintained, and it often does not engage the person's maximal talent or effort.

Whereas externally regulated behaviors are initiated and regulated by contingencies outside the individual, some controlled forms of behavior are initiated and regulated within the person. This means that internal regulation is not necessarily autonomously regulated, and it is certainly not necessarily intrinsically motivated. People can take in or, in the parlance of developmental psychology, *internalize* controlling regulations from their environments that were initially external to them and that remain controlling. Some of these internalized values and regulations may initially be in conflict with the individuals' desires, but it is possible that people will accept them as their own and make them part of their sense of self. Stated differently, people can internalize values or regulations to differing degrees, and this will have quite different consequences for motivation, behavior, persistence, and well-being.

First, there is a type of behavioral regulation in which people take in the regulations but don't really own them as their own, so the regulations have to be enforced by internal pressures, referred to as *introjection*. *Introjected regulations* are buttressed by guilt, shame, anxiety, pride, and the desire for feelings of self-worth. In other words, with introjection, people's self-esteem has become contingent on living up to the internalized external standards, so the people feel pressured and controlled by these internal contingencies.

In contrast, *identification* describes a more fully internalized form of behavioral regulation in which an external contingency is taken in as a new personal value. People will have identified with the importance of the behavior and thus will have accepted it as their own. When regulated by identifications, they will act with personal conviction and feel a sense of volition and willingness. Identified regulation therefore represents a type of autonomous extrinsic motivation. Finally, when identifications have been assimilated with people's sense of self—with

their needs, values, and other identifications—the regulation is considered *integrated*, and represents the most mature form of extrinsic motivation. Identified and integrated regulations are not considered intrinsically motivated because the behaviors are still done for instrumental reasons and not out of interest and enjoyment of the activity itself.

To summarize, external and introjected regulation are considered controlled forms of regulation, whereas identified, integrated, and intrinsic regulation are consider autonomous. The first four types of regulation are forms of extrinsic motivation and the fifth is intrinsic motivation. These five types of regulation line up along a continuum of relative autonomy in the order presented in the previous sentence. All five of these are bases for people's motivation, although they are of different types, and they stand in contrast to *amotivation*, which refers to a lack of motivation, intentionality, and regulation.

Factors That Affect Autonomous Motivation

A second important aspect of SDT, in addition to the differentiation of motivation, is the proposition that all human beings have basic psychological needs, the satisfaction of which are essential for psychological health, well-being, and effective functioning. The theory specifies three such needs—the needs for competence, autonomy, and relatedness. These needs were not just proposed on the basis of personal experience or intuition; rather, they were found to be the most effective way of providing a meaningful account for the many phenomena that were emerging from the research on intrinsic and extrinsic motivation. Hundreds of empirical investigations, including cross-cultural research, have found that these needs are in fact universal and that their satisfaction is associated with optimal functioning because their presence versus absence has predicted increases versus decreases in well-being, self-regulation, and performance. *Competence* refers to taking on stimulating challenges and mastering aspects of one's environment; *autonomy* refers to feeling volitional and willing in the regulation of one's behavior, as opposed to feeling heteronomous and pawn-like; and *relatedness* refers to having meaningful social interactions, to feeling cared for by other, and caring for them.

One of the important functions served by specifying these psychological needs is that it allows people to make predictions about what aspects of the environment—for example, task characteristics, management styles, and interpersonal factors—will facilitate intrinsic motivation, internalization, well-being, and performance. Simply stated, environmental factors that support satisfaction of the basic psychological needs are expected to promote autonomous motivation and its consequences, whereas factors that diminish or thwart satisfaction of the needs are expected to undermine autonomous motivation, promoting either controlled motivation or amotivation, and therefore having more negative consequences.

More specifically, in work environments where the selection of personnel is based on skills, abilities, acquired knowledge, and the capacity of employees to feel optimally challenged by the job, where training and developmental opportunities are offered, and where constructive feedback is given, the employees are more likely to feel competent. In work environments where strategic goals are explained to employees, participative management is used, and employees are allowed to take initiative and have a voice, they will be more likely to experience autonomy. Finally, in work environments where interactions are fostered by the design of jobs, teamwork is fostered, and managers listen to and respect their employees, the employees are more likely to feel high relatedness.

Among the most striking and controversial discoveries that have emerged from SDT research is that tangible rewards can often undermine intrinsic motivation, and they do so under quite clear and predictable conditions. Numerous laboratory studies have shown that when rewards are administered contingent on engaging in a particular task, completing the task, or achieving a certain level of performance on it, people are likely to become less intrinsically motivated for the task because their engagement in it depends on the rewards and they experience a sense of pressure. These experiences decrease satisfaction of the individuals' need for autonomy, which diminishes their interest and enjoyment in the rewarded tasks they initially found to be fun. In effect, rewards can turn a pleasurable task into drudgery. But because rewards can also function as feedback, they can also serve to enhance feelings of competence when that feedback is positive. This means that rewards can both provide competence need satisfaction and deprive autonomy need satisfaction, and it

is the net effect that determines the rewards' effects on intrinsic motivation. Often, this is influenced by whether the general ambience of the workplace is supportive versus controlling. Other events in the environment, such as deadlines, surveillance, and competition, have also been shown to undermine intrinsic motivation, especially when they are used to pressure or control people's behavior. These findings have important implications for management as workplaces are often fraught with such means for controlling behavior or performance.

Individual Differences

Individual differences focused on how people appraise their environments and regulate their behaviors are referred to as *causality orientations* and are crucial determinants of their motivation. Some people are more sensitive to environmental controls and consequently feel more readily controlled than others. These people who are high in the control orientation look for cues in the environment that will tell them what is expected of them, and they tend to feel pressured by those cues when initiating and regulating their behaviors. Indeed, they rely on environmental controls such as deadlines or reward contingencies to regulate their behavior; their internal controls (i.e., introjects) are easily stimulated, and they tend to select jobs based on status and pay. They also tend to evidence the Type A behavior pattern, which is related to health problems, and to be controlling and critical when in managerial positions. In contrast, some people tend to experience a sense of autonomy and choice when initiating and regulating their behavior, even in situations where others might experience control. These people are high in the autonomy orientation, and they tend to be quite proactive. Such individuals are more likely to select jobs that allow initiative, to interpret feedback as informational, and to make choices based on their own interests and values. They tend to behave in ways that are more coherent with their values and attitudes and, as such, are likely to make better managers. The different strengths in the autonomous and controlled orientations emerge out of developmental experiences with the environment, such as with parents, teachers, and peers who tend to be autonomy supportive versus controlling. Indeed, when the ongoing environment has supported satisfaction of the basic needs for autonomy, competence, and relatedness, people tend to be more autonomously orientated in their lives.

Other research examines how individual differences in people's life goals or aspirations develop and affect their lives. People who have strong *extrinsic aspirations* or goals, such as amassing wealth, having an attractive image, and being popular and well-known, generally report lower well-being than people who hold strong *intrinsic life goals,* such as meaningful affiliations, community involvement, and personal growth, regardless of the levels of success or efficacy at the goals. People with strong extrinsic goals also tend to be more Machiavellian and less cooperative, to act more prejudicially, and to take more health risks. The development of intrinsic and extrinsic aspirations depends on the satisfaction versus deprivation of the basic psychological needs: When the needs are more satisfied, people tend to adopt more intrinsic life goals. Education can also have an impact on the development of aspirations, even among adults. It has been found that students in law and business schools tend to develop more extrinsic life goals, whereas undergraduate students in arts and science tend to develop more intrinsic life goals during their educational years, largely as a function of internalizing the ambient values they see around them.

Evolution

Motivation concerns the forces that move people into action. Many earlier theories of motivation located the moving forces of human behavior in external sources—most notably, rewards and punishments. But SDT has been a central paradigm that has changed that vision and promoted the understanding that, although rewards and punishments are one source of human motivation, they are not the exclusive, or even the most effective, drivers of behavior. Instead, SDT has focused on the sources of volitional motivation and people's autonomous engagement within work, play, and relationships.

The theory has been developed over the past 40 years by Edward L. Deci and Richard M. Ryan at the University of Rochester, along with many collaborators from around the world. SDT has organized much basic, applied, and translational research in fields as diverse as management, health care, education, sport and exercise, religious motivation, and virtual environments. This breadth of application stems from the fact that a central focus of SDT is on factors that support volition and choice, which is central in each of these domains because people's willing participation in such endeavors is associated with maximal persistence, quality of performance, and positive experience.

Richard M. Ryan and James P. Connell developed an approach to measuring the different types of motivations that has been used with many ages, activities, and domains. The approach involves asking people why they do a behavior or set of behaviors (e.g., doing their homework, taking prescribed medications, or doing their jobs) and providing them with reasons representing the different forms of motivation that participants respond to on a Likert-type scale indicating the degree to which each reason applies to them. This method has been used in hundreds of studies in the fields of work, education, sport, exercise, parenting, leisure, and health behavior change. All in all, research has shown that these same types of motivation can be applied to the different activities and that the more autonomous types of motivation (identified, integrated, and intrinsic) tend to be associated with more positive outcomes, such as coping strategies, mental health, effort, enjoyment, or quality of learning and performance than do the controlled types (external and introjected), across domains, genders, socioeconomic status, and cultures.

Importance

Self-determination theory is increasingly being used to understand the effects of management practices on employee motivation, engagement, performance, and well-being. Not only has it been used to show how managerial behaviors that support the three psychological needs influence performance and well-being across cultures, but it has also been applied to show why transformational leadership behaviors influence performance, commitment to organizations, and job satisfaction. It has even recently been applied to show that occupational health and safety inspectors who support psychological needs when dealing with workplace conflicts are more effective in getting organizations to adhere to regulations. In short, managers who provide a vision or goals with a good rationale for them, who consider their employees' needs and empathize with them, who provide them with choices and opportunities for initiative, and who believe in their capacities have employees who are more autonomously motivated. This in turn translates into greater employee loyalty and satisfaction, job persistence versus turnover and burnout, and higher quality job engagement and performance.

One might ask whether this is trainable, and the answer is yes. Studies have shown that training managers to be more supportive of the three needs enhances employee motivation, trust in management, commitment to the organization, and job satisfaction. But training is not enough. Managers also need to experience less pressure themselves if they are to be autonomously motivated and supportive of subordinates' psychological needs. Therefore, organizational structure, culture, and practices are also important.

Jobs that provide variety, challenge, feedback, and decision latitude also foster more autonomous work motivation. This can be achieved through motivational job design, teamwork, and participative management. It has also been shown that employees who feel in sync with the goals and requirements of the organization, group, and task challenges are more likely to experience high need satisfaction, which in turn is associated with their performance and commitment to the organization. Need satisfaction and autonomous motivation are associated with better job performance than controlled motivation. These motivational factors have also been associated with better workplace mental health, decreased risk of burnout, commitment to the organization, and personnel retention.

Individual differences have been shown to influence worker outcomes as well. Autonomy orientation has been related to higher work-related well-being, performance, and engagement. Intrinsic work values have been related to interest in training, the ability of unemployed people to find a job, job satisfaction, engagement, and positive work adjustment. More recently, core self-evaluations, another individual difference whereby people vary in terms of four traits (self-esteem, self-efficacy, internal locus of control, and low neuroticism), have been positively related to autonomous motivation toward work goals, which in turn was associated with job satisfaction and goal attainment.

What is ironic is that the means most frequently taken to promote worker motivation in organizations, such as rewards, surveillance, and competition, often do not have the intended effects. The controlled motivation fostered through these means is generally unrelated or even negatively related to the outcomes desired by organizations: energized performance, sharing, and well-being. Although not all work is intrinsically motivating, even for uninteresting tasks, the person needs to feel competent, autonomous, and related in order to engage in those tasks and develop an autonomous type of extrinsic motivation for them. Therefore, it is management practices such as adequate selection, training opportunities, constructive feedback in performance evaluations, decision-making power, transparent communication, teamwork, and good leadership that foster autonomous work motivation. To conclude, self-determination theory offers very useful advice on how to ensure employee engagement, performance, and retention, which ultimately lead to organizational effectiveness.

Marylène Gagné, Edward L. Deci, and Richard M. Ryan

See also Empowerment; Job Characteristics Theory; Organizational Commitment Theory; Reinforcement Theory; Transformational Theory of Leadership

Further Readings

Deci, E. L., Koestner, R., & Ryan, R. M. (1999). A meta-analytic review of experiments examining the effects of extrinsic rewards on intrinsic motivation. *Psychological Bulletin, 125,* 627–668.

Deci, E. L., & Ryan, R. M. (2008). Facilitating optimal motivation and psychological well-being across life's domains. *Canadian Psychology, 49,* 14–23.

Gagné, M., & Deci, E. L. (2005). Self-determination theory as a new framework for understanding organizational behavior. *Journal of Organizational Behavior, 26,* 331–362.

Kasser, T. (2002). *The high price of materialism.* Cambridge, MA: MIT Press.

Pink, D. (2010). *Drive.* New York, NY: Riverhead Books.

Ryan, R. M., & Deci, E. L. (2000). Self-determination theory and the facilitation of intrinsic motivation, social development, and well-being. *American Psychologist, 55,* 68–78.

SELF-FULFILLING PROPHECY

The self-fulfilling prophecy (SFP) occurs when the expectation that an event will happen increases the likelihood that the event does indeed happen.

A common economic example is when our expectations that prices will rise lead us to buy more or sooner, contributing to aggregate demand: The collective "we" then witnesses price rises that we abetted, most often without any awareness of our own role in making it happen. The Pygmalion effect is a special case of SFP in which raising a manager's expectations regarding worker performance boosts that performance. The Pygmalion effect debuted in educational psychology when psychologists experimentally raised elementary school teachers' expectations toward a randomly selected subsample of their pupils and thereby produced greater achievement among those pupils than among control pupils. Subsequent research has replicated this phenomenon among supervisors and subordinates in military, business, industrial, and service organizations and among all four cross-gender combinations; both men and women lead male and female subordinates to greater success when they expect more of them. Interpersonal expectancy is inherent to most leader-follower interactions, and the Pygmalion effect characterizes many manager-worker relationships. Stated simply, the theory's central management insight is that managers get the employees they expect; managers' can boost effectiveness by expecting more of their subordinates. This entry describes the ubiquity of several varieties of SFP, explains the psychological mechanisms through which it works, and suggests practical applications in management.

Fundamentals

Several theories have been proposed to explain *how* raising leader expectations boosts subordinate performance. Common to all is a causal chain that begins with the impact of the leader's expectations on and his or her *own* behavior toward subordinates (i.e., his or her leadership), which arouses a motivational response among the subordinates, and culminates in subordinate performance that accords with the leader's expectations. Self-efficacy is the key motivational mediator in this process. Self-efficacy is an individual's belief in his or her own ability to execute the behaviors needed to perform successfully. Ample research shows that self-efficacy is a major determinant of motivation and performance. When individuals believe they have what it takes to succeed, they try harder. Conversely, those who doubt they can succeed refrain from exerting the requisite effort to apply such ability as they do have and end up underachieving. The manager-as-Pygmalion model posits that high expectations move the leader to treat followers in a manner that augments their self-efficacy, which in turn motivates the followers to exert greater effort, culminating in enhanced performance. Thus, the Pygmalion effect is a motivational phenomenon initiated by the high performance expectations held by a leader who believes in followers' capacity for success. In a largely unconscious interpersonal process, managers with high expectations lead their followers to success by enhancing their self-efficacy, thus fulfilling their prophecy.

However, SFP is a double-edged sword: Just as high expectations boost performance, low expectations depress performance in a negative SFP dubbed the "golem effect." *Golem* means dumbbell in Hebrew and Yiddish slang. Managers who expect dumbbells get dumbbells. Experiments have shown that golem effects can be mitigated by informing supervisors that subordinates with relatively low qualifications have fair potential to succeed.

Another variant of SFP is the "Galatea effect." Named after the statue that the mythical Pygmalion sculpted, this is an *intra*personal expectancy effect involving only the employee. Self-starters fulfill their own prophecy of success; believing in their own capacity to excel, they mobilize their internal motivational resources to sustain the effort needed for success without any external source (e.g., a supervisor) of high expectations. However, Galatea effects can also be golem-like. Individuals who harbor a negative self-image expect to fail; they refrain from using their abilities and thereby, tragically but unintentionally, they fulfill their own gloomy prophecy.

Self-efficacy concerns what individuals believe about their own internal resources that they can bring to bear to accomplish their goals. Beyond the motivating impact of boosting employees' self-efficacy, research has shown the positive impact of boosting external efficacy, or "means efficacy." Without influencing self-efficacy, simply getting workers to believe in the utility of the tools (i.e., means) at their disposal for performing the job motivates intensification of effort and produces improved performance. The means could be a computer, a weapon, a teammate, a subordinate, or a training course. Belief in the quality of the means, like belief in one's own ability, creates high expectations for success and triggers a fruitful SFP process.

Another variant of external efficacy refers to sources of expectations of success that are divorced from means and, instead, relate to beliefs about favorable or unfavorable external conditions. This is "circumstantial efficacy." Examples include home-court advantage and winning the opening coin toss in sporting competitions. Circumstantial efficacy also includes one's evaluation of a competitor's ability or of the relative ease or difficulty of a particular sales territory. Expecting the competition to be tough, the territory to be inimical, and the weather conditions to be inimical to our kind of operations reduces our circumstantial efficacy. Expecting favorable conditions, easy competition, and sensing positive omens, our circumstantial efficacy would be high and we would perform better.

To clarify the nuances, consider a job applicant. He might ask himself, "Am I cut out for this kind of job?" This is the self-efficacy question. He might further wonder, "Will they provide me with the tools I need to succeed?" This is the means efficacy question. Finally, he might consider who else is applying for the job, how many candidates there are, how qualified they are, and how many openings there are. These would be questions regarding circumstantial efficacy. The latter concerns neither the applicant's own ability nor the available tools; rather, they involve external factors not encompassed by self-efficacy or means efficacy that may affect his expectations for success and motivation to exert effort and, in the end, lead to success or failure. Research has shown that boosting competitors' circumstantial efficacy by merely informing them that they had an advantage nearly doubled their likelihood of actually winning; conversely, competitors who were told that they were at a disadvantage had a seriously diminished likelihood of winning.

Like the other sources of efficacy beliefs, circumstantial efficacy affords managers opportunities for getting SFP to work for them and their subordinates rather than against them. Managers can persuade their subordinates that the competition is not so tough or that operating on someone else's turf may be a contrary circumstance for us, but we've got countervailing resources that give us the advantage. "On balance, circumstances favor us."

Finally, research has shown group-level expectancy effects in which raising a manager's expectations for a whole group, as distinct from expectations toward particular individuals, causes that group to outperform control groups. This is especially important in team sports as well as in the teamwork that has emerged as a defining feature of modern organizations.

A fascinating but elusive aspect of interpersonal SFP involves the communication of expectations. Some of this communication is verbal and conscious, but much of it is not. Managers exhibit numerous nonverbal behaviors by which they convey their expectations, whether high or low, to their subordinates. When they expect more, they unwittingly more often nod their heads affirmatively, draw nearer physically, maintain eye contact, speak fast, and show great patience toward those they are supervising. These nonverbal behaviors "warm" the interpersonal relationship, create a climate of support, and foster success. Being subconscious, these nonverbal behaviors penetrate employees undetected "below their radar." Thus, SFP operates beyond the awareness of both parties. This explains why managers and employees know little or nothing about it.

Other ways in which leaders favor those of whom they expect more include providing them with more input, more feedback, and more opportunities to show what they can do, while those of whom less is expected are left, neglected, "on the bench." In short, managers invest their best leadership in subordinates whom they expect will succeed and withhold such treatment from the others. They do it unintentionally—but they do it and thereby unwittingly make their prophecies come true. Debriefing after Pygmalion experiments reveals how subconscious the process is; leaders insist that those randomly designated as having higher potential actually were more capable and that the leaders did nothing to produce the result. It often takes considerable effort to persuade participating leaders that the designations of potential had been random.

Fortunately, the high expectations that motivate enhanced performance also augment subordinate satisfaction. In every Pygmalion experiment in which satisfaction was measured, it was significantly increased. This is not surprising. High expectations and the resulting superior performance are satisfying because, by and large, employees want to succeed, and they are more satisfied when they do. Thus, all the news is good news, so far as the Pygmalion effect is concerned.

Importance

Meta-analyses have confirmed that the magnitude of the Pygmalion effect in management is medium to large. The Pygmalion research is unique in being entirely based on field experimentation, lending it extraordinary internal and external validity. Experimental design confirms the causal flow from leader expectations to follower performance, and the field settings confirm its generalizability. What remains to be shown is the *practical* validity of the Pygmalion effect. Although abundant replications have produced the effect in various organizations, attempts to train managers to *apply* it have been less successful. Managers' prior acquaintance with their subordinates appears to be a major barrier to widespread applicability. Virtually all the successful SFP replications have been among newcomers whose managers had not previously known them. Familiarity apparently crystallizes expectations because managers do not expect their subordinates to change much. Therefore, the most effective applications may be made among managers and their new subordinates.

Organizational innovations and other deviations from routine that unfreeze standard operating procedure are particularly conducive to SFP effects. Organizational development interventions or profound changes in organizational structure or function resulting from, say, mergers and acquisitions or personnel transitions open a window of opportunity. Savvy managers piggyback on these unsettling events and raise expectations to promote successful change and productive outcomes. In one classic industrial example, introducing simple job rotation and job enrichment produced significant improvements in productivity when accompanied by information that raised expectations from the new procedures, but neither innovation improved productivity when expectations were not raised. The practical upshot is clear: Change—any change—presents managers with opportunities for creating productive SFP. It is incumbent on those who want to lead individuals, teams, and organizations to success to convey high expectations whenever the opportunity presents itself. Conversely, cynical expressions of doubt about reorganizations, innovations, or developmental interventions condemn them to failure. Thus, the SFP agenda for managers is twofold: They must implant high expectations and they must counteract manifestations of contrary expectations.

A potential ethical dilemma may arise with regard to intentionally creating SFP effects. Some may question the admissibility of communicating high expectations as a management ploy in the absence of the manager's true belief in the subordinate's potential. Anyone who insists on strictly authentic communication and absolute truthfulness in interpersonal relations may be reluctant to convey any message that is not totally frank. However, such reluctance may amount to forfeiting a highly effective tool for enhancing subordinates' motivation and performance. Worse still, if total openness in communication means informing subordinates of their shortcomings and expressing genuine expectations of failure, the result inevitably will be suboptimal use of the available human resources. Few managers will be so foolish as to express such doubts, but many will refrain from pronouncements that exceed their actual assessments just to produce positive SFP. Unfortunately, refraining will cost them dearly because they will not reap the boost in subordinates' output that conveying high expectations would. The larger truth is that conveying high expectations—even when in doubt—is likely to produce better performance.

The essence of SFP in management is that managers get the employees they expect. Expect more and you will get more. However, the converse is true, too: Expect less and you will get less. All managers should strive to play a Pygmalion role by communicating high expectations regarding their subordinates' potential, thereby fostering in their subordinates high self-efficacy and high expectations for their own success. High expectations are too important to be left to chance or whim; they should be built into all manager-worker relationships and should be part of all managerial training and development programs.

Dov Eden

See also Appreciative Inquiry Model; Authentic Leadership; Goal-Setting Theory; Leadership Practices; Positive Organizational Scholarship; *Practice of Management, The;* Social Cognitive Theory; Transformational Theory of Leadership

Further Readings

Eden, D. (1992). Leadership and expectations: Pygmalion effects and other self fulfilling prophecies in organizations. *Leadership Quarterly, 3,* 271–305.

Eden, D. (2001). Means efficacy: External sources of general and specific subjective efficacy. In M. Erez, U. Kleinbeck, & H. Thierry (Eds.), *Work motivation in the context of a globalizing economy* (pp. 73–85). Mahwah, NJ: Lawrence Erlbaum.

Eden, D. (2003). Self-fulfilling prophecies in organizations. In J. Greenberg (Ed.), *Organizational behavior: The state of the science* (2nd ed., pp. 91–122). Mahwah, NJ: Lawrence Erlbaum.

Eden, D., Ganzach, Y., Granat-Flomin, R., & Zigman, T. (2010). Augmenting means efficacy to improve performance: Two field experiments. *Journal of Management, 36,* 687–713.

Eden, D., Geller, D., Gewirtz, A., Gordon-Terner, R., Inbar, I., Liberman, M., . . . Shalit, M. (2000). Implanting Pygmalion leadership style through workshop training: Seven field experiments. *Leadership Quarterly, 11,* 171–210.

Eden, D., & Sulimani, R. (2002). Pygmalion training made effective: Greater mastery through augmentation of self-efficacy and means efficacy. In B. J. Avolio & F. J. Yammarino (Eds.), *Transformational and charismatic leadership: The road ahead* (pp. 287–308). Oxford, England: Elsevier.

McNatt, D. B. (2000). Ancient Pygmalion joins contemporary management: A meta-analysis of the result. *Journal of Applied Psychology, 85,* 314–322.

Merton, R. K. (1948). The self-fulfilling prophecy. *Antioch Review, 8,* 193–210.

Rosenthal, R. (2002). Covert communication in classrooms, clinics, courtrooms, and cubicles. *American Psychologist, 57,* 838–849.

Stirin, K., Ganzach, Y., Pazy, A., & Eden, D. (2012). The effect of perceived advantage and disadvantage on performance: The role of external efficacy. *Applied Psychology: An International Review, 61*(1), 81–96.

SENSEMAKING

Sensemaking, an idea pioneered by the social psychologist Karl Weick, involves developing retrospective images and words that rationalize what people are doing; it seeks to capture the kinds of verbalizing and writing about situated action in organizational context. In effect, it is a process that makes meaningful social action take place in an organization. The terms *enactment* and *sensemaking* are joined in organizational studies to connect individual cognitive and affective processes with organizational structures. They are powerful "bridging concepts" that enable analysts to attribute meaning and negotiated order to the domain of "organization," and as such, they are designed to illuminate how organizations work, change, and even grow. The utility of the ideas is revealed in qualitative case studies, in statistically based research, and in the frequency with which they are cited. The approach has been applied to many kinds of organizations and has stimulated abundant research, although the primary application has been to analyze organizational change in corporations. It is perhaps less a theory than a frame of reference within which qualitative studies of organizations can be cast. The value of this for management theory is that it addresses the question of how actors feel attached to the organization and how the organization presents itself to those who work there. The entry proceeds as follows: Sensemaking is defined and the evolution of the ideas outlined; the ideas of Karl Weick are highlighted, and the importance of the ideas for organizational theory noted. Some of the critical issues that remain to be clarified in the approach end the entry.

Fundamentals

Sensemaking begins in situations in which people define, elaborate, identify, and name something. Sensemaking is transactional and interactional, collective, and shared. While individual actors struggle to create order, it is through the discourse and written texts that collective meaning arises and is sustained. Weick's foundational concern is how people make sense and how this is done in organizational context. The base for analysis might be called a *field*—a taken-for-granted world of assumptions and tacit meanings that cannot be captured easily or directly. As soon as it is noticed, it is no longer out of sight and may be questioned. The taken-for-granted field contrasts with what might be called *the ground* or what is noticed. Ambiguity and uncertainty with the accompanying emotional arousal produces responses, interpretation, or enactment. *Enactment* leads to *selection* among cues. *Retention* of some cues takes place, while others fade in importance. *Remembering* has both an individual and social aspect. These processes somehow become refined by feedback and amplification and are then part of generic sensemaking of the organization. The organization's view of itself, its identity and image, are reflected in the actor's sense of placement, or not. It is essential to understand the taken-for-granted culture of an organization to understand its resistance to change. On the other hand, change is incipient in sensemaking, because responses to new events are contrasted with memory of consequential past events. Practices then may be found wanting and adjusted. The richness of the ideas is found in the capacity to understand change as well as stability. This is a unique feature of a frame of reference since most are used to examine cross-sectional patterns of stability rather more than change. Failure, dissonance, confusion, and doubt are features of organizational life.

The sensemaking process is sometimes misunderstood. Sensemaking is not interpretation because it involves noting, noticing, picking, and plucking out cues that are then interpreted. People generate what they interpret. Sensemaking is not a metaphor: It is literally how people make sense. It is a process that is grounded in identity construction; it is retrospective, enacted in sensible environments, social, ongoing, focused on, patterned by extracted cues, and driven by plausibility. Because all deciding is fraught with ambiguity, making sense may only require that the deciding be plausible and acceptable. It does not begin with or produce "selves" and thus is *not* "symbolic interaction." While drawing on phenomenological ideas and Gestalt psychology, it moves beyond perceptions and cognitions into *collective social processes*. Two linked patterns are individual sensemaking and organizational sensemaking. Individually oriented sensemaking parallels and is connected to organizational or "generic sensemaking," a product of routines, tasks, and communications, especially technologies. These organizational processes sustain identity, image, or "who we are as an organization." The environment and the organization are not two entities but one. Subject and object are linked in transactional processes. In some sense, the organization projects a meaningful environment for its members and they act to sustain it. It is a way the organization dramatizes itself to its members through their own talk. While this is an abstraction, it goes to explain how the members of the organization see the organization, its role,

its history, and even its future. From a strategic or management perspective, changing organizational imagery, stated core values, and the organizational culture are linked loosely, but they are connected. They reinforce each other in feedback loops, so change is problematic. While the connections made between values, organizational segments, and units may be malleable, they are also rooted in the everyday life of the participants and contribute to their sense of connectedness.

The sensemaking approach seeks to understand both the sources of stability and change. In many respects, the problem of social science is to explain change and reactions to change; sensemaking directs attention to situations and processes that "don't make sense," and both indicate and produce more change. One might urge in a shorthand fashion: Watch for anomalies.

Evolution

Any theory, paradigm, or frame of reference will change as a result of new research concepts, techniques, and findings, as well as "rethinking" the frame of reference itself. Weick's compact and persuasive book, *The Social Psychology of Organization,* was published in 1969 and appeared in a second edition in 1979. Here, the scheme is laid out in diagrammatic form, emphasizing loose coupling and the processes of enactment, selection, retention, and feedback. The idea of loose coupling was a way of capturing the linkages between the salient processes within the model. Sometimes the entire scheme is called a model based on loose coupling, a sensemaking paradigm, or even a method. It is certainly a process-oriented framework for organizational/management theory.

The sensemaking approach attracted much attention following the publication of the "Loose Coupling" paper in the *Administrative Science Quarterly* in 1976. The loose coupling essay argued that the connections between actions and thought, between variables, between organizations as intersubjective constructions as individual cognitions, and within and between segments of organization were indeterminate, erstwhile, transitory, interpreted, and in every way subtly interconnected. The essay contains some examples from schools but is primarily an imaginative speculation about the articulation of organizational action. There is a tantalizing insubstantiality about it, in part because it captures two quite distinction processes: (a) those that link actors and organizations and (b) descriptions of how actors are linked or connected to organizational action itself. These are two problems that call out for integrated approaches. Loose coupling was used as a mode of capturing connections within and between organizational segments, but the larger paradigm was labeled as sensemaking, in which enactment was one phase of organizing.

Perhaps the most widely available examples of sensemaking analysis are found in the second part of Weick's 2001 edited book. This contains the classic papers on ecological change—on the Mann Gulch fire, the Tenerife air controller disaster, and the playful paper on technology as an equivoque. These illustrate the richness and complexity of sensemaking through detailed case studies. These case studies illustrate the locus of change, the disturbing anomaly that leads to reflection and reassessments, and a fruitful sequence that may imply the need for organizational change. From response follows enactment, or setting the cues in context, only to lead to selection among the cues to shape some sort of "collective mind." The collective mind is his version of how a consistent configuration of meaning is settled on, making possible repeated routines and technology and communication that sustains the necessary order. Once in place, this enables retention of the necessary to enable high-reliability practices in organizations. In a recent programmatic essay written with Kathleen Sutcliffe and David Obstfeld, Weick argues the need for the approach to be more future and action oriented, more macro, more closely tied to organizing, meshed more boldly with identity, more behaviorally defined, less sedentary, more infused with emotion and with sensegiving and persuasion.

Importance

Sensemaking has appeal because it makes imaginative claims about how people define events and act within the constraints of organized activity. It appeals neither to attitudes and values nor to structural characterizations such as "contingency theory," "rational choice," or the "iron cage" to explain organizational behavior. It explores meaning making. It is an approach to management theory that begins with experienced situations and works

to assemble them as a window into organizational structure. Because organizations combine order and disorder regularly, Weick, for example, uses stylized writing to suggest the kinds of experience he wants readers to recognize. The aim of his stylistic writing is to capture the appearance of complexity, whether in poetry, organizational analysis, or current affairs, and point to similar phenomena in the organizational world. This is theorizing by analogy. In some sense, the play on and with ambiguity, uncertainty, information overload, and turbulence command a rich, expressive, and often poetic language. Perhaps this "play" on words best captures sensemaking. To understand sensemaking as the basis for action one must feel it. Tables and graphic presentations do not produce much feeling. For example, Weick makes counterintuitive statements; constructs lists that, though intriguing, are not Aristotelian—that is, linear, mutually exclusive, and exhaustive; reverses the center and periphery of his concern and stretches definitions beyond easy recognition. Connotation, what is suggested, often rules denotation or precise reference. Perhaps context, what the reader brings to the reading, makes a text "work." Think of sensemaking in yet another way. Knowing the role of sensemaking should caution against employing top-down commands, massively orchestrated management strategies, and draconian reorganizations, because they erode and may explode what ordering guides the going concern.

Although widely used, the term *sensemaking* is subject to considerable debate; there is no consistent pattern of use, and its spongelike quality enhances its appeal. The most accessible iconic or miniature versions of sensemaking as a process are the diagrams featured in Weick's publications that chart the connections between ecological change, enactment, selection, retention, and remembering. At the same time, it is certainly ironic to introduce ideas that dance out of their linear frames of reference in boxes and arrows, lists, categories, and diagrams. As the ideas have become more popular, they have been used to describe statistically generated findings that cannot probe and reveal such meanings.

The matter of concern to sensemaking theorists is how organizations cope with events, incidents, and happenings that stand out: those that are ambiguous, uncertain, and turbulent—in short, in which deciding is consequential but impossible to anticipate consistently. There is a deep contradiction in this formulation, in that inability to maintain an eye on the variety that threatens the assumed *status quo ante* (my terms) may lead to ritualistic responses. One might say that anomalies processing is the basis for crises in dangerous occupations, firefighting, policing, and war. These occupations need reliable routines in the face of danger, and the work can spiral into destruction and death as Weick's work on disasters, fighting forest fires, routines on aircraft carriers, and nuclear power stations vividly illustrate. It is the uneasy combination of responses to routine events and emergency events that sustains organizational vitality. One can make the case that such organizations are classic examples of how environment and organization become one.

Consider organizations as shifting configurations of sensing and sensemaking. Once in place, imagery stabilizes action. Such imagery and rhetoric are the data used in survey research. Such research elicits rationalizations for what has been done. The shaping of these images and rhetoric is subtle. The configuration or image of an organization rests on several processes: talk, awareness of the distinction between a map (the logic) and the territory (what is done), minimal sensible structures, ideologies, organizational language, vocabularies of work or coping, and tradition and stories. These might be called *pins* that connect and secure meaning; they are ordering resources that hang together in some way. Given this substance, generic subjectivity, or the organization's sense of itself, rests on arguing, expecting, committing (to the organization), and manipulation. Revealing them requires ethnographic work. The first two, arguing and expecting, seem to point to unification and overt calls for organizational team work, while the second two, committing and manipulating, are the arenas in which managers work given the canopy of the organization's constraints. In some sense, interlocking organizational routines and tasks with interpretation (sensemaking) and communication are the yoke that pulls the organization along. Another way of stating this is that the intersubjective sensemaking occurs and is patterned or shadowed always by the generic sensemaking that is the organization's sense of itself.

Research in the sensemaking tradition has had enormous influence. It is certainly one of the most frequently cited organizational theories and is required reading in graduate programs in sociology, business, political science, and policy studies. They are unique for their literary and poetic style, detail, and consistent counterintuitive insights. Research by Dennis Gioia and colleagues on the impact of a "spin-off" on corporate executives richly documents the impacts of change at both the individual and the organizational level and is a detailed example of sensemaking research.

Four major questions arise about the further value of the approach. First, sensemaking captured in flowcharts outlines at a high level of abstraction a sketch of organized action in which routines, technology, and communication are said to bring together collective action. If all connections between phases are *problematic*, why are arrows and boxes used to represent them? Mixed evidence is provided of this in published research: snippets from media events; poems; brief commentaries, vignettes; lists; epigrams; diagrams, including boxes and arrows of causal flows of effects and occasional reflections on the argument, and tables from surveys. This stylistic mode or trope makes the claims tentative and subject to doubt, or "plausibility." In some sense, the arguments cry out for detailed ethnographic materials of a linking sort that would hone putative connections. Given this, of course, one might argue immediately "it depends on context," and that both loose and tight coupling can take place at the same time within any organization. Second, rationality, planning, and policy are made salient in a given organizational context and do not speak with a single "voice." The sensemaking of individuals, segments, groups, managers, top command, or line workers can clearly differ from the generic sensemaking of the articulated rhetoric of management in regard to an organization's view of itself. The research using this approach is devotedly managerial and articulates the paradoxes of upper management, not the workers, supervisors, or middle-level executives. Actors interpret, produce, and reproduce the patterns of risks they most fear. The "environment" is constituted—with others, for others, and by others. In organizations in which risk is both sought and a fundamental aspect of its mandate—such as firefighting, emergency medical services, policing, and other federal regulatory bodies—a rationing conservatism arises from the need to buffer demand on the organization, while innovation comes from interpreted responses to externally generated crises. All such high-risk organizations live in the shadow of death, yet routine, reliable procedures and backup systems mitigate this existential fact.

Heedful interactions, joint representations of mutual relations, and skillful responses to events within systems requiring highly reliable responses to complex and sometimes incomprehensible occurrences make for subtle forms of human sharing and cooperation. Rationality emerges from sensible, mutual responses to complex situations. Through and by mutual sense-making, reliability obtains under such circumstances. Technology, especially in high-risk organizations, is always embedded in the sensemaking of the organization and cannot stand outside of it. In short, top management does not create consensual meaning. The approach begins with the actor but seeks to explain collective organizational actions. There is an individual actor at the center of this theory: the person who notices an anomaly, makes sense of it, selects out cues and retains some, and in effect engages in the generic sensemaking of the organization. Even though cues are taken from the cues of others, the unit is the actor, not the dyadic unit, the group, or the network. This provides flexibility in the theorizing in that anomalies reinterpreted can make organizational change possible. But the boxes-and-arrows diagrams create a pride of associations, analogies, similarities, and resemblances that, although crucial in turning points, cannot be specified in such diagrams. In effect, these, too, produce apparent conflict between a list that can be seen as either metonymic (a sequence, one at a time, in some order), synecdochical (parts of a larger whole), or metaphoric (similar to or like something else). Fourth, a basic assumption in sensemaking research is that people in the course of responding must trust each other: managers, their employees; top management, their managers; and stakeholders, their management and employees. Questions of strategic management and planning hinge on trust, yet it remains a most difficult idea to measure and pin down.

Peter K. Manning

See also Behavioral Theory of the Firm; High-Reliability Organizations; Information Richness Theory; Learning Organizations; Organizational Culture Theory; Organizational Learning; Tacit Knowledge

Further Readings

Gioia, D. A., & Thomas, J. B. (1996). Identity, image, and issue interpretation: Sensemaking during strategic change in academia. *Administrative Science Quarterly, 41,* 370–413.

Manning, P. K. (2004). *Narcs' game* (2nd ed.). Prospect Heights, IL: Waveland Press.

Van Maanen, J. (1995). Style as theory. *Organization Science, 6,* 133–143.

Weick, K. E. (1976). Educational organizations as loosely coupled systems. *Administrative Science Quarterly, 21,* 1–19.

Weick, K. E. (1979). *The social psychology of organizing* (2nd ed.). Reading, MA: Addison-Wesley.

Weick, K. E. (1995). *Sensemaking in the organization.* Thousand Oaks, CA: Sage.

Weick, K. E. (2001). *Making sense of the organization.* Malden, MA: Blackwell.

Weick, K. E., Sutcliffe, K., & Obstfeld, D. (2005). Organizing and the process of sensemaking. *Organization Science, 16,* 409–421.

SERVANT LEADERSHIP

It can easily be argued that leadership is the most critical element of management; through leadership, the climate of the organization, attitudes and motivation of employees, and strategic direction of the organization are established. Although servant leaders have emerged throughout history, servant leadership is a theory that is especially well-suited for 21st-century management. To an increasing extent, the vast majority of organizations face turbulent environments characterized by fierce global competition and severe social, political, and economic pressures. An empowered, creative, and motivated workforce is best able to handle such unstable environments. In addition to environmental turbulence, the activities of organizations are more visible and under closer scrutiny than ever before, making corporate responsibility a critical goal. Servant leadership theory, defined as leadership based on serving followers first with ethical, supportive, and empathetic behaviors, directly addresses these challenges. Whereas other leadership theories, such as transformational leadership, focus on aligning follower behavior with the goals of the organization, servant leadership has a strong focus on providing followers with the tools and support they need to reach their full potential. When followers are empowered, and supported and can trust their leaders, their engagement in required, especially discretionary, behaviors naturally follows. Thus, servant leadership is unique among approaches to leadership in that it accentuates meeting the needs of followers.

Servant leadership is also unparalleled among leadership theories for its contention that leaders cannot be true servants unless they focus on serving others in *all* realms of life (work, family, community). Servant leadership is based on the premise that when leaders place serving followers above everything else, followers gain self-confidence and develop trust in the leader; they proceed on a journey toward realizing their full potential. Followers respond to support from leaders by reciprocating with behaviors that benefit the leader, coworkers, the organization, and the community in which the organization is embedded. In addition, servant leadership is alone among leadership approaches for advocating the grooming of select followers into servant leaders, a practice, which across many leaders, culminates in the creation of a servant leadership culture that promotes helping others. This entry introduces the key tenets of this emerging theory of leadership, with a focus on illustrating the potential that the theory has for enhancing knowledge of leadership as well as serving as a model for practicing managers. The measurement of servant leadership and the importance of developing the theory and empirically researching servant leadership at multiple levels of analysis are discussed. Finally, several topics for future study and development of the theory are outlined.

Fundamentals

Although introduced in 1970 by Robert Greenleaf and quickly attracting attention among practitioners, it was not until the 2000s that empirical research on this approach to leadership began to be published in scientific journals. Thus far, the findings of this research have supported the validity of servant leadership theory at both the individual and team levels. Specifically, the research has demonstrated that servant leadership, even when controlling the effect of popular leadership theories, such as transformational leadership and leader–member exchange, is related to important outcomes.

Critical to the commencement of empirical research on servant leadership was the development of a measure. The first scale to be developed based on rigorous scale development procedures culminated in a measure that captures seven independent

dimensions that define the domain of servant leadership, with all dimensions contributing toward overall or global servant leadership:

1. *Emotional healing*—being sensitive to the personal setbacks faced by followers

2. *Creating value for the community*—serving as a role model to followers by being active in helping the community as well as encouraging followers to also provide service to the community

3. *Conceptual skills*—the task knowledge and problem-solving abilities necessary for being able to provide help to followers

4. *Empowering*—providing followers with the autonomy, decision-making influence, and self-confidence critical for enabling followers to realize their full potential

5. *Helping subordinates grow and succeed*—providing emotional support and guidance to help followers develop professionally and to accomplish personal goals

6. *Putting subordinates first*—captures the essence of servant leadership, involves prioritizing fulfillment of follower needs above one's own needs

7. *Behaving ethically*—the demonstration of fairness, honesty, and integrity both at work and outside work, critical for gaining the trust and respect of followers

Although the initial validation of this servant leadership measure revealed that the dimensions uniquely related to outcomes, most researchers have tended to collapse the dimensions into a global servant leadership measure.

At the individual level, a positive association has been found between servant leadership and organizational commitment, commitment to the leader, self-efficacy (one's confidence in being able to perform specific tasks well), job performance, organizational citizenship behaviors (behaviors that extend beyond what is expected based on the employment contract), creativity, and participation in activities that benefit the community. Helping to explain how servant leadership influences outcomes—such as helping citizenship behaviors, creativity, and community service behaviors—is the finding that servant leadership cultivates within followers a desire to fulfill one's inner potential by seeking opportunities that help develop skills and abilities. Also contributing to the positive influence of servant leadership is the follower self-confidence and trust in leaders that grows in followers because of the empathy, support, mentoring, and concern shown by servant leaders toward their followers. Despite the overall positive findings for servant leadership at the individual level, it has been found that followers differ in their desire to be led by a servant leader. Although research has not uncovered any followers who are opposed to servant leadership, a range of responses from indifference to great enthusiasm for servant leadership has been found. Moreover, followers who express indifference toward servant leadership express less positive work attitudes and engage in lower levels of job performance and organizational citizenship behaviors the more their leader engages in servant leadership behaviors.

At the team level, servant leadership has been shown to be positively related to team psychological safety, which refers to team climates in which people trust, respect, and care for one another and as a result feel safe in expressing their viewpoints and personalities. Furthermore, servant leadership relates positively to team procedural justice climate, which depicts settings in which team members perceive that the processes followed to make decisions regarding team members are fair. Servant leadership has also been shown to cultivate strong service climates, which have direct implications for customer satisfaction. Servant leadership also positively relates to team potency, defined as a team's confidence in its ability to perform well, as well as team performance and team engagement in organizational citizenship behaviors.

Servant leadership has also been shown to moderate important relationships in team settings. Especially noteworthy is a study of five banks in which it was discovered that goal and process clarity positively related to team potency *only* in the presence of a servant leader. These results suggest a critical qualifying condition for the long-accepted belief that goal clarity has a beneficial effect on team potency and subsequent team performance. Specifically, the results indicated that when leaders tend not to engage in servant leadership behaviors, teams actually experience significantly higher levels of team potency and team performance when they are *unclear* about the goal. It appears that teams are frustrated when they know exactly what the goal is but cannot reach it because they are not getting the support that they need from the leader. However, in the presence of a servant leader, goal and process clarity showed a strong positive association with team potency and team performance.

Importance

The encouraging research results suggest that it may be advantageous for practicing managers to develop a full repertoire of servant leadership behaviors. This represents a challenge, however; it is considerably more difficult to be a servant leader than a "traditional" leader. Directing and controlling followers via formal power and authority is relatively easy compared to treating each follower as a unique individual and taking the time and effort to ensure that all followers reach their full potential. Given this formidable challenge, it becomes necessary for those in leadership roles to be patient in developing their servant leadership skills. Becoming an outstanding leader by engaging in servant leader behaviors requires devotion and practice. Just as a concert pianist or star athlete must practice incessantly build and maintain necessary skills, servant leadership similarly requires considerable practice, and maintaining the skill requires continued attention over the course of a career as a leader.

Given that scientific research on servant leadership is in its infancy, much remains to be learned about this theory of leadership, especially the antecedents of servant leadership and the specific processes through which it influences individual and team outcomes. And as with virtually all topics in management, the cross-cultural effects on servant leadership and its relationships with antecedents and outcomes also need more research.

A number of antecedents of servant leadership have been identified but remain untested empirically. Perhaps the most central antecedent is for the leader to have a desire to serve others. Personality characteristics, such as altruism, conscientiousness, and agreeableness might be explored as antecedents of servant leadership. Emotional intelligence likely plays a critical antecedent role because of the importance of (1) being aware of one's own emotions before attempting to understand the emotions of others, (2) listening to and empathizing with followers to determine how to best serve each follower, and

(3) being able to regulate one's emotions to enhance the chance that followers will trust and respect the leader. And from the follower side of the leader-follower relationship, a desire for servant leadership is necessary.

In terms of the process through which servant leadership affects outcomes, much needs to be explored. Servant leadership's focus on helping followers to attain their full potential suggests the critical importance of the dyadic relationship between leader and follower. It has been proposed that servant leaders endeavor through one-on-one communication to understand the abilities, needs, desires, goals, and potential of followers. Especially with respect to individual outcomes, servant leadership most likely takes place within the dyadic relationship between leader and follower. Research over the past few decades has suggested that the relationships employees develop with their leaders are foremost in importance in understanding the way in which employees can fulfill their potential and become self-motivated. When leaders nurture self-efficacy and self-motivation, employees become more committed to organizational values and become more inclined to "go the extra mile" in serving the organization's constituents. Much of this research argues that leaders foster these important attitudes and behaviors by forming social exchange relationships with their followers rather than relying solely on the economic incentives tied to the employment agreement or the authority vested in their positions. This suggests that examination of the interplay between leader-follower dyadic interactions as fully articulated by leader–member exchange theory and servant leadership may be fruitful. Indeed, it has been shown that servant leaders tend to form more high-quality leader–member exchange relationships with followers than leaders who do not engage in servant leadership. Research is therefore needed on the role that leader–member exchange relationship quality plays in the process through which servant leadership influences individual outcomes.

Finally, more needs to be explored with respect to the way in which servant leadership unfolds in different cultural contexts. Thus far, research has shown consistent results across the countries in which servant leadership has been studied, including Africa, mainland China, Hong Kong, and the United States. To more fully understand the cross-cultural implications of servant leadership antecedents, process, and outcomes, the role of key cultural variables—such as collectivism, power distance, and the salience of context—needs to be investigated.

In sum, servant leaders build trust by selflessly serving others first. The theme of serving others before oneself extends from the workplace to home and community. In all aspects of life, servant leaders serve others first. But perhaps most important, servant leaders instill in followers the self-confidence and desire to become servant leaders. Through the transformation of followers into servant leaders, a culture of servant leadership can be created. A culture of helping strives to assist all members of the organization and the community to realize their full human potential.

Robert C. Liden

See also Authentic Leadership; Emotional and Social Intelligence; Empowerment; Ethical Decision Making, Interactionist Model of; Fairness Theory; Leader–Member Exchange Theory; Social Exchange Theory; Transformational Theory of Leadership

Further Readings

Ehrhart, M. G. (2004). Leadership and procedural justice climate as antecedents of unit-level organizational citizenship behavior. *Personnel Psychology, 57,* 61–94.

Graham, J. W. (1991). Servant-leader in organizations: Inspirational and moral. *Leadership Quarterly, 2,* 105–119.

Greenleaf, R. K. (1977). *Servant leadership: A journey into the nature of legitimate power and greatness.* New York, NY: Paulist Press.

Hu, J., & Liden, R. C. (2011). Antecedents of team potency and team effectiveness: An examination of goal and process clarity and servant leadership. *Journal of Applied Psychology, 96,* 851–862.

Keith, K. M. (2008). *The case for servant leadership.* Westfield, IN: Greenleaf Center for Servant Leadership.

Liden, R. C., Wayne, S. J., Zhao, H., & Henderson, D. (2008). Servant leadership: Development of a multidimensional measure and multilevel assessment. *Leadership Quarterly, 19,* 161–177.

Neubert, M. J., Kacmar, K. M., Carlson, D. S., Chonko, L. B., & Roberts, J. A. (2008). Regulatory focus as a mediator of the influence of initiating structure and servant leadership on employee behavior. *Journal of Applied Psychology, 93,* 1220–1233.

Schaubroeck, J., Lam, S. S. K., & Peng, A. C. (2011). Cognition-based and affect-based trust as mediators of leader behavior influences on team performance. *Journal of Applied Psychology, 96,* 863–871.

Van Dierendonck, D. (2011). Servant leadership: A review and synthesis. *Journal of Management, 37,* 1228–1261.

Walumbwa, F. O., Hartnell, C. A., & Oke, A. (2010). Servant leadership, procedural justice climate, service climate, employee attitudes, and organizational citizenship behavior: A cross-level investigation. *Journal of Applied Psychology, 95,* 517–529.

Seven-S Framework

The Seven-S (7S) framework is a managerial tool for analyzing and diagnosing organizational performance and effectiveness. The framework was jointly developed by Tom Peters, Robert Waterman, Richard Pascale, and Anthony Athos in the late 1970s. Tom Peters and Robert Waterman were both management consultants at McKinsey & Company, a well-known consultancy firm whose management consulting activities were based on applied research in business and industry. The 7S framework was adopted as a main analysis tool by McKinsey; hence, the framework became known as McKinsey's 7S framework. The framework consists of seven key organizational and managerial variables/elements categorized as either soft or hard variables. Soft variables are *staff, styles, skills,* and *shared values,* and hard variables are *strategy, structure,* and *systems.* The framework is based on the assumption that to achieve organizational effectiveness, focusing merely on the rational aspects of organizations such as structure and strategy are not enough. Organizations are complex unities, and to deal with the complexity in any organizational improvement project or program, all seven variables have to be considered simultaneously because they are interdependent and mutually reinforcing. Since the framework was introduced, it has been widely adopted by practitioners as well as by academics for multiple purposes, such as an analytical framework of organizations, as a diagnostic framework of organizational effectiveness and efficiency, as a strategic improvement tool, and so on. Hundreds of organizations have been analyzed using the framework, which remains still popular. The framework's simplicity and memorability/recognizability are also contributing factors to its popularity. This entry reviews the contents of each variable of the framework as well as its historical background and concludes with descriptions of the relevance and importance with some managerial applications.

Fundamentals

As described earlier, the seven variables are considered key organizational factors that are interdependent. These factors interact, dynamically influence each other, and determine the way organizations perform. The factors' interdependency is well illustrated in the way the model is designed.

The *shared values* variable is considered to be the interconnecting center of all other variables. Shared values were originally called *superordinate goals* of organizations. Shared values refer to the guiding concepts and meaning or the purpose of organizations' existence that are shared among all organizational members; hence, shared values provide the foundation of the corporate culture. Normally, shared values do not include "materialistic" and measurable goals such as financial results or return on investments. Rather they refer to "spiritual"/ethical elements that can touch peoples' hearts deeply and can provide a deeper meaning for their work.

Structure is defined as the main skeleton of the organizational chart. Structure is the way in which work tasks are organized and the way various organizational units are linked to each other. Organizations can be structured in a variety of ways—for example, in a hierarchical way, as a matrix, a network, centralized, decentralized, an adhocracy, a hub, a chain, and so forth.

Strategy refers to plans or course of action for allocating scarce resources to achieve the identified goals over time. Strategic decisions are about the long-term as well as the short-term direction of an organization to achieve competitive advantage over competitors. It is about the way to transform an organization from the present position to the desired position described by its goals. Hence, strategy affects the tactical and operational activities of an organization.

Systems are defined as the formalized procedures, processes, and routines to be followed within the organization. Financial systems, promotion and reward systems, recruitment systems, and information systems are some examples of the internal systems. Through these organizational systems, all the processes and information flows and key activities are carried out.

Staff is described in terms of personnel, the composition of the workforce within the organization. Some will say that an organization is nothing but its people and only through its people can the organization carry out activities and achieve its goals. In fact, many leading organizations emphasize the importance of the people dimension.

Skills are the distinctive capabilities possessed by individuals, groups, and the organization as a whole. The skills variable can be referred to as the core competencies of the organization, and hence, it is a strong component of competitive advantages.

Style refers to the issues of how key managers behave in achieving organizational goals, and hence, this variable is also considered to encompass the cultural style of the organization. All organizations have their own specific culture and management style. The styles/culture includes the dominant values, beliefs, norms, and traditions that are relatively enduring features that permeate organizational life.

Importance

The 7S framework was formally introduced in the June 1980 issue of *Business Horizons,* in an article titled "Structure Is Not Organization," by Tom Peters, Bob Waterman, and Julien Phillips. One year later in 1981, the framework was adopted by Richard Pascale and Anthony Athos in their book *The Art of Japanese Management,* in which they documented how and why Japanese industry had been so successful. Using the 7S framework as a conceptual analysis tool in the 34 case studies of Japanese organizations, Pascale and Athos could identify the characteristics of successful Japanese companies. They found out that the Japanese companies excelled in combining both the "soft" and "hard" variables of the organizations, whereas Western companies generally ignored the soft dimensions and concentrated on the hard ones. The critical findings from their study were that the Japanese companies were not only good in combining soft and hard, but they were particularly excellent in the soft dimensions. The findings were in line with the main message of the initial article "Structure Is Not Organization."

Pascale and Athos' book was remarkable in several aspects. First, the book was one of the earliest to identify and describe the critical success factors of Japanese companies and stress the importance of the soft variables. Second, the book was the first to adopt the 7S framework as a conceptual analysis tool for those studied Japanese companies and proved the usefulness of the framework for explaining and analyzing organizational performance and effectiveness. However the 7S framework became famous worldwide not through the Pascale and Athos book, but through the book *In Search of Excellence* written by Peters and Waterman in 1982; the book became a best seller in the United States, with 1.2 million books sold, as well as a best seller worldwide.

In the book, Peters and Waterman used the 7S framework for studying and analyzing 62 of America's most successful companies. Like the findings of Pascale and Athos, Peters and Waterman concluded that the key success factors of American companies were the four soft *S*'s of *shared values, staff, style, and skills.* The study revealed that American companies generally ignored these four variables and tended to focus on the three hard variables: *strategy, structure, and systems.* The reason was that the hard *S*'s are relatively easier to identify and to understand and hence also easier to deal with because they are more tangible factors compared with the four soft ones. Most companies have well-documented organizational charts and strategy formulation. However, when it comes to the soft factors such as skills, styles, or shared values, there are no such documents. These soft factors are not only of intangible character, but they are also diversified greatly among organization members. For instance, peoples' competences are differentiated and are changing constantly. Owing to these reasons, changing organizational structure and strategy are much easier than changing skills, styles, or shared values. Those soft factors are mostly intangible and hence difficult to observe and to measure. The famous six words of Peters and Waterman, "Hard is soft. Soft is hard," symbolically illustrate the paradoxical characteristics of the hard *S* and soft *S* factors. The real competitive advantage of organizations lies in their capability to combine both factors, as was manifested in the successful Japanese and American companies.

By using the 7S framework as a diagnosing tool, Peters and Waterman could identify the following eight key attributes that characterized excellent companies: (1) a bias for action; (2) close to the customer; (3) autonomy and entrepreneurship; (4) productivity through people; (5) hands-on, value driven; (6) stick to the knitting (i.e., focus on what you do best), (7) simple form, lean staff; and (8) simultaneous loose-tight properties (balance between centralized and decentralized organization). These identified eight key attributes are related to all seven organizational factors.

The 7S framework with its four soft S and three hard S factors was introduced when most Western companies had a tendency to focus only on strategy and structure. Although the framework does not include any external/environmental factors, it provided a broad and comprehensive understanding of an organization. The framework's simplicity and ease of recognition made it popular for practitioners to use.

The recognition of, and emphasis on, the soft S factors contributed to a shift in the direction of organization and management theory toward greater awareness of organizational culture. The growth of interest in organizational culture among academics and practitioners beginning in the 1980s was largely influenced by the findings from successful Japanese and American companies where the 7S framework was used as a diagnostic tool. The power of the 7S framework was the distinction between hard and soft S factors and the recognition of the importance of the soft S. The latter would become a cornerstone for a new managerial movement called the "culture-excellence school."

Su Mi Dahlgaard-Park

See also Balanced Scorecard; Contingency Theory; Excellence Characteristics; Meaning and Functions of Organizational Culture; Organizational Culture and Effectiveness; Organizational Development; Strategy and Structure

Further Readings

Dahlgaard-Park, S. M., & Dahlgaard, J. J. (2007). Excellence—25 years evolution. *International Journal of Management History, 13*(4), 371–393.

Pascale, R., & Athos, A. (1981). *The art of Japanese management.* London, England: Penguin.

Peters, T., & Waterman, R. (1982). *In search of excellence.* New York, NY: Harper & Row.

Waterman, R. Jr., Peters, T., & Phillips, J. R. (1980). Structure is not organization. *Business Horizons, 23*(3), 14–26.

SITUATIONAL THEORY OF LEADERSHIP

The situational theory of leadership defines four styles of leadership and states that managers should use the style that is most appropriate for the level of ability and the degree of commitment of each subordinate. This is one of a number of theories describing how different styles of leadership may be appropriate in different contexts; it has a particular focus on the manager's role in developing the abilities of his or her subordinates. The behaviors of leaders and managers toward those they supervise have been an enduring subject for research and inquiry among both academics and practitioners. There is broad agreement that certain styles of leadership are likely to be more effective than others in guiding, motivating, and developing subordinates, but leadership theorists have put forward different descriptions of these effective styles. The following sections summarize the main elements of the theory of situational leadership, explain the relationship of the theory to other theories of leadership styles, and assess the validity and usefulness of the theory in practice.

Fundamentals

The situational theory of leadership has demonstrated enduring appeal since it was first put forward by Paul Hersey and Ken Blanchard in 1968. The authors have made minor refinements to the theory since its first appearance. The following summary is based on the current version of the theory, known as Situational Leadership II. The theory proposes four styles of supervisory leadership, based on a mixture of directive behavior and supportive behaviour. The four styles are

- directing (high directing, low supporting)
- coaching (high directing, high supporting)
- supporting (low directing, high supporting)
- delegating (low directing, low supporting)

According to the theory, each style is appropriate for a particular stage of a subordinate's competence and commitment to perform a task. As the subordinate's levels of ability and commitment change, the manager's leadership style should also change, to achieve the best performance from the subordinate.

People approaching a new task for which they have enthusiasm but no knowledge or skills will benefit from a *directing style* of supervision, where the manager sets out in detail what is entailed and teaches and demonstrates how to undertake the task.

After some experience and some learning, subordinates may have grasped the basics of the task, but their competence level is not yet very high, and their earlier enthusiasm and confidence for the new task may have declined. They will then benefit most from a *coaching style* of supervisory leadership, where the manager invites contributions but retains control over the decisions (the manager is still highly directive) and is also highly supportive, providing praise and encouragement for the subordinate's efforts.

Over time, subordinates' skill level grows, but they may still lack confidence and at times feel insecure. They will benefit most from a *supporting style* of supervision, which involves encouragement, praise, and other forms of support. The manager may act as a sounding board for a subordinate's ideas but will rarely take over decisions.

Finally, as the subordinate's skill level and confidence grows, a *delegating style* is the most appropriate approach. The manager hands over responsibility for the task to a subordinate, while still providing some support, praise, and acknowledgement for that person's achievements.

The theory of situational leadership is based on a positive view of people—a belief that they wish to learn and develop. Hence the expectation that over time, with the correct support and direction, subordinates will develop their skills and that one style of supervision should give way to the next style in the sequence. The ultimate aim is to develop empowered, autonomous subordinates, performing to a high level.

The appropriate style depends on the commitment and competence of the subordinate. The level of development of the subordinate and the appropriate leadership style can be summarized as follows:

- Stage 1: low competence, high commitment—a directing style
- Stage 2: low to some competence, low commitment—a coaching style
- Stage 3: moderate to high competence, variable commitment—a supporting style
- Stage 4: high competence, high commitment—a delegating style

It is important to note that the appropriate style of supervision is specific to a particular task rather than to particular individuals. Thus, for any one subordinate, a delegating style may be appropriate for some tasks, a supporting style for others, and so on. While the theory describes manager-subordinate relationships, the styles can also be applied in an education or training context, to describe teacher-learner interaction.

To be effective as situational leaders, managers need to (1) assess the competence and the confidence of their subordinate in relation to a specific task; (2) use each of the four leadership styles, which may entail overcoming the manager's own preferences for one or two of the styles; and (3) discuss and explain the use of the different styles with subordinates so that they understand and accept the process.

The theory was originally designed to describe supervisory styles a manager could adopt toward an individual subordinate but was later expanded to encompass leadership of teams and of organizations. While the original focus concerns training a subordinate to carry out a specific task or tasks, the theory can also accommodate situations when decisions must be made that affect a whole team, depending on the competence and commitment of the team members.

Relationship With Other Theories of Leadership Styles

Several other popular theories of leadership styles that predated the situational theory of leadership also focused on the extent to which leaders are directive or participative in tackling the decisions that face them and their teams.

One view, put forward by Robert Tannenbaum and Warren H. Schmidt, was that managers could adopt any one of a spectrum of approaches to decision making, from directive at one extreme of the scale to fully participative at the other. In this theory, the most effective style would depend on the nature of the decision and the characteristics (the knowledge, skills and attitudes) of the subordinates.

Other views built on research that had identified two broad categories of supervisors' behaviors—people-oriented behaviors and task-oriented behaviours. One popular theory, put forward by Robert R. Blake and Jane S. Mouton, was that managers could consistently apply a style of leadership that had a high regard for task achievement and also a high regard for the needs of the subordinate. This assumed that subordinates could be self-directing, responsible, and motivated to achieve results in their work.

Paul Hersey and Ken Blanchard's situational theory of leadership is similar, in broad outline, to the ideas of Blake and Mouton and can be traced to the same antecedents. The unique contribution of the situational theory of appropriate leadership style is to advocate different styles, depending on the changing needs of subordinates in relation to specific tasks.

Later theories of leadership styles include path-goal theory, which also suggested that leaders should adopt one of four different styles toward their subordinates, depending on the circumstances. Path-goal theory, however, focused on choosing a style that best suited a subordinate's motivational needs rather than the person's capability and commitment. In selecting a style, leaders were expected to take into account the factors that will motivate the subordinate, and the characteristics of the task they are undertaking.

Many of the more recent theories of leadership have been influenced by the idea of transformational leadership, which is also concerned with how to develop subordinates and with subordinate motivation and has emphasised the role of leaders in inspiring their followers. However, the idea that leaders must balance concern with task achievement with concern for supporting their staff is still very much a part of current thinking about leadership.

Importance

The situational theory of leadership has proved enduring; it is well known and is widely used in training programs in leadership and supervision. The basic elements of the model, of matching style to subordinate readiness, are easily understood, and the theory provides straightforward guidance on how to behave toward subordinates at different stages of development. The journey to competence of the individual subordinate and the changing styles of leadership that help bring about self-reliance and empowerment seem naturally complementary, and the model has an intuitive appeal. In addition, the emphasis on the role of managers in developing their subordinates is appealing and, logically, leads not only to individual growth but also to sustainability for the organization.

A number of criticisms have been made of the situational theory of leadership, however, indicating some limitations and areas where the theory is less than clear.

There have been few independent, peer-reviewed studies of the theory. Those studies that have been carried out offer only limited support for its application in practice, other than the advisability of detailed instruction when subordinates undertake new tasks, with the benefit of a reduction in this directive style as they become more experienced. There is thus little empirical support from independent studies for the accuracy or effectiveness of the situational leadership model.

A particular issue giving rise to criticism has been the description of subordinates' levels of development—a key component in the model. The readiness of the subordinate is defined in terms of ability to carry out the task (competence) and motivation to do so (commitment). The combination of these two elements indicates which leadership style should be practiced. However, the combinations included in the model are not comprehensive. For example, at the first stage for each new task the subordinate is said to be committed but not competent (at this stage, the subordinate has been described by Blanchard as "an enthusiastic beginner"). But not all beginners are enthusiastic. Similarly, the fourth stage contemplates competent and committed subordinates, but some competent subordinates may not be committed. The theory does not explain what leadership styles should be applied in these situations. While we might expect variation in both competence and commitment from subordinates, the four combinations included in the model do not cover every common possibility, and therefore the application of the model is less straightforward than it may first appear.

A second issue is that the amount of support that a leader should provide at each phase of the model is not entirely transparent. The directing and the delegating styles are designated as "low support" styles, but the detailed explanation of the theory (and also experience of managing others) indicates that some support is needed as part of both of these styles.

Another difficulty with the theory concerns the style(s) the manager should adopt when leading a group discussion about decisions facing the whole group, when group members are at different levels of competence and commitment.

A further limitation is that the full range of the theory applies only when the manager has more capability than the subordinate and is therefore in a position to direct and coach: In modern organizations, where managers have responsibilities for specialists and knowledge workers outside their own area of expertise, this is not always the case.

Despite these limitations and areas of lack of clarity, the descriptions of the four styles provide valuable guidance on different ways in which leadership can be exercised—particularly when the detailed descriptions are studied—and this can help managers reflect on the ways in which they behave toward their staff and the areas in which they could develop their leadership skills.

George Boak

See also Contingency Theory of Leadership; Path-Goal Theory of Leadership; Transformational Theory of Leadership

Further Readings

Blake, R. R., & Mouton, J. S. (1964). *The managerial grid.* Houston, TX: Gulf.

Blanchard, K. (2010). *Leading at a higher level.* London, England: FT Press.

Hersey, P. H., Blanchard, K. H., & Johnson, D. E. (2009). *Management of organizational behavior* (9th ed.). Saddle River, NJ: Prentice Hall.

Northouse, P. (2010). *Leadership: Theory and practice.* London, England: Sage.

Tannenbaum, R., & Schmidt, W. H. (1958). How to choose a leadership pattern. *Harvard Business Review, 36*(2) 95–101.

Thompson, G., & Vecchio, R. P. (2009). Situational leadership theory: A test of three versions. *Leadership Quarterly, 20,* 837–848.

SIX SIGMA

The term Six Sigma was first coined by Motorola in the United States during the mid-1980s as a quality improvement process or methodology whose purpose was to improve quality by reducing variation. Motorola called the process "The Six Steps to Six Sigma"—a process that, they claim, saved billions of dollars during the following years. In fact the Six Sigma methodology was first introduced in the United States in 1985 at Florida Power and Light (FPL) when the company decided to apply for the Japanese Quality Award called the Deming Prize. FPL learned the Six Sigma methodology from the JUSE (Japanese Union of Scientists and Engineers) counselors who helped FPL prepare for the Deming Prize application. Six Sigma became widely known by Motorola's and other well-known companies' successful implementation—such as GE and Samsung—and today the Six Sigma methodology has spread all over the world and is used in various sectors—private and public—manufacturing and services. This entry reviews some alternative methodologies or roadmaps to Six Sigma. The entry begins with a review of the fundamentals of Six Sigma, which includes tools and methods as well as impacts of implementing Six Sigma. The entry ends with a discussion of the importance and limitations of Six Sigma.

Fundamentals

Motorola's Six Sigma process was first developed and implemented in the 1980s for manufacturing, and from 1990 the process was adapted to the non-manufacturing areas of the company. The content of Motorola's "Six Steps to Six Sigma" in *nonmanufacturing* is as follows: (1) Identify the product you create or the service you provide to external or internal customers; (2) identify the customer for your product or service and determine what he or she considers important (your customers will tell you what they require to be satisfied; failure to meet a customer's critical requirements is a defect); (3) identify your needs (including needs from your suppliers) to provide product or service so that it satisfies the customer; (4) define the process for doing the work (map the process); (5) mistake proof the process and eliminate wasted effort and delays; and (6) ensure continuous improvements by measuring, analyzing, and controlling the improved process (establish quality and cycle time measurements and improvement goals; the common quality metric is number of defects per unit of work).

It follows from the Six Steps to Six Sigma methodology that the aim is to improve the quality of process outputs, improving customer satisfaction and at the same time reducing waste, time, and costs. To achieve that ambitious aim, Six Sigma focuses on identifying and removing the causes of failures and defects, reducing variation by applying a set of statistical methods and other methodologies of quality management. It follows also that the methodology is a data-driven improvement approach that step-by-step is minimizing failures and variations in a structured and systematic way. The methodology is used on well-defined projects such as a product, a service, or a process, and each Six Sigma project established has clear goals in terms of failure, cost, or time reduction.

The term *Six Sigma* is related to statistical modeling of variation in any process or any product and indicates a degree of *process capability.* When a process for example is *"in statistical control,"* which means that only *system* or *common causes* affect the variation, then it is known that process output with a high probability will vary within +/–3 sigma where sigma is the standard deviation of the measured output characteristic. This interval is also called the *natural variation.*

To reduce variation means that the natural variation of process output is reduced by reducing sigma (= the standard deviation). When improvement projects have been done systematically for a while, the natural variation of the process output may have been reduced to half of the acceptable variation as specified by design engineers or the customers. In this case, the "final goal of Six Sigma" has been achieved—a goal characterized with having the manufactured products mostly free of defects. Under those assumptions, we can expect that 99.99966% of the products will be free of defects, which corresponds to 3.4 defects per million outputs produced. In this case, the process is called "a six sigma process."

The Evolution and Tools of Six Sigma

In the previous paragraphs, we introduced and discussed Motorola's "Six Steps to Six Sigma quality"—that is, Motorola's roadmap to achieve six sigma quality (= 3.4 defects per million). These six steps were later replaced by General Electric (GE) when Jack Welch, chairman and CEO of GE, at the annual meeting April 24, 1996, declared the *Six Sigma process* to be GE's corporate strategy for improving quality and competitiveness. The change of road map follows directly from the following extract from his speech:

> Motorola has defined a rigorous and proven process for improving each of the tens of millions of processes that produce the goods and services a company provides. The methodology is called the Six Sigma process and involves four simple but rigorous steps:

First, *measuring* every process and transaction,

then *analyzing* each of them,

then painstakingly *improving* them, and

finally, rigorously *controlling* them for consistency once they have been improved.

Later on, GE developed further the sigma improvement process to follow the so-called DMAIC process—design, measure, analyze, improve, and control. But for the important areas of innovation and new product development, it was soon realized in GE and other companies that the DMAIC methodology was not suitable to use. Hence, an adapted methodology was suggested that gradually evolved into the so-called Design for Six Sigma methodology (DFSS) where the following *DMADV project methodology* was recommended:

- *Define* design goals based on customer needs and the company's strategy for new product development.
- *Measure* and identify CTQs (Critical To Quality characteristics), product capabilities, production process capability, and risks.
- *Analyze* to develop and design alternatives, create a high-level design, and evaluate design capability to select the best design.
- *Design* details, optimize the design, and plan for design verification.
- *Verify* the design, set up pilot runs, implement the production process, and hand it over to the process owner(s).

Within the individual steps of DMAIC or DMADV, many well-established quality management tools are used, such as flowcharting, cause-and-effect diagram, histograms, Pareto analysis, affinity diagram, quality function deployment (QFD), design of experiments, control charts, process capability analysis, analysis of variance, and regression analysis. The tools used are a combination of simple tools for data selection/analysis and advanced statistical tools.

Importance

Six Sigma Training, Education, and Implementation

Successful implementation of Six Sigma requires leadership together with education and training in the Six Sigma principles, tools, and methods. For that reason, clear leadership roles have been defined for people participating in the implementation process, and ambitious educational and training programs have been developed for each role as shown below.

- *Executive leadership* includes the managing director and other members of the top management team. These top managers are responsible for setting up a clear vision for Six Sigma implementation, and they also support their subordinates with the necessary resources both for education and training and for running the improvement projects.
- *Champions* have the responsibility for Six Sigma implementation across the whole organization and are nominated by the top management team from the managers at the first level under the top management level.
- *Master Black Belts,* identified by champions, act as in-house coaches on Six Sigma principles, tools and methods. Master Black Belts devote 100% of their time to Six Sigma, and they assist champions and guide Black Belts and Green Belts.
- *Black Belts* operate under Master Black Belts to apply Six Sigma methodology to specific projects, and they devote 100% of their time to Six Sigma. Black Belts primarily focus on Six Sigma project execution, whereas Champions and Master Black Belts are focusing on identifying projects/functions for Six Sigma.
- *Green Belts* are the employees who take up Six Sigma implementation along with their other job responsibilities, operating under the guidance of Black Belts.

Education and training programs vary from company to company, and several organizations and consulting companies offer education programs to qualify for the above roles. This is perhaps the most important part of Six Sigma programs.

Impact of Six Sigma

The success of Six Sigma became a reality in most companies that succeeded in implementing the methodology. Research articles, newspaper articles, and books on Six Sigma were published, informing the readers about the successes and the many results that successful companies could show. Here, we focus on some reported results from Motorola and GE.

According to Stephen George, the savings at Motorola from 1986 to 1990 by using the Six Steps to Six Sigma were as large as $1.5 billion in manufacturing, and they estimated in 1990 that it could save an additional $1 billion a year in nonmanufacturing. It has been reported that Motorola managed to save $5.4 billion in nonmanufacturing processes from 1990 to 1995. In 1999, GE reported savings of $2 billion attributable to Six Sigma, and in their 2001 annual report, GE claimed that the completion of over 6,000 Six Sigma projects probably had resulted in more than $3 billion in savings by conservative estimates.

The Importance and Limitations of Six Sigma

The importance of a new management methodology can be measured in various ways, and maybe the best way is to analyze if the methodology has been accepted within the management fields—within academics as well as by companies around the world—and how was it spread and accepted. Here especially, GE had an important role after Motorola.

After having experienced the first success of this methodology inside GE companies, and also from an increasing number of supplier companies, the methodology spread rapidly all over the world. The expansion of the Six Sigma methodology easily reached supplier companies because GE requested companies that wanted to do business with GE to implement the methodology.

In academia also, the topic of Six Sigma became popular because leading scholars in the field declared that the Six Sigma methodology was based on sound scientific principles. Hence, it is not surprising that journals in fields such as quality management, production management, operations management, process management, and service management suddenly were publishing a great number of research articles showing case studies where the Six Sigma methodology had been used.

The DMAIC (as well as the DMADV) process may be regarded as a short version of the quality story, which was developed in Japan in the 1960s as a standard for quality control circle presentations, but later on became an important quality improvement standard within the Japanese version of *total quality control* (TQC), which later evolved into the holistic management philosophy called *total quality management* (TQM).

Compared with Motorola's original road map to Six Sigma quality, some explicit and important details are missing. The most important difference is that "the customer" has not been explicitly included in GE's DMAIC process. This may be no problem if the users regard DMAIC as one of several alternative TQM road maps building excellent companies (see the entries for Total Quality Management and Excellence Characteristics). However, several people (managers, consultants as well as academics) seem to have misunderstood what Six Sigma is, and hence they may argue that Six Sigma is the successor of TQM or a stand-alone management philosophy competing with TQM and also lean production (see entry for Lean Enterprise).

However, going through systematic analyses such as the comparisons above between GE's DMAIC process and Motorola's original six-step methodology, it can be concluded that Six Sigma quality as well as lean production comprise management and manufacturing philosophies, concepts and tools that have the same origin as the management philosophy called TQM—namely, Japan's quality evolution.

By such systematic comparisons, it can also be concluded that the principles, concepts, and tools of Six Sigma quality (as well as lean production) should not be seen as alternatives to TQM but rather as a collection of concepts and tools which support the overall principles and aims of TQM. Hence it may not be surprising to observe that the latest evolution of Six Sigma has been to combine with lean production, which in the beginning of this century ended up with a lean Six Sigma road map to excellence. This combined road map is the result of an understanding that there can never be one and only one road map for excellence. Sometimes companies can best benefit by focusing on improving quality through reduction of variation (the Six Sigma approach), and later on it can be more meaningful and effective to focus on reduction of waste (the lean approach), and sometimes it may be meaningful to combine the two approaches under an overall management philosophy such as TQM and business excellence.

Su Mi Dahlgaard-Park

See also Excellence Characteristics; *Kaizen* and Continuous Improvement; Lean Enterprise; Quality Circles; Quality Trilogy; Total Quality Management

Further Readings

Breyfogle, F., & Salvekar, A. (2004). *LEAN Six Sigma in sickness and in health—An integrated enterprise excellence novel.* Austin, TX: Smarter Solutions.

Dahlgaard, J. J., & Dahlgaard-Park, S. M. (2006). Lean production, Six Sigma quality, TQM and company culture. *TQM Journal, 18*(3), 263–281.

Furterer, S. L. (2012). *Lean Six Sigma for the healthcare enterprise—Methods, tools and applications.* New York, NY: CRC Press, Taylor & Francis Group.

George, S. (1992). *The Baldrige quality system,* New York, NY: Wiley.

Park, S. H. (2003). *Six Sigma for quality and productivity promotion.* Tokyo, Japan: Asian Productivity Organization.

Pyzdek, T. (2003). *The Six Sigma handbook: A complete guide for green belts, black belts and managers at all levels.* New York, NY: McGraw-Hill.

Social Cognitive Theory

The failure to fully consider the psychological determinants of human behavior is often the weakest link in organizational initiatives. Social cognitive theory is founded on an agentic conception of human development, adaption, and change. To be an agent is to influence the course of events by one's actions. People exercise their influence through different forms of agency. In personal agency exercised individually, people bring their influence to bear on what they can control directly. However, in many spheres of functioning, people do not have direct control over conditions that affect their lives. They exercise proxy agency. This requires influencing others who have the resources, knowledge, and means to act on their behalf to secure the outcomes they desire. Children work through parents to get what they want, marital partners through spouses, employees through labor unions, and the general public through their elected officials. In the corporate world, proxy agency takes the form of outsourcing services and production of products to agents elsewhere. People do not live their lives in individual autonomy. Many of the things they seek are achievable only by working together. In the exercise of collective agency, they pool their knowledge, skills, and resources and act in concert to shape their future. The distinctive blend of individual, proxy, and collective agency varies cross-culturally. But one needs all three forms of agency to make it through the day, wherever one lives. This entry presents the causal structure on which social cognitive theory is founded, explains the origins and forms that human agency takes, and describes the mechanism through which it operates interdependently with sociostructural influences.

Fundamentals

Social cognitive theory subscribes to a causal structure grounded in triadic reciprocal causation. In this triadic codetermination, human functioning is a product of the interplay of intrapersonal influences, the behavior individuals engage in, and the environmental forces that impinge on them. Because intrapersonal influences are part of the determining conditions in this triadic interplay, people have a hand in shaping events and the course their lives take. The environment is not a monolithic force. The agentic perspective distinguishes among three types of environments—imposed, selected, and constructed. The imposed environment acts on individuals whether they like it or not. However, they have some leeway in how they construe it and react to it. For the most part, the environment is only a potentiality that does not come into being unless selected and activated. The activities and environments individuals choose influence, in large part, what they become and the course their lives take. And finally, people create environments that enable them to exercise better control of their lives. Gradations of environmental changeability require increasing levels of agentic activity.

Social cognitive theory rejects the duality that pits personal agency against social structure as a reified entity disembodied from individuals. In social cognitive theory of self and society, personal agency and social structure function interdependently. Social systems are the product of human activity. The authorized rules and practices of social systems implemented by social agents, in turn, influence human development and functioning.

Mechanisms of Agency

Among the mechanisms of human agency, none is more central or pervasive than people's beliefs in their efficacy to influence events that affect their lives. This core belief is the foundation of human motivation, performance accomplishments, and emotional well-being. Unless people believe they can produce desired effects by their actions, they have little incentive to undertake activities or to persevere in the face of difficulties. Whatever other factors serve as guides and motivators, they are rooted in the core belief that one has the power to effect changes by one's actions.

People's belief in their efficacy is developed in four principal ways. The most effective means is through mastery experiences. Development of a resilient sense of efficacy requires experience in overcoming obstacles through perseverant effort. The second way of developing personal efficacy is by social modeling. Seeing people similar to oneself succeed by perseverant effort raises observers' beliefs in their own capabilities. Social persuasion is the third way of strengthening efficacy beliefs. If people are persuaded that they have what it takes to succeed, they exert more effort that promotes success than if they harbor self-doubts and dwell on personal deficiencies when difficulties arise. People also rely on their physical and emotional states in judging their efficacy.

Self-efficacy beliefs affect the quality of human functioning through cognitive, motivational, emotional, and decisional processes. People's beliefs in their efficacy affect whether they think optimistically or pessimistically, in self-enhancing or self-debilitating ways. Such beliefs affect people's goals and aspirations, how well they motivate themselves and their perseverance in the face of difficulties and adversity. Self-efficacy beliefs also shape people's outcome expectations on whether they expect their efforts to produce favorable outcomes or adverse ones. In addition, self-efficacy beliefs affect the quality of emotional life and vulnerability to stress and depression. And last, but not least, people's beliefs in their efficacy determine the choices they make at important decisional points. A factor that influences choice behavior can profoundly affect the course lives take because it determines the social reality in which one becomes deeply embedded.

Self-efficacy beliefs operate in concert with other self-regulatory mechanisms through which agency is exercised. These mechanisms involve the temporal extension agency through forethought. The future cannot be a cause of current behavior. However, cognitive representations of future states, whether desired or undesired, bring the future into the present as guides and motivators. When projected over a long time, a forethoughtful perspective provides direction, coherence, and meaning to one's life.

People motivate themselves and guide their behavior by the goals and challenges they adopt. The motivating potential of goals lies in affective self-reactions to one's performances. Goals motivate by enlisting self-investment in the activity rather than directly. Once people commit themselves to certain goals, they seek self-satisfaction from fulfilling them and intensify their efforts by discontent with substandard performances.

Most goals are ineffective. This is because they are too general, too distant, and noncommitting. The goals that are motivating are the ones that enlist self-investment in the activity. They include explicitness, level of challenge, and temporal proximity. Explicit goals create motivational involvement by specifying the type and amount of effort needed to succeed. General goals leave uncertainty about how much effort one needs to mobilize. There is little satisfaction in easy successes. Interest and engrossment in activities are fostered by challenging goals within one's reach by sustained effort.

The effectiveness of goals in regulating motivation depends on how far into the future they are projected. Long-range goals provide the vision of a desired future. However, having a vision is not enough. There are too many competing influences in the present for distant futures to regulate current behavior. Under distant goals, people put off what needs to be done until looming deadlines spur them into a flurry of activity. Short-term goals provide the guides, strategies, and motivators in the here and now to get to where one is going. Self-motivation is best sustained by attainable subgoal challenges that lead to the realization of valued long-term goals.

People also anticipate likely outcomes of prospective actions to guide and motivate their efforts anticipatorily. The outcome expectations take several forms. They include the material costs and benefits of given courses of action. Behavior is also partly regulated by the anticipated approving and disapproving social reactions it evokes. People are not just reactors to external influences. The human capacity for evaluative self-reaction is another core feature of agency. People adopt standards and react self-approvingly or self-disapprovingly to their performances. The interplay among these different outcome expectations produces different types of adaption.

Expected external material and social outcomes wield significant influence when they are compatible with self-evaluative ones. People commonly experience conflicts of outcomes when they are rewarded socially or materially for behavior they personally devalue. When self-evaluative consequences outweigh the force of external rewards they have little sway. If, however, the allure of rewards outweighs self-devaluation, the result can be cheerless accommodation.

Another type of conflict of outcomes arises when individuals are chastised for activities they value highly. Principled dissenters and nonconformists often find themselves in such predicaments. The relative strength of self-approval and external censure determine whether the courses of action will be pursued or abandoned. In some situations, external support and reward for given activities are minimal or lacking, so individuals have to sustain their efforts largely through self-encouragement. For example, innovators persevere despite repeated failures in endeavors that provide neither rewards nor recognition for long periods, if at all during their lifetime. To persist, innovators must be sufficiently convinced of their efficacy and the worth of their pursuit to self-reward their efforts.

How people perceive the structural characteristics of their environment—the impediments it erects and the opportunity structures it provides—also influences the course of human action. Those of low self-efficacy are easily convinced of the futility of effort when they come up against institutional impediments, whereas those of high self-efficacy figure out ways to surmount them.

People are not only forethinkers and self-regulators in the exercise of agency. They are also self-examiners of their own functioning. They reflect on their personal efficacy, the soundness of their thoughts and actions, and the meaning of their pursuits and make corrective adjustments if necessary. The metacognitive ability to reflect on oneself is the most distinctly human core property of agency.

Evolution

When I began my career, behaviorism had a stranglehold on the field of psychology. I found this view of human nature at variance with the proactive, self-regulatory, and self-reflective nature of humankind. I devoted my efforts to further our understanding of this alternative conception of human nature.

Theory building is necessarily an incremented process. The evolution of social cognitive theory centered on clarifying the nature, development, and function of the core features of agency reviewed in this entry. The current extension of the theory focuses on the exercise of moral agency. This adds an important moral dimension to the workplace and other aspects of everyday life. Future research directions will be aimed at clarifying how individual, proxy, and collective agency operate in concert in different types of social system and cultural milieus. Extension of the theory to collective agency makes it generalizable to collectivistically oriented societies.

Importance

Modes of Self-Development and Change

An important feature of social cognitive theory is its research into the mechanisms through which competencies, attitudes, values, and styles of behavior are acquired and changed. For the most part, traditional psychological theories were formulated long before the revolutionary advances in communication technologies. They emphasized learning by direct experience via influences operating in one's immediate social and physical environment. Learning from the consequences of one's actions is a tough and laborious process. Moreover, the constraints of time, resources, and mobility impose severe limits on the situations and activities that can be directly explored for the acquisition of knowledge and competencies.

Humans have evolved an advanced capacity for learning by observation that enables them to develop their knowledge and competencies rapidly from information conveyed by modeling influences. Social modeling shortcuts trial and error. Indeed, virtually all types of behavioral, cognitive, and affective learning resulting from direct experience can be achieved vicariously by observing people's behavior and its consequences for them. In everyday life, people adopt the functional patterns of behavior they see modeled and refine them by enactive experiences to fit particular circumstances.

Some of the human learning occurs either deliberately or inadvertently by observing the behavior of others in one's social environment. However, much

of the observational learning is now based on the patterns of behavior portrayed symbolically through the electronic media. The growing importance of symbolic modeling lies in its tremendous scope and multiplicative power. A single model can transmit new ways of thinking and behaving to multitudes of people in widely dispersed locales. By drawing on the modeled patterns of thought and action, observers transcend the bounds of their immediate environment.

People now spend much of their waking life in the cyberworld. The revolutionary advances in electronic technologies are transforming the nature, reach, speed, and loci of human influence. Life in the rapidly evolving cyberworld transcends time, place, distance, and national borders and alters our conceptions of them. These evolving realities present new challenges and vastly expanded opportunities for people to exercise some measure of control over how they live their lives and the social systems in which they do so.

There were a number of misconceptions about the nature and scope of modeling. One such misconception was that modeling, construed as "imitation," could produce only response mimicry. This is not the case. Exemplars usually differ in content and other details but embody the same underlying principle. To cite a simple example, the passive linguistic form may be embodied in any variety of sentences. Modeling involves abstracting the information conveyed by specific exemplars about the structure and the underlying principles governing the behavior rather than mimicking the specific exemplars. Once individuals learn the guiding principle, they can use it to generate new versions of the behavior that go beyond what they have seen or heard. They can tailor the behavior to suit changing circumstances. Thus, for example, generic managerial skills, developed through modeling and guided enactments, are tailored to improve functioning in particular organizational settings.

There was another misconception regarding the scope of modeling. Many activities involve cognitive skills on how to acquire and use information for solving problems. Critics argued that modeling cannot build cognitive skills because thought processes are covert and are not adequately reflected in modeled actions, which are the end products of the cognitive operations. Cognitive skills can be readily acquired by verbal modeling in which models verbalize aloud their reasoning strategies as they engage in problem-solving activities. The thoughts guiding their decisions and actions are thus made observable. Cognitive modeling is more powerful in enhancing perceived self-efficacy and building innovative and other complex cognitive skills than the commonly used tutorial methods.

Still another misconception held that modeling is antithetical to creativity. Quite the contrary. Innovation can emerge through modeling. Modeled unconventional ways of thinking increase innovativeness in others. Creativity usually involves synthesizing existing knowledge into new ways of thinking and doing things. Organizations engage in a great deal of selective modeling of what is found to be effective. They adopt useful elements, improve on them, synthesize them into new forms, and tailor them for particular circumstances. Clever selective modeling can, indeed, be the mother of innovation.

Exercise of Moral Agency

In areas of functioning involving achievement and productivity, the personal standards that serve as the mark of adequacy are progressively altered as knowledge and skills are acquired and performances are improved. However, in many areas of social and moral conduct, the internal standards are relatively stable. People do not change from week to week in what they regard as right or wrong or as good or bad.

In the development of a moral self, individuals adopt standards of right and wrong that serve as guides and deterrents for conduct. In this self-regulatory process, people monitor their conduct and the conditions under which it occurs, judge it in relation to their moral standards and perceived circumstances, and regulate their actions by the consequences they apply to themselves. They do things that give them satisfaction and a sense of self-worth. They refrain from behaving in ways that violate their moral standards, because such conduct will bring self-condemnation. Moral agency is thus exercised through the constraint of negative self-sanctions for conduct that violates one's moral standards and the support of positive self-sanctions for conduct faithful to personal moral standards.

Adoption of moral standards does not create an immutable internal moral control system, however. The self-regulatory mechanisms governing moral conduct do not come into play unless they are activated, and there are many psychosocial mechanisms by which moral self-sanctions can be selectively disengaged from harmful practices. At the *behavior locus,* worthy ends are used to sanctify harmful means by social, economic, and moral justification, by exonerative comparison that renders the practices benign or even righteous, and by sanitizing any convoluted language that disguises what is being done. At the *agency locus,* people obscure personal responsibility by displacement and diffusion of responsibility. This absolves them of accountability for the harm they cause. At the *outcomes locus,* perpetrators minimize, distort, or dispute the injurious effects of their actions. At the *victim locus,* perpetrators dehumanize and blame recipients for bringing the maltreatment on themselves. Through selective moral disengagement, good people do harmful things without any loss of self-regard. These psychosocial mechanisms operate at both the individual and organizational levels.

Agentic Management of Fortuity

There is much that people do designedly to exercise some control over their personal development and life circumstances. But there is a lot of fortuity in the courses lives take. Indeed, some of the most important determinants of life paths occur through the most trivial of circumstances. People are often inaugurated into new life trajectories, marital partnerships, and occupational careers through fortuitous circumstances.

Fortuitous events are unintended intersects of persons unfamiliar with each other. The separate paths have their own determinants, but they are causally unconnected until their intersection. At that point, the encounter creates a unique confluence of influences. Most fortuitous events leave people untouched, others have some lasting effects, and still others branch people into new trajectories of life. Fortuitous occurrences may be unforeseeable, but having occurred, the conditions they create operate as contributing factors in causal processes in the same way as do prearranged ones.

Fortuity does not mean uncontrollability of its effects. People can bring some influence to bear on the fortuitous character of life. They can make chance happen by pursuing an active life that increases the number and type of fortuitous encounters they will experience. Chance favors the inquisitive and venturesome, who go places, do things, and explore new ideas and activities. People also make chance work for them by cultivating their interests, enabling beliefs, and competencies. These personal resources enable them to make the most of opportunities that arise unexpectedly. Pasteur put it well when he noted that "chance favors only the prepared mind." By developing their interests and talents and pursuing an active life, people can influence how they play the hand that fortuity deals them.

Albert Bandura

See also Corporate Social Responsibility; Empowerment; Entrepreneurial Effectuation; Expectancy Theory; Goal-Setting Theory; Innovation Diffusion; Moral Reasoning Maturity; Self-Determination Theory; Social Network Theory

Further Readings

Bandura, A. (1986). *Social foundations of thought and action: A social cognitive theory.* Englewood Cliffs, NJ: Prentice Hall.

Bandura, A. (1997). *Self-efficacy: The exercise of control.* New York, NY: Freeman.

Bandura, A. (1999). Moral disengagement in the perpetration of inhumanities. *Personality and Social Psychology Review, 3,* 193–209.

Bandura, A. (2006). On integrating social cognitive and social diffusion theories. In A. Singhal & J. Dearing (Eds.), *Communication of innovations: A journey with Ev Rogers* (pp. 111–135). Thousand Oaks, CA: Sage.

Bandura, A. (2008). The reconstrual of "free will" from the agentic perspective of social cognitive theory. In J. Baer, J. C. Kaufman, & R. F. Baumeister (Eds.), *Are we free? Psychology and free will* (pp. 86–127). Oxford, England: Oxford University Press.

Bolton, M. K. (1993). Imitation versus innovation: Lessons to be learned from the Japanese. *Organizational Dynamics, 21,* 30–45.

Latham, G. P., & Saari, L. M. (1979). Application of social learning theory to training supervisors through behavioral modeling. *Journal of Applied Psychology, 64,* 239–246.

Locke, E. A., & Latham, G. P. (1990). *A theory of goal setting and task performance.* Englewood Cliffs, NJ: Prentice Hall.

Zimmerman, B. J., & Cleary, T. J. (2006). Adolescents' development of agency: The role of self-efficacy beliefs and self-regulatory skill. In F. Pajares & T. Urdan (Eds.). *Self-efficacy beliefs of adolescents* (Vol. 5., pp. 45–69). Greenwich, CT: Information Age.

SOCIAL CONSTRUCTION THEORY

The premise of social construction theory is that many aspects of our world that are taken for granted as objective facts of life have actually arisen from patterns of social interaction that have become institutionalized. The purpose of the theory is to recognize and emphasize the power of these social facts in enabling and constraining our day-to-day lives. A pervasive example is the convention of time of day. Our system of time zones radiating from Greenwich Mean Time is a socially constructed system. On a daily basis, however, we take for granted that when the New York Stock Exchange bell sounds at 9:30 a.m. Eastern Standard Time in the United States, it is 9:30 a.m. everywhere in the EST zone. We know that the London Stock Exchange has already been open for six and a half hours, and the Tokyo Stock Exchange is already closed. Imagine the vast substantive impact of these social facts. Their socially constructed nature is salient to us only when something changes—for instance when the United States changes to daylight savings time during summer months. The theory is relevant to management because organizations are social institutions and behavior in and among them is governed by institutionalized patterns of behavior. Thus, it can be applied to any aspect of management, from human resource management to competitive strategy to global markets. As we will see in this entry, the concepts from social construction theory first influenced the management field through the work of organizational sociologists, who observed that organizational structures and routines often persisted even when they were no longer optimal given technological and competitive conditions. The following section of this entry describes the fundamental characteristics of social construction theory. The next section provides background on the history and development of the theory, and the final section assesses the importance of the theory to management.

Fundamentals

The core element of social construction theory is social knowledge, or what has been referred to as "knowledge in everyday life." What is meant by this is the knowledge about how to be a member of a social group and society. Although social construction theorists don't often use the terms *culture* or *cultural knowledge,* the idea is much the same. What is the appropriate way to interact with other members of the social group? How do we organize our day? How do we organize our work?

Socially constructed knowledge emerges through interactions among members of the social group. This is most obvious in the transmission of social knowledge from experts (adults) to novices (children), but it also occurs in many day-to-day interactions and activities. Thus, *interaction* is a key element of social construction. Interaction among people leads to an *intersubjective* set of beliefs and behaviors about what is true and appropriate. Appropriate ways of doing things in a social group become *habitual* over time. That is, behaviors and interactions take on a script-like character. Appropriate ways of organizing activities, such as work, in the social group become *reified* over time. That is, they take on the character of objective reality. They also become *legitimate;* that is, not only are practices taken as fact but also as correct, valid, and desirable.

The key assumptions on which social construction theory rests are as follows: First, knowledge is *socially distributed* among members of a family, community, organization, or society. This moves the concept of knowledge from something that exists within our minds to something that is created, understood, and changed through social interaction. The foundation of socially distributed knowledge is the objectification of subjective processes and meanings by which the intersubjective commonsense world is constructed. In other words, interpretation and meaning are created through webs of social interaction. Second, knowledge and its meaning are negotiated and constructed by actors who interact within a community with which they identify and who share the practices of the community. *Negotiation of meaning* in this context includes both the meaning of negotiation as in "negotiating a price" (competing interpretations) *and* "negotiating a sharp curve" (steering and staying on track). Third, because interaction is more frequent within social groups, there is higher agreement about the meaning of knowledge and practice within a community than across communities. Thus, socially constructed knowledge about which activities are appropriate and how to perform them has *boundaries* which coincide with the boundaries of a particular social group. Shared histories of learning within communities create boundaries between those who participate in a community and those who do not.

Fourth, as members of a social group perform the practices of their community, they engage in *mutual engagement and learning* and develop a shared repertoire of knowledge and activities. This shared repertoire includes terminology, stories, tools, and symbols. It reflects a unique and contextualized history of learning, and yet remains inherently ambiguous, because meaning in the community is continuously negotiated and renegotiated through interaction. Fifth, for periods of time, however, socially constructed knowledge and meaning in a community becomes *reified;* that is, abstract concepts are treated as substantially existing, real, and true, like a concrete material object. Examples include concepts such as "the economy" or "the rule of law" or "democracy." From the point of view of management, concepts such as reputation and market capitalization are socially constructed and yet have substantial material implications.

Of course, not all knowledge is socially constructed. With the exception of solipsism, social construction theory does not deny the existence of a physical reality—the Earth does spin on its axis resulting in what we experience as the approximately 24-hour day, with alternating periods of light and dark. Societies have not always possessed this objective knowledge and have at various times had developed socially constructed explanations for the pattern of light and dark. Though we now understand the objective reality that causes this pattern, we still create socially constructed institutions to help us organize our activities within and among social groups, such as the time zones described initially. Thus, the boundary conditions of social construction theory are considered to be the realm of the social rather than physical and mathematical fact. Social construction theory is closely related to the symbolic interactionism, ethnomethodology, sociology of knowledge, institutional theory, structuration theory, the social construction of technological systems, and perspectives on enactment and sensemaking.

Evolution

The roots of the theory come from a field known as the sociology of knowledge. The sociology of knowledge was first raised by philosophers concerned about both the epistemology (sources, nature, and limits of knowledge) and ontology (nature of being) of knowledge, or what are considered to be facts, causal relationships, and how we know such things. The term was first coined by German philosopher Max Scheler in the 1920s, but the germ of the ideas as we understand them today can be attributed to Karl Mannheim's work from the 1930s through the 1950s. Mannheim's writings helped bridge the philosophical question of "how do we know what we know?" to the sociological question of how social interaction and social context create all knowledge that is not physically or mathematically determined. Even Max Weber, the father of rational bureaucracy, alluded to the importance of subjective meaning in guiding action. American sociologists Talcott Parsons and Robert Merton brought the ideas fully into the sociology literature in the 1950s. Still, the focus in all these writings was primarily on the formation of ideology—that is how do we come to believe what we do?

It was not until sociologists Peter Berger and Thomas Luckmann's book, *The Social Construction of Reality: A Treatise in the Sociology of Knowledge,* in 1966 that a treatment of the sociology of knowledge moved decidedly away from an emphasis on philosophy and ideology to a concern with all knowledge that is used everyday life, and how social interaction creates much of what we experience as objective reality. This work drew from phenomenological sociology—both ethnomethodology (Harold Garfinkel) and symbolic interactionism (George Herbert Mead)—to focus on how everyday interactions create what we take for granted as knowledge of social facts and how to act in the context of these facts. Of particular importance are the concepts of objectification and signification.

Objectification refers to the way in which an object takes on a subjective meaning and intention. It is useful to consider the way in which knowledge is embedded in objects. Tools, such as a hammer, embody knowledge of leverage and force and material. They also embody an action or intention—to strike an object—perhaps a nail into a wall—in order to hang a picture. When we see a hammer, we understand its purpose. Taken out of its historical and cultural context, however, a hammer may not have the same meaning or be understandable at all. A wonderful illustration of this is in the movie *The Gods Must Be Crazy* in which an empty Coca-Cola bottle is construed by the Bushmen who discover it as a gift from the gods. Having no conception of its original purpose as a container for a sugary soft drink, they discover that it can be used for all manner of useful functions, from flattening snake skin to a child's toy.

Signification is a crucial example of objectification. Language is the most obvious and sophisticated form of signification, in which signs "stand for" intention and meaning. Language is also a good example of the basic assumptions of social construction, as described above. Language is socially distributed, meaning is negotiated and evolves through social interaction, and shared histories of learning create boundaries of meaning between languages and the communities in which they have evolved. Mutual engagement and learning create the shared repertoire of terminology, stories, and symbols that characterize social groups and their language.

Berger and Luckmann also elaborated on the way in which societies and their institutions are socially constructed. They defined the term institutionalization as "the reciprocal typification of habitualized actions by types of actors" (p. 54). To understand what they meant by this, let us examine an example. When I am staying at a hotel and call the front desk to ask for extra towels, both the clerk and I mutually understand that I am a guest and he is a clerk. Guests are types of actors in a hotel who request things. Clerks are types of actors who take requests and fulfill them. Neither of us is surprised by the request and response. If I call again tomorrow, the interaction will be much the same. Thus, in institutionalized situations, certain types of actors will expect and be expected to behave in certain ways in the course of their interactions (reciprocal typification), and these behaviors are repeated across numerous interactions (habitual). Through this process, behaviors become predictable and coordination of behavior becomes possible.

In 1977, an article by John Meyer and Brian Rowan in the *American Journal of Sociology* moved the ideas of social construction squarely into the domain of organizations and management. They argued that as organizational routines and structures become institutionalized, they become taken for granted as legitimate and appropriate; we then experience these features as objective facts about the ways things are in organizations. Indeed, they argue that the pervasiveness of organizations as a means of coordinating economic activity can be attributed not only to reasons of effectiveness and efficiency but to the socially constructed status of organizations as the appropriate and legitimate way of organizing economic activity. This article laid the foundation for what is called *institutional theory*, one of the most important and pervasive theories in the management field. The persistence and reproduction of legitimate ways of organizing has been explored extensively by scholars of institutional theory.

In 1979, the work of social psychologist Karl Weick applied ideas from social construction to his writings on the *social psychology of organizing*. Key to his argument is the notion of enactment, which suggests that the world that we experience and react to is not independent of our own actions. For instance, managers of organizations, by acting in a way that is consistent with their beliefs, actually help create a reality that is consistent with these beliefs. Weick elaborated on two points raised by Berger and Luckmann: Our experience of reality becomes structured through social interaction, but individuals differ in their interpretations of this reality. Weick argued that interpretations differ because individuals actually experience different realities. They do so because individuals enact their reality; that is, phenomena being perceived are also created by the perceiver. Weick's work had a tremendous influence on the management field, by emphasizing that managers were not just interpreting their organizational environments and adapting to them, but rather, through their own actions, they were actually creating the environments to which they needed to adapt. This notion spurred the development of several new areas of management research, including managerial sensemaking and sensegiving; the construction of managerial and organizational identity, reputation, and legitimacy; the social construction of technology; and the construction of competitive communities, markets, and organizational fields. The section below elaborates on these schools of management research and highlights the importance of this research to managers and managerial practice.

Importance

The application of social construction to theories of technologies, organizations, and institutions helped move these ideas beyond philosophy to sociology and eventually to management theory. Social construction theory has influenced management scholars and educators through its contributions to at least four key schools of thought: *institutional theory, the social psychology of organizing, the social construction of competitive environments,* and *the social construction of technology.* Because of the highly philosophical and conceptual nature of the theory, it is difficult to study empirically. However, each of the four schools of thought noted above do have solid support that lends credibility to their predictions. The theory has influenced managers primarily through the recognition of the way institutionalized practices both enable and constrain their activities and how their own organizations influence features of the environment to which they are trying to adapt.

Institutional theory developed first within the field of organizational sociology, with the work of John Meyer and Brian Rowan noted above, and later Paul J. DiMaggio and Walter W. Powell. Institutional theory developed into one of the most influential theories in management, focused primarily on the question, Why are organizations so similar in the way they organize work? At its core, institutional theory addresses this question by investigating why certain ways of organizing are considered legitimate, with the roots of legitimacy coming from socially constructed beliefs and practices. Numerous scholars adopted these ideas from organizational sociology and applied them to important managerial questions, such as how to maintain legitimacy in the eyes of stakeholders and how to adapt strategically while operating within the constraints of established institutionalized environments. More recently, management scholars have pushed institutional theory to consider how institutionalized practices emerge in the first place. Researchers in this area have explored the emergence of new institutional fields and industries and have coined the term *institutional entrepreneurs* to refer to those actors who help establish the socially constructed practices in a new field. A related area of research explores how leaders and organizations can attract resources by recognizing and managing the social construction of reputation, legitimacy, and assessments of value.

A number of researchers have drawn on *the social psychology of organizing* and explored the sensemaking and sensegiving activities of managers within organizations. This area of work explores how leaders and managers influence organizational decisions and actions, from the day to day to its strategic direction, through their ongoing interactions with others in the organization.

Also drawing closely on Weick's work on enactment, another group of researchers has explored the question of how managers' beliefs influence their competitive environment and developed a school of thought referred to as the *social construction of competition*. This body of research explores how behavior among competing organizations becomes institutionalized, much like the way institutional theory explored how ways of organizing become legitimate and taken for granted. This research suggests that even competitive behavior in the marketplace is, in part, socially constructed.

In 1987, *The Social Construction of Technological Systems* by Wiebe Bijker, Thomas P. Hughes, and Trevor Pinch integrated the ideas from the sociology of scientific knowledge with studies of technology and demonstrated that even knowledge that we take as solid, physical, objective certainty, such as physical technology, has, in fact, been socially constructed as legitimate and appropriate. A classic example of the persistence of a technological system beyond the effectiveness of its technological function is the QWERTY keyboard, which is the standard layout of the letter keys on the keyboard of typewriters and computers. It was adopted as the standard layout for manual typewriters in order to prevent the mechanical arms of the typewriter from sticking together. The layout has persisted, however, long after the demise of the manual typewriter. In the management field, researchers studying the social construction of technology have brought the concepts of social construction to the adoption and use of technology within and among organizations. This area has gained prominence as the role of information technology has become both essential and central to the functioning of organizations.

Even though social construction theory is derived from century-old philosophical explorations of the nature of knowledge, it is still relevant to the challenges faced by managers today. To manage the challenges and opportunities from globalization and technological change to shifting economic and political systems, managers must be adept at recognizing and influencing the way in which social interaction within and among organizations shapes knowledge, practices, and structures of doing business.

Theresa Lant

See also Actor-Network Theory; Adaptive Structuration Theory; Institutional Theory; Management Symbolism and Symbolic Action; Narrative (Story) Theory; Sensemaking; Structuration Theory

Further Readings

Berger, P., & Luckmann, T. (1966). *The social construction of reality.* New York, NY: Doubleday.

Bijker, W. E., Hughes, T. P., & Pinch, T. (1987). *Social construction of technological systems.* Cambridge, MA: MIT Press.

Chen, C. C., & Meindl, J. R. (1991). The construction of leadership images in the popular press: The case of Donald Burr and People Express. *Administrative Science Quarterly, 36,* 521–551.

Gergen, K. (2009). *An invitation to social construction.* Thousand Oaks, CA: Sage.

Giddens, A. (1984). *The constitution of society.* Berkeley: University of California Press.

Meyer, J., & Rowan, B. (1977). Institutionalized organizations: Formal structure as myth and ceremony. *American Journal of Sociology, 83,* 340–363.

Orlikowski, W. (1992). The duality of technology: Rethinking the concept of technology in organizations. *Organization Science, 3,* 398–427.

Porac, J., & Thomas, H. (1990). Taxonomic mental models in competitor definition. *Academy of Management Review, 15,* 224–240.

Rindova, V. P., & Fombrun, C. J. (1999). Constructing competitive advantage: The role of firm-constituent interactions. *Strategic Management Journal, 20,* 691–710.

Weick, K. (1979). *The social psychology of organizing.* New York, NY: McGraw-Hill.

SOCIAL ENTREPRENEURSHIP

Social entrepreneurship, broadly defined, is value creation in which opportunities are explored and exploited to meet social needs or enact social change in new ways. This general definition can be further broken down for greater clarity. *Value creation* refers to benefits generated when resources are combined to create new means, new ends, or new means-ends combinations. Social entrepreneurship generates rents that are invested back into society rather than being appropriated solely by the entrepreneur. It goes beyond economic value to place relatively greater emphasis on additional forms of value creation. Economic value creation is important for the long-term viability of the enterprise, yet it is a mission that focuses on social and/or environmental value creation that is the enterprise's reason for existence. *Opportunity exploration and exploitation* have reference to seeking out, and taking advantage of, situations in which new products, services, processes, organization methods, or raw materials may generate entrepreneurial rents, which situations are not generally known by all parties at all times. *Social needs* are human necessities such as food, shelter, or employment required for life or to improve its quality. These necessities are sometimes left unsatisfied by traditional market mechanisms for a segment of a population, which is then targeted by social entrepreneurs so that those social needs can be satisfied. Like social needs, *social change* is change targeted at rectifying some social injustice that traditional market mechanisms do not address. The final phrase, *in new ways,* refers to the innovativeness, proactiveness, and risk taking in social entrepreneurship. In this entry, the fundamentals of social entrepreneurship are presented, including its content, how content elements are related, rationale, domain, and context with other management theories. This is followed by the importance of social entrepreneurship to both management research and practice. The entry concludes with a cross-reference to other entries in the encyclopedia and a list of key suggested readings that provides seminal and contemporary articles in social entrepreneurship theory and research.

Fundamentals

Social entrepreneurs seek to alter the landscape in which social value is created and deployed. Social entrepreneurship may occur through the creation of new organizations or within existing organizations. While early studies modeled social entrepreneurship as an outcome, scholars tend to view it more recently as a process. Social entrepreneurship is generally thought to be a subset of traditional entrepreneurship, yet research in social entrepreneurship has not been limited to entrepreneurship theories. Research in this stream has drawn from theories commonly used in management and public policy research, such as agency theory, Austrian economics, discourse theory, institutional theory, organizational identity theory, the resource-based view, social network theory, social capital theory, and stakeholder theory. One outcome of this diversity is that neither a widely accepted definition nor one theory of social entrepreneurship has emerged.

The key factors in social entrepreneurship may be divided into antecedents and outcomes. Antecedents that seek to predict or explain social entrepreneurship include social motivation and mission, opportunity identification, access to resources and funding, multiple stakeholders, and the presence of a certain social ill or market failure. Outcomes of social entrepreneurship in the literature revolve around social value creation, sustainability of solutions, and satisfying multiple stakeholders. Alternate models of social entrepreneurship borrow from other theoretical perspectives and frameworks, such as entrepreneurial orientation or the people-deal-context-opportunity model. While these models generally portray the positive potential or impact of social entrepreneurship, scholars have given much less attention to its potentially negative side effects.

Process models of entrepreneurship suggest that the antecedents to the entrepreneurial process result in certain outcomes. Thus, a venture's social motivation and mission, opportunities identified by the social entrepreneur, resource availability, salient stakeholders, and the type of social ill being addressed all affect the way in which the venture goes about entrepreneurship, for better or for worse. For example, greater resource availability may allow for greater risk taking, and having a greater number of salient stakeholders could improve proactiveness as the venture draws from their knowledge and experience to act on opportunities. Likewise, the entrepreneurial process unique to social entrepreneurship may result in certain outcomes related to social value creation, sustainability, and satisfying stakeholders. Innovative social ventures should be more likely to arrive at lasting solutions to social problems, while excessive risk taking may jeopardize long-term venture viability.

Social entrepreneurship borrows from other underlying logics to explain these relationships. It draws from the strategic choice perspective in assuming that social entrepreneurs can identify and take advantage of opportunities that others do not, while presently leaving broader ecological questions of industry attractiveness and growth, maturity, and decline relatively unaddressed. It is based on the idea that a variety of stakeholders play a vital role in the venture meeting its mission because of relationships that transcend those based solely on economics. Many of the ills plaguing society are not remedied by traditional market mechanisms in which transactions between a buyer and seller maximize profits. Rather, social entrepreneurship adjusts the market mechanism such that some third party in society receives a portion of the value created. In this way, a social venture provides economic, social, and/or environmental returns.

The theoretical boundaries of who, when, and where in social entrepreneurship are still being defined. Initially viewed in light of public policy in the 1990s, social entrepreneurship has grown to encompass nonprofit contexts and presently includes for-profit organizations as well. Contextual boundaries have thus expanded, settling on a distinctly social mission or purpose regardless of organizational form. At the individual level, the social innovation school is interested in how social entrepreneurs enact social change through processes such as bricolage. At higher levels of analysis, the U.S. social enterprise school examines revenue generation by nonprofits, while the European social enterprise school is interested in the broader idea of a social economy. One critical contextual factor that is presently overlooked is the temporal nature of social entrepreneurship, or how it is expected to change over time.

As indicated in the cross-references, social entrepreneurship has clear connections to a variety of other management theories and perspectives. The emphasis on economic, social, and/or environmental value creation has clear reference to the triple bottom line, and the frequent inclusion of both market and nonmarket stakeholders as vital factors demonstrate a link with stakeholder theory. The importance of "scaling"—or rapid growth of social impact—in social entrepreneurship research is an indication of its relationship with innovation diffusion theory. Finally, the idea that social entrepreneurs are interested in multiple forms of value creation suggests an association with stewardship theory, in which the entrepreneur as an agent acts in the welfare of the organization (and society) as a whole rather than out of opportunism.

Importance

Research in social entrepreneurship is still in a nascent state. Accordingly, there have been a multitude of studies that improve scholarly understanding and explanation of the phenomenon. The majority of studies from 1991 to 2009 have relied on case-based research, which provides thick description and insight into processes and motivations of entrepreneurs and ventures. What has been less frequent are studies that predict relationships, although the large number of recent special issues in leading entrepreneurship journals on the topic are one indication that this trend is changing. Few empirical studies of social entrepreneurship have been published, in part because of the difficulty in identifying these individuals and their ventures. However, increases in the number of foundations and other grant-making entities that support social entrepreneurs, coupled with websites that compare their ventures, are beginning to improve scholarly access to much-needed data.

The influence of social entrepreneurship on management scholars and educators continues to grow. Again, the large number of journal special issues dedicated the phenomenon, as well as the rapid growth in the number of articles in the literature, demonstrates its increasing popularity in academe. Scholars now have a theory-based rationale to explain the emergence of new types of organizations that have new purposes and missions, which did not fit in the traditional profit-maximizing model. The lines between nonprofit and for-profit organizations, and their competitive boundaries, are beginning to blur and shift. Nonprofits increasingly generate earned-income activities and create for-profit subsidiaries, while for-profits continue to compete with nonprofits for public services contracts. Social entrepreneurship provides a rationale that improves our understanding of these changes. Educators are likewise responding to the increased emphasis on social entrepreneurship. Many universities now offer courses at both the undergraduate and graduate levels, with some even offering degrees in or emphases on social entrepreneurship. Whereas in the past, these courses have had to rely on cases, guest speakers, and books from the popular press, a number of textbook options are now available to educators. Fortunately, these texts provide different perspectives on social entrepreneurship, giving educators the option to use the text that best fits their needs.

One of the benefits of research in this area is its clear applicability to management practice. Scholars of social entrepreneurship have been disseminating their findings through books and education aimed at making managers in the social sector more entrepreneurial and students of entrepreneurship more attuned to social issues and opportunities. Indeed, many social entrepreneurship books are filled with examples and practical tools for analysis, decision making, and implementation within the context of social ventures. Universities, such as New York University's Stern School of Business and the Harvard Business School/Kennedy School of Government, sponsor workshops and conferences on social entrepreneurship that target practitioners. These workshops integrate key research findings with practitioner-generated best practices to improve outcomes. Practitioners and researchers are able to collaborate during these types of conferences to generate project ideas that have real meaning.

Two popular examples of social entrepreneurship are presented in works by Muhammad Yunus and C. K. Prahalad (see Further Readings). Yunus, winner of the Nobel Peace Prize, started the microcredit Grameen Bank in his native Bangladesh in response to traditional banks refusing to make loans to the poor. Yunus found that local basket weavers were not the credit risks that others assumed them to be. Prahalad has written about Aravind Eye Care in India, founded by Dr. Govindappa Venkataswamy. Aravind uses principles such as specialization of labor and 24-hour-a-day service to provide ophthalmic surgeries. Aravind's success allows it to provide free surgeries to the poor while still earning a profit. The low default rates on the loans from Grameen Bank and the high success rates and throughput of Aravind Eye Care are examples of social entrepreneurship. They directly address social ills through innovative, long-term sustainable business models that have dramatically improved quality of life for others who are traditionally excluded from market transactions. Both of these organizations are now applying their business models to other complementary products and services to broaden their impact.

There is an increasing emphasis on and awareness of social issues in Generation Y students now in universities and entering the workforce. Social entrepreneurship has grown with this awareness and is providing undergraduate and graduate business students with new perspectives on value creation. For instance, Brigham Young's Marriott School of Management and Texas Christian's Neeley School of Business sponsor social venture competitions that mirror similar competitions for traditional entrepreneurship students. Social entrepreneurship is thus well-positioned to provide frameworks for future managers to create and maintain lasting social change.

Todd W. Moss

See also Corporate Social Responsibility; Entrepreneurial Opportunities; Entrepreneurial Orientation; Innovation Diffusion; Stakeholder Theory; Stewardship Theory; Triple Bottom Line

Further Readings

Austin, J., Stevenson, H., & Wei-Skillern, J. (2006). Social and commercial entrepreneurship: Same, different, or both? *Entrepreneurship: Theory and Practice, 30*(1), 1–22.

Dacin, P. A., Dacin, M. T., & Matear, M. (2009). Social entrepreneurship: Why we don't need a new theory and how we move forward from here. *Academy of Management Perspectives, 24*(3), 37–57.

Mair, J., & Marti, I. (2006). Social entrepreneurship research: A source of explanation, prediction, and delight. *Journal of World Business, 41*(1), 36–44.

Prahalad, C. K. (2010). *The fortune at the bottom of the pyramid.* Upper Saddle River, NJ: Prentice Hall.

Short, J. C., Moss, T. W., & Lumpkin, G. T. (2009). Research in social entrepreneurship: Past contributions and future opportunities. *Strategic Entrepreneurship Journal, 3*(2), 161–194.

Tracey, P., & Jarvis, O. (2007). Toward a theory of social venture franchising. *Entrepreneurship: Theory and Practice, 31*(5), 667–685.

Waddock, S. A., & Post, J. E. (1991). Social entrepreneurs and catalytic change. *Public Administration Review, 51,* 393–401.

Weerawardena, J., & Sullivan Mort, G. (2006). Investigating social entrepreneurship: A multidimensional model. *Journal of World Business, 41*(1), 21–35.

Yunus, M. (2007). *Creating a world without poverty.* New York, NY: PublicAffairs.

Zahra, S. A., Gedajlovic, E., Neubaum, D. O., & Schulman, J. M. (2009). A typology of social entrepreneurs: Motives, search processes and ethical challenges. *Journal of Business Venturing, 24*(5), 519–532.

Social Exchange Theory

Social exchange theory is an old and venerable framework for understanding human social behavior. For decades, this theory has been explored by anthropologists, sociologists, and social psychologists, as well as being extensively applied to management theory. This long tradition of social exchange—buttressed by the wide-ranging disciplinary perspectives of interested scholars—has added richness to our understanding of interpersonal transactions. However, this diversity has also come with a cost. Social exchange theory has evolved considerably over time. It is no longer a single "theory" but rather a family of conceptual models that are not always closely aligned. Commensurate with this historical evolution, contemporary social exchange theory has branched considerably, with researchers exploring human interactions from a number of distinct perspectives. With this in mind, our purpose here is to provide a broad overview of social exchange for the general reader. The entry continues with a brief review of social exchange theory's defining attributes. We then turn to a historical review, which discusses the evolution of this conceptual framework. Finally, the entry closes with a consideration of considering social exchange theory's impact on management research.

Fundamentals

Four major themes of social exchange theory remain the subject of much analysis and discussion: interdependent interactions, self-interest, rules of exchange, and the formation of interpersonal relationships.

Interdependent Interactions

During the modern period, models of social exchange were concerned with individual choices in interpersonal situations, with special attention to mutual fate dependence among social actors. For example, in their well-known interdependence theory, Harold Kelley and John Thibaut illustrated each party's available options and potential consequences with an "outcome matrix." Outcome matrices illustrate how closely the consequences for each party depend on the choices made by the other. The power that one holds in a relationship can be limited by another person's resource control. Conversely, power can be enhanced through the availability of alternative options.

This quality of outcome interdependence between parties can be accounted for in terms of four attributes. The first is the *degree of dependence*. To the extent that each party's outcomes are controlled by the other, then degree of dependence is high. When such control is lacking, then degree of dependence is low. The second property is the *mutuality of dependence*. This concerns whether individuals need to cooperate to the same degree to achieve their desired outcomes. The third is the *correspondence of outcomes*. Roughly, high correspondence implies that the two parties share interests in common, and low correspondence suggests that this is not the case. The fourth property is the *basis for dependence*. This involves whether control for outcomes is shared rather than dominated by a single party. By analyzing the pattern among these four attributes, researchers can predict choices made in social situations, such as the potential for conflict or for cooperation.

Independence theory and it heirs continue to inspire research, though the original theory has been somewhat superseded by more recent extensions and new innovations, such as Caryl Rusbult's investment model. Regardless of the specific theoretical framework that one employs, this tradition of research has proven highly influential because these models are reasonably comprehensive yet conceptually flexible. For example, the interactive decision-making approach has been applied to romantic relationships as well as to bilateral negotiations. The breadth of this generalizability provides a practical illustration of the importance of social exchange in everyday life.

Self-Interest

In 1958, George Homans published an influential article in the *American Journal of Sociology*, which was followed in 1961 with a book-length explication of his ideas. Consistent with the economic thinking of his day, Homans was primarily concerned with individual exchanges that were transacted in order to achieve self-interested goals. Subsequent to Homans, this notion was not uncommon within social exchange theory and was adopted by other scholars. Still, universal self-interest remained controversial. Interdependence theory, for one, did not take a strong position as to the underlying motives that drive exchange interactions and was open to the possibility that choices could be made for altruistic reasons. More recent thinking has also taken a broader view of human motivation.

Reciprocity and Other Rules of Exchange

Roughly speaking, reciprocity is the tendency of people to respond to a beneficial action by returning a benefit and to a harmful action by returning a harm. In this way, positive and negative outcomes would approximately balance. A misalignment would be viewed as an injustice. Reciprocity, though borrowed from earlier social exchange traditions, continues to be actively investigated. For example, Linda D. Molm and her colleagues have found that exchange relationships that develop from reciprocal exchanges, as opposed to relationships negotiated in advance, tend to show less inequality, fewer power abuses, greater trust, and higher commitment. Reciprocity seems to encourage greater social harmony.

Though reciprocity remains a critical concept, other rules of social exchange have also emerged. For example, Meeker proposes six: (1) *reciprocity,* which we have already discussed; (2) *rationality,* an exchange rule that suggests an exchange partner should maximize his or her own benefits (i.e., instrumental logic); (3) *altruism,* an exchange rule that stipulates individuals seek to benefit the other exchange partner, even if it comes at personal cost; (4) *group gain,* an exchange rule that suggests individuals seek to maximize benefits for a community of individuals who hold common interests; (5) *status consistency* or *rank equilibration,* an exchange rule that suggests deference be given to individuals of prestige or formal rank; and (6) *competition,* an exchange rule suggesting that individuals seek the maximum possible *difference* between their benefits and those assigned to other people.

Without gainsaying the prevalence of reciprocity in human interaction, the inclusion of additional exchange rules provides a much richer description of social exchanges.

Interpersonal Relationships

In 1964, the sociologist Peter Blau published his influential volume, *Exchange and Power in Social Life.* Drawing explicitly from Bronisław Malinowski's earlier work, Blau asserted that there were at least two types of transactions—economic exchanges and social exchanges. Economic exchanges are quid pro quo, expect quick repayment, and characterized by individual self-interest. Social exchanges are more open-ended and longer term. To Blau's thinking, the most important distinction between these two sorts of exchanges is the issue of obligations. Economic exchanges tend to specify the terms and form of repayment, whereas social exchanges tend not to do so. Likewise,

negotiation of repayment is more allowable in economic exchanges, less so in social transactions. Blau's observations about economic and social exchanges were often interpreted in relational terms. That is, researchers distinguished social exchange *relationships,* which are relatively close and longer-term, from economic exchange relationships, which are relatively less committed. We shall return to this point in the next section when we take up research in organizational behavior.

Given this new emphasis, scholars began to explore the formation of social exchange relationships. A good example of this can be found in a series of investigations by Edward Lawler and Jeongkoo Yoon. In their experimental studies, Lawler and Yoon found that successful agreements produced positive affect. This affect, in turn, enhanced the relationship between the two parties. These benefits were most likely to accrue when the individual shared responsibility for both the exchange agreement and the resulting outcomes.

Social Exchange Theory and Interpersonal Relationships

During the 1980s and early 1990s, organizational behavior researchers sought to explain the motivation bases of organizational citizenship behavior (OCB). At the time, OCB was viewed as voluntary activity, not part of regular job duties, which served the interests of work groups and organizations. Dennis W. Organ argued that OCB could be accounted for in terms of Blau's work. Specifically, if an employee had a social exchange relationship with an employer, then she or he would exert extra effort with the confidence that, over the long run, things would "even out." Organ's view proved very influential. Besides OCB, Blau's conceptual model has since been applied to endeavors such as workplace fairness, leadership, organizational commitment, and organizational support, among others. This approach to social exchange theory de-emphasizes certain features of the paradigm but emphasizes others. On one hand, this approach attends less to social power, decision interdependence, and the specific pattern of outcomes exchanged over time. On the other hand, this approach underscores the central role of close working relationships and their importance to organizational success. As thinking about social exchange relationships has evolved, there has been a tendency for theorists to treat interpersonal attachments in three distinct fashions: relationship-formation models, relational-attribute models, and relationship-context models.

Relationship-formation models emphasize the development of social exchange relationships. Research on trust formation by Roy J. Lewicki and his colleagues takes this view. According to these scholars, trust develops through three stages. Stage 1 is calculus-based trust. Calculus-based trust is grounded in the balance between the costs and benefits of the relationships. If the latter outweighs the former, then this sort of "trust" exists. The second stage is knowledge-based trust. Knowledge-based trust is predicated in the understanding and predictability of the behavior of another person. If all goes well, this gives way to the third stage, identity-based trust. Identity-based trust, which can be thought of as the highest form of a social exchange relationship, is based on an appreciation of the other person's needs and desires.

Relational-attribute models treat attributes of the relationship as benefits to be exchanged. For example, Sternberg's theory of romantic love contains three components, at least two of which (commitment and intimacy) are amenable to exchange. Likewise, Uriel Foa and Edna Foa present six classes of goods that can be transacted. Two of these goods, status and love, are treated as attributes of relationships in other theoretical models. Relational-attribute models have also made an appearance in macro-organizational sciences. Some work that focuses on executives or interorganizational dynamics has explored exchange attributes and their impact on organizational outcomes. For example, this research shows that attributes such as interdependence or "know-how" (acquired competitive knowledge) are important qualities for relationship development and reciprocity patterns.

Relationship-context models examine how aspects of the relationship alter the way that goods are exchanged. John Hollander's well-known work on idiosyncrasy credits is a good example of this tradition. According to Hollander, leaders earn these credits by treating their subordinates well. As the stock of credit expands, a manager improves his or her relationship with employees. Later, leaders can draw on these credits when making a controversial decision. In essence, the good relationship means that workers will give their leader the benefit of the

doubt when something has gone wrong or has the potential to go wrong. Similarly, within the macro-organizational sciences, researchers have found that executives doing favors for key stakeholders yields important reciprocal patterns that affect organizational performance and firm reputation. This work is consistent with the relationship-context model. Specifically, doing favors generates an obligation in the other exchange partner to reciprocate favorably. Not doing favors may generate retaliation.

Evolution

The founding, or at least the original inspiration, for social exchange theory can be attributed to Adam Smith's *An Inquiry Into the Nature and Causes of the Wealth of Nations*. In Book I, Chapter 2 Smith famously outlined his theory of the "invisible hand." According to this framework, individual economic transactions provide an efficient means for allocating society's resources. By extension, communities are bound together in a "bottom-up" fashion, as the result of a spontaneously emerging market. In this regard, Smith foreshadowed the emphasis on reciprocity that would become central to social exchange theory as the paradigm developed.

The long-standing debate on the meaning of Smith's work continues. However, it can be said with some confidence that, insofar as the economic system was concerned, Smith focused on individual self-interest as a key motivational principle behind his "invisible hand." Self-interest included strictly commercial considerations, of course, but it also concerned a desire for social approval. This is not to say that Smith rejected all motives other than self-interest (see, for example, his *Theory of Moral Sentiments*), only that self-interest plays a central role in his economic thinking. This concern with self-interest would be a point of contention in later social exchange research, as we shall see.

While Smith's outline of social exchange anticipates much later work, it is noteworthy that the "invisible hand" is grounded primarily in the domain of economics. Roughly a century later, the sociologist Albert Chavannes began to give social exchange theory its modern hue. Chavannes accepted Smith's notion of an emergent order generated through individual social exchanges. However, he criticized Smith on two points. First, Chavannes believed that economic self-interest did not exhaust the range of human motives, even in economic settings. He recognized other reasons for action, such as a sense of duty. Second, Chavannes was interested in individual relationships, which he argued developed from beneficial exchanges. People may begin to trade based on their pecuniary interests, but over time, they often experience a sense of affection and loyalty toward one another. With Chavannes's critique and extension of Smith, we can see the foundations of modern social exchange theory's core metatheoretical positions: (a) exchanges of goods, (b) which are based on considerations in addition to economic self-interest, (c) that spontaneously build relationships, which can then (d) provide the infrastructure for stable societies and business organizations

While Chavannes had identified the major themes of social exchange theory, his "arm chair" approach to the topic lacked empirical data. Additionally, Chavannes theorizing, like that of Smith, was based largely on Western nations. Non-Western and pre-industrial cultures were deemphasized. Early in the last century, scholars began to address these limitations through fieldwork in non-Western societies. One such thinker was the influential anthropologist Bronisław Malinowski. Reciprocity, though mentioned by Smith and Chavannes, placed an especially important role in Malinowski's work. He argued that reciprocity involves the tendency to "repay" the provision of a good or service based on obligations that people felt were owed to one another. Reciprocal exchanges tie people together. Interestingly, Malinowski also provided an early description of what would later be called a "social exchange relationship." He argued that people supported one another with the general assumption that exchanges would balance over the long run. This idea was central to later organizational behavior research.

Marcel Mauss held similar views. Mauss stressed that gift exchanges had symbolic value within the context of particular cultures. Certainly, some gifts held economic value, but others went beyond monetary worth. Transactions involving such gifts could build social ties that allowed societies to function harmoniously, even in the absence of a central government or "top-down" administration. As was the case with Chavannes and Malinowski, Mauss argued that individual transactions, which were not exclusively economic, built relationships among individuals. He stressed that these reciprocal exchanges often resulted from felt obligations and shared ethical norms.

During the late 1950s and early 1960s social exchange theory took on its now familiar look. Quite of bit of contemporary research still draws heavily on the theoretical perspectives that were originally laid out, though in seminal form, during this era.

Importance

Social exchange theory emerged early in the industrial revolution with the thinking of Adam Smith. Over the years, it has borrowed from major social and behavioral science disciplines, such as anthropology, psychology, and sociology. Given its richness, it should come as no surprise to learn that social exchange theory has had a profound influence on much of the conceptual thinking that underlies management. For example, there are social exchange models of leader–member exchange (LMX), trust formation, organizational commitment, organizational justice, and organizational citizenship behaviors. Despite this attention, or perhaps because of it, the specific paradigms explored under the rubric "social exchange" are quite diverse and not always closely integrated. As a result, there are many insights from social exchange theory that remain unexplored by organizational scientists and could be more broadly applied to work settings. There is reason to suspect that research on this fascinating conceptual paradigm will keep scholars busy for many decades to come.

Social exchange theories hold many applications for practitioners and managers. As we have outlined, social exchange principles explain the nature of social interactions among organizational members and between organizations. They help describe what motivates employees to work at high levels and also what motivates them to sabotage and undermine workplace goals. While differing models of social exchange have emerged in the literature, a consistent theme among them is that behavioral patterns demonstrated within exchange relationships can take on the reciprocal nature of beneficial and harmful contributions that are exchanged among organizational members and between organizations. Such exchanges can foster cooperative relations or end them. Thus, social exchange principles are important for managers to consider as they seek to produce benefits and limit costs associated with their work.

Russell Cropanzano and
Marie S. Mitchell

See also Group Development; Leader–Member Exchange Theory; Organizational Commitment Theory; Psychological Contracts Theory; Resource Dependence Theory

Further Readings

Blau, P. M. (1964). *Exchange and power in social life.* New York, NY: Wiley.

Cropanzano, R., & Mitchell, M. S. (2005). Social exchange theory: An interdisciplinary review. *Journal of Management, 31,* 874–900.

Fiske, A. P. (1991). *Structures of social life: The four elementary forms of human relations.* New York, NY: Free Press.

Homans, G. C. (1961). *Social behavior: Its elementary forms.* New York, NY: Harcourt Brace.

Knox, J. B. (1963). The concept of exchange in sociological theory: 1884 and 1961. *Social Forces, 41,* 341–346.

Lewicki, R. J., Tomlinson, E. C., & Gillespie, N. (2006). Models of interpersonal trust development: Theoretical approaches, empirical evidence, and future directions. *Journal of Management, 32,* 991–1022.

Molm, L. D., Peterson, G., & Takahashi, N. (2000). Power in negotiated and reciprocal exchange. *American Sociological Review, 64,* 876–890.

Nord, W. A. (1973). Adam Smith and contemporary social exchange theory. *American Journal of Economics and Sociology, 32,* 21–436.

Rusbault, C. E., & Van Lange, P. A. M. (2003). Interdependence, interaction, and relationships. *Annual Review of Psychology, 54,* 351–375.

Westphal, J. D., & Zajac, E. J. (1997). Defections from the inner circle: Social exchange, reciprocity, and the diffusion of board independence in U.S. corporations. *Administrative Science Quarterly, 42,* 161–183.

SOCIAL FACILITATION MANAGEMENT

How does the presence of others impact employee performance? The construct *social facilitation* was coined in an attempt to answer this question, and more than 90 years of research has sought to better understand the answer. In organizations, the social facilitation effect represents the extent to which an employee's performance increases or decreases when the employee performs his or her work in the presence of others. In organizations attempting to maximize performance, a better understanding of social facilitation is imperative. The following entry provides a succinct summary of what social facilitation is, how and when it impacts performance, and its managerial implications for teams, workplace design, and employee monitoring.

Fundamentals

While the social facilitation construct has important implications for the management of individuals, teams, and organizations, the construct's deep roots are anchored in basic psychology and sociological observations. For example, near the beginning of the 20th century, it was observed that bicyclists recorded faster times when riding with others compared to riding alone. Later, it was found that people generating lists of ideas produced a higher number of ideas when in a group context. These observations spawned a century of investigation of research into the social facilitation effect. This article highlights several of the tenants and findings of this theory and the implications it has for modern management practice.

Despite its name, research has revealed that the social facilitation effect is not always positive. That is, there are times when having other people present has a detrimental effect on employee performance. The evidence suggests that one primary factor that determines if the social facilitation effect is positive is the type of task being completed. For physical tasks, the social facilitation effect tends to be positive, with the presence of others leading to higher performance. For complex or unfamiliar tasks, however, the social facilitation effect tends to be negative, with the presence of other reducing task performance. Thus, the nature of the organization's work is an important factor that determines whether the social facilitation works for or against the organization's performance goals.

Along with task type moderation, current research is converging with research on social loafing. Social loafing research has demonstrated that in group contexts individuals may have a tendency to reduce the effort they expend on the group's work. While this would seem to contradict the social facilitation effect, research has shown that both effects can simultaneously operate if the individual inputs are distinguishable. Said another way, whether or not the social facilitation effect is positive or negative may also depend on the identifiability of individual (vs. team) contributions. If individual efforts are identifiable, then the social facilitation effect is present and positive. If individual inputs cannot be distinguished from group inputs, however, the social loafing effect or negative social facilitation effect is more likely to appear.

There are three interrelated mechanisms by which social facilitation works: drive, comparison, and cognitive resources. The drive mechanism suggests that the "mere presence" of other individuals creates a greater arousal state in employees. This instinctive increase in energy results in greater motivation for task performance. The comparison mechanism states that employees naturally tend to compare themselves to others and have an apprehension of being evaluated. Thus, employees will have a tendency to increase their efforts in order to improve the evaluation that others have of them and the evaluation they have of themselves. Finally, the cognitive resources mechanism states that the presence of others creates attention conflict as employees try to pay attention to both the task and the people. This conflict creates a degree of arousal that can augment performance on simple tasks. For complex tasks, however, where more cognitive resources are required for performance, conflict reduces the cognitive resources available for task performance and therefore reduces that performance.

Social Facilitation and Implications for Management

The many years of research on the social facilitation effect have important implications for modern management. Three of these major implications include work teams, workplace design, and electronic performance monitoring.

The use of work teams is one area where the task type moderation of the social facilitation effect has clear implications. Managers and organizations routinely make choices about how to structure the work in the organization, with work teams representing one such structure that has been gaining in popularity in recent years. The clear implication of social facilitation effect is that if the underlying work to be accomplished is physical in nature or relatively simple, then the use of work teams with identifiable individual accountabilities would be likely to yield benefits because of the social facilitation effect. Conversely, when the work is more cognitive in nature and relatively complex with individual-level accountabilities that are not specified, a negative social facilitation effect may occur along with a potential social loafing effect. This is not to say that teams should never be used to complete complex work; on the contrary, teams are often the structure of choice for managing complex tasks. Rather, managers in organizations need to ensure individual-level accountability within teams and consider whether the performance gains as a result of integrated expertise, complexity management, and synergy are greater than the performance decrements as a result of the social facilitation effect, social loafing, and other process losses.

The social facilitation effect mechanisms also have implications for the management of organizations' physical space. For example, a trend in organizations is moving from traditional office space to one of cubicles or shared work space. While this removal of physical barriers is intended to increase communication and collaboration as well as reduce infrastructure costs, the literature on the social facilitation effect suggests that although it may produce benefits such as increased physical activity because of evaluation apprehension, it may also increase distraction on more complex cognitive tasks and reduce performance. Thus, organizations should also consider the social facilitation effect in their workplace design decisions.

Finally, the social facilitation effect has clear connections to the organizational practice of electronic performance monitoring. Electronic performance monitoring involves tracking employee behaviors and productivity via their interactions with computer-based technologies. Applied research on social facilitation in this context illustrates that the monitoring does tend to increase stress levels, which results in higher performance for employees skilled at the task and lower performance for employees inexperienced at the task.

Thus, the social facilitation effect has stood the test of time but has also become more nuanced in its predictions. Managers should consider this nuance and their specific context in determining its likely impact on performance in their organizations.

Troy V. Mumford

See also High-Performing Teams; Human Resource Management Strategies; Job Characteristics Theory; Virtual Teams; Work Team Effectiveness

Further Readings

Aiello, J. R., & Douthitt, E. A. (2001). Social facilitation from Triplett to electronic performance monitoring. *Group Dynamics, 5,* 163–180.

Aiello, J. R., & Kolb, K. J. (1995). Electronic performance monitoring and social context: Impact on productivity and stress. *Journal of Applied Psychology, 80,* 339–353.

Bond, C. F., & Titus, L. J. (1983). Social facilitation: A meta-analysis of 241 studies. *Psychological Bulletin, 94,* 265–292.

Guerin, B. (1993). *Social facilitation.* Cambridge, England: Cambridge University Press.

Mumford, T. V., & Mattson, M. (2009). Will teams work? How the Nature of work drives synergy in autonomous team designs. In G. Solomon (Ed.), *Academy of Management Best Paper Proceedings.*

Weber, B., & Hertel, G. (2007). Motivation gains of inferior group members: A meta-analytical review. *Journal of Personality and Social Psychology, 93,* 973–993.

Zajonc, R. B. (1965). Social facilitation. *Science, 149,* 269–274.

Social Identity Theory

Social identity theory (SIT) is important to management research and practice by informing the development of an individual's self-concept within the context of social groups, in particular, to address questions related to "Who am I?" SIT explains how self-classification in group membership shapes an individual's self-concept by creating, defining, and locating his or her position within an intergroup system of meaning derived from social categorizations and comparisons. Henri Tajfel developed the seminal work for SIT when he first defined social identity as a person's knowledge of belonging to particular social categories that become meaningful in shaping behaviors, beliefs, and values when compared to other social groups. The theory relates to numerous management concerns, such as group dynamics, intergroup relationships, team development, leadership, social networks, human resources, diversity management, and organizational culture. The following discussion summarizes the major ideas of SIT, reviews its key developments, and highlights some of its main influences on management research and practice.

Fundamentals

The SIT Model

The SIT model identifies a process in which individuals' social identification with perceptually salient, distinctive social categories drives self-evaluative and subjective classifications and identifications that can create internal in-group prototypes and depersonalized out-group stereotypes that often result in enhanced self-esteem, reduced uncertainty, self-reinforcing intragroup assimilation and congruency, and potential conflict stemming from intergroup differences.

SIT maps a system of relational meaning derived from membership in social categories of intergroup relationships between in-group versus out-groups. Identity refers to the meanings and attributes that individuals have for their self-concept. Multiple identities are generated from membership in different social groups. Membership in social groups includes gender, age, religion, organizational membership, ethnicity, and many others. Within organizations, social groups may be the organization itself, departments, shared professional occupations, committees, status, and other types of social groups in organizations. Key factors that lead individuals to identify with a particular social group include (1) the distinctiveness of the group's values and practices relative to comparable group, (2) prestige of the group's status, (3) awareness of the out-group, and (4) traditional factors of group formation— interpersonal interactions, proximity, shared goals, liking, common history, and so on. Turner defines a social group based on perceptions of sameness where two or more individuals see themselves as sharing a common social identification. Thus, membership in a social group is a self-directed process along with self-evaluation in identifying shared similarities.

Focus. Belonging to a social group enables uncertainty reduction and consensual validation afforded by the in-group prototype as well as the positive value for self-esteem based on in-group distinctiveness compared to out-group differences. People would normally choose the different social categories that are salient in terms of providing positive attributes that can be extrapolated for their own self-concept. The choices for memberships are based on subjective perceptions of connections or classifications. While social identification focuses on membership in different social categories, it is distinctly different from internationalization, which involves integration of values, attitudes, and related features. Although one may belong on a team, one may not necessarily share the particular values, strategy, vision, or other characteristics.

Group dynamics. Developing a positive social identity requires beliefs about the nature of intergroup relationships, such as legitimacy, status, permeability, and stability. Tajfel and Turner extended social identity theory with self-categorization theory to account for how individuals express prototypical behaviors and attitudes of their social group over their distinctive individuality. In particular, self-categorization theory focuses on specific microprocesses of developing a social identity within an individual in relation to classification within social groups.

Self-categorization emphasizes the perceived similarities within group. At the same time, a parallel process of depersonalization occurs in reference to those in out-groups. Prototypical characteristics integrate attributes of the in-group while at the same time differentiating it from out-groups. But optimal distinctiveness theory describes how some individuals create a balance between their shared characteristics and individual uniqueness. Nevertheless, the cognitive assimilation of self into the in-group prototype produces a number of outcomes, including positive in-group attitudes and cohesion, cooperation and altruism, collective behavior, shared norms, stereotyping, and ethnocentrism. As a result, in-group favoritism occurs even with minimal to no interaction along with discrimination against out-group members.

Consequences. A central premise of SIT is that achieving a positive self-concept relies on evaluating in-group more favorably than out-group. This results in disparate treatment of members in an out-group that includes unfair discrimination, stereotyping, and

prejudice. Consequences of social identification are that (1) individuals choose social groups salient with their individual identities; (2) group formation has cohesion, cooperation, and altruism; and (3) antecedents of identification become reinforced. An important contribution of SIT is that identification can occur without the necessary interpersonal cohesion, similarity, or interaction.

SIT and Management

SIT draws heavily from social psychology to focus on work-related identities. Daily work interactions help create a composite of self from different roles, groups, tasks, and activities. Blake Ashforth has applied SIT to processes such as organizational socialization, role conflict, and intergroup relations. Newcomers to an organization need orientation to integrate their self-concept with a positive and distinct organizational identity that may involve storytelling, symbolism, and related identity work. SIT applied to role conflict indicated that cognitive resolution can be achieved with ordering, separating, and buffering as well as compartmentalizing identities, with possibilities of double standards, apparent hypocrisy, and/or selective forgetting. Hence, SIT accounts for two motivations in processes of social identity: (1) self-enhancement with positive favorable attributes and (2) uncertainty reduction to simplify and organize a complex social environment.

Identity work can take place internally with inward cognitive processes for identity creation and maintenance as well as externally with negotiating image and reputation. Being able to avoid the challenges of both "underidentification" and "overidentification" is necessary to mitigate socially deficient or excessive identification. The internal and external processes tend to be complex with tensions between individual distinctiveness and social connectedness in groups. Identity salience helps sort out which identities are more central to an individual's self-concept and aspirations to an ideal self. Social identity complexity refers to how much perceived overlap exists between an individual's different social groups. When the different groups have similarities in membership and prototypical characteristics, the degree of social identity complexity is reduced. Cultural identity formation involves a three-stage model—exploration, resolution, and affirmation. For example, becoming an American requires exploring what cultural practices and meanings are involved; resolving conflicts between different identities, such as being an immigrant to being an American; and affirming to see oneself as an American. Similar identity work processes are likely to occur with career transitions, promotions, and mergers and acquisitions.

Integration into an in-group not only benefits an individual with positive support, but also one is more likely to contribute to the social group and freely assist its members. This cooperation has important implications for productivity in work organizations with effectively bringing new employees on board or building high-performance teams. Identity orientations are personal, relational, or collective. The three identity orientations recognize how individuals vary in their degree of willingness to engage with others to collaborate

Further research into the positivity of work-related identity by Jane Dutton and her colleagues described four theoretical perspectives that allow organizational members to access and build their social resources. The four articulated perspectives of "positive" work-related social identity are virtue, evaluative, developmental, and structural. These lenses recognize that individuals may have different needs for social resources to strengthen the development of their self-concept. They also represent different sources or pathways that managers can facilitate to support and shape the identity development process in a particular direction to achieve desirable organizational outcomes.

Finally, it is also important to note that the social structure of groups does not establish equal status for all groups. Dominant groups seek to legitimate the status quo by exercising their power and status, whereas subordinate groups become involved in social change to improve the positive position of their group, as in the case of women and minorities in management. Some in-groups have negative distinctions. Members of negatively distinct groups such as lower class to upper class achieve positive social identity by exercising various strategies. If access to a higher-status group is possible, individuals may increase positive values for their social identity with social mobility without altering the in-group's status. Individuals may also exercise other strategies to leave a negatively distinctive in-group, including psychologically leaving by decreasing identification, decreasing perceived similarity to

in-group, increasing perceived similarity to a higher-status out-group, decreasing time spent with in-group, and decreasing physical and/or behavioral similarities to in-group. At a group level, collective strategies can be used to change negatively distinct in-groups to shift toward more positive orientations. One is social creativity by shifting from a negative orientation on a dimension toward a more positive one and/or changing the dimension to a different one that is more positive. Another is social change or social action that involves collective actions to change the status quo by confronting out-group members to alter the in-group status.

Evolution

Henry Tajfel is a major intellectual figure who shaped the post–World War II development of European social psychology in terms of the professional infrastructure, new intellectual movement in the field, and seminal concepts in intergroup relations that were integrated in SIT during the 1970s. Tajfel's major contributions were social perception and intergroup relations based on the premise that social psychological functions at the individual level are interrelated in a reciprocal manner with the large-scale social context and processes. Tajfel and Turner's collaboration continued to extend the development of SIT with Turner's contribution of self-categorization theory. *Minimal group paradigm* (MGP) developed from a methodology used to conduct research on the minimal conditions leading to intergroup discrimination. Tajfel developed psychological experiments that stripped away as much noise as possible to focus on minute differences between groups to identify favorability of in-group behavioral dynamics, norms, and attitudes. Recently, researchers employed MGP to examine prejudice against immigrants.

The volume of social psychology research grew rapidly from Tajfel and Turner's ideas. While many of their key ideas evolved from within a context of the Cold War, management researchers began to integrate SIT to examine work-related identities in the 1980s. Blake Ashforth and Michael Hogg are two prominent researchers who articulated the relevance of SIT in a range of organization workplace issues. Developments of SIT in organizations examined intergroup and individual state of social identity and processes of social identity development by accounting for multiple social group memberships within the context of workplace issues. Important contributions from an organizational perspective for SIT include the conflicts arising from social identity complexities, tensions from dual identities, and processes of social change at a group level to alter the status of negative distinctiveness. In contrast, processes of decline with increasing negative distinctiveness have not been addressed but require investigation that is relevant for organizations facing stress in the face of bankruptcies or scandals.

Today, SIT research is taking place as organizations are challenged to develop more diverse workforces related to a multicultural agenda and demands from an increasingly global marketplace. For example, within the conceptual space of relational demography and diversity management, SIT examines how people compare their own demographic characteristics such as age, gender, race, ethnicity, and others to those in other demographic groups. A particular work unit provides the context for daily interactions within which in-group versus out-group comparisons of behaviors occur. Diverse organizations need to develop a context that enables frequent interactions across demographic groups to create a shared identity, leverage the talent of different individuals, and create a multicultural organizational environment. Self-management by leveraging relational demography likely involves micro role transitions and managing boundaries.

Research in SIT continues to extend in both depth and breadth with a wide range of organizational topics in varied settings. Some of the organizational studies related SIT to topics including identity management, identity conflicts, identity threat, team diversity management, decision making, conflict management, leadership, motivation, sexual orientation, stereotypes, commitment, group performance, physical environment, emotions, role transitions, boundary spanning, careers, social injustice, boundary management, and performance feedback. Hence, SIT holds significant relevance for the field of management that is expected to continue into the future.

Importance

SIT is critically important in management research and practice for a number of different reasons. First, SIT helps explain the significance of how the social context shapes one's sense of self where the relationship between individuals and social groups entails reciprocal dynamics. Researchers related SIT to organizations to illuminate work-related identities where members engage with a composite of multiple group memberships that may span their immediate work groups to the superordinate group. The sense of belonging to organizational groups matters to shape its membership's self-concept. A positive organizational image and reputation contributes to a positive self-concept that in turn motivates individuals to behave in ways that reinforce the positive features. For management practitioners, SIT provides directions for managing the balance between harmonious work groups and commitment to the superordinate group at an organizational level.

Second, SIT outlines intergroup relations, especially with social identities related to demographic diversity and cross-cultural groups. This is increasingly important with increasing diversity in the workplace. Tajfel's earlier work on stereotypes and prejudice provides leads to understanding both positive and negative distinctiveness of groups. Subsequently, management researchers identified key strategies for managing negative distinctiveness, dealing with threats to identities, and bullying behaviors in the workplace. With each one of these issues, researchers developed further depth and understanding into the phenomenon by building on SIT and developing further depth and breadth in understanding how social identities engage with challenges to in-group favorability.

Third, SIT provided relevant insights into organizational processes such as individual development, leadership identities, group processes, and intergroup relationship dynamics. Social cultural settings contribute to these processes that lead to prejudice and discriminatory practices between in-group and out-group dynamics. In-group favoritism bias is a central concept in these processes as well as situations of selecting and hiring new employees, allocating rewards to team members, appointment of directors to boards, leadership development, different mentoring relationships, minority recruitment, and many other related topics. Positive treatment of in-group members and negative treatment of out-group members can lead to intergroup discrimination. But instances of reversals of in-group favoritism also take place when members are biased against others in their own in-group. As a result, a variety of concepts helps extend the process of self-concept in SIT.

Fourth, SIT is being applied by researchers to innovative concepts such as group fault lines and relational demography. The term *fault lines* refers to the hypothetical dividing lines subdividing a group as a result of multiple differences, often demographic ones. The division impacts group processes in terms of conflict management and cohesiveness, employee satisfaction, and performance outcomes. Dynamics of fault lines become salient when they raise the issue of identity threat, which is defined at the individual level as experiences considered as potentially harmful to the values, meanings, or enactment of an identity. Additional definitions of identity threat include questioning an individual's sense of self; stigma-relevant stressors that exceed the ability of an individual to cope with them; and when the process of identity is disabled from its continuity, distinctiveness, and self-esteem. Responses to identity threat are classified into two categories—(1) identity protection with derogation, concealment, or positive distinctiveness or (2) identity restructuring with identity exit, meaning change, and importance change. While derogation and concealment result in an outcome of the identity threat being maintained, the remaining four have the potential to eliminate the threat. Moreover, attention is just starting to be focused on understanding strategies to alter relational dynamics of in-group and out-group relationships based on social identity. In addition to examining the micro- and meso-processes, researchers are examining SIT from a critical theory perspective to raise the issues of power and gender in intergroup relations.

Overall, the research contributions of SIT are substantial and extensive to address a wide range of work-related identity issues with both breadth and depth. Because of its explanatory power and provocative theoretical and empirical range, SIT continues to grow as a referential framework with significant research and management implications and applications in the context of daily work interactions in organizations

Diana J. Wong-MingJi

See also Group Development; Interactional Model of Cultural Diversity; Norms Theory; Organizational Identification; Organizational Socialization; Organizationally Based Self-Esteem; Positive Organizational Scholarship; Self-Concept and the Theory of Self

Further Readings

Ashforth, B. E., & Mael, F. (1989). Social identity theory and the organization. *Academy of Management Review, 14*(1), 20–39.

Brown, S. D., & Lunt, P. (2002). A genealogy of the social identity tradition: Deleuze and Guattari and social psychology. *British Journal of Social Psychology, 41,* 1–23.

Calas, M. B., & Smircich, L. (2000). Ignored for "good reason": Beauvoir's philosophy as revision of social identity approaches. *Journal of Management Inquiry, 9*(2), 193–199.

Dutton, J. E., Roberts, L. M., & Bednar, J. (2010). Pathways for positive identity construction at work: Four types of positive identity and the building of social resources. *Academy of Management Review, 35*(2), 265–293.

Hogg, M. A., & Terry, D. J. (2000). Social identity and self-categorization processes in organizational contexts. *Academy of Management Review, 25*(1), 121–140.

Kreiner, G. E., & Sheep, M. L. (2006). Where sit the "me" among the "we"? Identity work and the search for optimal balance. *Academy of Management Journal, 49*(5), 1031–1057.

Tajfel, H. (1974). Social identity and intergroup behavior. *Social Science Information/Information sur les Sciences Sociales, 13*(2), 65–93.

Tajfel, H. (1981). *Human groups and social categories.* Cambridge, England: Cambridge University Press.

Tajfel, H., & Turner, J.C. (1986). The social identity theory of intergroup behavior. In W. G. Austin & S. Worchel (Eds.), *Psychology of intergroup relations* (2nd ed., pp. 7–24). Chicago, IL: Nelson-Hall.

SOCIAL IMPACT THEORY AND SOCIAL LOAFING

Social impact theory was introduced by social psychologist Bibb Latané in 1981 as a potentially unifying theory of social influence processes. It provides a framework for analyzing the impact of social influence attempts or situations in terms of social and situational factors that can influence the relative power of various potential sources and targets of influence. In the case of a group of people trying to influence a specific individual, the theory proposes that the magnitude of social influence will be a multiplicative function of the strength (e.g., status or expertise), immediacy (i.e., physical or psychological distance), and number of people in the influencing group. In the case of an individual attempting to influence other people, his or her influence should be divided across those others as an inverse function of the strength, immediacy, and number of people in the target group. The theory has been applied to a range of group, interpersonal, and organizational phenomena. One prominent area of application has been in the development and growth of research on social loafing, which refers to the tendency for individuals to work less hard on group or collective tasks than on individual tasks. This entry explains key elements of social impact theory, illustrates the variety of phenomena it has been applied to, discusses its prominent role in social loafing research, traces its recent development into a dynamic model, and briefly highlights its contributions to research and practice.

Fundamentals

Social impact theory represents a broad, integrative perspective with the potential for understanding a range of social influence situations from a limited set of common principles. Latané considered social impact in terms of any influence that the real, implied, or imagined presence or behavior of others could have on the physiology, emotions, motivations, cognitions, or behavior of individuals. This broad scope encompasses a wide range of potential social or interpersonal phenomena.

Latané grounded his perspective within the general metaphor of social forces (analogous to physical forces such as gravity, light, or sound) that operate within a social structure or social force field. He reasoned that individuals and groups are capable of exerting social influences on one another as a function of their relative size and the prominent social factors that influence the power or magnitude of their respective social influences. In particular, social impact theory posits three key principles about the dynamics of social influence.

First, the theory predicts that the social impact experienced by an individual is a function of the strength, immediacy, and number of influence sources, as represented by the equation

$$I = f(SIN)$$

Strength refers to the power or importance of an influence source, which might be affected by

factors such as one's status, prestige, or position of authority. Immediacy refers to physical or psychological closeness in space or time, which might be affected by physical distance or by the presence versus absence of barriers, filters, or delays to communication or visibility. Number refers to how many people are attempting to exert influence.

Second, the theory suggests that increases in the number of sources should have more impact on targets when groups are small rather than large. Specifically, it posits the existence of a psychosocial law, represented by the equation

$$I = sN^t$$

wherein the amount of impact experienced by an individual is equal to some power, t, of the number of sources present, N, multiplied by a scaling constant, s. Moreover, the value of the exponent t is predicted to be less than one. Therefore, the social impact experienced by the individual should increase as the number of influence sources increases, but this incremental increase in impact should diminish as N gets larger and larger. Thus, the increase in experienced social impact should be larger when the number of sources increases from two to three rather than from 20 to 21 and so on.

The third key principle concerns the multiplication versus division of impact based on the number and nature of influence sources (i.e., those exerting influence) and targets (i.e., those being influenced) present. Namely, multiple influence sources intensify the magnitude of social impact, whereas multiple influence targets diminish it. In the case of a group's influences on a single individual, this influence is predicted to be a multiplicative function of the strength, immediacy, and number of group members. Inversely, in the case of an individual attempting to influence a group, this impact is predicted to be divided across the group members. Overall, the influence exerted within a given social force field is based on the strength, immediacy, and number of influence sources divided by the strength, immediacy, and number of influence targets.

Social Loafing

Perhaps most relevant to managerial contexts, social impact theory has been a driving force behind the development and maturation of research on social loafing. Social loafing refers to the tendency for individuals to work less hard on group or collective tasks than on individual tasks. On collective tasks, social impact theory predicts that the request from an outside source of influence (such as one's boss) to work hard on the task should be divided among the group members, resulting in less effort than if these same individuals were working alone. Moreover, consistent with the psychosocial principle, this reduction in effort should be more evident as group size increases. These hypotheses were supported in a seminal 1979 research article by Latané, Kipling D. Williams, and Stephen Harkins that coined the term *social loafing* and provided an influential example of how to study the phenomenon in a way that allows motivation losses to be separated from mere lack of coordination of members' efforts.

Research on social loafing has since evolved into a rich and mature literature consisting of more than 100 studies that have examined a wide variety of populations and tasks. A 1993 meta-analysis of 78 studies by Steven J. Karau and Williams concluded that social loafing is moderate in magnitude and replicates across most tasks and studies, yet it is also influenced by a variety of moderating variables that can reduce or even eliminate the effect. For example, social loafing can be reduced when individual inputs are easier to identify, when the group is cohesive, when group size is small rather than large, and when the individual identifies with the group can make more distinctive contributions or views the task as high in meaningfulness or importance. Although the bulk of studies have been conducted in laboratory settings, field studies of social-loafing perceptions within teams in business organizations and classroom settings have generally produced results highly consistent with those from laboratory studies.

Dynamic Social Impact Theory

Social impact theory was originally fairly static in nature, focusing on a specific influence situation or event. However, several later analyses in the 1990s and beyond by Latané and colleagues have proposed dynamic modifications of the theory that extend its basic assumptions to their iterative implications over time. Dynamic social impact theory considers groups as complex systems of individuals who interact in some manner to jointly influence their social environment. It proposes that, through the repeated interaction within the system of individual-level social influences, large groups tend to show four patterns of self-organization over time: (a) consolidation—a reduction in the number and diversity of attitudes or judgments within the group; (b) clustering—the formation of coherent subgroups within the larger group, especially as influenced by geography or communicative proximity; (c) correlation—the association of originally unrelated opinions, in part through the impact of particularly influential members; and (d) continuing diversity—the persistence of some minority viewpoints or judgments, largely because clustering processes prevent consolidation from fully eliminating minority attitudes. Dynamic social impact theory has received initial support from complex computer simulations, as well as from studies of attitude formation and change within large classroom, electronic discussion, or community groups. It represents a promising source of hypotheses and insights for future research on the dynamics of social influence patterns within groups over time.

Importance

Social impact theory represents a prominent perspective for understanding a wide range of social influence phenomena. It has proven useful both in integrating prior research in areas such as persuasion, minority influence, and social anxiety and in stimulating new research in areas such as group motivation and influence patterns in large social networks and communities. The theory was also very influential in driving early and continuing research on social loafing. The diversity of phenomena to which the theory has been applied makes a full assessment of its research support somewhat challenging and tentative. Yet evidence to date appears largely encouraging. Hypotheses regarding the number of influence sources and the psychosocial principle have received the strongest support, with evidence for strength and immediacy of sources generally supportive, albeit sometimes weak or mixed when comparing across individual studies. The theory has been particularly influential among social psychologists and has enormous potential (largely unexploited) for future organizational research.

Social impact theory is potentially applicable to any situation involving social influence. Indeed, the theory has been applied to a host of social influence phenomena, including conformity, persuasion, aggression, attitude formation and change, bystander intervention, voting behavior, motivation, group performance, and social anxiety. The theory has been deployed in a number of instances to help organize existing research literatures. For example, Latané and Sharon Wolf provided a compelling integration of past research on major and minority influence processes in groups. Social impact theory has also been used to derive testable hypotheses in a variety of social influence domains. The theory's potential for producing novel insights and clever methodological choices has been evident in dozens of empirical studies. In one example, an interesting field study by Constantine Sedikides and Jeffrey M. Jackson examined social influence processes at a zoo. Requests for visitors to refrain from leaning on exhibit railings were found to be more successful when delivered by an individual wearing a zookeeper's uniform (high source strength) rather than casual dress, within a short duration of the request (high immediacy) rather than at a later exhibit, and in small rather than larger visitor group sizes (number of targets). In another example, an experiment by Karen B. Williams and Kipling D. Williams examined the inhibiting role that concerns with being evaluated negatively by others could have on seeking help. Groups of eight students were asked to take exams on computers that had been rigged to malfunction. Individuals were slower to seek help from high- rather than low-status test givers and when there were three rather than one test giver, supporting social impact theory's hypotheses about strength and number.

Regarding managerial practice, the theory has some relatively straightforward implications. Namely, influence can potentially be increased by enhancing the leader's strength and immediacy (such as by increasing one's status, credibility, or physical proximity) or by increasing the size of the influencing group and is potentially diminished by an increase in these same factors among targets of influence. The theory also highlights the potential for group tasks to reduce the effort of individual members, especially in larger groups and when individual efforts are difficult or impossible to identify. Finally, dynamic social impact theory suggests that patterns of attitude formation and change across large communities or social networks typically evolve predictable emerging properties over time.

Steven J. Karau

See also Asch Effect; Brainstorming; High-Performing Teams; Influence Tactics; Social Cognitive Theory; Social Facilitation; Social Information Processing Theory; Systems Theory of Organizations

Further Readings

Karau, S. J., & Williams, K. D. (1993). Social loafing: A meta-analytic review and theoretical integration. *Journal of Personality and Social Psychology, 65,* 681–706.

Latané, B. (1981). The psychology of social impact. *American Psychologist, 36,* 343–356.

Latané, B., Williams, K., & Harkins, S. (1979). Many hands make light the work: The causes and consequences of social loafing. *Journal of Personality and Social Psychology, 37,* 822–832.

Latané, B., & Wolf, S. (1981). The social impact of majorities and minorities. *Psychological Review, 88,* 438–453.

Nowak, A., Szamrej, J., & Latané, B. (1990). From private attitude to public opinion: A dynamic theory of social impact. *Psychological Review, 97,* 362–376.

Sedikides, C., & Jackson, J. M. (1990). Social impact theory: A field test of source strength, source immediacy and number of targets. *Basic and Applied Social Psychology, 11,* 273–281.

Williams, K. B., & Williams, K. D. (1983). Social inhibition and asking for help: The effects of number, strength, and immediacy of potential help givers. *Journal of Personality and Social Psychology, 44,* 67–77.

Social Information Processing Model

Social information processing (SIP) theory hypothesizes that people's attitudes and motivations—at work or, for that matter, other places—are a function not just of the objective situations they face but also of the attitudes and motives held by others in their immediate environment; they are also a result of the effect of others to cause individuals to rationalize and make sense of past behavior. Because of the importance of these processes, one of the major tasks of management is to affect the informational context so that people come to see the world in particular ways. SIP theory developed in part in reaction to the large literature on job characteristics that spoke to the motivating potential of jobs and the importance of objective job characteristics. SIP theory argued that job characteristics were not merely objective properties of particular work arrangements but rather were socially constructed through a process of collective perception and agreement. And perceptions of job attributes were also created by the choices people made and their need to make sense of those choices. Thus, people in an employee's environment influenced what job dimensions the person focused on, what information the person used in assessing those dimensions of the work environment, and what attitudes and perceptions to hold. As a consequence, management could intervene in the workplace not just by changing the objective features of the job but also by affecting how people thought about and talked about their work. This entry reviews the arguments and predictions of SIP and also places the theory in the context of other ideas that emphasize the importance of context for understanding behavior.

Fundamentals

SIP posits that, as adaptive organisms, individuals modify their attitudes and behavior to accommodate to the social environment in which they exist, as well as to their own past behaviors. The most commonly studied dependent variables have been perceptions of job characteristics—autonomy, variety, and so forth—and job attitudes such as overall satisfaction with the job and with particular facets of satisfaction, such as pay and the quality of supervision. In fewer instances, the dependent variables have included actual behaviors, particularly turnover (e.g., voluntarily quitting).

The first prediction is that social information affects perceptions of job attributes and job attitudes. The prediction has been tested using both field data and experiments. One experimental paradigm involved designing tasks that varied in their characteristics as assessed by others and then randomly assigning people to either enriched (more interesting and challenging) or unenriched (routine activities with little variety or autonomy) tasks and also exposing subjects to information that suggested that the tasks they were working on as part of the experiment were either enriched and challenging or not. Social information not only affected task perceptions but had an effect larger than the actual job characteristics. A typical field study design assessed the extent to which people working together and in frequent contact with each other shared perceptions of task characteristics and job attitudes. One study design asked whether people in contact had a higher degree of consensus on perceptions of job attributes and their job attitudes than others doing similar work but located in different units that had less (or even no) contact.

With respect to the effect of social information on behaviors, the prediction was that people would be influenced by what others with whom they were in contact did. So some research asked whether behavior was contagious within work units. For instance, in a study of turnover in fast food restaurants, once people began to leave, did others connected in their social interactions with those people also tend to leave at a higher rate? If those in contact with people who had quit also quit at a higher rate, this would indicate that turnover was influenced by social information; when others left, it would cause those still in the organization to reevaluate the work and job conditions and their own choices about staying or leaving.

The second main class of predictions from SIP theory was that, when called on by cues in their social environment to make sense of their choices, individuals would use logical inferences from their past behavior to infer their attitudes and perceptions about their work environment. In some sense, this prediction from SIP theory builds on and is a direct extension of the research literature demonstrating the effects of commitment in creating attitude-behavior consistencies. But SIP theory added the element of salience; specifically, the social environment, information provided by others, and even the particular framing of questions made some past choices and aspects of past behavior more or less salient and thereby differentially influenced how people constructed explanations for their actions.

As one example of this effect, consider a study of how students constructed attitudes toward a particular course. Some students were primed by the questions asked by the experimenter to think of pro-course behaviors, activities that would reflect interest in the class. Other students were primed to recall anticourse behaviors, actions that would be reflective of not enjoying or being interested in the class. Those study participants who were primed to recall pro-course activities subsequently expressed more favorable attitudes toward the class than did those influenced to recall anticourse actions.

Evolution

The idea that people are influenced in their attitudes, perceptions, and motivations by the social context is a very old one in the social sciences. Leon Festinger argued that when confronted with uncertainty and ambiguity, people looked to what others were doing, thinking, and saying as a way of helping resolve that uncertainty. One intriguing manifestation of this social influence effect appears in the literature on bystander intervention. The original incident that stimulated that literature was a case of numerous people watching without doing anything while a woman was stabbed on the streets of New York City. The initial puzzle was, How could so many people stand by and do nothing while someone was brutally attacked? But the very fact that there were so many people watching was precisely the reason that no one intervened. Not only was responsibility diffused across the many witnesses so that no single individual felt the need to take action, the fact that many others weren't doing anything made inaction normative, expected, and accepted. Doing nothing was what others, similarly situated, were doing. All those others could not be wrong.

The enormous literature on conformity pressures and adherence to group judgments also is consistent with ideas of attitudinal and behavioral uniformity with respect to the work environment but for a different reason. As social creatures, people want to be accepted and liked by their peers. Indeed, social ostracism is very stressful and punishing. Because a fundamental basis of interpersonal attraction is similarity, including similarity in attitudes, the argument is that people would conform to the attitudes and judgments of others as a way of ensuring their acceptance by and into peer groups.

A third foundation for attitudinal and perceptual similarity among interacting peers comes from the idea of social proof. Robert Cialdini and others have argued that people have limited information-processing capacity and, moreover, are miserly in their cognitive efforts. People don't want to expend time thinking about something if they don't need to. If others, and particularly similar others, have come to a judgment or taken some action, the simplest and most straightforward thing to do is to assume these others must be right and not to spend a lot of time and effort revisiting the question. Thus, a third mechanism explaining the uniformity of opinions and beliefs in the workplace is a motivation to avoid cognitive load and effort, taking the beliefs of others as informative about the state of the world.

For purposes of developing SIP theory, which of these explanations—and, of course, they are not mutually exclusive—is correct is irrelevant. The point is that many social science theories posit attitudinal consistency among interacting individuals, with such consistency increasing over time. The increase in uniformity over time results because dissimilar others would come to be excluded and possibly leave as a result and because a shared consensus about the definition of the situation would emerge as people mutually influence each other through a process of informational social influence.

For people to influence others' perceptions, for instance, about job characteristics, it must be the case that not only is there social influence but also that the reality of the work and task environment itself is and can be socially constructed. Once again, numerous social science writings are consistent with this idea. Here are just some examples. The large literature on the durability of first impressions posits that initial information, about someone else as an example, maintains its hold because new information is assimilated in ways to be consistent with the initial judgments, people stop seeking additional information once they have formed a judgment about another, and discrepant information is dismissed as being not valid. If initial impressions matter and if initial impressions can be based on information provided by others, then the "facts" about a given individual may matter less than the socially constructed image. And what is true for individuals is also true for particular jobs and organizations—initial reputations and perceptions can and do become stable, self-fulfilling, and self-reinforcing over time.

The literatures on the self-fulfilling prophecy and organizational performativity also provide mechanisms that would account for how reality becomes socially constructed. The self-fulfilling prophecy literature shows that expectations matter because expectations influence what people *do,* in that people not expected to perform well don't expend as much effort and don't do as well because of the anxiety aroused by the anticipation of failure. The literature on organizational performativity demonstrates that when institutional arrangements are constructed in ways consistent with social beliefs and theories, these very institutional arrangements can cause the beliefs and theories to be true because such arrangements *make* them or *cause them to come into being.*

One classic study in this tradition showed that originally the Black-Scholes option pricing formula had a number of theoretical rivals and did not do a particularly good job of predicting the prices at which options actually traded. However, once the model became operationalized on sheets showing option pricing and even in a software program, the advantage of this formulation, which relied on only one variable rather than several, and the availability of the prices it produced, increased the use of Black-Scholes's predicted prices. In the process, the predictions of the model became true because the model affected institutional arrangements and the actions of traders that made it become true.

In the case of jobs and organizations, if a specific job or organization is perceived as "cool" or good, there will be many applicants and the quality of the applicant pool will be higher. Able to hire better people, the organization will be more successful. Moreover, people will flock to places where everyone else wants to be. Thus, what is a good place to work or a desirable sort of job depends on the beliefs of others and their acting on those opinions.

As a final example of the social construction of organizational reality, there is a large literature in ethnomethodology and sociology that also illustrates how the process unfolds. One important mechanism is measurement, with the measurement of something creating the reality of what is measured and potentially signaling its importance. Discourse and conventions of everyday conversation help frame what we see and how we see it. The definition of "mental illness" and what is "criminal activity" are obviously socially constructed by the agencies and professions that decide what normal behavior is and what is acceptable or illegal. In a similar fashion, talking about and measuring job variety or task autonomy signals that these are important dimensions of work. And the particular ways of measuring these or other organizational or job characteristics primes individuals to assess work environment dimensions in some ways using some measures rather than others.

And as originally formulated, SIP theory had a third important foundation: Interactions with others would, in many instances, compel people to have to explain their past decisions, and this process would cause them to rationalize and increase their commitment to those choices. For instance, someone might take a job that pays less than others for numerous

reasons or for no reason at all, as behavior is sometimes automatic and practically free from thought. But other individuals in the social environment might ask about this choice, and this form of social influence would cause the individual to make sense of the choice and, by so doing, become more committed to working for this organization and also more committed to the reasons for the choice.

These ideas of social influence, the social construction of reality, and the presence of others causing people to rationalize and thereby increase their commitment to decisions, form the (well-established) theoretical foundations out of which SIP theory emerged.

Importance

Social information-processing ideas have been important in the first place because they have received substantial empirical support. In the years immediately following the publication of the theory, many studies found that the most important determinant of perceptions of jobs, as measured by instruments such as the Job Diagnostic Survey, was informational influence about the nature of the tasks as being enriched or unenriched. The studies showed that, for the most part, social influence on perceptions of job characteristics and job satisfaction provided by the opinions expressed by others was stronger than the actual characteristics of the jobs themselves. And it was not just peers but managers, too, who could influence the evaluation of job environments. An influential field study of actual job changes and managerial informational influence interventions reported that both informational influence and job redesign affected employee perceptions of job attributes, job attitudes, and even productivity. That study and others suggested that intentional managerial interventions directed at changing job perceptions, not just the beliefs and comments of coworkers, could be used to affect employees' perceptions of and reactions to their work environment.

SIP theory was also important and has been influential over time because many of its fundamental ideas linked naturally to other emerging themes in management research. SIP theory was, at its core, an argument about the importance of the environment in affecting people's perceptions and choices. In that sense, the theory nicely tapped into the growing influence of situationism and the social psychological idea that situations, including the information conveyed and primed by situations, matter in affecting people's behavior. Recently, for instance, research has found that people are more likely to vote in favor of school bonds when they cast their vote in a school compared with, for instance, a church basement, or another public building that is not a school.

As another example, the theory's main argument concerned the importance of social influence on perceptions, attitudes, and decisions. The development and increasing importance of network ideas and methods made the investigation of how influence traveled through structures of interactions empirically more rigorous and demonstrated network influences on behavior and attitudes. And network imagery was quite consistent with the idea of social influences on behavior.

The theory's emphasis on the social construction of attitudes and judgments and the role of management in structuring perception formed a natural precursor to the importance of the symbolic and meaning-creating functions of leadership and to the argument that, to use Louis Pondy's apt phrase, leadership was essentially a "language game." That one of the critical functions of leadership is to influence how people make sense of their activities and see the organizational environment has now come to be almost taken for granted and is a natural outgrowth of SIP's emphasis on management's role as a creator of the perceived environment.

It is important to note that SIP theory does not maintain that the objective conditions of job and work have no influence. Rather, the theory argues that reality is filtered through and affected by the influence of others and by the person's own past behaviors and commitments.

Jeffrey Pfeffer

See also Management Symbolism and Symbolic Action; Self-Fulfilling Prophecy; Sensemaking; Social Construction Theory; Social Network Analysis

Further Readings

Cialdini, R. B., Wosinska, W., Barrett, D. W., Butner, J., & Gornik-Durose, M. (1999). Compliance with a request in two cultures: The differential influence of social proof and commitment/consistency on collectivists and individualists. *Personality and Social Psychology Bulletin, 25,* 1242–1253.

Festinger, L. (1954). A theory of social comparison processes. *Human Relations, 7,* 117–140.

Griffin, R. W. (1983). Objective and social sources of information in task redesign: A field experiment. *Administrative Science Quarterly, 28,* 184–200.

Ibarra, H., & Andrews, S. B. (1993). Power, social influence, and sense making: Effects of network centrality and proximity on employee perceptions. *Administrative Science Quarterly, 38,* 277–303.

Krackhardt, D., & Porter, L. W. (1986). The snowball effect: Turnover embedded in communication networks, *Journal of Applied Psychology, 71,* 50–55.

O'Reilly, C. A., & Caldwell, D. F. (1979). Informational influence as a determinant of perceived task characteristics and job satisfaction. *Journal of Applied Psychology, 64,* 157–165.

Pfeffer, J. (1981). Management as symbolic action: The creation and maintenance of organizational paradigms. In L. L. Cummings & B. M. Staw (Eds.), *Research in organizational behavior* (Vol. 3, pp. 1–52). Greenwich, CT: JAI Press.

Salancik, G. R. (1975). Attitude inferences from salient and relevant cognitive content about behavior. *Journal of Personality and Social Psychology, 32,* 829–840.

Salancik, G. R., & Pfeffer, J. (1978). A social information processing approach to job attitudes and task design. *Administrative Science Quarterly, 23,* 224–253.

Social Movements

Social movement theory considers how challengers to the status quo mobilize collective action supporting change and examines the conditions in which these bottom-up efforts are likely to be successful. Management often finds itself confronted by challengers—actors with competing, conflicting agendas who seek to compel reform. These actors exercise influence by coalescing into groups that take collective action to influence managers to amend contested practices or policies. We refer to those organized, purposeful attempts at reform as social movements. A new vein of research has focused on the role of social movements in instigating organizational change. This research contends that movements, although often small in size, are capable of generating significant influence and are an important source of innovation in industries and organizations. This entry looks at the various forms that movements take and assesses their potential for creating organizational change.

Fundamentals

Corporate management is naturally inclined to resist change and maintain the status quo for number of reasons. Organizations are designed to be stable and self-reproducing. As their guardians, managers are sensitive to the uncertainty and cost of change, which tends to make them cautious and conservative when considering radical reforms. Cognitive constraints and political alliances within the organization can also make managers politically vested in the status quo.

In contravention to organization's static tendencies, social movements form when actors share a common vision of the future that is in some way directly opposed to the status quo. Reasons for pushing reform include seeking to implement innovative products or organizational forms, changing companies' employment practices, or altering top management's philosophy or governance policies. These movements may take several forms. Employee-led movements manifest through a steady process of coalition building among employees and managers around particular issues. Movements mobilized by external stakeholders, on the other hand, are typically more disruptive and oppositional. For example, anticorporate campaigns often use coercive tactics such as boycotts or protests to force their organizational targets to reform.

Different types of movements face different opportunities and challenges. Employee-led movements are most likely to produce innovative reform when they work within existing channels and develop favor with elite allies in top management. Because of their internal positioning, these movements can draw on their knowledge of organizational rules and procedures to foster political advantages and build support for emerging coalitions. However, employee movements may be somewhat constrained to push for radical reforms because their members naturally depend on management for their jobs, which may limit their ability to take risky actions. Moreover, employee activists experience an identity trade-off, being both reformers and caretakers of the organizations. Thus, employee-led movements may be unwilling to voice their concerns in the public sphere, where their actions could harm the organization's reputation. These constraints could pose higher costs on employee-led movements, which may deradicalize them and make their proposed reforms less innovative.

In contrast, movements led by external stakeholders do not suffer the same constraints on behavior or tactics. Outsider movements are free to use subversive tactics, such as street demonstrations or lawsuits, that create negative media attention for the firm. These disruptive practices potentially stigmatize the firm and hurt its reputation. As public support builds and more media attention focuses on the movement, the movement leverages its influence, and firms may feel pressured to adopt reformative practices against their will. Past research shows that firms suffering from previous reputation declines, even those due to completely unrelated reasons, are the most vulnerable to activist pressure because they are already concerned about their faltering public image.

Although externally led movements may be better equipped to leverage their influence by escalating their claims to the public sphere, they also face their own challenges. First, because external activists have no formal affiliation with a firm, management may assume that they do not have the best interests of the firm at heart and, therefore, be more reticent to listen to them. Also, these movements depend on the media to notice and give air to their grievances. If the media are preoccupied with other events, they should have weaker influence. Similarly, firms facing external activist pressure may symbolically concede to the movement without actually implementing internal changes. If not followed up with accountability mechanisms, promises to reform may be hollow. Because of their lack of access to the organization's day-to-day operations, external movements may be incapable of monitoring the firm's substantive response to their demands. Thus, external movements may be more effective when they simultaneously develop allies within the firm that share their vision of reform.

While managers may be tempted to ignore or quash movements targeting their organizations, failure to be receptive to activists' demands can sometimes be detrimental to a firm. Failing to heed changing social expectations about corporate action can lead to market risks, as entrepreneurs may use a movement's claims to create new, innovative competitors. Frustrated movements may also go over managements' head by targeting the state or international trade associations to encourage the adoption of new regulations. Firms forced to change because of new competitors or regulations may experience higher costs than they would have paid by initially complying with the movement. Additionally, firms that refuse to change contested practices could find themselves chronically targeted, which could have negative financial consequences. One recent study showed that a firm targeted by a single protest event could experience a 0.4% to 1% decline in stock price.

And finally, although movement reform efforts may seem threatening and disruptive to managers, research suggests there are good reasons for managers to engage with them. Entrepreneurial leaders may use movements to overcome natural inertia and introduce otherwise risky practices, especially when there is growing internal support for reform. Movements' claims also could be construed as bellwethers of shifting consumer values, which signal growing demand for new products, new marketing opportunities, or burgeoning niche markets. Newly contested social issues indicate changing social expectations, which could aid firm leaders in creating appealing corporate social responsibility platforms to provide their organization with a valuable reputational advantage. Thus, movement threats can unearth new opportunities and sources of value for savvy managers who are willing to think outside the box and embrace innovative practices.

Brayden G. King and
Mary-Hunter Morris McDonnell

See also Analytical and Sociological Paradigms; Business Policy and Corporate Strategy; Corporate Social Responsibility; Institutional Theory; Patterns of Political Behavior; Process Theories of Change; Social Entrepreneurship; Strategies for Change

Further Readings

King, B. G. (2008). A political mediation model of corporate response to social movement activism. *Administrative Science Quarterly, 53*, 395–421.

King, B. G., & Soule, S. A. (2007). Social movements as extra-institutional entrepreneurs: The effect of protest on stock price returns. *Administrative Science Quarterly, 52*, 413–442.

Rao, H. (2009). *Market rebels: How activists make or break radical innovations.* Princeton, NJ: Princeton University Press.

Scully, M., & Segal, A. (2002). Passion with an umbrella: Grassroots activists in the workplace. *Research in the Sociology of Organizations, 19*, 125–168.

Social Network Theory

Social network theory is an interdisciplinary approach to understanding social phenomena based on the relationships between actors and the patterns of connectivity and cleavage those relationships create when taken as a whole. Two characteristics of organizations that make the social network perspective particularly relevant to management theory are that (1) organizations generally exist for the express purpose of establishing interaction and exchange with other entities, whether that exchange is economic (e.g., corporations), social influence (e.g., nongovernmental organizations), humanitarian (e.g., charities), or another currency, and (2) they do so by bounding and coordinating the interactions of multiple individuals to achieve ends not achievable separately. Within the realm of organization and management theory, social network research animates several streams of fruitful research. This entry first summarizes the fundamental characteristics of social network theory and the major streams of research in this domain before considering some of the unique challenges of conducting research in this tradition. It then delineates several substantive contributions social network theory has made to organization theory more broadly by identifying insights common to those streams of research. Finally, a short bibliography of articles and books is provided representative of social network research within the domain of management and organization management.

Fundamentals

The fundamental difference between the social network perspective and most other approaches to management research is social network theory's dual assertions that *relationships matter* and *structure matters*. Relationships matter because they provide individual actors (people, teams, organizations, etc.) with channels through which social interactions and exchanges occur. Structure matters because the particular arrangement of those relationships creates opportunities and constraints not only for actors occupying specific positions in the network but also for the network as a whole and for different regions within the network.

Social networks comprise a set of actors and the collection of ties among those actors. Generally, a single type of tie (e.g., friendship, advice, sales) reflects one network, but research often considers multiple networks (relationships) at the same time. Theories concern outcomes for the actors themselves as individuals (What are the consequences of having many ties?), outcomes for each pair of actors (Does having a friendship tie lead to creating a business tie?), for groups of actors within the network (Do departments with more internal trust ties perform better?), or for networks as a whole (Do companies with more social interaction outperform those with less?). In each example above, "actors" in the network were individual people, but research questions considered them individually, in pairs, in groups, or as a single collective, respectively. However, actors can also be collectives (e.g., teams, organizations), which can also be aggregated. For example, in a network where actors are organizations, they can be considered as a single collective making up an industry (e.g., Do industries with denser alliance networks adapt more or less quickly to exogenous shocks?).

While an exhaustive list of the prominent social network research related to management theory would likely require a volume of its own, a significant majority can be characterized as relating to one of three approaches: *relatedness and topology, embeddedness,* and *egonet composition.* A brief summary of each approach, with some characteristic findings, constructs, and operationalized variables follows.

Relatedness and topology. Although relatedness here refers to immediate connections of individual actors in the network and topology refers to the shape of the network when taken as a whole, they are typically considered simultaneously. However, the most basic approach is investigating the power of direct relationships among actors. Being connected or not connected creates both opportunities and constraints that impact the behaviors of organizations and the people they comprise. Organizationally relevant relationships run the gamut from physical proximity of individuals (closer proximity increases chances of information sharing) to board interlocks (companies who share board members exhibit similarities in certain governance behaviors) and a host of other relationships ranging from providing the potential for interaction (such as physical proximity or demographic

similarity) through realized exchanges (such as the flows of personnel among companies in an industry).

Because individual connections form structural patterns (a social system), where a particular actor's specific constellation of connections position it within the network as a whole also creates opportunities and constraints. Thus, although some work focuses on direct relationships (individuals with more ties within an organization have higher job satisfaction), considerable work assesses the structural implications of those connections (occupying a bridging position in the friendship network decreases job satisfaction). These types of analyses consider individual actors, subgroups, or the entire network. For example, within networks capturing personnel flows between organizational actors in two different regions (two networks), the variance in flows across the two regions offered insight into the relative success of each.

There are many different measures to assess relatedness in social networks. At the actor level, the most common and concise ways to measure these are through the concept of *centrality.* There are many measures of centrality but most operationalization of one of four constructs: (1) the number of direct or immediate connections the actor has (*degree centrality*), (2) the extent to which the actor is connected to other highly connected actors (e.g., *eigenvector centrality* and *Bonacich power*), (3) the extent to which the actor can reach other actors in the network (e.g., *closeness centrality*), and (4) the extent to which the actor is an intermediate between other actors in the network (e.g., "*betweenness*" *centrality*). There are group-level analogs to some of these, but *density* (the percentage of possible ties that actually exist) is commonly used to measure relatedness at the group and network level.

Although some of the centrality measures capture characteristics about the actor's position in the global network structure (e.g., betweenness), other research focuses on the topologies of actors' local networks. In an influential stream of work, Ron Burt has identified various advantages to being a broker by occupying what he terms a *structural hole.* Specifically, when a focal actor (called *ego*) is connected to two other actors (called *alters*) and those alters are not connected to each other, ego has comparatively more information, more control over that information, and more autonomy than if those alters are connected to each other. Research links occupying structural holes to many positive outcomes for the individual. The primary constructs in this stream of research are operationalized as *effective size* (which is effectively degree centrality discounted to account for connections among ego's alters) and *constraint* (which is the extent to which ties among ego's alters constrain ego's ability to pull out of the network). Although the structural holes perspective is perhaps the most influential stream of management based on network topology, other structural research (e.g., identifying abstracted social roles based on patterns of structural positions) has also made important contributions to management theory.

Embeddedness. While the structural hole perspective typically focuses on individual actors, another stream of research focused more on interorganizational network structures points to the value of embeddedness, though both approaches are used with individual and collective actors. Embeddedness holds that interactions and exchanges (particular economic ones) generally happen within the context of (or are embedded in) a larger social context. Two implications of this are *mutiplexity* and *cohesiveness*. Multiplexity means that exchange partners typically have multiple types of interactions; for example, economic transactions are accompanied by social interactions, which might influence the way they are handled. Cohesiveness refers to the tendency to establish new ties or strengthening existing ties within a defined community rather than establishing ties outside the community. By becoming embedded with each other in these ways, organizations reduce uncertainty, develop trust, and share information better, all of which lower transaction costs through decreased monitoring or surveillance and less formalized contracts. Thus, being embedded in a tighter-knit community creates normative pressures on behavior, enabling a form of network governance that simultaneously produces economic benefit for members of the community while limiting exploitation. In addition to *density* and the identification of these communities with *cliques* and *clusters,* embeddedness is also operationalized through *tie strength* (assessing the number of transactions or degree of trust rather than just the presence or absence of a relationship) and *multiplexity* (the number of different types of ties between any two actors).

Egonet composition. While the work above focuses on the relationships and their aggregated structure, social network theory recognizes that actors also bring specific characteristics with them and these characteristics interact with and may influence or be influenced by patterns of ties. For example, research repeatedly shows friendship ties are more prevalent within than between specific demographic categories (e.g., gender, ethnicities) across various settings. This phenomenon, *homophily,* accounts for the selection of new ties based on existing similarity. The mechanism can also work in the opposite direction through influence, as when adopting attitudes or technologies similar to one's existing alters. In either direction, the construct is typically modeled using tools testing for *autocorrelation* (e.g., *Moran's I*) or adoption and other changes in state (e.g., *logistic regressions* and *survival analyses).*

When autocorrelation is the result of influence, the network ties are conceived of as pipes through which influence flows from alters to the ego. This metaphor animates much research in this category where an actor's (or ego's) ties serve as a channel through which ego accesses its alters' tangible and intangible resources. In addition to adopting the same technologies as an alter, ego can also procure money, gain the benefits of experiences, or borrow the status of its alters. Thus, ego can be characterized based on the attributes available through its alters, at least in part. Thus, an entrepreneur whose alters have a combined $100,000 in capital available for investment can be distinguished from one whose alters have $5,000 available. Research on *egonet composition* adopts this perspective and ascribes ego attributes based the aggregation or distribution of its alters' attributes, including aggregations of quantitative data (e.g., *sums* or *averages*) as well as measures of qualitative variance (e.g., *heterogeneity*).

Importance

In addition to the specific theoretical contributions outlined above, social network theory has made other very important contributions to organization and management theory more broadly.

Informal networks. One contribution that cuts across the various theoretical approaches outlined above is the role it has played in solidifying the importance of informal networks in organizations, and providing a rigorous methodology to represent them and analyze their impact. For example, in a frequently cited study, David Krackhardt demonstrates that a unionization attempt in a small high-tech company failed, at least in part because the union representative was very isolated in the informal (friendship) network, despite being central in more formal (reporting, advising) networks. In another highly cited study relating to topology, Rob Cross, Stephen Borgatti, and Andrew Parker found that although a virtual team was assembled within a large consulting organization, it did not act as a team because there were many structural holes in the informal information-sharing network, and one person brokered information between two informal groups that emerged among two distinct skill sets. These types of disconnects between the formal and informal networks frequently explain unexpected organizational outcomes. Yet in practice, such outcomes can often *only* be understood by understanding both types of networks.

Perception and reality. Although far from being the exclusive advocate, social network theory has nonetheless made substantial cross-cutting contributions to improving our understanding of the relative importance of perception in social systems. Network research in this area has shown that perception has clear effects, both for actors as the object of perception (e.g., individuals perceived to be friends with powerful people have a reputation for good performance) and as the perceiver (e.g., better perceiving the network is a source of power). Again, this work applies across the different approaches outlined above, and research is furthering our understanding of why, when, and how both perceived and actual networks impact behaviors and outcomes.

Structure and agency. A final contribution of social network research to organizational theory is in advancing the debate around structure and agency. Although social network theory derives largely from a structural perspective, it has long recognized the effects of individual differences in the creation of social structures. Perhaps the richest tradition here is around effects for gender across a range of theoretical insights (e.g., gender homophily has a long tradition, and Ron Burt's work on structural holes found gender moderated the effects of occupying structural holes). More recently, Ajay Mehra and others have advanced the case for individual agency through work showing that other personality characteristics (e.g., self-monitoring) affect not only the positions individuals occupy in the network (e.g., high self-monitors occupy more structural holes) but that they occupy those different positions because of deliberate choices they make. Additionally, as far back as 1985, Mark Granovetter, perhaps best known for the "strength of weak ties" theory (which fits into the relatedness and topology category and relates to Ron Burt's work on structural holes), suggested social network theory could navigate between the under- and oversocialized views of actors in social systems. Network research has made important contributions here by providing exemplars that disentangle systemic and structural influences from actors' individualistic agency.

Finally, it is important to note that the three fundamental approaches listed above (and the specific theories they represent) and the three broader contributions represent a larger body of research that has improved our understanding of organizational phenomena and had practical impact for managers. In fact, social network theory has been applied by managers across many settings to improve a variety of organizational outcomes. For example, because of the work of Rob Cross, Steve Borgatti, and Andrew Parker mentioned above, the organization was able to implement structural and policy changes to successfully encourage more cohesion in the virtual group, as evident when evaluated 9 months later. Likewise, Ron Burt's work on the moderating effect of gender on structural holes discussed above has led to practical implications for how senior managers should engage in different forms of networking when mentoring women and men. And David Krackhardt has demonstrated that there are real benefits for managers who are knowledgeable about their organizational networks. Consequently, managers who invest time in both assessing their networks and learning how to do so well have been able to increase their power in the organization. These three examples give just a sampling of the power of social network theory in use in organizations and management.

Rich DeJordy

See also Complexity Theory and Organizations; Innovation Diffusion; Interorganizational Networks; Resource Dependence Theory; Social Exchange Theory; Structuration Theory

Further Readings

Borgatti, S. P., & Foster, P. (2003). The network paradigm in organizational research: A review and typology. *Journal of Management, 29,* 991–1013.

Borgatti, S. P., Mehra, A., Brass, D., & Labianca, G. (2009). Network analysis in the social sciences. *Science, 323,* 892–895.

Burt, R. (1995). *Structural holes: The social structure of competition.* Cambridge, MA: Harvard University Press.

Burt, R. (2007). *Brokerage and closure: An introduction to social capital.* New York, NY: Oxford University Press.

Granovetter, M. (1985). Economic action and social structure: The problem of embeddedness. *American Journal of Sociology, 91,* 481–510.

Kilduff, M., & Brass, D. (2010). Organizational social network research: Core ideas and key debates. *Academy of Management Annals, 4,* 317–357.

Kilduff, M., & Krackhardt, D. (2008). *Interpersonal networks in organizations: Cognition, personality, dynamics, and culture.* Cambridge, England: Cambridge University Press.

Labianca, G., Brass, D., & Gray, B. (1998). Social networks and perceptions of intergroup conflict: The role of negative relationships. *Academy of Management Journal, 41,* 55–67.

Mehra, A. (2005). The development of social network analysis: A study in the sociology of science. *Administrative Science Quarterly, 50,* 148–151.

Mehra, A., Kilduff, M., & Brass, D. (2001). The social networks of high and low self-monitors: Implications for workplace performance. *Administrative Science Quarterly, 46,* 121–146.

Social Power, Bases of

Power is an essential element in any managerial theory that attempts to account for the dynamics of behavior in organizations. A widely held notion is that leadership is inextricably related to the concept of power. Indeed, leadership is the exercise of power, and power is the "reason" why subordinates comply with their manager's directives. Hence, it is critical for managers to understand the bases of power available and how to acquire and use them effectively. The longest-standing theory on the bases of social power was developed by John French and Bertam Raven and published in 1959. They defined five bases of power—referent, expert, legitimate, reward, and coercive. This entry explains the fundamentals of the model, provides definitions of the bases of social power, and reviews how the theory and research have evolved over the last half century.

Fundamentals

To begin, we must note that power has played a central, important, and ubiquitous role in the study of social phenomena. That some people in organizations have more power than others is obvious, and it is also clear that power can be used in many ways—some positive and some negative. Mention the word *power* and people have very different reactions to it. For some, power conjures up images of negative leaders, such as Adolf Hitler or Muammar Gaddafi, or a boss who has belittled them. Others think of positive leaders such as John F. Kennedy, Gandhi, Martin Luther King Jr., or a boss whom they really respected. This range of reactions makes the point that power in and of itself is neither bad nor good. How it is used can be for bad or good, but power is simply the capacity one person has to influence another individual, group, or organizational entity. It is also possible for individuals to use their power to make other people more powerful (stronger, more influential). Oddly enough, it is the lack of power or a feeling of powerlessness, rather than power itself, that may be more harmful to organizational productivity, employee morale, and managerial effectiveness.

Every management textbook devotes attention to the topic of power, because it is critical for managers who want to be effective to understand how to gain and use power. It is also important to understand the reactions of people when power is being used by others toward them. For example, when managers use their power, the response from others can vary from compliance to a calculative response (what can one get in return for following the manager?), or it can be a positive, emotional response that results in high levels of commitment to the task. Clearly, managers need to understand how power can be used to achieve the response they want from their direct reports, their colleagues, and others in the organization (even their own managers). As Jeffery Pfeffer notes in his 1992 book, *Managing With Power,* managers need the skills to get things done as much as the skills to determine what needs to be done, and bases of power are essential skills for getting things done.

Succinctly put, *leadership* is the process of influencing the behavior of others, presumably toward the achievement of organizational goals. For influence attempts to have an impact, a person must have the *capacity* to influence others. Without some reason for people to be influenced by an individual, influence attempts will fail. *Power* is the resource behind the leader's attempt that makes influence possible. Without power, people cannot lead. While there have been many frameworks of power offered by various scholars, the most widely accepted, still today, is the framework of bases of social power developed by French and Raven in 1959. Most every management textbook includes their theory, in which they defined social power as the *potential* influence one person can have to change the actions or beliefs of another person. The social power bases they conceptualized define the capacity one person can draw on to influence another person.

In their original article, French and Raven proposed five conceptually different bases of social power that are socially dependent on continued interaction between two people. They defined two personal sources of power (*referent* and *expert*) developed by the person and three based in one's position that is granted by the organization (*legitimate*, *reward*, and *coercive*). The other variable that French and Raven used to distinguish the bases of power was whether surveillance of the influencee was an important factor for the power base to have impact. They felt that surveillance was important for coercion and reward power but unimportant for legitimate, expert, and referent power. In other words, the influencer does not have to be watching the influencee for these power bases to result in successful influence. Let us now define the five bases of social power.

Referent power is a personal source of power that derives from the admiration, respect, and identification one person feels for another. A person can develop a reputation for integrity, have a personal attractiveness, or exhibit charisma that makes others want to follow him or her voluntarily. For example, when subordinates see managers with referent power, they are drawn to them and want to follow. To develop referent power, a person must behave with integrity on the job and demonstrate respect for others. For example, President John Kennedy did not oversee passage of nearly as much legislation as did his successor, Lyndon Johnson, but he was far more revered and admired because of his leadership in times of crisis. It was less his technical ability on the job and more that he had that "something" to which others were drawn. He exuded a great deal of confidence that many people admired and respected, and this referent power allowed him to have significant influence with his cabinet and with the public.

Expert power is another personal source of power that derives from a person's abilities, skills, and talents. For example, people gain expert power by education, training, and performing well in key aspects of their job. Perhaps someone is especially good with numbers and analysis. As this fact becomes known to others, this person can influence others in math-related matters. Expert power is normally limited in range to specific areas of the job, whereas referent power is wide in scope. For example, a master programmer may have a great deal of expert power in the design of new software, to which others will yield when this person offers ideas. However, if the issue switches to a focus on marketing of new software, this person will have less expert power from which to draw. Normally, for expert power to develop, a person must exhibit greater expertise than others over time.

It is important to note that both referent and expert power are earned by the person through direct or indirect experience with others. People learn to admire and respect a person through interaction. They also come to recognize a person's expert power through interactions related to the expertise on a particular type of work. The point here is that "personal power" is earned over time and essentially granted by others. Hence, it is possible for people to lose these types of power. For example, if a manager does something morally wrong, it may damage his or her referent power, and if a manager offers expert advice that proves to be wrong, the manager may lose some or all of his or her expert power.

Legitimate power is a positional (as opposed to personal) source of power granted to a person usually via their hierarchical position in an organization. It is based on the perception that a person has the legitimate right to influence the behavior of others because of the person's position in the organization.

Thus, legitimate power is the purest form of position power. For example, it is normally recognized that an Army drill sergeant has the "right" to tell a trainee what to do and the trainee has an obligation to obey the sergeant. Since legitimate power is grounded in the hierarchy of an organization, it will grow as a person moves up the organizational hierarchy. A captain in the Army has more legitimate power than a sergeant. And if a person is demoted in an organization, his or her legitimate power will decrease. In addition, legitimate power has a zone of influence associated with it. As long as people remain in that zone, their legitimate power remains the same, but it can decrease if they move out of the area. For example, a manager may have the legitimate power to require employees to work overtime, but the manager may not have the power to require employees to use the company's products. For example, some people who work for Honda drive Fords, and vice versa.

Reward power is another position source of power based in the ability the person has to reward others for desired behaviors. For example, if a manager is granted control over the pay and performance evaluation of others, subordinates will be inclined to do what their manager wants in order to receive these rewards. This is a calculative or "contractual" relationship. If the subordinate does certain things desired by the manager, the subordinate can receive rewards from the manager. However, the reward must be valued by the subordinate if it is to be useful in influencing his or her behavior. And if the company encounters a period when these desired rewards are not available, the manager loses some of this reward power that is granted by the organization. In such times, it is still possible for a manager to use nonmonetary rewards, such as praise of good work as a substitute for monetary rewards.

Coercive power is another position-related source of power that is essentially the opposite of reward power. It is based in the ability of a person to punish others for not doing what the person wants done. For example, if a manager can withhold granting organizational resources (such as pay, promotion, discretionary time off, and the like), their subordinates will be inclined not to do things that would result in the manager using this coercive power. It is important to note that coercive power is often most useful in stopping an undesired behavior, and it can lead to unintended consequences, such as resentment.

Also, once the undesired behavior is stopped, it may be necessary to use reward power to promote desired behaviors. And oddly enough, sometimes the punishment can actually work as a reward. For example, suppose a manager reprimands an employee's behavior and the employee views it as "at least I got some attention from my manager." The result may be continuation of the undesired behavior. Hence, coercive power must be used with caution and not used too often, lest it lose its value.

A sixth base of power that was originally debated by French and Raven has at times made its way into the literature on social power. **Information power** is conceptually different from the other five in that it is "socially independent," meaning that it could be maintained without continued interaction. Some have combined it with expert power. Information power derives from the person providing information so compelling that it can lead others to change their behaviors. This form of power is essentially persuasion, and it is transitory—that is, it can move from one person to the other and create a motivation to change in the person being influenced. For example, in the empowerment literature, providing information to people is suggested as one of the things a manager can do that will create the intrinsic motivation in others to act in a more empowered fashion, using their knowledge, experience, and motivation to take responsibility for problem solving and making decisions. For example, if employees understand that the company is in financial trouble, they may be more likely to suggest ideas that can either generate more revenue or reduce costs. Unlike the other power bases, information power can and does move from one person to another rather easily.

Evolution

As explained in a 2008 article by Steven Elias in the *Journal of Management History*, French and Raven's theory of bases of social power began its evolution at the University of Michigan's Research Center for Group Dynamics in the late 1950s. The topic of social power in work organizations was a hot topic at the time, but there was no widely accepted theoretical model. There was a great deal of discussion about bases of power other than position power—that is, legitimate power—that were also socially dependent, and the issue of whether surveillance was important or not helped frame elaboration of the six bases of social power defined above. While there have been other attempts to create a model of social power in workplaces, they are typically still rooted in the French and Raven model, which explains why it has continued to be viewed as the most useful of the frameworks.

The initial framework of the five bases of social power (leaving aside information power) has, itself, been expanded, refined, and included in a power/interaction model developed by Raven and his colleagues at UCLA in 1992. At one point, the number of bases of social power grew to 14 through refinement of the original list, but time and time again, the number used in research and reported in textbooks has reverted to the original five bases of referent, expert, legitimate, reward, and coercive.

The most significant extension of the five bases framework has been the development of the power/interaction model by Raven. It places the social power bases in the context of leadership actions—that is, how one attempts to influence the behavior and beliefs of others. It moves the discussion beyond the capacity to influence another person to actually making the effort to influence another. There are five steps to this framework:

1. The influencer must determine the motivation to influence—that is, why does he or she want to influence the other person? Is it to attain a goal, to satisfy internal needs, to satisfy role requirements, to motivate the influencee, or to attain desired status?

2. Next, the influencer must assess which power bases are available to the influencer in relation to the target person of influence, plus power preferences and inhibitions. For example, does the influencer have expert or referent power available to use? Does he or she have legitimate, reward, or coercive power available to use? The influencer must also assess the likelihood of success using the various power bases available.

3. Next, the influencer must prepare for the influence attempt by setting the stage, enhancing the power bases so the influencee knows they might be used, and thus preparing the influencee to be influenced.

4. Next, is the actual action step wherein the influencer uses the chosen power bases in the method of choice to make an influence attempt.

5. Finally, the effects of the influence attempt can be addressed. Did the attempt result in the desired outcomes or not? Was the outcome positive or negative? What was the impact on other power bases not used, and were there any side effects?

This framework can be useful in extending beyond just a look at what power bases a person may have. For example, to successfully use power, a manager must not only assess what power bases he or she has but must also decide what power bases to use and develop a strategy for using them. Then it remains to be seen what impact transpires, and the model can be iterative in nature as the manager recycles through it in a relational basis with his or her subordinates.

Importance

Prior to the mid 1980s, efforts to assess the utility of the French and Raven taxonomy were limited, at best. The many methodological problems in published studies made interpretation of findings difficult. Philip M. Podsakoff and C. A. Schreisheim in 1985 published a review of various field studies of the framework in *Psychological Bulletin*. They offered a number of suggestions for improving future research on the model. In 1989, Timothy Hinkin and Schreisheim developed a measure of the power bases. Then in 1998, Raven, along with Joseph Schwarzwald and Meni Koslowsky, published another instrument in the *Journal of Applied Social Psychology*, called the Interpersonal Power Inventory (IPI). The IPI measures 11 bases of power, the original five, plus information power and refinements of reward, coercive, and legitimate power bases. Their research found that these 11 bases of power clustered together in seven factors, which only added confusion around the instrument. Neither of these measures has achieved traction in the literature. Scholars, including Raven, himself in 2008, are still calling for better measures of the French and Raven taxonomy.

Nevertheless, the continuing interest in understanding power, as applied especially to current leadership models, compels researchers to explore the underpinnings of the original French and Raven taxonomy. Using a variety of methodologies, efforts are ongoing to develop more robust instruments, as well as expanding investigations across cultures and linking power to important leadership issues. For example, a study by Mainuddin Afza n 2005, reports similar findings in India to U.S. studies in that use of power bases is related to employee commitment, satisfaction, intention to leave, and compliance. Another study in R & D departments by Li-Fen Liao in 2008 found a relationship between use of power bases and knowledge sharing. A multi-organizational study by W. Alan Randolph and Edward Kemery in 2011 found that managerial use of power bases (as perceived by employees) fully mediated the relationship between manager empowerment practices and employee perceptions of psychological empowerment.

Interest in the French and Raven taxonomy of social bases of power remains strong. Researchers continue to add new knowledge, even while working to develop a measure that can gain traction in the literature. The model also continues to find appeal in management textbooks because it offers practical insight for managers in learning ways to enhance their influence effectiveness.

To have influence, managers must acquire and use their bases of social power. Clearly, legitimate, reward, and coercive power are granted by the organization. Hence, managers must work to achieve positions that offer these sources of power. On the other hand, referent and expert power are sources that managers can develop on their own. Once acquired, the bases of social power can be used to gain influence. Managerial practice suggests that it may be best to rely more on the personal sources of power (referent and expert) rather than the position sources (legitimate, reward, and coercive) if the desired outcome is a positive emotional response from one's followers. Finally, let us not forget that influence can be bidirectional. People at lower levels of an organization can also acquire and use bases of power, especially the personal ones.

W. Alan Randolph

See also Empowerment; Leader–Member Exchange Theory; Leadership Practices; Needs Hierarchy; Organizational Culture and Effectiveness; Situational Theory of Leadership; Theory X and Theory Y; Work Team Effectiveness

Further Readings

Elias, S. (2008). Fifty years of influence in the workplace: The evolution of the French and Raven power taxonomy. *Journal of Management History, 14*(3), 267–283.

French, J. R. P., & Raven, B. (1959). The bases of social power. In D. Cartwright (Ed.), *Studies in social power* (pp. 150–167). Ann Arbor, MI: Institute for Social Research.

Hinkin, T. A., & Schreisheim, C. A. (1989). Development and application of new scales to measure the French and Raven (1959) bases of social power. *Journal of Applied Psychology, 74*(4), 561–567.

Podsakoff, P. M., & Schreisheim, C. A. (1985). Field studies of French and Raven's bases of power: Critique, reanalysis and suggestions for future research. *Psychological Bulletin, 97*(3), 387–411.

Randolph, W. A., & Kemery, E. R. (2011). Managerial use of power bases in a model of managerial empowerment practices and employee psychological empowerment. *Journal of Leadership & Organizational Studies, 18*(1), 95–106.

Raven, B. H. (1992). A power/interaction model of interpersonal influence: French and Raven thirty years later. *Journal of Social Behavior and Personality, 7*(2), 217–244.

Raven, B. H. (2008). The bases of power and the power/interaction model of interpersonal influence. *Analyses of Social Issues and Public Policy, 8*(1), 1–22.

Raven, B. H., Schwarzwald, J., & Koslowsky, M. (1998). Conceptualizing and measuring a power/interaction model of interpersonal influence. *Journal of Applied Social Psychology, 28*(4), 307–332.

Sociotechnical Theory

Sociotechnical theory is a term often used to describe the complex interplay between people and technology, in which neither the social (people, relationships, structure, etc.) nor technology (devices, process, materials, etc.) can be considered in isolation if performance is to be optimized. This term, also referred to as sociotechnical systems and sociotechnical design, has had far-reaching influence on management principles and theories, by incorporating principles of self-management and empowerment in management techniques and organizational change initiatives. It has also greatly impacted how the innovation process is managed and how product design is carried out. In providing a brief description of this concept, this entry first covers some of the fundamental aspects and considerations, including a further explanation of its principles. This is followed by a brief synopsis of its evolution in management thought and its importance to the field.

Fundamentals

As implied by its name, sociotechnical theory is concerned with the interaction of the social and technical aspects of a system, as well as the interaction between these and the environment. These two components, the interaction of the social and the technical and the influence of the environment on these social and technical aspects, make up essential elements of the theory. The theory is explicit in that the term *technical* is not limited to the specification of devices or machines but, rather, is a much broader term used to describe work processes and material flows as well as equipment. Similarly, the term *social* describes not only the implications for how a device, machine, or work flow impacts an individual but also how it affects the whole set of skills, knowledge, attitudes, social relationships, and network of connections and interactions between individuals and groups within the organization. *Social* in this sense denotes worker relationships related to task functioning and interdependence and not friendships per se. Additionally, the term *social* comprises individuals and groups at all levels of the organization and encompasses reward systems and authority structures, which are naturally a prime concern to managers.

Sociotechnical theory is grounded in the realization that the characteristics of a device, machine, or work flow have implications for how employees conduct their work, how they view the work itself and their role in the work organization, and how employees relate to each other both professionally and socially. In this way, a particular technology is not considered simply as a piece of equipment that workers must be trained to use, but rather, the equipment is considered in terms of its implications for the pattern of social relationships impacted by the equipment's introduction into the system. For example, considering the case of electronic mail being introduced into a work organization, the e-mail software is not considered merely in terms of how employees must be trained to use the software and policies for how e-mail is to be used but also, more important, how the introduction of e-mail might alter the social relationships and networks among employees and their pattern of interaction. Some possible considerations might include how people might communicate differently and if their relationships might be as effective as the traditional face-to-face type of interactions. E-mail lacks immediate feedback and does not provide for nonverbal cues such as gestures or the tone of one's voice, and these are important aspects of communication that might be lost with the introduction and reliance on e-mail in an organization. This could lead to greater misunderstandings, frustration, lower satisfaction, and the like, which may be made worse when e-mail is used as a primary communication mode. Hence, sociotechnical theory would be concerned not just with how to change work flows by using e-mail, but also with how it changes the social fabric and overall effectiveness of the work unit.

Sociotechnical theory is based on the premise of joint optimization between social and technical considerations rather than emphasizing one over the other. Optimization is achieved by explicitly considering the interactions between social and technical aspects and determining how these two subsystems or considerations can best be maximized together. The theory's main emphasis, then, is that it is not enough to merely consider introducing a piece of equipment and adapting people to fit how the equipment operates, without also considering how the equipment and its requirements might disrupt the interactions between employees and their view of their work and the organization. The theory stresses that maximum performance in any work flow, process, or from the use of machinery or a device can be achieved only if the intricate interdependence and interaction between social and technical aspects are jointly considered.

A second main component of sociotechnical theory considers the interdependence and interaction of social and technical aspects with the environment. The theory proposes that any sociotechnical work system is inherently embedded within its environment, which requires continual adaption and reaction to changing external influences. Even in relatively stable surroundings, environmental changes evolve and occur that impact both the social and technical aspects of the work system, requiring continual adaptation by both. In a business, advances in product design by competitors, or evolving consumer preferences for the use of products, alter the internal processes of a business as well as product design characteristics. As a result, managers therefore need to pay special attention to the interface between internal and external conditions and how one might influence the other. This has led to greater importance being placed on boundary-spanning roles, in which individuals carefully account for fluctuations between the internal and external conditions and strive to reconcile changes that need to occur to restore balance in the overall system.

This coupling of social and technical aspects, and the embedded nature of these considerations within the overall environment, has led management practices and theories to evolve in the form of direct participation by workers. Most notably perhaps, these have occurred in the form of self-managed work teams and employee participation in innovation processes. In these approaches, management gives employees greater responsibility and discretion for completing work projects and empowers them to make choices about the products and processes without necessarily seeking managerial approval. In effect, managers give employees greater decision-making authority and place greater reliance on their judgment. In many instances, employees may run their department or portion of the business as if they own it, planning and measuring the impacts of their decisions for maximum performance and profitability. The rationale behind this is that employees who are intricately involved in their product or process on a day-to-day basis are best suited to understand what changes need to be made for maximum efficiency and effectiveness. Moreover, their intricate and personal involvement with both internal and external constituents and customers places them in a particularly advantageous vantage point for gathering this information and for realizing the implications for how changes in one aspect might impact elsewhere in the processes or system. In part, this has led to the worldwide proliferation of self-managed teams; this form of structuring in an organization allows for continual adaption and adjustment and for mutual accommodations to be made as one aspect of team functioning influences another.

An important aspect of sociotechnical theory, often referred to as *minimum crucial specification,* suggests that managers provide direction to employees about only essential aspects of their jobs or projects rather than about things that are not critical. In other words, managers should direct employees only in the things that are necessary and then only to the degree that is needed rather than overspecifying and therefore constraining the worker's innovation and creativity to make the process more efficient and effective. Overspecifying may squelch employee innovation and insights, which

is undesirable because it often provides unique and valued improvements. This aspect then differentiates *what* should be done, from *how* it should be done. Managers can and should generally be precise in specifying what should be accomplished, yet specifying exactly how it should be accomplished is often unnecessary. As noted by Albert Cherns in 1987, in most organizations there is "far too much specificity" about how work should be accomplished, and employees often contrive to accomplish their job despite the detailed rules and procedures.

From a job design standpoint, sociotechnical theory's emphasis that jobs and processes ought to rely on worker insights and initiative implies that this autonomy in these jobs is inherently more motivating and satisfying. Since individuals are given greater discretion and control to carry out responsibilities as they see fit to best accomplish work objectives, their greater sense of freedom and control enhances the motivation they feel and the likely energy they devote to work activities. By specifying only the minimum required rather than micromanaging, managers empower employees and therefore tap internal psychological processes that are self-motivating and internally driven. Employees therefore work and devote energy to solving work problems because they want to rather than because they were told to do so. In this way, employees are viewed as important resources for improving the effectiveness and efficiency of the organization. Moreover, the autonomy and self-control instill a sense of ownership of the product and processes within the individual, thereby generating a willingness to persevere despite any setbacks that may occur and a sense of commitment to the job and organization.

Evolution

Sociotechnical theory was originally developed in the 1950s by a group of researchers at the Tavistock Institute in London. Although it has evolved since this early period, the seminal work in this area is an article published in 1951 by Eric Trist and Ken Bamforth titled "Some social and Psychological Consequences of the Longwall Method of Coal-Getting." This article is a case study on a coal mining operation, in which the production of coal was mechanized and "mass production" techniques were instituted in the expectation that productivity in the form of coal harvesting would increase. Miners were distributed into specialized shifts: cutting the coal in the first shift, shoveling the coal onto a new conveyor in the second shift, and constructing gateways and roof supports in the third shift. Miners were spread out beside a long wall in the mine, each shift conducting the one task. At the time, this was thought to be more efficient than smaller groups of miners in each shift who conducted each of the three tasks among their group and independently allocated the tasks among their own group members. In the new "mass production" techniques with specialized shifts, miners experienced less variety in their work and challenge in their job, and as a result morale decreased and productivity fell as well. In brief, what the researchers concluded was that although a technological change (such as introducing mass production techniques) appears quite rational when considered from an engineering viewpoint, it is based on only a limited view of the production system that ignores the workers needs in the social system and thus may actually reduce the benefits that had been expected from the new technology. The researcher's insight of the interdependent nature of technical and social systems led to the term *sociotechnical systems*.

Sociotechnical theory evolved in direct contrast to Frederick Taylor's concept of scientific management, which was dominant at the time. In this approach, "mass production" techniques were implemented and people were adapted to fit the technology. Notably in production or assembly lines, people were organized to fit the design and capabilities of the machines and the work flow rather than accounting for people and how workers experience their work. According to Taylor's principles of scientific management, specialized jobs on an assembly line were more efficient and could raise production and although they were repetitive and monotonous tasks that provided little job variety or intrinsic value for the worker, workers would conduct their work with appropriate inducements such as money and other rewards. In contrast, sociotechnical theory introduced the idea that maximum production can be achieved only by considering the interplay between the technology and the people who work with the technology.

Since the early days of sociotechnical theory, many tests and some refinements of the theory have been offered. A review of the literature reveals literally thousands of studies and articles published on the topic up to the present day. These have been carried out by leading scholars and thinkers in the field, such as Cherns, Fred Emery, Louis Davis, Albert Rice, Philip Herbst, H. F. Kolodny, Enid Mumford, William Pasmore, and others. The main emphasis has been on developing effective ways to apply the concepts of sociotechnical theory to work organizations. Along these lines, Emery and others have written numerous elaborations on how the theory can be applied to business organizations, detailing the "nine-step model" for implementing sociotechnical principles. A challenge has been implementing sociotechnical concepts in the workplace, principally on turning control and power over to workers rather than maintaining it with managers. Although implemented on a widespread basis in concept, moving beyond title and name changes to the actual self-management in teams and structure has at times proved difficult to achieve.

The main emphasis of these elaborations of sociotechnical theory involves meaningful participation in decision making and design. The democratic design principle, as it has been called, involves assigning responsibility for control and coordination of work to be placed with the employees who actually conduct the job tasks. Rather than more bureaucratic approaches whereby managerial control is centralized and vested in hierarchy, participative design involves truly empowering employees to make decisions over the work assigned to them. Such delegation and empowerment can come with significant risk for the manager, and this had led to some managerial reluctance to enact sociotechnical principles. According to the sociotechnical perspective, empowering employees and teams to make their own decisions, and having managers truly serve as coaches and facilitators, involves removing hierarchy as well as centralized power and control that have been a premise of managerial thinking. Such changes are no doubt difficult to make.

An additional outgrowth of sociotechnical theory has been the evolution of learning organizations and the popularization of self-discovery. Grounded in the view that workers are best able to make decisions about their work, the learning organization is viewed as one in which workers are best able to respond to changing and turbulent external environmental conditions. The constant adaptation and alignment to changing environmental conditions is facilitated by employees who understand their jobs and are able to make informed decisions over how best to conduct and adapt their work to meet organizational objectives. The rapid and turbulent nature of environmental changes that occur in business places new emphasis on this approach and on the need to have workers make autonomous decisions about how best to conduct their work in order to adapt process and product designs.

Importance

The influence of sociotechnical theory has been far-reaching. Sociotechnical theory's coupling of social and technical aspects and the need to optimize both to achieve maximum performance, including the embedded nature of these within the environment, has had dramatic impacts on management practices and product design approaches. Perhaps most important, it has centered attention on the important role that people play in implementing new processes or using new devices.

From a product design standpoint, rather than considering how technology can be best designed in isolation, true performance according to sociotechnical theory depends on how people might use the technology and the overall implications of how the technology is used for the organization and social system. In other words, simply because a technology has an elegant design does not mean it will be used as intended, nor does it mean that all the ramifications of using the technology can possibly be anticipated by the product's designers. As a result, managers and product designers must consider the many potential implications (both people and technology related) of how the technology might change the behaviors of those individuals who use the new product or technology. As one example, consider the texting ability of cell phones today. While originally conceptualized as a quick means to convey brief and truncated messages, it is today used by some as a substitute for voice communication. Moreover, the texting ability of cell phones has been implicated in many traffic fatalities caused by accidents whereby drivers were distracted by texting. As a result, many states have now begun to implement laws forbidding texting while driving. As this texting example illustrates, there are many implications of how technology is used that impact behaviors and the social system that are encompassed within sociotechnical theory.

Another commonly acknowledged outcome of sociotechnical theory concerns the widespread implementation of self-managed teams to conduct work, as well as other management practices that embody autonomy and internal self-regulation. Self-managed teams, because they operate at the level where social and technical changes occur in real time, can more easily react and make modifications than more senior management who are further removed in time and space. In this way, with the acknowledgment of the dynamic interplay between teams and technology came the realization that small autonomous units are best able to adapt to changing conditions, leading to improved responsiveness and performance. Self-managed teams proliferated as a result, with many industries, organizations, and departmental units adopting this way of organizing in an effort to improve efficiency and competitiveness. Self-managed teams today are a fundamental way of organizing that have been implemented in myriad applications, from professional level employees to hourly workers on factory floors to customer-centric organizations around the world.

The implications of sociotechnical theory can also be seen in new forms of organizing and working, such as telework, telecommuting, virtual teams, social networking, wikis, distance or e-learning, and many other innovations. In each of these, people interact with and through technology, which has profound implications for the way in which they are able to work together and for the nature of the jobs and tasks undertaken. For example, teleworkers or telecommuters who work from home several days per week instead of at the office may have different relationships with coworkers and supervisors than if they worked in the office full-time. It may be that a greater reliance on e-mail and phone calls and the absence of face-to-face interactions affects how coworkers view them or how strong their relationships are with coworkers and supervisors. Moreover, research shows that electronic communication is less rich in social cues and hampers the ability to interpret others when the topic is complex or socially sensitive. These considerations in-turn have important implications for their ability to collaborate on projects and produce group products.

As these examples illustrate, the implications of sociotechnical theory been widespread and have important implications for managers in their efforts to maintain and improve individual and organizational performance. The implementation of sociotechnical techniques have led to more rewarding and fulfilling jobs for employees, enhanced product quality and efficiency, and reduced absenteeism and turnover. Sociotechnical concepts have been used to design factory production floors, structure organizations, initiate team-based management initiatives, and design new devices and software systems. Management concepts that have their roots in sociotechnical theory include job enlargement, job enrichment, empowerment, autonomous groups, and team-based management approaches, to name a few. Sociotechnical theory has also led to a trial-and-error approach, often referred to as action research. As the foregoing suggests, sociotechnical theory has been and continues to be highly influential in management theory and practice.

Timothy D. Golden

See also Action Research; Empowerment; Job Characteristics Theory; Scientific Management; Systems Theory of Organizations; Technology Acceptance Model; Technology and Interdependence/Uncertainty; Total Quality Management

Further Readings

Beekun, R. (1989). Assessing the effectiveness of sociotechnical interventions: Antidote or fad? *Human Relations, 42*(10), 877–897.

Cherns, A., (1976). The principles of sociotechnical design, *Human Relations, 9*(8), 783–792.

Cherns, A. (1987). Principles of sociotechnical design revisited. *Human Relations, 40*(3), 153–162.

Cummings, T. (1994). Self-regulating work groups: A sociotechnical synthesis. In W. French, C. Bell, & R. Zawacki (Eds.), *Organizational development and transformation* (4th ed., pp. 268–277). Burr Ridge, IL: Irwin.

Emery, R. E., & Trist, E. L. (1965). The causal texture of organizational environments. *Human Relations, 18,* 21–32.

Kolodny, H., & Kiggundu, M. (1980). Towards the development of sociotechnical systems model in woodlands mechanical harvesting. *Human Relations, 33*(9), 623–645.

Pasmore, W. (1995). Social science transformed: The sociotechnical perspective. *Human Relations, 48*(1), 1–21. doi:10.1177/001872679504800101

Pasmore, W., Francis C., Haldeman, J., & Shani, A. (1982). Sociotechnical systems: A North American reflection on empirical studies of the seventies. *Human Relations, 35*(12), 1179–1204.

Rousseau, D. M. (1977). Technological differences in job characteristics, employee satisfaction and motivation: A synthesis of job design research and socio-technical systems theory. *Organizational Behavior and Human Performance, 19,* 18–42.

Trist, E. L., & Bamforth, K. W. (1951). Some social and psychological consequences of the longwall method of coal-getting: An examination of the psychological situation and defences of a work group in relation to the social structure and technological content of the work system. *Human Relations, 4,* 1–38.

STAGES OF CREATIVITY

To consider how creative ideas/outcomes arise, it is necessary to provide a definition of creativity. There are as many definitions of this term as there are authors providing these definitions. For our purposes, *creativity* will be defined as outcomes or processes that are not only new/different but also perceived as useful to those in an organizational setting. Usefulness is crucial in this definition, since many creative ideas may be proposed, but only those useful to an organization are of concern here. Similarly, there are as many answers to the question of how creative ideas/outcomes arise as there are those who ponder this question. One set of answers to this question argues that creativity results from individuals moving through a set of stages—from the motivation to develop creative outcomes to the actual implementation of these outcomes. This stage approach to creativity suggests that although some believe creative outcomes, such as new products, strategies, and the like, appear full-blown in the minds of their "creators," a more likely explanation holds that individuals and organizations work through a process or a set of stages to arrive at new and useful outcomes. It is a managerial truism that the successful development of innovative and creative ideas/outcomes is crucial to the survival and growth of nearly every organization. Innovations bloom from the creative seeds sown by those in organizations. Without these innovations, organizations can grow stagnant, overtaken in their marketplace by more innovative firms with bolder, better, and more creative ideas and products. Managers work to bring forth their own news ideas as well as ideas from those working with them and for them.

Well-known organizations, such as Apple, Google, and Procter & Gamble (P&G) prosper by developing innovative and creative products and services. To the extent that managers and their organizations have an appreciation of how various stages and their ordering can lead to creative outcomes, the more likely it is that these organizations will continue to develop the creative grist for their innovation mills. With a basic understanding of the topic of interest and its importance to managers and their organizations, the second section of this entry considers two of these stage approaches to creativity. With this as foundation, the third section of this entry evaluates these approaches to creativity and provides managers with several recommendations for encouraging the beneficial activities for each stage of the creative process. The bottom line, of course, is to increase the probability that valued creative outcomes will result from the implementation of some creative process.

Fundamentals

In 1950, in his presidential address to the American Psychological Association, J. P. Guilford talked about creativity as an important focus for future research. He suggested that in looking at previous research on the nature of the creative process there was fairly good agreement that there were four stages in the process, first proposed in 1926 by Graham Wallas. These stages were labeled (a) preparation, (b) incubation, (c) illumination, and (d) verification. Thus, over 60 years ago, there was some consensus concerning the process followed to develop creative ideas relevant to a particular area of interest. One needed to have the necessary skills and abilities in that domain of interest (preparation), to be able to step away from the conscious evaluation of the issue of interest, allowing one's mind to engage in subconscious or even unconscious consideration of this issue (incubation) to facilitate the "lightbulb going off" (illumination) to reveal the creative idea, and finally, to determine whether this idea will satisfy the demands of the original area of interest (verification). However, Guilford also concluded that while this stage model provides a useful heuristic for thinking about the creative process, the approach failed to reveal the motivation, skills, and abilities needed to work within each stage to move from stage to stage.

More recently, Teresa Amabile introduced her componential model of creativity, which consisted of four stages associated with creative outcomes: (a) problem/task identification, (b) preparation, (c) response generation, and (d) response validation and communication. As part of her stage model, she suggested that at each stage individual intrinsic motivation, domain-relevant skills (skills necessary to think creatively within a particular domain), and creativity-relevant skills (skills necessary to think creatively) are necessary to ensure that the outcomes of this process are new and useful.

Further considerations of these stage models of the creative process suggest that the stages (however labeled) are not discrete but likely overlap in their timing and may reflect a recursive process. Obstacles arising in later stages may require that individuals return to the activities associated with earlier stages. It has also been proposed that while this heuristic approach is helpful to visualize the creative process, more attention needs to be paid to the subprocesses that likely occur within each of these stages. These subprocesses include activities such as problem definition, divergent thinking, intuition, idea generation, and idea evaluation, among others.

Although this entry is not the place to consider these subprocesses in detail, two additional stages can usefully be added to the models above. These two additions might well be contained within several of the stages already considered, but by making these particular additions explicit, their inclusion may offer managers additional leverage points that might further encourage a successful creative process. The first of these additions is "motivation," and it is necessarily the first step in explaining any behavior. In particular, an individual who is not motivated (intrinsically or extrinsically) to behave in a creative fashion, will be unlikely to develop any useful creative outcomes. It is possible that motivation is assumed or subsumed in the first stage of any stage model of creativity, but making this a separate, explicit stage allows for the suggestion of specific actions managers can/should take to encourage pursuit of creative outcomes by organizational members.

The second addition to the four-stage models above is a stage where creative thinking is most directly brought to bear on the problem at hand—often called "manipulation," this stage refers to those processes that might generate creative ideas *before* incubation is necessary. Incubation is that stage that occurs when attempts at creative thought have been frustrated. Again, this new stage might be contained in the preparation or the response-generation stages considered above, but it would appear to demand organizational systems/resources different from those needed in other stages in this process.

Importance

There is empirical evidence to support these stage models of creativity, as well as their value in exposing the various subprocesses that might encourage creative outcomes. However, one valuable function of these models is to provide indicators of where organizations can leverage certain systems/activities to increase the likelihood that creative outcomes will obtain from organizational members. The final section of this entry offers several ideas to facilitate each particular stage.

Motivation. As a general rule, organizations with a creative culture (à la Apple, Google, and P&G) will have employees who believe that the pursuit of creative outcomes is an organizational good. No stage model of creativity will be successful if employees do not believe that one of the most important values guiding employee behavior is the desire to produce creative and innovative products or services. Employees really have to want to be creative. Not surprisingly, evaluation and reward systems are key determinants of employee behavior. A second managerial truism might be, "What gets evaluated/rewarded is what gets done." Thus, if managers want employees to be creative, evaluation and reward systems must reinforce those behaviors leading to creative outcomes.

Preparation. Employees must have the necessary skills and abilities to engage in creative thought and behavior. This means employee education, experience, and training must provide them the appropriate domain-relevant skills. Preparation can be a double-edged sword, however. Too much education, experience, and training focused on a particular domain might reinforce the accepted way of doing things. This makes "outside the box" thinking more difficult. This possible obstacle to creativity could be overcome by exposing employees to other employees with different experiences/training and allowing them to offer different perspectives on the question at hand.

Manipulation. Here is where the initial attempts at creativity are pursued. Here is where the creativity-relevant skills that Amabile included in her model creativity become more important. Divergent thinking, fluency, and flexibility are all skills that can be learned and are most valuable in attempting to see things in different ways. The development of collaborative efforts in producing creative ideas also provides opportunities for employees to see how others from different functional areas might deal with a particular issue. Collaborative efforts can be quite valuable in moving the manipulation stage along.

Incubation and illumination. These stages are paired, since it is often difficult to tell where the incubation stage ends and the illumination stage begins. It is likely that you, the reader, have experienced roadblocks that have hampered your efforts to generate that creative solution—a solution you know is there but that you just can't quite put your finger on. Organizations that allow employees time away from the active pursuit of creative outcomes are encouraging the incubation and illumination stages. Some organizations do this in formal ways with time off, sabbaticals, quiet hours, and the like. Additionally, a tolerance for uncertainty or ambiguity as outcomes are pursued and an appreciation of importance of employee intuition in these stages of the creative process are quite valuable.

Verification. Many creative ideas perish in this final stage of the creative process. It is at this point that new ideas are offered for public perusal and comment. It is also the nature of most humans to criticize that which is new and different. Consider your reactions the first time you were confronted with a new idea. It is up to the employee and the organization to provide protection for creative ideas from the onslaught of criticisms too often thrown at new approaches. Some creative individuals have personalities (self-confidence and courage, in particular) that afford them the willingness to fight to protect their creations from criticism. To protect ideas from those without these traits, organizations should develop verification approaches that reduce levels of criticism of creative ideas until the full nature of the idea has been explained and is more fully understood and perhaps even appreciated. Not every new idea will survive this step, but even those ideas that do not may provide the fodder for an even more creative outcome in the future.

In summary, these two models explaining the stages of creativity have good research support and have been responsible for creating a variety of research programs aimed at a better understanding of what contributes to the development of new and useful organizational ideas and outcomes. This entry has described the creative stages in these models expanding the number of stages from four to six. A stage approach to creativity may be somewhat simplistic, since within each stage there are a number of subprocesses that likely occur. In fact, one could argue that there are similar minicreative processes at work within each of the macrostages. Certainly, taking this reductive approach too far is not terribly helpful to the practicing manager. Thus, the six-stage model discussed above was the foundation for suggestions as to how each stage might be facilitated. It is hoped that the modern manager will find these suggestions beneficial as they strive to increase levels of personal and professional creativity.

Richard S. Blackburn

See also Brainstorming; BVSR Theory of Human Creativity; Componential Theory of Creativity; Interactionist Model of Organizational Creativity; Investment Theory of Creativity; Stages of Innovation

Further Readings

Amabile, T. M. (1988). A model of creativity and innovation in organizations. *Research in Organizational Behavior, 10*, 123–167.

Amabile, T. M. (1996). *Creativity in context*. Boulder, CO: Westview.

Amabile, T. M., & Kramer, S. (2011). *The progress principle: Using small wins to ignite joy, engagement, and creativity at work*. Boston, MA: Harvard Business School Press.

George, J. M. (2007). Creativity in organizations. In J. P. Walsh & A. P. Brief (Eds.), *Academy of management annals* (pp. 439–477). New York, NY: Lawrence Erlbaum.

Guilford, J. P. (1950). Creativity. *American Psychologist, 5*, 444–454.

Lubart, T. (2000–2001). Models of the creative process: Past, present and future. *Creativity Research Journal, 13*, 295–308.

Wallas, G. (1926). *The art of thought*. New York, NY: Harcourt, Brace.

Woodman, R. W., Sawyer, J. E., & Griffin, R. W. (1993). Toward a theory of organizational creativity. *Academy of Management Review, 18*, 293–321.

Stages of Innovation

An innovation is the creation and implementation of a new idea. The new idea may pertain to a technological innovation (new technical artifacts, devices, or products), a process innovation (new services, programs, or production procedures), or an administrative innovation (new institutional policies, structures, or systems). The idea may be a novel recombination of old ideas, an invention that challenges the present order, or an unprecedented formula or approach. As long as the idea is perceived as new and entails a novel change for the actors involved, it is an innovation. Innovations can vary widely in novelty, size, complexity, and temporal patterns of development. Some innovations involve small, quick, incremental, lone-worker efforts. They are unplanned and emerge by chance, accident, or afterthought. On the other hand, the innovations examined in this entry are larger in scale and scope. They consist of planned, concentrated efforts to develop and implement a novel idea that reflects substantial technical, organizational, and market uncertainty; entails a collective effort of considerable duration; and requires greater resources than are held by the people undertaking the effort. Most studies of innovation have focused on the causes and consequences of innovation. Very few have examined the process of how innovations develop from concept to implementation or termination. Understanding the process of innovation is critical for entrepreneurs and managers who seek advice in developing their innovations. In practice, the majority of new and seemingly useful inventions fall by the wayside during the innovation development process and never get implemented. Some of these ideas are terminated for good reasons because during the development process they are found not to work, be feasible, or solve a problem. However, many good ideas are never implemented because of complexities and dynamics of the innovation process (i.e., the sequence of events and challenges that unfold to initiate, develop, and implement an innovative idea). Therefore, understanding the innovation process provides important insights to practitioners and scholars. This entry presents a model of the stages of idea creation, development, and implementation during the innovation journey.

Fundamentals

Perhaps the most widely known model of the innovation process was proposed by Everett Rogers. It represents four decades of Rogers's own research and a synthesis of over 4,000 published innovation studies. This model portrays the process of innovation as consisting of three basic stages: (1) *creation or invention* of novel idea, which comes from a recognition of market or user needs and advances in basic science or technology; (2) its *development,* or the sequence of events in which the new idea is transformed from an abstract concept into an operational reality; and (3) *implementation,* or the adoption and diffusion of the innovation by users. A major longitudinal study that tracked how these stages unfolded in a wide variety of new technologies, products, services, and programs was conducted by the Minnesota Innovation Research Program (MIRP). In this research program, Andrew Van de Ven and his colleagues found a dozen common characteristics that occurred during the initiation stage (dealing with innovation gestation, shock, plans), the development stage (proliferation, setbacks, shifting assessments, fluid participation of organizational personnel, relationships with investors/top managers and others, infrastructure development), and the implementation stage (adoption by integrating the new into the old, and termination). The following section elaborates on processes in each stage of innovation.

Idea Creation or Invention Stage

Studies of the innovation process have found the initial period to be characterized by gestating ideas, shocks, and planning. Innovations are usually not initiated on the spur of the moment, by a single dramatic incident or by a single entrepreneur. An extended gestation period often lasting several years unfolds in which seemingly random events occur before innovations are initiated. Many events may not be intended to start an innovation. Some trigger recognition of need for change; others, awareness of technical possibilities. Some of these events "shock" entrepreneurs to mobilize plans and resources for developing an innovation.

Amabile summarizes many research studies indicating that individuals are more likely to be creative (come up with novel ideas) and innovative (develop and implement new ideas) in organizations that both enable and motivate innovation. The design of an organization's structure, culture, and practices influence the likelihood that innovative ideas will be surfaced and that once surfaced they will be developed and nurtured toward realization. Several features of organizational structure are empirically related to innovative activities. The more complex and differentiated the organization, and the easier it is to cross boundaries, the greater the potential number of sources from which innovative ideas can spring. However, as organizational size and complexity increases, organizations tend to segment tasks and develop bureaucratic procedures. These often constrain innovation unless special systems are put in place to motivate and enable innovative behavior.

Key motivating factors include providing a balance of intrinsic and extrinsic rewards for innovative behaviors. Incentive pay (i.e., monetary rewards contingent on performance and in addition to base salary) seems to be a relatively weak motivator for innovation; it more often serves as a proxy for recognition. Individualized rewards tend to increase idea generation and radical innovations, whereas group rewards tend to increase innovation implementation and incremental innovations.

In addition to these motivating factors, the following components have also been found to enable and constrain innovative behavior in organizations:

- Resources for innovation (e.g., financial, technical, human resources)
- Frequent communications across departmental lines, among people with dissimilar viewpoints
- Moderate environment uncertainty and mechanisms for focusing attention on changing conditions
- Cohesive work groups with open conflict resolution mechanisms that integrate creative personalities into the mainstream
- Structures that provide access to innovation role models and mentors
- Moderately low personnel turnover
- Psychological contracts that legitimate and solicit spontaneous innovative behavior

Innovation Development Stage

The initiation stage usually concludes when an innovation (or entrepreneurial) team is formed and funded to develop the innovation based on a plan and budget approved by resource controllers (top managers or venture capitalists). This developmental process is characterized by proliferating innovation events, setbacks, shifts in assessment criteria, fluid participation of organizational personnel, conflicting involvements of investors/top managers, changing relationships with others, and involvements in developing an industrial infrastructure to commercialize or implement the innovation. An intensive real-time study of innovation development conducted by the MIRP found that soon after work begins to develop the venture, the process proliferates from a simple unitary sequence of activities into divergent, parallel, and convergent progressions. Some of these activities are related through a division of labor among functions, but many are unrelated in any noticeable form of functional interdependence. Ideas and paths that were perceived as relevant and congruent at one time become viewed as being independent and disjunctive at another time when the innovation idea or circumstances change. Problems, mistakes, and setbacks frequently occur as these developmental paths are pursued, and they provide opportunities either for learning or for terminating the developmental efforts.

Maneuvering these common characteristics of the innovation development journey emphasize the importance of learning and leadership. Learning is critical in pursuing those courses of action that appear successful and in avoiding or terminating those actions that do not work or lead to apparent failure. During the initial period of development, an innovation team must learn by discovering what innovation goals, courses of action, and contexts are feasible before it can learn through a trial-and-error process of testing which courses of action achieve desired goals in different contexts.

The innovation development process is also guided by four different leadership roles: a sponsor, mentor, critic, and institutional leader. These four leader roles often serve as checks and balances on each other in directing innovation entrepreneurs. A sponsor is typically a high-level manager who can command the power and resources to push an innovation idea into good currency and thus procures and advocates the innovation. A mentor is usually an experienced and successful innovator who assumes the responsibility for coaching and counseling an entrepreneur. On the other hand, a critic serves as a "devil's advocate" by challenging

innovation investments, goals, and progress. An institutional leader is often an executive who is less involved in the innovation and who settles disputes between the pro-innovation leaders (i.e., sponsor, mentor, and entrepreneur) and the critic.

Innovation Implementation (Adoption) Stage

The implementation stage begins when activities are undertaken to adopt and implement an innovation. When the innovation is created and developed within the organization, implementation processes include introducing the innovation in the market, transferring it to operating sites, or diffusing it to potential adopters. If the innovation is developed elsewhere, the implementation process centers on the activities undertaken by a host organization to introduce and adopt the innovation. Through diffusion, the innovation is communicated through communication channels (e.g., mass media, experts, and peers) over time among the members of an adopting community or market.

Rogers points out that it is misleading to assume that development of an innovation is completed during the implementation period because much reinvention occurs during the implementation process. Reinvention is a process in which adopters modify an innovation to fit their local implementation setting. It facilitates the transition of innovation ownership from developers to implementers. This is true whether the innovation was developed within the organization that uses it or was imported from the outside. In either situation, implementation deals with adopting and tailoring an innovation to the organization's specific local needs and constraints.

In organizations where innovations are "homegrown," researchers found that implementation activities often occur throughout the developmental period by linking and integrating the "new" with the "old," as opposed to substituting, transforming, or replacing the old with the new. Because of limited organizational resources, an important implication of this finding is that implementing innovations can seldom be simple additions to existing organizational programs. Substituting the old with the new is also often not possible for political reasons. People are reluctant to replace existing organizational programs, because of the history of investments and commitments they have made to them. Implementation proceeds more smoothly in those cases where the "new" overlaps with and becomes integrated into existing organizational arrangements.

Evolution

Early conceptions of the innovation process viewed it as consisting of a linear sequence of invention, development, and implementation stages that can be controlled by managers or entrepreneurs. Subsequent studies have found that the innovation process is considerably more complex than the commonplace view of the creation, development, and implementation of a core novel idea by a stable and full-time set of people operating within a stable context. Overall, the process is linear in that it evolves from invention, development, and implementation of an idea. However, closer examination of activities within each of these stages reveals more complex nonlinear processes. For example, during the innovation development stage, the core innovative idea tends to proliferate into many ideas. There is not only invention, but there is reinvention as well, with some ideas being discarded as others are reborn. Many persons are involved in innovation, but most of them are only partially included in the innovation effort, as they are distracted by very busy schedules because they perform many other roles unrelated to the innovation. The network of stakeholders involved in transactions is constantly being revised. The various parties to an innovation create a multiple enacted environment. Rather than a simple, unitary, and progressive path, we see multiple tracks, spin-offs, and the like, some of which are related and coordinated and others that are not. Rather than a single after-the-fact assessment of outcome, we see multiple, in-process assessments. The discrete identity of innovation may become blurred as the new and the old are integrated.

As these observations suggest, most innovation processes do not unfold in sequential stages and orderly steps. The process is often highly unpredictable and uncontrollable. Yet it is not a random process either. Van de Ven and colleagues conclude that the innovation journey is a nonlinear dynamic cycle of divergent and convergent activities that unfold over time. Organizations often use stage gate processes to manage the stages of new product development, including idea screening, concept development, product design, testing and validation, and product launch. While stage gate processes provide a useful discipline for reviewing and investing in multiple periods often required to develop innovations, they do not necessarily increase the predictability of the process. Indeed, studies of the nonlinear innovation process suggest that managers cannot control innovation; instead, they can learn to maneuver the journey by practicing and learning routines for dealing with challenges and setbacks when they arise.

Recent studies of the management of innovation have expanded to examine the external environment of innovation. Using the population (of organizations) in an industry, researchers can examine the sources of technological variation among firms and the rates of innovation emergence over time. Studies find that the development and diffusion of innovations is highly dependent on a community or industrial infrastructure for innovation. This infrastructure includes basic resource endowments of scientific knowledge, financial resources, and competent human capital, enabling institutional rules, standards, and norms, as well as market demand and educated potential consumers of the innovation.

Specialized fields of study have examined the stages of innovation with different perspectives. Psychologists investigate individual and group creativity, intrinsic and extrinsic motivation to develop innovation, and cooperative working environment to implement innovation. Sociologists explore the social networks of knowledge transfer and their impact on innovation initiation and the pressure toward social conformity. For example, an organization adopts innovations or imitates other organizations to follow fads and fashion in its population and to appear legitimate. Economists explain the initiation of innovation using "technology push" versus "demand pull." They also argue that rational actors should implement effective innovation or otherwise become inefficient and weeded out from the population.

Importance

Building on the three stages of innovation, a number of studies have explored enabling and constraining factors. Studies have found that organizational age, size, incumbency, and interorganizational networks have both enabling and constraining effects on innovation. As organizations age, they generate more innovations (or patents), but these gains in competencies and efficiencies come at the price of a decreasing fit between organizational capabilities and environmental demands as organizations age. In terms of size, research programs located within larger firms are significantly more productive than rival programs located within smaller firms because the advantages large firms realize from economies of scale and scope (e.g., diverse portfolios of research projects that capture internal and external knowledge spillovers) outweigh the efficiency losses attributable to market power of large firms. With regard to incumbency, firms established in a product domain fail to adopt new technologies as a result of inertia in the decision-making processes induced by powerful customers. However, the advantages that established firms have over new entrants—investment resources, technical capabilities, and complementary assets—generally offset their handicap of introducing inferior or competence-enhancing product designs in comparison to rival or competence-destroying designs of new entrants.

The position and connections of an innovation within larger social networks can facilitate and constrain innovation by providing access to valuable information and knowledge for innovation initiation or development and by diffusing the developed innovation through the networks. In a similar vein, research based on cluster theory found that innovation diffusion is geographically bounded within a firm's cluster. Studies have shown that complementary innovations in technical and institutional arrangements are usually required to develop and commercialize a technology. This has been demonstrated in studies of innovations as diverse as in agriculture, cement, minicomputers, glass, biotechnology, and biomedical devices. The roles of public and private sector actors have also been found to be important in the development of an industrial infrastructure for innovation.

Directions for Future Research

The pioneering work of Schumpeter called practitioners' and academics' attention to the importance of innovation in management, and many studies of innovation have been conducted since then. Nonetheless, there is still enormous room for research in the process of innovation both theoretically and methodologically. Despite the multilevel or cross-level interactions that occur during the innovation process, studies that incorporate such interactions are

rare. The increasing number of international collaborations for innovation also requires cross-cultural examinations in innovation research. Moreover, future studies should be free of the positive bias that pervades the study of innovation. Innovation is often viewed as a good thing because the new idea must be useful—profitable, constructive, or solve a problem. New ideas not perceived as useful are often called "mistakes." However, the usefulness of a new idea can be determined only after the innovation process is completed and implemented.

Methodologically, the complexity of the innovation process and the diverse range in every innovation (i.e., duration, scale, scope, etc.) make it difficult to empirically examine innovation from the initiation to the implementation, especially with large-sample data. Most studies so far thus have focused on one stage or the other, leaving a handful of studies that follow through the entire stages. Even so, some valuable research is done through case studies and simulation models. In addition, studies of patents and patent citations have demonstrated that the knowledge and resources relevant to the development of many innovations transcend the boundaries of individual firms, industries, and nation states.

*Yoonhee Choi and
Andrew H. Van de Ven*

See also Innovation Diffusion; Patterns of Innovation; Process Theories of Change; Stages of Creativity; Strategic Entrepreneurship

Further Readings

Amabile, T. M. (1996). *Creativity in context: Update to the social psychology of creativity.* Boulder, CO: Westview.

Cooper, R. G. (1990). Stage gate systems: A new tool for managing new products. *Business Horizons, 33*(3), 44–53.

Nelson, R. R. (1993). *National innovation systems: A comparative analysis.* New York, NY: Oxford University Press.

Rogers, E. (2003). *Diffusion of innovations* (5th ed.). New York, NY: Simon & Schuster.

Ruttan, V. W. (2001). *Technology, growth, and development: An induced innovation perspective.* New York, NY: Oxford University Press.

Schumpeter, J. (1942). *Capitalism, socialism, and democracy.* New York, NY: Harper & Row.

Van de Ven, A. H., Polley, D. E., Garud, R., & Venkataraman, S. (2008). *The innovation journey.* New York, NY: Oxford University Press.

STAKEHOLDER THEORY

Stakeholder theory advances the notion that organizations that take particularly good care of a broad group of their stakeholders (i.e., customers, suppliers, employees, communities) will function more effectively and create more value. This value may then be used to sustain and grow the organization, and to give back to the stakeholders who helped create it. This type of firm behavior will be referred to herein as managing for stakeholders. Stakeholder theory is both managerial and prescriptive because it deals very specifically with manager behavior and the relationships between a firm and its constituencies. The theory also rests on a strong ethics foundation. This entry begins with a detailed elaboration of some of the fundamental concepts of stakeholder theory, followed by a description of its evolution and importance.

Fundamentals

The description provided in the introduction contains several concepts that require further explanation and elaboration: Who are an organization's stakeholders? What does it mean to take particularly good care of them? What is "value"? How does taking care of stakeholders help an organization create more of it?

Defining Who Is and Is Not a Stakeholder

Stakeholders are groups and individuals who have an interest in the activities and outcomes of an organization and on whom the organization relies to achieve its own objectives. For instance, customers are a stakeholder because they acquire goods and services from the firm in exchange for money that is then used to continue the firm's operations. This is an example of an economic stake. Suppliers and employees are other examples of stakeholders with an economic stake in the organization. Stakeholders might also have an equity stake in the firm, such as shareholders. In addition, stakeholders may simply have an interest in what the firm does because it influences them in some way, even if it is not a direct market effect. In the early stakeholder literature, these stakeholders were sometimes referred to as *kibbutzers*. Special interest groups, for instance, try to influence firm decisions in conformance with

their own agendas. Of course, stakeholder interests also tend to be interconnected, which means that stakeholder coalitions often form around particular issues and any particular organizational action could be received either favorably or unfavorably across a variety of stakeholder groups.

The third type of stake, the influencer or kibbutzer stake, highlights an important point: Just because a stakeholder has an interest in the organization does not necessarily mean that the organization is particularly interested in that stakeholder. Although there is no universally accepted definition of who merits classification as a legitimate stakeholder from the organization's perspective, in general, stakeholders are considered salient to the managers of an organization if they have power and legitimacy. Stakeholders have power if they possess critical resources that the firm needs or if they have the ability to influence outcomes through political, coercive, or other means. Legitimacy pertains to cultural and societal norms. For instance, a stakeholder may be considered salient to a manager because doing so is considered desirable, proper, or appropriate given the circumstances. In addition to power and legitimacy, a stakeholder that might not normally be considered very important could become important in urgent situations, where urgency means that a particular stakeholder's claim is time sensitive or critical to the stakeholder.

Another way to determine which stakeholders should receive primary attention from an organization is the principle of fairness. This principle suggests that the organization's legitimate stakeholders should include those from whom the organization has voluntarily accepted resources. Primary stakeholders would include employees, customers, financiers, suppliers, and local communities. They might also be considered primary because they are integrally linked to the value-creating processes of the organization. Secondary stakeholders can dramatically influence an organization but typically are not a part of the firm's operating core. Examples of secondary stakeholders include the government, the media, special interest groups, consumer advocate groups, and competitors.

Stakeholder theory received criticism early in its development from people who claimed that it advances the position that all stakeholders should have equal standing with the firm. While it may be true that stakeholder theory advocates for moral and just treatment of all a firm's stakeholders, it does not argue that all stakeholders are equal. This is especially pertinent with regard to the resources an organization devotes to serving particular stakeholders and the value it allocates back to them. Fairness would suggest that more value and attention should be allocated to stakeholders who are central to the organization's objectives and who contribute the most to the firm's value creation processes.

Stakeholder Treatment and Business Ethics

Treatment of stakeholders is central to stakeholder theory. Although there is no consensus on exactly what it means to treat stakeholders well, certain principles exist regarding treatment of stakeholders that are widely accepted among those who advance the theory. These principles rely primarily on ethical thinking, which means, in part, that the actions of a firm with regard to its stakeholders are judged by core rules based on socially accepted norms of behavior (i.e., lying is wrong). Firm behavior, from a stakeholder perspective, may also be judged based on outcomes. That is, firms are expected to produce favorable outcomes based on achievement of goals that are morally important. For instance, a for-profit corporation is expected to create products and/or services that satisfy consumer needs and wants, to provide a means for employees to take care of the physical needs of themselves and their families, to help in the communities in which they operate, and to provide fair returns to stockholders, among other things.

Organizational justice theory is a helpful tool for judging firm behavior with regard to stakeholders and for understanding how particular behaviors can influence firm outcomes. *Distributional justice* occurs when a stakeholder perceives that its allocation of value from the firm is fair relative to what the firm's other stakeholders receive or what the stakeholders of other firms receive. For instance, an employee might feel that his or her salary and benefits are fair compared to what other employees receive within the firm or compared to what people who perform similar tasks in other firms receive. *Procedural justice* pertains to a stakeholder's perception of the fairness of an organization's decision-making processes. A supplier, for example, may not like the fact that a bid was rejected but can handle the rejection much better if the selection process was perceived as fair. Interactional justice deals with

fairness in the way stakeholders are treated in day-to-day transactions and communications with the firm. Firms that exhibit organizational justice can expect most of their stakeholders to reciprocate with similar behaviors. Thus, cooperative relationships are developed based on trust.

Stakeholder theory's inclusion of ethical considerations increases its practicality because business and ethics are inseparable in real life. All business decisions contain ethical dimensions because they all influence outcomes for multiple stakeholders. The attempt to consider business decisions in the absence of ethical considerations is referred to as the separation fallacy.

Stakeholder Theory and the Value Created by an Organization

Much of the business literature is founded on the notion that financial profits (and associated shareholder returns) are the primary objective of the corporation. This obsession with the bottom line is easy to understand because financial profits are easily measured, whereas other types of value are difficult to measure. Also, a very popular stream of thought called *agency theory* argues that managers have a fiduciary responsibility to maximize returns to shareholders and that any manager behavior that works to reduce those returns represents an agency problem. Further, some authors have argued that shareholders are the only firm stakeholder who receives residual returns; that is, shareholders do not have a well-defined contract with regard to the returns they will receive, and they receive returns only after all other stakeholders with explicit contracts are paid. The ensuing shareholders versus stakeholders debate has filled many thousands of journal pages, with stakeholder advocates arguing that managers (and boards of directors) have legal responsibilities as well as moral obligations to all their stakeholders and not just to the shareholders. This treatment of the debate is oversimplified, but it will suffice for purposes of this entry.

Value is defined much more broadly in the stakeholder literature. An organization creates value by providing utility to a wide range of stakeholders. Customers and clients receive utility as they make use of the products and services of the firm, employees in a positive work environment may receive personal enrichment and growth from the work they perform, communities may benefit from a cadre of organizational volunteers who provide services to local charitable organizations, and so forth. Voluntarism is one of the defining characteristics of stakeholder theory. That is, the organization, through its managers and employees, behaves in certain ways because of an organizational culture that is based on a set of widely understood principles, not because of compulsion.

According to stakeholder theory, organizations that manage for stakeholders provide more value to their stakeholders than they need to provide just to keep them engaged with the organization. This type of behavior, when combined with trust stemming from organizational justice and adherence to ethical principles, leads to trusting, respectful, and mutually beneficial relationships with stakeholders—and a high level of reciprocation. Stakeholders are more likely to share valuable information with such a firm, which can lead to both efficiency and innovation. These sorts of firms have excellent reputations, which makes their products and services more attractive to existing and new consumers. Resources are easier to obtain because stakeholders expect to be treated well in exchange for what they provide to the firm. Contracting costs are reduced because stakeholders are more trusting of the firm and therefore fewer features of the contracts between a firm and its stakeholders have to be written down and carefully monitored. All this leads to firm growth, efficiency, flexibility, and therefore, an increased ability to both plan and carry out plans. Basically, these types of firms just run better. Firms of this type are also much less likely to become victims of negative stakeholder actions such as walkouts, boycotts, lawsuits, and bad press. Consequently, their securities may be seen as less risky (and thus more valuable) to investors.

Evolution

Stakeholder theory rests on some easily understood concepts and principles whose origin it is impossible to trace with precision; however, practically everyone who works in the stakeholder area acknowledges R. Edward Freeman, currently of the Darden School at the University of Virginia, as its intellectual leader. By Freeman's own account, many of the ideas contained in his landmark book, *Strategic Management: A Stakeholder Approach*, were developed at the Wharton Applied Research Center at the University of Pennsylvania in collaboration with colleagues including James R. Emshoff, Arthur Finnel, Ian Mitroff (and Richard Mason), Thomas Saaty, Russel Ackoff, and Eric Trist. Nonetheless, from among this group of scholars, it was Freeman who in 1984 published the book that provided an intellectual framework on which an entire stream of management inquiry and debate was built.

Freeman thought he was writing a textbook for the strategic planning process that could be used by both students and executives. The book is very applied. It was written with the express purpose of helping managers (and future managers) to effectively guide their organizations in an environment that had become increasingly complex, turbulent, and interconnected. The book's greatest influence on academia was first felt in the business ethics literature. Business ethics scholars embraced the stakeholder approach to management because of its moral foundation. In particular, social responsibility scholars found it especially helpful as a means to defend socially responsible firm behaviors. Ironically, the emerging strategic management discipline for whom the book was intended largely ignored Freeman's work, in spite of the fact that many of its early thought leaders advocated for a strategic management process that incorporated morality and social responsibility. Early neglect of stakeholder theory by strategists was perhaps at least partially a result of the field's obsession with economic models from the 1980s forward.

Interest in stakeholder theory has blossomed in recent years, to the point that it might now be called a field of scholarship, albeit a field that is very diverse. Its popularity is probably a function of several forces: an increasingly complex and interconnected external environment that stakeholder theory is especially well suited to address, acknowledgment among business scholars and managers that too much emphasis on short-term financial returns has led to unfavorable outcomes for businesses and society, numerous highly visible business scandals that have raised public awareness of ethical issues, and a global sustainability movement. The diversity of the field is demonstrated in a book published in 2010 called *Stakeholder Theory: The State of the Art* that contains nearly a thousand references, including references from the economics, strategic management, finance, marketing, management, accounting, information technology, health care, law, business ethics, social responsibility, environmental policy, and public policy/administration disciplines. A conference on stakeholder theory in Barcelona in 2011 attracted scholars and practitioners from 25 nations, and the Strategic Management Society just formed a special interest group on stakeholder strategy intended to promote research and debate.

Much of the literature on stakeholder theory thus far has been devoted to either defining and justifying the stakeholder perspective or, from an empirical perspective, proving that seeking to satisfy a broad group of stakeholders is economically justifiable. Moving forward, stakeholder theory offers the opportunity to redefine capitalism as a way to create value for stakeholders, as well as a lens through which best practices for stakeholder engagement can be identified.

Importance

Managing for stakeholders is associated with higher costs in some areas. A firm that gives more value back to its stakeholders than is absolutely needful to ensure their continued involvement with the firm might pay more to employees in wages and benefits than its competitors pay and is likely to offer a more attractive value proposition to its customers for its products and services than the market might otherwise demand. Surrounding communities tend to be beneficiaries of philanthropy and service from firm employees in a variety of ways. Furthermore, firms that manage for stakeholders will incur human and financial costs associated with higher levels of communication with and concern for stakeholders. Although stakeholder theory embraces a much broader view of value creation than mere financial returns, many management scholars have expressed the opinion that the financial benefits associated with managing for stakeholders are likely to exceed the financial costs. Consequently, they argue that managing for stakeholders should be associated with higher financial performance.

The bulk of the empirical and anecdotal evidence to date supports the notion that firms that manage for stakeholders tend to have higher financial performance. Even some of the theory's most ardent detractors have come around to the idea that this type of management is congruent with shareholder value creation. Consequently, the shareholders versus stakeholders debate is not particularly important—if the stakeholder approach leads to high shareholder returns, then why should shareholder advocates object to it?

Causality is an issue that requires more empirical research. Some researchers argue that managing for stakeholders is a luxury that follows financial success and that this is the source of the positive correlation. This may be true in part, but some research indicates that causality works in the opposite direction is well. That is, excellent stakeholder treatment can enhance firm performance. Nevertheless, it is important to understand that since stakeholder theory measures value more broadly than merely financial returns, even a firm with average financial returns may be creating substantially more value by providing more utility to a wider range of its stakeholders. Research that supports a positive financial correlation with the managing-for-stakeholders approach may be useful in silencing the shareholder advocates that have tended to be its most vocal critics, but leading stakeholder scholars tend to be more interested in the bigger picture of the total impact of firms that practice this sort of management and in defining a set of best practices for increasing the total value a firm creates.

Stakeholder theory has had an enormous impact on business practice. Most of the annual reports of the largest companies in the United States and many other industrialized nations include some version of the stakeholder concept or at least stakeholder terminology. The popularity of the concept is part of a global trend toward more socially responsible or sustainable management practices. Many companies are now taking the concept seriously and make very deliberate efforts to satisfy their primary stakeholders, whereas other companies may simply use the terminology as a sort of "window dressing" because it is politically fashionable.

Stakeholder theory has also found its way into the political arena, with politicians in some nations now using its principles and terminology when debating public policy issues. A global movement to make businesses more responsible to a larger number of stakeholders is reflected in the U.N. Global Compact that includes ten principles built around human rights, labor, the environment, and anticorruption. Many other groups have emerged on a global scale to promote stakeholder-friendly business practices, such as the Caux Round Table, a global network of business leaders, and the Conscious Capitalism Institute, which includes scholars, corporate executives, consultants and thought leaders who engage in stakeholder-oriented research, teaching, and practice.

Jeffrey S. Harrison

See also Corporate Social Responsibility; Human Capital Theory; Leadership Practices; Learning Organization; Organizational Effectiveness; Stewardship Theory; Strategic Alliances

Further Readings

Donaldson, T., & Preston, L. E. (1995). The stakeholder theory of the corporation: Concepts, evidence, and implications. *Academy of Management Review, 20,* 65–91.

Freeman, R. E. (1984). *Strategic management: A stakeholder approach.* Boston, MA: Pitman.

Freeman, R. E., Harrison, J. S., & Wicks, A. C. (2007). *Managing for stakeholders: Survival, reputation, and success.* New Haven, CT: Yale University Press.

Freeman, R. E., Harrison, J. S., Wicks, A. C., Parmar, B., & de Colle, S. (2010). *Stakeholder theory: The state of the art.* Cambridge, England: Cambridge University Press.

Harrison, J. S., Bosse, D. A., & Phillips, R. A. (2010). Managing for stakeholders, stakeholder utility functions and competitive advantage. *Strategic Management Journal, 31,* 58–74.

Jones, T. M. (1995). Instrumental stakeholder theory: A synthesis of ethics and economics. *Academy of Management Review, 20,* 404–437.

Jones, T. M., & Wicks, A. C. (1999). Convergent stakeholder theory. *Academy of Management Review, 24,* 206–221.

Mitchell, R., Agle, B. R., & Wood, D. J. (1997). Toward a theory of stakeholder identification and salience: Defining the principles of who and what really counts. *Academy of Management Review, 22,* 853–886.

Phillips, R. A. (2003). *Stakeholder theory and organizational ethics.* San Francisco, CA: Berrett-Koehler.

Phillips, R. A., Freeman, R. E., & Wicks, A. C. (2003). What stakeholder theory is not. *Business Ethics Quarterly, 13,* 479–502.

STEWARDSHIP THEORY

Stewardship is defined as caring and loyal devotion to an organization, institution, or social group. From a managerial perspective, it can explain settings where organizational leaders serve the organization's objectives, its greater good, and its shareholders. In contrast to agency theory, which suggests organizational "agents" are self-serving, economically motivated, and have interests that may diverge from those of the principals/shareholders, stewardship theory suggests "stewards" have interests beyond purely economic motivations and these noneconomic motivations can cause them to pursue cooperative, pro-organizational behaviors in service to others, which is consistent with the interests of principals/shareholders. In contrast to agency theory, where "agents" seek to optimize their personal economic gains at the expense of others, stewardship theory suggests "stewards" gain greater utility by pursing actions that increase their own intrinsic rewards and by putting the interests of the organization, and others, above their own. By drawing on sociological and psychological perspectives, stewardship theory offers a broader, complementary view to agency theory. It also suggests some of the agency theory-based control and governance mechanisms intended to ensure that the alignment of agents and principals—such as compensation schemes (e.g., stock ownership, stock options, or pay for performance) or boards of directors—need to be reconsidered to reflect individuals' noneconomic motives. The next section describes the theoretical assumptions and mechanisms on which stewardship theory was founded and concludes with a discussion of the domain of stewardship theory.

Fundamentals

While agency theory is based on the economic model of man, stewardship theory is based on the self-actualizing model of man. A fundamental belief of stewardship theory is that, given a choice, stewards will choose to pursue pro-organizational, collectivist behaviors over individualistic, self-serving behaviors because of the greater utility they will receive from the former, making stewardship behavior a completely rational choice. The assumptions of stewardship theory differs from those of agency theory in that the motivations of stewards stem not only from their own psychological mechanisms and motivations but also from the situational mechanisms that exist within their organizations. Three psychological mechanisms and three situational mechanisms uniquely define how stewardship theory differs from agency theory. The psychological mechanisms are

(1) intrinsic motivation, (2) identification with the organization, and (3) use of power. The situational mechanisms are (1) involvement orientation, (2) the extent to which the organization values individualism versus collectivism, and (3) the level of power distance accepted within the ranks of the organization.

Psychological Mechanisms

While agency theory assumes that agents are extrinsically motivated by lower order needs—economic and tangible rewards (e.g., physiological and security needs)—stewards are assumed to hold higher order needs, meaning they will be intrinsically motivated and will actively seek opportunities for personal growth and achievement. These motives will direct them to work harder on behalf of the organization. Identification with the organization occurs when stewards define themselves as members of their organization and accept the organization's mission and objectives as their own. In this instance, stewards are motivated to help the organization overcome problems and obstacles and gain satisfaction from the firm's successes, which will align their interests with those of shareholders. In terms of use of power, stewards are assumed to prefer personal power (i.e., expert power—power based on knowledge—and referent power—power based on someone liking you) as opposed coercive, legitimate, and rewards powers, which are the bases of power central to agency theory. Reliance on personal power creates a setting that emphasizes long-term relationships as opposed to short-term, transactional relationships.

Situational Mechanisms

Organizations can be classified as either control oriented, which is an agency-based perspective, or involvement oriented. Involvement-oriented organizations can be described as having work climates of self-control and self-management where employees are challenged to take responsibility, generate novel ideas, and develop new approaches to solve organizational problems, a condition that aligns with the interests of shareholders. Organizations can also be viewed as having either an individualistic, agency-based culture or a collectivist culture. Collectivist cultures emphasize the accomplishment of organizational goals, and members have a strong sense of belonging to the organization. *Power distance* is defined as the extent to which less powerful members of the organization expect and accept that power is unequally distributed throughout the organization. In high-power-distance organizational cultures, status and special privileges are given to those in higher ranks, which may foster agency-based behaviors. However, low-power-distance organizational cultures are more egalitarian, and organizational members are treated equally, which would foster stewardship behaviors within the organization.

Domain and Application

Stewardship theory is most often discussed in the corporate governance literature. Because stewardship behaviors require long-term, cooperative, trusting, mutually dependent relationships, stewardship theory is often applied within the context of family businesses, where these types of collective relationships are most likely to emerge. Thus, stewardship behaviors are proposed to provide family businesses with a competitive advantage because they experience reduced opportunism and lower agency costs compared to nonfamily business firms. Stewardship theory is also important to all managers because it suggests that by establishing a pro-stewardship climate (e.g., by relying on referent power or emphasizing a collectivist culture), managers can improve individual and organizational performance. For example, investments in R & D or new product development might have a greater positive effect on financial performance in organizations with a strong stewardship climate. Although there is growing interest in stewardship theory, few empirical studies have tested stewardship-based relationships because of the difficulty of measuring stewardship at an individual and organizational level.

Donald O. Neubaum

See also Agency Theory; Management Control Systems; Organizational Identification; Servant Leadership

Further Readings

Craig, J. B., Dibrell, C., Neubaum, D. O., & Thomas, C. H. (2011). Stewardship climate scale: Measurement and an assessment of reliability and validity. *Academy of Management Annual Meeting Proceedings*, 1–6.

Davis, J. H., Schoorman, F., & Donaldson, L. (1997). Toward a stewardship theory of management. *Academy of Management Review, 22*, 20–47.

Donaldson, L. & Davis, J. H. (1991). Agency theory and stewardship theory: CEO governance and shareholder returns. *Australian Journal of Management, 16*, 49–64.

Le Breton-Miller, I., Miller, D., & Lester, R. H. (2011). Stewardship or agency? A social embeddedness reconciliation of conduct and performance in public family businesses. *Organization Science, 22*, 704–721.

Pearson, A. W., & Marler, L. E. (2010). A leadership perspective of reciprocal stewardship in family firms. *Entrepreneurship Theory and Practice, 34*, 1117–1124.

STRATEGIC ALLIANCES

In recent decades, strategic alliances have become a widely accepted competitive tool in business. Broadly defined, strategic alliances refer to interfirm cooperative arrangements aimed at pursuing mutual strategic objectives of the partner firms. The two or more partners forming such alliances remain competitors. Examples of strategic alliances include joint ventures, research and development (R & D) agreements, research consortia, joint manufacturing and marketing agreements, buyer-supplier relationships, licensing, franchising, and so on. Strategic alliances seem to be proliferating with increasing competition and globalization. The rationale for entering into alliances typically include market access, economies of scale, risk and cost sharing, and learning. However, notwithstanding this popularity, strategic alliances have inherent instabilities and quite often end up as failures. We should note, though, that alliance failures refer to major changes (such as a merger/acquisition not originally intended) or dissolutions of alliances that are unplanned from the perspective of one or more partners. Planned terminations of alliances, with time-bound agreements, should not be considered as failures. Estimates of instabilities have ranged between 40% and 70% within a period of a few years of the formation of alliances. Overall, given the relatively high likelihood of failure, strategic alliances must be considered as a high-risk strategy, and alliance managers would need to develop a facility beyond handling single-firm strategies in to judiciously cope with the unique complexities and risks in alliances. This entry discusses the basic types of strategic alliances, their developmental stages, and the complexities relating to their management, such as those concerning resources, risks, trust, control, and internal tensions.

Fundamentals

Strategic alliances can be divided into two groups—equity and nonequity. Equity alliances are generally in the form of equity joint ventures, which are separately incorporated entities jointly owned by the partners. Equity joint ventures are created to substantially integrate the joint efforts of partner, and are the most instrumental among various alliance forms in the transfer of tacit knowledge between the partners, because of the significant extent to which partners are exposed to each other. In minority equity alliances, one or more partners take an equity position in others.

Nonequity alliances may be differentiated between unilateral contract-based alliances and bilateral contract-based alliances. Alliances are unilateral contract-based when there are well-defined transfer-of-property rights, such as in R & D and licensing agreements. Such unilateral alliances are based on contracts that tend to be complete and specific, and partners carry out their obligations independently of each other, without much coordination or collaboration. Bilateral contract-based alliances, however, require partners to work together on a constant basis, as in joint R & D, joint production, and joint marketing and promotion. These alliances involve the sustained joint creation of property and knowledge for the partners. Bilateral contracts are usually incomplete and more open-ended than the unilateral type, and the partners generally have to let their cooperative relationship unfold with experience.

For managing alliances effectively, it may be useful to keep in mind the three developmental stages of alliance formation, operation, and outcome. The *formation* stage comprises the formulation of an alliance strategy, selection of partners, negotiation of contractual provisions, and setting-up of the alliance. An alliance is a viable option only if it is substantially beneficial after the partial integration with another firm; otherwise, it should be avoided because of its managerial complexity. In selecting the alliance partner, the ideal would be to seek one with strategic compatibility, complementary resources, a certain level of interfirm trust, and a mutual understanding of value creation and value appropriation. A tentative partner selection would be followed by the negotiation of the alliance agreement. Here, the choice of an appropriate governance structure is a key feature. The next step is, of course, setting up the alliance. The partners should not pursue predominant managerial control in the alliance; rather, more attention should be given to committing the best personnel, keeping alliance personnel for a long term, and the blending of their cultures. The second of the three stages is that of *operation,* in which the negotiated agreement is implemented and the partners begin working together. Here, the partners should always regard cooperation and competition as dual roles in a strategic alliance. Cooperation should be emphasized in operational areas, while competition should mostly be capitalized through interfirm learning. The third stage is that of *outcome,* where the alliance performance is evaluated, resulting in either some degree of stabilization or a decision to modify arrangements. A comprehensive evaluation of an alliance's performance should use various kinds of measures, such as financial indicators as well as the state of the alliance (e.g., harmony, morale, productivity, and learning).

Importance

The complexities of managing alliances are well known and can be appreciated from the roles, discussed below, of critical factors such as resources, risks, trust, control, and internal tensions.

Resources

Alliances enable partners to gain access to each other's resources temporarily and with more flexibility than mergers and acquisitions. The two related but distinct motives for a firm to consider forming a strategic alliance are to obtain resources of others and to retain and develop its own resources by combining them with others' resources. Resources are sometimes classified as property-based resources, which have clear property rights and in which a firm's ownership is absolute and protected by law, and as knowledge-based resources, which cover tacit skills and knowledge involved in technological, managerial, and organizational resources. The management of resources includes optimally using one's existing resources, developing new resources, protecting one's resources, and gaining access to other firms' resources. Hence, the key challenge for firms in strategic alliances is effectively protecting themselves from losing critical resources at the same time as they attempt the fullest use of their contributed resources.

Risks

There are many types of risk in strategic alliances, arising not only from external sources such as competition, economic fluctuations, environmental factors, and government policy, but also internal sources such as lack of competence and the deceitful behavior of the partners. The concept of risk in alliances can be separated into two types—relational risk and performance risk. Relational risk is the probability that a partner firm does not commit itself to the alliance in a cooperative manner, leaving open the possibility that the partner may behave opportunistically, thereby undermining alliance performance. Perceived relational risk is high when it is difficult to protect one's proprietary know-how, the pay-off inequity expected by partners is high, and the number of previous alliances is small. Performance risk is the probability that the objectives of the alliance may not be achieved, given full interpartner cooperation. In other words, performance risk is the probability that an alliance may fail even when partner firms commit themselves fully to the alliance. Perceived performance risk is high when there is a shared R & D component, cross-border alliances are involved, and the nonrecoverable investments are high. Whereas relational risk is the risk of unsatisfactory interfirm cooperation, performance risk is all other factors that impact adversely on alliance performance.

Trust

The concept of trust has special significance in the dynamics of alliance management because of the central role of a cooperative relationship between the partners. Trust has been defined in terms of being vulnerable to the actions of trusted others in situations that involve risk. According to a popular formulation, trust has two dimensions—namely, goodwill trust and competence trust. Goodwill trust refers to the good faith, good intentions, integrity, and reputation for fair dealing of the partner. It reduces the perceived likelihood of opportunistic behavior occurring, which in turn contributes to low transaction costs. Competence trust refers to the expectation of competent performance. Competence is based on the various resources and capabilities of a firm. Firms that have been successful in previous alliances tend to build a reputation for competence.

Interpartner trust can be developed in alliances in several ways, including from risk taking, equity preservation, communication, and interfirm adaptation. Trust and risk taking are believed to form a reciprocal relationship: Trust leads to risk taking, and risk taking, in turn, buttresses a sense of trust, given that the expected behavior materializes. Trust can also be developed from equity preservation, as a high level of trust tends to encourage partners to tolerate short-term inequity and exercise mutual forbearance. Given a certain trust level among partners, extended periods of inequity will create tension and strain existing trust. Communication can generate trust by ironing out the potential kinks in daily operations, to make for a satisfactory working relationship. Last, trust may be fostered by interfirm adaptation. Being flexible enough to respond positively to the changing needs of a partnership demonstrates that the firm not only values the alliance but is also willing to make considerable efforts toward a desirable accommodation.

Control

Control is generally viewed as a process of regulation and monitoring for the achievement of organizational goals. The more critical control mechanisms in strategic alliances are goal setting, structural specifications, and cultural blending. Establishing specific and challenging goals in organizations ensures discipline of both partners to strive cooperatively in operations. Structural specifications, including rules and regulations, consist of both *ex ante* and *ex post* deterrents designed to minimize partners' incentives for opportunism, deceit, and misbehavior. As to cultural blending, it is generally accepted that managing alliance culture is a challenging task because it is about blending and harmonizing two different organizational cultures.

Internal Tensions

One of the reasons for the high failure rates of strategic alliances is the difficulty of managing the unique complexities of alliances. An explanation of this inordinate instability lies in the tricky problem of having to balance, on a continuing basis, the interactions among the partners in terms of the dialectical

forces or internal tensions within an alliance. These opposing force pairs are cooperation versus competition, rigidity versus flexibility, and short-term versus long-term orientation. *Cooperation* refers to the pursuit of mutual interests and common benefits in the alliance, whereas *competition* is the pursuit of one's own interest at the expense of others and private benefits in the alliance. *Rigidity* is the degree of connectedness of partner firms with each other in the alliance, and *flexibility* is the degree to which partner firms are able to modify the structural arrangements in the alliance to adapt to changing conditions. *A short-term orientation* is evident when alliances are viewed as transitional in nature, with a demand for quick and tangible results, whereas a *long-term orientation* is manifest when alliances are considered as at least semipermanent entities so that more patience and commitment are exercised.

When, in the course of managing an alliance, there is a movement toward the dominance of competition, flexibility, and a short-term orientation, the likelihood increases that the alliance will tend toward dissolution, because these forces mimic the attributes of market transactions. In this case, the internal transactions of alliances are effectively transferred to the marketplace. In the reverse situation, if the dominance encompasses cooperation, rigidity, and a long-term orientation, all associated with hierarchies, an alliance will tend toward a merger or acquisition. Alliance transactions, then, would in effect be transferred to a hierarchy or single organization. The continuing challenge in managing alliances is to reasonably preserve a balance among the internal tensions while carrying out the usual transactions.

T. K. Das

See also Interorganizational Networks; Resource-Based View of Firm; Theory of Cooperation and Competition; Trust

Further Readings

Bleeke, J., & Ernst, D. (Eds.). (1993). *Collaborating to compete: Using strategic alliances and acquisitions in the global marketplace.* New York, NY: Wiley.

Contractor, F. J., & Lorange, P. (Eds.). (2002). *Cooperative strategies and alliances.* Oxford, England: Elsevier Science.

Das, T. K. (Series Ed.). (2008–). *Research in strategic alliances.* Charlotte, NC: Information Age. (The only book series exclusively dedicated to alliance research.)

Das, T. K., & Teng, B. (1998). Between trust and control: Developing confidence in partner cooperation in alliances. *Academy of Management Review, 23,* 491–512.

Das, T. K., & Teng, B. (2000). Instabilities of strategic alliances: An internal tensions perspective. *Organization Science, 11,* 77–101.

Das, T. K., & Teng, B. (2000). A resource-based theory of strategic alliances. *Journal of Management, 26,* 31–61.

Doz, Y. L., & Hamel, G. (1998). *Alliance advantage: The art of creating value through partnering.* Boston, MA: Harvard Business School Press.

STRATEGIC CONTINGENCIES THEORY

Strategic contingencies theory is a theory of intraorganizational power that was proposed in 1971 by some members of the Aston group: David Hickson, Bob Hinings, C. A. Lee, Rodney Schneck, and Johannes Pennings. The theory assumes that subunits, or departments, within a firm necessarily exert power over one another because the organizational division of labor creates strategic contingencies. Control of these contingencies serves as the basis of intraorganizational power. This entry describes the fundamentals of the theory, support for the theory, a critique, and a comparison of the theory to resource dependence theory. It concludes with an assessment of the theory's importance.

Fundamentals

An assumption of the theory is that the organization is an open system of interdependent subunits (i.e., intraorganizational units) that rely to varying degrees on one another to complete the organization's task. The underlying concept of power, based on work by Richard Emerson, views power as derived from structural relationships that create situations of dependence and power. Subunits can be dependent on each other to varying degrees. However, the most dependent subunit is also the least powerful subunit.

A contingency occurs when one subunit's activities are affected by the activities of another subunit. A contingency becomes strategic when it is critical to workflow interdependencies among subunits and, consequently, affects the power distributions in an organization. A subunit can gain control over a strategic contingency if it is able to help other subunits cope with uncertainty; if it is non-substitutable, or not easily replaced; and if it is pervasive, or central to the other subunits. Each of these three conditions is necessary but not sufficient for the control of strategic contingencies.

Uncertainty is defined by the Aston group as a lack of information about future events that renders alternatives and their outcomes unpredictable. It is a "raw situation" that often must be dealt with so that the subunit can execute its tasks. There are a number of ways that a subunit can reduce uncertainty and help other departments cope with uncertainty:

- Prevention: For example, a marketing department provides a steady stream of orders so there is no fluctuation in the operations of the production department.
- Information: For example, a marketing research department provides forecasts that predict fluctuations.
- Absorption: For example, a marketing department adopts novel selling approaches if there is a problematic drop in sales.

A subunit becomes non-substitutable if there are no other alternatives available that can ensure the effective performance of its activities. This could be because the subunit's staff members are so highly trained or knowledgeable about the organization's processes, needs, or environment that a replacement within or outside the organization cannot easily be found.

Subunit centrality is defined by the Aston group as the degree to which its activities are interlinked within the organization. A highly central subunit is both pervasive and immediate: It is pervasive if it is connected to the activities and workflows of many other subunits in the organization. It is immediate if the operations of the organization would be quickly and detrimentally affected if the subunit's activities were to cease.

Although subunits may display varying degrees of coping with uncertainty, non-substitutability and centrality, Hickson and his colleagues assumed that a multiplicative combination of the three are necessary to gain control of strategic contingencies. The extent to which a subunit controls the strategic contingencies of other subunits can be used to explain different levels of power.

Routinization may reduce intraorganizational power in two ways. When routinization promotes coping with prevention, uncertainty can be avoided or reduced. Routinization by coping with information or absorption encourages standards that make it easier to replace a subunit and, consequently, make it more substitutable.

Importance

Hickson and his colleagues reported the first test of strategic contingencies theory in 1974 using a sample of 28 subunits in seven small manufacturing organizations. They operationalized their constructs using questionnaire, interview, and archival data and recognized three types of power: position, perception, and participation. In each organization, they assessed the relative power of the engineering, marketing, production, and accounting departments, as well as their ability to cope with uncertainty, non-substitutability, and centrality. With few exceptions, the independent variables positively correlated to the power measures based on perception and participation (though no significance levels were reported). In their sample, the production subunits had the most power and the accounting subunits had the least. Their theory explained 24 of the 28 subunit power rankings. Different subunits apparently obtained power by using different strategies that varied over time.

Subsequent tests of the theory have been limited to less than a dozen published studies. However, the context of those studies has been rather wide-ranging. That is, the theory has been tested in Canadian, American, Singaporean, Israeli, and multinational organizations in a number of settings: manufacturing firms; universities and colleges; medical clinics and information-intensive firms (i.e., marketing and sales, insurance, and transportation firms). Most of the studies used small samples with 10 or fewer organizations. The theory has been supported to some extent in all studies. In virtually all tests of the theory, at least two of the three conditions for power (i.e., coping with uncertainty, non-substitutability, and centrality) were related to one or more operationalizations of power. The theory has been used by disciplines other than management to assess the power of information systems departments, libraries, and brand managers.

Only two sets of studies explored power over time. One noted temporal inconsistencies in the theory. In particular, Ran Lachman found support for the theory when he looked at each of two temporal periods separately. However, when he looked across time, power was not found consistently to be a function of any of the theory's three major independent variables measured 2 years earlier. He found that those subunits that had high power tended to hold on to it, while those that had low power did not necessarily remain powerless. Hence, Lachman concluded that the ability to cope with uncertainty, non-substitutability, and centrality are strongly associated with power, but they may not be determinants of power.

Critique

The theory has a number of strengths. First, it is among the earliest to adopt a systemic view of intraorganizational power. In particular, it considers organizations to be integrated systems of complexly interrelated subunits whose activities are coordinated to achieve the organization's objectives. Second, it is parsimonious. Its developers focus on structural sources of power and not on either the nature of social relationships or the psychological attributes of members of those organizations. It incorporates only those constructs hypothesized to affect power by their contribution to the control of contingencies exercised by a subunit. Third, the developers went to considerable effort to define constructs and propose multimethod operationalizations that could be used by others to test the theory.

While the authors did an excellent job overall in defining strategic contingencies theory, they did not adequately operationalize what is meant by "control of a strategic contingency." Consequently, others who have sought to test the theory have struggled with how to incorporate and measure this important construct in their studies. Several, including Lachman and Sze Sze Wong and colleagues, introduced constructs called *criticality* and *knowledge criticality*, respectively. However, these constructs do not really address the nature of control of strategic contingencies. Carol Saunders operationalized control of strategic contingencies and concluded that it should be considered as a moderator in the relationships between power and coping with uncertainty, non-substitutability, and pervasiveness. Her findings have not been replicated, and an essential aspect of the model remains unclear after several decades of testing.

Further, the theory is a variance model that does not adequately address process issues. This could be why Lachman did not find support for the model when looking across temporal periods. To their credit, the theory's developers did attempt to show how the three basic conditions could be used to capture power.

Comparison With Resource Dependence Theory

Often, strategic contingencies theory and resource dependence theory are cited together as theories of intraorganizational power. Jeffrey Pfeffer himself treats the two theories as "variants of each other." Graham Astley and Edward Zajac, however, argue that the two theories actually have different power bases. The strategic contingencies theory is based explicitly in dependencies resulting from task processes created by the division of labor. Power is derived from the structure of relationships that constitute an organization's system of work flow interdependencies. As such it is built on a rational model in which subunit goals are subordinated to those of the organization. In contrast, resource dependence is a coalitional model in which subunits participate in exchanges that reflect their varying preferences and interests. Dependence is generated through transactions or exchanges of resources between organizational subunits. These resources may be used in performing tasks, but the resource dependencies do not parallel work flow interdependences. Strategic contingencies theory is not based on exchange since the structural dependencies (i.e., task performances and roles) created by division of labor are not transferable resources using standard definitions of resources.

At the time that this entry was written, a search by Google Scholar indicates that the theory has been cited by 1,224 articles. That's not bad. However, the seminal work of resource dependence theory which appeared around the same time frame has 13,375 citations. Why has one of these seminal works been cited 11 times more than the other? Most likely there are a variety of factors. One might be that resource dependence theory was described in more detail in a widely read book. Or it might be that the resource dependence theory covers a broader spectrum of types of power. It can be applied to departmental, organizational, and interorganizational levels of analysis since resources can be exchanged at each of these levels. In contrast, strategic contingencies theory has been limited to the departmental level, probably because of the requirement that it focus on interdependencies created by work flows. A final reason might be that the loose coupling inherent in resource dependence theory might make it more suitable for today's highly dynamic environment than strategic contingencies' more tightly coupled model.

Practical Application

It is not obvious that the theory has influenced managers directly. It has, however, been applied by management scholars to understand power distributions in a range of organizations around the globe. This suggests that the theory still has salience for researchers, but it has not been well-leveraged by practitioners. Practitioners can use the theory to develop strategies for gaining and maintaining power in dynamic environments. Using the theory, practitioners can position their departments to perform important and not easily imitable tasks needed by other departments in their organization, or even by other companies within their complex corporate networks.

Carol Saunders

See also Contingency Theory; Environmental Uncertainty; Resource-Based View of the Firm; Resource Dependence Theory

Further Readings

Astley, W. G., & Zajac, E. (1991). Intraorganizational power and organizational design: Reconciling rational and coalitional models of organization. *Organization Science, 2*(4), 399–411.

Hickson, D. J., Hinings, C. R., Lee, C. A., Schneck, R. E., & Pennings, J. M. (1971). A strategic contingencies' theory of intraorganizational power. *Administrative Science Quarterly, 16,* 216–229.

Hinings, C. R., Hickson, D. J., Pennings, J. M., & Schneck, R. E. (1974). Structural conditions of intraorganizational power. *Administrative Science Quarterly, 19,* 22–44.

Lachman, R. (1989). Power from what? A reexamination of its relationships with structural conditions. *Administrative Science Quarterly, 34,* 231–251.

Saunders, C., & Scamell, R. (1982). Intraorganizational distribution of power: Replication research. *Academy of Management Journal, 25,* 192–200.

Saunders, C. (1990). The strategic contingencies theory of power: Multiple perspectives. *Journal of Management Studies, 27*(1), 1–18.

Wong, S. S., Ho, V., & Lee, C. H. (2008). A power perspective to interunit knowledge transfer: Linking knowledge attributes to unit power and the transfer of knowledge. *Journal of Management, 34,* 127–150.

STRATEGIC DECISION MAKING

Strategy is about making decisions—decisions such as which industry to enter, how to position the firm and its products, which resources to develop or to buy, who to hire, and which organizational structure to use. It is no surprise, then, that much research within the strategy field has studied how strategic decisions are made and how they can be improved. The literature addressing these two questions falls under the rubric of strategic decision making (SDM). This literature focuses on the processes leading to a decision (e.g., how different opinions are taken into account) rather than on the content of the decision (e.g., which strategy framework to use to devise the firm's positioning). This entry presents some of the fundamental concepts and tools studied in SDM and ways in which they might be applied by managers.

Fundamentals

Nature of SDM

Before discussing the research on SDM, it is fair to ask how strategic decisions differ from other kinds of decisions, thus addressing why SDM research is useful and necessary. To do so, we start by looking at the two main bodies of literature that inform SDM—decision theory and the psychological research on judgment and decision making—and show that one must be careful when interpreting findings in the context of SDM because of several characteristics inherent to strategic decisions.

Decision theory is a mathematical approach to making decisions. According to this theory, the decision maker must make a choice among various actions ($a \in A$); the world can be in one of many states ($x \in X$), and each of these states has a probability of occurring, which may depend on the chosen action ($P[x|a]$). Finally, the decision maker experiences a payoff or utility, depending on the state of the world and the decision taken ($U(x,a)$). The goal of decision theory is to select the action that maximizes the expected utility (i.e., $\max_a E[U(x,a)|a]$). However, strategic decisions are difficult to analyze using this approach because (1) strategic decisions are usually made under ambiguity (the probabilities $P[a|x]$ are unknown); (2) the set of possible actions (A) is not known a priori but it is discovered "on the way" via a search process, usually over a vast solution space; (3) strategic decisions are usually not made by a unique decision maker but by a group of people, such as the top management team, board of directors, or a chain of employees along which a proposal is passed and evaluated, so there may not be one utility function ($U(a,x)$) but many; (4) because there may be several utility functions, decisions are made by a process fraught with politics and power, considerations out of the scope of decision theory; and (5) even if there is agreement regarding the utility function, the different decision makers may have different assessments about the possible actions, states of the world, and probabilities, so the problem of how to best aggregate these perspectives becomes paramount.

The other body of literature that informs SDM is the psychological research on judgment and decision making. This research has been highly successful in identifying the ways in which humans systematically deviate from the perfect rationality benchmark set by decision theory. The research on judgment and decision making has mostly been developed via lab experiments involving test subjects facing simple choices. The applicability of the judgment and decision-making literature to SDM is hampered by a number of additional issues: (1) Strategic decisions are unstructured, nonroutine, high stakes, and difficult to reverse, which is quite different from the typical decision experiments used in the judgment and decision-making literature. (2) Unlike most decisions in a lab setting, strategic decisions are complex, involving many subdecisions and constraints, and thus the task of the decision maker is to make some key architectural choices that will determine waves of other interdependent choices. (3) Many problems are unclear or ill-defined, and thus the formulation of the problem (usually a given in the judgment and decision-making literature) becomes central; (4) because of their complex nature, strategic decisions are difficult to implement, thus SDM pays particular attention to the determinants of implementation, which is outside the scope of most studies on judgment and decision making; and (5) strategic decisions are made within organizations, thus notions of power, incentives, expertise, and organizational structure, conditions difficult to replicate in lab settings, play important roles.

These differences and limitations of scope and focus reveal some of the distinctive characteristics of strategic decision making and suggest that conceptual frameworks are necessary beyond those provided by either decision theory or by studies on judgment and decision making.

Some Factors Influencing SDM

Following the work of Herbert Simon, researchers generally agree that SDM is a process with three main stages: (1) identifying a problem, (2) developing potential solutions to the problem, and (3) selecting (ideally) the best solution. One implication of this process is that once a problem has been identified (e.g., how should our firm expand internationally to maximize profits?), the chances of making a successful decision depend on coming up with many potential solutions and on having effective tools for evaluating these solutions. Perhaps the main point of agreement among SDM researchers is that how decisions are made impacts the outcome of these decisions. Accordingly, the rest of this section summarizes how different characteristics of the individuals and the processes used to make strategic decisions affect the outcome of these decisions. The summary is structured according to increasing levels of analysis: It progressively moves from individual-level to organizational-level characteristics. Given that this is a huge literature, this brief summary cannot do justice to all the findings, so priority is given to widely accepted findings with direct managerial application.

The role of individual biases. For most of its history, the human brain has evolved to deal with the daily tasks of hunter-gatherers, not with the challenges of managing a multibillion dollar corporation. Thus, it is not surprising that untrained individuals make systematic errors when dealing with complex strategic decisions. Some of the biases that are most pervasive in SDM are overconfidence (being overly optimistic), availability (focusing on data that has recently been observed), and confirmation (favoring evidence that supports the decision maker's preferred theory).

The role of the information aggregation process. Making good strategic decisions involves much information, all of which is unlikely to be available in just one mind. For instance, because of their different backgrounds, managers may assess a given strategy differently. Further, managers may have different ideas about what strategies are available to the firm, and some strategies may be discovered only if the knowledge of different managers is combined. All this emphasizes how relevant it is to aggregate information that resides in the minds of different decision makers. Otherwise, some valuable strategies may be inaccurately analyzed or not analyzed at all.

The role of organizational structure. One key characteristic of organizational structure that affects SDM is the degree to which an organization is centralized or decentralized. In a centralized structure, top management makes decisions, communicates them to the rest of the organization, and monitors their implementation. In a decentralized firm, top management lets the strategy emerge from different parts of the organization by acting as a facilitator or sponsor. Centralization is useful when decisions are interrelated, when information from disparate sources must be aggregated to make good decisions, and when a few high-stakes decisions are relevant. Decentralization is helpful when the information and decisions of different parts of the organization are not interrelated, when decisions must take into consideration local information, and when many fast-paced decisions must be made. Another way in which centralization and decentralization affect SDM is in the types of projects that get to be accepted. In a centralized firm, projects must pass several screens before being accepted (e.g., the whole chain of command) limiting errors of commission, while in a decentralized firm, decisions are accepted locally (e.g., by the engineer and her closest supervisor) limiting errors of omission. The choice of which structure to use depends on which type of error is costlier. For instance, decentralization may be the right structure for organizations where innovation is important (e.g., R & D labs), because accepting a few bad projects may be a low cost to pay when compared to the cost of missing many good projects.

The role of politics. Because strategic decisions are usually made by multiple individuals who may have competing interests, conflict may emerge among the decision makers. When there is conflict, decision makers usually engage in political tactics (such as coalition formation, bargaining, agenda control, and strategic use of information) and the preferences of the most powerful tend to win. Since the preferences of the most powerful do not necessarily reflect what is best for the organization, political conflict constrains the search process and thus decreases the effectiveness of SDM. Additionally, because most people dislike politics, politics increase frustration and animosity among managers, which further reduce organizational effectiveness.

Importance

Because the most important job of top executives is to make strategic decisions, the study of SDM can have vast implications. Even small improvements in a few decisions can have a large impact on outcomes such as profitability, innovation, and economic development. The following addresses some of the ways in which managers might productively use insights from the SDM literature at various levels of the organization.

Individual level. Managers should be on the watch for biases and should put in place mechanisms to avoid these common errors of individual judgment. Techniques aimed at minimizing the effect of individual biases include the following: (1) Use formal analysis tools such as decision trees, influence diagrams, and mathematical models (e.g., spreadsheets, simulations, game-theoretic analyses). (2) Use frameworks (such SWOT or Porter's five forces) and checklists. (3) Take an outsider's perspective; try to remove the actual decision maker from the narrow confines of their situation and consider how an outsider would make the decision. (4) Educate the decision makers on SDM, statistical thinking, and decision-making biases.

Group level. Some of the techniques aimed at effectively combining information across individuals include the following: (1) Expand the pool of ideas. Before delving into the details of a given decision, spend time and resources on expanding the set of potential options. Tools here include brainstorming sessions, scenario planning, the Delphi method, asking decision makers to "consider the opposite," using experts, and crowdsourcing. (2) Increase the critical analysis of ideas. Tools here include assembling a team with a diverse set of expertise, increasing the number of decision makers, introducing outside experts, designating a devil's advocate, and encouraging an open and frank communication atmosphere that encourages cognitive (not political) conflict.

Structural level. In general, organizational structure offers a powerful way to "hard-wire" decision-making processes in the organization. For example, if the goal is to minimize errors of commission, then employing centralization, a hierarchical organization structure, and granting veto power to some key parties seem good ideas. If the goal is to increase the number of alternatives considered before making decisions, it could make sense to create a planning department, institute the role of devil's advocate, and create a strategic committee that includes people from different parts of the organization. In addition, a "perfect" decision is worthless if it is not well implemented. Thus, implementation is inextricably linked to SDM. One finding here is that successful implementation is more likely when the implementers agree with the decision being implemented. Thus, mechanisms such as consensus building and selecting implementers from the decision-making team improve the chances of success.

Felipe A. Csaszar

See also Behavioral Theory of the Firm; Brainstorming; Decision Support Systems; Groupthink; High-Reliability Organizations; Managerial Decision Biases; Organizational Structure and Design; Strategy and Structure

Further Readings

Baron, J. (2007). *Thinking and deciding* (4th ed.). Cambridge, England: Cambridge University Press.

Bazerman, M. H., & Moore, D. A. (2008). *Judgment in managerial decision making* (7th ed.). New York, NY: Wiley.

Berger, J. O. (1985). *Statistical decision theory and Bayesian analysis* (2nd ed.). New York, NY: Springer.

Csaszar, F. A. (2012). Organizational structure as a determinant of performance: Evidence from mutual funds. *Strategic Management Journal, 33,* 611–632.

Cyert, R. M., & March, J. G. (1963). *A behavioral theory of the firm.* Englewood Cliffs, NJ: Prentice-Hall.

Eisenhardt, K. M., & Zbaracki, M. J. (1992). Strategic decision making. *Strategic Management Journal, 13,* 17–37.

Hammond, J. S., Keeney, R. L., & Raiffa, H. (1998). *Smart choices: A practical guide to making better decisions.* Boston, MA: Harvard Business School Press.

Mintzberg, H., Raisinghani, D., & Théorêt, A. (1976). The structure of unstructured decision processes. *Administrative Science Quarterly, 21*(2), 246–275.

Schwenk, C. R. (1995). Strategic decision making. *Journal of Management, 21*(3), 471–493.

Simon, H. A., Dantzig, G. B., Hogarth, R., Plott, C. R. Raiffa, H., Schelling, T. C., . . . Winter, S. (1986). *Report on the research briefing panel on decision making and problem solving* (Research briefings 1986). Washington, DC: National Academy Press.

Strategic Entrepreneurship

Strategic entrepreneurship (SE) is a newly recognized field that draws, not surprisingly, from the fields of strategic management and entrepreneurship. The field emerged officially with the 2001 special issue of the *Strategic Management Journal* on "strategic entrepreneurship"; the first dedicated periodical, the *Strategic Entrepreneurship Journal,* appeared in 2007. SE is built around two core ideas: (1) Strategy formulation and execution involves attributes that are fundamentally entrepreneurial, such as alertness, creativity, and judgment, and entrepreneurs try to create and capture value through resource acquisition and competitive positioning. (2) Opportunity seeking and advantage seeking—the former the central subject of the entrepreneurship field, the latter the central subject of the strategic management field—are processes that should be considered jointly. This entry explains the specific links between strategy and entrepreneurship, reviews the emergence and development of the strategic entrepreneurship field, and discusses key implications and applications.

Fundamentals

The links between strategy and entrepreneurship can be understood in several ways. First, entrepreneurs need strategy, across all stages of product and firm life cycles, and insights from strategic management about capturing value through resource acquisition, industry positioning, capability development, the creation of real options, and the like are critical to our understanding of the emergence of new products, firms, and industries. In other words, the domain of SE includes those entrepreneurial phenomena that can be best explained and understood using concepts normally associated with the field of strategic management. Second, strategic management theory can be improved by thinking about the origins of competitive advantage. Resource attributes such as value, rarity, imitability, and substitutability do not exist *ex ante,* but must be created or discovered through human agency. Entrepreneurial action is thus prior to value creation and capture. Hence, there are obvious gains from trade between the two fields. SE in fact draws opportunistically on both fields.

A basic idea of strategic entrepreneurship is that concepts from strategy designed to answer the question, Why do some firms outperform others? may apply in a more entrepreneurial setting. (By *entrepreneurial* here we mean not only the creation of new firms and the introduction of new products but creativity, alertness, and discovery more generally.) The dependent variable in strategic management research is usually taken to be sustained competitive advantage—that is, a firm's ability to create and appropriate more value than the competition on a sustained basis. This is often addressed in terms of established economic theories of applied price theory, industrial organization theory, game theory, and bargaining theory. In fact, most modern strategic management theory (whether resource-based theory or the positioning approach) is based on a logic of "competitive imperfection": ultimately, *some* deviation from the ideal of the perfectly competitive model, leading to imperfect factor and/or product markets, explains strategy's central dependent variable—sustained competitive advantage. Indeed, the latter is very often taken as synonymous with earning rents in equilibrium. Various lists have been compiled of the criteria that resources must meet to yield rents in equilibrium. However, there is a retrospective character to such lists: Their main function is to perform a kind of sorting among the firm's resources to see if any conform to the criteria.

SE research typically takes the creation and capture of firm value as the phenomenon of interest. This allows SE scholars to use constructs, theories, and methods well established in the two fields. For example, among the antecedents of value creation and capture are established variables such as entrepreneurial orientation and dynamic capabilities.

However, focusing on value creation and capture implies that SE research is not committed to the strategy scholar's traditional emphasis on sustained competitive advantage; wealth creation may be a matter of discovering and exploiting a few large, but short-lived opportunities, or it may be a matter of many small, long-lived ("sustainable") opportunities. Competitive advantages may thus be fleeting and need to be created and created anew. SE asks how firms can use strategic intent to continuously leverage entrepreneurial opportunities for advantage-seeking purposes.

There is currently no list of key assumptions made by those engaging in strategic entrepreneurship research. However, some of these assumptions include the following:

- Wealth creation is not automatic but results from the creative actions of individuals.
- Economic action takes place under conditions of Knightian uncertainty.
- Under Knightian uncertainty, decision making is poorly described by the models of rational, utility-maximizing agents borrowed from mainstream economics. Judgment, satisficing, biases and heuristics, experimentation and learning, and the like are critically important.
- Entrepreneurship involves the assembly and deployment of heterogeneous capital resources, which may (but does not necessarily) result in the establishment of a new firm.
- Resource characteristics are not given, *ex ante*, but must be created or discovered through entrepreneurial action.

Building on these assumptions, strategic entrepreneurship can then be conceived as the study of individuals building economic institutions to create wealth under conditions of Knightian uncertainty, where traditional profit-maximizing decision-making criteria may be replaced with other kinds of decision rules. This definition of this specialized field is both strategic and entrepreneurial, focuses both on individuals and institutions, is not limited to the study of just firms as an institutional form, focuses on the centrality of wealth creation, and addresses the challenges associated with forming opportunities whose exploitation can lead to wealth. Like any good definition, this proposed definition of the field of strategic entrepreneurship

also eliminates certain phenomena from the field. For example, decision making under risk—an undoubtedly important topic—is not included in this proposed definition. Also, firms that are formed for reasons besides the creation of wealth are not included in this definition—although it is important to recognize that this does not necessarily eliminate not-for-profit firms or social entrepreneurship. Whether this more integrated approach to the definition of strategic entrepreneurship will emerge as the dominant definition is yet to be seen. However, as a matter of theory and discipline development, the integrated approach seems to hold more promise than the other approaches discussed here.

Evolution

Anticipations of SE can be found in several earlier contributions. For example, Edith Penrose coined the notion of the firm's "subjective opportunity set," the set of opportunities the firm's top-management team perceives and believes it can seize, and Richard Rumelt linked entrepreneurship and the creation of competitive advantage. Moreover, work on corporate entrepreneurship, corporate venturing, organizational learning, innovation research, hypercompetition, real options, and dynamic capabilities theory each in various ways anticipates SE theory. Yet those streams needed to be explicitly pulled together and focused. Understood as a relatively concerted research effort, SE is a very young field that has existed for only a decade or so.

Most strategic management theory has until recently been surprisingly silent about where competitive advantage comes from. However, over the last decade or so, building, accumulating, transforming, managing, learning about, combining, and recombining resources has become a central theme in strategic management. Thus, scholars increasingly emphasize, following Joseph Schumpeter, the inherently *temporary* nature of competitive advantages. This focus has substantial support in the relevant empirical literature, which broadly suggests that firm-specific returns that can be linked to specific competitive advantages regress to the industry mean, and that, moreover, the pace of regression has accelerated over the last few decades. A tradeoff arises under these circumstances, because on the one hand, hypercompetition provides incentives to accelerate investments in discovering new entrepreneurial opportunities that can be turned into temporary advantages, while on the other hand driving investment costs up (because of time-compression diseconomies).

Thinking on the origins of competitive advantage was also furthered by real options theory, which has influenced strategic management scholars since in the 1990s. The reason is not difficult to understand: Strategic management has choices between flexibility and commitment at its very core. Real options allow strategic managers to take specific actions now or postpone them to a future point in time. They thereby provide flexibility in uncertain markets. Strategic managers may invest in a host of different real options to accommodate speedy and flexible reaction to changes in the environment. The link to firm-level entrepreneurship and competitive advantage is straightforward: As environments change, so do competitive advantages. Given that future competitive advantages are highly uncertain, it may pay to continue developing and keep several options open. Internal corporate venturing is a means to such option creation. When uncertainty resolves, the firm can then call the option most likely to lead to an advantage in the relevant environment. However, the most direct precursor of SE is probably the "dynamic capabilities" view associated with David Teece and colleagues. This view argues that superior performance comes from a firm's capacity to change its resource base in the face of Schumpeterian competition and environmental change. Dynamic capabilities are defined as the firm's ability to integrate, build, and reconfigure internal and external competences to address rapidly changing environments. Importantly, dynamic capabilities reflect past learning processes, as they are a learned pattern of collective activity through which the organization systematically generates and modifies its operational routines in pursuit of improved performance. Superior dynamic capabilities enable firms to adapt more quickly and effectively to a changing business environment, creating a stream of temporary competitive advantages over time. More or less explicitly, these approaches emphasize the value of putting entrepreneurship into strategic management.

Seeing it from the other side, the notion that concepts from strategic management can inform research and practice in entrepreneurship is, perhaps, best exemplified in some of the most popular undergraduate entrepreneurship textbooks. In many of these books, the link between strategic management and entrepreneurship is almost explicit. For example, these textbooks often recommend that entrepreneurs need to begin with a purpose, an idea very close to strategic management's concept of a mission. In analyzing industries to identify opportunities and threats, these entrepreneurship texts often advise using the "five forces framework" and other tools that were originally developed in strategic management. The identification of entrepreneurial strengths applies resource-based logic; the strategic alternatives available to a firm parallels the list of "generic strategies" found in most strategy textbooks.

Of course, there is much that can be said about importing well-developed theories and tools from a discipline such as strategic management into the study of entrepreneurship. After all, the history of strategic management has been to import theories and tools developed elsewhere—primarily economics—and then to adapt them to strategic management. And this model has served the field of strategic management well. However, this first approach to defining strategic entrepreneurship essentially subsumes this new field as a special case of strategic management and assumes away any special attributes that entrepreneurship—as a phenomenon—possesses. This seems problematic since the study and practice of entrepreneurship seems to involve issues, including, for example, decision making under Knightian uncertainty, that have not received much attention in the strategic management literature.

Importance

The Entrepreneurial Foundation of Competitive Advantage

Although many of the conceptual building blocks used in SE have been operationalized and used empirically in either the entrepreneurship or strategic management literature, as a distinct research field, SE has yet to produce its own robust literature of empirical tests of dominant conceptual models and their main mechanisms. Conceptually, SE has been rather quick to converge on an overall theoretical model with wealth creation as its dependent variable; however, lower-level causal mechanisms underlying this relationship are not clearly defined and operationalized. Appropriate tests of the underlying mechanisms of SE would appear to require longitudinal examination of how exactly firms' strategic intent affects their ability to transform the recognition of opportunities into wealth. What are the underlying mechanisms? Specifically, what is the interplay between organizational members with specific abilities and skills, interacting within an administrative framework (broadly conceived), that make some firms capable of continuous wealth creation? This calls for an approach to SE that highlights organizational design and behaviors in a multilevel framework. Some, including the authors of this entry, view the absence of such a framework as a major gap in extant SE research.

The strategic entrepreneurship literature can also be organized around a series of research questions or research topics of interest to both entrepreneurship and strategic management scholars and that are, so far at least, understudied. This seems to be the approach to defining the field adopted by Michael Hitt and Dan Schendel in their editorial essay announcing the formation of the *Strategic Entrepreneurship Journal*. In particular, these authors identified 10 topic areas that overlap strategy and entrepreneurship that deserve further study. Examples of these topic areas include the study of creativity, imagination, and opportunities; the study of risk and uncertainty; the study of the behavioral attributes of entrepreneurship; and the study of the social role of entrepreneurship. However, while defining strategic entrepreneurship in this manner has certain advantages—not the least of which is to establish the editorial boundaries of a new journal as widely as possible—it ultimately has limitations. Indeed, defining the field in this way in an important sense avoids defining the field—it provides little or no guidance to young scholars interested in contributing to an emerging field but is unclear as to what is and is not included within those field boundaries.

Another way to think about the literature begins by recognizing that strategy and entrepreneurship have several things in common. Among these are emphases on wealth creation, decision making, operationalizing decisions, and assembling resources to create wealth. Such commonalities suggest that these two fields could inform one another. However, despite these common features, there are important differences between the two fields that suggest possible points of conflict but also possible points of integration. For example, while both fields focus

on decision making, strategic management looks at decision making under conditions of risk, whereas entrepreneurship also looks at decision making under Knightian uncertainty. Also, although both fields focus on wealth creation, strategic management theory generally adopts the assumption that opportunities to create wealth already exist and the task facing managers is how to best accomplish this. Entrepreneurship, on the other hand, focuses on the processes by which opportunities are formed.

This way of thinking about strategic entrepreneurship imagines a robust dialogue between the two fields, where questions that are important in strategy but difficult to answer given current theory—for example, where does resource heterogeneity come from?—can be addressed using concepts and ideas taken from entrepreneurship scholars, and vice versa.

Practical Implications

SE has emerged over the last decade as a new focus in the intersection between the individual-centric and start-up-focused entrepreneurship field and the strategic management field with its traditional emphasis on established firms and firm-level performance variables. The defining characteristic of the field is a sustained attempt to link opportunity seeking (i.e., opportunity discovery and evaluation) with advantage seeking—an endeavor that is related to work on dynamic capabilities, hypercompetition, and real options. Like these research streams, SE appears to have dropped strategic management's search for the conditions of sustainability of (any single) competitive advantage and instead focused on the entrepreneurial pursuit of a string of temporary advantages, often encapsulated under the label of "wealth creation." SE research has identified a large set of variables that may drive such firm-level entrepreneurship, for example, borrowing (from strategic management) notions of "strategic intent" or (from entrepreneurship) "entrepreneurial orientation."

We have argued, however that SE is still mainly a rather loose amalgam of a number of insights from strategy and entrepreneurship. Whether it will morph into a distinct and cumulative research stream seems dependent on the development of clear(er) research models around which research can build and also on gradually building a body of distinct SE empirical knowledge. The foregoing discussion offers what we think are important components of such a development. Is the emergence of SE a positive development? Some scholars have expressed concern that SE represents a takeover attempt by a more developed field (strategic management) against a less developed counterpart (entrepreneurship). We see things in a more positive light, because each field has much to learn from the other. Consistent with this, the modern manager would be advised to think carefully about entrepreneurial alertness, innovation, and judgment, even within the context of existing practices, products, and business units. Uncertainty and novelty are hardly the domain of a few industries or business practices but are ubiquitous in an advanced industrial economy. Likewise, managers of new and small firms must consider the core questions of strategic positioning, organizational design, and contracting that are central to processes of creating and capturing economic value. The strategist needs the entrepreneur, and the entrepreneur needs the strategist.

Peter G. Klein, Jay B. Barney, and Nicolai J. Foss

See also Business Policy and Corporate Strategy; Competitive Advantage; Dynamic Capabilities; Entrepreneurial Opportunities; Entrepreneurial Orientation; Hypercompetition; Resource-Based View of the Firm

Further Readings

Ahuja, G., & Lampert, C. M. (2001). Entrepreneurship in the large corporation: A longitudinal study of how established firms create breakthrough inventions. *Strategic Management Journal, 22,* 521–543.

Alvarez, S., & Barney, J. (2004). Organizing rent generation and appropriation: Toward a theory of the entrepreneurial firm. *Journal of Business Venturing, 19*(5), 621–635.

Baker, T., & Pollock, T. G. (2007). Making the marriage work: The benefits of strategy's takeover of entrepreneurship for strategic organization. *Strategic Organization, 5,* 297–312.

Burgelman, R. A. (1983). Corporate entrepreneurship and strategic management: Insights from a process study. *Management Science, 29,* 1349–1364.

Foss, N. J., & Klein, P. G. (2012). *Organizing entrepreneurial judgment.* Cambridge, England: Cambridge University Press.

Hitt, M. A., Ireland, R. D., Camp, S. M., & Sexton, D. L. (2002). *Strategic entrepreneurship: Creating a new mindset.* Malden, MA: Blackwell.

Ireland, R. D., Hitt, M. A., & Sirmon, D. G. (2003). A model of strategic entrepreneurship: The construct and its dimensions. *Journal of Management, 29,* 963–989.

Rumelt, R. P. (1987). Theory, strategy, and entrepreneurship. In D. Teece (Ed.), *The competitive challenge* (pp. 11–32). Cambridge, MA: Ballinger.

STRATEGIC FLEXIBILITY

The idea of strategic flexibility has been discussed in various areas, including, economics, strategic management, organization theory, decision analysis, and information technology. Strategic flexibility can be defined as an organization's capability to identify major changes in the external environment (e.g., introduction of disruptive technologies), to quickly commit resources to new courses of action in response to the change, and to recognize and act promptly when it is time to halt or reverse such resource commitments. Here, strategic flexibility is discussed in relation to a fundamental dilemma managers are faced with: commitment versus change. Understanding the dilemma and how to deal with it and maintain strategic flexibility is critical for managers.

Fundamentals

Key Ideas of Strategic Flexibility

Strategic flexibility is composed of three key components: attention, assessment, and action. To the extent that an organization and its top managers are (1) paying attention to information that indicates change of the external environment, (2) objectively assessing the implication of the information, and (3) timely initiating an action corresponding to the assessment of the information, an organization is likely to avoid making too slow or too hasty decisions.

Under a rapidly changing and globalizing environment, it is increasingly important for an organization to change its strategy and adapt to new environments quickly. However, organizations, particularly those that have experienced success, are often slow to respond to change because of organizational inertia. In this sense, strategic flexibility is frequently associated with ideas such as agility, quickness, and responsiveness.

However, quickness per se will not provide an organization a competitive advantage. New initiatives encounter various types of problems and challenges in their implementation that must be overcome for success to be achieved. Only with strong commitment and patience can an organization enjoy the fruits of its success. Thus, strategic flexibility should not simply be equated with rapid change. Instead, strategic flexibility is an organization's capability to deal with the dilemma of commitment versus change. Correctly balancing commitment and timely change should contribute to sustainable positive performance. At the same time, achieving the correct balance is undoubtedly challenging. Abandonment of an initiative too quickly because of initial problems may result in the loss of future potential benefits, while overly strong commitment to a money-losing project will only exacerbate problems. Even if a strategy is successful at one point in time, current success does not guarantee the long-term success of an organization. This is partly due to organizational inertia, which we discuss below.

Commitment and Organizational Inertia

Once a particular strategy becomes successful, an organization can develop consistent structures and systems to further enhance the implementation of the successful strategy. By accumulating knowledge (or know-how) from experiential learning, an organization is able to implement the strategy more effectively and efficiently. The organization, its outputs (i.e., services and products), and financial performance will become more reliable and predictable. This organizational self-enhancing tendency to further commit to a current strategy and a current way of doing things is often referred to as *organizational inertia*.

Although organizational inertia has positive effects on performance when the environment is stable and the strategy is successful, organizational inertia also becomes a barrier to change. Two major factors cause an organization's resistance to change: psychological commitment and institutionalized structures and systems. The former, which

is often called *cognitive inertia,* is a mental schema or perspective that managers develop through their experiences. The perspective is self-reinforcing such that successful experience leads to an understanding of information consistent with the developed perspective and compels managers to ignore new but potentially important information. In many cases, the perspective of top management is shared and taken for granted within the organization.

The second factor, a more structural and organizational factor that causes resistance to change, is called *structural inertia.* When organizations become older and larger, the organizational structures and systems become more complex. The structures and systems also become tightly interrelated over time, developing a set of structure that is hard to untangle. Moreover, under such structures and systems, the same type of information is collected using the same methods, and the information collected will be analyzed using the same taken-for-granted assumptions. In this way, cognitive inertia and structural inertia reinforce each other. It is difficult and costly to change such structures and systems once these are institutionalized.

In this sense, an organization faces an ongoing dilemma in relation to commitment and change. First, an organization needs to commit itself to implementing a new strategy that almost always accompanies unexpected problems and challenges. Without commitment, even a potentially great strategy may be regarded as defective. Yet commitment to a wrong strategy leads to a waste of resources and future deterioration of performance. Second, once a strategy is successful, an organization reinforces its structures and systems to more efficiently implement the successful strategy. In this process, both cognitive inertia and structural inertia often arise and make the organization insensitive to new information derived from changing environments. To overcome this problem and strike a fine balance between commitment and change, an organization needs strategic flexibility.

Importance

How can an organization obtain strategic flexibility? Although there is no panacea for such a fundamentally crucial dilemma, researchers provide various suggestions. Such suggestions can be categorized into four major approaches: (1) strategic approach,

(2) structural approach, (3) contextual approach, and (4) top management approach. These are not mutually exclusive, and an organization can adopt multiple approaches simultaneously. The basic assumption behind these approaches is that an organization has a natural tendency to become short-sighted, rigid, and efficiency oriented by decreasing the number of alternatives. Organizations inherently prefer stability and certainty to uncertainty; thus new initiatives and changes are often undercommitted or postponed. To counter such a tendency, an organization proactively needs to set mechanisms to encourage new trials (experiments) and increase the number of alternatives.

Strategic Approach

By investing a small amount, an organization can buy future options (i.e., postpone a decision) to further commit or abandon the small investment until uncertainty becomes lower; these are called *real options*. For example, developing a joint-venture with a certain partner can be a real option because it maintains the possibility of acquiring the partner later. Instead of gambling on one decision, an organization can learn from the small-decision outcomes and use the learning for subsequent decisions. It is notable that assessing a particular option objectively and deciding to abandon is difficult. Comparing multiple alternatives will help managers decide resource allocation. Thus, the real value of this approach will be realized when an organization has a diverse set of alternatives that can not only be compared with each other but that also are responsive to various environmental changes and conditions.

Structural Approach

An organization can set a structure to obtain strategic flexibility—that is, simultaneously efficient in the management in the current business environments while also sensitive to changes in the environment. An organization with such a structural capability is sometimes called *structurally ambidextrous*. As discussed, structural inertia is enhanced when an organization becomes large. Moreover, the relationship between individuals' roles and performance is often ambiguous in a large organization, which results in less ownership and creative thinking. By making organizational units smaller and providing autonomy, each unit

will become less complicated, and it is easier to initiate something new. With autonomy, each unit is encouraged to take a risk and try something new, in addition to what they have now. Obviously, to enjoy economies of scale, such small units need to be coordinated by headquarters when necessary. When an organization needs to focus on implementing current strategy, it is difficult to spend time and energy on something new simultaneously. One way to deal with the problem is to set a different entity, such as a subsidiary or a joint venture with other firms. Such a different entity can be set to explore new strategic opportunities. Although it is also possible to set autonomous units dedicated to new and explorative work within the current organization, existing organizational systems such as culture and reward systems may create conflicts between the autonomous unit and other units. Rather than fully institutionalizing organizational structures and systems, an organization can maintain strategic flexibility by intentionally allowing some room or redundancy for new actions. Some examples of such semi-structures are temporary assignments, prototyping rather than formal planning, and forming alliances rather than relying on internal development.

Contextual Approach

Besides formal structures and systems, informal contexts also matter by setting organizational climate. To encourage organizational members to be both efficient/exploitation oriented and effective/long-term explorative, a context that is both tight and loose should be developed. An example is an organization in which achieving performance goals is absolutely a must, but the means to achieving the goals can be totally up to individual members. To develop such a climate, researchers suggest there are two important factors. One is discipline and stretch. Unless higher goals are strongly expected, individual members will neither pursue performance vigorously nor think creatively and take new risky alternatives. To share such high expectations among organizational members, strong discipline is needed, for example, by replacing managers who cannot meet the expectations. The other factor is support and trust. To demand high performance and risk taking, an organization needs to provide various types of support for individuals. Moreover, unless trust is developed, individual members will behave independently, failing to cooperate and come up with organizational-level alternatives. Given that new initiatives involve many unexpected problems, support and trust also help organizational members to share information and learn from each other's problems and mistakes.

Top Management Approach

It is important for top managers to be open to new ideas while rigorously implementing the current strategy. Many organizations use team-based decision making that enhances the opportunity to incorporate different perspectives into decisions. Team-based decision-making processes also create means for a check-and-balance process to the chief executive officer's opinions. However, teams are subject to groupthink whereby team members focus more on harmony and consensus within the group than on the quality of the decisions. Accordingly, team decision-making processes need to be carefully designed to avoid this problem and to achieve maximum effectiveness. Researchers have suggested two methods to assist team decision making. First, the value of a team-based approach can be best derived from the diversity of the members' perspectives and experiences. This diversity is formally emphasized when a member of the top management team is designated as a devil's advocate. The role of the devil's advocate is to question the assumptions and alternatives presented. In this way, alternative solutions are analyzed more completely and from many different vantage points. Such an approach can be particularly effective when a decision-making team is relatively homogenous. The CEO should build a nurturing organizational culture that encourages open communications. Second, establishing an organizational system that regularly receives new ideas and infuses new perspectives from outside the firm can provide a "wake-up call" to managers. An external perspective helps managers to be more sensitive to negative feedback by questioning assumptions regarding previous successful experiences, to change the group dynamics within the top management team, and to stimulate the development of new routines. Such systems include obtaining managers from outside and creating a joint venture with other organizations.

Katsuhiko Shimizu

See also Behavioral Theory of the Firm; Escalation of Commitment; Managerial Decision Biases; Strategic Decision Making

Further Readings

Adner, R., & Levinthal, D. L. (2004). What is not a real option: Considering boundaries for the application of real options to business strategy. *Academy of Management Review, 29,* 74–85.

Eisenhardt, K. M., Furr, N. R., & Bingham, C. B. (2010). Microfoundations of performance: Balancing efficiency and flexibility in dynamic environment. *Organization Science, 21,* 1263–1273.

Gibson, C. B., & Birkinshaw, J. (2004). The antecedents, consequences, and mediating role of organizational ambidexterity. *Academy of Management Journal, 47,* 209–226.

Hannan, M., & Freeman, J. (1984). Structural inertia and organizational change, *American Sociological Review, 49,* 149–164.

March, J. G. (1991). Exploration and exploitation in organizational learning. *Organization Science, 2,* 71–87.

Shimizu, K., & Hitt, M. A. (2004). Strategic flexibility: Organizational preparedness to reverse ineffective strategic decisions. *Academy of Management Executive, 18*(4), 44–59.

Tushman, M. L., & O'Reilly, C. A. III. (1996). Ambidextrous organizations: Managing evolutionary and revolutionary change. *California Management Review, 38*(4), 8–30.

STRATEGIC FRAMES

A cognitive frame organizes individual thought and influences action. It directs attention in a world of overwhelming stimuli and potentially influences further analysis and action by the framer and those the frame affects. A *strategic* frame is intended to similarly organize and affect a collective. Frames are the product of both invention and experience, and thus, they are influenced by social structures and situated history. They also reflect individual and group will and values. The concept cannot account for action by itself, but it is an important construct for understanding cognition's role in purposeful individual and organizational activities. It is especially useful for considering how new opportunities are developed and contested. This entry summarizes key aspects of strategic frames and makes the case for the construct's usefulness to theory and practice. It discusses the difference between schema theories and frame theories and draws a distinction between sensemaking and entrepreneurial frames. Strategic frames found in recent discussions about and by entrepreneurs are used to illustrate how the theory can be used. We particularly emphasize strategic framing as fertile ground for research and practice because of its capacity for prospective reasoning.

Fundamentals

It is important to distinguish frame and framing from two other cognitive concepts: schema and sensemaking. We believe that there is necessary overlap among these concepts, but confusion has been created by changes in academic emphasis over time and overlapping definitions that blur important distinctions.

Helpful clarification comes from linking the academic definition of a frame to the way the word is used in day-to-day conversation. A picture frame protects and draws attention to something interesting and valuable. The frame of a new building establishes its dimensions and is a scaffold to which other components are added over time. Speeches, political publications, and other communications are said to be more or less successful in framing convincing arguments. Many people reframe their plans as they consider such appeals, perceive changes in available resources, or analyze outcomes of their own and others' activities.

Organizational actors similarly protect and advance individual and group interests by proactively framing issues and events. Over time, the proffered frame is elaborated in an effort to more effectively influence other actors' activities. As with physical structures, it is difficult to change such strategic frames, but it is possible. Some frames are adopted and further developed by others, while many other efforts languish. Thus, framing is an ongoing strategic process, made complex and interesting by the interaction of purposeful intellectual activity with other phenomena (content decisions, social structures, available resources, emotions, etc.) of interest to researchers in strategic management and other areas of management research.

While early work sometimes defined frames and framing as delimiting attention and leading to bias in a way that is consistent with research on schema, recent research on frames and framing in different disciplines has emphasized agency. In the authors' view, this effort to define frame theory is still in process, but a promising metalogic is being developed across fields of inquiry that can be applied at different levels of analysis with varied methods. Those interested in the creation of social movements, for example, are paying attention to how frames are developed and aligned to mobilize individuals and groups with varied interests. The ethics and impact of framing by the media is an important topic in communication research and journalism. In addition, activists interested in affecting political decision making have used ideas about framing to change public and legislator opinions.

Some commonalities between older schema theories and frame theory still remain. Both theories address the difficulties of dealing with overwhelming information. The resulting frame or schema is conceived as strongly influenced by experience, especially experience interacting with others, and in both cases the phenomena is of interest because it guides perception and interpretation.

But there are also important differences in emphasis. Frame theories tend to focus on explicit knowledge; they are often used to understand agency's successes as well as failures. Frames are an interactive effort that changes over time, evoking the idea of the framework that helps organize the construction of a building. In contrast, schema theories tend to focus on less conscious social and cultural commonalities and search for bias and error that result from tacit assumptions.

In short, a frame is a distinct cognitive concept that (1) helps describe the genesis of efforts to protect and develop a desired state of affairs and (2) provides a scaffold for agency that can be modified over time. This work frequently addresses the requirements for change, including the need to bend or destroy existing frames. Many efforts also link cognition to other phenomena of interest. Research has shown, for example, that competitors have an impact on strategic frames. Other studies suggest that interactions with information technology, product prototypes, and other artifacts affect the way opportunities are framed.

Much of this research has important overlaps with research on sensemaking. Karl Weick's work is very influential in defining this domain, along with research on sensegiving initiated by Dennis Gioia and Kumar Chittipeddi. Both sensemaking/ sensegiving and framing are about purposeful labeling, not only for individual understanding but often for attempts to influence others. The distinctive contributions of framing, however, are apparent when actors try to create something novel.

The distinction between sensemaking and framing in an entrepreneurial context is exemplified by contrasting the sensemaking perspective presented by Karl Weick and his colleagues with work on "effectuation" by Saras Sarasvathy and her colleagues, which we believe is an important example of framing. A distinction in these two bodies of research and theory development involves their focus. Sensemaking and sensegiving focus on dealing with ambiguity by bracketing stimuli; effectuation emphasizes experimentation that creates opportunity. As a result of these differences, an important effect of entrepreneurial framing is that it reinforces and creates flux, while sensemaking organizes flux.

More generally, these and other comparisons lead us to suggest that theories about strategic framing are especially important for understanding invention and innovation. Theories about schema and sensemaking are rooted in the past. While the past has a role to play in most cognition, the more unique contribution of framing theory is to direct attention to future agendas for action.

Importance

Examples of Strategic Framing

It is interesting to illustrate the process of framing new ideas with a short look at studies of entrepreneurship. Early work in this area struggled to differentiate the field from strategic management, organizational behavior, and other areas of inquiry. Arguably, entrepreneurship began to coalesce as a separate area of research in response to the strategic framing proposal by Sankaran Venkataraman and others that its distinctive domain was the discovery, evaluation, and exploitation of opportunities and, more specifically, the role of individuals in opportunity development.

Entrepreneurship research (in fact, all research) can be summarized as the result of continuing framing "contests." One contest involves the further definition of opportunities and whether they are created or discovered. Yolanda Sarason and her colleagues suggest these disagreements are based on opposing ontological stands. One group argues that opportunities are features of the environment; the other group believes that opportunities are inseparable from the entrepreneur.

A further framing contest can be found in the emerging domain of social entrepreneurship. Tina Dacin and her colleagues argue that social entrepreneurship is not significantly different from financially focused entrepreneurship, and thus established definitions and theories are sufficient. These scholars suggest that the definition of entrepreneurship encompasses social entrepreneurship and that value creation and institutional efficiency explain all successful entrepreneurship. In contrast, Tom Dean and his colleagues have argued that social entrepreneurship represents conditions of market failure or institutional voids and that the focus should be on the prioritization of social value over personal wealth. Both frames are discussed by social entrepreneurs themselves; some argue that doing good is the best way of doing well, whereas others pay little attention to financial reward.

Clearly, each strategic frame we have identified will, if accepted, guide further action by either researcher or manager. They highlight and protect key ideas, just as a picture frame would. But they are also open enough to invite addition and even related modification, just as the framework of a building in process would. Shared experience, including experience by those with little patience for intellectual argument, is an important backdrop. Frames are not primarily about organizing "facts." They tend to consider multiple subjects and involve multiple levels of analysis. In the words of Gregory Bateson, a pioneer in the field, frames are "messages about messages." Disagreements are important in the further evolution of messages/frames.

Implications of Strategic Framing

The nature of different agendas and possibilities for resolving them, if any, can be better understood by considering the relationship between schema, sensemaking, and frames. Many largely unacknowledged schema act as the necessary backdrop for strategic framing. If the actors involved have some social links and are operating in contexts with some overlap, there will be some overlap in schema. This overlap supports the likely overlap in sensemaking and strategic frames as well. We propose that sensemaking about surprise and the unsatisfactory are important but distinct from strategically framing arguments for action.

Even the passive cannot avoid using schema, whether they are recognized or not, because schema facilitate simplifying interpretation of a world that offers overwhelming stimuli. The more conscious processing that sensemaking and framing require builds on but goes beyond schema. Sensemaking research on the actions of firefighters, emergency room doctors, airline pilots, and others leads to suggestions for more effective action. But this work essentially puts a black box around the move to action. Recent discussions of framing in various social science disciplines help us understand volition and its agendas.

Framing is necessary to act because of limited cognitive capacity but also because of the requirements for organizing action. The more novel the situation, the more distracting and biasing schemas and sensemaking can be for individuals in organizations. Frames are about interpretations that proactively protect and advance the interests of a specific individual or group. They are about efforts to change not just understanding but also activity.

Attention to the frame is especially important when actors try to develop the new opportunities widely sought by individuals, companies, industries, and governments. Radical innovations require taking a significant step away from past experience. Strategic frames and the process of strategic framing inform this process.

Anne Sigismund Huff and
Yolanda Sarason

See also Entrepreneurial Cognition; Entrepreneurial Effectuation; Schemas Theory; Sensemaking; Social Cognitive Theory; Social Entrepreneurship

Further Readings

Bateson, G. (2000). *Steps to an ecology of mind*. Chicago, IL: University of Chicago Press. (Original work published 1955)

Dacin, P. A., Dacin, M. T., & Matear, M. (2010). Social entrepreneurship: Why we don't need a new theory and how we move forward from here. *Academy of Management Perspectives, 24*(3), 37–57.

Dean, T. J., & McMullen, J. (2007). Toward a theory of sustainable entrepreneurship. *Journal of Business Venturing, 22*(1), 50–76.

Gioia, D., & Chittipeddi, K. (1991). Sensemaking and sensegiving in strategic change initiation. *Strategic Management Journal, 12,* 433–448.

Huff, A. S. (1982). Industry influences on strategy reformulation. *Strategic Management Journal, 3,* 119–130.

Kaplan, S. (2008). Framing contests. *Organization Science, 19*(5), 729–752.

Sarason, Y., Dean, T., & Dillard, J. (2006). Entrepreneurship as the nexus of individual and opportunity: A structuration perspective. *Journal of Business Venturing, 21,* 286–305.

Sarasvathy, S. (2001). Causation and effectuation: Toward a theoretical shift from economic inevitability to entrepreneurial contingency. *Academy of Management Review, 26*(2), 243–263.

Venkataraman, S., Sarasvathy, S. D., Dew, N., & Forster, W. R. (2012). Whither the promise? Moving forward with entrepreneurship as a science of the artificial. *Academy of Management Review, 37,* 1.

Weick, K., Sutcliffe, K. M., & Obstfeld, D. (2005). Organizing and processes of sensemaking. *Organizational Science, 16*(4), 409–421.

STRATEGIC GROUPS

A strategic group, as defined by Michael Porter in 1979, is a set of firms within an industry that compete based on a similar set of strategies. There could be several strategic groups within an industry. For example, in the automotive industry, there could be strategic groups based on compact cars, luxury cars, electric cars, and so on. Likewise, in the pharmaceutical industry, there could be strategic groups based on whether firms compete in the market for generic drugs or branded drugs. There is a greater level of competition between firms within a strategic group than between strategic groups. Thus, strategic groups are important because they define the domain of competition within an industry. This entry discusses the origin of strategic groups in the management literature, the key theoretical approaches used to explain strategic groups, and the implications of strategic groups for firm behavior.

Fundamentals

The term *strategic group* was first coined in 1972 by Michael S. Hunt, who suggested that firms within an industry use heterogeneous survival strategies. Since then, a number of studies from the industrial organization (IO) economics stream have examined the existence of strategic groups in different industries. More recently, scholars have used managerial cognition and organizational ecology as the theoretical foundations to study strategic groups. The managerial cognition theory suggests that managers tend to focus on certain firms in an industry most similar to their own firms, resulting in a strategic group. Organizational ecology scholars suggest that the patterns of competition and population dynamics within an industry vary for different groups of firms. In spite of these advances, the theoretical foundation for study of strategic groups remains weak.

On the basis of the managerial cognition theory, some scholars have suggested the concept of strategic group identity to explain the emergence of strategic groups in an industry and the consequences of the same for firm behaviors and outcomes. According to Margaret Peteraf and Mark Shanley, strategic group identity refers to a set of mutual understandings, among members of a cognitive intraindustry group, regarding the central, enduring, and distinctive characteristics of the group. The strategic group identity is developed based on the interactions among social learning, social identification, economic forces, and historical and institutional forces. The emergence and persistence of a strategic group depends on the strength of the strategic group identity.

Based on the IO literature as outlined by J. Lee, K. Lee, and S. Rho, scholars have identified four sets of factors that make the basis to analyze the emergence and persistence of strategic groups: mobility barriers, strategic interactions, firm rivalry, and dynamic capabilities. Mobility barriers across strategic groups limit the extent of imitation and entry by members of different strategic groups. As a consequence, some strategic groups are able to maintain a higher level of profitability compared to others. The mobility barriers could arise as a result of huge investments in innovation and advertising and the path of dependency in developing such capabilities. Strategic interactions occur by way of collusion between firms within a strategic group and may help sustain the group by limiting entry by imitators. With respect to firm rivalry, there are two competing views. One view suggests that there is less rivalry between firms within a group than across groups. This is because firms within a strategic group have mutual dependence and use tacit collusion to maintain the entry barriers and superior performance. The other view suggests that there is a greater level of rivalry between firms within a group than with firms outside a group. The very existence of mobility barriers implies that firms within a strategic group do not need to be concerned about competition with firms outside the strategic group. There is no conclusive empirical evidence about which of the above holds true. Finally, dynamic capabilities are the capabilities that firms need to sustain their competitive advantage. For a strategic group to remain differentiated from another strategic group and maintain a higher level of performance, the firms within this strategic group need to rely on dynamic capabilities.

Strategic groups can be used to analyze the competitive structure within an industry. Formation of a strategic group within an industry is hindered by high mobility barriers, high level of rivalry, and low resources. However, once formed, strategic groups tend to persist, making them a useful tool for industry analysis. Firms within a strategic group may consider multiple dimensions in their strategic decision making. These include product range and quality, pricing and promotion strategies, distribution channels, innovation, and customer service. Firms within a strategic group may be similar to others in one or more of these dimensions, which in turn determine the strategies that firms adopt to compete and survive.

One can develop a map of a firm's competitive actions and reactions along one or several of the strategic dimensions identified above to understand an industry's competitive structure. Such a map for multiple firms can help identify a group of firms that use similar strategies to compete with each other, thus forming a strategic group. Using this map, one can also identify the dimensions on which multiple strategic groups within an industry differ with each other. A commonly used statistical technique for such analysis is cluster analysis, which groups firms in different clusters based on pre-identified criteria.

Strategic groups have several implications for firm behavior. By identifying the set of firms most closely related to each other and analyzing each other's strategic actions, members of a strategic group can formulate their own strategies to remain competitive. These firms usually serve the same set of customers, with similar product and service offerings. Firms can also identify the strategic distance between their own strategic group and other strategic groups and predict future competitors. Finally, strategic group mapping can be used to find unexplored opportunities for growth and potential challenges in sustaining competitive advantage.

Ajai Gaur

See also Hypercompetition; Interorganizational Networks; Social Cognitive Theory; SWOT Analysis Framework; Theory of Cooperation and Competition

Further Readings

Hunt M. (1972). *Competition in the major home appliance industry 1960–70* (Unpublished doctoral dissertation). Harvard University, Cambridge, MA.

Lee, J., Lee, K., & Rho, S. (2002). An evolutional perspective on strategic group emergence: A genetic algorithm-based model. *Strategic Management Journal, 23,* 727–746.

McNamara, G., Deephouse, D. L., & Luce, R. A. (2003). Competitive positioning within and across a strategic groups structure: The performance of core, secondary, and solitary firms. *Strategic Management Journal, 24*(2), 161–181.

Peteraf, M., & Shanley, M. (1997, Summer). Getting to know you: A theory of strategic group identity. *Strategic Management Journal, 18*(Special issue), 165–186.

Porter, M. E. (1979). The structure within industries and company performance. *Review of Economics and Statistics, 61,* 214–227.

Strategic Information Systems

Although information technology (IT) first entered organizations in the early 1950s, it was only in the late 1970s that IT, or more specifically information, began to emerge as a resource that could be considered strategic and harnessed in the pursuit of competitive advantage. Driven on by this realization, organizations began to proactively seek out opportunities to exploit information using IT in ways that enabled them to differentiate themselves from competitors. Early examples were American Airlines (with their SABRE booking and airline seat inventory management system), Baxter Healthcare (with their ASAP online ordering system permitting hospitals to place orders electronically), and Otis Elevators (with Otisline, where problems with elevators were automatically diagnosed and elevators automatically "phoned" an engineer dispatch center) that deployed IT in ways that enabled Otis to enjoy a competitive advantage over their competitors. These applications of IT were referred to as *strategic information systems* (SIS). In this entry, the fundamentals of SIS are outlined. How the concept has evolved is described, the life cycle of IT investments is illuminated, and the latest contemporary thinking is presented.

Fundamentals

Early applications of IT in organizations automated existing work practices and processes, particularly clerical work in the accounting area (e.g., payroll and general ledger). Because they processed transactions (debits, credits, hours worked, tax deductions, orders, invoices, etc.), they were typically referred to as *transaction processing systems* (TPS). There was also a realization that such systems generated information (data) as a by-product—sometimes vast amounts—that could be potentially of value to the management of an organization, particularly if aggregated. This led to the concept of a management information system (MIS) emerging. This was also the time when organizations looked to develop what they referred to as decisions support systems (DSS) to support the decision-making processes of management. Rather than merely presenting information from TPS as an MIS did, these systems enabled managers to combine this information with emerging modeling capability to ask "what-if" questions, build financial and operational models, and simulate scenarios. Despite these developments, IT was generally considered as a tool to support ongoing business operations.

In contrast, SIS are fundamental to the execution of a business strategy. Indeed, they provide the organization with the basis for competitive advantage. Any application of IT underpinning an organization's business model can be considered as a strategic information system. This is particularly true where executing the business model would not be possible without IT. It is important to note that strategic does not mean using leading-edge technology: What is crucial is the purpose for which technology is applied. There are many examples of SIS that use technology that has been around for many years but apply it in a novel way.

To capitalize on the potential of information and IT, and to identify SIS, executives seek to align their organizations, investment in IT with the strategy of the organization. Often referred to as strategic information systems planning (SISP), this is a systematic process that usually begins with the strategy of the organization and seeks to determine its information and systems requirements. There are many proprietary approaches to SISP, particularly those developed by management consultancy practices, as well as tools to support the process for building the information systems (IS) strategy. Research has also identified the factors that contribute to alignment, and these include senior executive support for IT, chief information officer (CIO) involved in strategy development, strong business-IT partnership, and well-prioritized IT investments.

The problem with alignment is that as a process it begins with the business strategy, where the challenge is to align the IT investment portfolio to this strategy. It typically doesn't take into account that technology could potentially drive strategy—that is, create a strategy that would not be possible without IT. This is where IT becomes the source of innovation: business model innovation, product/service innovation, process innovation, innovation in the customer experience, or management innovations.

Not exploiting the innovative opportunities provided by IT reflects the fact that in many organizations, the CIO/IT director may not be directly involved in the strategy formulation process. Additionally, the low level of "digital literacy" within the leadership team building the strategy generally results in its being unable to conceive of strategic opportunities provided by IT. The duality of IT is that it not only *enables* the strategy of an organization, it can also *shape* the strategy. Coevolution rather than alignment is the more contemporary proposition that seeks out alignment as well as innovation, with both the business and IS strategies coevolving with each other.

Of course, organizations will make different kinds of investments in IT, not all of which will be strategic. One way to categorize these investments is to consider the contribution they make to achieving the strategy of the business. Each investment will fit into one of four categories:

- *Strategic*—investments in IT applications that are *critical* to sustaining future business strategy. Strategic investments are often confused with large and expensive. The definition relates to the contribution to strategy; as a result, what is positioned here will differ from organization to organization.
- *Key operational*—investments in IT applications on which the organization *currently depends* for success. That is, if they were switched off, significant and immediate loss would result. These are often referred to as the systems: electronic point-of-sale, warehousing, credit card authorization, website for ordering, supply chain, and so on.
- *Support*—investments in IT applications that are *valuable but not critical* to success. There may be dozens or hundreds of these, and they often soak up far too much time and money.
- *High potential*—investments in IT applications that *may* be important in achieving future success. These are often neglected. Included here are business R & D and technology experimentation to identify potentially applications.

Investments in *strategic* and *high potential* applications are about gaining advantage. IT investments in *key operational* and *support* applications are about avoiding disadvantage.

It is unlikely that an SIS will stay strategic for very long. Although organizations may gain some "first-mover advantage" with an innovative application, it can be quickly copied and does not produce an advantage that is sustainable, particularly when patent protection for IS applications is almost nonexistent and where keeping an IS innovation secret is difficult, especially for systems used by customers or suppliers. Applications thus have a life cycle that often sees them begin in high potential, where the idea and innovation and its potential is identified and piloted, through to strategic, where the advantage is achieved, and then to key operational and/or support were they no longer provide any competitive advantage as competitors have made similar investments, but can be still fundamental to the workings of the organization.

Few organizations continuously derive advantage from their IT investments and most examples that one reads about tend to be one-offs, which the organization fails to repeat. Even the early examples of SIS quoted above were often due to luck rather than any rigorous analysis. Consequently, there is a realization that organizations today must develop an IS capability: an ongoing ability to both harness IT as well as leverage competitive opportunities to identify SIS. This capability is less about technology and more about the quality of management and the processes that they put in place.

Joe Peppard

See also Decision Support Systems; *Practice of Management, The;* Strategies for Change

Further Readings

Earl, M. J. (1993). Experiences in strategic information systems planning. *MIS Quarterly, 17,* 1–24.

Keen, P. G. W. (1993). Information technology and the management difference: A fusion map. *IBM Systems Journal, 32*(1), 17–39.

Kettinger, W., Grover, V., Guha S., & Segars, A. H. (1994). Strategic information systems revisited: A study in sustainability and performance. *MIS Quarterly, 18,* 31–58.

King, W. R., & Teo, T. S. H. (1996). Key dimensions of facilitators and inhibitors for the strategic use of information technology. *Journal of Management Information Systems, 12*(4), 35–53.

Mata, J. F., Fuerst, W. L., & Barney, J. B. (1995). Information technology and sustained competitive advantage: A resource-based analysis. *MIS Quarterly, 19,* 487–505.

Peppard, J., & Ward, J. (2004). Beyond strategic information systems: Towards an IS capability. *Journal of Strategic Information Systems, 13,* 167–194.

Piccoli, G., & Ives, B. (2005). IT-dependent strategic initiatives and sustained competitive advantage: A review and synthesis of the literature. *MIS Quarterly, 29,* 747–776.

Porter, M. E., & Miller, V. (1985). How information gives you a competitive advantage. *Harvard Business Review, 63*(4), 149–160.

Ward, J., & Peppard, J. (2002). *Strategic planning for information systems.* Chichester, England: John Wiley.

Wiseman, C. (1985). *Strategy and computers: Information systems as competitive weapons.* Homewood, IL: Dow-Jones Irwin.

Strategic International Human Resource Management

Broadly speaking, strategic international human resource management (SIHRM) is about the management of human resources consistent with the strategic direction of the multinational enterprise in a dynamic, interconnected, and highly competitive global environment. More specifically, SIHRM is about understanding, researching, applying, and revising all human resource activities in their internal and external contexts since they impact the processes of managing human resources in organizations throughout the global environment to enhance the experience of multiple stakeholders. The purpose of SIHRM is to enable the firm, the multinational enterprise (MNE) regardless of size, to be successful globally. SIHRM for many firms can be critical to their success, and effective SIHRM can make the difference between survival and extinction for many MNEs. The following sections of this entry review the fundamentals of the components of SIHRM.

Fundamentals

Because SIHRM reflects so many components, it is helpful to use an integrative framework to describe the five major factors of SIHRM: (1) strategic MNE factor; (2) exogenous factor; (3) endogenous factor; (4) SIHRM policies, practices, and issues; and (5) MNE effectiveness. Taken as a whole, this framework incorporates the numerous contributions of the frameworks, models, and theoretical perspectives of many authors in SIHRM.

Strategic MNE Factor

As is true for firms operating in a single country or region, MNEs strive to develop SIHRM systems that fit the contours of the realities of MNEs and their present context—a global context that is much more complex, multifaceted, uncertain, and even chaotic than ever before. This implies that strategic international human resource management involves an understanding of the environments of MNEs and the management of the MNE's inter-unit linkages as well as the concern for alignment. Understanding the environments requires that SIHRM continually monitor the external and internal contextual

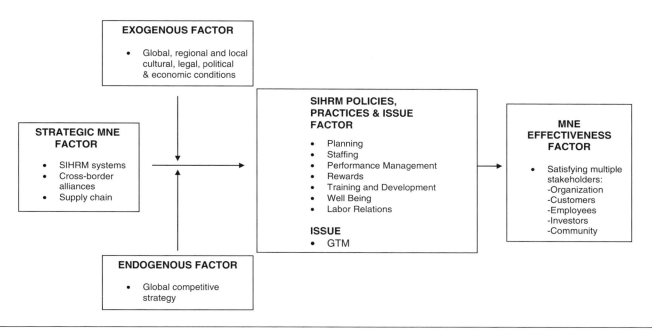

Figure 1   Integrative Framework of Strategic International Human Resource Management

Source: Adapted from Schuler, R. S., Dowling, P., & DeCieri, H. (1993). An integrative framework of strategic international human resource management. *International Journal of Human Resource Management, 4,* 722.

factors. Managing inter-unit linkages is needed to integrate, control, and coordinate the units of the MNE scattered throughout the globe. Concern for alignment includes concern for how the SIHRM policies and practices fit together and for the way the MNE and its units operate in concert with the laws, culture, society, politics, economy, and general environment of particular locations. This is developed further in the discussion under "Exogenous Factor."

As shown in Figure 1, an important strategic MNE factor is cross-border alliances (CBAs). An important challenge for MNEs and SIHRM is developing and managing CBAs. CBAs in general involve two or more firms agreeing to cooperate as partners in an arrangement that is expected to be mutually beneficial. Such an alliance can take the form of a complete merger or a creation of a third entity, an international joint venture (IJV).

As suggested earlier, all types of CBAs share varying amounts of complexity, which can become a barrier to three needs common to all forms of CBAs; the needs for organizational learning, economies and efficiencies, and control. Prior research suggests

that organizational learning is a key building block and major source of developing and sustaining a competitive advantage for MNEs as well as CBAs.

Another important need for CBAs is to develop and maintain managerial and organizational efficiencies and economies. These economies and efficiencies can result from combining operations, building upon the experiences of existing management, and taking advantage of the latest in technologies, such as when establishing a new facility. The third significant need for CBAs is to develop the ability to exercise control. In the absence of control, it can be challenging for partner firms to build conditions that maximize learning for itself and its partners. All three of these needs are served by effective SIHRM. As such, CBAs are no longer a peripheral activity of SIHRM, but a mainstay of competitive strategy and competitive advantage.

Other issues that have become increasingly important to MNEs and SIHRM and that could be discussed in detail include supply chain management and global talent management. Because of space constraints, we discuss only global talent management (see "SIHRM Policies, Practices, and Issues," below).

Exogenous Factor

SIHRM professionals are becoming more sensitive to variations in country conditions. Understanding and using this sensitivity are necessary challenges for MNEs, particularly in aligning their SIHRM systems with other elements of the global external environment, specifically, the legal, economic, cultural, political conditions in each country of operation.

A related challenge in SIHRM is developing a global approach to managing human resources that embraces a few universal principles that give the entire global system consistency while also allowing local and regional autonomy. Achieving the right balance between consistency and autonomy requires continual evaluation and discussion about which policies and practices can be global and which can or should be regional or even local. This can be a challenge because local conditions relevant to SIHRM practices vary so greatly. Thus as local units align their practices with local conditions they invariably find themselves having different HR practices across local and even regional units. Thus in attempting to get consistency across all units in how they manage their employees they either need to develop a common set of HR policies that can guide development of local HR practices, or develop a multilevel set of HR practices, some of which are common globally, such as performance management, and some of which are unique locally, such as labor relations. These considerations are further reflected in the section on "SIHRM Policies, Practices, and Issues."

Endogenous Factor

While a great deal of the earlier discussion of competitive advantage was most applicable to a domestic context, a more recent discussion of gaining competitive advantage in the global context has emerged. These authors suggest that "lasting" global competitive advantage from human resource management comes from developing SIHRM practices appropriate for an organization's specific context, including its culture, legal and political systems as presented under the Exogenous Factor. Additional bases of global competitive advantage come from (1) effectively using economies of scale and scope, (2) relocating operations around the world, and (3) transferring learning and knowledge across operations worldwide. All these bases of gaining global competitive advantage have distinctive implications for SIHRM.

Other endogenous factors that could be discussed here for their SIHRM implications include: headquarters decision-making orientation (centralization to decentralization), structure of international operations (regional to global), and the experience of management in operating an international enterprise (limited to extensive).

Importance

SIHRM Policies, Practices, and Issues

The several SIHRM policies and practices listed in Figure 1 represent those activities that multinational firms use in managing their human resources in the dynamic and interconnected global environment. The policies of these activities can be developed by SIHRM professionals to guide the units of an MNE around the world in their development of more specific SIHRM practices that reflect the local cultural, social, economic, legal, and political conditions. With the growing concern for talent management, MNEs around the world have developed many of these SIHRM policies and practices in a systematic, coordinated way in order to more effectively manage their global talent. Because of the importance of managing global talent effectively, it has become a major SIHRM issue over the past decade, and is likely to remain one in this decade.

The SIHRM issue of global talent management (GTM) is about planning, staffing, developing, appraising, compensating, reducing, locating, and even relocating human resources to obtain the right talent, at the right place, at the right time, and at the right price consistent with the strategic direction of the MNE. Besides GTM, other SIHRM issues that could be discussed here include managing relationships between headquarters and the globally dispersed units (high control to high autonomy), and balancing the need to blend in with the local conditions with the needs to have policies and practices consistent with the strategic and technological imperatives of the business (local sensitivity to strategic fit).

MNE Effectiveness

The importance of developing SIHRM systems that address the concerns of all key stakeholders is now becoming recognized around the world. Certainly, the organization itself, including all its subsidiary units, is a primary stakeholder, so it is appropriate to assess the impact of the SIHRM system against objectives such as improving productivity, improving profitability, sustainability and capability, and ensuring the organization's long-term survival in a multiple-country context.

Employers also recognize that organizational strategies that depend on total quality, innovation, and customer service cannot be met unless employees are willing to strive for the same goals on the organization's behalf

The effectiveness of a SIHRM system can also be assessed by showing its effects on customers. SIHRM practices can influence the quality and variety of products available to customers, the price at which those products can be purchased, the service received and so on. In a multiple-country context, analyzing and responding to customers' needs in several environments can constitute a successful competitive strategy in being local and global at the same time.

Other major stakeholders who can be affected by an MNE's SIHRM practices include suppliers and alliance partners in a multiple-country context. Through various forms of cooperative alliances, a company seeks to achieve goals common to all members of the alliance. Finally, the effects of an MNE's SIHRM practices on the local community and the broader society are being taken into account when assessing the effectiveness of SIHRM, moving beyond the sole concerns embodied in laws and regulations. An organizational assessment of SIHRM effectiveness that fails to consider its ability to reduce or prevent unethical or corrupt business practices in a multiple-country environment or to incorporate the impact on the environment may be inconsistent with today's thinking on SIHRM.

Overall, the framework offered here seems to be supported by the empirical work that has been done over the past twenty years. In considering their worldwide operations, managers would be well advised to include a methodological analysis of a variety of human resource management issues, for surely these will impact the success of the firm. Using the framework provided can be a helpful way to go about this analysis.

Randall S. Schuler

See also Balanced Scorecard; High-Performance Work Systems; Human Resource Management Strategies; Human Capital Theory

Further Readings

Briscoe, D., Schuler, R., & Tarique, I. (2012). *International human resource management* (4th ed). New York, NY: Routledge.

Budhwar, P., Schuler, R. S., and Sparrow, P. (Eds.). (2009). *Major works in international human resource management* (Vols. 1–4). London, England: Sage.

Schuler, R., & Jackson, S. (2005). A quarter-century review of human resource management in the U.S. The growth in importance of the international perspective. *Management Revue, 16,* 11–35.

Sparrow, P., Brewster, C., Budhwar, P., & DeCieri, H. (2013). *Globalizing human resource management* (2nd ed.). London, England: Routledge.

Tarique, I., & Schuler, R. (2010). Global talent management: Literature review, integrative framework, and suggestions for further research. *Journal of World Business, 45,* 122–133.

STRATEGIC PROFILES

Many firms, especially successful ones, have a clear and persistent manner of addressing their markets and broader environment. In this sense, the firm can be said to have a "strategy." Coupling strategy with other key organizational features such as capabilities, structures, processes, and management philosophies results in a firm's strategic profile. Having an accurate and comprehensive strategic profile is particularly useful in strategic planning and decision making when the firm evaluates its competitiveness in existing businesses while considering those businesses it might enter in the future. This entry describes how the profile concept originated, and how strategy and industry profiles are used to craft competitive strategies that fit their industrial circumstances.

Fundamentals

Research and writing about strategy moved to the fore in the management literature when improvements in planning and forecasting methods, quantitative operations management, and computers found their way into business firms. A number of academic books and articles were published in the post–World War II period that helped firms formulate effective business strategies. Three of the most prominent books were by H. Igor Ansoff (*Corporate Strategy*), Raymond E. Miles and Charles C. Snow (*Organizational Strategy, Structure, and Process*), and Michael E. Porter (*Competitive Strategy*).

Ansoff introduced the concept of a *profile*, which, he argues, can be useful in strategic decision making and planning. Specifically, he describes how a firm can use capability and competitor profiles to help determine the kinds of businesses the firm should seek to enter. By analyzing both the firm's internal and external environments, management can determine the gap between what the firm is currently doing and what it wants to do in the future, and a strategic plan can be formulated to close the gap.

Miles and Snow, whose studies included industries as diverse as college textbook publishing, hospitals, electronics, and food processing, identified three firm strategies that were effective in each of those industries: prospectors, defenders, and analyzers. Subsequent studies by other researchers showed that those strategies also were effective in a variety of other industries. As numerous researchers have documented, prospectors, defenders, and analyzers each have a specific profile (configuration) of key organizational characteristics such as capabilities, structures, and processes.

- *Prospectors* are firms that continually develop new products, services, technologies, and markets. They achieve success by moving first relative to their competitors, either by anticipating the market based on their research and development efforts or by building a market through their customer-relating capabilities. Prospectors compete through continuous innovation supported by managerial approaches that emphasize collaborative knowledge sharing within and across organizational levels.
- *Defenders* are firms with stable product or service lines that leverage their competence in developing process efficiencies. They search for economies of scale in markets that are predictable and expandable. Successful defenders tend to be the low-cost, high-volume producers of a limited product or service line.
- *Analyzers* are firms that use their applied engineering and manufacturing skills to make a new product better and cheaper, and they use their marketing skills to improve product sales.

Analyzers search for proven technologies with significant potential for generating new products and services. Analyzers' innovations tend to follow those of prospectors and usually result in higher quality and/or lower prices.

Various scholars have examined the Miles-Snow strategy typology's validity and reliability, the effectiveness of the typology compared to other prominent typologies, the functional attributes and performance of the strategy types in different industries and countries, the relationship of each strategy type to the firm's marketing orientation, and the extent of the typology's use.

Porter contributed to strategic planning and decision making by emphasizing the need for a firm to have an in-depth understanding of both its industry structure and competitors' behavior. His *five forces model* focuses on the competitive dynamics produced by interactions among a firm's customers, suppliers, competitors, and substitute products or services as well as the potential for new firms to enter the industry. Each of these forces affects a firm's ability to compete in a given market. Together, they determine the profit potential of an industry. Porter used industrial organization economics theory to develop a set of concepts and tools managers can use to perform industry and competitor analyses. Such analyses are the basis of the firm and competitor profiles used in strategic planning and decision making.

Using insights from these and related sources, managers can analyze their firm's current profile to determine the extent of the firm's internal and external *fit*. Internal fit is achieved when the firm's strategy is supported by appropriate capabilities, structures, and processes. External fit is achieved when the firm's strategic intentions have value in its industries and markets. Research shows that the dominant strategic profiles may shift as industries mature, with prospector strategies dominating when industries are new and analyzer and defender strategies dominating as the industry grows and matures.

Raymond E. Miles and Charles C. Snow

See also Behavioral Theory of the Firm; Business Policy and Corporate Strategy; Modes of Strategy: Planned-Emergent; Strategic Contingencies Theory; Strategic Frames; Strategy and Structure; Strategy-as-Practice

Further Readings

Ansoff, H. I. (1965). *Corporate strategy*. New York, NY: McGraw-Hill.

Ketchen, D. J., Thomas, J. B., & Snow, C. C. (1993). Organizational configurations and performance: A comparison of theoretical approaches. *Academy of Management Journal, 36,* 1278–1313.

Miles, G., Snow, C. C., & Sharfman, M. P. (1993). Industry variety and performance. *Strategic Management Journal, 14,* 163–177.

Miles, R. E., & Snow, C. C. (2003). *Organizational strategy, structure, and process* (with new foreword and introduction). New York, NY: McGraw-Hill. (Original work published 1978)

Porter, M. E. (1980). *Competitive strategy*. New York, NY: Free Press.

Snow, C. C., Fjeldstad, Ø. D., Lettl, C., & Miles, R. E. (2011). Organizing continuous product development and commercialization: The collaborative community of firms model. *Journal of Product Innovation Management, 28,* 3–16.

Strategies for Change

With an increasingly integrated global economy, the speed of change required for most organizations, particularly businesses, is greater than in the past. The ability to lead change is something now seen as a necessity for managers. Strategies for change can be defined as how to effectively lead/manage change within an organization. Undoubtedly, the leading change model has been the eight-stage framework developed by Harvard Business School (HBS) professor John Kotter. This entry focuses on the Kotter model as well as related key ideas about change that have proven themselves valuable to practicing managers.

Fundamentals

Leading Change: An Eight-Step Process of Change

During the 1980s and 1990s, John Kotter studied a number of leading techniques of the day used by managers to adapt to a changing market: quality management, reengineering, rightsizing, restructuring, cultural change, and turnaround. Their success rate was low; Kotter's question was, Why is it so low? From this work, Kotter identified the eight most common mistakes made during change that get in the way of success and, by turning them on their heads, came up with his eight-stage model:

1. *First and most important, establish a sense of urgency.* Although this may sound easy, many companies do not communicate sufficiently in the early stages to help their people understand the considerable need to change. Encouraging people to get out of their comfort zone also requires time; therefore, executives have to display patience in creating that sense of urgency. Another element is to help people see that they are on a "burning platform," metaphorically referring to an oil platform in the North Sea, where the only reason to jump into the frigid waters would be to avoid the worse fate of an oil platform fire. Over many years of working with firms with his model, Kotter came to see that this was the most critical step and published a book, *A Sense of Urgency,* in 2008, to help explain how to help people understand the need for change.

Communication is a big part in creating urgency. Kotter underlines that playing it too safe is risky because it will not drive people to see the need to change. He sums this idea up with a simple statistic: when 75% of all managers are convinced that the current state of affairs is no longer tolerable, the sense of urgency is sufficient.

A key part of the model is to distinguish between managing change and leading change: whereas management needs to keep control of the systemic consequences of the change process, the business's leadership needs to drive forward the organization to a different place. Change is doomed if there are only change managers and no change leaders.

2. *Create a powerful guiding coalition.* Here, we should not limit the change process to a handful of selected individuals. To be successful, the change process needs to be influenced by a number of key people across the hierarchy. It may well include powerful members of the union or even customers. Effective change teams often cut across the silos of an organization, such as marketing, research and development, manufacturing and service, and what Henry Mintzberg calls "slabs": that is, the different levels of hierarchy in an organization—frontline, middle, and executive management. Cross-functional and cross-hierarchy teams are very helpful.

3. *Develop a vision and strategy.* Going beyond the typical business plan, change needs an appealing vision. It often takes time to establish that vision, which needs to be followed by a strategy to implement it. Failure at this step often results from a multiplicity of plans and programs that lack vision. In contrast to mere methods and procedures, a vision rallies and inspires people.

4. *Communicate the vision widely, throughout the organization.* To implement the vision, considerable efforts of communication must be undertaken. The communication must be credible, shared by the whole senior executive team, and spread repetitively. It is easy for a vision to get lost in the clutter of organization life if it is not communicated again and again.

5. *Empower people to start to make it happen.* Obstacles can be everywhere: in the organizational structure of the company, in the minds of people, or in the form of one person blocking the way to renewal. These obstacles must be removed by change agents or the entire effort could potentially lose its credibility, and the organization will revert to its old way of doing things.

6. *Generate short-term wins.* To keep motivation up, the long-term goal needs to be attainable by setting a couple of short-term goals. When change takes a long time to implement, people's sense of urgency drops. Therefore, it is necessary to keep the pressure on by insisting on reaching multiple short-term goals. Achieving short-term wins encourages those on the fence to see that the need for change is real and to more fully commit their energy to the change effort.

7. *Consolidate change and do not let up.* Some declare victory too soon. Change takes time to become part of the organizational culture. Hence, declaring the effort a success too early can threaten the fragile progress. Even when the results seem clear, it takes years to ensure that the transformation will last. It is helpful to use the credibility earned with early wins to tackle the bigger problems right away. One cannot help thinking of former president George W. Bush on an aircraft carrier declaring "Mission Accomplished" too early in the process.

8. *Anchor change in the organization's culture:* The change process must result in an attitude of "that's the way we do things around here." Only if the transformation is no longer tied to a particular person who implemented and represented the effort will it be followed by future generations of executives. Therefore, even the next generation must be champions of change because they need to take over the legacy. The hardwiring of the organization's reward and motivational system, of who gets promoted, who gets featured in organizational magazines, the kind of new hires, and so on, reflect the anchoring of change in the organization.

The Beer Model: Harnessing the Power of the Middle

One of Kotter's colleagues at Harvard, Michael Beer, has developed a related model for managing change. Beer argues that some of the most effective change comes from middle management and frontline managers and troops through their informal efforts to solve business problems. The model is effectively a five-step model: First, they mobilize commitment to change through joint diagnosis of business problems. Second, based on their join diagnosis, they develop a shared vision of how to organize and manage for competitiveness. Third, over time, the organization develops competence to enact the shared vision. At this juncture, the fourth step, senior management plays a key role by deciding which of these from across the organization should be scaled up and spread throughout the organization. Not all will be; in fact, many of these new innovations will remain the part of the organization that created them or may even die out if it turns out to not stand the test of time. For the few that are scaled up, similar to the Kotter model, they are institutionalized over time through formal policies, systems, and structures and made part of the organizational culture, the fifth and final step.

This model makes a lot of sense. Some old-fashioned executives see themselves as the prime source of innovative ideas, approaches, and business models. But this "big brain" approach relies too much on one person or a handful of people. So executives shouldn't try to be the source of all innovation but instead harness the wisdom of crowds by engaging their frontline troops and middle managers. Frontline troops are boundary spanners; they have a foot in the organization and a foot in the turbulent, changing, demanding world of customers, suppliers, and competitors. Too often, executives spend most of their time locked away in internal meetings. That's not necessarily a bad thing, but they should recognize the downside: They become out of touch with the external world of the firm.

With the proper encouragement, frontline employees can be an outstanding source of new ideas to grow your business. Perhaps even more important are middle managers. Research has demonstrated again and again that change initiatives originating with middle managers are the most powerful force for successful change in larger organizations. These days, many recommend using these two groups to produce new approaches to reducing costs—always good in challenging times—but more fundamentally, to spot and experiment with new ways of getting growth from existing and new potential customers. What role do executives play? They create a culture where this occurs, encourage it through their own actions, and choose which growth possibilities to scale up.

An Emerging Idea: Nudge Your Way to Transformation

A more recent model of managing change is the nudge model, popularized in a book, *Nudge*, by economists Richard Thaler and Cass Sunstein. This approach looks at using small changes to have a big impact on the organization and hence leading to considerable change. This approach argues that it is much easier to alter just one or two constraints to release change than to identify and manage every factor, every aspect, and every bit of commitment, belief, skill, knowledge, and communication. But when you intervene in a complex system, you want to be sure you are taming the tiger, not simply poking it with a stick. Advocates admit it isn't easy to find that one perfect nudge to release exactly the change desired. Often, the nudge is used in areas seemingly irrelevant to the problem at hand. One observer dubbed this approach "minimalist intervention." The actions designed must be highly leveraged. If they fail, no one notices. If they succeed, no one notices how it was done or even who was responsible.

Let us consider three examples designed by consultants: A company desperate to preserve retail prices in the face of widespread discounting by competitors reenergized its sales force and preserved prices on over 80% of all business written. What was the nudge? The CEO delivered a powerful metaphor at a sales meeting that changed the way the sales force members viewed their relationships with their customers. A sector-changing merger was in jeopardy because of turf wars between the finance functions of the merger partners. Special incentives and threats proved useless. The merger succeeded only when the CFO nudged the situation away from fear and distrust by sending a simple e-mail request inquiring after local schools. A third example: Top-producing salespeople paid lip service to the company's policy of aggressive internal cross-selling, while lining their pockets via side deals with competitors. The nudge to finally get internal cross-selling to take off? It was getting the most conspicuous violator to become a sudden champion by having the CEO offer him a special assignment. In each case, what it took was a carefully designed, small, nudge-like intervention that rapidly led to dramatic improvement.

Importance

Kotter's change model is probably the most widely used in the world. It has been criticized by Michael Beer of HBS and Henry Mintzberg of McGill, among others, for being too CEO-centric and for failing to recognize the power and role of middle management in bringing about success change strategies. A considerable amount of academic research conducted since then has suggested that most CEO-led change fails and that most effective change comes from middle managers who are closer to the action than senior executives. Even so, unlike first-level managers, they generally have greater credibility with senior executives who control the resources of the organization. In a recent interview with the author of this entry, Kotter readily admitted that he agreed with the importance of middle management and included this in his teaching and consulting work. Kotter believes that his model is one that is equally applicable to every well of management of an organization.

In the experience of those who have led change, there is no question that change almost always produces emotional reactions, whether the change seems small or big, important or trivial. These emotional reactions are brought forward in different ways, passively or aggressively, and it is important to understand why people resist change so that one can predict the impact that the announcement of change might have. Three common triggers for resistance are these: (1) *Self-interest, misunderstanding, and lack of trust:* People resist when they do not trust the change leaders, when they do not grasp the consequences that can be expected, and when rumors circulate. (2) *Different assessments:* Resistance can be met when management and employees assess risks differently, hence draw different conclusions and then stand in opposition to each other about the change that must be implemented. Often, this results from assumptions and a lack of communication. This doesn't mean necessarily these people are "stick-in-the-mud" types; they may honestly feel that the change leader is making a mistake, and they need to fight the leader who is taking the organization is an unhealthy direction. (3) *Low tolerance for change:* Although people may realize the need to change, they may be incapable emotionally to implement it because of their unconscious and low tolerance to change. Also, some may resist because they feel that their previous work will lose credibility and that they may therefore lose face.

In recent years, the theme of the importance of emotions in change has received much attention, for example in the 2010 book *Switch: How to Change Things When Change Is Hard,* by brothers Chip and Dan Heath. They argue that it is difficult to make lasting change because there is a conflict built into the human brain. They go on to suggest our minds are ruled by two different systems, the rational mind and the emotional mind, and these two minds compete for control. This best-selling book highlights in a populist way the importance of emotions. Many outstanding scholars have done serious academic work on the importance of emotions. A good summary of recent research in the area is *Research on Emotion in Organization* (Vol. 8), edited by Neal Ashkanasy and colleagues.

All in all, we conclude that strategies for change are critical in a world where change seems the only constant. Modern managers should use these models to help their organizations gain greater alignment with changes in their external environment. Many organizations are working toward being more agile, which seems what is required of many organizations in today's world.

Karl Moore

See also Appreciative Inquiry Model; Charismatic Theory of Leadership; Hypercompetition; Learning Organization; Organizational Culture Model

Further Readings

Ashkanasy, N., Zerbe, W. J., & Härtel, C. E. J. (Eds.). (2012). *Research on emotion in organization* (Vol. 8). Bingley, England: Emerald Group.

Beer, M., Eisenstat, R., & Spector, B. (1990). Why change programs don't produce change. *Harvard Business Review, 68*(6), 158–166.

Beer, M., & Nohrai, N. (2001). *Breaking the code of change.* Boston, MA: Harvard Business School Press.

Kotter, J. (1996). *Leading change.* Boston, MA: Harvard Business School Press.

Kotter, J. (2008). *A sense of urgency.* Boston, MA: Harvard Business School Press.

Heath, D., & Heath, C. (2010). *Switch: How to change things when change is hard.* New York, NY: Crown Business.

Thaler, R., & Sunstein, C. (2008). *Nudge: Improving decisions about health, wealth and happiness.* New Haven, CT: Yale University Press.

STRATEGY AND STRUCTURE

The idea that "structure follows strategy" is generally associated with the American business historian Alfred DuPont Chandler. Chandler's proposition does not constitute a theory but rather a conclusion drawn from his case analyses of the development of large American companies since the mid-19th century. However, this observation resonated with a contingency perspective according to which a firm would achieve its full performance potential only if its organizational structure optimally supported the pursuit of its objectives and could adapt this structure in response to the strategy chosen to achieve these objectives. In discussing the relationship between strategy and structure, Chandler was among the first to use the term *strategy* in a business context and to portray both strategy and structure as results of managerial choices rather than treat them as givens. These ideas were a strong catalyst to the development of strategy as a field of academic study and are widely considered to be among the most influential ones that emerged in management literature during the 1960s and 1970s. The following outlines the academic debate about the relationship between strategy and structure in greater detail. Thereafter is a discussion of the empirical evidence related to this relationship and an assessment of the influence the notion that "strategy and structure" has had on managerial practice.

Fundamentals

In his early work, Chandler suggested that the design or structure of an organization results or follows from its strategy for achieving its objectives, specifically its growth objectives. He defined strategy as the determination of the basic long-term goals and objectives of an enterprise, and the adoption of courses of action and the allocation of resources necessary for carrying out these goals. Although he did not formally distinguish between different types of strategy, the examples used in his work suggest that Chandler referred primarily to corporate-level strategies, in contrast to strategic decisions typically taken at the business unit level, such as product design and pricing. With respect to the structure of an organization, he referred to the design of its hierarchy (e.g., lines of authority and communication) and the information flow within this hierarchy. Among other arguments, he suggested that the introduction of the multidivisional organization under the management of a corporate head office constituted an organizational response to facilitate diversification and internationalization strategies.

While not constituting a theory in its own right, the idea of a contingency relationship between strategy and structure has been integrated in a diverging set of theoretical perspectives. However, the exact nature, directionality, and temporal dimension of this relationship, the factors underlying it, and—to a lesser extent—the conditions under which it holds, have been subject to an ongoing debate that was at its most intense during the 1970s and 1980s. Chandler saw the causal link between strategy and structure primarily in the need for organizational efficiency. His view that strategy precedes structure in a temporal sense is rooted in the belief that top management formulates relatively stable, long-term strategic objectives, then aligning the organization to facilitate the most efficient attainment of these objectives—a perspective also found in what Henry Mintzberg called the design school of strategic management. In contrast, organizational ecology does not invoke the realization of managerial intentions

or objectives as a driving force but derives the temporal ordering between strategy and structure from an organization's need for peripheral features of (such as its administrative structure) to adapt to its core features (such as its strategy).

During the 1970s, authors began to question the directionality of the strategy-structure relationship, both in the temporal and in the causal sense. Several reasons as to why structure may precede, constrain, and inform strategy have been proposed. First, particular organizational structures may influence repertoires, cognitive processes, and individual or organizational-level skills and competencies that affect the way managers develop and formulate strategies. In this context, organizational structures are characterized as highly pervasive so that they may exert subtle effects on strategic decision making. They do so at least in part by limiting the set of strategic choices available to managers. Second, many strategic ideas and initiatives may emerge from lower levels of the organizational hierarchy rather than be defined by top management. The organizational setting provides an incentive structure for these strategic ideas to be proposed in the first place and affects the information flows through which they are reported and the way in which they are being processed. In this way, structures may influence both strategy processes (e.g., the adoption and the nature of strategic planning processes) as well as the content of the strategy pursued by an organization. Third, organizational structures may not only influence the efficiency with which given strategic objectives are implemented but also the effectiveness of the choice of these objectives. In particular, transaction cost economic approaches suggest that structures such as the multidivisional organization reduce opportunism among division managers and incentivize the pursuit of strategies in support of overall corporate goals. Fourth, structures may precede strategy in situations of rapid environmental change. In these conditions, swift strategic response to both threats and opportunities may be more conducive to performance than are the formulation of long-term strategies. Therefore, the role of top management is to create organizational conditions (including structures) that facilitate (and thus precede and inform) the rapid formulation and implementation of strategies.

The conclusion to be drawn from the above-summarized debate is that the relationship between strategy and structure is a reciprocal one, a point made even by Chandler himself in his later writings. The definition of temporal and causal ordering depends, at least in part, on the specific elements considered (i.e., whether corporate or business unit strategies are being analyzed, and which aspects of organizational structures are included in this analysis), where the focus is (i.e., on top versus lower-level management as organizational actors), as well as the environmental conditions of the organizations under study.

In contrast to the perspectives outlined above, configuration approaches are not primarily concerned with establishing a causal or temporal ordering between strategy and structure but rather with their adherence to overarching organizational configurations, archetypes, or "gestalts." Configuration approaches have proposed a variety of reasons why different characteristics or elements of strategy and structure tend to coalesce in such configurations. The more classical contributions in this stream of literature emphasize the notion of "fit"—that is, the idea that different organizational features may mutually support and reinforce one another. Tight coupling of multiple features helps maximize these benefits and reduces the threat of imitation by competitors. Other approaches introduce the notion of deeply embedded organizational norms, values, or "interpretive schemes" that drive the adoption of both strategic objectives and organizational characteristics so that these characteristics cluster together in stable configurations.

More recent analyses of fit between strategy and structure have concentrated on the complementarities between (particular aspects of) these two factors. A relationship between two elements is defined as complementary if an increase in the level of any one element enhances the marginal benefits of the other element. The presence of complementarities between two elements may be contingent on other conditions, such as a particular environmental setting. The complementarity perspective does not constitute a theory in that it does not provide specific predictions regarding the factors between which complementary relationships may exist or the boundary conditions under which such complementarities may hold. However, modeling the relationship between structure and strategy as a complementary one provides tractability to the idea that they may mutually reinforce one another, without the need for a unidirectional cause-effect relationship.

Importance

Since its original formulation, three types of empirical work have investigated the nature of the relationship between strategy and structure. A first group of authors have applied Chandler's historical perspective to other geographies—in particular to Western Europe—and also expanded it to more recent time periods. This literature, prominent in the 1970s, largely confirmed the idea that structure would follow strategy.

In the 1980s, a second group of authors began to use regression-based and choice-theoretic approaches to test propositions on the relationship between strategy and structure. Whereas some of the earlier contributions to this literature used cross-sectional data to investigate the nature of this relationship, an increasing number of publications began to employ longitudinal designs to address the sequence and causal interplay between strategy and structure. Overall, this evidence clearly attests to the reciprocal nature of the strategy-structure relationship. However, the majority of these investigations find that the effect of strategy on structure tends to be stronger and more direct than the effect of structure on strategy—hence, providing a fairly positive assessment of Chandler's original proposition that structure follows strategy. Furthermore, the strategy-structure relationship appears to hold even in relatively turbulent environments.

A third group of authors has investigated the firm performance effects of fit between strategy and structure (or dimensions thereof). Relatively few studies in this category have focused on the interaction of specific, relatively well-defined aspects of strategy and structure. A slightly larger number of contributions have investigated complementarities or fit in entire organizational systems involving multiple dimensions of strategy and structure. Overall, the evidence produced in both approaches sheds positive light on the proposition that the optimal matching between the strategy and the structure of an organization enhances its performance. However, some authors also caution that a tight coupling of multiple elements creates barriers to organizational change.

The idea that strategy and structure should fit one another optimally has had a significant influence on applied management literature, in particular during the 1980s. The two terms feature prominently in the

"Seven-S framework" proposed by Tom Peters and Robert Waterman, according to which the alignment among an organization's strategy, structure, skills, staff, systems, style, and superordinate goals (respectively "shared values") determine its performance. They also play a role in Peter Drucker's writings on management. However, the importance of the strategy-structure relationship in management literature has gradually declined since the mid-1990s.

Anna Christina Littmann and
Ansgar Richter

See also Diversification Strategy; Firm Growth; Organizational Structure and Design; Seven-S Framework; Strategic Decision Making

Further Readings

Amburgey, T. L., & Dacin, T. (1994). As the left foot follows the right? The dynamics of strategic and structural change. *Academy of Management Journal, 37,* 1427–1452.

Burgelman, R. A. (1983). A model of the interaction of strategic behaviour, corporate context, and the concept of strategy. *Academy of Management Review, 8,* 61–70.

Chandler, A. D. (1962). *Strategy and structure: Chapters in the history of the industrial enterprise.* Boston, MA: MIT Press.

Hall, D. J., & Saias, M. A. (1980). Strategy follows structure! *Strategic Management Journal, 1,* 149–163.

Milgrom, P., & Roberts, J. (1995). Complementarities and fit strategy, structure, and organizational change in manufacturing. *Journal of Accounting and Economics, 19,* 179–208.

Miller, D. (1986). Configurations of strategy and structure: Towards a synthesis. *Strategic Management Journal, 7,* 233–249.

Mintzberg, H. (1990). The design school: Reconsidering the basic premises of strategic management. *Strategic Management Journal, 11,* 171–195.

Rumelt, R. P. (1974). *Strategy, structure, and economic performance.* Cambridge, MA: Harvard University Press.

Waterman, R. H., Jr., Peters, T. J., & Phillips, J. R. (1980). Structure is not organization. *Business Horizons, 23,* 14–26.

Whittington, R., Mayer, M., & Curto, F. (1999). Chandlerism in post-war Europe: Strategic and structural change in France, Germany and the UK, 1950–1993. *Industrial and Corporate Change, 8,* 519–551.

STRATEGY-AS-PRACTICE

Strategy-as-practice is a perspective within the broader field of strategic management that considers strategy as something people *do* rather than simply something organizations *have.* From this perspective, strategy is a kind of work ("strategizing") that managers, consultants, planners, and others perform with the support of various tools. These tools may be analytical (e.g., Porterian analysis), discursive (e.g., strategy rhetoric), social (e.g., strategy workshops) or material (e.g., PowerPoint presentations and the like). Many such strategy tools are institutionalized widely in society at large, as well as specific to particular organizations. Thus, strategy-as-practice departs from the organizational focus of much strategy research in two respects. Strategy-as-practice concerns itself not just with organizational performance but also with the performance—in terms of personal effectiveness—of strategists in their strategy work. At the same time, strategy-as-practice attends to the wider effects of strategy tools as they diffuse through societies, sometimes shaping strategies and strategy work in ways that are consequential far beyond particular organizations. This entry (1) outlines the core assumptions of the strategy-as-practice approach and distinguishes it from other approaches, (2) discusses some of the methodological implications of undertaking research using this perspective, and (c) offers some insights about where this relatively new field of inquiry is headed in the future and the lessons it might impart to managers.

Fundamentals

Strategy-as-practice takes its inspiration from a larger intellectual movement in the social sciences known as the "practice turn." This practice turn considers what people actually do in various social contexts as scientifically important because it provides insights into how individual agency links with social institutions. Strategy, as seen from a strategy-as-practice perspective, is thus conceptualized as a situated and socially accomplished flow of activity that occurs over time. Strategy-as-practice offers a novel lens for looking at the social phenomenon of developing strategy in organizations, one that promises distinctive advances in strategic management knowledge. Because it stays close to what strategists do on a day-to-day basis, its outputs tend to be more pragmatic and immediately relevant to practitioners than research at the organizational level. Strategy-as-practice directly addresses the managerial skills and tools involved in strategy rather than abstracting to the level of organizational performance. Because it recognizes the institutionalization of certain tools throughout society, it offers the possibility of critique and reform of strategy practices that may have widespread and sometimes unexpected consequences. Thus strategy-as-practice links day-to-day strategy work with key outcomes at multiple levels—personal, organizational, and societal.

The strategy-as-practice perspective emerged in the early 2000s out of a growing frustration with the mainstream strategy literature and its primary emphasis on organizational-level strategy. Strategy research was seen as focusing on what organizations have (e.g., strategies, market positions, or resources) and as limiting its concern to implications for organizational performance. Within this mainstream perspective, very little attention was given to the individuals who proposed, planned, organized, debated, and otherwise participated in the conception and implementation of strategies. These individuals were marginalized even though their skills and emotions had considerable impact on how successful any given strategy effort was likely to be. Scholars interested in the new strategy-as-practice perspective felt a need to refocus research on strategy practitioners, their tools, and their interactions, to better understand how the myriad activities associated with the "doing" of strategy are consequential both for organizations and for others with a stake in strategy outcomes.

Core Assumptions

Strategy-as-practice takes three interconnected elements as core. On the one hand, there are the *practitioners*, all those involved in strategy work. Next, there are the *practices* of strategy, the various tools, norms, and procedures of strategy work. Finally, there is strategy *praxis*, the activity involved in specific instances or "episodes" of strategy work. Praxis is where practices and practitioners are brought together in action. Thus, an important assumption of strategy-as-practice is that practitioners, practices, and praxis are closely interlinked. Episodes of praxis rely on institutionalized practices;

through praxis, practitioners express their agency; practices are produced and reproduced in praxis.

First, unlike many traditional views on strategy, strategy-as-practice does not assume that strategy work is the exclusive preserve of top management teams in organizations. On the contrary, a core assumption of this perspective is that strategy's practitioners are potentially many: All kinds of people may contribute to defining and enacting strategy in organizations. These people might be either internal to the organization (e.g., not just top managers and strategic planners but middle managers and below) or external (e.g., consultants, regulators or investment bankers). Strategy-as-practice is concerned with the skills, power, careers, and emotions of all those involved, or seeking involvement, in strategy work.

A second distinctive feature of strategy-as-practice is its concern not only for organizationally specific practices ("the way things are done here") but for strategy practices that are widely diffused and institutionalized in society ("the done thing generally"). These practices embody the way strategy work "ought" to be done, as articulated by management culture or prescribed by consultants, textbooks, and how-to manuals or defined by standard technologies and processes. Thus, these practices include standard social practices (such as board meetings, strategy workshops, away days, video conference calls, and so on), common analytical tools (SWOT [strengths-weaknesses-opportunities-threats] analysis, the BCG [Boston Consulting Group] matrix, Porter's five forces, to name only a few), influential discourses (e.g., the rhetoric of ecosystems, downsizing, or shareholder value), and those practices embedded in ubiquitous material artifacts and technologies (planning documents, flip charts, PowerPoint slides, e-mails, etc.). Many of these practices are so banal as to be taken entirely for granted in strategy work. But this very banality speaks to their pervasive influence. The concern here is not only with these practices' consequences for particular organizations but also with less obvious societal effects: for example, how they shape identity and authority for various kinds of practitioners and would-be practitioners, or favor some strategies while precluding others. A characteristic concern for strategy-as-practice, then, is how the spread of generic strategic technologies or discourses may systematically exclude certain kinds of issues and practitioners from strategy debate, with potentially widespread implications.

Third, strategy-as-practice is distinctive in seeking typically to understand practitioners and practices through close observation of specific episodes of praxis. These episodes of praxis might be particular strategy workshops, projects, conversations, or presentations. Praxis takes us to concrete, local moments of strategy work, where practitioners translate practices into action. Here, strategy-as-practice recognizes there is an important performance aspect to practices: generic practices are rarely employed as prescribed or intended. They are typically adapted, improvised, and tweaked by skillful practitioners making do with the resources and circumstances they have to hand in the moment. The focus on praxis recognizes that the real-life performance of a generic practice typically departs from the textbook. Praxis is the "situated doing" or "localized instantiation" of practice(s). Close study of praxis is worthwhile because in these specific episodes, skill is displayed, subtle power and identity effects are revealed, and practice innovations are often made.

A final distinctive feature of strategy-as-practice is the diversity of theoretical resources it draws on. Because strategy-as-practice is oriented toward an empirical phenomenon (the work of strategy) rather than a particular frame or method, it embraces multiple theories. Theoretical inspirations for studies so far include structuration theory, activity theory, actor-network theory, sensemaking theory, situated learning theory, discourse theories, theories of practice (notably those of Pierre Bourdieu and Michel de Certeau), and institutional theory. Each theory contributes in its own unique way to a more general understanding of how strategy gets accomplished in organizations.

Importance

Differences With the Process Tradition

Even though there are similarities with some of the foundational work in the strategy process tradition, strategy-as-practice sees itself as being distinct. In particular, strategy-as-process scholars disagree with the forced dichotomy between content and process that continues to characterize much of the strategy discipline. Both content and process theorists in strategy stem from different schools of thought, each harboring distinct ontological and epistemological beliefs about the reality of what constitutes strategy. Strategy-as-practice scholars argue on the

contrary that content and process are inextricably intertwined. Their view is that content is an inherent part of process and that processes are constituted by practical activities. Although they laud the process tradition for opening up the black box of organization, their sense is that it has not been opened enough to fully understand what actually goes on inside these processes. Strategy-as-practice scholars see value in the study of the actual activities that constitute strategy processes and believe that such study will provide a better understanding not only of the processes themselves but also of how strategizing activities contribute to various outcomes both at the level of the organization and wider society.

Methods

Strategy-as-practice's interest in praxis, including the ordinary day-to-day activities of strategists, calls for methods amenable to such study, the majority of which are qualitative. Typical approaches include ethnography (and video-ethnography), in-depth cases studies, interviewing, discourse analysis, and conversation analysis. The concern to simultaneously consider both localized activities and the organizational and institutional contexts in which they are embedded presents particular challenges from a methods perspective because it calls for methodologies and research designs that are both broad in scope and close to the phenomenon under study. This challenge explains recent calls within the strategy-as-practice perspective for new and different methodological approaches that make it easier to capture the complexity of making strategy at all three levels of the individual, the organization, and wider society. Some of the more novel approaches proposed include interactive discussions groups (with informants), self-reports by informants (in the form of diaries, for example), and practitioner research (inviting informants to collect data on and reflect on their own practice). Almost all approaches require expanded data sets, and increasingly, there are calls to experiment with combined methods (qualitative and quantitative).

Challenges

Interest in strategy-as-practice as a field has grown considerably over the past decade. Several leading journals have published special issues on the topic, a number of books on the topic have appeared, and more recently a handbook has been published. All the main international conferences in management and strategy now have interest groups dedicated to advancing scholarship within the field.

The strategy-as-practice perspective faces two challenges, however. For one, strategy-as-practice's focus on the situated and the particular, and its leaning toward qualitative studies has so far restricted its ability to contribute to a strategic management discipline that is preoccupied with explaining general patterns of organizational performance. To participate more fully in the mainstream, strategy-as-practice needs to offer more on the organizational performance implications of strategic practices—which practices link to successful strategic outcomes and which do not. A second challenge similarly harks on the detailed praxis focus characteristic of much strategy-as-practice research, but here the concern is at the societal level. Strategy-as-practice has been fascinated by "micro" episodes of praxis but has relatively neglected the general implications of certain practices for the empowerment of employees and the strategic orientations of influential corporations in society. Responding to both these organizational and societal-level challenges implies an enlarging of the research focus for strategy-as-practice: The lens needs to zoom out from the micro to encompass organizational and societal concerns. Much remains to be accomplished in this still nascent field, therefore—both a criticism and an invitation to further research.

Implications

One of strategy-as-practice's principal appeals is its direct relevance to managerial practice. Traditional strategy research's focus on strategy content—for example, which strategies managers should pursue under what conditions—is frequently of limited practical use for managers who must deal with an ever-changing environment, limited organizational resources, internal politics, and recalcitrant staff, to name only a few of the usual barriers to strategy formation and implementation. Given that strategy-as-practice research considers these realities as part and parcel of the process of strategizing (and not as externalities, problems, or exceptions) and seeks to understand them directly, its outputs are more likely to be practically relevant to managers. Indeed, strategy-as-practice's theorizing on strategy

practice does not help managers make sense from a strategy perspective of *what* they should do, but rather, it helps them understand *how* and *why* they do what they do and, by association, what works and what doesn't.

Charlotte Cloutier and Richard Whittington

See also Actor-Network Theory; Dramaturgical Theory of Organizations; Institutional Theory; Narrative (Story) Theory; Neo-Institutional Theory; Process Theories of Change; Structuration Theory

Further Readings

Balogun, J. A., Huff. S., & Johnson, P. (2003). Three responses to the methodological challenges of studying strategizing. *Journal of Management Studies, 40,* 197–224.

Golshorkhi, D., Rouleau, L., Seidl, D., & Vaara, E. (Eds.). (2010). *Cambridge handbook of strategy as practice.* Cambridge, England: Cambridge University Press.

Jarzabkowski, P., Balogun, J., & Seidl, D. (2007). Strategizing: The challenges of a practice perspective. *Human Relations, 60,* 5–27.

Johnson, G., Melin, L., Langley, A., & Whittington, R. (2007). *Strategy as practice: Research directions and resources.* Cambridge, England: Cambridge University Press.

Johnson, G., Melin, L., & Whittington, R. (2003). Micro-strategy and strategizing: Towards an activity-based view. *Journal of Management Studies, 40,* 3–22.

Whittington, R. (2006). Completing the practice-turn in strategy research. *Organization Studies, 27,* 613–634.

Vaara, E., & Whittington, R. (2012). Strategy-as-practice: Taking practices seriously, *Academy of Management Annals, 6*(1), 285–336.

STRUCTURATION THEORY

Like many of their counterparts in the human and social sciences, management theorists are skilled in creating dichotomies: agency/structure, meaning/cause, relativism/objectivism, and micro/macro. Yet once established, these dichotomies often end up obscuring the emergence of other ways of thinking, sometimes more creative and/or opportune and sometimes just different. To make sense of—or perhaps to deconstruct—such dichotomies, a number of theoretical frameworks have appeared. Regarding the agency/structure relationship, management literature over the last 30 years has been strongly influenced by a number of nondichotomist logical schemata, which deserve recognition as valuable attempts to purposively explore new understandings of human agency and organizational structures rather than continue to fuel dualistic debates. Among the many approaches that have avoided dichotomies, the propositions of British sociologist Anthony Giddens have been adopted by a number of management researchers since the 1980s. How do individual agents' actions relate to the structural properties of societies and social systems, and vice versa? How is action structured in everyday contexts? How are the structured features of action reproduced? One of the most pervasive and difficult issues in social theory is the relationship between agency and structure. In the late 1970s and early 1980s, Giddens addressed those fundamental problems in the social sciences in a way that was unconventional at the time in a number of articles, culminating with the publication of *The Constitution of Society* in 1984. The central purpose of structuration theory is a distinct conceptualization of structure and agency: While structural properties of societies are real, they depend on regularities of social reproduction; structure exists only in and through the activities of human agents. A complete overview of Giddens's structuration theory will not be undertaken in this entry because a number of comprehensive and authoritative texts on the topic already exist. What is offered here is an outline of some of the most important elements of structuration theory and how they have been interpreted, along with their implications for management research.

Fundamentals

The notions of structure and agency were deeply reformulated by Giddens, who emphasizes that although action has strongly routinized aspects, not only is it conditioned by existing cultural structures but it also creates and re-creates those structures through the enactment process. To position his examination of the dualism between agency and structure, Giddens departed from the conceptualization of structure as a particular given or external form. Structure is that which gives form and shape to social life but is not itself the form and shape: It exists solely in and through the activities of human

agents. Giddens also departed from the idea of agency as something merely "contained" within the individual; he posited it as referring to the flow or pattern of people's actions rather than to people's intentions in doing things. Although structural properties of societies and social systems are real, they have no physical existence. Rather, they depend on regularities of social reproduction. Consequently, the basic area of study in the social sciences consists of social practices ordered across time and space.

Therefore, besides the agency-structure duality, the notions of time and space are central to structuration theory. How people conceptualize time and space and how they manage to organize themselves across time and space are key issues in understanding the properties of social systems. The importance of studying the contextualities of institutionalized patterns of interactions across time and space is stressed by Giddens, whose views invest them with an inherent role in the investigation of social reproduction. He argues that cultural, ethnographic, or anthropological dimensions, which necessarily exist in all social research, are nonetheless frequently neglected in social studies. An analogous claim could easily be made with regard to organization studies: although the analysis of time/space is inseparable from the study of organizational change, context, history, and process were given only limited attention in literature on organizational change until quite recently. Although there have been considerable advances made in these areas, the field of management studies is still far from a mature understanding of the dynamics and effects of time, process, discontinuity, and context.

Complementary to the aforementioned notions of duality of structure and time/space is the concept of knowledgeability, the competence of agents. Giddens holds that all actors are socially competent, with the core idea being reflexivity: The capacity of humans to be reflexive—to think about their situation—entails the ability to change it. There is a strong interrelation between the concepts of duality of structure and knowledgeability. Indeed, competent and reflexive actors are required by the structurationist way of interpreting the interplay between structure and action. Other pivotal concepts in structuration theory are structures of signification, domination, and legitimation; structuring modalities (interpretive schemes, facilities, and norms); elements of interaction (communication, power, and sanction); and consciousness (discursive and practical) and unconsciousness.

Evolution

Structuration theory drew significant attention with its account of the constitution of social life—an account that departed from and challenged established theoretical positions and traditions and that prompted the appearance of numerous books and papers in which it was discussed, scrutinized, supported, or criticized. Management studies have emerged as an especially rich arena for theoretical discussion of the use of Giddens's social theory in the study of societal and organizational phenomena. In 1997, Stephen Barley and Pam Tolbert discussed the similarities between institutional and structuration theory, developing an argument for why a fusion of the two would enable institutional theory to significantly advance and proposing methodological guidelines for investigating the process empirically. In 2002, Udo Staber and Jörg Sydow revisited conventional approaches to organizational effectiveness and survival by using structuration theory's political, cognitive, and normative aspects of managing change and offering an innovative framework for understanding adaptive capacity. More recently, in 2011, William McKinley focused on organizational adaptations to environmental conditions, challenging some of the structuration theory tenets by proposing extensions that might help improve its application.

A number of articles have drawn on previously published case studies to illustrate the structurationist framework. For instance, Ernest Alexander used the rich description of four cases dealing with air pollution abatement, river basin management and other environmental issues to illustration the structuration of interorganizational coordination structures in their natural settings. Finally, the variety of research domains integrating structuration theory as a theoretical lens is also noteworthy. For example, in accounting several researchers, including Cristiano Busco, Alan Coad, and Ian Herbert, recalled that the use of structuration theory has made a distinctive contribution to management accounting research as its new developments in the area have a potential to provide new insights. In the electronic commerce area, Md. Dulal Hossain and his colleagues developed a theoretical model grounded on structuration theory to investigate the impact of organizational assimilation of electronic government systems on business value creation. In entrepreneurship, Rich Huebner and Margaret Britt focused on the behavioral and social aspects of security and used emotional intelligence, structuration theory, and social network analysis to offer a new model to help entrepreneurs. In marketing, Calin Gurau investigated the complex relationship between the various elements that shape consumption experience and market institutions by developing a theoretical model based on structuration theory. Finally, in public administration, Eun Gee Yun used structuration theory to improve the understanding of administrative culture changes and the formation of a contemporary administrative culture in a globalized world.

Importance

Instead of counterposing objective/subjective or voluntarist/determinist dimensions, in proposing the theory of structuration, Giddens challenged the premise of mutual exclusivity and assumed the duality of structure and action. But Giddens has not been the only one to propose alternative forms of social analysis that avoids dualistic logic. Other examples are Pierre Bourdieu's interplay between objectivism and subjectivism, Richard Bernstein's trajectory bypassing objectivism and relativism, Roy Bhaskar's account of positivism and postmodernism, and Béatrice Fay's discussion of science versus hermeneutics. Such a debate has made its way into management and organizational studies, as illustrated by Hugh Willmott's break from paradigm thinking, Gary R. Weaver and D. A. Gioia's juxtaposition of incommensurability and structurationist inquiry, and Michael I. Reed's discussion of duality and dualism. These alternative approaches seek to overcome narrow dualistic thinking and to explore new interpretations of well-known sociological dilemmas. As argued by Marlei Pozzebon, most of these represent not competing but alternative vectors, with the choice among them often being resolved on the basis of ontological affinity.

While offering great theoretical promise, Giddens's concepts encounter difficulty in being applied. In the discussions that followed publication of Giddens's ideas about social theories, certain issues regarding their applicability have been raised.

Structuration theory is conceptually complex, drawing on ideas from psychoanalysis, phenomenology, ethnomethodology, and action theory, among others. The high level of abstraction that structuration theory operates on has given rise to diverse and occasionally contradictory interpretations. Moreover, Giddens claims that structuration theory is not intended as a method of research or even as a methodological approach, and the extreme difficulty in applying it to empirical research is widely recognized. Any theory must be empirically applied to be relevant, and structuration theory is not easily coupled with any specific method. Nonetheless, authors such as J. B. Edwards, Lisa Jack, Ahmed Kholeif, and Pozzebon and Alain Pinsonneault represent attempts to explore the empirical application of structuration theory.

The obstacles and criticism notwithstanding, structuration theory has played a relevant role in research concerning organizations and their management, and individuals and their choices. In both conceptual discussions and empirical inquiries, since the publication of *The Constitution of Society*, researchers in diverse fields have made use of concepts drawn from structuration theory. However, much work clearly remains to realize structuration theory's potential contribution to understanding of management issues.

Marlei Pozzebon

See also Adaptive Structuration Theory; Institutional Theory; Multilevel Research; Neo-Institutional Theory; Process Theories of Change

Further Readings

Cohen, I. J. (1989). *Structuration theory: Anthony Giddens and the constitution of social life*. New York, NY: St. Martin's Press.

De Cock, C., Rickards, T., Weaver, G. R., & Gioia, D. A. (1995). A rejoinder to and reply from Weaver and Gioia. *Organization Studies, 16*(4), 699–705.

Giddens, A. (1984). *The constitution of society*. Berkeley: University of California Press.

Held, D., & Thompson, J. B. (1989). *Social theory of modern societies: Anthony Giddens and his critics*. Cambridge, England: Cambridge University Press.

Jones, M. R., & Karsten, H. (2008). Giddens's structuration theory and information systems research. *MIS Quarterly, 32*(1), 127–157.

Pozzebon, M. (2004). The influence of a structurationist perspective on strategic management research. *Journal of Management Studies, 41*(2), 247–272.

Pozzebon, M., & Pinsonneault, A. (2005). Challenges in conducting empirical work using structuration theory: Learning from IT research. *Organization Studies, 26*(9), 1353–1376.

Ranson, S., Hinings, B., & Greenwood, R. (1980). The structuring of organizational structures. *Administrative Science Quarterly, 25*, 1–17.

Reed, M. I. (1997). In praise of duality and dualism: Rethinking agency and structure in organizational analysis. *Organization Studies, 18*(1), 21–42.

Turner, J. H. (1991). *The structure of sociological theory*. Belmont, CA: Wadsworth

Substitutes for Leadership

The substitutes-for-leadership theory concentrates on contextual factors that enhance, neutralize, or substitute for leadership. For example, members of a work team communicate and manage their task responsibilities very effectively, which essentially takes the place of a formal team leader. In this case, team members' ability to self-manage effectively substitutes for team leadership. The substitutes-for-leadership theory was developed by Steven Kerr and John M. Jermier and has received considerable attention within the field of management. The study of leadership is central to the field of management as it is likely the most frequently discussed and researched topic. The following sections on the substitutes-for-leadership theory begin with a brief review of key approaches to the study of leadership and where substitutes for leadership fit into the overall study of leadership. Next, key elements of the substitutes-for-leadership theory are reviewed. This is followed by an analysis of the theory's validity and overall impact.

Fundamentals

There is a rich history of studying leadership in the field of management. In fact, it may be the field's most frequently examined topic. Leadership is essentially the process through which a leader influences the behavior of others to advance the strategic goals of the organization. One of the earliest assumptions in the study of leadership was that effective leaders possessed a specific set of traits. Commonly identified traits were intelligence, charisma, assertiveness, and conscientiousness. However, researchers were not able to identify leadership traits that consistently improved organizational performance across multiple contexts. In the late 1940s, researchers begin focusing on the relationship between leadership behaviors and performance. Surprisingly, no robust, consistent relationships were found between particular leader behaviors and organizational performance. Leadership researchers in the 1950s turned away from leader traits and behaviors and considered the situation within which they operated as the most important factor affecting leadership effectiveness. This, in the 1970s, led to a variety of contingency theories of leadership that hypothesized the fit between the situation and a leader's style/approach matters most. That is, a leader's approach may be very effective in one situation but not work at all in another context. This new focus led to Steven Kerr and Anne Harlan's first mention of substitutes for leadership as factors that lessened a leader's impact on subordinate outcomes. This paper and several others led to Kerr and Jermier's paper, published in 1978, that introduced the substitutes-for-leadership theory.

Substitutes-for-leadership theory states that multiple situational factors (i.e., subordinate, task, and organizational characteristics) can substitute for, neutralize, or enhance the impact of a leader's behavior. These factors can reduce or increase a leader's ability to influence the job attitudes and effectiveness of subordinates and serve as moderators of the relationship between leader behavior and employee outcomes.

Factors and Characteristics

A variety of different variables have been identified as possible substitutes, neutralizers, or enhancers of leader behavior across the three categories of subordinate, task, and organizational characteristics: (1) the subordinate's ability, experience, training, or knowledge; professional orientation; need for independence; and indifference toward organizational rewards; (2) intrinsically satisfying tasks; routine, methodologically invariant tasks; and task feedback; and (3) the degree of organizational formalization; rule inflexibility; work group cohesiveness; amount

of staff and/or advisory support; organizational rewards outside the leader's control and spatial distance between the leaders and their subordinates.

Specific characteristics impact relationship-oriented versus task-oriented leadership. For example, a subordinate's need for independence, professional orientation, and indifference toward organizational rewards tend to neutralize *relationship-oriented* leadership. Regarding tasks, intrinsically satisfying tasks, cohesive work groups, no control over rewards, and spatial distance between subordinate and superior also would neutralize relationship-oriented leadership. *Task-oriented* leadership is more likely to be neutralized by subordinate characteristics such as the need for independence, professional orientation, indifference toward rewards, and ability and experience. Regarding tasks, routine tasks, highly standardized tasks, tasks that provide their own outcome feedback, cohesive work groups, no control over rewards, spatial distance between subordinate and superior, highly specified staff functions, and organizational formulization and inflexibility also neutralize task-oriented leadership. Some of these examples in the review of substitutes, neutralizers, and enhancers below.

Categories and Functions

Substitutes are factors that essentially take the place of a leader by decreasing his or her ability to influence subordinates. For example, air traffic control teams are continually and intensively trained and are taught to do whatever is necessary to keep air travel safe, including ignoring directions from superiors. Members of these teams often rely heavily on fellow team members because of the regular intensity of this type of job. In this case, the combination of experience, extensive training, and interdependence substitute for directive leadership. Technology represents another example of a substitute. Many organizations use technology to perform many of the functions formerly conducted by managers. For example, in a high-tech manufacturing firm, employees continually interact with a networked computer system that monitors quality, errors, productivity, and a number of other important variables. The system regularly communicates this information to employees who respond by inputting additional information. All this information is used to provide continually updated performance goals and even rewards for goal attainment. Yet another example of a leadership substitute is advanced training and/or education. Consider the example of surgeons who are supervised by hospital administrators. Surgeons possess a high level of education and a significant amount of training in performing the surgical procedures necessary within their specific area of specialization. Surgeons have a high degree of autonomy in performing their job because of their specialized education and training, and this often substitutes for the leadership of a hospital administrator who has little ability to provide guidance or feedback on performance.

Neutralizers are variables that stop or counteract actions taken by the leader. They make it very difficult or even impossible for leaders to make a difference. For example, when leaders are physically separated from their subordinates, many recommended leadership practices are not useful and/or difficult to perform. This can be seen with virtual work teams whose members are not located in the same place. Reward systems represent another neutralizer when leaders don't have the control necessary to provide the most appropriate rewards to their subordinates. Lacking control over the reward system neutralizes a leader's ability to motivate subordinates. A different type of leadership neutralizer can be seen when leaders ignore the hierarchical structure of their organization. For example, a leader communicates directly with a manager's subordinates without working through the manager. This bypasses the manager completely and neutralizes his or her ability to influence subordinates. Neutralizers typically have a negative influence on organizational outcomes when those who are being "neutralized" are high-quality leaders. However, neutralizers can have positive organizational consequences when dysfunctional leaders are neutralized.

Enhancers are factors related to employees, tasks, and organizations that magnify a leader's impact on employees. For example, highly functional work groups with norms of candid communication, cooperation, and organizational citizenship behavior can augment the performance of a leader who fails to provide consistent, candid, and constructive feedback. An organization's culture can also serve as a leadership enhancer. That is, organizations with cultures emphasizing norms of principled ethics and high-level performance often enhance a leader's ability to impact subordinates. Another leadership enhancer is related to the amount and accuracy of information to which leaders have access. Consider the leader of a new product development team comprised of members from multiple areas within the organization (e.g., design, manufacturing, marketing, sales, etc.). Access to accurate information about the goals, limitations, and budget flexibility within each of these areas will likely enhance the team leader's ability to influence the team and move the project forward. Increasingly, a well-developed internal organizational network serves as a leadership enhancer. Well-developed networks of relationships serve to increase access to information, influence across the organization, and access to power. Moreover, leaders who have extensive relationship networks are typically interpersonally skilled and provide this positive example to their followers.

Importance

While the substitutes-for-leadership theory has a significant amount of intuitive appeal, it has been challenged on multiple fronts. The key challenges to the substitutes-for-leadership theory can be reviewed across two primary areas: (1) theoretical relevance and empirical support and (2) practical application.

Theoretical Relevance and Empirical Support

The substitutes-for-leadership theory was originally motivated by Steven Kerr's frustration with available leadership theories and the reality that there were a number of different factors involved with leadership effectiveness. This highlights one of the conceptual shortcomings of the substitutes-for-leadership theory, the generality of the substitutes identified. The theory fails to identify substitutes that are relevant for specific leadership behaviors. Instead, it focuses on broad categories of behavior, making it less applicable and relevant for managers' day-to-day challenges. Researchers, such as Philip M. Podsakoff and his colleagues, have advanced the theoretical relevance of the substitutes-for-leadership theory. However, the lack of identifying substitutes that are relevant for more specific leadership behaviors remains a key theoretical issue.

Overall, there has been a lack of robust empirical support for the substitutes-for-leadership theory.

The research that has demonstrated empirical support likely suffers from several methodological shortcomings. First, prior studies with supportive findings may suffer from common-source bias. That is, when all the data in a study is collected from the same source (e.g., team members), relationships among those key study variables may not be accurate because of inflated results. Another common criticism of the substitutes research is the prevalence of cross-sectional studies. In other words, most of the studies examining the substitutes-for-leadership theory collected all their data at the same point in time, making it much more difficult to establish causal relationships between the variables being studied. A primary remedy for this is to conduct more longitudinal research. A final issue that may have led to the lack of empirical support for the substitutes-for-leadership theory is that the original measurement scale developed by Kerr and Jermier has been challenged in accurately assessing substitutes for leadership.

Practical Application

The substitutes-for-leadership theory suggests that subordinate, task, and organizational characteristics affect the relationship between leader behavior and subordinate outcomes. This central idea highlights several important, practical considerations for managers and leaders in today's competitive business landscape. First, leaders should appreciate the multitude of factors that have an impact on leadership effectiveness in addition to their own capabilities. Some of these include subordinates (e.g., personal goals, future leadership capacity, personality, etc.), the task (e.g., complexity, degree of autonomy involved, decision making required, KSAs needed), and organization (e.g., culture, current climate, competitive position, financial strength, top leadership). Consistently assessing these factors would contribute to a more accurate picture of what the leader must do to succeed at the individual, team, and organizational levels. Finally, another related yet critical insight from the substitutes-for-leadership theory is that leaders can't do it *all* themselves. While it is important to assess the factors above, leaders must also learn to rely on some of them to assist in the leadership process.

Tjai M. Nielsen

See also Attribution Model of Leadership; Charismatic Theory of Leadership; Contingency Theory of Leadership; Leader–Member Exchange Theory; Path-Goal Theory of Leadership; Situational Theory of Leadership

Further Readings

Kerr, S., & Jermier, J. M. (1978). Substitutes for leadership: Their meaning and measurement. *Organizational Behavior and Human Performance, 22,* 375–403.

Howell, J. P., Bowen, D. E., Dorfman, P. W., Kerr, S., & Podsakoff, P.M. (1986). Substitutes for leadership: Effective alternatives to ineffective leadership. *Organizational Dynamics, 19,* 21–38.

Howell, J. P., & Dorfman, P. W. (1981). Substitutes for leadership: Test of a construct. *Academy of Management Journal, 24,* 714–728.

Howell, J. P., & Dorfman, P. W. (1986). Leadership and substitutes for leadership among professional and non-professional workers. *Journal of Applied Behavioral Science, 22,* 29–46.

Jermier, J. M., & Kerr, S. (1997). Substitutes for leadership: Their meaning and measurement—Contextual recollections and current observations. *Leadership Quarterly, 8,* 95–101.

Podsakoff, P. M., & MacKenzie, S. B. (1997). Kerr and Jermier's substitutes for leadership model: Background, empirical assessment, and suggestions for future research. *Leadership Quarterly, 8,* 117–125.

Podsakoff, P. M., MacKenzie, S. B., Ahearne, M., & Bommer, W. H. (1995). Searching for a needle in a haystack: Trying to identify the illusive moderators of leader behavior. *Journal of Management, 21,* 422–470.

Podsakoff, P. M., MacKenzie, S. B., & Bommer, W. H. (1996). Meta-analysis of the relationships between Kerr and Jermier's substitutes for leadership and employee job attitudes, role perceptions, and performance. *Journal of Applied Psychology, 81,* 380–399.

Stewart, G. L., Courtright, S. H., & Manz, C. C. (2011). Self-leadership: A multilevel review. *Journal of Management, 37,* 185–222.

SWOT ANALYSIS FRAMEWORK

In setting strategies or future directions for a firm, it is important to understand the general or macro-environment surrounding the organization as well as its industry and competitive environment. It is also important to assess the firm's internal strengths and weaknesses. A tool used to facilitate this understanding is the SWOT analysis framework. Researchers in strategic management agree Strengths, Weakness, Opportunities, and Threats analysis provides the foundation for realization of the desired alignment of organizational variables. By listing favorable and unfavorable internal (strengths and weaknesses) and external (opportunities and threats) issues in the four quadrants of a SWOT analysis grid, which resembles simply drawing a vertical and an intersecting horizontal line in the center of a piece of paper and labeling each of the four squares for one of the letters of SWOT analysis, planners can better understand how strengths can be leveraged to realize new opportunities and understand how weaknesses can slow progress or magnify organizational threats. In addition, it is possible to postulate ways to overcome threats and weaknesses or future strategies, from SWOT analysis. This entry addresses the fundamentals of SWOT, including how to prepare a thorough analysis; discusses its importance in practice and criticisms in usage; and finally, suggests alternatives to use with or in place of SWOT analysis.

Fundamentals

A SWOT analysis can be constructed quickly and can benefit from multiple viewpoints as a brainstorming exercise. Typically managers first consider internal strengths and weaknesses (at the top row of the 2 × 2 grid) which can include image, structure, access to natural resources, capacity and efficiency, marketing, operations, and financial resources. At the bottom row of the SWOT grid, external opportunities and threats, including customers, competitors, trends in the market, partners and suppliers, social changes and new technology, and various environmental economic, legal, social, political, and regulatory issues are included. When SWOT is used to analyze a country and not a single organization, classification of variables is different. Macroenvironmental forces that would be an external threat or opportunity for a company are components that would exist within a country and are thus classified as internal strengths and weaknesses.

Strengths are assets often unique to the organization that competitors may not possess and could include marketing skills, critical human resources,

or even a product patent. *Weaknesses* may include pressing problems, including lack of cash flow or high debt, little market recognition, a weak website, or not using industry standard software. Externally, *opportunities* are ways to gather new business, often relying on an organization's strengths and could include ideas such as expanding internationally, marketing an "add-on" product or service, or pursuing a new major supplier. *Threats* may face the entire industry but could become opportunities if a firm quickly takes advantage of them. Examples of threats include new legislation, changes in the demographic makeup of the customer base, new technology, depressed economy, or an unstable political environment.

The idea behind SWOT analysis is to complete the list of variables under each of the four headings through brainstorming with company managers, employees, customers, consultants, or other knowledgeable parties and then developing strategies or future directions for an organization. The tool reminds managers that strategies must create an internal and external match. SWOT is used by business students, consultants, practitioners, marketing researchers, and academicians alike. The term was first described in the late 1960s, although the exact origin of the term is unknown.

Importance

SWOT's simplicity and catchy acronym perpetuates its usage in business and beyond as the tool is used to assess alternatives and complex decision situations. In the business arena, the grouping of internal and external issues is a frequent starting point for strategic planning. SWOT analysis is one of the most prevalent tools of strategic planning. The traditional SWOT analysis can be reconceptualized in terms of the direction and momentum where the market can still be changed. This provides insight into teaching marketing strategy and competitive rationality skills. It is a traditional means for searching for insights into ways of crafting and maintaining a profitable fit between a commercial venture and its environment. SWOT is used to identify cultural impediments and advantages and external governmental roles as well as internal company issues.

While SWOT analysis is primarily used to help an organization plan future strategies, the framework can also be applied to individuals or groups of individuals. Studies report use of the tool for individual organizations, for comparing two companies, and for assessing several companies. In studies of individual organizations, SWOT's use can be found in the subcategories of education; health care, government, and not-for-profit and for-profit companies. Industry studies have also benefited from SWOT analysis, and studies have even used the popular methodology to compare two or more industries.

More recently, SWOT analysis has been used to focus on countries or country pairs as well as entire industries. In the academic research, studies using SWOT range from assessing political correctness to career counseling to time management for builders. In cases published in various academic teaching journals or strategic management and business policy textbooks, students are often directed to use the SWOT analysis framework to profile an organization as they first begin to craft and defend new strategic alternatives. Outside the business setting, the framework can be used to evaluate any complex, personal decision.

Criticisms

The SWOT framework, with its vagueness, oversimplified methodology, and limitations, is often seen as a victim of its own success. SWOT analysis does not provide a sufficient context for adequate strategy optimization, and the simplicity may lead managers to use it incorrectly, producing short lists of nonprioritized, generalized bullet points. It is a good starting point, according to many managers, but it does not provide guidance on where new strategies will or should come from nor how to implement or achieve them.

The framework does simplify a complex internal and external environment into a shorter list of more manageable issues. Yet the reduction does require human judgment, which may vary and may not be comprehensive or parsimonious. The quantity and timeliness of information used in preparing the SWOT analysis is as important as the variety and dependability of the various perspectives involved. These experts must also be involved in assessing the reliability of the data as they interpret the information provided. Top managers emphasize financial strengths, whereas middle and lower managers tend to focus on technical issues suggesting a high potential for differences related to the level of management conducting the analysis. Perceptions can also be influenced by culture, so it is important to have

a diverse, multilevel group of internal and external stakeholders involved in the analysis.

The strengths may not lead to an advantage even though they are important to the firm. They may not provide a lasting advantage. Also, as environments change rapidly and life cycles of products and services continue to decrease, the environmental opportunities may be short-lived or may be too narrowly focused. Adequate benchmarking of competitors and the industry are also keys for a strong external analysis. Vetting and subjecting the findings to additional "due diligence" is needed to ensure that the information and the interpretation of the SWOT evidence is clear and appropriate. These processes can help reduce some of the subjective nature of SWOT analysis.

In addition, categorization of variables into one of the four SWOT quadrants is also challenging. Strengths that are not maintained may become weaknesses. Opportunities not taken, but adopted by competitors, may become threats. The differences between internal and external issues may be difficult to spot. Also, threats acted on quickly and effectively may be rally opportunities. Emerging technologies too have often not yet proved themselves as strength or a weakness.

Another potential problem with SWOT analysis is its circularity. We spot strengths because they allow organizations to capitalize on opportunities, and we identify opportunities by reflecting on an organization's strength.

SWOT is a moving target given the dynamic nature of strategy, and this may be only a situational analysis without a diagnostic capacity. SWOT is only one dimension of strategy and should also be combined with more innovative, creative brainstorming techniques to develop new products and services in new markets or market segments for long-term sustainability.

Alternatives for Improvements

Alternatives for SWOT include reorganized or repackaged lists of issues. In WOTSUP (weaknesses, opportunities, threats, and strengths, underlying planning), UP stands for "underlying planning" and in SOFT (strengths, opportunities, faults, threats), weaknesses have been re-identified as "faults." Others are the TOWS (threats, opportunities, weaknesses, and strengths) strategic matrix and the VRIO (value, rarity, imitability, and organizational) framework (which identifies resources by value, rareness, immutability, and organizational characteristics to recognize competitive advantages). Goals Grid has categories labeled achieve, preserve, avoid, and eliminate. Yet each alternative is a repackaged list of issues.

Resource-based SWOT analysis focuses on systemic causal issues that afford more perceptive, reliable, and actionable insights. The resource-based view categorizes SWOT variables only after the business has been carefully examined for both defensive and offensive goals.

Without ranking or weighting, planners may assume each of the SWOT variables is equal in scope and importance. Current research suggests the use of a quantifiable SWOT method that adopts the concept of multiple-criteria decision making (MCDM) or a multihierarchy scheme to simplify complicated problems. The indices of SWOT are voted on and weighted to assess the competitive strategy, and the total weighted scores method is then used to identify the best strategic alternatives.

SWOT can easily be combined with a number of other strategic models and techniques to organize qualitative data. For example, SWOT is useful in analyzing the organizational environment while value chain analysis or strategic mapping helps managers understand the value-generating components of the core activities. The Boston Consulting Group product portfolio matrix can assist in identifying the nature of the products offered by the industry. SWOT can be combined with Robert S. Kaplan and David P. Norton's *balanced score card* as well as used in organizations pursuing quality function deployment (QFD) methodology or for identify critical successful strategic perspectives prior to using the Malcolm Baldrige National Quality Award criteria. Michael E. Porter's *five forces analysis* moves beyond the internal analysis to focus on the organization's external environment, including the five competitive forces external to the organization. Porter's *diamond analysis* is also useful to shape strategy to reflect national strengths and weaknesses. Other complementary analyses include scenario analysis for exploring different futures, McKinsey's *Seven-S framework* to ensure that all parts of the internal organization work in harmony, Porter's generic strategies, for the best choice for competitive advantage, and

benchmarking to compare performance against external competitors or industry leaders.

Marilyn M. Helms

See also Balanced Scorecard; Diamond Model of National Competitive Advantage; Resource-Based View of the Firm; Strategic Decision Making; Strategic Profiles; Strategies for Change; Value Chain

Further Readings

Coman, A., & Ronen, B. (2009). Focused SWOT: Diagnosing critical strengths and weaknesses. *International Journal of Production Research, 47*(20), 5677–5689.

Dey, P. K., & Hariharan, S. (2008). Managing healthcare quality using combined SWOT and the analytic hierarchy process approach. *International Journal of Healthcare Technology & Management, 9*(4), 392–409.

Duarte, C., Ettkin, L. P., Helms, M. M., & Anderson, M. S. (2006). The challenge of Venezuela: A SWOT analysis. *Competitiveness Review, 16*(3/4), 233–247.

Evans, C., & Wright, (2009). How to conduct a SWOT analysis. *British Journal of Administrative Management, 24*, 10–34.

Grant, R. M. (2008). Why strategy teaching should be theory based. *Journal of Management Inquiry, 17*(4), 276–291.

Helms, M., & Nixon, J. (2010). Exploring SWOT analysis—Where are we now? A review of academic research from the last decade. *Journal of Strategy and Management, 3*(3), 215–251.

Helms, M. M., Rodriguez, M. A., De Los Rios, L., & Hargrave, W. (2011). Entrepreneurial potential in Argentina: A SWOT analysis. *Competitiveness Review, 21*(3), 269–287.

Kong, E. (2008). The development of strategic management in the non-profit context: Intellectual capital in social service non-profit organizations. *International Journal of Management Review, 10*(3), 281–299.

Mishra, R. P., Anand, G., & Kodali, R. (2008). A SWOT analysis of total productive maintenance frameworks. *International Journal of Management Practice, 3*(1), 51–69.

SYSTEMS THEORY OF ORGANIZATIONS

A common attribute claimed for an organizational science theory is that it is a systems theory. Indeed, most modern theories of organizations can be classified as systems theories, making it more of a general paradigm than a specific theory. In fact, systems theories expand well beyond theories of organizations to include theories of individuals, of which organizations are composed, down to theories of the cells of which individuals are composed. This generalizability was intentional. That is, early proponents of systems theories sought to describe a general set of principles that would be applicable to a wide range of phenomena across many levels of analysis. Interestingly, the approach has become both differentiated and reintegrated—two processes often described in systems theories—into various manifestations that make describing a single entity very difficult. Moreover, the principles are often paradoxical. Nonetheless, this entry attempts to describe some of the core principles, processes, and management insights arising from the systems perspective and their evolution and impact today, as well as to describe possible resolutions to the paradoxes stemming from the principles.

Fundamentals

Systems Theory

In its most general form, a systems theory describes its unit of inquiry (e.g., organizations) as a recognized whole composed of interrelated, interacting parts. The paradox arising from this description is that because the principle is so general, it can refer to nearly any unit of inquiry and thus appear not helpful in understanding any particular type of unit. The resolution of this paradox is the notion that many units of inquiry share properties and processes that can be ported from one type of unit to others—that strong analogies can be made—that inform theories across the units of inquiry. The major differences among systems theories are largely in terms of the fundamental observations that motivate theorizing and the properties and processes emphasized within the particular theory.

Two fundamental observations generally motivate systems theories. The first observation is that changes in one part of a system can have effects, often unexpectedly, on other parts of a system (i.e., the law of unintended consequences), and the second observation is that attempts to change a system often result in no change. Again, these observations form a paradox, but both can potentially be explained by the nature of the subsystems, interconnections among them, and the dynamics arising from the subsystems' operation. Thus, the systems theorist is interested in developing this explanation to create interventions that work but that do not lead to adverse side effects. Often, these types of interventions include many elements (i.e., describe changes in numerous parts of an organization) in order to effect the desired change while minimizing undesired change.

One property often emphasized in systems theories is that most systems have variables within them whose state at one time is at least partially a function of the previous state of the variable (i.e., $x_{1t} = f(x_{1t-1}, x_n)$). This relationship appears to hold because of one of two conditions. One condition is that some variables have "memory." That is, they retain their value over time and change by forces that move the variable from one state to another. These types of variables are called *dynamic, stock,* or *level variables.* If some specific force is applied to such a variable, the new state of the variable is a function of that force *and* the previous state of the variable (e.g., the new state of the variable is 2 plus the previous state of the variable). Moreover, the degree of the force's effect can be a function of the previous state of the variable (e.g., the new state of the variable is 2 times the previous state of the variable plus the previous state of the variable). The importance of this principle is highlighted with research that finds that humans, even ones well-trained in scientific principles, have trouble predicting the states of variables with memory, particularly when the effects take time to be realized.

A more complex but apparently ubiquitous condition that leads to the observation that the state of a variable at one time is a function of the state of the variable at a previous time is that changes to a variable's state at one time can feed back to influence subsequent states for the variable. Thus, changes to a variable might increase or decrease the likelihood or direction of future changes to the variable. An example of a specific type of system that demonstrates this property is a control system. Control systems include a mechanism for comparing the state of a variable with a desired state and acting on the variable when the state deviates from the desired state. A thermostat within a temperature control system is a classic example of this mechanism. These types of systems are also called *negative feedback loops* and the study of them is referred to as *cybernetics*. They are also the structure that describes the notion of a goal, whether an individual's, a group's, or an organization's. That is, a goal can be represented as a control system where the desired state of a variable is the goal. Finally, the control system is a primary explanation for the observation that attempts to change properties of a system often result in no change. In control theory language, such an attempt is considered a *disturbance*, which is exactly what control systems counteract (i.e., dampen).

Systems Theory of Organizations

W. R. Scott sought to categorize the vast array of organizational theories, all of which he considered systems theory. Specifically, Scott referred to systems theories that focus on an organization's goals and the control systems attempting to achieve and maintain those goals as *rational systems* theories. One example of a rational systems theory is Tannenbaum's control theory. This theory as well as earlier rational theories by sociologists (e.g., Talcott Parsons; Charles Perrow) focused on the goals of the organization. Scott contrasts rational systems theories with what he called *natural system* theories that emphasize the goals of the parts (i.e., the individuals in the organization) that may, or may not, be held in common or include the goal of maintaining the organization. Perhaps the most extreme of these is Richard Cyert and James March's garbage can model of organizational decision making, where the results of actions are evaluated after the fact rather than determined by a rational process of forethought. Finally, theories that focused on the interplay between the system and its environment (e.g., how the system obtains energy and information from the environment) Scott called *open systems* theories. Daniel Katz and Robert Kahn's social psychology theory, Eric Trist's sociotechnical systems theory, James D. Thompson's organizations in action theory, and Paul Lawrence and Jay Lorsch's contingency theory of organizations are classic open systems theory. A slightly more recent open system's theory is Jeffrey Pfeffer and Gerald Salancik's resource dependence theory, which focuses on the relevance of managing resources from the environment and the social aspects of this process. Scott's classification scheme is still popular today.

To give a flavor of the differences between the theories, consider that rational systems theories describe goals as their core concept. Specifically, they describe hierarchies of goals such that higher level goals are served by lower level goals. Moreover, one might use different subgoals, or means, to achieve a given goal. This leads to the property of *equifinality*, which is the notion that goals may be achieved via different means regardless of initial states. The implication of the principle is that analysis of a system involves focusing on the states a unit might be striving for as opposed to the behaviors used to get there. In contrast to this rational approach, Katz and Kahn described a comprehensive open systems theory of the organization. Their theory focused heavily on the individuals within organizations and how they interacted with each other. The theory barely mentioned goals, and indeed, when it did, it was to disparage them (i.e., the espoused goals of executives should not be taken on faith). Interestingly, other theories have since argued that both approaches share a strong tie to the control subsystem conceptualization. They merely differ regarding how centrally coordinated these networks of control subsystems are assumed to be. Clearly, one resolution of these paradoxical descriptions is that the degree of central coordination is a variable on which organizations vary.

Evolution

As mentioned, numerous systems theories have been developed and numerous types of systems are described in system's terms. Several theorists have attempted to create systematic taxonomies of systems. For example, the control systems described above represent the third level of a hierarchy of systems described by K. E. Boulding. In this hierarchy, levels in the hierarchy are a function of complexity, and complexity varies as a function of the composition (i.e., parts) of each system in each level. That is, each level becomes more complex by describing systems composed of the lower level systems. The levels include frameworks (i.e., static structures), clockworks (i.e., simple dynamic structures), thermostats (i.e., control systems), cells (i.e., open systems), plants, animals (adds mobility), human beings, social organizations, and transcendental systems. Many of the properties of lower level systems (e.g., goal striving found in control systems) are represented in the higher levels, while new properties *emerge* from the interaction among the lower level systems. For example, control systems are the third level, but the process they represent can be found in control theories of humans (seventh level) and organizations (eighth level). Between Boulding's third level and fourth level, open systems, he delineates life. Specifically, open systems have the critical property of negative entropy, which means the systems can acquire energy from the environment to organize and maintain their functioning.

One particularly ambitious systems theorist was J. G. Miller. Miller focused on living systems. For Miller, this included cells at the first level, followed by organs, organisms (e.g., humans), groups, organizations, societies, and finally supranational systems (e.g., the United Nations, the Internet). All these types of systems are conceived as containing 19 critical subsystems to sustain life (e.g., an ingestor that transforms energy from the environment into the system) and one (i.e., the reproducer) that is critical to the species or type of system, though the level of complexity of the subsystem depends on the level in the hierarchy. The bulk of Miller's approach can be found in a 1,102-page tome published in 1978 titled *Living Systems*. In that book, he attempted to support the conceptualizations put forth and to identify weaknesses in knowledge at that time.

The Boulding and Miller efforts represent integrative processes (i.e., processes seeking to organize or coordinate the parts of a system). Systems also engage in differentiation, which is the increased specialization that occurs as systems grow in complexity. In this case, numerous less grand systems theories arose from these grander efforts. For example, one review of systems theories identified 49 systems theories emerging between 1983 and 1994 that might be relevant to organizational scholars. For example, L. R. Beach's image theory is an example of a dual-level theory where the less than optimal decision-making processes of individuals and organizations are described within a single, systems perspective. Another influential but more comprehensive example is neoinstitutional theory described by Meyer and Scott in their 1983 book on organizational environments.

Importance

A major purpose of theories is to provide protocols for examining the unit of inquiry. Systems theories have provided numerous insights into the kinds of analysis one might do to understand an organization's function or how organizations function in their environments. For example, a common "systems" approach to studying organizations is to identify the environmental inputs (i.e., signals, material, and energy sources) that impinge the system and the outcomes that emerge from the system. However, such an approach is actually inconsistent with the principles of systems theories because it (a) ignores feedback processes and (b) treats the throughput processes as a black box.

More sophisticated analytic strategies include substantial qualitative research regarding networks, process tracing, and structural elements (e.g., technology, procedures, and policies). Also, several branches of systems theories use sophisticated quantitative methodologies. For example, a branch of systems theories called *system dynamics* focuses on representing the dynamically interacting parts of a system computationally so that simulations can be run to predict future behavior of the system. These models can become very complex, though they can often be decomposed into repetitions of the simple subsystems and structures. Yet they are necessary because the nonlinearities and dynamic processes described within the system and environment preclude logical analysis.

Other branches of systems theory also use computational modeling to predict the emerging effects of the interacting parts. The models are called *agent-based models* because they are composed of multiple, simple, rule-based systems (i.e., agents) placed in an environment and allowed to interact. For example, the agents might represent automobile drivers on a highway or people in a crowded room trying to escape through a single exit. These models can then help engineers design highways and rooms to minimize injury or maximize movement given the assumption that the rules represented in the models match the rules real systems (e.g., people) would use to govern their behavior in similar situations—a testable proposition in some cases. These types of models are particular useful for exploring the properties that emerge from (i.e., exists only at the level of the whole, but not the parts) interacting parts.

A relatively new branch of systems theories called dynamical systems also uses mathematical modeling and simulations to represent theoretical propositions and identify underlying simple structures that can account for complex behavior. This discipline has identified specific, frequently reoccurring data patterns common in dynamic data (i.e., longitudinal data).

In general, the quantitative modeling techniques represent a realization of the initial promise of systems theories. That is, they use general mathematically represented structures and processes put together in ways described by beliefs regarding the systems under investigation. These models can then be used to test the internal consistency of the beliefs (i.e., Can the theory "work"? Does it account for the phenomena observed or presumably explained by the theory?). The models can also be used to test elements of the theory without necessitating experimentation on the units themselves. This can be particularly important in the case of organizational theories where experimental control over hypothesized independent variables is difficult.

For managers, the systems perspective provides several, nonintuitive insights. For instance, S. A. Snell and P. M. Wright published several papers describing the implications of a systems perspective on strategy human resource management, and P. M. Senge describes creating learning organizations via embracing a systems perspective. These treatments acknowledge the difficulty of applying a rational approach to organizing, but they use tools from the systems perspective to facilitate sensemaking and intelligent institutionalization of effective actions (e.g., managing creativity and environmental diversity via personnel diversity coupled with institutional practices that optimize smooth interaction among participants). They also highlight when organizational decision makers can get into trouble, such as when lags in information motivate overreactions to noisy environmental conditions, but how overconfidence in effectiveness can result in slow reactions to true environmental change.

In conclusion, consider one final paradox. That is, if one were to peruse the organizational theory literature or vast majority of corporate communications these days, one might have a difficult time finding a reference to a systems theory of organizations. This is somewhat surprising given that in the latter half of the 20th century, it was difficult to find a theory of organizations that was not labeled a systems theory. However, the systems theory perspective is not gone; it is merely hidden within the assumptions of most modern theories of organizations. Moreover, the systems theory approach has provided a language for talking about organizations and sophisticated methods for analyzing organizations and organizational processes. Thus, systems theories have submerged as an assumption (or set of assumptions) rather than a point of inquiry. Said another way, the systems theory approach is not controversial; it is widely accepted and, when properly applied, critical to organizational success. The down side of this acceptance is that fewer theorists or executives are inspired by the progress made in understanding systems in other domains of inquiry—for example, in applying advanced knowledge of biological systems to better manage teams, corporations, and institutions. Moreover, the grand theorists of the heyday of systems theories are largely gone. Yet if these theorists are correct, the differentiation currently on the rise will lead to increased efforts at integration. Perhaps this is happening now.

Jeffrey B. Vancouver

See also Complexity Theory and Organizations; Human Resource Management Strategies; Image Theory; Learning Organization; Management Control Systems; Neo-Institutional Theory; Resource Dependence Theory; Role Theory

Further Readings

Ashmos, D. P., & Huber, G. P. (1987). The systems paradigm in organizational theory: Correcting the record and suggesting the future. *Academy of Management Review, 12,* 607–621.

Bertalanffy, L. von (1968). *General systems theory, foundations, development, and application.* New York, NY: George Braziller.

Boulding, K. E. (1956). General systems theory—The skeleton of science. *Management Science, 2,* 197–208.

Buckley, W. (1967). *Sociology and modern systems theory.* Englewood Cliffs, NJ: Prentice-Hall.

Katz, D., & Kahn, R. L. (1978). *The social psychology of organizations.* New York, NY: John Wiley.

Miller, J. G. (1978). *Living systems.* New York, NY: McGraw-Hill.

Millett, B. (1998). Understanding organizations: The dominance of systems theory. *International Journal of Organisational Behaviour, 1,* 1–12.

Richardson, G. P. (1991). *Feedback thought in the social science and systems theory.* Philadelphia: University of Pennsylvania Press.

Scott, W. R. (1998). *Organizations: Rational, natural, and open systems* (4th ed.). Upper Saddle River, NJ: Prentice Hall.

Vancouver, J. B. (1996). Living systems theory as a paradigm for organizational behavior: Understanding humans, organizations, and social processes. *Behavioral Science, 41*(3), 165–204.

TACIT KNOWLEDGE

Tacit knowledge is the central construct in Michael Polanyi's explanation of human knowing expressed in acts of interpretation and skillful performance. Whether knowledge is tacit or not turns on how individuals draw upon it as they think and act. Tacit knowledge remains outside a person's focal attention but is essential to reasoning and action. Tacit knowledge has been an important construct in research on knowledge creation and transfer, although the associated meaning in knowledge management research differs from that proposed by Polanyi. The following section of this entry, Fundamentals, clarifies the meaning of tacit knowledge. The next section, Importance, indicates (a) the tacit/explicit dichotomy in knowledge management research, (b) challenges to tacit knowledge as a construct, and (c) the connection between tacit knowledge and practices in organizations.

Fundamentals

Prompted by Polanyi's famous aphorism, "We can know more than we can tell," discussions of tacit knowledge in the management literature have pointed toward people's inability to articulate what they know or their never having done so (even if they could) as the defining characteristic of tacit knowledge. Although inarticulability or nonexplicitness frequently characterizes tacit knowledge, neither is the general criterion for qualifying knowledge as tacit in Polanyi's presentation. The essential consideration defining knowledge as tacit is that the knower draws upon the knowledge *subsidiarily* (i.e., nonfocally) in cognitive and physical activity. By definition, knowledge that is used subsidiarily is tacit.

The appropriate descriptor for the category of knowledge that contrasts with tacit knowledge is not *codified, articulated, theoretical,* or *explicit,* which indicate knowledge that has been put into words or written symbols. Neither is the appropriate label *codifiable, articulable,* or *explicable,* which indicates the *potential* for people to render knowledge in words or writing. The complement to tacit knowledge—telling us what tacit knowledge is not—is *focal* knowledge. Thus, the characterization of knowledge as tacit turns on how it is used, not on whether it has been verbalized or codified or on the difficulty of verbalizing or codifying it.

When we humans attend to knowledge expressed in verbal or written form, we do so on the basis of personal background knowledge. Although our focus is on what a speaker or document expresses, our interpretation draws upon our background understanding of words and contexts. Likewise, the act of speaking or writing expresses some aspect of a person's knowledge, yet it relies upon subsidiary knowledge. When people express, receive, or put to use knowledge, tacit knowledge always is involved.

Many actions make no direct use of formulaic (verbal or written) knowledge. Humans simply act, and we demonstrate our knowledge through our performances. The focus of our attention is on performing within a particular situation, and we have no need to consider directly or articulate the knowledge implicit in our action. When we humans act skillfully, we rely upon knowledge already internalized through practice. We give no consideration to how or whether this knowledge could be expressed in words or symbols; such considerations are irrelevant. People could attempt to put this subsidiary knowledge into words, but doing so is a fundamentally different activity from the skillful performance itself. Whereas in doing the activity, our focus is on performing within the situation (i.e., doing the task at hand), when we want to identify and articulate the knowledge involved, we shift to a reflective stance focused on how we perform.

Here is the key point in a nutshell. Skillful performances—be they acts of reasoning or bodily action—involve both relying upon one's own knowledge and attending to situations. As we humans attend *focally* to a subject or activity, other pertinent aspects of our knowledge become subsidiary. We attend *from* our background knowledge *to* the object of our focal awareness. Knowledgeable reasoning and acting always have this from-to structure. Any act of *attending to* is also an act of *attending from*. The knowledge from which we attend remains subsidiary and therefore tacit. Tacit knowledge includes the embodied capabilities and cognitive schema that are the background for our perceptions and actions. People can shift their focal awareness to that which was previously subsidiary and in so doing make focal that which was tacit, yet doing so does not undermine the inherent from-to structure of knowing. Knowledge always has a tacit dimension regardless of the subject of our focal awareness.

Keeping the particulars of our tacit knowledge outside our focus of attention aids skillful performance, whereas focusing on knowledge that previously operated subsidiarily introduces a distraction that undermines skillful performance. Focusing on the physical mechanics or implicit theories involved in actions, such as speaking, riding a bicycle, or playing a musical instrument, impairs proficiency. Focusing on how to perform, rather than simply acting, makes performing awkward. Tacit knowledge must remain subsidiary for us to perform proficiently.

An actor drawing upon tacit knowledge *indwells* such knowledge while the actor focuses elsewhere. We humans dwell in our knowledge just as we do our own bodies; indeed, tacit knowledge is an implication of embodiment. We rely upon our bodies as we attend to the world around us and act within it. In so doing, we relate to our own bodies subsidiarily as tools and sources of data. By implication, all knowing is personal. Our unavoidable reliance upon subsidiary knowledge undermines efforts to achieve impersonal objectivity.

Tacitness is a dynamic property, identifying how knowledge is used, rather than a stable property of the knowledge itself. A way of knowing—subsidiarily (or nonfocally)—is the basis for categorizing knowledge as tacit. How a particular actor in a particular situation accesses particular knowledge determines whether it is tacit. This is a process-oriented, rather than an object-oriented, way to classify knowledge as tacit. Knowledge that can be used focally or nonfocally in different situations defies general categorization as *tacit*. Nevertheless, if we observe people's consistent tendency to access particular knowledge nonfocally, we can—following Polanyi—reach a general characterization of such knowledge as tacit.

Importance

Three topics are central to assessing the validity and importance of tacit knowledge for organizations: (a) the tacit/explicit dichotomy applied to knowledge management, (b) tacit knowledge exhibited in practices, and (c) the research challenges associated with identifying tacit knowledge.

Tacit/Explicit Dichotomy

Researchers generally have addressed the implications of tacit knowledge for organizations by working from a tacit/explicit dichotomy. In this framing, *tacit knowledge* refers to uncodified or uncodifiable knowledge, whereas explicit knowledge is codified or codifiable in documents or other artifacts. The general claim motivating this research is that the tacit/explicit distinction carries implications for creating, storing, transferring, coordinating, and applying knowledge. Furthermore, the difficulties associated with transferring tacit knowledge between firms make it a potential source of sustainable competitive advantage.

In *The Knowledge-Creating Company,* Ikujiro Nonaka and Hirotaka Takeuchi explained *organizational knowledge creation* in terms of social interactions involving tacit and explicit knowledge. They described four knowledge conversion processes in organizations: (a) from tacit knowledge to tacit knowledge, or *socialization;* (b) from tacit knowledge to explicit knowledge, or *externalization;* (c) from explicit knowledge to explicit knowledge, or *combination,* and (d) from explicit knowledge to tacit knowledge, or *internalization.* In this explanation, organizational knowledge creation is the cumulative result of sequentially and repeatedly applying these four processes.

Strong interpersonal ties and dense social networks facilitate the transfer of tacit knowledge within and across organizations. Experience working together, trust, frequent communication, and proximity appear to be more important for facilitating the transfer of tacit knowledge than explicit knowledge. Furthermore, the transfer of tacit knowledge is associated with organizations' successful product and process innovation.

Using the tacit/explicit dichotomy facilitates empirical research by introducing a construct that is amenable to observation and measurement—explicit knowledge—and making tacit knowledge a residual category for all other knowledge. However, research applying the tacit/explicit dichotomy misses Polanyi's distinction between focal and subsidiary knowledge. Other complications arise from working from the tacit/explicit dichotomy because (a) the use of explicit knowledge always relies upon tacit knowledge—that is, we use codified knowledge in noncodifiable ways—and (b) the articulation of knowledge is necessarily incomplete; in other words, knowledge can never be fully explicit. Hence, although we can make a meaningful conceptual distinction between tacit and explicit knowledge, the two kinds of knowledge function complementarily when put to use.

Connection to Practices

Simply put, practices are shared ways of acting that are given meaning by a social context. By expressing knowing through action, practices manifest both focal and tacit knowledge. Because tacit knowledge is integral to practices, studies of practices and tacit knowledge are mutually informing. Practices have the same from-to structure that characterizes all tacit knowing. Learning and performing practices involve the cognitive, somatic, and social aspects described by Polanyi.

Participating in a community of practitioners facilitates learning by affording opportunities to observe, imitate, experiment with, reflect upon, and discuss new skills. Key processes for developing the tacit knowledge associated with practices include mentoring and repetition. Experts demonstrate skills and instruct apprentices thereby providing a focus of attention for early learning. Repeated personal experience is essential to shifting focal awareness from how to do the task to doing the task with proficiency. Tacit knowledge is demonstrated by experts and then generated anew by apprentices as they gain experience.

Research Challenges

The key challenges to tacit knowledge as an explanation for individuals' performative capabilities and organizational phenomena stem from (a) conflicting uses of the term and (b) the construct's unobservability.

Management researchers have used the term *tacit knowledge* in various ways, and the most prevalent meanings—noncodified knowledge and noncodifiable knowledge—conflict with Polanyi's understanding. The distinction between noncodified knowledge and codified knowledge is quite relevant to knowledge management, but noncodified knowledge is not synonymous with tacit knowledge. As explained above, the term *tacit* applies to knowledge that is used nonfocally. Polanyi understood *tacit knowledge* (a type of knowledge) as an implication of *tacit knowing* (a process). Confusion regarding tacit knowledge in the management literature may be due to neglect or misunderstanding of Polanyi, or, focusing on particular aspects of Polanyi's explanation to the neglect of others.

In view of the confusion surrounding tacit knowledge, Stephen Gourlay argues that researchers should shift their attention and efforts toward the streams of research that examine underlying aspects of the phenomenon. Studies of human neurology, motor skills, and implicit learning provide possible leads for explaining tacit knowledge. However, by breaking tacit knowledge into its particular components, we may lose sight of the multilevel dynamic process that Polanyi described. Tacit knowledge may be best understood holistically, and its relevance to management and organizations may be found through exploring both its intrapersonal and interpersonal dimensions.

Determining the tacit knowledge involved in an action is unavoidably problematic because tacit knowledge is not directly observable. In trying to figure out what knowledge is relevant but nonfocal, outside observers suffer from the inherent deficiency that they cannot observe the internal cognitive and somatic processes of practitioners. As insiders, practitioners may be able to reflect on what was focal during their actions, yet their ability to recall and articulate the subsidiary knowledge enabling what they do is limited. Outsiders can try to become insiders in order to gain this insightful perspective. Nevertheless, even the insider has no direct access to the knowledge that remains subsidiary (i.e., outside any practitioner's focal awareness) in the act of performing.

Scholars postulate the nature of tacit knowledge as an inference responding to this question: Given what we know about the focal attention of the actor, what other knowledge must be in use subsidiarily to account for a performance? Answers to this question rely upon practitioners' introspective reflections and researchers' reflections on comparable personal experiences. Dialogue can enhance practitioners' awareness of their tacit knowledge and elicit efforts to articulate that knowledge. Articulation does not make the knowledge any less tacit when the practitioner returns to performing and the knowledge reverts to being subsidiary.

For many research purposes (e.g., explaining the difficulty of transferring knowledge), it suffices to identify that there is more knowledge demonstrated in action than can be accounted for by what is focal for the performer, while the precise nature of the tacit knowledge necessarily remains unidentified.

Kent D. Miller

See also Knowledge-Based View of the Firm; Knowledge Workers; Organizational Culture Theory; Organizational Learning; Social Network Theory; Strategy-as-Practice

Further Readings

Baumard, P. (1999). *Tacit knowledge in organizations.* London,: Sage.

Collins, H. (2010). *Tacit and explicit knowledge.* Chicago, IL: University of Chicago Press.

D'Eredita, M. A., & Barreto, C. 2006. How does tacit knowledge proliferate? An episode-based perspective. *Organization Studies, 27,* 1821–1841.

Gourlay, S. (2007). An activity centered framework for knowledge management. In C. R. McInerey & R. E. Day (Eds.), *Rethinking knowledge management: From knowledge objects to knowledge processes* (pp. 21–63). Berlin, Germany: Springer.

Miller, K. D. (2008). Simon and Polanyi on rationality and knowledge. *Organization Studies, 29, 933–955.*

Nonaka, I., & Takeuchi, H. (1995). *The knowledge-creating company: How Japanese companies create the dynamics of innovation.* New York, NY: Oxford University Press.

Nonaka, I., & von Krogh, G. (2009). Tacit knowledge and knowledge conversion: Controversy and advancement in organizational knowledge creation theory. *Organization Science, 20,* 635–652.

Oğuz, F., & Şengün, A. E. (2011). Mystery of the unknown: Revisiting tacit knowledge in the organizational literature. *Journal of Knowledge Management, 15,* 445–461.

Polanyi, M. (1962). *Personal knowledge: Towards a post-critical philosophy.* Chicago, IL: University of Chicago Press.

Tsoukas, H. (2011). How should we understand tacit knowledge? A phenomenological view. In M. Easterby-Smith & M. A. Lyles (Eds.), *Handbook of organizational learning and knowledge management* (2nd ed., pp. 453–476). Chichester, England: Wiley.

TECHNOLOGICAL DISCONTINUITIES

A technological discontinuity (TD) is a novel and paradigm-inconsistent concept of creating and capturing value in a given industry. For instance, digital imaging (relative to film-based imaging), online news (relative to printed news), low-cost airlines (relative to flag carriers), quartz watches (relative to analog watches), and Voice over Internet Protocol (relative to traditional landline telecommunication) have been described as archetypal cases of TDs in their respective industries. TDs are a particularly challenging type of external change as they require established organizations to drastically modify internal processes. As exemplified by the stumbling of Polaroid and Kodak—incumbent firms in the photographic industry that lost their market dominance to new entrants whose businesses were based on digital imaging—TDs can engender drastic shifts in market structures. In the following section, the fundamental concepts underlying the prevailing theory on TDs are summarized. Thereafter, the historical evolution of research on TDs is explored. The final section discusses the impact of research on TDs on overall management theory and practice, as well as the limitations of existing approaches to the phenomenon of discontinuous change.

Fundamentals

Technologies

Much of the extant literature on TDs builds on a broad definition of the term *technology,* which is best summarized as "any given concept of how to create and capture value." The creation and capture of value encompasses three core dimensions. The first, *use value,* refers to the types and combinations of benefits that are proposed to customers. For instance, "ease of use," "shopping atmosphere," or "24/7 access to goods and services" are dimensions of use value. The second, the *process of value creation,* denotes how use value is created by transforming such inputs as labor, capital, materials, and information into outputs of higher value. Finally, the *process of value capturing* describes how companies capture the value they create in the form of economic surplus.

Paradigm-Consistent Versus Paradigm-Inconsistent Technological Change

Also underlying the concept of TDs is the assumption that technological change is either paradigm-consistent or paradigm-inconsistent. This notion dates back to Thomas Kuhn's description of the development of scientific knowledge. As Kuhn observed, scientific knowledge usually develops within a certain paradigm. In phases of what Kuhn calls "normal science," scientific research basically aims to actualize and extend a given set of accepted focal laws and logics. For example, the geocentric paradigm of cosmology drove scientific observation and progress for several hundred years. During this period, the goal of researchers was to match astronomic observations with Ptolemy's view of Earth as the center of the world.

In the history of science, there are also periods of nonparadigmatic change. At the beginning of such extraordinary periods, scholars become insecure about the fundaments of their science because they make observations that contradict established assumptions. These researchers subsequently challenge established assumptions and then establish a new paradigm that is incompatible with the previous, widely accepted, approach. For example, the generations of astronomers working around the time of Copernicus, Galileo, and Kepler collected observations that falsified the Ptolemaic model. These astronomers then developed a heliocentric cosmology that allowed for more precise explanations and predictions of astronomical phenomena.

The theory of discontinuous technological change assumes that technologies generally function similarly to scientific paradigms. Under "normal" circumstances, improvements in goods and services remain within established criteria of use value, and they fulfill the basic logic of how inputs are transformed into goods of higher value and how companies capture this value in the form of profits. In such phases, industries develop into stable systems of (often oligopolistic) players. Under extraordinary circumstances, however, industries become unstable because "Schumpeterian" entrants use discontinuous technologies to challenge established players.

Analogously, technological evolution has been conceptualized by Philipp Anderson and Michael Tushman as encompassing two cyclically repetitive phases: an *era of ferment* and an *era of incremental change.* An era of ferment begins with the appearance of a technological discontinuity that deviates dramatically from the established paradigm of innovation (e.g., the automobile in comparison to horse carriages). The appearance of this revolutionary concept is followed by a design competition between different technologies, all of which are incompatible with the established technology (e.g., different types of motors). As a number of new technologies are competing for dominance, decision makers become highly uncertain about which technology to adopt. An important feature of an era of ferment is that the established technology still exhibits a residual fit with the market environment (e.g., people continued to use carriages for many decades after the automobile was introduced). In other words, even though the old technology is increasingly substituted with a new technological paradigm, market segments remain in which a company can create and capture value utilizing established resources and capabilities.

An era of incremental change begins with the establishment of one *dominant design.* Technological progress during this second era includes elaborations of the dominant design, but, as in Kuhn's normal science phase, no revolutionary designs (e.g., improvements of the dominant petrol engine). The era of incremental design ends with the appearance of a new technological discontinuity and the cyclical process starts again.

Categories and Measures of Technological Discontinuities

While TDs and their consequences are the topic of a multitude of articles and books, there is no widely accepted scale for measuring the degree to which an innovation is discontinuous. Nevertheless, it is possible to integrate the different types of discontinuous technological change described in the literature by categorizing a given occurrence of technological change as a TD if that change falls into at least one of the following three domains: (a) a discontinuous change in the use value offered, (b) a discontinuous change in the value-creation process, and (c) a discontinuous change in value capturing.

Discontinuous change in the use value offered. Historically, innovation research has focused on changes in perceived use value. For instance, Richard Foster's *technology S-curve* model posits that the performance evolution of a technology is an S-shaped function of the cumulated resources spent on developing that technology. This model implies that, at the end of a technology life cycle, even significant resource commitment cannot yield substantial increases in technological progress because the technology has reached its natural performance limit. At this point, a new technology may begin to compete against the old technology. Even though the new technology may initially perform worse than the established technology, it develops and ultimately exceeds the established technology's performance level.

Clayton Christensen takes the S-curve approach one step further. As he points out in his theory on "disruptive innovations," TDs often underperform relative to existing technologies early in the innovation life cycle. However, this is only true when performance is measured based on established performance criteria. With regard to other performance criteria, TDs often outperform old approaches. In fact, TDs alter the basis for competition by introducing new performance metrics along which firms compete. For example, such innovations are often simpler, smaller, more convenient to use, and cheaper. Consequently, technological discontinuities are typically more attractive to low-end or new

customers. Furthermore, as proposed by Tushman and Anderson, discontinuous innovations are "competence-destroying" innovations: They render old resources and capabilities less important. Most importantly, established social capital and relational resources, such as knowledge about the purchasing behaviors of existing high-end customers, become less relevant relative to knowledge about low-end or new customer segments.

Christensen uses the example of personal computers (PCs), such as the Apple II, to explain technological discontinuities in the context of perceived use value. When they were first sold, PCs had much lower storage capacity than minicomputers—the leading devices at the time. Therefore, PCs appeared unattractive to the mainstream customers in the minicomputer market. However, PCs met other performance criteria that the established technology did not. For instance, they were smaller, easier to use, and cheaper than minicomputers. As a result, consumers outside the group of mainstream minicomputer users valued PCs. Over time, PC manufacturers were able to increase the storage capacity of personal computers until PCs became an attractive alternative to minicomputers, even for customers of minicomputer manufacturers.

When faced with paradigmatically different concepts of perceived use value, established companies are required to significantly change their mental models of how to succeed in their business. For instance, engineers at Digital Equipment Company (DEC), the world's leading manufacturer of minicomputers in the late 1970s, consistently focused their efforts on increasing the storage capacity of their machines because this was the most relevant performance attribute for DEC's main customers. As such performance characteristics as size or convenience were unimportant to their customers, they could be neglected by DEC's research and development department. However, when the TD emerged, the same engineers were asked to focus on previously irrelevant performance attributes. Thus, engineers at minicomputer manufacturers had to change their mental model of how the computer business functioned.

Discontinuous change in the value-creation process. TDs are not only product related. They also include discontinuous developments within the processes that create value. Process innovations are important because they can increase the use value offered by a company and lower the costs a company incurs when creating that value. Low-cost airlines, such as Southwest Airlines or Ryanair, are a good example of a discontinuous process innovation relative to the established concept of flag carriers. In fact, the purely technical part of the two technologies was not much different. Low-cost airlines built on the same components as established carriers. However, the architecture of the internal value chain of low-cost airlines was leaner and less complex than those of large flag carriers and contradicted fundamental assumptions about value creation held by the traditional players.

Discontinuous change of process architectures significantly affects the value of the different parts of an organization's internal value chain. Such TDs make existing organizational and procedural structures obsolete, destroy the value of established core competencies, or diminish the value of existing knowledge bases. While the value created can remain the same, the processes of creating this value are systematically altered.

To some degree, Dell's direct-sales model in the PC industry is another illustrative example of a competence-destroying discontinuous process innovation. While the value chain of Dell's peers relied on pushing pre-configured products in the market, Dell's model built on a *pull approach* whereby customers could configure the computer by themselves, pay, and receive a highly customized machine only a few days later. Dell's business model fundamentally differed from the traditional concept of value creation in the computer industry. Furthermore, value creation traditionally flowed from procurement through production, assembly, and sales to the end customer. Accordingly, demand forecasting was an important competence in the established business model. In Dell's paradigm, however, competencies, such as demand forecasting, were of much less importance than in the established paradigm.

Discontinuous change in value capturing. The value captured by a company, or producer surplus, is the difference between the price charged for goods sold by that company and the incurred costs. Recent research in the field of strategic innovation, business model innovation, and disruptive strategic innovation emphasizes the importance of discontinuous change to the way that companies capture the value they create. This literature points out that such discontinuities often entail a reconceptualization of the value network in which a company is active. As a result, old streams of income become substantially less important than new streams of income. For instance, the incumbent Microsoft captures value directly from end customers by selling its software package MS Office at a given price. In contrast, Google captures value indirectly: It provides customers with the office software Google Docs for free. To capture the value created, Google sells advertising space and other services on its platform to business customers. Thus, Google has redefined the value network in which the company operates by focusing on maximizing the value created for advertising customers instead of concentrating on maximizing the value created for consumers. In Google's business model, the traditional source of income, namely, sales of software packages, is less important than new streams of income.

Evolution

The evolution of research into TDs can broadly be separated into three overlapping phases. During the initial phase, scholars primarily built on the work of Joseph Schumpeter. Schumpeter used the originally Marxist term of *creative destruction* to describe the pattern in which small, but innovative, new entrants are repeatedly able to use TDs to take market leadership from large incumbent firms. In particular, scholars focused on the inertia of established organizations in response to TDs and showed that incumbents often myopically overlook or misinterpret these radical shifts and therefore adopt them too late and too timidly. For instance, Theodore Levitt provided a classic account of the failure of North American railroad companies to adapt to the changes triggered by the advent of new technologies such as airplanes.

In the second phase, scholars were primarily devoted to explaining incumbent inertia by applying various theoretical lenses. Michael Hannan and John Freeman's application of population ecology is particularly influential in this regard. These scholars theorized that incumbent inertia is rooted in a dilemma inherent in any organization: to succeed in stable circumstances, organizations work toward reliability, efficiency, and stability; however, efficient routines are dysfunctional in times of discontinuous change. Other prominent advances include institutionalist explanations of inertia by Paul DiMaggio and Walter Powell, research by Richard Gilbert and

David Newbery describing the effect of companies' inherent avoidance of cannibalization, and disruptive innovation theory by Christensen.

Current research on TDs is characterized by a more nuanced account of technological change and organizational adaptation and a study of factors that might cause an established organization to resist the prevailing pattern and to overcome organizational paralysis. Many of these researchers adopt the lens of cognitive organizational psychology and show that how decision makers make sense of and interpret TDs can lead to substantial differences in how they respond. For instance, Clark Gilbert showed that organizations that perceive a given TD as a threat are more likely to invest aggressively in that innovation than organizations that perceive the TD as an opportunity. Mary Tripsas recently highlighted the role of organizational identity in the context of organizational adaptation, and Sarah Kaplan showed that CEOs' varying levels of attention to discontinuous change can lead to differences in their companies' response behaviors. Other recent research has focused on the influence of external constituents on incumbent reactions to TDs. In particular, Mary Benner has shown that securities analysts tend to penalize incumbents for leaving established technology trajectories. Finally, a larger body of research, kindled by Charles O'Reilly and Tushman, focuses on organizational design. These studies demonstrate that ambidextrous structures are a dynamic capability that helps organizations to capture value from TDs. Ambidexterity provides those organizational units that explore and market TDs with independence from established business routines, which is necessary to succeed in radically shifting environments.

Importance

Research into TDs and their effects on industrial change belong to the core of current management theory. This is not surprising given the increasing pace and amplitude of technological change in national and global economies. Many models of technological change have been corroborated by rich sets of qualitative and quantitative data. Nevertheless, theory on TDs remains a subject of debate. In particular, critics have argued that most change is continuous rather than discontinuous and that the importance of discontinuous change for managers is largely overemphasized. Others have scrutinized the dialectical notion underlying the model of discontinuous change and questioned whether the degree of discontinuity of a technology can ever be objectively measured. Finally, some opponents disapprove of the normative position of many studies on technological change, which implicitly envision the stability of industrial structures—and, as such, the dominance of established quasi monopolists—as the ultimate goal.

Research on TDs is also highly relevant for management practice. In particular, scholars in this area provide recommendations on how established organizations can work to prevent failure. Most importantly, incumbents should create ambidextrous structures, build up broad networks with diverse sets of outsiders, and enter into alliances to strategically use complementary assets to leverage the economic potential of TDs. For instance, incumbent organizations in the pharmaceutical sector have benefited greatly from alliances with new entrants when adapting to the changes triggered by the emergence of biotechnology. In these partnerships, the incumbent companies primarily contributed to the capturing of value through their knowledge and resources in the area of marketing and sales. The biotech companies, on the other hand, allowed the partnership to maximize value creation by providing the necessary know-how and skills of biotechnology-based research and development.

Similarly, research on TDs has implications for entrepreneurial start-ups. Most importantly, new entrants can exploit the generic weaknesses that incumbent organizations fall prey to when responding to discontinuous change. For instance, start-ups are more likely to succeed if they are able to launch products in market areas that are unattractive, or even systematically disregarded, by established players (for example, due to small market size, lower margins, or different performance metrics). Entrepreneurs should also systematically aim to develop innovations that contradict the tried-and-true method of value capturing, for example, by introducing modular, razor-blade business models (such as Apple's App Store) or by disintermediating existing steps in the value chain (such as Amazon's attempts to enter the publishing business).

Overall, however, the biggest challenge underlying all of these recommendations is that it is still difficult for managers to know whether a new technology is going to pan out in the future, or not. Research, particularly in the area of disruptive innovation theory, suggests that certain situations improve the odds for a discontinuous technology to appear (for instance, an overserving of customer needs by established offerings or the inability of potential customers to use an existing technology). Other recent research, primarily that conducted by Ron Adner, recommends executives to take a more inclusive look at innovation by integrating the entire innovation ecosystem (specifically the innovations of complementors and suppliers that are necessary to allow your own inventions to succeed) into the equation. All scholars unanimously agree though that staying flexible and being ready to execute at the same time is paramount for long-time firm survival.

Andreas S. König

See also Dynamic Capabilities; First-Mover Advantages and Disadvantages; Innovation Diffusion; Innovation Speed; Schemas Theory; Sensemaking; Strategic Flexibility; Technology S-Curve

Further Readings

Adner, R. (2012). *The wide lens: A new strategy for innovation*. New York, NY: Penguin.

Ahuja, G., Lampert, C. M., & Tandon, V. (2008). Moving beyond Schumpeter: Management research on the determinants of technological innovation. *Academy of Management Annals, 2*, 1–98.

Benner, M. J. (2010). Securities analysts and incumbent response to radical technological change: Evidence from digital photography and internet telephony. *Organization Science, 21*, 42–62.

Christensen, C. M. (1997). *The innovator's dilemma*. Boston, MA: Harvard Business School Press.

Hill, C. W. L., & Rothaermel, F. T. (2003). The performance of incumbent firms in the face of radical technological innovation. *Academy of Management Review, 28*, 257–274.

Kaplan, S. (2008). Cognition, capabilities and incentives: Assessing firm response to the fiber-optic revolution. *Academy of Management Journal, 51*, 672–695.

Tripsas, M., & Gavetti, G. (2000). Capabilities, cognition and inertia: Evidence from digital imaging. *Strategic Management Journal, 21*, 1147–1161.

Tushman, M. L., & Anderson, P. (1986). Technological discontinuities and organizational environments. *Administrative Science Quarterly, 31*, 439–465.

TECHNOLOGY ACCEPTANCE MODEL

The technology acceptance model (TAM) is a theory that seeks to explain how users of a technology come to accept and use a technology. Most prevalent in information systems literature, the theory, TAM, has been applied across a wide variety of organizational and national contexts and in many respects parallels the diffusion of innovation interest in the field of information systems. In this field, the need to reliably predict failures of system implementations in terms of adoption and use remains an understudied, yet critical, area of the information systems field. This entry provides in-depth fundamentals and history of the TAM, including its validity and criticism, as well as use in management research and in applied domains.

Fundamentals

TAM is an extension of the theory of reasoned action, introduced by Fred Davis in 1989, that has found a prominent place in the information systems literature as a reliable and parsimonious theory of technology acceptance. The latter characteristic, parsimony, is not just extant in the paucity of constructs and linking relationships of the theory but also in its theoretical transparency to the average person. Thus, TAM can be easily explained and accepted at face value by a lay audience, while simultaneously passing the rigor of theoretical and empirical testing fairly well. The use of TAM findings in a prescriptive manner is chief among its shortcomings.

The TAM posits that when a user is considering use of a new technology, the user forms two key perceptions (beliefs) regarding the technology: *perceived usefulness* and *perceived ease-of-use*. These beliefs are formed from external and internal influences at the individual (i.e., experience) and social level (culture, organizational policy, group norms, etc.). From these beliefs, an *attitude toward using* is formed by the user. Finally, *intention to use* is theorized as a key determinant of *actual use*. External variables, such as specific technology characteristics and individual attributes, are posited to be mediated by, and even antecedents to, beliefs. Perceived usefulness was originally defined by Davis in 1989 as "the degree to which a person believes that using a particular system would enhance his or her job performance" and perceived ease-of-use as "the degree to which a person believes that using a particular system would be free from physical and mental effort" (p. 320). Thus, the more an individual believes that a technology will enhance their job performance and the less they believe the effort will be in using the technology, the greater the intention to use it. The original theory also included the specification of external variables that would have influence on perceived usefulness and perceived ease-of-use. In early studies, these external variables were chiefly technology characteristics, but that would change quickly.

Over the past two decades, the TAM has been empirically tested and has evolved from its initial model to incorporate greater breadth of external influences, antecedents of the principal independent variables, and testing of theoretical relationships between constructs. Researchers would find that intention to use (i.e., behavioral intention) was a better predictor of actual use and that attitude toward use was neither empirically or theoretically necessary in the model. Furthermore, comparisons of the TAM to the theory of planned behavior and the theory of reasoned action showed that the TAM was equally as predictive, and greatly more parsimonious, than either of the more sophisticated models at predicting intention to use. A new model, TAM2, introduced by Viswanath Venkatesh and Davis a decade after TAM, incorporated social influence (e.g., subjective norms, voluntariness, image, etc.) and cognitive process (e.g., job relevance, output quality), related constructs that had been explored and validated by researchers over the first decade of empirical and theoretical refinement. TAM2 was found to be a valid expanded specification of the original TAM model in a series of four longitudinal studies in both voluntary and involuntary implementation settings. TAM2's incorporation of additional construct antecedents, systems characteristics, and contextual measures responded well to the oft-stated criticism of theoretical simplicity. A final revision by Venkatesh and Hillol Bala in 2008, called TAM3, further specified antecedents to perceived usefulness from TAM2 and included work introduced on anchoring and adjustment from research on framing in decision making as antecedents of perceived ease of use, which fully specified and merged the preceding two decades of research of TAM into a single model.

In all, the TAM has been well cited, studied across a diverse set of technologies from voicemail to presentation software to decision support systems, in a broad range of cultures from the United States to Europe to Asia and among a cross section of users from students to doctors, programmers, and brokers. While providing ample evidence to support the validity of the TAM, this research also demonstrated that perceived usefulness was a more powerful predictor of intention to use, thus, sparking more focused study on the possible antecedents of perceived usefulness. TAM2 was found to be valid in environments of either mandatory or voluntary use and extended the antecedents of perceived usefulness, while TAM3 further included expansion with respect to ease-of-use and social context. Ironically, the TAM in all its forms has failed to provide more than a descriptive view of technology adoption and remains locked at the micro level of individual use. Nonetheless, the TAM holds promise in the area of information systems research as it has matured sufficiently for prescriptive strategies to be proposed.

Importance

Despite its high citation rates, extensive reliability testing, and overall robustness across contexts, the TAM is not without criticism. The number and sophistication of these criticisms varies wildly, but there are some common themes. Among these are the criticisms of the deterministic specification of technology use predicted by only two belief constructs (perceived usefulness and ease-of-use) leading to intention to use leading to actual use. The root of these criticisms stems from the individual behavior level of analysis which effectively negates an understanding of the strategizing that is often the context of technology adoption where the actualization of intention is constrained, or even blocked, because of an external constraint or social processes. For example, the intention-actual use link may be modified by a preferred vendor agreement, a marketing campaign, or the implementation strategy of the technology itself. This criticism also rises above a purely theoretical criticism pointing to a broader effect on prescriptive strategies born of the research using the model. This is due to the fact that any effective strategy for improving technology adoption, in even a small scale, requires a level of analysis above the individual. Even if the summation of individual intentions is employed as a surrogate for collective behavior, the overall prediction confidence is likely below 50%, well short of engineering desires, but nonetheless useful to improving on the success rates of modern information systems implementations.

Despite the theoretical limitations that may lead to prescriptive faults, criticism of the TAM's lack of application in mitigating a surprisingly low implementation success and intended adoption rates are common. In many respects, the context in which the TAM is studied is often a single adoption and not a series of adoptions or adoptions in which the strategy of attaining a certain level of adoption is the goal. The consequence is that learning and social influence remain relegated to preadoption beliefs alone. The theoretical criticism leveled above reenters here in that all technology use is adopted in a social context and so too must the prescriptive strategies leading to more successful adoption.

Notwithstanding the limitations, there has been limited progress on the prescriptive implications by Venkatesh and his colleagues in the form of a proposed *unified theory of acceptance and use of technology* and TAM3. In one case, the TAM constructs were conceived of in more prescriptive fashion, which gleaned a somewhat prescriptive strategy that is in line with the impetus of the original research. This research adapted the TAM measures into a usefulness/ease-of-use two-by-two model of attributes conceiving of and testing four implementation strategies for a technology in the human computer interface context.

The impact of TAM, in all its forms, lies in two areas. The first is the pursuit of understanding how users select which technology to use. In this respect, TAM is a parsimonious theory with a relatively rich history and robustness of application. Although perhaps simplistic and obvious, a managerial takeaway from this is that one should carefully balance the management of perceived usefulness and ease-of-use in technology implementations, perhaps even equally with budget changes, deadlines, and other project management considerations to better ensure intended use. The relative cost of efforts to influence or understand perceptions to the financial cost of modern technology projects can thus yield significant returns or savings in any given project.

The second is the ability to provide sufficient understanding and predictive power such that user intentions can be incorporated fruitfully into and implementation and adoption strategies. In this respect, the TAM falls short. Development in this area would further solidify the TAM in the information systems adoption field and would likely allow the theory to find application and connection to broader innovation diffusion and technology literatures. Nonetheless, managers should solicit and value user intentions, perceptions of usefulness, and ease-of-use in their implementation planning and implementation. This consideration also serves in reducing counterimplementation efforts by users as well as reducing time to technology adoption. Again, the financial costs of enterprise implementations and the pervasiveness of their impact to an organization may compound the negative effects of ignoring basic TAM prescriptions.

Edward W. Christensen

See also Decision-Making Styles; Innovation Diffusion; Theory of Reasoned Action

Further Readings

Bagozzi, R. P. (2007). The legacy of the technology acceptance model and a proposal for a paradigm shift. *Journal of the Association for Information Systems, 8*(4), 244–254.

Davis, F. D. (1989). Perceived usefulness, perceived ease of use, and user acceptance of information technology. *MIS Quarterly, 13*(3), 319–340.

Davis, F. D., Bagozzi, R. P., & Warshaw, P. R. (1989). User acceptance of computer technology: A comparison of two theoretical models. *Management Science, 35,* 982–1003.

Lee, Y., Kozar, K. A., & Larsen, K. R. T (2003). The technology acceptance model: Past, present and future. *Communications of the Association for Information Systems, 12,* 752–780.

Silva, L. (2007). Post-positivist review of technology acceptance model. *Journal of the Association of Information Systems, 8*(4), 255–266.

Venkatesh, V., & Bala, H. (2008). Technology acceptance model 3 and a research agenda on interventions. *Decision Sciences, 39*(2), 273–315.

Venkatesh, V., & Davis, F. D. (2000). A theoretical extension of the technology acceptance model: Four longitudinal field studies. *Management Science, 46*(2), 186–204.

Technology Affordances and Constraints Theory (of MIS)

Information systems are combinations of devices, software, data, and procedures designed to address the information processing needs of individuals and organizations. Examples include electronic mail and social networking tools as well as enterprise-level applications for financial management, decision making, production planning, and so forth. The pervasiveness of information systems in organizational practices and daily life makes their study increasingly critical for management theory. There is no single theory of *management information systems* (MIS). Rather, the term refers to a broad class of conceptual frameworks developed to understand and explain the design, use, administration, and consequences of information systems. One framework that is used increasingly to study how people and organizations use information systems and how the use of information systems affects individuals, organizations, and their performance, is a framework we refer to as *technology affordances and constraints theory* (TACT). TACT's essential premise is that to understand the uses and consequences of information systems, one must consider the dynamic interactions between people and organizations and the technologies they use. In this entry, we first explain the major theoretical constructs and focus of TACT and then discuss its importance for management theory.

Fundamentals

The concept of technology affordance refers to an action potential, that is, to what an individual or organization with a particular purpose can do with a technology or information system; technology constraint refers to ways in which an individual or organization can be held back from accomplishing a particular goal when using a technology or system. Affordances and constraints are understood as *relational concepts,* that is, as potential interactions between people and technology, rather than as properties of either people or technology. Affordances and constraints are best phrased in terms of action verbs or gerunds, such as "share knowledge" or "information sharing." Other examples include "working anywhere anytime" and "introducing

like-minded people to each other" and "preventing proscribed organizational practices." Affordances and constraints are distinct from *technology features,* which are functionalities built into information systems either by design or by accident. For example, "a shared communication space accessible by all users" and "the automatic calculation of raw material orders from data about a new sale" are examples of technology features and functionality. Affordances and constraints are also distinct from *human and organizational attributes,* such as tasks, needs, and purposes. Finally, a distinction is made between affordances and what was afforded by the use of the technology: Affordances refer to action *potentials* that technologies represent for users with certain characteristics and purposes, while "afforded by" is employed when examining use that *occurred* for a particular purpose within a particular context.

The value of having the relational concepts of technology affordances and constraints that are distinct from both technology features and human purposes is that they help explain two common empirical observations. First, people and organizations do not always realize the apparent potential of a technology when they use it. Second, people and organizations sometimes or often use technology in ways that designers never intended. As relational concepts, affordances and constraints facilitate the scholarly understanding that what one individual or organization with particular capabilities and purposes can or cannot do with a technology may be very different from what a different individual or organization can do with the same technology. For instance, social networking software may afford different patterns of technology use and consequences in organizations with cultures that reward information sharing than in organizations with cultures that reward information hoarding. At the same time, patterns of technology use and consequences cannot be understood solely by reference to human and organizational attributes, such as culture, but must also be understood in relation to the features of particular technologies. For example, the uses and outcomes of social networking technology in organizations may depend on differences in the social-networking software they use (text-based messaging software versus a virtual reality system).

TACT can be used to study either the unique technology-involved practices of particular individuals or organizations or the patterns of similarity and difference in technology uses and consequences across individuals or organizations. Scholars employing TACT can come at technology uses and consequences from either direction. That is, they can hypothesize about affordances and constraints by first analyzing the features and functionalities of a technology, such as asynchronous message transmission. Or they can start by analyzing human and organizational purposes, such as the desire to have effective teams with geographically distributed members. However, scholars employing TACT do not stop either at features or purposes, but rather, they continue by examining interactions among them. Thus, one TACT researcher may describe how an organization uses the affordances of electronic communication technology to keep projects going nonstop: At the end of a workday, one co-located team "passes" the project to another co-located team just starting its workday elsewhere in the world. Another TACT researcher may determine that electronic communication technology affords development of shared identity in some virtual teams, while affording the development of enhanced individual self-efficacy in another.

Regardless of whether a scholar's focus is on the unique practices observed in particular settings or in transcontextual patterns, researchers who employ TACT emphasize the potential actions that technologies with particular features afford (or hinder) for people and organizations with particular purposes and characteristics. TACT scholars then use the concepts of affordances and constraints to interpret or explain people's technology uses and consequences. Again, affordances and constraints are understood as conceptual relations between people and organizations and their technologies—they are the action potentials or potential stumbling blocks that people can draw on or may encounter when using a particular technology.

Importance

Management scholars commonly explain technology uses and consequences with psychological, sociopsychological, or sociological theories. When they consider technology at all, they use simplifying assumptions, for instance, about communication being "synchronous" or "asynchronous" or about media being "rich" or "lean." These theories have several limitations for scholars interested in the role of technologies in human and organizational behavior. First, existing theories may privilege "natural" human behavior over behavior that involves or is mediated by technology. For example, face-to-face communication is considered to be the baseline against which all mediated communication seems impoverished or diminished in some way. This privileging of the natural ignores the possibility that humans using technology can often enact new practices or achieve outcomes that could not occur without the use of technology. An example is the ability of people using social media to find and develop intense personal relationships with like-minded others whom they have never met face-to-face.

Second, existing theories may assume that technology is fixed and immutable. This assumption blinds researchers to the possibility of people using technology in "unintended" ways. For instance, electronic mail is commonly understood as a technology that supports asynchronous and cross-location communication. However, people sometimes use electronic mail to communicate synchronously with people sitting right next to them. They may do so because email affords them creating a written record of the communication that can be shared with third parties and referred to later to follow up on requests and promises. Alternatively, they may do so because email affords them the opportunity to engage in organizationally required communication with people they do not like. In addition, people and organizations often modify apparently fixed technologies, such as by combining them with other technologies and practices. For instance, some organizations combine enterprise software with "business intelligence" technology in ways that afford dramatic changes in their decision-making processes and performance.

By contrast to most existing management theories, TACT avoids both limitations discussed above by explicitly focusing attention on the nondeterministic interactions between people or organizations and the technologies they use. On the other hand, TACT itself has a few disadvantages. First, because TACT is a relatively new framework for the study of individual and organizational technology uses and outcomes, there is inconsistency in the terminology used by TACT scholars, and controversies exist over some core concepts and assumptions. For example, some scholars refer to what we call TACT using the label of *sociomateriality*. One core controversy concerns the ontological status of "technology." Some TACT scholars assert that technology is inseparable from (that is, has no ontological existence apart from) the ways in which people and organizations use it. These scholars refer to "technology-in-use" and consider the distinction between technology and human or organizational use of technology to be analytical only. Other TACT scholars accept an ontological distinction between technology and individual or social practices; that is, they believe that technologies have features and functionalities regardless of whether humans recognize or use them. These scholars acknowledge, however, that technology and social practices are tightly intertwined in a way that is sometimes called "imbrication."

A second limitation of TACT attributable to its relative newness is that there are as yet few empirical studies, and most TACT studies to date are individual case studies. As a result, TACT scholars have not made much progress toward consensus about the existence, nature, and naming of technology affordances and constraints across contexts or technologies. In part, this is a function of the granularity of analysis. If technology analysis is fine-grained and each setting is treated as unique, there are virtually infinite combinations of technology and human or organizational behavior. Conversely, if the scope is broad enough, that is, if all instances of a class of technologies (e.g., enterprise systems) or even all information technologies are considered at once, the "general" affordances and constraints may be so few in number and so abstract that they are not useful to other scholars. For instance, for the class of decision support systems, the accepted affordances and constraints ("guidance" and "restrictiveness") are quite general and can be interpreted as synonyms for *affordance* and *constraint*. Similarly, "simplification" has been proposed as an essential affordance or constraint of information technology as a whole. The abstractness of such concepts seems likely to hinder efforts by other scholars to apply them. Over time, an accumulation of TACT studies may enable scholars to agree on the most productive levels of abstraction and generality for the identification and description of affordances and constraints.

In sum, for TACT to generate testable predictions about human and organizational behavior and outcomes, the concepts of affordance and constraint should be concretely examined for particular categories of technologies and use settings. While examining technologies and uses concretely may deter some scholars, it actually makes TACT appealing to some scholars, including those who aim to build theory, those who aim to interpret human and organizational technology-use behavior, those who aim to construct post hoc explanations of behaviors and outcomes in individual case studies, and those who are interested in more precisely defining *alignment*, or *fit*, between people and technology.

Despite its recentness and current limitations, technology affordances and constraints theory holds great promise for contributing to the scholarly management literature. TACT overcomes the limitations of theories that focus only on psychological or social behavior thereby ignoring the features and functionalities of information technology altogether and of theories that make simplistic and deterministic assumptions about the effects of information technology on human behavior and organizational outcomes. TACT overcomes these limitations by advancing technology affordances and constraints as relational concepts linking people and technology.

TACT also has significant implications for improving management practice. Specifically, insights from TACT can help managers achieve more successful technology implementations, that is, higher levels of expected uses of technology, beneficial innovations in technology use, positive outcomes, and fewer unintended negative consequences. Using TACT gives managers guidance about what to do before technology implementations: how to assess users' needs and capabilities, modify technology features (e.g., by disabling some capabilities and setting default parameters), make changes in work practices and processes to achieve greater alignment, and provide proper support structures (e.g., training, communication, and help services). In short, considering the relationships between people and information technology, using TACT makes better "systems thinkers" of today's managers.

Ann Majchrzak and
M. Lynne Markus

See also Actor-Network Theory; Adaptive Structuration Theory; Decision Support Systems; Information Richness Theory; Sociotechnical Theory; Structuration Theory; Systems Theory of Organizations

Further Readings

Gibson, J. L. (1977). A theory of affordances. In R. Shaw & J. Bransford (Eds.), *Perceiving, acting and knowing: Toward an ecological psychology* (pp. 67–82). Hillsdale, NJ: Lawrence Erlbaum.

Kallinikos, J. (2011). *Governing through technology: Information artifacts and social practice.* New York, NY: Palgrave Macmillan.

Leonardi, P. M. (2011). When flexible routines meet flexible technologies: Affordance, constraint, and the imbrication of human and material agencies. *Management Information Systems Quarterly, 35*(1), 147–167.

Majchrzak, A., & Meshkati, N. (2001). Aligning technological and organizational change. In G. Salvendy (Ed.). *Handbook of industrial engineering* (3rd ed., pp. 948–974). New York, NY: Wiley.

Markus, M. L., & Silver, M. S. (2008). A foundation for the study of IT effects: A new look at DeSanctis and Poole's concepts of structural features and spirit. *Journal of the Association for Information Systems, 9*(10/11), 609–632.

Orlikowski, W. J., & Scott, S. V. (2008). Sociomateriality: Challenging the separation of technology, work, and organization. *Academy of Management Annals, 2*(1), 433–474.

Zammuto, R. F., Griffith, T. L., Majchrzak, A., Dougherty, D. J., & Faraj, S. (2007). Information technology and the changing fabric of organization. *Organization Science, 18*(5), 749–762.

TECHNOLOGY AND COMPLEXITY

The increasing pace of globalization; unrelenting innovation in technology; pressure for sustainable management of ecological, human, and technological resources; and the need to manage associated complex interrelationships are creating a challenging organizational environment for managers. Such challenges have been well documented around efforts to create order, predictability, and efficiency in heavy change. The globalization of new technologies and the alignment of economic, social, political, and cultural systems are generating simultaneously new forms of order, while also increasing complexity for managers. The word *technology* derives from the Greek word *technologia* combining *téchnē* (art, skill, craft) and *logia* (study of). It can be used as

a general term or to refer to specific areas, such as information and computer technology, biotechnology, and so on. Technology can be defined narrowly as the development, usage, and knowledge of tools, techniques, or machines to perform specific functions or solve problems, or, broadly to include organizational design and culture, including procedures, systems, and methods used to achieve specific outcomes. Under this latter definition, managing the design of a sociotechnical interface would be an application of technology itself. Such a broad interpretation also illustrates the dynamic, iterative, and interactive relationship between technology and complexity; each concept invokes the other to frame the nature and scope of the managerial challenge. Complexity theory provides insights into this dynamic. Constituting a critique of multiple theories derived mainly from the natural and social sciences, it is concerned with understanding how order appears to emerge rather than be imposed in complex environments. Leadership and management theorists suggest that this body of literature provides insights into effective management philosophies, mind-sets, and practices in dynamic, complex, and uncertain environments. This entry identifies critical constructs to explain dynamic interactions between technology and complexity systems that raise issues for management theory and practice.

Fundamentals

Change, Technology, and Complexity

The need to accommodate constant and dynamic change in and between organizations has challenged linear systems thinking, particularly reductionist and narrow views concerning the roles of the human and the technical in effecting change. Following World War II, debates highlighted differences between the effects of controlled (cybernetics) and uncontrolled systems on change processes. Management science, still influenced by Newtonian thinking, strove to determine systems inputs and transformations to move systems toward equilibrium, the latter seen as both desirable and achievable. Technology was often seen as a means of standardizing rules and processes around interventions toward this end.

Since that time, management theory has increasingly questioned the extent to which such equilibrium states can be achieved through top-down control-based technologies, increasingly recognizing the disruptive and discontinuous nature of change associated with technology. An understanding of core management concepts associated with technology and complexity introduced here include models of complexity theories, an exploration of dynamic interactions between complexity and technology, and the impact of technology on organizational design, including the structure of work.

Characteristics of Complexity Theories

Complexity theories attempt to exemplify how order emerges in nonlinear, complex, dynamic systems characterized by conditions of high uncertainty and ambiguity, often described as "the edge of chaos." In complex systems, causes and effects are difficult to identify, and order emerges unpredictably through iterative processes of self-organization, guided by the operation of simple order-generating rules to meet contextual challenges. Models identified as useful analogies for leading and managing in complexity include the following:

> *Chaos theory*—Describes dynamic systems connected nonlinearly in constant states of irreversible change, very sensitive to changes in initial conditions with amplification of initial differences creating impetus for unique change reactions.

> *Dissipative structures*—Constitute systems that spontaneously transform into new structures under pressure. However, whereas in the natural sciences water will transform predictably into steam under high temperatures, in the social sciences, characteristics of the future ordered state of the system is unknowable, reacting to diverse and shifting pressures that can impact differently on individuals and groups.

> *Complex adaptive systems* (CAS)—Describes order that emerges through the actions of agents (i.e., semiautonomous units, groups, systems, or individuals) within or on the system as they seek to maximize their fitness of purpose in response to dynamic environments. Developments within a CAS are unpredictable and irreversible.

> *Complex responsive processes*—View changes in the complexity of open ended, unpredictable human interactions as iterative exchanges produced outside rigidly defined system boundaries, producing innovation and increasing learning, knowledge creation, and novelty.

Complexity Theory and Technology

Complexity theory is useful in conceptualizing the relationship between technology and underpinning social processes. Sociological theory suggests that technology is socially located in that it undergoes a process of transformation based on its actual use; that is, the relationship between technology and complexity is not necessarily discrete, linear, static, or even rational. Rather, it is seen to be dynamic, unpredictable, iterative, and interactive. Effective deployment and management of technology requires understanding what constitutes a technological solution, its purposiveness, and how skills, perceptions, and utilization of technological initiatives influence the design and emergence of order-generating processes that will affect its nature and ultimately its outcome. These critical interactions are deliberate but not fully structured.

Technological innovation has been instrumental in redesigning business models to create dynamic organizational structures and related systems design for achieving sustainable, nimble, and adaptive organizational responses to complex environments. Managerial decision making around technology is complex as it concerns economic, social, and political choices around allocation of resources and power. A key concern for academics and practitioners has been the impact of technological innovation on organizational structure as well as the labor process itself.

Perrow's Model of Technological Complexity

Numerous studies have investigated the complex relationship between technology and organizational structure. In the 1960s, Joan Woodward suggested three levels of technological complexity associated with small batch production (customized), mass production (e.g., the auto industry), and continuous process (e.g., chemical plants). Also, James D. Thompson suggested that different technologies raised organizational design issues of varying levels of complexity that concerned the extent of their interdependence and coordination to fulfill organizational tasks effectively. Different types of technologies underpinned mediating roles (e.g., between lenders and borrowers by banks), long-linking roles (e.g., assembly lines), and complex interdependencies of intensive technologies (e.g., construction projects). In 1967, Charles Perrow identified two features of technology which he claimed influenced organizational structure: (a) variability, determined by the level of routine embedded in the task and uncertainty in the environment; and (b) analyzability, reflecting the extent to which task-related problems are analyzable because there is an existing body of knowledge that can also inform assessment of employee performance. The interactions between these dimensions allowed him to identify four types of technologies: routine technologies, such as those in manufacturing (analyzable with low variation); engineering or planned contingency technologies (analyzable but with many exceptions); craft technologies (unanalyzable but with low variability); and nonroutine technologies, such as research that is both unanalyzable and has high variability. Each of these categories had different implications for the level of formalization and centralization of management control.

Importance

Technological complexity impacts management research and practice from both a structuralist-functionalist as well as interpretivist perspective.

Perrow's structuralist-functionalist approach purports organizational structure as being the outcome of technology choices and operations to get work done. His categorization of technology types provides key insights into organizational features, such as centralization and spans of control, levels of management, and formalization of processes and roles. However, his model might also be seen as accommodating a dynamic appraisal of the relationship of structure to other contingency factors affecting organizational design, such as organizational goals, strategy, culture, and environmental pressures.

A broader perspective suggests that complex and dynamic technologies have produced both positive and negative "externalities," or spill-over effects, for the broader community. Although benefit has been derived from specific technological innovations, such as increasing telecommunications access through the global Internet or accessing life-saving technologies and drugs, the deployment of technology can also result in unwanted by-products such as pollution, toxic waste, depletion of finite and precious natural resources (sometimes spanning generations), costly accidents in high-risk systems with interactive complexity in the presence of tight coupling, as well as dehumanizing and de-skilling the work process itself.

Technology choice and its application can influence and be influenced by societal values, often raising tension-ridden ethical questions. For instance, while the ethics associated with technologies, such as embryonic stem cell research, may be easily perceived, communities may be less able to identify value conflicts associated with technology as an instrument to increase human productivity. For example, Frederick W. Taylor's pursuit of machine-like efficiency in human productive effort, while producing significant output gains, was claimed to have dehumanized workers through breaking labor tasks into minute processes controlled by detailed instructions. Fordism's system of mass production, while delivering initial gains in output, was also deemed to dehumanize workers through standardization of automated processes in continuous assembly lines that increased absenteeism. In response, the Ford Motor Company claimed to have redressed worker boredom and alienation through monetary incentives and stability of employment. The advent of the Internet has seen a resurgence of scientific management technologies in customer service call centers, raising similar issues around ethical and sustainable work practices.

In the 1970s, Harry Braverman rejuvenated critical scholarship on the labor process debate within the social sciences. Applying the Marxist theory of surplus value, he rejected an analysis of work effort from the perspective of only individual and management practice, highlighting the consistent diminution of control by labor over the labor process under capitalism. He concluded that technology could be used both as a tool to achieve erosion of worker influence over their productive processes, and, to upgrade worker skills. More recent critique has resurfaced concerning the de-skilling of workers by subdividing and automating tasks through, for example, content management systems.

In the late 20th century, Peter Checkland's soft systems methodology emphasized the need to understand holistically how systems work. This was a precursor to agile software development methodology in which a range of stakeholders are involved in iterative processes from specification through to acceptance testing of software solutions. Technology as a homogeneous and stable concept has also been challenged by Jonathan Sterne, who saw it as an alternative and specific form of social practice subject to constantly changing power relations and agency influences. He argued that technologies are cocreated by designers, implementers, and end users, incorporating historical perspectives on social structure embodied in spontaneous and creative initiatives of stakeholders.

Organizations benefit economically from the development of new technologies and the implementation of existing technologies that facilitate increased efficiencies in resource deployment. It is also important that management understands to what extent technology leads to improvements in human well-being and benefits society, or is diminishing physical and human resources thereby alienating stakeholders.

Literature and research that has recognized the contribution of technology to organizational complexity has highlighted the management challenge in interpreting an appropriate level of holism in the design, application, and adaptation of technology, acknowledging the complexity of social process. Considerations might include organizational design to facilitate improved interaction between designers, implementers, and users of technologies; responsible leadership facilitating adaptive systems and processes rather than reproducing hierarchical and autocratic structures; acceptance that multiple stakeholder interactions will shape a culture of sustainable and effective technological solutions; and motivating and rewarding contributions derived from structure, spontaneity, and creativity as appropriate.

Dianne Bolton

See also Complexity Theory and Organizations; Environmental Uncertainty; Quantum Change; Systems Theory of Organizations; Technology and Interdependence/Uncertainty

Further Readings

Burnes, B. (2005). Complexity theories and organizational change. *International Journal of Management Reviews, 7*(2), 73–90.

Goldstein, J., Hazy, J. K., & Lichtenstein, B. B. (2010). *Complexity and the nexus of leadership.* London, England: Palgrave MacMillan.

Orlikowski, W. J. (2007). Sociomaterial practices: Exploring technology at work. *Organization Studies, 28*(9), 1435–1448.

Perrow, C. (1967). A framework for the comparative analysis of organizations. *American Sociological Review, 32*(2), 194–208.

Perrow, C. (1999). *Normal accidents: Living with high risk technologies.* Princeton, NJ: Princeton University Press.

Stacey, R., & Griffin, D. (2005). Leading in a complex world. In D. Griffin & R. Stacey (Eds.), *Complexity and the experience of leading organizations* (pp. 1–16). New York, NY: Routledge.

Sterne, J. (2003). Bourdieu, technique and technology. *Cultural Studies, 17*(3/4), 367–389.

Wheatley, M. (2006). *Leadership and the new science* (3rd ed.). San Francisco, CA: Berrett-Koehler.

Winston, M. E., & Edelbach, R. D. (2006). *Society, ethics and technology* (3rd ed.). Toronto, Ontario, Canada: Thomson Wadsworth.

TECHNOLOGY AND INTERDEPENDENCE/UNCERTAINTY

James D. Thompson proposed a theory of management that focuses on the critical role of uncertainty in determining organizational action. His 1967 book *Organizations in Action: Social Science Bases of Administrative Theory* is considered one of the classic works of organizational theory and has inspired later theories of organizations, such as contingency theory, institutional theory, and resource dependence theory, among others. Some of the concepts developed by Thompson, such as the role of interdependence, uncertainty, and technology in organizational structure and action, are at the core of management theories even today. Therefore, it is essential for students, scholars, and practitioners of management theory to understand the ideas proposed in *Organizations in Action*. The following entry first describes the theory as developed by Thompson in his 1967 book, then the subsequent evolution of the theory, and finally its importance.

Fundamentals

Thompson developed a sophisticated and detailed theory that is concerned with the explanation of the structure and functioning of modern complex organizations. He created multiple typologies and many propositions. These typologies and propositions are valid for any organization, including corporations, universities, nonprofits, and governmental organizations.

Core Concepts and Typologies

The core concepts in the theory are uncertainty, technical rationality, organizational rationality, interdependence, structure, and task environment. Also, two typologies are central to Thompson's theory: types of organizational *technologies* and types of internal *interdependence*. These concepts and typologies are explained below followed by the relationships among these concepts and the rationale behind these relationships.

Uncertainty can be understood as the opposite of determinate: Under conditions of uncertainty, there are more variables in the system than the actor can make sense of, or at least, some of the variables are not predictable or controllable by the actor.

Technical rationality is a system of cause-effect relationships which leads to a desired result, whereas *organizational rationality* also involves input and output activities to the technical rationality.

Structure is the internal differentiation and patterning of relationships.

Task environment, as proposed by William Dill, refers to the parts of the environment which are relevant or potentially relevant to goal setting and goal attainment. There are four elements of a task environment: (a) customers; (b) suppliers of materials, labor, capital, equipment, and work space; (c) competitors; and (d) regulatory groups.

Interdependence refers to the dependence of units within an organization to each other (i.e., internal interdependence) and also the dependence of an organization and its environment to achieve a common goal (i.e., interdependence with the task environment). There are three types of internal interdependence. *Pooled interdependence* refers to the condition under which each part makes a discrete contribution to the whole, and each is supported by the whole. It is illustrated by two different geographical branches of a bank. *Sequential interdependence* refers to the condition under which part X has to complete its part successfully before part Y can act, and part X cannot find use for its output if part Y does not act. It is illustrated by a production plant for tires and another plant for cars. *Reciprocal interdependence* refers to the condition under which the outputs of each unit are inputs for the other. It is illustrated by the operations and maintenance units of an airline company. The operations unit's output is an aircraft needing maintenance and is an input for the maintenance unit, whereas the maintenance unit's output is a usable aircraft which is the input for the operations unit. All organizations have pooled interdependence, more complex ones have sequential interdependence, and the most complex ones have all three types.

The purpose of complex organizations is to operate *technologies* which are impossible or impractical for individuals to operate. Thompson creates a typology of technologies for complex organizations which includes three different types. The first type is the *long-linked technologies* which include serial interdependence in the sense that action Z can be performed only after the successful completion of action Y, which can be performed only after action X, and so on. An example of long-linked technology is the mass production line. The second type of technology is the *mediating technology* which involves the linking of clients or customers who are or wish to be interdependent. For example, banks link lenders and borrowers. The third type of technology is *intensive technology* which involves bringing together a variety of techniques in order to achieve a change in some specific object. The selection, combination, and order of application of the techniques are determined by feedback from the object of interest. A general hospital is a good example of intensive technology: Each emergency admission requires some combination of dietary, X-ray, laboratory, medical specialties, pharmaceutical, and other services, and the choice depends on the condition of the patient.

Main Arguments

The first fundamental premise of Thompson's theory is that organizations are not only open systems, hence indeterminate and facing uncertainty, but also subject to criteria of rationality and therefore need determinateness and certainty. An organization's technical core is subject to technical rationality and should be protected from uncertainty by reducing the number of variables operating on it. At the same time, at the institutional level, uncertainty is found to be greatest, and an organization has to deal with its environment over which it has no formal authority or control. The purpose of the managerial level is to mediate between the closed-system perspective at the technical level and the open-system perspective at the institutional level.

The second fundamental premise is the existence of two different types of "rationalities": technological rationality and organizational rationality. According to Thompson, organizational rationality is different from technological rationality since it operates within open-systems logic. When the organization is open to environmental influences, this organizational rationality is a result of (a) *constraints*, which the organization must face; (b) *contingencies*, which the organization must meet; and (c) *variables*, which the organization can control.

Building on these premises, Thompson argues that organizations seek to reduce uncertainty stemming from the task environment through strategic actions. These actions can be internal to the firm (e.g., forecasting) or aimed at reducing dependency on external elements (e.g., seeking alternatives). Structure of the organization is determined by (a) the organization's response to external uncertainties, (b) interdependencies within the technical core, (c) the needs of boundary spanning units to adjust to environmental constraints and contingencies, (d) and finally by the relationship between the technical core and the boundary spanning units. Uncertainty is also critical in determining how organizations measure their performance, for the relationship between the individual and the organization, and also in how decisions are made in organizations. These arguments are explained in more detail below.

Rationale

Organizations seek to reduce the uncertainty around their technical core by sealing it off from environmental influences, since the efficient functioning of the technical core requires certainty. However, organizations also have to deal with input and output activities to the technical core, which are interdependent with the technical core and also with the larger environment. As a result of this interdependency, organizational rationality demands the logic of an open system, and therefore, achieving a complete isolation is never possible. In order to deal with this dilemma, organizations follow multiple strategies. First, organizations seek to buffer their technical core by managing their input and output components. For example, in an unstable market, organizations stockpile supplies in order to guarantee a steady flow of inputs, and at the demand side, they maintain inventory in order to allow the technical core to function at a steady rate. The second strategy is that they aim to reduce fluctuations in the environment by smoothing out the input and output

transactions. For example, utility companies offer inducements for low-usage periods, while charging premiums during peak periods. The third strategy is that organizations seek to forecast and adapt to environmental changes, which cannot be buffered or smoothed out. If there is a pattern to the changes, such as peak sales before holidays or seasons, they adapt to this patterned increase in demand. When the changes in the environment are not patterned, but they result from a combination of many factors and are complex in nature, then organizations seek to forecast the changes through the use of different forecasting methods. Finally, when all else fails, organizations resort to rationing. An example of rationing is seen clearly in emergency situations when hospitals ration beds by establishing priority systems for nonemergency admissions.

Organizations and their task environments are interdependent, and as a result, the actors in the task environment have power over the organization. Organizations seek to minimize the power of these actors by different strategies. The first strategy is maintaining alternatives to each actor. For example, a firm will have multiple suppliers for a certain input. The second strategy is to seek prestige, which is the "cheapest" form of power according to Thompson. The logic behind this argument is that the environment can find exchange with a prestigious organization to be beneficial, which gives a certain degree of power to the focal organization. The third strategy is that organizations seek power relative to those on whom they are dependent, which can be achieved by contracting, co-opting (e.g., acceptance of representatives of other organizations into the board of directors), or coalescing (i.e., forming a joint venture). Finally, if an organization is constrained in some areas of the task environment, it will seek more power in the remaining areas, and if that is not possible either, the organization will seek to extend its task environment.

Organizations may remove or reduce contingencies through organizational design. Boundaries of organizations are determined by activities, which would be critical contingencies if they were left to the task environment. Different types of technologies are associated with different kinds of crucial contingencies, and therefore, the type of technology affects boundaries. Organizations with long-linked technologies seek to expand their domains through vertical integration, those with mediating technologies by increasing the populations served, and those with intensive technologies by incorporating the object worked on. Also, organizational growth is seen as a dynamic process. Organizations extend their boundaries to incorporate the sources of contingencies, which leads to excess capacity compared to the planned goal. In this case, the organizations seek to grow until the capacity is filled. When this is not possible, they will seek to enlarge their domains (i.e., horizontal diversification).

The structure of the organization depends on the types of interdependence across organizational units of an organization. Organizations aim to minimize coordination costs when grouping positions. Pooled interdependence is coordinated by standardization, which is the least costly form of coordination. Sequential interdependence is coordinated by planning. Reciprocal interdependence is coordinated by mutual adjustment, which is the most expensive form of coordination. Since mutual adjustment is the most costly, organizations will group the reciprocally interdependent positions together, followed by sequentially interdependent positions, and finally, they will group positions homogeneously to achieve standardization. After this grouping, following the same logic, organizations will link these groups into higher order groups thus creating a hierarchy.

Structure is affected not only by the coordination of interdependent parts in the technical core but also by the need of boundary-spanning units to adjust to environmental constraints and contingencies. Thompson identifies two critical dimensions of the task environment that are relevant: degree of stability and degree of homogeneity. When organizations face heterogeneous task environments, they identify homogenous segments and establish structural units to deal with each. Organizations facing stable environments will rely on rules to adapt to this environment. When the range of instability in the environment is known, organizational units will first treat this as a constraint and adapt multiple sets of rules for different conditions. When the instability is too large or unpredictable, the organizational units will monitor the environment and plan responses, which require decentralization.

Furthermore, the relationship between the technical core and the boundary-spanning organizational components affect the organizational structure. When they can be removed from each other except for scheduling, organizations will be centralized with

a structure based on functional divisions. When the components are reciprocally interdependent, these components will be segmented and arranged in clusters dedicated to a specific domain, creating a decentralized structure based on product divisions.

Uncertainty also plays a crucial role in how organizations measure their performance. The two important criteria here are the standards of desirability and the understanding of cause-effect relations. Standards of desirability (of multiple goals) can vary from crystallized to ambiguous, while understanding of the cause-effect relationships can be complete or incomplete. In stable task environments, organizations are measured against past performance, while in dynamic environments, they are measured in comparison to other similar organizations. Organizations also will emphasize criteria that are most visible to important task-environment elements and the criteria that are extrinsic rather than intrinsic. Similarly, organizations assess their own components in terms of efficiency when technologies are perfected and task environments are stable or well buffered. If those conditions are only met to some extent, then organizations seek to account for interdependence and assess each unit in efficiency terms. But if cause-effect relationships are not well understood, organizations will measure their components in terms of organizational rationality.

Evolution

The organizational theory field developed two conflicting world views in the early 20th century: closed-system perspective and open-system perspective. *Closed-system perspective* included the scientific management theory of Frederick W. Taylor, the administrative management theory of Luther Gulick and Lyndall Urwick, and the bureaucracy theory of Max Weber, whereas open-system perspective included studies of informal organizations by Fritz Roethlisberger and W. J. Dickson and administrative theories of Chester Barnard, Philip Selznick, and Burton Clark. One of the fundamental conflict points between these two perspectives was the treatment of uncertainty. Closed-system perspectives have a high need for predictability and are inclined to get rid of all uncertainty or treat it as exogenous as a determinate system helps with predictability, and uncertainty makes things unpredictable. On the other end of the spectrum of uncertainty, the open-system perspectives takes uncertainty as a given and assumes the system is indeterminate. The theory of Thompson addresses this dilemma directly through a synthesis of these two conflicting views about organizations by building on Talcott Parsons's three distinct levels of responsibility and control: *technical, managerial, and institutional*. The *technical* level refers to the suborganization in which the technical function or the technical core of the organization functions. A typical example of this level is the assembly line, and the central problem at this level is the effective and efficient performance. The *managerial* level services the technical suborganization by mediating between the technical organization and those who use its products and also by supplying the necessary resources to it. Finally, the *institutional* level refers to the larger environment in which the organization is embedded and is the source of the legitimacy for the organization's goals.

Thompson also extended and integrated the work of Richard Emerson on power, the works of J. March, H. Simon, and Chester Barnard on bounded rationality, coalition building, and inducement and contributions to look at the dynamics of the relationship between the individual and the organization. There are two fundamental issues here. First is how organizations reduce the uncertainty from the behavior of their individual members. Second is how organizational members exercise discretion. To explore the first question, Thompson builds on the inducements and contributions theory. The contract that is signed between the individual and the organization is determined through a political power process. This process varies from collective action and collective bargaining in routinized technologies and early-ceiling occupations in intensive technologies, to the relative power of the task-environment elements, individual abilities, and individual visibility at the contingent boundaries of the organization and late-ceiling occupations. Individuals will try to avoid discretion when they believe that their understanding of the cause-effect relationships is not adequate or the consequence of error in discretion is high. When options are available, individuals will choose to select tasks which promise to improve their scores on assessment criteria and seek to report successes but not failures. Furthermore, coalition building is an important part of the discretionary process, since highly discretionary jobs involve a political process and individuals in these jobs need to maintain power equal to or greater than their dependence.

The foregoing discussion forms the background for exploring the second question on power and coalitions. It suggests that the discretion in organizations is taken by a dominant coalition, and the more numerous the areas needing decision making, the larger the dominant coalition will be. If the dominant coalition gets too big, then it becomes very difficult to make decisions, and a smaller inner circle composed of the most critical members of the coalition will conduct coalition business. In an organization with dispersed power, the most powerful actor will be the individual who can manage the coalition.

There have been subsequent attempts to build on the ideas of Thompson, but they are scattered across multiple disciplines and do not coherently form a complete theory. However, many subsequent theories of organizations have been inspired by Thompson's work or at least have many commonalities with it. Contingency theory is built on the premise that there is no single organizational structure that is equally effective for all organizations, but the optimal structure varies according to *contingency factors*—such as size, strategy, uncertainty, or technology. In order to be effective, the organization should fit its structure to the contingency factors. Resource dependence theory focused on the interdependence and uncertainty among organizations and particularly the element of power in this relationship. Organizational design perspective focused on the characteristics of tasks (e.g., complexity, interdependence) and the matching structural characteristics. Institutional theory focused on the institutional environment and how legitimacy is created within an organizational field. Thompson's model has been extended by J. C. Spender and Eric H. Kessler to explain innovation process, where innovation is treated as a source of internally generated uncertainty. Thompson's typology of three technologies have been extended by Charles B. Stabell and Oystein D. Fjeldstad to argue that there are three corresponding value configuration models (the value chain, the value shop, and the value network) which will help us to understand the firm-level value-creation logic much better across industries and firms.

Importance

Later empirical studies have tested the 86 propositions in Thompson's book and found substantial support. The work of Andrew Van de Ven, Andre Delbecq, and Richard Koenig Jr. found that both task uncertainty and task interdependence have an effect on the use of different coordination mechanisms in terms of both quantity and quality. A review of the empirical work on technology-structure relationship between 1965 and 1980 by Louis W. Fry showed that technology has a significant effect on structure and the effects of interdependence is one of the critical factors in this relationship. The work on organizational design based on Thompson's theory has helped practitioners to design more effective organizational structures. Furthermore, subsequent theories built on these propositions also provide support for Thompson's arguments. Findings of the contingency theory show that both uncertainty and technology determine the optimal structure, while the findings of the resource dependence perspective show that organizations co-opt other organizations to reduce their dependency to the environment. Overall, there is strong evidence that uncertainty and interdependence from technology and the environment determine the structure of the organizations, which is the central argument in Thompson's book.

Thompson's model can be helpful to managers for designing effective organizational structures, decision making, and incentive systems. It is essential for the managers to realize that both internal technology and the inter-unit interdependence and the external dependence to the environment should be considered while designing organizations. If they are not considered during the design process, they should be expected to exert their influence in the organization over time, causing significant conflict and forcing later changes; therefore, understanding these relationships and designing organizations accordingly may save time and resources. Furthermore, studying and implementing the strategies to deal with reducing dependence and uncertainty will allow the managers to be more effective in helping their organizations achieve their goals.

Remzi Gözübüyük

See also Bounded Rationality and Satisficing (Behavioral Decision-Making Model); Contingency Theory; Institutional Theory; Organic and Mechanistic Forms; Organizational Structure and Design; Resource Dependence Theory; Value Chain

Further Readings

Emerson, R. M. (1962). Power-dependence relations. *American Sociological Review, 27*(1), 31–41.

Fry, L. W. (1982). Technology-structure research: Three critical issues. *Academy of Management Journal, 23*(3), 532–552.

Kamps, J., & Polos, L. (1999). Reducing uncertainty: A formal theory of *Organizations in action. American Journal of Sociology, 104*(6), 1774–1810.

Spender, J. C., & Kessler, E. H. (1995). Managing the uncertainties of innovation: Extending Thompson (1967). *Human Relations, 48*(1), 35–56.

Stabell, C. B., & Fjeldstad O. D. (1998). Configuring value for competitive advantage: On chains, shops, and networks. *Strategic Management Journal, 19*, 413–437.

Thompson, J. D. (1967). *Organizations in action: Social science bases of administrative theory.* New York, NY: McGraw-Hill.

Van de Ven, A. H., Delbecq, A L., & Koenig, R. J. (1976). Determinants of coordination modes within organizations. *American Sociological Review, 41*(2), 322–338.

TECHNOLOGY AND PROGRAMMABILITY

Joan Woodward has had a significant and lasting impact on the study of organizations, conducting pioneering empirical research into the relationship between technology, organizational structure, and firm performance. Her framework for assessing technology and programmability achievements, particularly given the time and place, represents a significant and original contribution to our knowledge of organizations and forms an important part of the foundations of modern contingency theory. Woodward's work was a springboard for much subsequent research. Her ideas have been widely debated, empirically tested and challenged, and still remain an important part of the foundation of organizational theory. Not everything that Woodward originally propounded back in the 1950s as part of the turn to the "technological imperative" in organizational sociology has stood the test of time. However, there is still much to be gained from a critical engagement with her work. This entry will discuss the central contributions of her work and reflect on the lasting impact of her ideas regarding technology and organization.

Fundamentals

Joan Woodward is best known for her book *Industrial Organization: Theory and Practice.* This volume marked an important turning point in the history of organizational theory, establishing the important links among technology, organizational structure, and business success. First published in 1965, it challenged classic scientific management principles and theories, revealing findings that represent a major contribution to the foundation of contingency theory. Contingency theory scholars moved organizational theory beyond the "one best way" view of scientific management and began to explore how organizational outcomes are contingent on various characteristics of the organization and its environment, in this case, the technology used in production.

Woodward's groundbreaking field study was conducted while she was part of the Human Relations Research Unit at the South East Essex Technical College. The Human Relations Research Unit had been set up in 1953 with support from a number of national agencies, with the aim of enhancing the performance of industry and commerce in Great Britain through the application of social science. Through the field study, Woodward examined the relationship between technology and organizational structure using a sample of 100 small and medium manufacturers in South East Essex. The preliminary results of this research were first published by the British government's Department of Scientific and Industrial Research in 1958 in a 40-page booklet. Although she is now best remembered for her 1965 book, this 1958 volume had already exerted a considerable influence on key U.S. scholars by the time *Industrial Organization: Theory and practice* appeared.

In her research, Woodward first investigated the organizational structure of the selected firms and proposed a new typology of production systems, locating the firms on an 11-point scale of production systems, according to the complexity of technology representing the degree to which the production system was controllable and predictable, what she referred to as "programmable." She distinguished three main categories in ascending order of technological complexity: (a) unit and small batch production, (b) large batch and mass production, and (c) the most complex process production and continuous flow. These three categories were then subdivided into nine subcategories of production systems from least to most complex.

She then ranked firms' degree of business success based on a range of different economic criteria,

dividing the firms into three broad categories of success: above average, average, and below average success. She then analyzed whether firms' success was correlated to common organizational characteristics. According to Woodward herself, the most important finding the research team revealed was that firms with similar organizational structure and other administrative characteristics could present substantial variations in outcomes; there was no one best way. Furthermore, they found that differences in technology and manufacturing techniques account for many differences in organizational structure.

A number of organizational characteristics varied significantly among the firms studied and were not independently predictive of economic success: communication forms, levels of authority and span of control, numbers of levels in the line of command, proportion of direct and indirect labor, labor costs, and the number and proportion of managers to the total workforce. In fact, the commercially successful firms were the ones that aligned function and form, since different technologies need appropriate organizational structures. Successful firms from a commercial standpoint were not the ones implicitly following abstract classic management theories but the ones that choose the organizational structure according to the logic of their production technology. Woodward showed that technology influences organizational behaviors and that there seemed to be a "particular form of organization" which was most appropriate to "each technical situation."

Classic management theory did not therefore appear to be adequate as a practical guide to those responsible for the organization of industry. This observation—that successful manufacturing organizations did not always conform to the prescriptions offered by the management textbooks of the day but rather responded to the demands of their unique operative circumstances—became popularized through its role as a foundational assumption of contingency theory.

Importance

It is, of course, important to keep in mind that ideas that seem obvious today may have been remarkably radical when they were proposed. At the time her research was first released, Woodward was challenging the fundamental orthodoxy of the time: that "classical management theory" derived from Frederick

Winslow Taylor, Henri Fayol, or Mary Parker Follett did indeed offer a universal set of principles that would lead to a convergence of organizational structures and practices. According to Woodward, by applying these principles, scholars ought to find three characteristic configurations of authority relations: (a) line organization where authority flows directly from the chief executive to subordinate managers and onto employees in a traditional bureaucratic manner, (b) functional organization where individual employees were directed by a number of specialist supervisors, and (c) hybrid line-staff organization where a direct line of authority is retained by senior managers as employees are assigned to functionally specialized departments. Little advice was ever offered, however, by advocates of these respective organizational structures about how a manager should go about choosing which one would best guarantee their organization's success. After first wrestling with the problem of defining success, the consternation felt by the research team was palpable when they reported that, of the 100 manufacturing firms studied, no relationship of any kind had been established between business success and what is generally regarded as sound organization structure.

Reading contemporary North American reviews of *Industrial Organization: Theory and Practice*, one is struck by how perplexed many of the reviewers are to discover that a theoretical and inductive research enterprise could yield such profound and influential results. Some of the reviewers reacted quite negatively, feeling that Woodward's research findings were undermining the underlying principles of classic management theory and regarding her work as an attack on traditional management education. More sympathetic reviewers, however, (including people of the stature of Charles Perrow in the *American Sociological Review*, Arthur Stinchcombe in the *Journal of Business*, and Terence Hopkins in the *Administrative Science Quarterly*) had the perspicacity to see her work as a diamond in the rough with an intrinsic value that shone through despite its flaws.

Looking back on *Industrial Organization: Theory and Practice* 5 years after its publication, Woodward noted in 1970 that "patient and detailed exploration of what really happens inside industrial firms was a prerequisite to the development of an organization theory comprehensive enough to provide managers with a reliable basis for their decisions and actions"

(1970a, p. 234). Her principal achievement challenged the ideological basis of 20th-century management theory that made it, as she stated in her 1965 book, "impossible for managers to be detached and impersonal enough to be conscious of the nature of their own achievements" (p. 256). In this sense, her championing of an empirically based research program stands alongside her inspiration of the "technological turn" as a major aspect of her legacy.

It was not until the emergence of the Aston school that her work was to be subjected to its first major empirical test in the strategic contingencies theory of intraorganizational power. Here, Woodward's observation that you could explain a firm's success by the status and influence it afforded to its "critical function" (be it design, marketing, or production) is taken as a foundational assumption of a sophisticated model that links the power of a subunit with its centrality in the organization's work flow.

Certainly *Management and Technology* and *Industrial Organization: Theory and Practice* are today remembered for their claims about the way in which technology appears to be an independent variable that predicts human behavior or organizational properties. However, the accusation of "technological determinism" has endured, with a number of writers considering her positions to be overly unidirectional and deterministic—that is, understanding the details of technical systems of production provides us with the key to unlock the secrets of the social organization of work. As an alternative perspective in considering Woodward's continuing legacy, it is useful to remember the intellectual, economic, social, and theoretical milieu in which Woodward operated. Thus, the finding for which her research is best remembered—that the way a manufacturing firm is socially and technically organized depends on the nature of its production process—can be seen as a serendipitous by-product of an original objective to determine what makes an organization successful or not in terms of its structure. Consequently, her perceived technological determinism aside, Woodward provided a framework for understanding the interaction of the technical and social aspects of work that did not pretend that managers were benign and disinterested servants of everyone in the organization. Woodward's now largely forgotten great insight was that whoever had ultimate control over the inception, design, and operation of new technical systems exerted a great deal of subsequent influence over employees' activities regardless of whether those employees were consulted about (or even participated in) the change process itself. This interest in technical change and its relationship to the social relations of work and organization can therefore be considered the most enduring aspect of Woodward's work, and it remains a fruitful and critically important area of study in the organization and management field. It is an area that, despite the large existing literature, continues to attract the attention of a large group of scholars working from a diverse range of perspectives.

Woodward's focus on technology and organization continues to have resonance today as the development of new technologies challenge current approaches to organizing. Whether the technologies are technologies of production or communication, Woodward's work highlights the need to continually rethink assumptions about what constitutes the best way to organize and reminds us that the effectiveness of even well-proven theories of organization may change as technologies evolve. As technologies change, organizations must change with them to ensure continued success. Complacent firms that try to adopt new technologies without adjusting structures and management practices will find their performance decline.

Francesca Bria and Nelson Phillips

See also Bureaucratic Theory; Contingency Theory; Scientific Management; Strategic Contingencies Theory

Further Readings

Flanders, A., Pomeranz, R., & Woodward, J. (with Rees, B. J.). (1968). *Experiments in industrial democracy: A study of the John Lewis Partnership*. London, England: Faber.

Perrow, C. (1967, April). A framework for the comparative analysis of organizations. *American Sociological Review, 32,* 194–208.

Woodward, J. (1958). *Management and technology: Problems of progress in technology* (No. 3). London, England: HMSO.

Woodward, J. (1960). *The saleswoman: A study of attitudes and behavior in retail distribution*. London, England: Isaac Pitman & Sons.

Woodward, J. (1965). *Industrial organization: Theory and practice*. Oxford, England: Oxford University Press.

Woodward, J. (1970a). *Industrial organization: Behaviour and control*. Oxford, England: Oxford University Press.

Woodward, J. (1970b). Technology, material control and organizational behavior. In A. R. Negandhi & J. P. Schwitter (Eds.), *Organizational behavior models* (pp. 58–68). Kent, OH: Kent State University Press.

TECHNOLOGY S-CURVE

The theory of the technology S-curve explains the improvement in the performance of a technology through the collective efforts of multiple actors over time within an industry or technological domain. The technology S-curve helps managers understand the complexities and contingencies associated with how to best manage the development and improving performance of a technology and when to transition from one technology to another. The remainder of this entry is structured to answer the following questions in-depth in order to help readers understand technology S-curve theory: What is a technology S-curve? What factors influence the shape of a technology S-curve? When should a firm switch to a new technology S-curve? These are all valid and important questions that those interested in the management of technology and innovation often ask when confronted with this concept.

Fundamentals

What Is a Technology S-Curve?

Before a discussion of what a technology S-curve is can begin, a particular point of common initial confusion by new scholars must be addressed. Specifically, there are two technology management related S-curves: *technology S-curve* (the focus of this entry) and the *technology adoption S-curve* (also known as technology adoption curve or technology adoption life cycle). These S-curves are very different in regard to their focus and subsequent insights offered. However, unfortunately, both are sometimes referred to simply as technology S-curves and, thus, a discerning manager or scholar must recognize and understand their distinctions before appropriate insights can be gleaned. The technology S-curve, which is elaborated in more detail below, is focused on technology performance improvement and maturity as a function of consistent R & D (Research & Development) effort. The technology adoption S-curve is focused on market share capture via various adopter groups for a technological innovation.

What Factors Influence the Shape of a Technology S-Curve?

The key concepts associated with the technology S-curve are performance and effort. The technology S-curve displays the improvement of performance of a technology through the collective efforts of multiple actors (e.g., firms, individuals, institutes, universities, associations, etc.) over time within an industry or technological domain. Some research also suggests technology improvements can be firm dependent although the ever-increasing practice of open innovation suggests that the inclusion of diverse actors beyond firm boundaries will continue well into the future. The shape of the S-curve reflects the dynamics of the slow initial improvement of the technology as part of the uncertain fluid stage where the fundamentals of the technology are poorly understood. But as the technology diffuses to more actors and is better understood and improved upon, the extent and rate of technological improvements specific to the technology increases and, subsequently, performance increases, creating a significant rise in slope of the S-curve. Finally, maturity of the technology is reached when further performance improvements slow or cease to materialize due to actual or perceived physical constraints of the technology. Initial models of the technology S-curve suggested that technology performance improvement occurs over time, but more recent research has shown that R & D efforts are a better determinate of improved technological performance than time. Thus, older models of the technology S-curve will show time on the x-axis, while more recent models will reflect effort instead. It should also be noted that the term *technology* is contextually defined to include various technological domains, such as information technology, engineering, sciences, and so on, and can exist in differing forms, such as a product (e.g., pharmaceutical drug), process (e.g., biotechnology assay), component (e.g., silicon wafer), or system (e.g., smart phone) technologies.

As noted previously, the technology S-curve shape reflects technology performance that is a function of the extent of R & D effort made by multiple actors. However, performance and effort indicators are not universal but are technology specific. The performance and efforts to improve a smart phone clearly differ from the performance and improvement efforts of a biotechnology assay. Thus, a keen awareness of critical areas to focus effort for technological improvement and an understanding of market desired performance are crucial. In the following paragraphs, several examples in differing industries are offered for insights on what key indicators were identified to develop a technology S-curve and how valuable insights were gleaned.

Moore's law is an established theory in the information technology industry that reflects a technology S-curve specifically in the context of integrated circuits, which is a system technology. According to Moore's law, the continual improvements via R & D of key performance enhancing technologies that are embedded within the integrated circuit (identified as manufacturing, design, and chip size technologies) will continually improve performance (identified in the market as speed, reliability, and cost) until the physical constraints of these embedded technologies are reached. Each of these embedded technologies can also be exhibited through their own S-curve. Moore predicted in 1986 that the then-current pace of improvements in integrated circuit technologies would result in a doubling of transistors on a chip every 18 months. His prediction was reflective of the projected steepness of the S-curve slope. While some have argued that Moore's law has become obsolete, the dynamics behind his predictions are clearly aligned with the technology S-curve theory and simply reflect that the maturity of the technology has likely neared.

When Should a Firm Switch to a New Technology S-Curve?

Up to this point, we have viewed technology S-curves as individual and independent curves that can be compared across the dimensions of performance and effort within the same technological or industrial context but do not necessarily influence one another. From this perspective, a new technology S-curve would be identified and followed when the prior technology reaches maturity. In a noncompetitive and/or noncannibalistic market, this tactic may be appropriate. However, the reality is that new, discontinuous technologies can emerge making an existing technology obsolete before maturity is reached, resulting in what Joseph Schumpeter has referred to as *creative destruction*. This disruption is sometimes caused by new entrants into an industry, since large industry incumbents tend to focus on improvements of existing technologies—more comfortably seeking to extend existing S-curves by refining their current base of knowledge—rather than learning new technological areas, opening the door for an "attackers advantage." However, incumbents can also thwart attackers with continued improvements on existing technologies. As a result, predicting the emergence of a new technology and its related S-curve and determining if and when to shift to the new technology is a significant and potentially costly challenge for firms.

New, discontinuous technologies fulfill a similar market need as an existing technology but are based upon an entirely new knowledge base and may involve a new system of components. Thus, incremental improvements on an existing technology do not prepare a firm for discontinuous technologies. Initially, this new technology may offer lower performance than the current technology in the market. But, as effort is expended on the new technology, the returns to performance can increase and may exceed prior technologies. The firm that hesitates to switch may be left behind competitors with the ability to stay on the front edge of the technological improvement and performance due to learning curve dynamics, negatively influencing the firm's competitiveness in the market. Switching decisions are complex and based upon multiple factors such as (a) advantages the new technology offers to the firm, (b) the fit of the new technology with the firm's existing capabilities, (c) the fit of the new technology with the firm's strategic positioning in the market including complementary resources, (d) the fit of the technology as a component within the larger technological system, and (e) the expected rate of diffusion of the technology.

Clayton M. Christensen offers an example of this switching decision dynamic within the disk drive industry. International Business Machines Corporation (IBM) invented the first disk drive technology in 1956 involving multiple components, such as rotating disks, spindle, ferrite read/write-heads, actuator motor, electromagnets, and electronic circuitry with a real recording density (megabits per square inch) as the measure of product performance. A critical juncture in this industry was the switch of technologies from ferrite heads to thin-film technology. However, the predicted maturity of this ferrite component technology differed both among and within firms. Some firms began thin-film technology development in anticipation of the switch, sometimes at the expense of ferrite-head improvement efforts. However, in this case, there was no attacker or first-mover advantage for firms that switched to the new technology since the overarching disk drive system was not changed, only a component technology, and component technologies offered multiple avenues for improved performance of the technological system for firms since the system design remained unchanged.

However, when new technologies require a new system architecture or design where component improvements require changes in other components as part of the larger system, attackers advantage emerges. Christensen offers the example of disk drive size from 18 inches to 2.5 inches diameter requiring reconfiguration of the entire system of components and their relation to one another. These new technologies and their new design were often entered into the industry by new competitors rather than incumbents. And because these new architectural systems often involve different performance measures from other technologies on the market, they are sometimes dismissed as inferior by incumbents. Thus, understanding the dynamics of component versus architectural technologies, the capabilities and strategic position of the firm, and the related S-curve predictions enables better competitive technology decisions by firms.

Importance

The validity of the technology S-curve theory has been supported over time and across technological contexts beginning with empirical evidence in the information technologies of integrated circuits and disk drives to new empirical and anecdotal evidence in industries such as energy, software, agricultural chemistry, and cloud computing. This continued evidence of the technology S-curve theory has strengthened the premise of the theory as a valuable and powerful tool for technology managers seeking to understand the development of technologies and predicting their eventual maturity.

Recently, Melissa Schilling and Melissa Esmundo applied the technology S-curve to a very current topic: the energy industry. They developed S-curves for fossil fuels, such as coal, oil, and natural gas, as well as renewable energy sources, such as hydroelectric, geothermal, solar, wind, and biomass, to predict which of these technologies offers the greatest potential for performance per unit of effort. In their work, they identified cumulative R & D dollars across nations as the key indicator for technological improvement effort, reflecting global actors contributing to technology development, and kilowatt per dollar as the key indicator for market valued performance. Their S-curve findings suggest that although the largest amount of R & D dollars were spent on fossil fuels, wind and geothermal energy sources offer the greatest potential kilowatt-per-dollar performance per R & D dollar.

Managers seeking to understand and compete, utilizing the technology S-curve theory, must gain a clear understanding of the development and evolution of technologies from their initial, growth, and maturity phases and as well work with technologists to understand critical areas and valid measures of effort and performance, stay aware of discontinuous technologies that may emerge from within or beyond their industry, and understand the dynamics of component versus architectural designs in technological improvements—including when attackers advantage is most likely to exist.

With the ever-increasing technological advancements of today that either serve as a core foundation or as a significant facilitating or complementary technology that influences the competitive advantage of a firm, understanding the S-curve of these technologies can have a significant impact on the survival and profitability of firms.

Joanne L. Scillitoe

See also Architectural Innovation; Competitive Advantage; Innovation Diffusion; Open Innovation; Technological Discontinuities

Further Readings

Bowden, M. J. (2004, Winter). Moore's law and the technology S-curve. Stevens *Alliance for Technology Management*, 8(1), 1–4. Retrieved from http://howe. stevens.edu/fileadmin/Files/research/HSATM/newsletter/v08/v8i1/bowden.pdf

Chesbrough, H. (2003). *Open innovation.* Boston, MA: Harvard Business School Press.

Christensen, C. M. (1992). Exploring the limits of the technology S-curve: Part 1 Component technologies. *Production and Operations Management, 1*(4), 334–357.

Christensen, C. M. (1992). Exploring the limits of the technology S-curve: Part 2 Architectural technologies. *Production and Operations Management, 1*(4), 358–366.

Foster, R. N. (1986). *Innovation: The attackers advantage.* New York, NY: Summit Books.

Rogers, E. M. (1995). *Diffusion of innovations* (4th ed.). New York, NY: Free Press.

Schilling, M. A., & Esmundo, M. (2009). Technology S-curves in renewable energy alternatives: Analysis and implications for industry and government. *Energy Policy, 37,* 1767–1781.

Tushman, M. L., & Anderson, P. (1986). Technological discontinuities and organizational environments. *Administrative Science Quarterly, 31*(3), 439–465.

Utterback, J. M. and Abernathy, W. J. (1975). A dynamic model of process and product innovation. *Omega, 3*(6), 639–656.

THEORY DEVELOPMENT

Within the field of management and organizational studies, an author's precise meaning of the term *theory* is often difficult to grasp, even for experienced readers. With the goal of informing the reading of this literature, this entry is divided into three sections. The first provides an overview of theory within the field of organizational and management scholarship, focusing on two broad topics: what is and isn't considered theory and different kinds of theory. It then focuses on the development (including by way of graphical modeling) of one kind of theory—referred to as middle-range—characterized as answers to questions of, Why? The second section traces the evolutionary nature of different "stages" of theorizing and theory enhancement. The final section provides a practical template for readers who wish to assess the nature of a theory as well as to construct better management theory themselves. Throughout the entry, the term *development* is used in both a descriptive (how to) and a prescriptive (making something better) manner. The first treatment focuses on the building blocks of middle-range theorizing; the second focuses on the improvement of middle-range theories.

Fundamentals

What Is and Isn't "Theory"?

In their classic 1995 article, Robert Sutton and Barry Staw specified "what theory is *not*." Included in their list were references, data, variables, diagrams, and hypotheses. At the end of their treatise, the authors briefly addressed what theory is. Their depiction represents a fairly wide consensus within this field, and social science more generally:

> Theory is the answer to queries of *why*. Theory is about the connections among phenomena, a story about why acts, events, structure, and thoughts occur. Theory emphasizes the nature of causal relationships, identifying what comes first as well as the timing of such events. (p. 378)

Some scholars consider theory as the answering of any question, while others focus on "process" questions pertaining to *how* something happened. In line with the view expressed by Sutton and Staw, the focus of this entry will be on questions of why, generally characterized as causal explanations. This naturally invites the follow-up question: What is and isn't an explanation?

One way to address this question is by comparing *explanation* (Why is it? How does it come to be?) with *description* (What is it?)—two complementary forms of scholarship used widely in this field. While descriptions focus on "a single thing" (What is *it?*), explanations necessarily encompass "multiple things"—often signified as an X → Y relationship. This leads to a second distinction. While descriptions of Y might use "arrows" to signify what things Y is related to (X is correlated with Y), it is customary and preferable to use arrows for causal explanations of Y (X is a cause of Y). Indeed, it has been argued that the "strength" of a particular theory depends on how well the causal mechanism implied by an arrow is specified. A third distinction involves the scope of an explanation: Whereas a description can apply to a single case (one manager, group, or organization), it is expected that an explanation applies to multiple cases—that is, it is expected that a theory is "broadly applicable."

Different Kinds of Theory

Within this broad domain of theory-as-explanation, there are various kinds or types of theories. One of the most important distinctions is between *general* and *middle-range* theory. Although this distinction is rarely mentioned in organizational scholarship, it can help readers reconcile varied and seemingly inconsistent treatments of organizational *theory*. For example, calls for "new theory" typically refer to general theory, whereas admonitions to "improve theory" more often refer to middle-range theory. While, as their names suggest, these two types of theory vary in scope and breadth, they have other noteworthy differences.

General theories operate like paradigms—broad explanations that might help explain a variety of different outcomes. For example, "agency," "need," or "expectancy" theory might help explain why individuals make a variety of decisions. The promise of general theory is that if you look at a particular outcome-of-interest through this "lens," your attention will focus on one possible explanation (cause). The paradigmatic quality of general theory is reflected in its pattern of usage. Specifically, general theories are intended to be applied, not systematically tested and improved—except to clarify boundary conditions (e.g., does agency theory operate the same way in different cultures?). Note that if everyone who applied a general theory did so with the intent of changing it, soon it would lose its utility as a common frame of reference.

Whereas general theories can be used to explain a variety of outcomes, *middle-range theories* are explanations of a particular outcome (Why Y?). In this way, middle-range theory is consistent with the goal of organizational leaders: increase or decrease specific kinds of performance or performance-related outcomes, such as organizational efficiency, product quality, group creativity, and employee satisfaction. If one thinks of general theories as "omnibus Xs" looking for particular Ys to explain, middle-range theories can be thought of as "particular Ys" looking for suitable explanations. As this comparison suggests, the Xs used to explain a particular Y are often inspired by relevant general theories. For example, X1 might be inspired by agency theory, X2 by need theory, and so forth. An additional feature of the best middle-range theories is that they specify the conditions under which they are likely to apply—the scope conditions. This characterization of middle-range theory can be summarized as, What causes what and why, and under what conditions. In the following sections, readers will notice that "and why" is a distinctive feature of *strong* theory and "under what conditions" is the hallmark of *useful* (high utility) theory.

Middle-Range Theory Development

With the benefit of this brief overview of the distinctive domain of theory, this entry now turns the readers' attention to the process of theory development. Inasmuch as general theories are not assembled piece by piece and, once formulated, their function is incompatible with an ongoing process of testing and improvement (development), this section is limited to middle-range theorizing—inspired, if you will, by relevant general theories. The bulk of what follows introduces a structured approach, referred to as "modeling-as-theorizing." It can be used to guide the initial articulation of posited answers to Why Y? questions, as well as their subsequent enhancement by others. Following this discussion of middle-range theory modeling is an outline of the evolution traced by concept-focused scholarly conversations.

Everyday experience tells us humans that the quality of a product, whether created by our hands or our minds, depends on how well it was made. Aristotle famously set forth a dual standard for evaluating a body of knowledge: Is it complete? Is it systematic? The use of X → Y propositions, expressed as simple or complex graphical (box and arrow) models, offers a simple and universally understood medium for the long-term development of middle-range theory that becomes more and more complete and systematic. One of the benefits of using graphical models to both generate and communicate causal arguments is that they focus attention on the essential ingredients of middle-range theorizing: what causes what, and why, and under what conditions. These conventions can also aid the evolution of thinking within scholarly conversations, seeking to explain outcomes requiring complex explanations, for example, turnover, job satisfaction, mergers, and acquisitions. Thus, adapting a familiar adage, within the realm of middle-range theorizing, "a 'picture' is worth *at least* a thousand words."

To begin, imagine a simple theory: X and Y in individual square boxes, an arrow pointing from one to the other, and these three elements circumscribed by a larger rectangular box, signifying relevant boundary conditions. One of the nice features of graphical modeling is that it can be used to convey a simple or highly complex theory, and the meaning of boxes (concepts) and arrows (causal relationships) remains constant, regardless of scale and complexity. In addition, an understanding of the basic structure of causal modeling helps those interested in improving a particular proposition identify a suitable intervention strategy. In what follows, the building blocks of middle-range theorizing—boxes, arrows, and boundary conditions—are briefly described.

Boxes or Concepts. One might think of the boxes composing a middle-range-theory model as the nouns in a sentence, or, as the main characters in a play. Recalling our definition of middle-range theory (what causes what and why, and under what conditions), the boxes are the whats. The simplest middle-range theory contains two boxes (an X and a Y). The more boxes included in a model the more complex the theoretical argument. While the addition of new elements doesn't necessarily improve the quality of a theory, it is clear that within the social realm, models containing a single X are always incomplete explanations of Y. Thus, each box within—and the large rectangular box circumscribing—any size of causal model is a salient visual invitation to "think outside the box" (what's missing?)

Experience has shown that the modeling-as-theorizing process works best when authors follow three key specifications for the selection and naming of boxes. First, they should be expressed as nouns or brief noun phrases (e.g., group composition, task interdependence, organizational size). Second, for theorizing intended for scholarly publication, it is best to use concepts (sometimes called constructs) utilized with the targeted body of literature, rather than everyday terminology—such as organizational reputation, rather than outsiders' opinions. Third, every box must be capable of being operationalized as a variable (a measureable range, from high to low, or, even on and off) and functioning as a cause or an effect. Importantly, these specifications caution against the use of broad categories (environment, leadership, culture) from middle-range theorizing. In these cases, the addition of an adjective to these categories often allows them to be operationalized as variables and incorporated into testable propositions (e.g., perceived environmental uncertainty, charismatic leadership style, individualistic culture).

Arrows or Causal Relationships. Graphically, the answer to what *causes* what, and *why* is signified by arrows. Building on earlier analogies, arrows can be thought of as the verbs in a sentence or the plot of a play. There are basically three kinds of causal relationships utilized in middle-range theorizing: direct, mediated (indirect), and moderated. Direct causes are the easiest to describe. Regardless of the number of X-antecedents included in a model, each one with an arrow pointing directly at a Y-outcome is considered a direct cause. To clarify the causal mechanism signified by an arrow—the "and why" component of our definition—the relationship might be described in the text as, X causes Y, because . . . The extent to which an arrow signifies a specific causal mechanism, rather than simply a correlation, is a distinguishing characteristic of *strong* (not weak) theory. Completing this sentence is much easier when the selection of X-antecedents reflects an investigator's interest in applying one or more relevant general theories. In these cases, the arrow in a proposition signifies a distinctive causal mechanism associated with a particular general theory (X causes Y, because [general theory mechanism]). Examples of such ties between concepts used as X-antecedents and related general theory mechanisms in this field include the following: in institutional theory, legitimacy (concept)—and isomorphism (mechanism); in social identity theory, organizational identification (concept)—and social identification (mechanism); in social justice theory, perceived fairness (concept)—and expectations of fairness (mechanism).

A mediated causal argument contains three boxes, connected by two arrows, signifying a "two-stage," causal sequence. A simple analogy might help illustrate how a mediated cause works. Imagine three balls lined up in fairly close proximity. The first ball represents an X, the third ball represents a Y, and the middle ball operates as the *mediator.* In what's called a "fully mediated" relationship, the effect of the first ball on the third ball goes entirely through the middle one. For example, it might be argued that the effect of leadership style on group performance is mediated by (goes through) the motivation level of group members. It is worth noting that when a mediator is introduced into an existing Why Y? proposition, the focus typically shifts from the existing X-antecedent to the Z-mediator, as the direct cause of Y.

The third type of relationship "looks different," because the arrow of a moderator points to another arrow, not to a box. Using yet another analogy, if we think of the arrow in an X → Y proposition as representing an electrical current moving from X to Y, then a *moderator* can be thought of as a switch, controlling the current's flow. This might be a simple on-off switch, a rheostat, or one that is capable of reversing the current's polarity (+ or –). In statistics, Z-moderators are used to create interaction variables, combining in some specified manner the effects of an X-antecedent and a Z-moderator on a Y. Conflicting results from multiple empirical tests of an X → Y proposition, involving different samples of individuals or organizations (from different cultures, for example), often prompt further theorizing about possible moderating factors.

An important implication of this brief overview of the three kinds of relationships utilized in causal modeling is that, as a set, they delineate the logical possibilities for improving an existing Why-Y? explanation. That is, we can add X-antecedents (direct causes), Z-mediators (indirect causes), or Z-moderators (moderated causes). Inspiration for these enhancements comes from imagining key elements of a better, more complete explanation that have been overlooked. This process can be thought of as bringing what was previously outside (the rectangular box) into the model as new boxes and arrows. An important source of this information is the model's contextual boundary conditions.

Contextual Boundaries. As noted earlier, a large rectangular box circumscribing a middle-range theory can be used to signify the theory's boundary conditions. Inasmuch as all explanations must apply to more than a single condition, the *utility* of a particular X → Y argument is to a large extent based on the specification of its applicable conditions: when, where, and for who it does or does not apply. To be clear, failure to enumerate a theory's contextual boundaries does not qualify it as a universal theory. Instead, this common oversight actually limits a theory's value as a guide for both scholars interested in theory testing, and practitioners interested in theory application. The systematic assessment of a theory's boundaries often extends over a long period of time. In the end, the goal is to produce "useful theory" containing an up-to-date "users guide," describing suitable who, when, and where applications.

Evolution

Broadening the scope of our focus, from a discrete theory-development contribution to the evolution of a theory over time and across contributors, it is instructive to consider different "stages" of theorizing. Herein, *stages* is used loosely to connote different forms or types of middle-range theory development that are depicted, more or less, as a series of enhancements. (Note: One stage doesn't necessarily lead to another, and as a set, the stages are not necessarily linear.) Equipped with this heuristic, readers of a particular theory-based literature within organizational scholarship might better understand the focus of current and past theorizing and recognize opportunities for further theory development.

The initial stage in this framework is technically speaking pre-theory, in that the *introduction* of a new concept focuses attention on a single *what* (though often enriched by description of its surrounding [proposed] conceptual and empirical context). This stage often entails debates about the concept's meaning and proposed measures. These discussions often include efforts to logically distinguish the new concept from a network of related extant concepts (what it is similar to and how it differs from similar others). Subsequent uses of the concept (stages 2–4) are likely to prompt refinements in its initial introduction, possibly leading to the specification of multiple meanings, interpretations, or applications.

Once there is some agreement about what *it* is, a recently introduced concept might, in Stage 2, be combined with an existing concept to form a novel X → Y proposition. Unless the new concept is generally considered an outcome (e.g., employee turnover), its first appearance in middle-range theorizing is likely to be as an X-antecedent. Further, it will most likely be deliberately paired with what like-minded scholars view as a very important Y-outcome (e.g., organizational commitment, firm performance), forming a Why X? proposition (Why is X an important concept?). This supposition about the initial casting of a new concept as an X-antecedent reflects the following logical argument: Something is worth explaining (cast as a Y-outcome) if it is a proven explanation of something else, of greater perceived importance. Thus, a hallmark of Stage 2 propositions is the *justification* of a new concept as theoretically relevant—something whose utility in middle-range theorizing

has been demonstrated. If and when a body of scholars agrees that a new concept is a significant direct cause of one or more important outcomes, the X → Y proposition in which it is embedded often becomes the subject of further theory development.

One option, referred to here as Stage 3, is for the X and the Y in a Stage 2 proposition to remain the same, while the possibility of "expanding the middle" by adding suitable mediators or moderators is explored. (Think of a Stage 2 proposition becoming a 3+ column model, with the X on the left and the Y on the right, and 1+ mediators and/or moderators in the middle.) When appropriate, the *specification* of a direct cause argument is enhanced by the addition of a mediated relationship—dividing it into a two-step causal sequence. In a similar manner, enhanced *contextualization* comes from the addition of one or more moderators. This is an important step in the evolution of Why Y? explanations in that it focuses attention on the important qualifiers in our definition of theory: (a) why and how exactly does X cause Y, and (b) under what conditions. Reinforcing a point made earlier, the need to add a mediator is more likely when the X-antecedent in a Stage 2 proposition does not explicitly invoke the causal mechanism of a specific general theory.

An even greater transformation of a Stage 2 proposition occurs when, in Stage 4, a "proven X" is recast as a "promising Y" and becomes the focus of a new Why Y? investigation. In other words, what was an X-antecedent in Stage 2 becomes a Y-outcome in Stage 4. What is referred to as the *explanation* stage of middle-range theorizing typically features "tall models," depicting posited direct causes of the new Y. (Imagine a model with two columns: The column to the right consists of a single Y and the one to the left contains a vertical list of proposed Xs, each connected with an arrow to the Y.) Consistent with the objective of formulating "complete" explanations of Y, it is advisable to build Stage 4 models mostly using X-antecedents that are unrelated to each other. Said differently, it is important to distinguish Stage 4 models from multiple-X Stage 2 models, in which additional (presumably weaker) Xs are used to justify the merits of the favorite X, or, in which a cluster of related Xs are used to demonstrate their value (e.g., various types of personality). Recalling an early distinction, one way to ensure the selection of unrelated X-antecedents is to link each one to a different general theory.

Importance

The elements of the preceding discussion suggest four "levels of theoretical utility" for evaluating specific middle-range theories. First, building on an earlier distinction, when authors use arrows to merely signify a correlation between X and Y, the X → Y proposition can be categorized as a *non-theory*. Second, when it seems reasonable to assume that X causes Y, but authors offer no specifics about how and why this occurs, the proposition is a *weak theory*. Third, propositions that signify a clearly specified causal argument (X causes Y, because . . .) qualify as *strong theory*. Fourth, when the contextual conditions of a strong theory are delineated, it becomes a *useful theory*—in the sense that it can be confidently tested and applied.

Several points from this entry can be applied to enhance strength of theorizing. Theory is answering a specific question with an explanation—usually about what causes what and why. Scholars must take care not to substitute references, data, variables, diagrams, and hypotheses *in place of* rather than *in support of* underlying (theoretical) explanation. Often, general theories aid and inspire the process of explaining, while middle-range propositions provide precision and empirically verifiable clarity. Management scholars can make contributions "of" theory—by applying a theory downstream to particular contexts and phenomena; or scholars can make a contribution "to" theory—by applying empirical findings upstream to enhance or extend extant theoretical arguments. (Junior scholars will likely spend more time applying theories downstream.) Either way, graphical models of theory are a powerful method for enhancing lucidity, insight, and communicability throughout the theorizing process. By considering the evolutionary stages of theory, the theoretical arguments at the core of many scholarly conversations can be better understood and "grafted" into.

While we have not discussed how to select "what to explain" in this entry, it is equally crucial to explain the right things as it is to explain them well. *Interesting* theory is likely to be important to managers and theorists, alike. Important aspects of the causal what(s)-being-explained condition include novelty, an answer to the so what/who cares? question, impact, timing, and applicability to actual management situations—are managers seeking explanations for the individual, group, or organizational outcome my theory purports to provide? In the end, the goal of theory-based management scholarship is to enhance managers' efforts to facilitate good outcomes and to minimize bad outcomes, by better understanding what causes what and why, and under what conditions.

In conclusion, Kurt Lewin's dictum, "There is nothing quite so practical as a good theory," nicely frames this brief overview of theory and theory development. Although unstated, Lewin's praise of theory presumes a shared understanding of what theory is and isn't and what kind of theory we're talking about. Of greater significance, we can infer from this statement that only "good" theory has practical value—this is consistent with our everyday observations that "bad" theory is not only impractical but also often causes harm. Focusing on the formulation of good theory, the second part of this entry depicted a structured, cumulative theorizing process and set of principles that can over time yield more complete and systematic explanations of important management and organizational outcomes.

David A. Whetten and
Zachariah J. Rodgers

See also Academic-Practitioner Collaboration and Knowledge Sharing; Action Research; Analytical and Sociological Paradigms; Appendix: Central Management Insights; Bad Theories; Engaged Scholarship Model; Evidence-Based Management; Multilevel Research; Organizational and Managerial Wisdom; Process Theories of Change; Theory of the Interesting

Further Readings

Bacharach, S. B. (1989). Organizational theories: Some criteria for evaluation. *Academy of Management Review, 14*(4), 496–515.

Christensen, C. M., & Raynor, M. E. (2003, September). Why hard-nosed executives should care about management theory. *Harvard Business Review,* 66–74.

Colquitt, J. A., & Zapata-Phelan, C. P. (2007). Trends in theory building and theory testing: A five-decade study of the *Academy of Management Journal. Academy of Management Journal, 50*(6), 1281–1303.

Corley, K. G., & Gioia, D. A. (2011). Building theory about theory building: What constitutes a theoretical contribution. *Academy of Management Review, 38*(1), 12–32.

Sutton, R. I., & Staw, B. M. (1995). What theory is *not*. *Administrative Science Quarterly, 40,* 371–384.

Van de Ven, A. H. (2007). *Engaged scholarship: A guide for organizational and social research.* Oxford, England: Oxford University Press.

Weick, K. E. (1989). Theory construction as disciplined imagination. *Academy of Management Review, 14,* 516–531.

Whetten, D. A. (1989). What constitutes a theoretical contribution? *Academy of Management Review, 14,* 490–495.

Whetten, D. A. (2009). An examination of the interface between context and theory with applications to the study of Chinese organizations. *Management and Organizational Research, 5*(1), 29–55.

Whetten, D. A. (2009). Modeling theoretical propositions. In A. Huff (Ed.), *Designing research for publication* (pp. 217–250). Thousand Oaks, CA: Sage.

THEORY OF CONSTRAINTS

The theory of constraints (TOC) is a managerial framework for continuous improvement developed by Eliyahu M. Goldratt. Part of the novelty of this managerial framework is that Goldratt presented his ideas in a 1984 novel, *The Goal: A Process of Ongoing Improvement,* rather than presenting his theory as a set of equations or in an academic paper. Using this narrative device, Goldratt and Jeff Cox (his coauthor) provided several examples of how TOC works in practice. The central premise of TOC is that operational performance of an organization or system is only as successful as its "weakest link," a theme that Goldratt builds upon. All systems comprise a collection of interrelated and independent processes through which parts and the produce flow to create value. The weakest link is considered to be the largest constraint to the throughput of the system. Thus, in order to improve operational performance, the largest constraint posed by the weakest link must be addressed. Another key concept in TOC is the importance of considering variation when examining system performance. In his book *The Goal,* Goldratt illustrates the flaw of using average component performance to determine the performance of the system, particularly when there are interrelated components. TOC is a relevant topic for this encyclopedia because *The Goal* has become a

mainstay and perhaps even classic in the pedagogy of teaching operations management to master of business administration, or MBA, students and, as a result, has become a part of the vernacular of many analysts and managers. The remainder of this entry is devoted to describing TOC in more detail and then assessing the impact of TOC.

Fundamentals

The theory of constraints proposes a holistic rather than local consideration of organizational performance—with profits being the ultimate metric of success. The primary measures of that performance are (a) *throughput*—the rate at which money is made from sales, (b) *inventory*—the costs associated with purchasing and holding items that will ultimately become products (or services) for sale, and (c) *operating expenses*—the costs associated with turning inventory into sales.

Once the goal of the organization has been articulated, the TOC indicates a set of five iterative focusing steps to identify and address the constraints (also known as "bottlenecks") in the system in an effort to enhance organizational performance and achieve its goal. Throughput may be increased by focusing on the constraints and increasing the flow through the system, thereby increasing sales.

The five focusing steps are as follows:

1. *Identify the system constraint.* A constraint may be a physical limitation that restricts flow in the system (e.g., the maximum capacity of a critical piece of machinery), a human performance limitation (e.g., inadequately skilled or unmotivated workforce), or even a policy that impedes optimal performance (e.g., worker work-rest schedules that may limit utilization of some part of the system).

2. *Exploit the constraint.* Once the constraint has been identified, all efforts must be made to maximize throughput capacity at that particular bottleneck. This might include continuous operation or eliminating unnecessary work.

3. *Subordinate all other activities to the above decision.* In other words, this step requires that the entire operating system is tuned to the weakest link in order to reduce unnecessary inventory and operating expenses.

4. *Elevate the system's constraint.* Once you have gotten the most out of the constraint in the second step and tuned the system to that constraint in the third step, implement significant improvements and/or changes to release the constraint so that it will no longer be the weakest link. At this point, another constraint will likely emerge.

5. *Repeat.* If a new constraint has emerged as a result of the efforts from the previous steps, identify the new weak link that constrains system throughput and work through the five focusing steps once again.

In conjunction with the five focusing steps of the overarching continuous improvement framework, the TOC also offers a series of "soft" tools referred to as the *logical thinking processes.* Taken together, these thinking processes provide managers an ability to diagnose why an organization or system may not be achieving its goals. The suite of logical thinking processes includes the following logic diagrams: concurrent reality tree, evaporating cloud, future reality tree, prerequisite tree, and transition tree.

The concurrent reality tree and the evaporating cloud provide analytic processes for problem identification—what to change? The evaporating cloud and future reality tree provide strategic processes for constructing solutions—what to change to? The prerequisite tree and the transition tree provide tactical processes for designing the implementation—how to cause the change to happen? The thinking processes also include a set of logic rules called the *categories of legitimate reservation.*

While this TOC has been specified in a particular manner and has been widely deployed, its underlying rationale is that of many iterative, continuous improvement frameworks and methods—with the goal of continuously and iteratively identifying limitations and waste so that they may be eliminated. Goldratt suggests that TOC holds up in a variety of domains and, in *The Goal,* he illustrates this both in a manufacturing setting, as well as in the protagonist's personal life. Basically, the TOC may be applied when a system comprises a set of interrelated processes such that any one process (i.e., the constraint) may limit system performance.

Additionally, Goldratt noted that variance in subsystem performance must be considered when examining the performance of the entire system. For example, if a system comprises two serial subsystems, the mean system throughput is additive of the subsystems. TOC deals with this by subordinating the system to the constraining constraint or subsystem.

Other concepts related to TOC include what Goldratt has called *drum-buffer-rope* (DBR) scheduling. The drum refers to the steady beat of the system that sets the pace for throughput. In the TOC, this pace is dictated by the weakest link (or bottleneck) constraint. Buffer is an allowance to ensure a degree of protection against variability and uncertainty. This becomes particularly important in the second of the focusing steps when exploiting the constraint. A buffer (such as an inventory of work in progress before the constraint) helps ensure the constraint is never starved and always fully exploited. There are stock buffers, time buffers, and other types of buffers placed before and even after constraints. The rope is a reference to a scheduling system that pulls work through the system like a thread. The rope is dictated by the drum and the buffer and provides a mechanism for optimizing throughput. Often, the rope is realized as a communication process for monitoring and controlling workflow.

In relation to mathematical optimization, where there will be some objective function (e.g., profit maximization) subject to specific constraints (including resource constraints), the TOC focuses on the constraints as a mechanism of improving system or organizational performance. In some sense, TOC is comparable to dual problem for a constrained resource profit maximization optimization. Additionally, TOC has been compared and contrasted to other continuous quality improvement frameworks, namely, six sigma and lean thinking. Interestingly, all have five-step processes. However, whereas the constraint-focused TOC attempts to manage the constraints and improve throughput, the problem-focused six sigma attempts to reduce variation and provide uniform process output, and the flow-focused lean thinking attempts to remove waste and reduce flow time. Thus, each has similar goals and slightly different approaches.

Importance

Since the time of its original publication in 1984, *The Goal* has sold over 3 million copies. Additionally, in the subsequent decades since that original publication, many more books and articles have been written that expand the concepts and illustrate applications of TOC. A recent literature review for the 12-year period from 1994 to 2006 has demonstrated a growth in the number of academic papers and dissertations on the subject of TOC, particularly the so-called thinking processes. This literature review notes gaps, as well as opportunities, in the literature that would be reflective of a growing body of knowledge.

The TOC may be used in any managerial application that requires a method for identifying opportunities for continuous improvement. For example, if a manager needs to determine how to increase sales, that manager could use the TOC to evaluate his company's service function, supply chain, or manufacturing base to determine how to increase throughput, reduce inventory, and/or increase sales. In the 20th-anniversary third edition of *The Goal*, there are "case study interviews" that illustrate how some practitioners have embraced the TOC and have demonstrated process improvements, some transformational. There have been several studies that illustrate the potential benefits of applying TOC to actual organizational settings.

A 2005 review of the TOC, using a framework for classifying methodologies, found that TOC may be viewed as a complementary framework across the social, personal, and material dimensions. It further suggests that the TOC shares ontological and epistemological characteristics and assumptions of other existing management science methodologies (e.g., systems dynamics). On the other hand, there have been criticisms about the suboptimality that might result from TOC and the drum-buffer-rope scheduling. There are claims that TOC compares favorably to mathematical optimization techniques; there are also claims that TOC is inferior to mathematical optimization and produces suboptimal results.

Paul Szwed

See also Actor-Network Theory; Gantt Chart and PERT; *Kaizen* and Continuous Improvement; Process Consultation; Quality Circles; Quality Trilogy; Six Sigma; Systems Theory of Organizations; Total Quality Management

Further Readings

Cox, J. F., & Schleier, J. G. (2010). *Theory of constraints handbook*. New York, NY: McGraw-Hill.

Davies, J., Mabin, V. J., & Balderstone, S. J. (2005). The theory of constraints: A methodology apart?—A comparison with selected OR/MS methodologies. *Omega, 33,* 506–524.

Gardiner, S. C., Blackstone, J. H., & Gardiner, L. R. (1994). The evolution of the theory of constraints. *Industrial Management, 36*(3), 13–16.

Goldratt, E. M., & Cox, J. (2004). *The goal: A process of ongoing improvement* (3rd ed.). Great Barrington, MA: North River Press. (Original work published 1984)

Goldratt, E. M., & Fox, R. E. (1986). *The race.* Croton-on-Hudson, NY: North River Press.

Gupta, M. C., & Boyd, L. H. (2008). Theory of constraints: A theory for operations management. *International Journal of Operations & Production Management, 28*(10), 991–1012.

Theory of Cooperation and Competition

All management involves creating and facilitating cooperation among the organization's members while minimizing competitive and individualistic efforts. Since an organization is a set of interpersonal relationships structured to achieve established goals and cooperation is a joint effort to achieve mutual goals, cooperation is a necessary condition for organizations to exist and function. All management involves organizing people to work together (i.e., cooperate) in accomplishing goals, using available resources efficiently and effectively. In order to be an effective manager, therefore, it is helpful, perhaps necessary, to understand the nature of cooperation and social interdependence. This entry provides an overview of the theory of cooperation and competition.

Fundamentals

The roots of social interdependence theory lie in the early 1900s when Kurt Koffka (one of the founders of the Gestalt school of psychology) proposed that groups were dynamic wholes in which the interdependence among members could vary. In the 1920s, Kurt Lewin proposed that the essence of a group is the interdependence among members created by common goals and that interdependence results in the group being a "dynamic whole" so that a change in the state of any member or subgroup changes the state of any other member or subgroup. In 1949, Morton Deutsch asserted there are two types of social interdependence: cooperative and competitive. *Cooperation* exists when individuals' goal achievements are positively correlated; individuals perceive that they can reach their goals if and only if the others in the group also reach their goals. Thus, individuals seek outcomes that are beneficial to all those with whom they are cooperatively linked. *Competition* exists when individuals' goal achievements are negatively correlated; each individual perceives that when one person achieves his or her goal, all others with whom he or she is competitively linked fail to achieve their goals. Thus, individuals seek an outcome that is personally beneficial but detrimental to all others in the situation. The absence of social interdependence results in *individualistic efforts,* which exist when individuals work by themselves to accomplish goals unrelated to the goals of others. Thus, individuals seek an outcome that is personally beneficial without concern for the outcomes of others.

Interaction Patterns

The basic premise of social interdependence theory is that the type of interdependence structured in a situation determines how individuals interact with each other which, in turn, determines outcomes. Positive interdependence tends to result in promotive interaction, negative interdependence tends to result in oppositional or contrient interaction, and no interdependence results in an absence of interaction. *Promotive interaction* occurs when members help and assist each other, exchange resources, give and receive feedback, challenge each other's reasoning, and encourage increased effort. Two important aspects of promotive interaction are the appropriate use of individual and small group skills and group processing (reflecting on group efforts to describe what member actions were helpful and unhelpful in achieving the group's goals and maintaining effective working relationships among members and make decisions about what actions to continue or change). *Oppositional interaction* occurs as individuals discourage and obstruct each other's efforts to achieve. Individuals focus both on increasing their own success and on preventing anyone else from being more successful than they are. Competition tends to result in constructive consequences when it occurs

within a broader cooperative context, clear and fair rules and criteria for winning are present, the task is appropriate, the task may be completed individually, competitors have an equal chance of winning, and winning is of low importance. *No interaction* exists when individuals work independently without any interaction or interchange with each other. Individuals focus only on increasing their own success and ignore as irrelevant the efforts of others. Each of these interaction patterns creates different outcomes.

Deutsch noted that depending on whether individuals promote or obstruct each other's goal accomplishments, there is *substitutability* (i.e., the actions of one person substitute for the actions of another), *cathexis* (i.e., the investment of psychological energy in objects and events outside of oneself), and *inducibility* (i.e., openness to influence). Essentially, in cooperative situations, the actions of participants substitute for each other, participants build positive relationships with each other, and participants are open to being influenced by each other. In competitive situations, the actions of participants do not substitute for each other, participants generally develop negative relationships with each other, and participants refuse to be influenced by each other. When there is no interaction, there is no substitutability, cathexis, or inducibility. The relationship between the type of social interdependence and the interaction pattern it elicits is assumed to be bidirectional. Each may cause the other.

Outcomes

The investigation of cooperation and competition is one of the longest standing research traditions within social psychology. Since the late 1800s, over 1,200 research studies have been conducted on social interdependence. Since participants have varied widely, a wide variety of research tasks and measures of the dependent variables have been used, and since the research has been conducted by many different researchers with markedly different orientations, working in different settings and countries and in different decades, the overall body of research on cooperation and competition has considerable generalizability.

The numerous outcomes studied may be subsumed within three broad categories: (a) effort to achieve, (b) interpersonal relationships, and (c) psychological health. Meta-analyses of all available studies found that cooperative efforts, compared with competitive and individualistic efforts, promoted considerably higher productivity, more liking among individuals, greater social support, greater psychological health, and higher self-esteem. These outcomes of cooperative efforts form a gestalt where they are likely to be found together.

Application

While most managers may intuitively understand that their job is to structure and facilitate cooperation among organizational members, while discouraging competitive and individualistic efforts, knowing social interdependence theory allows managers to structure cooperation consciously and deliberately, thus, increasing their effectiveness. They do so through five steps. The first is to structure strong positive goal interdependence and supplement it with other types of positive interdependence, such as role, resource, identity, and outcome interdependence. The second is to ensure each individual is accountable for doing their fair share of the work. The third is to ensure that team members promote each other's efforts. The fourth is to help team members appropriately use small-group skills, such as leadership, decision making, trust building, communication, and conflict resolution skills. Finally, managers need to structure group processing sessions in which members discuss how well the team is performing and how its effectiveness may be improved. These five steps operationalize social interdependence theory into functioning teamwork.

David W. Johnson and
Roger T. Johnson

See also Fairness Theory; Goal-Setting Theory; Group Development; Organizational Effectiveness; Path-Goal Theory of Leadership; Social Construction Theory; Trust; Virtual Teams

Further Readings

Deutsch, M. (1949). A theory of cooperation and competition. *Human Relations, 2,* 129–152.

Deutsch, M. (1962). Cooperation and trust: Some theoretical notes. In M. Jones (Ed.), *Nebraska symposium on motivation* (pp. 275–319). Lincoln: University of Nebraska Press.

Johnson, D. W., & Johnson, R. (1989). *Cooperation and competition: Theory and research.* Edina, MN: Interaction Book.

Johnson, D. W., & Johnson, R. (1994). *Leading the cooperative school* (2nd ed.). Edina, MN: Interaction Book.

Johnson, D. W., & Johnson, R. (2005). New developments in social interdependence theory. *Psychology Monographs, 131,* 285–358.

Johnson, D. W., Johnson, R. T., & Holubec, E. (2008). *Cooperation in the classroom* (8th ed.). Edina, MN: Interaction Book.

Tjosvold, D., & Wisse, B. (Eds.). (2009). *Power and interdependence in organizations.* Cambridge, England: Cambridge University Press.

West, M. A., Tjosvold, D., & Smith, K. G. (2003). (Eds.) *International handbook of organizational teamwork and cooperative working.* Chichester, England: Wiley & Sons.

THEORY OF EMOTIONS

Over the past two decades, there has been an explosion of interest in the role of emotions in management, based largely on the intuitive belief that many phenomena within the workplace are driven as much by emotional dynamics as they are by so-called rational processes. In spite of the great enthusiasm, and unlike many theories within management, there is no single theory for emotion in organizations—however, this is underdevelopment. Attempting to integrate theories imported and adapted from psychology, this entry is focused on those most relevant to the management domain, with citations for readers to explore further. The overarching concept of *process models,* described below, attempts to combine these theories into a unified framework.

Fundamentals

Emotions are adaptive responses to the demands of the environment. Social function theories argue that emotions evolved to help individuals solve the problems of group living—that is, aiding cooperation and navigating conflict. Using the metaphor of an alarm system, emotions direct our attention to the most pressing issues in our environment and provide action tendencies that allow us to solve those pressing issues. Accordingly, *process models* empha-size that emotion is not a unitary phenomenon but an interrelated series of processes that unfold chron-ologically. Although common wisdom considers emotion to be chaotic and disorganized, the emotion process is orderly, carefully sequenced, and governed by empirical regularities. Integrating the various process models that have been proposed produces the set of steps below. All midrange theories within the area of emotions in management can be situated within this process model. Doing so provides guid-ance for how these midrange theories relate to each other and to a larger whole.

- A stimulus is an event or experience that sets the process in motion. This can be anything of relevance to the individual in their workplace. For example, a stimulus might be a colleague's behavior at a meeting, an announcement of downsizing, or even the thermostat being turned too high.
- Emotional registration is the interpretation, however minimal, of this stimulus with respect to its implications for the self. Basic emotions theorists argue that we humans are hardwired to code events automatically in terms of their meaning for the self. The cognitive appraisal process is an ordered sequence of checklists that direct our attention soonest to the most pressing emotional challenges. The checklist includes positivity-negativity, novelty, certainty, control, and fairness. For example, the distinction between anger and guilt is a matter of who controls a negative event: another party, oneself, or nobody, respectively. Although there is heated debate about whether emotion precedes cognition, cognitive appraisal typically begins without deliberate thought. *Primary appraisal*—that is, the first item on the checklist of distinguishing positivity-negativity—occurs first and largely automatically, which leads to the finding that emotion can precede cognition.
- Emotional experience is the resulting subjective feelings and physiological experience that we typically consider "emotion." *Affective events theory* was developed to distinguish emotional experience from emotion-driven attitudes, such as job satisfaction, as well as to emphasize chronologically that stimuli in work environments lead to emotional experiences.

Circumplex models portray emotional experience as a two-dimensional space with axes of positive-negative valence and high-low activation. This contrasts with *basic emotions theory*, which describes emotion as distinct categories, such as anger and fear. *Regulatory focus theory* argues that people can be motivated either to seek positive outcomes or to avoid negative outcomes, which indicates preferences for particular emotional experiences. Such preferences can differ not only across individuals, but also it can change over time. New work on *affective diversity* has theorized that management outcomes are influenced by the similarity in emotional experience among colleagues. Management research is split between work examining consistent individual differences in emotional experience and work examining variation over time for the same individual.

- Emotional expression is the outward display of cues that can convey our internal states. Whereas *neurocultural theory* argues that emotional expressions directly convey our internal states unless we regulate them, more modern evolutionary theories, such as *behavioral ecology theory*, emphasize that emotional expressions attempt to influence others. The *emotions as social information model* provides an integration of this work within a social functional framework. Dialect theory details how emotional expressions differ across cultures, akin to dialects of a universal language.
- Postemotional responses, simultaneous with emotional expression, consist of attitudes, behaviors, and cognitions influenced by one's emotional experience. This is the stage of the emotional process inspiring the greatest body of research in management—particularly around the finding that experiencing more positive emotion is associated with better job performance, as well as factors such as creativity, accurate analysis, and extra-role volunteer behaviors. Barbara L. Frederickson's broaden-and-build model emphasizes the role of positive emotion in freeing individuals to explore their environment and forge new connections. Barry M. Staw and colleagues have argued the positive emotion-performance link results from three mechanisms separately and in tandem: improved motivation and perseverance, biased

performance ratings from others, and the ability to receive greater cooperation from others. *Affect-as-information* theory emphasizes how people are guided by their emotional states to reach mood-consistent attitudes, even in domains that are irrelevant to the original emotional state. Joseph P. Forgas's *affect infusion* model details under what circumstances to expect greater influence of emotion on subsequent cognition.

- Emotion recognition, in which observers interpret a target person's emotional expressions, however minimally, is itself a stimulus that feeds into the observer's own chronological set of steps in the emotion process. Theories of emotional contagion emphasize that individuals can "catch" each other's emotions and feel the same way. Theories of emotional linkage emphasize the more nuanced influences that one person's emotion can have on another person, for example, when a supervisor's anger strikes fear in a subordinate.

- Emotion regulation can deliberately bring control to emotional processes—which occur automatically—by many distinct forms that act on each stage of the process. For example, *stimulus selection* involves avoiding negative stimuli and seeking out positive ones. *Reappraisal* involves changing how one registers a situation, and *suppression* involves changing the experience itself. Theory on *emotional labor* and its consequences emphasizes the role of regulation in social influence, and particularly emphasizes the different outcomes of reappraisal versus suppression.

As an especially active area of management research, new theoretical perspectives on emotion are continually being developed and refined. These are typically midrange theories that benefit from being situated within the larger process framework—toward the goal of a unified theory of emotion in management. Such a model could be useful in helping to integrate together the various components of management theories that address emotional dynamics yet have been examined largely in the absence of each other. These areas include stress and burnout, counterproductive behavior, motivation, decision making, and many other topics of pressing concern to managers.

Hillary Anger Elfenbein

See also Affect Theory; Affective Events Theory; Emotional and Social Intelligence; Influence Tactics; Positive Organizational Scholarship; Social Construction Theory

Further Readings

Elfenbein, H. A. (2007). Emotion in organizations: A review and theoretical integration. *Academy of Management Annals, 1,* 371–457.

Ellsworth, P. C., & Scherer, K. R. (2003). Appraisal processes in emotion. In R. J. Davidson, K. R. Scherer, & H. H. Goldsmith (Eds.), *Handbook of affective sciences* (pp. 572–595). Oxford, England: Oxford University Press.

Feldman Barrett, L., & Russell, J. A. (1999). The structure of current affect: Controversies and emerging consensus. *Current Directions in Psychological Science, 8,* 10–14.

Fridlund, A. J. (1994). *Human facial expression: An evolutionary view.* San Diego, CA: Academic Press.

Frijda, N. H. (1986). *The emotions.* Cambridge, U.K.: Cambridge University Press.

Gross, J. (2001). Emotion regulation in adulthood: Timing is everything. *Current Directions in Psychological Science, 10,* 214–219.

Isen, A. M., & Baron, R. A. (1991). Positive affect as a factor in organizational behavior. *Research in Organizational Behavior, 13,* 1–53.

Schwarz, N., & Clore, G. L. (1983). Mood, misattribution, and judgments of wellbeing: Informative and directive functions of affective states. *Journal of Personality and Social Psychology, 45,* 513–523.

Staw, B., Sutton, R., & Pelled, L. (1994). Employee positive emotion and favorable outcomes at the workplace. *Organization Science, 5,* 51–71.

Weiss, H., & Cropanzano, R. (1996). Affective events theory: A theoretical discussion of the structure, causes, and consequences of affective experiences at work. *Research in Organizational Behavior, 18,* 1–74.

THEORY OF ORGANIZATIONAL ATTRACTIVENESS

Organizational attractiveness is defined as the degree to which an individual perceives the organization to be a place to work or the general desirability an individual has to work for an organization. This area of research asks what attracts an individual to apply for a position at an organization or why does an individual apply for a position at an organization. This research provides insight to managers of what variables influence an individual's perceptions of an organization and how these perceptions influence an individual's intention to apply for a job, pursue the job, and willingness to accept the job. Research in organizational attractiveness can be used by managers to enhance the strategies of recruitment. This entry first presents theoretical frameworks used in researching organizational attractiveness. Next the variables are examined, along with the research methods used in studying organizational attraction. The entry closes with implications for management practice.

Fundamentals

Research in organizational attractiveness has a long history. The roots of this field of inquiry can be traced to recruitment research. While research in organizational attractiveness is interrelated with recruitment, it is distinctively different than research on recruitment. First, research on recruitment focuses on the various processes an organization uses to recruit employees. Recruitment research is from the perspective of the organization. On the other hand, research in organizational attractiveness focuses on an individual and how this individual's perceptions of the organization influence the individual to seek a job with the organization. Recruitment is a means to attract a prospective candidate to an organization, but it is *not* what attracts the individual. In examining what attracts individuals to an organization, researchers have identified a number of factors that can be used in the recruitment process or other functions of human resource management (e.g., inducements, compensation) to increase the number of job applicants or even influence the characteristics of the individual who applies for the job. These factors are viewed from the perspective of the individual candidate and not the organization. In examining recruitment, it is assumed that organizational characteristics influence job attitude and behaviors of organizational members; while research in attractiveness assumes that organization, job or task, and individual characteristics affect the applicant's perceptions and ultimate attractiveness to the organization.

Research in organizational attractiveness further assumes that an individual selects and remains in an organization by choice. Job candidates use a satisficing decision-making process rather than a maximizing decision-making process. This decision model states that due to limited time, limited resources, and incomplete and/or inaccurate information, individuals, when making a decision, do not seek to maximize their outcomes but rather select that first solution that satisfies a minimum set of criteria in regards to that decision. One criterion that will be used in the employment decision process would be how attractive an organization is to the individual. A final assumption is that different kinds of people are attracted to different kinds of organizations. It becomes vital to understand how individual characteristics influence perceptions of the organization and ultimately the choice to join and remain with the organization.

Theoretical Frameworks

Four basic frameworks have been used to explore organizational attractiveness. The primary framework that has been used is the *interactional perspective* from psychology. Complementary explanations have also been provided through *theory of reason action, signaling theory,* and *social identity theory.*

Interactional perspective has its roots in interactional psychology and examines individual behavior as a result of the complex multivariable and multidirectional interaction between the individual and the organization. The basic propositions of interactional psychology state that actual behavior is a function of a continuous process of multidirectional interaction or feedback between the individual and the situation encountered. The individual is an intentional, active agent in this interaction process, being both changed by situations and changing situations. Cognitive, affective, and motivational factors and individual ability are essential determiners of behavior. The psychological meaning of situations for the individual and the behavior potential of situations for the individual are essential determiners of behavior. In applying the interactional perspective to research in organizational attractiveness, researchers focus on explaining the differences between organizations by studying the attributes of people. These attributes include personality characteristics, such as self-esteem, type A personality, and need for achievement, and the interaction with organizational characteristics, including reward systems, centralization, size, and geographical location. This research has been extended to include similarity-attraction effect in which individuals will be more attracted to organizations whose values are similar to their values and complementary-attraction in which people will be more attracted to organizations that are more likely to provide them with maximum need gratification. The interactional perspective further suggests different kinds of people are attracted to different types of organizations.

Theory of reasoned action argues that a person's intentions predict behavior, and these intentions are driven by the beliefs and attitudes of the individual. This theory has three basic components—behavior intention, attitude, and subjective norm. It is the combination of attitude and subjective norm that leads to behavioral intention (e.g., to apply for a job). The attitude of the individual is based on the individual's perception or value of applying for the job. Subjective norm involves how others would view this action if taken. Thus, the behavioral intention is influenced by both of these factors; however, these factors do not necessarily have equal weight in influencing intention. Research in organizational attractiveness that is based on this perspective examines how attitudes influence behavior intentions.

Signaling theory examines how to reduce the information asymmetry that exists between organizations and its various stakeholders. While this information asymmetry exists, stakeholders' ability to make good decisions regarding the organization is hindered. To reduce this asymmetry, organizations send signals, or messages, to its various stakeholders. These signals are then interpreted by the intended recipient as to the organization's intentions and actions. It is through the process of signaling that information asymmetry, which exists between an individual and organization, is reduced. One set of signals that organizations send is to prospective job candidates. Researchers in organization attractiveness examine how the prospective job candidates interpret these signals provided by organizations to form an opinion about the organization's intentions and actions.

Social identity theory states that individuals belong to a number of groups (e.g., school, religious, job), and these individuals not only identify with these groups but also use these groups to classify others. Social identification is a perception of belonging to the group. The perception stems from distinctiveness of the group and the salience of outgroups and leads to activities that are congruent with the values and norms of the group. Combining this perspective with the theory of reasoned action and signaling theory, scholars can draw the link that the group that the individual identifies with provides the subjective norms in evaluating the message (signal) that the organization sends to prospective applicants. Researchers in this area examine the affect that group identification has on the attractiveness of the organization.

Methodology

Over 60 articles which have organizational attractiveness as their dependent variable and were published in peer review journals and published between 2000 and 2011 were identified using Ebsco Host and ProQuest databases. The focus on this section is to illuminate the reader on the operationalization of organizational attractiveness, categories of independent variables, subjects, research methods, and statistical analyses used in researching organizational attractiveness.

Dependent variable of organizational attractiveness has been measured by a series of questions based on a Likert-type scale. Daniel Turban and Thomas Keon asked respondents the extent that they

A. would exert a great deal of effort to work for this company;
B. would be interested in pursuing their application with the company;
C. would like to work for the company;
D. would accept a job offer;
E. were no longer interested in the company (reverse score).

Burke and Deszca asked the following:

A. How attracted would you be to this organization?
B. How satisfied would you be in this organization?
C. How successful would you be in this organization?
D. How likely would you take a job in this organization?

Other studies asked similar questions regarding how respondents perceived the attractiveness of the organization as a place to work.

Independent variables used in research of organizational attractiveness can be divided into four basic categories. The first category is individual characteristics, including Type A and Type B personality type, cultural differences, ability to select job as defined by educational level, Myer Brigs Type indicator, and individual difference traits on exchange, communalism, equity sensitivity and uncertainty avoidance, and various demographic variables. The next category of independent variables can be classified as organizational characteristics. These characteristics included geographic dispersion, size, and age; organizational structural variables, such as decentralization, teams, reward systems, and so on; corporate social responsibility; and images and personality types of organizations. The final set is job and/or task characteristics. *Subjects* used were various groups of job seekers. These groups would include undergraduate and graduate students representing various disciplines and countries, high school students, and adults. *Multimethods and tools of statistical analysis* have been used. One method includes manipulation of organizational descriptive scenarios accompanied by surveys. Instead of manipulating descriptive scenarios, other studies used a survey to collect perceptions of organizations. Statistical analysis included ANOVA/MANOVA regression analysis and factor analysis.

Importance

Researchers have found consistent evidence that organizational characteristics, individual characteristics, and job or task characteristics do influence an individual's perception of an organization, which does ultimately impact the individuals desire to work for that organization. Since individuals are attracted to organizations that match their individual characteristics, human resource managers can capitalize on this information by being mindful of the image and message presented in recruitment advertisements and brochures. For example, "employment at will" clauses have a negative impact on organizational attractiveness, while discussion of performance standards and innovation have a positive impact on applicants.

Besides recruitment advertisements, managers must also strategically consider the message that is communicated to the general market. These messages have a secondary benefit of attracting applicants. For example, neutral to positive images of social responsibility increased attractiveness among job applicants.

The message that is developed needs to be consistent with the attributes of potential applicants that the organization wishes to attract. Examination of this research would assist managers in strategically auditing and composing the messages that are sent to applicants and the general marketplace. The theory coupled with the practical application indicates that organizational attractiveness has importance not only to researchers but also to practitioners.

Joann Krauss Williams

See also Attraction-Selection-Attrition Model; Big-Five Personality Dimensions; Bounded Rationality and Satisficing (Behavioral Decision-Making Model); Human Resource Management Strategies; Job Characteristics Theory; Sensemaking; Theory of Reasoned Action

Further Readings

Albinger, H. S., & Freeman, S. J. (2000). Corporate social performance and attractiveness as an employer to different job seeking populations. *Journal of Business Ethics, 28*(3), 243–253.

Anderson, M. H., Haar, J., & Gibb, J. (2010). Personality trait inferences about organizations and organizational attraction: An organizational-level analysis based on a multi-cultural sample. *Journal of Management and Organization, 16*(1), 140–150.

Backhaus, K. B., Stone, B. A., & Heiner, K. (2002). Exploring the relationship between corporate social performance and employer attractiveness. *Business and Society, 41*(3), 292–318.

Gomes, D., & Neves, J. (2011). Organizational attractiveness and prospective applicants intentions to apply. *Personnel Review, 40*(6), 684–699.

Kausel, E. E., & Slaughter, J. E. (2011). Narrow personality traits and organizational attraction: Evidence for the complementary hypothesis. *Organizational Behavior and Human Decision Processes, 114*(1), 3–14.

Lievens, F., & Highhouse, S. (2003). The relation of instrumental and symbolic attributes to a company's attractiveness as an employer. *Personnel Psychology, 56*(1), 75–102.

Lievens, F., Van Haye, G., & Schreurs, B. (2005). Examining the relationship between employer knowledge dimensions and organizational attractiveness: An application in a military context. *Journal of Occupational and Organizational Psychology, 78,* 553–572.

Rynes, S. L., & Barber, A. E. (1990). Applicant attraction strategies: An organizational perspect. *Academy of Management Review, 15*(2), 286–286.

Turban, D. B., & Keon, T. L. (1993). Organizational attractiveness: An interactionist perspective. *Journal of Applied Psychology, 78*(2), 184–184.

THEORY OF REASONED ACTION

The theory of reasoned action (TRA) as developed by Martin Fishbein and Icek Ajzen provides a means to understand the drivers of human behavior. It states that behavioral intentions are the most proximal and reliable predictors of whether a person will engage in a specific volitional act. Behavioral intent is influenced by one's attitude toward the specific act that is being contemplated and subjective norms, the social pressure to perform the act. The TRA is arguably the most widely used theory of its kind. It is used extensively in the literatures of marketing, business management, social psychology, and health care. In a recent search of the ProQuest database, it generated a list of nearly 8,000 research articles that referenced or used the theory. When searching for TRA and its extension, the theory of planned behavior, it generated a list of over 14,000 research articles. In the marketing literature, it is used to understand the influence of consumer attitudes toward products on buying decisions and to test how to influence attitudes and subsequent buying decisions that can be affected by marketing efforts. It is used extensively in the health care industry to study how patient attitudes influence decisions to use medication, use screening for various types of cancer, and use of disease prevention measures. In the management literature, it is used to study worker attitudes toward cooperation, motivated behaviors, safety, and other relevant management issues. This entry will explain the overall model and its component parts. Boundary conditions for use of the model, theories that are related to the TRA, and the importance of the theory to business are also discussed.

Fundamentals

The TRA is a very compact model of human behavior. It consists of attitude toward the act, subjective norms, behavioral intent, and the target behavior. Attitude toward the act is one's subjective evaluation of the desirability, or undesirability, of performing a specific action. It considers the consequences to the actor of performing the act and whether these consequences are favorable to the actor or unfavorable. Subjective norms represent the social pressure to engage in performing or not performing the act. The actor considers what others who are respected or important to them would do in the same situation. It considers peer pressure to conform. Behavioral intent is influenced by subjective norms and attitude toward the act and is the most proximal determinant of behavior according to the TRA. It represents the actor's intention to perform or not perform a specific act.

Attitude Toward the Act

Attitude toward the act involves three different categories of potential responses to the target person, object, or idea. These categories are cognitive, conative, and affective. A cognitive response is representative of the person's thoughts or ideas about the attitude object. *Cognitive responses* are categorized as verbal and nonverbal. A verbal response is demonstrated by beliefs about the attitude object. For instance, a student may believe that a particular faculty member is interesting and worthwhile to choose as an instructor or that a given class will be beneficial to learning relevant skills to use in his or her career. A nonverbal response is observable and attitude is inferred. If a student comes to a classroom on time and prepared to work, it is likely that she or he has a favorable attitude toward the class and/or the instructor.

Affective responses are relative to one's feelings about a particular attitude object. If a student admires a professor and appreciates her approach to teaching, the student can be said to "feel good" about taking a class with that professor. This would infer a favorable attitude about the class and/or the instructor.

Conative responses have to do with what the person actually does. These are behavioral tendencies and actions toward the attitude object. If the person says that he is eager to attend the next lecture, it may be inferred that he has a positive attitude about attending class. This would be a verbal response. The nonverbal conative indicators could be the person reading the material for the class and doing extra credit work or choosing to do research projects for the class. These would imply a positive attitude about the class.

Subjective Norms

These are a function of a person's beliefs regarding what she or he feels others who are important to them would do in the specific context under consideration or if the referent others would actually engage in the behavior under consideration. Referent others may be coworkers, peers, parents, friends, professional associates, or other social referents whose opinion may be relevant in the specific context involved. The relevant referent group will change with the context and the behavior under consideration. A decision regarding whether to go bowling with a group of friends will likely not be influenced by coworkers, but it will be influenced with the social group of friends. Conversely, a decision to hand in a white paper on time to support committee work at one's job will be likely to be influenced by coworkers' opinions and behavior but not by one's parents. These are referred to as normative beliefs.

In addition to normative beliefs, subjective norms involve motivation to comply. If most of the relevant referent group that is important to the person would perform the behavior in question, there is motivation to comply. This results in social pressure to perform the act. Conversely, if the referent group would not perform the act, there is motivation to comply with restraining from the behavior.

Behavioral Intent

This is a key distinguishing characteristic of the TRA that sets it apart from other behavioral theories. Behavioral intent mediates attitude and subjective norm influences on behavior. All other influences on behavior affect behavioral intent through their impact on attitudes and subjective norms. The theory states that behavioral intent is the most proximal determinant of behavior. It is a measure of the person's decision or intention to perform a specific act in a given context. The strength of behavioral intention is also a measure of how hard the person will try to actually perform the behavior. If behavioral intent is a large value, the person will exert significant effort to accomplish the behavior.

Boundary Conditions

While the theory has predictive value across numerous situations and contexts, there are some conditions that need to be observed to ensure correct application of the theory. The TRA is intended for use in situations where the behavior under consideration is volitional. That is, the person who will be performing the behavior has the skill, ability, and independence necessary to perform the behavior. For situations that do not meet these conditions, there is an extension of the theory called the *theory of planned behavior* (TPB). The TPB added perceived behavioral control to capture self-efficacy and other control beliefs regarding influences on one's actions that are essentially out of one's direct control.

To have the maximum predictive capability, the principle of compatibility must be followed. It states that when applying the model attitude, the subjective norms, behavioral intent, and behavior all need to be consistent in terms of time, target, context, and action. For example, to apply this principle, researchers could predict one's likely action of buying a car by looking at the decision to buy a specific car from a specific dealer, on a specific day, at a specific time. The more general the measures are and the less consistent the antecedents to the behavior are in terms of time, target, context, and action, the lower the predictive value of the model.

Other Related Theories

Two other theories are commonly used in the same or similar contexts as the TRA. These are *social cognitive learning theory* (SCLT) and the *health belief model* (HBM). The SCLT includes self-efficacy, outcome expectations, goals, and social structural factors as antecedents to behavior. The health belief model includes susceptibility, severity, benefit, barrier, and cues to action as antecedents to behavior. All three models include assessment of favorability of outcomes in some form. The concepts of self-efficacy and social structural factors of the SCLT correspond to perceived behavioral control in the extended version of the TRA, the theory of planned behavior, and subjective norms in the TRA respectively. The concepts of susceptibility, severity, and barrier in the health belief model relate to perceived behavioral control on the theory of planned behavior. The concept of benefit in the health belief model is related to the attitude component of the TRA.

Importance

The TRA and its extension theory of planned behavior are by far the most commonly used behavioral theories in the business literature today. As noted in the introduction, searching the major databases generates thousands of hits. The marketing field uses it extensively to predict consumer behavior and to understand how to influence consumer attitudes in order to increase demand for products and services. Research in the management literature has used it to understand employee motivation and other relevant behavioral issues.

The theory is robust and reliable. There have been numerous meta-analyses of research using the theory, and they consistently return large effect sizes for the variables demonstrating the predictive validity and power of the theory. For example, in a meta-analysis conducted in 1988 studying results of research using the TRA, the authors found that the attitude + subjective norms correlation with behavioral intention was 0.66 and the behavioral intention to behavior correlation was 0.53 across 87 studies. In another meta-analysis conducted in 2001 using 96 independent studies, behavioral intent was correlated 0.51 with behavior. Interestingly, in the same meta-analysis, the effective difference between the predictive value of the TRA and theory of planned behavior was significant, but small.

In sum, the TRA, and its extension, the theory of planned behavior, or TPB, have been shown to have very good predictive power in applications involving attempts to understand the drivers of behavior. The lessons learned have been used to formulate programs aimed at changing employee attitudes about work safety, increasing favorable attitudes and motivation in work settings, and changing consumer attitudes and behavior as it relates to purchasing decisions, among others. It has stood the test of time and has consistently remained the most often used behavioral model in the management literature since shortly after its inception.

Francis Jeffries

See also Equity Theory; Expectancy Theory; Goal-Setting Theory; Job Characteristics Theory; Social Cognitive Theory

Further Readings

Ajzen, I. (2005). *Attitudes, personality, and behavior* (2nd ed.). Berkshire, England: McGraw-Hill.

Armitage, C., & Christian, J. (Eds.). (2004). *Planned behavior.* New Brunswick, NJ: Transaction.

Bandura, A. (1986). *Social foundations of thought and action: A social cognitive theory.* Englewood Cliffs, NJ: Prentice Hall.

Fishbein, M., & Ajzen, I. (1975). *Belief, attitude, intention, and behavior: An introduction to theory and research.* Reading, MA: Addison-Wesley.

Forgas, J., Cooper, J., & Crano, W. (Eds.). (2010). *The psychology of attitudes and attitude change.* New York, NY: Psychology Press.

Herr, P. (1995). Whither fact, artifact, and attitude: Reflections on the theory of reasoned action. *Journal of Consumer Psychology, 4*(4), 371–380.

THEORY OF SELF-ESTEEM

Self-esteem involves an individual's own evaluation of his or her abilities and subsequent feelings of competence and worthiness stemming from those evaluations. William James, considered by many to be the grandfather of self-esteem, defined the construct simply as, "What we back ourselves to be and do." Self-esteem is a complex construct and is considered one element of an overall self-concept, with other connected and related elements such as self-efficacy and self-identity also being central to one's self-concept beliefs. At present, there is not an overall encompassing theory of self-esteem, as much debate exists as to its importance and causality in both the fields of clinical and applied psychology. Although self-esteem is a fairly frequently studied construct in the field of psychology and to a lesser degree in the field of management, its relevance and importance is a matter of some debate. Self-esteem has been found in some studies to be weakly to moderately positively related to work-relevant variables such as satisfaction and performance, but the causal nature of these relationships has not been supported. Therefore, while individuals with high self-esteem tend to have higher life satisfaction, for example, it has been argued that individuals may be deriving their levels of self-esteem from satisfactory lives, rather than the high self-esteem itself leading to high levels of life satisfaction. The following sections explore the theoretical foundation, measurement, development, and importance of self-esteem.

Fundamentals

The origins of self-esteem can be traced back over a hundred years to two classic psychologists: William James and Charles Cooley. James (1842–1910)

believed that self-esteem was a reflection of how adequate an individual felt he or she was in areas that he or she viewed as important. This deceptively simple explanation actually reflects the complexity of the self-esteem construct, as it suggests that self-esteem is not simply about one's feelings of competence—it is rather about our feelings of competence only in the areas that matter to us personally. Cooley (1864–1929) first spoke of self-esteem in his description of what he called the "looking glass self," which stated that it is *others'* opinions of us that were of central importance to our development. These viewpoints, when taken together, comprise the underlying core constructs of self-esteem. In short, self-esteem appears to be based on whether people feel competent to face the obstacles in life, and to be healthy, these assessments must be based in reality. In terms of development over the life span, young children tend to have universally high levels of self-esteem, and these levels begin to change differentially as they get older. Both the ideas of James and Cooley combine in the idea of a *symbolic interactionist* perspective, which states that we humans develop our self-esteem over time through our interactions with other people. If we perceive these interactions with others as being positive, we develop higher regard for ourselves.

Self-esteem is a complex construct, representing both self-efficacy (an individual's belief that he or she is competent to accomplish something) as well as self-respect (belief that he or she is worthy and deserving of respect, love, admiration, etc.). Self-determination theory (SDT) also provides a useful mechanism to understand the underpinnings of self-esteem. This theory states that all individuals are born with an innate desire to experience and master their surroundings and that self-esteem is achieved when the basic needs of life (defined by SDT as relatedness, competency, and autonomy) are all in balance. Self-esteem is rooted in one's internal feelings about their competence as well as their worthiness. SDT postulates that there may be two different types of self-esteem to consider: (a) *contingent self-esteem,* which is comparative and based on criteria defined in the external world (how you believe you compare with others on externally defined measures of success); and (b) *true self-esteem,* which is argued to be the healthiest and most important kind, defined as one's sense of self as worthy, based not on what one has accomplished but rather as a given, stable belief.

Rosenberg's Self-Esteem Scale is the classic method for assessing one's self-esteem levels. This measure consists of 10 items scored on a Likert scale. Rosenberg believed that substantial social structural experiences, such as race and ethnicity, education, and family experiences, create strong social forces that help to shape one's self-esteem over a lifetime.

Self-esteem has been conceptualized on three levels: *global self-esteem* (also known as generalized self-esteem), *state self-esteem,* and *domain-specific self-esteem.* Global, or generalized, self-esteem is the most frequently studied level, and it can be best thought of as trait-based self-esteem, or one's overall evaluation and judgment about him or herself. Global self-esteem operates much like other personality variables, developing early in life and remaining relatively stable over time and situations. State self-esteem, in contrast, involves an individual's judgment of competence at a particular point in time, usually in reaction to a specific event, and is more temporary in nature than global self-esteem. Finally, domain-specific self-esteem involves one's assessment of his or her competence toward a particular subject, rather than a more universal assessment of worth.

Much debate exists as to whether self-esteem can be taught, or whether clinical intervention occupationally-relevant training may successfully increase self-esteem levels. The conflict among researchers about the malleability of self-esteem may lie in the lack of clarity about which level or domain of self-esteem is being investigated. Global self-esteem is not easily modified, as it is relatively stable across one's life span. State self-esteem, by definition, can be more easily manipulated, as could domain-specific self-esteem, because of their more temporary nature. However, skepticism exists in the literature regarding the value of such interventions, as they are not likely to have substantial or lasting impact on the dependent variables often associated with high levels of global self-esteem.

Clinical psychologists have developed interventions designed to increase self-esteem. It has been postulated that there are six "pillars" for nurturing self-esteem: (a) living consciously, (b) self-acceptance, (c) self-responsibility, (d) self-assertiveness, (e) living purposefully, and (f) personal integrity. However, efforts to increase self-esteem, using external methods, such as training or counseling, are considered questionable. The more universal value of increasing self-esteem through such methods, even if it is possible, is also questioned.

How much self-esteem is optimal? It appears that too little or too much self-esteem can have less than desirable results. Researchers have examined whether extremely high levels of self-esteem can be dangerous or detrimental to healthy human functioning. If levels of self-esteem are not rooted in reality, they may lead to delusions about competence or ability. These delusions may cause individuals to persist in the face of extreme challenges or failures, past the point where such behavior is wise. Failures may then result in the individual with inflated self-esteem to blame others for their lack of success, rather than assuming necessary personal responsibility. Individuals with extremely low levels of self-esteem, in contrast, may limit their efforts and not take advantage of opportunities at all, believing they are neither competent nor worthy enough to make much of them.

Self-esteem is one component of the larger concept of self-concept. Positive self-concept, also called core self-evaluations by Timothy Judge and colleagues, is composed of self-esteem, generalized self-efficacy, locus of control, and emotional stability. These four components, when combined, have been shown to yield a positive relationship to job satisfaction, work motivation, and job performance. Self-esteem is similar in nature to the construct of self-efficacy, but they differ in fundamentally important ways. Whereas self-esteem is one's overall assessment of value as a person, assessments of self-efficacy focus more on one's belief that he or she can be successful. These also differ from the other two components of core self-evaluations. Internal locus of control is the belief that one has control over a range of factors in life (and seems arguably similar to self-determination theory's idea of "true self-esteem"). Finally, emotional stability is one's level of confidence and security.

The lack of a universally accepted theory of self-esteem, as well as conflicting research about its causality, has resulted in questions about the relevance of the construct to applied workplace psychology. While some researchers and practitioners remain hopeful that interventions and training may increase levels of self-esteem (and consequently, work satisfaction and performance), there is not strong research support for this notion.

Importance

Self-esteem has been found through research to be related to a number of subjective constructs, such as positive affectivity, well-being, and life satisfaction. It is the best predictor of life satisfaction than any other known construct (with relationships ranging from 0.3 to 0.5), including such factors as marital status and health. Self-esteem is also positively related to self-confidence and positive self-belief, initiative, and happiness, and it is negatively related to anxiety and depression, as well as drug and alcohol use. However, the question of whether those who engage in negative behaviors do so *because* of low self-esteem, or, whether low self-esteem *causes* such detrimental behavior is a matter of empirical debate.

The relationships between global self-esteem and performance are weak to moderate at best, with some researchers refuting that self-esteem has any positive impact on achievement, performance, or leadership whatsoever. It seems that self-esteem is related to one's positive self-beliefs, but these positive self-beliefs do not appear to result in substantially stronger levels of management-related outcomes, such as job performance. Other researchers have argued that the strength of the relationships between self-esteem and performance are similar to those found with other stable individual differences, such as personality traits. Self-esteem, when considered on a global level, is a broad trait, and these researchers argue that it is not realistic that a broad trait would strongly predict more domain-specific behaviors, such as academic or job performance.

Without definitive evidence about causality, the importance or necessity of interventions or training designed to increase self-esteem is also in question. A key question of interest for management practitioners has been whether it is a beneficial use of resources to try to improve employees' self-esteem, and whether such an investment of time and energy may result in subsequent improvements in performance.

There has not been extensive research as to the importance of self-esteem to career development. Based on initial research, it appears that having positive early career experiences can generate positive self-esteem and having low self-esteem may limit one's opportunities by restricting one's view of what is possible, causing an individual to not act upon what he or she may be interested in pursuing. Once again, research in this area has determined that the relationship between career development and self-esteem is bidirectional.

Most recently, research has explored the concept of organization-based self-esteem (OBSE), or an employee's assessment of her worth and competence as a part of a specific organization. OBSE appears to stem from an interaction of the employee's disposition and the work environment itself. High levels of OBSE are positively linked to job satisfaction, organizational commitment, job performance, and organizational citizenship behaviors, beyond what can be predicted by generalized self-esteem. Research suggests that management should emphasize organic environmental structures, increased job complexity, and management and leadership practices that encourage participation and self-direction to increase employee OBSE.

Megan W. Gerhardt

See also Organizationally-Based Self-Esteem; Self-Concept and the Theory of Self; Self-Determination Theory; Social Cognitive Theory

Further Readings

Bowling, N. A., Eschelman, K. J., Wang, Q., Kirkendall, C., & Alarcon, G. (2010). A meta-analysis of the predictors and consequences of organization-based self-esteem. *Journal of Occupational and Organizational Psychology, 83*, 601–626.

Cooley, C. H. (1922). *Human nature and the social order* (Rev. ed.). New York, NY: Scribner's. (Original work published 1902)

Ferris, D., Lian, H., Brown, D. J., Pang, F. J., & Keeping, L. M. (2010). Self-esteem and job performance: The moderating role of self-esteem contingencies. *Personnel Psychology, 63*, 561–593.

Guindon, M. H. (2010). *Self-esteem across the lifespan: Issue and interventions.* New York, NY: Routledge.

Hewitt, J. P. (2002). The social construction of self-esteem. In C. R. Snyder & S. J. Lopez (Eds.). *Handbook of positive psychology.* Oxford, England: Oxford University Press.

James, W. (1999). *Principles of psychology* (Reprinted, Vols. 1–2). Bristol, England: Thoemmes Press. (Original work published 1890, New York, NY: Henry Holt)

Judge, T. A., & Bono, J. E. (2001). Relationship of core self-evaluations traits-self-esteem, generalized self-efficacy, locus of control, and emotional stability-with job satisfaction and job performance: A meta-analysis. *Journal of Applied Psychology, 86*, 80–92.

Kernis, M. (Ed.). (2006). *Self-esteem: Issues and answers.* New York, NY: Psychology Press.

Owens, T. J., Stryker, S., & Goodman, N. (2001). *Extending self-esteem theory and research.* Cambridge, England: Cambridge University Press.

Pierce, J. L., Gardner, D. G., & Cummings, L. L. (1989). Organizational-based self-esteem: Construct definition, measurement, and instrument validation. *Academy of Management Journal, 32*, 622–648.

Theory of the Interesting

Sociologically speaking, Murray Davis considered that what is interesting to an audience (experts or laypeople) is something that stands out in their attention in contrast to their normal life. It constitutes an attack on some (not all) of their everyday assumptions about their ongoing activities. Analogously, an *interesting* theory is one that stands out for an audience by attacking some (not all) of the taken-for-granted propositions that make up the conceptual structure of their daily lives. Psychologically speaking, interest is an emotion that stimulates curiosity and fosters exploration for its own sake. It encourages growth in knowledge and competence.

The term *interesting* is important in management circles because it is used often by academic journal editors who wish to stimulate the production of novel arguments and novel research questions in articles in their journals. Their expectation is that such articles will be much more influential and much more generative of other research than non-interesting papers no matter how sound they are. The editors almost always base their arguments on Davis's sociological work, although Davis's theory of the interesting has not been developed very much. This entry first summarizes Davis's approach to the interesting and then summarizes contemporary psychological theorizing about what is interesting. Although this is not intentional, the approaches are somewhat complementary.

Fundamentals

Davis's Sociological Approach to the Interesting

Davis argued that interesting ideas motivate intellectual life much more than true ideas do, in part because they generate incomplete gestalts in people's minds and thus are dynamic. Truth, in contrast, though the final goal of knowledge, is static. Davis also contrasted what is interesting from what is obvious (does not challenge any assumptions) and from what is absurd (too strong a challenge to assumptions).

Davis's particular focus was on characteristics of interesting ideas and propositions. He originally described interesting propositions as articulating a phenomenological presumption about some aspect of the world and then denying it in the name of a more profound insight. Davis considered interesting ideas to have several characteristics: They are novel, often including dialectic properties. They are easily elaborated to apply to new topics, shifting what was on the periphery of awareness to the center. They are reorganizational; they create and interrelate categories in new ways (e.g., separate what was coupled and couple what was separated). They are reflexive, applying their theses to themselves. They are ambiguous, allowing multiple, sometimes contradictory, meanings. They are sociable for the group that holds them; they establish a social base that conveys developments of original ideas to current and potential members thus reproducing the ideas. Finally, they are transient, since they alter the background against which they first appeared interesting.

Psychological Approach to the Interesting

Psychologists' research on interest is derived from a focus on the importance of cognitive appraisals, the presumption that emotions arise from people's evaluations of events rather than from objective features of the events. Thus interest, like other emotions, is caused by how people appraise what is happening in a particular situation. Further, because people experience events differently, they will often have different emotions in response to what appears to be the same situation.

Interest is considered to foster intrinsic motivation and to be fundamental to motivated learning. By fostering intrinsic motivation, interest increases the likelihood that people will develop knowledge, skills, and experience.

For example, there is evidence that when they are interested, students spend more time on learning tasks, study more, read more, remember more of what they read, and consequently get better grades in classes. This type of outcome appears to happen

at least in part because interest stimulates deeper levels of processing of the meanings of textual material. Further, when people are faced with a boring task, they often attempt to make it more interesting. Thus, interest is likely a prime motivator for persistence and long-term engagement in tasks.

While interest is often associated primarily with the positive, this is not always the case. People might experience negative emotions even in the midst of interested engagement, for example, when they feel frustrated while trying to solve a particularly difficult problem.

What makes something interesting? More precisely, what types of appraisals cause interest? It appears that interest comes from two appraisals. The first appraisal is an evaluation of an event's novelty and related complexity, that is, evaluation of the event as new, unexpected, complex, mysterious, or obscure. The second appraisal is an event's comprehensibility, which refers to people believing that they have the skills, knowledge, and resources to deal with such new and complex events. Interest differs from confusion, in that confusing things stem from appraisals of high novelty but low comprehensibility.

The Complementarity of Sociological and Psychological Approaches

In some ways, the sociological and psychological approaches to interest complement and reinforce each other. The sociological approach emphasizes the types of characteristics that challenge the assumptions in which thought and practice are grounded. The psychological approach emphasizes that interest—and thus such challenges—have emotional components; what is going on in successful challenges is a stimulation of intrinsic motivation. The sociological approach does not consider characteristics of the audience in very much depth. The psychological approach emphasizes characteristics of the audience, discussing how audience members' appraisals of ideas as both novel and comprehensible affect whether they consider something as interesting. It may be that the perception of incomprehensibility is one reason that audiences consider some ideas as absurd. Both the sociological and psychological approaches emphasize that the outcomes of the experience of something interesting are likely to include desires to learn and explore in more depth. The psychological approach emphasizes these outcomes for individuals, while the sociological approach suggests how interesting ideas may have considerable impacts on scholarly thinking over extended groups and time periods.

Managers (and many other people) can learn from this theory about why being interesting is so crucial in terms of fostering attention and learning. They can also learn how to use appropriate novelty in conjunction with comprehensibility to create interest. This includes challenging some, though not all, assumptions even while fostering people's sense that they have the abilities to deal with the novelty appropriately.

Jean M. Bartunek

See also Achievement Motivation Theory; Role Theory; Social Cognitive Theory; Theory Development; Theory of Emotions

Further Readings

Alvesson, M., & Sandberg, J. (2011). Generating research questions through problematization. *Academy of Management Review, 36,* 247–271.

Bartunek, J. M., Rynes, S. L., & Ireland, R. D. (2006). What makes management research interesting, and why does it matter? *Academy of Management Journal, 49,* 9–15.

Davis, M. S. (1971). That's interesting! Towards a phenomenology of sociology and a sociology of phenomenology. *Philosophy of the Social Sciences, 1,* 309–344.

Davis, M. S. (1999). Aphorisms and clichés: The generation and dissipation of conceptual charisma. In J. Hagan & K. Cook (Eds.), *Annual review of sociology* (Vol. 25, pp. 245–269). Palo Alto, CA: Annual Reviews.

Sansone, C., & Thoman, D. B. (2005). Interest as the missing motivation or self-regulation. *European Psychologist, 10*(3), 175–186.

Silvia, P. J. (2006). *Exploring the psychology of interest.* New York, NY: Oxford University Press.

Silvia, P. J. (2010). Confusion and interest: The role of knowledge emotions in aesthetic experience. *Psychology of Aesthetics, Creativity, and the Arts, 4*(2), 75–80.

THEORY OF TRANSFER OF TRAINING

Transfer of training is the extent to which knowledge and skill acquired by trainees in a training setting are generalized, maintained, and adapted in a job setting. In organizational contexts, positive transfer of training is generally regarded as the paramount concern of training efforts—but it has proven to be a formidable challenge. Indeed, there is a widely recognized "transfer problem" whereby researchers and practitioners consistently conclude that the return on many training investments is low and organizational investments in training are too often wasted due to poor transfer. This is of particular concern in today's rapidly changing business climate, where organizational success often depends on the speed with which people can learn and transfer new ideas and information. The theory's central management insight is that learning and transfer are fundamentally different phenomena and learning is necessary, but not sufficient, for transfer to occur. To achieve transfer, training designers and trainees must actively pursue those training elements and activities known to foster generalization, maintenance, and adaptation of learned skills and knowledge. This entry synthesizes the most important advances in our understanding of transfer outcomes, highlights transfer antecedents most supported by empirical evidence, and identifies implications for management action.

Fundamentals

Within the domain of transfer of training, three recent conceptual advances are of particular importance. The first of these is overt recognition of the multidimensional nature of transfer outcomes and greater precision in describing those different dimensions. The second involves an expanded view of the antecedents of transfer beyond the design of learning events to include factors in the person, training, and work climate. The third directly acknowledges the importance of the type of *training content* on transfer outcomes.

Transfer Outcomes

Many traditional definitions stop at defining *transfer* as the application of learned skills to the workplace. *Application* is a very general term, however, and definitions that dimensionalize transfer more specifically as generalization, maintenance, and adaptability are preferred. Generalization involves more than merely mimicking trained responses to events that occurred in training. It requires trainees to exhibit new behaviors on the job in response to different settings, people, and situations from those trained. Maintenance focuses on the changes that occur in the form or level of skills or behaviors exhibited in the transfer setting as a function of time elapsed from the completion of the training program. Adaptability reflects the reality that, for many jobs today, trained individuals must not only deal with routine situations and issues but must also adapt to novel or nonroutine situational demands. The most critical point is that positive transfer is more than a function of original learning in a training experience. For transfer to have occurred, learned behavior must be generalized to the job context, maintained over a period of time, and be adapted to the particular work climate of interest.

As alluded to above, even within each dimension, there are levels or distinctions. For example, with respect to generalization, it is useful to think in terms of transfer *distance*. To illustrate, learning to drive a car and then finding oneself in a truck would be a situation that would demand generalization, but of a relatively short distance. On the other hand, learning principles of organizational change in a management development seminar and then attempting to practice behaviors stemming from those principles over time as head of a merger and acquisition team would represent much greater generalization distance. Depending on the type of transfer outcomes desired, closing the transfer "gap" can involve greater or smaller distances. It is important to have some degree of clarity about the nature of the transfer of interest before designing and evaluating training interventions.

Transfer Antecedents

Transfer of training has long been recognized as a complex challenge and was among the first issues addressed by early industrial psychologists. However, until fairly recently, the majority of efforts to improve transfer have focused solely on the design and delivery of the learning event. An important expansion in our understanding is that it is not just the training intervention itself but a system of factors in the person, training, and organization that ultimately influence transfer of training to job performance. Transfer can only be completely understood and influenced by examining the entire system of influences.

Considerable progress has been made in discovering the antecedents to transfer. Conventional wisdom is that three categories of factors will most impact transfer outcomes: (a) training design, (b) trainee

characteristics, and (c) work environment factors. Training design factors include the incorporation of learning principles, such as stimulus variability, active practice, and overlearning. Trainee characteristics consist of factors, such as ability, skill, motivation, and personality. Work environment factors include transfer climate and social support from supervisors and peers, as well as the opportunities to perform learned behaviors on the job.

Transfer and Type of Training

Although this was curiously neglected for many years, transfer researchers and training practitioners now more explicitly acknowledge that the type of skill being trained can impact transfer outcomes. One influential conceptualization of potential training content distinguishes between "closed" and "open" skills. Closed skills are those where trainees are trained to respond in one particular way on the job according to a set of rules—implemented in a precise fashion. For example, an auto mechanic changing turn lights on a car has a prescribed process and time to complete this task. On the other end of the scale are highly variable open skills—where there is not one single correct way to act but rather freedom to perform. With open skills, the objective is generally to learn *principles* and not solely discrete steps.

For example, a manager who is trying to motivate staff members cannot look up a "cookbook" of steps to take. A manager could, however, use motivational principles to accomplish the objective. The evolution of many military jobs, from what were once primarily physical roles with closed-skill requirements to now more cognitive open-skill demands, means that not only are the skills more difficult to train but also that tasks requiring high-level cognitive components are subject to greater and more rapid decay than are simpler motor skills.

The central point is that the linkage between a transfer antecedent and outcome may well vary depending on the nature of the training content. For example, the positive influence of a climate variable, such as peer support, may differ in its relationship to transfer depending on whether the skill being trained is an open or closed skill.

Importance

Notwithstanding, the consensus among scholars is that the traditional yield from organizational training has been disappointing and the transfer problem remains acute. Left to chance, the likelihood that significant transfer will occur from most learning initiatives is truly very small. The good news, however, is that the development and evaluation of active transfer interventions is still in its infancy and research evidence has grown significantly in the last two decades. To conclude that transfer is resistant to intervention is based on the assumption that interventions have regularly been designed and implemented and yet failed to yield transfer—but that is not the case. Although a number of exceptions exist, the reality is that transfer has generally *not* been actively pursued or managed with planned interventions. When it has been, the results are encouraging.

For example, there is emerging evidence that interventions focused on heightening trainee self-efficacy and readiness can improve ultimate transfer. Similarly, new training designs that focus on identifying existing knowledge frames, random practice, and error diagnosis are showing great promise. Further, post-training interventions that help trainees envision their use of the training, predict and manage relapses, and set transfer goals have demonstrated transfer gains. The most successful transfer-inducing interventions will be those based on the accumulating evidence of what affects transfer in organizational contexts.

For those managers faced with the challenge of improving transfer in organizations, the emerging research suggests that there is ample reason to believe that they *can* improve transfer but probably not in the ways training has often been designed and delivered. The most important lessons are to think of multiple domains of transfer intervention—not just training design—and to go beyond the classroom (e.g., trainee selection and pretraining program framing, supervisor support, post-training visioning, and goal setting) in seeking to enhance transfer. Explicitly articulating training objectives, involving managers and peers in the training process and linking transfer outcomes with traditional organizational reward systems, are the most promising strategies for improved transfer in today's organizations.

Timothy T. Baldwin

See also Action Learning; Learning Organization; Management (Education) as Practice; Organizational and Managerial Wisdom; Organizational Learning; Transfer of Technology

Further Readings

Baldwin, T. T., & Ford, J. K. (1988). Transfer of training: A review and directions for future research. *Personnel Psychology, 41,* 63–105.

Baldwin, T. T., Ford, J. K., & Blume, B. D. (2009). Transfer of training 1988–2008: An updated review and new agenda for future research. In G. P. Hodgkinson & J. K. Ford (Eds.), *International review of industrial and organizational psychology* (Vol. 24, pp. 41–70). Chichester, England: Wiley.

Barnett, S. M., & Ceci, S. J. (2002). When and where do we apply what we learn? A taxonomy for far transfer. *Psychological Bulletin, 128,* 612–637.

Blume, B. D., Ford, J. K., Baldwin, T. T., & Huang, J. L. (2010). Transfer of training: A meta-analytic review. *Journal of Management, 36,* 1065–1105.

Ford, J. K., & Weissbein, D. A. (1997). Transfer of training: An updated review and analysis. *Performance Improvement Quarterly, 10*(2), 22–41.

Yelon, S. L., & Ford, J. K. (1999). Pursuing a multidimensional view of transfer. *Performance Improvement Quarterly, 12*(3), 58–78.

THEORY X AND THEORY Y

Douglas McGregor's landmark book, *The Human Side of Enterprise,* advanced one of the most important theories in the history of management thought. According to McGregor, a manager's basic assumptive world, or cosmology, influences the managerial practices employed, which in turn shape the attitudes, work behavior, and performance of subordinates. After elucidating the fundamental (and pessimistic) assumptions managers tended to hold regarding human behavior in organizations, McGregor called on managers to engage in self-reflection and to consider alternative sets of assumptions. In the final analysis, McGregor hoped that increased self-awareness might prompt attitudinal and behavioral changes among managers. This entry first describes McGregor's theory x and theory y; next, the importance of McGregor's theorizing is discussed; and the final section delineates implications for practice.

Fundamentals

In its briefest form, McGregor's theorizing reflects the following six ideas. First, managers make assumptions about human behavior in organizations, even if they are unaware of doing so. Second, two broad categories of managerial assumptions can be identified: a pessimistic view (which McGregor labeled theory x) and a more optimistic view (theory y). Third, there are three primary dimensions pertinent to these assumptions, namely, whether people are seen as (a) inherently lazy versus industrious, (b) possessing a limited versus substantial capacity for useful contributions, and (c) being untrustworthy and requiring external control versus being responsible and capable of self-direction and self-control. McGregor also noted that people differ in their levels of ambition, willingness to accept responsibility, and desire for security, but the first three dimensions are of central importance. Fourth, differences in managerial assumptions result in corresponding patterns of managerial behaviors (such as close supervision and limited delegation of authority versus more general supervision and broad delegation). Fifth, enacted managerial practices influence employee motivation and work behavior. Thus, whereas opportunities for intrinsic satisfaction may spur employee interest and motivation, a distrustful style of management will likely produce employee disengagement. Sixth, because managers are typically unaware of the self-fulfilling nature of their assumptive worlds, there is often a misperception of cause and effect. The manager holding theory x beliefs may unwittingly engineer a low level of employee motivation. Completing the self-reinforcing cycle, upon observing low levels of employee engagement and motivation, the manager feels vindicated that his or her low expectations were warranted. Conversely, the manager who believes that employees are generally trustworthy, capable of contributing, and desirous of growth will facilitate such outcomes.

Questioning widely held and, at the time, conventional (theory x) assumptions about human behavior in organizations, McGregor outlined a new role for managers: Rather than commanding and controlling subordinates, managers should assist them in reaching their full potential. Clearly, McGregor was one of the first advocates of what is now referred to as the positive psychology movement. With good management practices, he argued, the potential for human achievement is vast, albeit largely untapped.

Importance

McGregor, a seminal figure in the field of management, was among the earliest humanistic psychologists whose theorizing developed in response to the perceived limitations of both scientific management and the human relations movement. McGregor himself was inspired by Abraham Maslow's prior work on the natural desire for psychological growth and self-esteem. Indicative of the impact of McGregor's work, John Miner in 2003 reviewed 73 established organizational behavior theories and found that theory x and theory y was tied for second place in terms of recognition and in 33rd place with respect to importance. By the time of the 25th year reprinting of *The Human Side of Enterprise* in 1985, it had become a classic with the dust jacket reading like a who's who in management. Accolades from Peter Drucker, Warren Bennis, and other luminaries used descriptors such as "most powerful" and "profound." A particularly eloquent and insightful commentary was subsequently provided by William L. Gardner and John R. Schermerhorn in their 2004 article in *Organizational Dynamics*:

> Douglas McGregor's message endures like a timeless melody, well worth listening to over and over again. . . . His respect for innate human capacities—talent, willingness to accept responsibility, creativity, and capacity for personal growth is well evidenced by many practices in our best-run organizations . . . self-directed work teams, employee involvement groups, job enrichment . . . [and these practices reflect] the essence of Theory Y assumptions McGregor espoused almost a half-century ago. (p. 270)

Further evidence of the impact of McGregor's work comes from an examination of the classic management texts that have been explicitly grounded in the prescriptions of theory y: Robert Blake and Jane Mouton's *Managerial Grid*, Edward Lawler's *High Involvement Management* and *The Ultimate Advantage*, and Chris Argyris's *Management and Organizational Development: The Path from XA to YB*. (Argyris proposed that organizations needed to shift from the pattern of behaviors associated with theory x—pattern a—to a pattern associated with theory y—pattern b.) McGregor has also been credited with contributing to the zeitgeist that fostered Frederick

Herzberg's motivator-hygiene theory and Rensis Likert's systems 1 through 4. McGregor's influence is also evident in leadership theories that emphasize the nature of the relationship between leaders and followers, including authentic leadership, ethical leadership, servant leadership, and transformational leadership.

A Paucity of Validity Evidence

There have been very few direct tests of McGregor's theory x and theory y. McGregor himself conducted no research related to his formulations, nor did he attempt to make his variables operational in any kind of measurement procedures. McGregor did, though, identify management practices that he thought were consonant with theory y assumptions, such as participative leadership, delegation, job enlargement, and performance appraisals. For example, in his book *Leadership and Motivation*, McGregor devoted two chapters to the Scanlon plan, and other chapters suggested other types of management initiatives. Consequently— and unfortunately—tests of the efficacy of these management practices were often conflated with an assessment of the validity of McGregor's theorizing. Instead, a test of the substantive validity of McGregor's theorizing should begin by viewing theory x and theory y as reflecting fundamental individual differences in attitudes, which lead to variations in managerial behaviors and performance results. This distinction points to an issue that has seemingly eluded management scholars and researchers, to this day—namely, that theory x and theory y pertain to individual differences in assumptions about people at work—not the extent to which specific recommended management practices are enacted.

There are two primary explanations for why there has been so little research that directly tests McGregor's theorizing. First, a direct test of theory x and theory y is a difficult undertaking. The requisite data include managerial assumptions and behaviors, along with individual and work-unit level indicators of work behavior and performance. The central research question might be framed as follows: Do work groups led by managers with theory y assumptions demonstrate higher levels of employee engagement (motivation, commitment, and creativity) and higher levels of individual and work-unit performance, as compared to groups led by theory

x managers? Such a test would entail obtaining multilevel data (on managers, teams, and subordinates) and include a measure of performance that is comparable across groups. It would also entail examining data from intact (natural) work groups where differences in managerial attitudes and behaviors result from organic individual differences.

A second obstacle to testing McGregor's theory x and theory y has the absence of a validated and established measure of managerial x and y attitudes. Over a period of 40 years, about a dozen attempts have been made to measure managerial x and y assumptions, but most efforts have provided no construct validity evidence. Frequently, items have been assembled and published in textbooks for students to use in conducting a self-assessment. A few studies have reported limited psychometric data, such as reliability coefficients, but until recently, no research has been conducted to develop a construct valid measure of managerial theory x and y attitudes and behaviors. It is, therefore, not surprising that McGregor's theorizing has largely gone untested, given that the focal constructs have essentially gone unmeasured. In recent years, a few studies have been conducted by Richard Kopelman and his colleagues that focus on the development and validation of measures of managerial x and y assumptions and behaviors—see recommended readings.

To date, the most comprehensive direct test of McGregor's theorizing was conducted by Byron Fiman in a study published in 1973. He collected attitudinal and self-perception data from managers and their subordinates along with individual performance data. Managers' attitudes and behaviors were unrelated to either subordinate satisfaction or individual performance. Performance could not be assessed at the work group level due to outputs being incomparable. These results may have discouraged follow-up research. However, in a just completed, but as yet unpublished study (by Richard Kopelman and associates), managerial attitudes and behaviors were assessed along with individual and group-level performance data. Associations between managerial x and y behaviors and individual- and group-level performance were significant, and the effect sizes were medium and large, respectively. As anticipated, managerial behaviors were more strongly associated with performance than were managerial x and y attitudes.

Practical Implications

Several substantive questions might be researched given the recent development of construct valid measures of the focal variables in theory x and theory y. There are also implications for practice that flow from theory x and theory y.

Coaching and development. McGregor asserted that managerial attitudes reflect deep-seated (and possibly unconscious) beliefs. This may partially explain why brief workshops which attempt to "train" managers to adopt a more theory y perspective have not been particularly successful. A more modest, yet realistic, aim may be to provide diagnostic information to managers, so they might privately access and reflect on it. This information may yield heightened self-awareness regarding core attitudes and assumptions about managing people at work. Along these lines, research might examine the efficacy of direct and indirect methods of management development via theory x and theory y diagnostic data.

New management paradigm. There has also been general agreement among both academics and practitioners that a new social-psychological contract has been emerging—one that emphasizes new employer and employee responsibilities. Employers are now expected to provide training, educational, and skill development opportunities, involve employees in decision making, and foster challenging and stimulating work opportunities; for their part, employees are now expected to take initiative, participate in organizational decision making, and ultimately be responsible for developing their own careers. From this perspective, the new employment paradigm assumes a theory y view with respect to what employees are willing and able to contribute to the organization, with corresponding employer responsibilities.

Boundary conditions. There are boundary conditions that moderate the efficacy of theory y managerial assumptions. Organizational climate is one such boundary condition. A manager with theory y inclinations may be less successful in a command-and-control type of environment—that is, organizations with mechanistic structures and control-oriented cultures. At the other extreme, theory y may be difficult to enact in environments characterized by continuous, turbulent exogenous changes, and by powerful external complexities requiring interorganizational, global, virtual teams. The optimal set of circumstances for a theory y mind-set and approach to management would be where there are stable managerial-subordinate relationships among defined participants, where capabilities and trust can develop along with shared goals and norms, and where self-managed teams can flourish with managers serving more as coaches than as bosses.

Boundary conditions, of course, apply to all theories, serving to specify the realms of applicability. McGregor recognized that there are boundary conditions for theory y. In his words, "under proper conditions," there is the potential for "unimaginable resources of creative human energy" available to managers within organizational settings.

Richard E. Kopelman and
David J. Prottas

See also Authentic Leadership; Needs Hierarchy; Organizational Development; Positive Organizational Scholarship

Further Readings

Carson, C. M. (2005). A historical view of Douglas McGregor's theory y. *Management Decision, 43,* 450–460.

Eden, D. (1990). *Pygmalion in management: Productivity as a self-fulfilling prophecy.* New York, NY: Lexington Books.

Fiman, B. G. (1973). An investigation of the relationships among supervisory attitudes, behaviors, and outputs: An examination of McGregor's theory y. *Personnel Psychology, 26,* 95–105.

Gardner, W. L., & Schermerhorn, J. R., Jr. (2004). Unleashing individual potential: Performance gains through positive organizational behavior and authentic leadership. *Organizational Dynamics, 33,* 270–281.

Kopelman, R. E., Prottas, D. J., & Davis, A. L. (2008). Douglas McGregor's theory x and y: Toward a construct-valid measure. *Journal of Managerial Issues, 20,* 255–271.

Kopelman, R. E., Prottas, D. J., & Falk, D. W. (2010). Construct validation of a theory x/y behavior scale. *Leadership & Organization Development Journal, 31,* 120–135.

McGregor, D. M. (1960). *The human side of enterprise.* New York, NY: McGraw-Hill.

McGregor, D. M. (1966). *Leadership and motivation.* Cambridge, MA: MIT Press.

McGregor, D. M. (1967). *The professional manager.* New York, NY: McGraw-Hill.

Schein, E. H. (1975). In defense of theory y. *Organizational Dynamics, 4,* 17–30.

Schein, E. H. (2011). Douglas McGregor: Theoretician, moral philosopher or behaviorist? An analysis of the interconnections between assumptions, values and behavior. *Journal of Management History, 17,* 156–164.

Total Quality Management

Total quality management (TQM) has been one of the most widespread management approaches for improving products and/or services and processes for achieving higher customer satisfaction and higher competitiveness of organizations during the last 25 years. Even though quality management approaches have been recognized and utilized by industry since the 1930s, the "arrival of TQM" in the last part of the 1980s opened a new era in the quality movement. However, during the first 10 years of the new millennium, the term *total quality management,* or *TQM,* seems to have lost its attractiveness in the industrialized parts of the world, and instead, new terms such as *business excellence, organizational excellence, six sigma,* and *lean* seem to have taken over its position even though the contents of these new terms can be understood within the framework of TQM. Parallel with these tendencies, scholars observe that the "TQM wave" is hitting eastern European countries, as well as newly emerging industrial countries in Asia. In those countries, numerous dynamic activities exist for learning, disseminating, promoting, and implementing TQM. The next section of this entry reviews definitions, scope, and core principles of TQM. After that, the evolutional aspect is reviewed, and the entry ends up with a discussion of the importance and limitation of TQM, including some TQM implementation issues.

Fundamentals

A large number of books, articles, and scientific journals cover the subject of TQM, but there are very few books and articles published before 1990 that use this term. The first book with the title *Total Quality Management* was published in 1989 by John Oakland, and the definition of TQM is formulated as follows:

> TQM is quality in all functional areas. . . . TQM is an approach to improving the effectiveness and flexibility of businesses as a whole. It is essentially a way of organising and involving the whole organization; every department, every activity, every single person at every level. For an organization to be truly effective, each part of it must work properly together, recognizing that every person and every activity affects, and in turn is *affected by other.* (pp. 14–15)

When reviewing various definitions of TQM, it can be said that TQM is a management philosophy with a vision aiming at building a corporate culture characterized by increased customer satisfaction through continual improvements in which all employees actively participate. To achieve the TQM vision is not a quick fix. The company's management has year by year to set up business and image goals, which when achieved will give a satisfactory balance between customer satisfaction and the various stakeholders' satisfaction. Stakeholders are here defined as employees, suppliers, business partners, society, and owners.

Drawn from various definitions, the key *principles* of TQM can be summarized as the following: (a) a strong management commitment and leadership; (b) focus on the customers and the employees; (c) customer driven continuous improvements; (d) everybody's participation; (e) focus on facts (processes and measurements); (f) focus on training, learning, and education; (g) building partnership with suppliers, customers, and society; (h) building a quality culture.

The implication of these eight key principles is that in order to build a quality organization, there must be a strong leadership commitment to provide necessary training and education for employees so that they can be empowered and be involved in continuous improvement processes. When carrying out continuous improvements, the objective should be to increase customer satisfaction, and the improvement methodology should be based on quantifiable and reliable facts rather than assumptions or anecdotes. An organizational wide approach for improving quality is only possible when there are trustworthy partnerships between suppliers, customers, and other stakeholders. Building a quality culture is assumed to be a result of practicing the first seven key principles.

Evolution

The birth of modern quality control has its origin in the time of mass production and specifically during the 1930s with the industrial application of statistical control charts suggested by Walter A. Shewhart from Bell Laboratories. Shewhart's presentation of control charts into industry and his publication of the book *Economic Control of Manufactured Product* in 1931 are generally viewed as marking the birth of modern quality control.

The Second World War provided rich opportunities for the application of control charts in various military industries, and by application of the control charts, the United States was able to produce large quantities of military supplies at a relatively low cost. During the war, thousands of quality specialists had been trained. In 1946, these specialists established the American Society for Quality Control (ASQC).

Although quality control methods were applied in the military industries during the wartime and quality control was established as a recognized discipline by the late 1940s, there were very few efforts to apply the methods in general. The U.S. managers generally ignored quality control methods for several decades until Japanese products gained a good reputation for quality in the world market and gradually became dominant, not only in world markets but also on the American market.

The circumstances in Japan, however, were quite different after the Second World War. All of its industries had been destroyed, and people lacked almost everything. Under these circumstances, the most important and urgent task for Japan was to determine "how to survive." In this almost hopeless situation, the only way to survive was to produce superior industrial products, which could be accepted by, and exported to, foreign countries. For this purpose, the Japanese Standard Association (JSA) was founded in 1945 and, in the following year, the Union of Japanese Scientists and Engineers (JUSE). Since then, these two organizations—JUSE and JSA—have played the central roles in the training and promotion of various quality control principles, tools, and methods.

The Japanese people confronted quality issues as their challenge, and in the following few decades, they revolutionized the quality of their products and thereby became recognized as the world leader in quality. Some major contributions in the revolutionizing process were the result of the role of the U.S. quality experts William Edwards Deming and Joseph M. Juran.

In recognition of Deming's contribution to and encouragement of quality development in Japanese industries, JUSE established in 1951 the Deming Prize, which became not only the first prize in quality in Japan but also the role model for numerous other quality prizes in the world several decades later.

Another influential person from the United States was J. M. Juran, who, by giving lectures in 1954, influenced the Japanese to change the quality direction from an emphasis on the technique-oriented ASQC to an emphasis on managerial aspects and a broader approach to quality control. The impact of Juran's visit resulted in a transition of the quality control concepts from the narrow technology-based approach to an overall management philosophy.

Under these circumstances, the special Japanese model for everybody's involvement in QC—the so-called quality control circle—was born in 1962, which laid a foundation for company-wide quality control (CWQC). During the 1960s the CWQC approach spread to all major Japanese companies, and it was decided officially to use the term *company wide quality control* in 1969.

As a consequence of the committed implementation of company wide quality control, the market share of Japanese products increased rapidly during the 1960s and 70s in many industrial sectors. America and other relatively rich European countries did not pay serious attention to the gradual dominance of the Japanese products in world markets in spite of some "warning signals."

During the 1980s, many American companies were to experience the loss of jobs and market share to Japanese competitors even in their home market of automobiles. In winning by quality rather than by any other single issue, the Japanese were able to achieve a massive market share which gradually became a serious threat to many Western countries, including the United States, during the 1970s and 1980s.

A remarkable turning point was provided in America and other Western countries when W. E. Deming, after three decades, was "rediscovered" in his home country in June 1980 by the National Broadcasting Company (NBC) television documentary *If Japan Can, Why Can't We?* Since then, this documentary has been widely cited as a wake-up call to U.S. managers to focus on quality and on customers' needs.

The 1980s became a revolutionary era for quality management in the United States and in other Western countries. An increasing number of companies adopted quality management, and parallel with that, numerous publications concerning quality management were published. In this period, many theoreticians attempted to develop a holistic or synthetic theory of quality management with all the relevant theories and practical experience taken in particular from the Japanese case. The term *total quality control* (TQC) and, later, *total quality management* (TQM), was often applied to these synthesizing theoretical attempts.

Another accelerating push toward the quality movement in this period was the establishment of the Malcolm Baldridge National Quality Award in 1987 in the United States, the Australian Quality Award in 1988, the birth of European Foundation for Quality Management (EFQM) in 1988, and the birth of the European Quality Award in 1991. In the following years, most western European countries established similar national quality awards as well as countries outside Europe such as China. It is assumed that today there are more than 90 national and regional quality awards in the world.

As seen from the evolution, the concepts used within the framework of quality evolved gradually, for instance the word *control* was gradually replaced with *management*. We can also observe the gradual change of wording for various quality awards. For instance, during 1992 to 1997, The EFQM model was termed "the European Model for TQM" or just "the European Quality Award Model." During 1997–1999, the wordings changed significantly to "the European Model for Business Excellence." The change was a systematic one which comprised not only the name of the model but also the text describing how to use the model for assessing a company's level of business excellence or for award application purposes. This change of wording initiated by European Foundation for Quality Management (EFQM) in 1997 followed the change in the U.S. quality award model (the Malcolm Baldrige Quality Award) a year before. This change of wordings is a kind of evidence that people's understanding and paradigms in relation to the theoretical scope and application of TQM changed significantly during the 1990s.

This change in attitudes is also reflected in the EFQM definition of *business excellence:* The overall way of working that results in balanced stakeholder (customers, employees, society, stakeholders) satisfaction is increasing the probability of long term success as a business (see also Kanji, 2006).

The above definition of business excellence indicates that TQM has moved from being a relatively narrow engineering or quality discipline which top management did not bother about too much, to a holistic management philosophy which has to be integrated in the daily management of all areas of any business.

Importance

During the last 10 to 15 years, several case studies have indicated that companies which have succeeded in investing and implementing TQM have improved their competitiveness as well as their profitability. Such case studies have, however, been regarded as weak indicators or no proofs of the potential impacts of TQM because other not-shown causal factors may have been disclosed in the case presentations and discussions. For that reason, more comprehensive studies on the financial impacts of TQM have been done in several regions of the world.

One example was a huge 1999 study in the United States in which researchers compared financial results and stock prices for more than 600 quality award-winning companies with a comparison company from the same industry over a period of 10 years. The results showed that during the implementation period (5 years before the first award was given), there were no significant differences in financial performance between the award-winning companies and the non-award-winning companies. But during the postimplementation period (5 years after the award), the award-winning companies outperformed the non-award companies, and the difference between the two groups of companies increased during this period. For example, it was documented that 5 years later, the award-winning companies had experienced an average increase in operational income of 86%, while the non-award-winning companies had only experienced an average increase of 43%.

Another example was a 2006 study in Europe where 120 companies, which had won the European Quality/Excellence Award or the national equivalence, were compared with 120 non-award-winning companies from the same country and the same industry as the award-winning companies. The research study design was the same as the U.S. study, meaning that financial results and stock prices were compared during a period of 10 years for each pair of award- and non-award companies. The result patterns resembled and hence supported the U.S. results.

The results showed that during the implementation period (5 years before the first award was given) there were—as in the U.S. study—no significant differences in financial performance between the award-winning companies and the non-award-winning companies, but during the post-implementation period (5 years after the award), the award-winning companies outperformed—as in the U.S. study—the non-award companies, and the difference between the two groups of companies also increased during this period. For example, it was documented that 5 years after the award, the award-winning companies had a significantly higher performance in terms of revenues.

Criticism of TQM

Parallel with TQM's appeal as being one of the most significant managerial approaches, TQM has also been subject to various criticisms especially during the last part of the 1990s.

First, the reliability of TQM as a successful managerial tool has been criticized by organizations that have tried to implement the principles and didn't get the expected results. Organizations have been disappointed with the implementation of TQM, because TQM could not deliver what they expected. Data and information concerning alleged TQM failure rates and description of particular cases gave rise to a new debate of whether the companies which experienced failure really adopted TQM or not.

Second, regarding a critical aspect of TQM's position as a general management theory, critics have stated that there is no consensus on terminology and definitions. TQM has also been criticized

on the point that its main tenets are not all unique to TQM but are also part of other organizational change initiatives or generally accepted "good management practices." Linkages between TQM and other management theories were lacking, organizational contingencies were not recognized, and organizational informal aspects such as power and politics were either completely forgotten or viewed as having little importance.

Implementation of TQM

Much of the critique of TQM is related to the high failure rate when private as well as public companies are trying to implement TQM. On the surface, it may seem surprising that failure rates of more than 70% have been reported in various research studies about the success of TQM. However, there may be several causes for such high failure rates. One simple cause may be that the companies' management teams have not understood that implementing TQM is not "a quick fix" but is about the transformation of the company culture, a transformation where employees gradually through education and training are empowered and motivated to take over the responsibility for the continuous improvement process within their work areas. This transformation is also about the management team's new role to build up a new organizational infrastructure where improvement teams are supported to take their own bottom-up initiatives, balanced with the strategic directions decided by management's strategic plans for improvements. The latter has also been called strategic quality management (SQM), which is a natural part of the company's yearly strategic planning process. To delegate the responsibilities for TQM implementation to an expert group—for example, the quality department—will inevitably lead to such high failure rates as reported in literature.

Another cause for high failure rates in TQM implementation may be related to the criticism mentioned above regarding the importance of organizational contingencies and informal aspects. This critique may especially be important if companies are trying to adopt so-called best TQM practices instead of adapting such best practices to the context where, for example, the national context may be quite different from the contexts where the "best TQM practices" worked. This issue seems not to have been raised too much among the Western quality professionals who have influenced the quality evolution, even if it was raised early in the 1950s in Japan by "the brain" behind just-in-time (strategy), the Toyota production system (TPS), and lean production (practice)—chief engineer Taiichi Ohno—who in 1950 declared, after his first study visit to the world's then most efficient automobile assembly factory, that mass production as running at Ford could never work in Japan. Without this skepticism to adopt best methods, we may not have seen and experienced lean production, and Toyota would not have grown to be one of the top three automakers in the world.

A similar case of adaptation instead of adoption can be found in the success story of Samsung in South Korea. The company developed its own unique quality culture throughout the 1990s and continued to refine management systems so that it fits to their needs and circumstances.

Another example of adaptation instead of adoption is also from the early quality evolution in Japan, where Professor Ishikawa in the beginning of the 1960s suggested the so-called quality control circles (QCCs) be promoted and implemented in Japanese companies. Promoting QCC was quite another way of involving people in quality improvements compared with the best practices from the United States where people involvement was based on control (the principles and methods of scientific management) instead of empowerment through study and learning through practice. The Japanese success with QCC became heavily studied in the 1970s and 1980s, and many Western companies experienced failures when they tried to copy (adopt) the Japanese way of implementing QCC circles because they did not understand that adaptation to the national and company context is a necessity for success.

These learning points, as well as many others, say clearly that Total Quality Management should not be copied from companies which have had success with the TQM implementation. Successful companies' TQM systems should be studied only for inspiration; then, each company should build up its own TQM framework based on the basic principles or generalized values characterizing TQM.

Su Mi Dahlgaard-Park

See also Excellence Characteristics; *Kaizen* and Continuous Improvement; Lean Enterprise; Organizational Learning; Quality Circles; Quality Trilogy; Six Sigma; Strategies for Change

Further Readings

Cole, R. E., & Scott, W. R. (1999). *The quality movement & organization theory.* London, England: Sage.

Dahlgaard, J. J., Kristensen, K., & Kanji, G. K. (2002). *Fundamentals of total quality management.* London, England: Chapman & Hall. (Original work published 1998)

Dahlgaard-Park, S. M. (2011). The quality movement—Where are you going? *Total Quality Management & Business Excellence, 22*(5), 493–516.

Deming, W. E. (1986). *Out of the crisis.* Cambridge, MA: Center for Advanced Engineering Study, MIT.

Garvin, D. A. (1988). *Managing quality: The strategic and competitive edge.* New York, NY: Free Press.

Kanji, G. (2006): *Measuring business excellence.* New York, NY: Routlege.

Kondo, Y. (1993). *Companywide quality control—Its background and development.* Tokyo, Japan: 3A Corporation.

Oakland, J. S. (1989). *Total quality management.* Oxford, England: Heinemann Professional.

TRAIT THEORY OF LEADERSHIP

Trait theory's central premise is that leadership emergence and effectiveness can be explained in terms of stable and consistent differences in how individuals behave, think, and feel. This begs the questions: Are leaders born or made, and is leadership an art or science? The answers to these questions are not quite as simple as leadership theorists perhaps would like. Consequently, researchers have spent many years studying and identifying traits associated with leaders and leadership. The following sections describe the core traits associated with leadership, the history and development of trait theory, and finally, the importance and implications of trait theory to managers in the workplace.

Fundamentals

In many different walks of life, social structures are formed, and within those structures emerges a leader, an "alpha male" or "queen bee." The universality of a construct like leadership reinforces the concept of individual differences in that not everyone can rise to the top. Indeed, the fundamental thesis of trait theory is that possession of certain traits allows individuals to ascend to leadership positions over the collective and to perform their roles well. Although conceptualizations of leadership have evolved, traits remain an enduring thread in the progression of leadership research. Individual differences matter across many contexts and, in light of contingency theories, also within context. In the realm of leader perception, traits form the basis by which one evaluates leader ability which in turn impacts the relationship between leaders and followers. Traits or individual differences in thought, feelings, and behavior, form the core of trait theory. Relevant to leadership, personality and intelligence are the two most frequently studied traits.

Personality and Leadership

Big five and leadership. The big five factor model was first developed in the 1930s, but with technological and statistical advances in the 1980s, it has become the indispensable framework of personality due to its explanatory strength. The big five consists of five distinct factors, including neuroticism (emotional stability), extraversion, openness, agreeableness, and conscientiousness. Neuroticism is associated with negative affect, anxiety, and insecurity. Extraversion is associated with positive affect, energy, and a tendency to be socially outgoing. Openness is associated with creativity, open-mindedness, and eagerness to learn. Agreeableness is associated with being accommodating, caring, and trusting. Finally, conscientiousness is associated with achievement and dependability. As a result of these five broad and inclusive categories, personality traits that once yielded only scattered and inconsequential findings in terms of leadership could be studied more systematically. Using this framework, researchers found higher levels of extraversion, conscientiousness, and openness and lower levels of neuroticism were related with both leader emergence and effectiveness exhibiting moderate effect sizes.

HEXACO and leadership. The big five framework has several strengths, including its relative parsimony and prevalence in organizational and psychological research studies on personality. Despite these strengths, some researchers believe more than five traits are necessary to capture the full extent of personality traits described in our lexicon. Consequently, the HEXACO Personality Inventory has

been developed which includes an honesty-humility factor in addition to the big five for a total of six underlying dimensions of personality. Research using the HEXACO Personality Inventory has shown both agreeableness and extraversion to be associated with leadership.

Charisma and leadership. Although the big five framework and HEXACO Personality Inventory examine personality and its relation to leadership in terms of multiple traits, charisma may be best understood as a combination of traits. Charismatic leaders are unconventional visionaries who are willing to take risks and challenge the status quo in an effort to bring about change in their organization. Additionally, charismatic leaders have excellent communication skills and know how to use emotion to make others feel competent while inspiring trust and hope. As a result, followers identify with charismatic leaders and go above and beyond what is normally required to help the leader achieve his or her goals. Past research shows charismatic leadership is associated with the big five's extraversion, openness, and agreeableness traits. In terms of the HEXACO, charismatic leadership is associated with high levels of extraversion, conscientiousness, agreeableness, openness to experience, honesty-humility, and low levels of emotionality.

GLOBE studies and leadership. While the majority of leadership research has taken place in North America and Western Europe, there has been a steady and increasing recognition that culture may also play a large role in leadership. To determine whether or not certain leadership traits were universal or culturally contingent, the Global Leadership and Organizational Behavior Effectiveness (GLOBE) Project examined cultural differences and/or similarities in leadership for over 60 countries around the world. Results of this project showed a universal belief that effective leaders possess charisma, integrity, and successful team-building skills. In addition, universal impediments to effective leadership were managers who were loners, asocial, non-cooperative, irritable, nonexplicit, egocentric, ruthless, and dictatorial. While these positive and negative leader attributes were considered to be universal, traits related to being self-centered and individualistic were viewed by some cultures to be positive and negative in others.

Intelligence and Leadership

General cognitive intelligence and leadership. Intelligence has long been identified as one of the most important traits in not only leadership but also job performance in general. Indeed, some of the earliest research in trait theory and leadership found that general cognitive intelligence was one of the only traits perceived to be possessed by all types of leaders and in all contexts. While more recent investigations continue to indicate intelligence is a strong predictor of leader emergence, intelligence is not as strongly associated with leadership effectiveness as other frameworks such as the big five of personality or models of specific intelligences.

Emotional and social intelligence and leadership. Research is starting to suggest there are limits to which traditional forms of intelligence can explain leadership effectiveness. More recently, emotional and social intelligence (ESI) has been investigated as an explanation for leadership effectiveness when traditional views of intelligence fail. Indeed, leaders who show empathy and attempt to understand the emotions of others are consistently rated as more effective leaders. ESI comprises two components, emotional intelligence and social intelligence, and refers to the ability of individuals to understand and use effectively not only their own emotions but those of others as well. As a result, ESI researchers feel that the best leaders are interested in promoting positive affect in followers.

Cultural intelligence and leadership. Related to emotional intelligence is the concept of cultural intelligence or CQ. Whereas ESI is mainly relegated to the domain of interindividual interactions, cultural intelligence deals with understanding the norms, traditions, and customs of a group. Those who have high levels of CQ are able to recognize shared beliefs, values, and attitudes of a group and are able to effectively apply this knowledge in order to achieve a goal. Researchers studied 2000 managers from 60 different countries and identified six profiles of CQ which reflect different combinations of cognitive, physical, and emotional-motivational dimensions of CQ. The six profiles include the provincial who prefers staying local, the analyst who exhibits strong cognitive skills, the natural who relies on intuition, the ambassador who has the motivation and confidence to belong, the mimic who mirrors others, and

the chameleon who has the ability to take on the persona of any of the other profiles.

WICS model and leadership. Leaders may possess different types of intelligence that matter for leadership yet fail because they do not utilize them effectively. The wisdom, intelligence, and creativity synthesized (WICS) model proposes that effective leadership is due in large to making good decisions and using all three of these attributes simultaneously. Effective leaders use creativity to generate ideas, intelligence to analyze and implement the ideas, and wisdom to ensure they represent the common good. WICS holds that the best leaders exhibit all three qualities of intelligence, creativity, and wisdom. It also holds that these skills can be developed.

Evolution

Just as our understanding about the relationships between personality, intelligence, and leadership has changed over time, the trait theory also has been revised and adjusted as a result of new research findings. Trait theory has not always been revered for its time and place in leadership research. Many texts narrate the rise, fall, and resurgence of trait theory. Trait theory research was once disdained as "futile," "atheoretical," and "simplistic" for inconsistencies in early findings. Trait theory was later restored with the aid of psychometric advances in personality assessment and meta-analytic reviews. The following section synthesizes the progression of trait theory ideology and findings.

The Rise and Fall of Trait Theory

The earliest conceptualizations of leadership are linked to the "great man" theory, which presumes great men are born not made. This necessitates that leaders possess heritable traits that distinguish them from nonleaders.

The great man theory evolved into the trait theory. Following from this perspective, systemic trait theory research commenced in the 1930s with the driving questions being, What characteristics differentiate leaders from nonleaders and effective from ineffective leaders? Many different individual differences were examined as predictors of leader emergence and effectiveness. Trait theory offered no strong distinctions about whether leadership abilities are innate or acquired. The dominant part of this literature, published between 1930 and 1950, was criticized as being futile due to lack of consistency in findings offering clear distinctions between leaders and nonleaders and moreover across situations. In light of the psychometric capabilities of the time, operationalization and measurement issues contributed to the downfall. Recent attempts to integrate the literature categorize individual difference variables as traitlike or statelike, offering some resolve to the question, Are leaders born or made?

The Resurgence of Trait Theory

Until the 1980s, trait theory was largely discredited as a theory of leadership. Advances in personality assessment ultimately led to its resurgence. In the 1980s, several seminal studies emerged that directly challenged the evidence leading to the rejection of the trait theory.

First, researchers statistically aggregated findings from many separate research studies investigating trait theory and found intelligence, masculinity, and dominance were significantly related to leader perceptions. They also concluded that much of the confusion surrounding leadership traits resulting from nonsignificant and inconsistent findings in the past might have occurred as a result of poorly defined personality constructs. For example, two different researchers approaching the same personality trait may actually define and measure the construct in very different ways. As a result, publications may refer to one specific personality trait and actually mean something entirely different.

Second, researchers have noted the difference in merits between the more distinct and specific personality traits that were originally the emphasis of trait research and the higher order, broader personality categories they create. Although specific personality traits may be more predictive in one instance, because they are more exact and relevant to the phenomenon of interest, broad personality traits may be easier to define and measure in some cases thanks to the big five personality framework. Recent research findings maintain positive relationships between leader emergence and effectiveness with extraversion, conscientiousness, openness, charisma, and negative relationships with neuroticism. Charisma, in particular, seems to be associated with leadership emergence and effectiveness; however, this concept is riddled with issues of definition and measurement.

There is some debate as to whether charisma is even a trait since many of the attributes associated with it, such as persuasive speaking, confidence, and dominant body language, can be learned and developed over time. Moreover, while charisma is typically associated with positive outcomes, such as increased follower motivation and commitment to the organization, it has no moral dimension. Hence, leaders who possess charisma can use their incredible influence for either moral or immoral ends.

Finally, new models of leadership that include general cognitive ability and emotional and cultural intelligences, as well as creativity, have bridged a gap in the literature left by traditional models. While general cognitive ability is associated mainly with leadership emergence, other forms of intelligence are associated with effectiveness. Specifically, the WICS model argues intelligence is important only to the extent that leaders are able to use its products (e.g., creativity, ideal implementation, and wisdom) successfully.

Models of Leader Attributes and Leader Performance

In addition to personality and intelligence, leadership researchers in recent years have focused on other categories of leadership skills and attributes beyond the contributions of the big five and intelligence. These models of leadership effectiveness include broad statelike attributes such as (a) motivation, (b) social skills, and (c) metacognitive skills.

Motivation. Just because an individual has the cognitive ability and personality to lead does not mean that they will actually accept leadership roles. Therefore, "motivation to lead" has been examined as a mediating variable, which determines whether those who have the cognitive ability and personality to lead actually take on a leadership role. Motivation, and a similar construct of responsibility, has been found to be associated with leader emergence, promotion, and effectiveness.

Social skills. The term *social skills* refers to the ability of leaders to understand themselves and others in terms of thoughts, feelings, and behaviors in a social context. The most predominant variable studied in the social skills arena is self-monitoring. Self-monitoring reflects the propensity to regulate and scrutinize one's presentation of the self as a result of the social setting.

Findings indicate high self-monitors are more likely to be promoted, and consequently, emerge as leaders.

Metacognitive skills. Metacognition involves planning, memory, attention, reasoning, motivation, and processing information. Specifically, those with high levels of metacognitive skills are thought to have the ability to reflect on the way in which they think and learn and, as a result, are better able to know what they need to do to learn and succeed in the workplace. Thus, metacognition is fundamental to problem solving and manifests itself as expertise. Therefore, those with higher levels of metacognitive skills are more likely to emerge as leaders.

A Theory of Leader Attributes and Followers' Perception

The power of the traits discussed thus far goes beyond their ability to predict leader emergence and effectiveness. Traits also form the basis by which we judge leadership ability. Leadership perception is inherent to the leadership process. One must be seen by others as a leader before she or he is able to lead. Furthermore, the extent to which an individual is perceived as a leader influences the relationship with followers and ultimately effectiveness. *Leader categorization theory* contends that as individuals interact with leaders over time, we develop a relatively stable idealized view of what a leader should be and use this view to judge leadership in ourselves and others. Traits are the basis of these judgments, specifically personality, intelligence, motivation, social skills, and metacognitive skills. Individuals categorize another as a leader or not based on whether the exhibited traits match those of the idealized view of a leader. Researchers have found when leaders match our idealized view of what a leader should be we are more likely to be influenced and rate those leaders as more effective. Findings suggest effective leaders achieve positive outcomes, not only as a function of their own traits and skills but also through the admiration and willingness of their followers to support them.

The Bright and Dark Side of Leadership

Leader perceptions have typically been studied in terms of effective leadership traits. Indeed, leadership has been synonymous with the best of human qualities. However, as business scandals demonstrating epic failures of leadership at the highest levels of the organization became ever prevalent in the early part of the century, e.g., Enron and American International Group (AIG), a burgeoning interest in destructive leadership and the traits composing it emerged.

Leadership researchers began to examine the possibility that ineffective leadership was the result of dysfunctional or destructive traits rather than the lack of prototypical or effective ones. Eleven traits have been identified as those possessed by "dark" leaders, including excitable, skeptical, cautious, reserved, leisurely, arrogant, dutiful, diligent, imaginative, colorful, and mischievous. It is thought these traits result in a high probability of leader derailment since they make the leader more likely to blow up, show off, or conform when under pressure. Consequently, hiring managers may be well advised to select for candidates that do not possess dark traits. Although this is a sound piece of advice, conflicting and confusing findings regarding these dark traits underscore the difficulty in implementing it. Specifically, narcissism and assertiveness seem to be two traits which have both a "bright side" as well as a dark side.

Narcissism. Narcissism refers to the level of egoism, selfishness, conceit, or vanity an individual feels. While many studies have reinforced the idea that narcissism leads to abuse of power and rule breaking, other work has shown that healthy levels of narcissism may be associated with positive leadership qualities, such as vision and creativity.

Assertiveness. Assertiveness describes the extent to which one proactively pursues self-interests, either by voice or action. Assertiveness, like narcissism, is a trait which has plagued leadership researchers. Despite numerous studies attempting to pin down the role of assertiveness in leadership, this construct is surrounded by confusion. Too much assertiveness is associated with ineffective leadership and is characterized by displays of hostility and competitiveness. On the other hand, leaders who display too little assertiveness are marked as pushovers and are unable to reach goals.

While one of the difficulties with the dark side is the challenge of understanding the role of certain dark traits in leadership, it has also been an opportunity for researchers to start examining traits in combinations rather than as sole determinants of effective leadership. Indeed, the value of assertiveness and narcissism cannot be described in terms of linear combinations. Rather, the impact of traits, both bright and dark, is best understood in terms of whole configurations or patterns where certain traits complement or detract from one another. The pattern approach is an alternative to the variable approach typically examined by trait theorists and ushers in the new age of leadership and trait research.

Taking a Pattern Approach to Leadership

Leadership is the result of a set of complex and multifaceted behaviors that are often reflected in a combination of skills and attributes, not just one trait. Despite this acknowledgement, a substantial amount of leadership research examines traits in isolation from one another rather than as a pattern.

Due to the strong focus on the individual, person-oriented approaches are useful for the study of leader emergence and effectiveness. Individuals are differentiated from one another into subgroups based on patterns determined by their standing on a set of characteristics or traits. Importantly, person-oriented approaches parsimoniously model interactions among variables at the person level as a pattern of characteristics, rather than as individual interactions among variables. Research shows that groups of people sharing similar patterns of personality interact and engage with the environment in similar ways. Over time, then, individuals within a cluster are growing and adapting in similar fashion, thus, providing a more realistic and holistic understanding of how leaders behave and more insight into what differentiates effective from ineffective leaders.

Recent studies taking a pattern approach have found that constellations of different leadership traits explain leader emergence and effectiveness better than taking the sum of the same leadership traits. Indeed, researchers have found that a pattern of high intelligence, dominance, general self-efficacy, and self-monitoring among military students resulted in higher levels of leader emergence, promotion, and effectiveness ratings. Additionally, effective leaders have been found to use a combination of transformational behaviors, exchange-based transactional leader behaviors, and a low-level of passive management-by-exception behavior. These optimal patterns were associated with the highest levels of subordinate satisfaction and commitment. Given findings from pattern-oriented research, hiring managers should consider patterns of traits rather than individual, isolated traits as well as patterns that are most likely to be optimal given the role or workplace.

Importance

Findings from studies examining patterns of traits as well as meta-analyses demonstrate unequivocally that traits do matter in leadership. Trait theory is the first theory of leadership and essentially underpins all others. Strengths of the trait theory include the fact it is rational, valid, and has stood the test of time. The theory is sometimes critiqued as being too simplistic; however, it is precisely this simplicity that makes the trait theory generalizable, applicable, and long standing. However, the paradox of traits is they ignore contexts. Specifically, a trait associated with leadership in one situation may become irrelevant, or worse, counterproductive, when a situation changes as noted in the discussion of the bright side and dark side of personality traits.

Trait theory can be used at all levels of the organization to both select and develop future leaders. Some traits, such as general cognitive intelligence and personality variables, should be selected for as they are theorized to be heritable and stable. Although useful, traits are not perfect predictors of leadership, and other important factors such as culture, organizational structure, and hierarchical level need to be considered.

Finally, other traits such as social skills, metacognitive skills, ESI, cultural intelligence (CQ), and WICS are viewed as flexible and dynamic rather than as rigid and static. They are, to some extent, modifiable forms of developing expertise that can be developed through training or experience.

All in all, trait theory findings are informative for managers in helping identify their own as well as their subordinates' strengths and weaknesses. Such assessments can help managers determine which employees to promote and which may require training before succeeding to leadership positions. Further, managers are encouraged to consider patterns of traits and how these patterns map on to the specific demands of different positions and situations, in making such decisions.

Roseanne J. Foti, Sarah F. Allgood,
and Nicole J. Thompson

See also Attribution Model of Leadership; Big-Five Personality Dimensions; Charismatic Theory of Leadership; GLOBE Model; Transformational Theory of Leadership

Further Readings

Antonakis, J. (2011). Predictors of leadership: The usual suspects and suspect traits. In A. Bryman, D. Collinson, K. Grint, B. Jackson, & M. Uhl-Bien (Eds.), *The Sage handbook of leadership* (pp. 269–285). Thousand Oaks, CA: Sage.

Bass, B. M. (1990). *Bass and Stogdill's handbook of leadership: Theory, research, and managerial applications.* New York, NY: Free Press.

Day, D. V. (2000). Leadership development: A review in context. *Leadership Quarterly, 11,* 581–613.

Foti, R. J., & Hauenstein, N. M. A. (2007). Pattern and variable approaches in leadership emergence and effectiveness. *Journal of Applied Psychology, 92,* 347–355.

Hogan, R., & Hogan, J. (2001). Assessing leadership: A view from the dark side. *International Journal of Selection and Assessment, 9,* 40–51.

Judge, T. A., Bono, J. E., Ilies, R., & Gerhardt, M. W. (2002). Personality and leadership: A qualitative and quantitative review. *Journal of Applied Psychology, 87,* 765–780.

Lord, R. G., De Vader, C. L., & Alliger, G. M. (1986). A meta-analysis of the relation between personality traits and leadership perceptions: An application of validity generalization procedures. *Journal of Applied Psychology, 10,* 402–410.

Zaccaro, S. J. (2007). Trait-based perspectives of leadership. *American Psychologist, 62,* 6–16.

TRANSACTION COST THEORY

Transaction cost theory emerged in the 1970s as a theory of vertical integration and buyer-supplier relations. It has since become a more general explanation for firm boundaries, organization, and governance, providing insight into vertical structure, complex contracting, regulation, financing choice, public-private interaction, and other important economic, legal, and organizational phenomena. Transaction cost economics (TCE) is foundational to many of the core questions in management and increasingly popular in research and teaching in strategic management, governance, international business, and regulation. This entry will explain the origin and nature of transaction costs, show how transaction costs influence organizational structure, review the development of transaction cost theory, and conclude with empirical evidence and managerial applications.

Fundamentals

Transaction Costs

Transaction costs entered the discussion about firms with Ronald Coase's influential 1937 article, "The Nature of the Firm." Coase argued that entrepreneurs internalize activities within firms to reduce the costs of search, communication, and bargaining. Absent these transaction costs, production could be organized though networks of independent contractors, with their interactions mediated by the price mechanism. In other words, without transaction costs, there is no reason for firms.

These arguments have been elaborated most forcefully by Oliver Williamson, who developed insights from Coase, John R. Commons, Herbert Simon, and others into a more general transaction cost theory of economic organization. Transacting is costly not only because of the problems described by Coase but also because complex transactions often require co-specialized investments, and investing in relationship-specific assets exposes trading partners to particular risks. Forward-looking agents will structure their relationships to minimize these risks. Unlike conventional economics treatments of firms and industries, the focus here is on transactions, not firms, and on the difficulties of contracting, not the technical aspects of production (scale, scope, etc.). Also, in contrast with industry and competitive analysis as developed by Michael Porter, the key to the firm's success is seen as its ability to organize transactions efficiently, not its ability to leverage market power. As in the resource-based view of the firm, TCE focuses on assets but is interested in how they are organized and governed, not their ability to generate rents.

A more detailed illustration will help. Consider vertical integration, the first problem to be studied systematically in transaction cost terms. Economists traditionally viewed vertical integration and other forms of vertical coordination as attempts by dominant firms to earn monopoly rents by gaining control of input markets or distribution channels, to engage in price discrimination or to eliminate multiple markups along the supply chain. TCE, by contrast, emphasizes that in-house production or procurement from particular suppliers in long-term relationships can be an efficient means of mitigating contractual hazards. However, vertical coordination brings other kinds of transaction costs, namely, problems of information flow, incentives, monitoring, and performance evaluation. The boundary of the firm, then, is determined by the trade-off, at the margin, between the relative transaction costs of external and internal exchange.

In a world of positive transaction costs, contracts are unavoidably incomplete—they provide remedies for only some possible future contingencies. This obviously applies to written contracts for all but the simplest forms of trade. It also applies to relational contracts, agreements that describe shared goals and a set of general principles that govern the relationship, and to implicit contracts—agreements that, while unstated, are assumed to be understood by all sides. Contractual incompleteness exposes the contracting parties to certain risks. Primarily, if circumstances change unexpectedly, the original governing agreement may no longer be effective. The need to adapt to unforeseen contingencies constitutes an additional cost of contracting; failure to adapt imposes what Williamson calls "maladaptation costs."

The most often-discussed example of maladaptation is the "holdup" problem associated with relationship-specific investments. The holdup problem figures prominently in the interpretations of the transaction cost theory. Investment in such assets exposes agents to a potential hazard: If circumstances change, their trading partners may try to expropriate the rents accruing to the specific assets. Rents can be safeguarded through vertical integration, where a merger eliminates any adversarial interests. Less extreme options include long-term contracts, partial ownership, or agreements for both parties to invest in offsetting relationship-specific investments. Overall, several governance structures may be employed. According to transaction cost theory, parties tend to choose the governance structure that best controls the underinvestment problem, given the particulars of the relationship.

Discriminating Alignment Hypothesis

The transaction cost approach to the firm sees economic organization primarily in economizing, not strategizing, terms. "Efficiency is the best strategy," as Williamson has said. This approach is manifest in the idea of *discriminating alignment* between attributes of transactions (asset specificity, uncertainty, frequency, etc.) and the characteristics of organizational modes or governance structures. Simply put, the transaction cost approach tries to explain how trading partners choose, from the set of feasible institutional alternatives, the arrangement that mitigates the relevant contractual hazards at least cost.

Transactions differ in the degree to which relationship-specific assets are involved, the amount of uncertainty about the future and about other parties' actions, the frequency with which the transaction occurs, and so on. Each matters for the preferred institution of governance, although the first—asset specificity—is particularly important. Asset specificity is durable investments that are undertaken in support of particular transactions. Investments that are specific to a particular transaction have a higher value to that transaction than they would have if they were redeployed in best alternative uses or users. This could describe a variety of relationship-specific investments, including both specialized physical and human capital, along with intangibles such as research and development (R & D) and firm-specific knowledge or capabilities.

Markets, hierarchies, and hybrids. The pure anonymous spot market suffices for simple transactions, such as basic commodity sales. Market prices provide powerful incentives for exploiting profit opportunities and market participants are quick to adapt to changing circumstances as information is revealed through prices. When relationship-specific assets are at stake, however, and when product or input markets are thin, bilateral coordination of investment decisions may be desirable, and combined ownership of these assets may be efficient. The transaction cost approach maintains that such hierarchies offer greater protection for specific investments and provide relatively efficient mechanisms for responding to change where coordinated adaptation is necessary. Compared with decentralized structures, however, hierarchies provide managers with weaker incentives to maximize profits and normally incur additional bureaucratic costs.

Much recent strategy literature has focused not on markets and hierarchies but intermediate, or "hybrid" forms, such as long-term contracts, partial ownership agreements, franchises, networks, alliances, and firms with highly decentralized assignments of decision rights. Hybrids attempt to achieve some level of central coordination and protection for specific investments while retaining the high-powered incentives of market relations.

Financial decisions. The firm's financial structure can also be interpreted in transaction cost terms. The choice between debt and equity is treated in this framework as a trade-off between rules and discretion. Debt represents a more rigid, rules-based financial mechanism, while equity is more flexible and discretionary. In the event of failure, control over the underlying asset reverts to the creditor, who might exercise liquidation of the assets. Although the creditor might choose to concede some discretion allowing the borrower to work things out, the advantage of equity reflects in its governance design the existence of administrative processes that can facilitate the practice of working things out. While the need to work things out would be low for financing of projects with redeployable assets, the demand to work things out increases as redeployability diminishes. Equity is much more intrusive and involves the active role of investors in the management of the project. In this setting, Williamson proposed that the condition of asset specificity is the primary factor to explain the use of debt versus equity finance.

Firms try to choose the financial mechanism that minimizes the costs of external funding. Debt is a low-cost governance arrangement for projects involving highly redeployable assets, because if the project is successful, interest and principal will be paid on schedule, and if the project fails, debt-holders can liquidate assets to recover their investments. The opposite applies when the assets involved in a project are highly specific (i.e., non-redeployable) and, hence, have lower value for other purposes in case the project is liquidated. Creditors may lack the skills or means to monitor projects actively involving few collateralizable assets. These projects involve high risk for banks, and even if banks were to make loans to high risk projects, the interest rate required would be extremely high, creating liquidity problems for the firm. Equity governance, by contrast, provides incentives for investors to monitor firms more closely.

Equilibrium and adaptation. The discriminating alignment hypothesis does not necessarily assume that trading partners behave "optimally" in every transaction. Indeed, Williamson, unlike other transaction cost theorists, such as Benjamin Klein, Robert Crawford, Armen Alchian, Sanford Grossman, and Oliver Hart, place particular emphasis on adaptation as a characteristic of organizational forms. In other words, particular organizational forms may be chosen because they facilitate sequential, coordinated adaptation.

Evolution

As noted above, transaction cost theory is rooted in the seminal work of Coase, Commons, and Simon. Coase was the first to explain that the boundaries of the organization depend not only on the productive technology but also on the costs of transacting business. Commons argued that the transaction, not the firm, should be the unit of analysis, directing researchers' attention to the behavior of contracting parties and emphasizing the role of law in influencing behavior. Simon developed the notion of bounded rationality, the idea that economic behavior is "intendedly rational, but only limitedly so"—the core idea of modern behavioral theories of management. These concepts were integrated into a comprehensive transaction cost theory of the firm by Williamson, Klein, Crawford, and Alchian in the 1970s.

The transaction cost literature of the 1970s and 1980s focused largely on vertical integration, or the "make-or-buy decision." More recently, transaction cost theories have sought to explain not only the choice between external and in-house procurement—"markets and hierarchies," to borrow the title of Williamson's hugely influential 1975 book—but also the rationale for hybrid forms, such as long-term contracts, franchises, joint ventures, alliances, and other intermediate forms. Hybrids represent a blend between the benefits of centralized coordination and control and the incentive and informational advantages of decentralized decision making. Of course, hybrids are increasingly important in the networked, knowledge-based economy, and transaction cost theory focused increasingly on the design and evolution of hybrid forms.

In the transaction cost literature associated with Coase and Williamson (often termed "transaction cost economics"), transaction costs are conceptualized as the costs resulting from the transfer of property rights. However, there is another transaction cost tradition, associated with economists such as Alchian, Harold Demsetz, Steven Cheung, and Yoram Barzel, which treats transaction costs as the costs of establishing and maintaining property rights. This concept is also important for strategic management. Value creation and capture often depend on defining and enforcing economic rights, meaning the enforceable residual income and control rights associated with ownership. For example, attempts to capture value through competitive positioning assumes that the focal firm's suppliers or customers cannot contract around competitive imperfections by forming coalitions, making side payments, and otherwise challenging attempts to build and sustain market power. Many resource-based arguments about value creation and capture depend on assumptions about transaction costs. Moreover, while transaction cost and capabilities approaches are typically seen as rival explanations for firm boundaries and internal organization, recent contributors proposed that these two approaches can be usefully integrated by viewing transaction costs as antecedent to capability development.

In addition, several important extensions to the theory should be noted. First, the governance of a particular transaction may depend on how previous transactions were governed, what Nicholas Argyres and Julia Liebeskind call "governance inseparability." Where governance inseparability is present, firms may rely on arrangements that appear inefficient at a particular time, but which make sense as part of a longer term process. This way, changes in governance structure affect not only the transaction in question but also the entire temporal sequence of transaction. Transaction inseparability also appears within firms. Consider, for example, the biotechnology industry, in which large pharmaceutical companies have been unable to achieve the research capabilities of small firms. An explanation is that large firms employ both traditional research scientists, who are accustomed to low-powered incentives such as restrictions on publication, and biotechnological researchers, who respond better to higher powered incentives. It is difficult for the large firm to use different governance structures for different groups of scientists.

Second, the capability to improve transactional performance through time is particularly important where contracts govern interfirm relationships. In this setting, firms with superior contract design capabilities might be faster to use the market to organize the marginal transaction, whereas firms with weaker contract design capabilities might tend to internalize those same marginal transactions. Moreover, learning to contract and learning to collaborate might have an intimate relationship. That is, firms might not learn to contract with each without also learning to contract with each other.

Importance

Empirical Research on Transaction Costs

One reason the transaction cost approach has become so popular in management is because it has inspired a large and diverse empirical literature. Much of the empirical work on transaction costs and firm structure follows the same basic model. The efficient form of organization for a given economic relationship—and, therefore, the likelihood of observing a particular organizational form or governance structure—is seen as a function of certain properties of the underlying transaction or transactions: asset specificity, uncertainty, frequency, and so on. Organizational form is the dependent variable, while asset specificity, uncertainty, complexity, and frequency are independent variables. Specifically, the probability of observing a more integrated governance structure depends positively on the amount or value of the relationship-specific assets involved and, for significant levels of asset specificity, on the degree of uncertainty about the future of the relationship, on the complexity of the transaction, on the frequency of trade, and possibly on some aspects of the institutional environment.

Detailed surveys of this literature are provided in the reference list below. Classic papers include Scott Masten's study of aerospace component procurement, a series of papers by Paul Joskow on long-term contracting for coal, and research by Erin Anderson and coauthors on marketing channels and several other industry case studies. In most of these studies, organizational form is often modeled as a discrete variable—make, buy, or hybrid, for example—though it can sometimes be represented by a continuous variable. Of the independent variables, asset specificity has received the most attention, presumably because of the central role it plays in the transaction cost approach to vertical integration.

Case studies compose the bulk of the studies on the make-or-buy decision, primarily because the main variables of interest—asset specificity, uncertainty, and frequency—are difficult to measure consistently across firms and industries. Although the evidence from individual cases may not apply to other cases, the cumulative evidence from different studies and industries is remarkably consistent with the transaction cost arguments. Nevertheless, there remain outstanding puzzles, challenges, and controversies. For example, many studies use a reduced-form model linking transactional attributes to organizational choices, without a detailed underlying structural model of what these attributes do, how they interact, and so on. Critics have suggested that alternative theories derived from social psychology, identity theory, organizational sociology, and the like could also be consistent with an observed relationship between (say) asset specificity and vertical integration. Put differently, the transaction cost literature has focused much more heavily on the transaction cost of market exchange than the transaction costs or organizational costs of in-house production.

Practical Implications

Transactions costs—both the cost of transferring existing property rights and the costs of defining and enforcing property rights—are highly important for firm strategy and organization. The transaction cost approach has become a standard part of the strategist's toolkit for explaining the choice of organizational form, and transaction cost considerations underlie many of the standard conclusions about competitive positioning and the development of capabilities.

Managers can find transaction cost theory particularly useful in designing and executing contracts, managing internal hierarchies, and dealing more generally with customers, suppliers, employees, and partners. The fundamental lesson of transaction cost theory is that the cost of governing transactions depends on their characteristics, such as asset specificity, and that organizational form should be chosen to match these characteristics. Failure to protect against opportunistic behavior by trading partners exposes firms to critical hazards that threaten profitability and sustainability. Relationship-specific investments, for example, should be protected with

appropriate formal or informal contracts, offsetting specific investments or joint ownership. Trading partners will not make desired investments specific to the focal firm without similar protection. Employees will be reluctant to learn idiosyncratic routines and procedures—that is, to invest in firm-specific human capital—without explicit or implicit long-term employment contracts. In general, firms should consider not only the technical aspects of production and distribution but also the costs of contracting, when considering organizational design.

Peter G. Klein and Mario P. Mondelli

See also Agency Theory; Behavioral Theory of the Firm; Bounded Rationality and Satisficing (Behavioral Decision-Making Model); Organizational Structure and Design; Resource-Based View of the Firm; Strategic Alliances

Further Readings

Argyres, N. S., & Liebeskind, J. P. (1999). Contractual commitments, bargaining power, and governance inseparability: Incorporating history into transaction cost theory. *Academy of Management Review, 24,* 49–63.

Coase, R. H. (1937). *The firm, the market and the law.* Chicago, IL: University of Chicago Press.

Grossman, S. J., & Hart, O. D. (1986). The costs and benefits of ownership: A theory of vertical and lateral integration. *Journal of Political Economy, 94,* 691–719.

Klein, B., Crawford, R. A., & Alchian, A. A. (1978). Vertical integration, appropriable rents, and the competitive contracting process. *Journal of Law and Economics, 21,* 297–326.

Klein, P. G. (2005). The make-or-buy decision: Lessons from empirical studies. In C. Ménard & M. Shirley (Eds.), *Handbook of new institutional economics* (pp. 435–464). New York, NY: Springer.

Lafontaine, F., & Slade, M. (2007). Vertical integration and firm boundaries: The evidence. *Journal of Economic Literature, 45*(3), 629–685.

Macher, J. T., & Richman, B. D. (2008). Transaction cost economics: An assessment of empirical research in the social sciences. *Business and Politics, 10*(1), 1–63.

Williamson, O. E. (1975). *Markets and hierarchies, analysis and antitrust implications: A study in the economics of internal organization.* New York, NY: Free Press.

Williamson, O. E. (1991). Strategizing, economizing, and economic organization. *Strategic Management Journal, 23,* 75–94.

Williamson, O. E. (1996). *The mechanisms of governance,* New York, NY: Oxford University Press.

TRANSFER OF TECHNOLOGY

Transfer of technology, often referred to as TOT, is a conceptual framework that integrates empirical generalizations and midrange theories about transfer of technical, organizational, and operational knowledge in a variety of forms and contexts between institutional providers and recipients. It articulates the attributes of technical knowledge, organizational mechanisms used for its transfer, characteristics of the provider and recipient, national policies and intellectual property rights law, and other contextual factors and how all these elements interact, to predict outcomes of improved technological capabilities of institutions and nations. The "not-invented-here" syndrome is a behavioral phenomenon that has been identified as a barrier to TOT for mainly tacit and informal technical knowledge. The following section of this entry describes the main elements of the conceptual framework, their interactions, and their organizational and national context, including theoretical antecedents and context and addressing the evolution of the framework. The final section reviews the impact this framework has had on management research and education and on management practice, consulting, and professional training.

Fundamentals

Technology and Transfer Mechanisms

The concept of technology transfer involves complexity and dynamism. Technology embodies machinery, tools, equipment, skills, and knowledge of personnel, technical information, organizational processes, and management practices. The interrelationships of these aspects of technology and the symbiotic integration of technology and the social, cultural, informational, and economic aspects of the organization are imperative for an effective transfer. Aggregated to the national level, the realization of the benefits of TOT is critical for economic development and international competitiveness.

Effectiveness of TOT is dependent on numerous factors, and technology is the central element of the framework. The technology life cycle model depicts technological performance trajectory as an S-curve, its logic related to the concept of technological paradigms, with theoretically defined limits of capabilities. A phenomenon that contradicts this theory was observed when mature technologies improved beyond the S-curve trajectory in response to the emergence of a new and better technology. Theory of learning and knowledge acquisition, such as stages of knowledge from art to science, in the context of process control, is relevant here. The emerging, progressing, and maturing stages are characterized by the evolution in the nature of the technology on the continua of codification, from tacit to codified; ambiguity, from high to low; and uncertainty, from high to low. Economists use the concept of stickiness of information or knowledge, and mature technologies are less sticky. Consequently, mature technologies are easier to assess, learn, integrate, and transfer. A basic principle is that *transfer mechanism* must fit the nature of the technology, from informal flow of uncodified know-how among individuals all the way to turnkey plants and complex equipment. A related theory of industrial evolution, on which the product life cycle model hinges, identifies the shift in the patterns of innovation from product focused to process focused.

TOT mechanisms are the nature of interaction between the technology provider and the recipient. Empirical studies suggest that noncodified parts of technology are not often traded because such firm-specific knowledge is of less importance in the perception of many technology recipients deterring the utilization of technology. The arms-length market mechanisms, such as licensing and subcontracting, are suited more for mature technologies, and progressing or emerging technologies are more inclined toward internalized mechanisms, such as foreign direct investment or strategic alliances. Both competitive and noncompetitive mechanisms carry the potential for yielding favorable benefits for partnering entities. The policy environment such as foreign investment and foreign exchange controls can dictate the choice between licensing and foreign direct investment mechanisms in international TOT.

Determinants of Effectiveness

The conceptual model of TOT consists of basic elements of *technology and transfer mechanisms*, *technology provider*, and *technology recipient*, interacting in the global context and the attributes of the country of the technology recipient. The interaction of these elements impacts the *effectiveness* of transfer, being contingent upon the nature of the technology being transferred. For emerging and tacit technologies, effectiveness depends on successful learning and integration with internal process and knowledge, such as new product and process development. For the mature end of the continuum, as the TOT activities are embodied in a specific project or program, effectiveness is project success, which includes process cost improvement or higher value-adding product features. On the national level, effective TOT improves international competitiveness in terms of factor productivity and export volumes, and consequently gross domestic product (GDP) per capita measures. Related outputs are also measured in national science, technology and innovation indicators.

Conceptually, *vertical technology transfer* is down the value chain, either interinstitutional between manufactures and suppliers or research and development (R & D) institute, or university to industry, or intrainstitutional from R & D design to production. *Horizontal technology transfer*, on the other hand, takes place inside a link in the value chain, such as between different manufacturers or universities. Another classification is geographic, with increased complexity in *international technology transfers*.

The process of TOT commences with the identification of technology requirements which arise from the external pressure—such as the market pushing technology or being pulled by firms with advanced technological capabilities—to pursue opportunities. The factors of business strategy, firm size, financial and nonfinancial resources, perceived benefits of technology acquisition, industry competitiveness and dynamism, market characteristics, and the need of emulating the competitors influence technology acquisition decisions. The degree of influence varies with the size of the firm and absorptive capacity accumulated through R & D, prior knowledge activities, appropriate knowledge structure, and the possession of skilled human capital stock. Firms with low levels of technological capabilities acquire technology from external sources in order to substitute for low technological capabilities while others do it to complement existing internal technological capacities.

A balance between the relative performance advantage of the new technology and the degree of operational novelty compared with existing technologies is crucial for successful implementation. The recipient must possess an accumulated advanced knowledge stock of research and design skills to absorb and extend emerging or progressing technologies. High codifiability of mature technologies lowers this requirement significantly. The model of innovation diffusion identifies relative advantage, compatibility, simplicity, trialability, and observability as positive attributes of an innovation. *Appropriateness* of technology refers to the fit between the technology and resources required for its optimal use and corporate strategies. The concept of appropriateness has become controversial in the context of international technology transfer, being seen as neocolonial because the construct can be interpreted as a policy that new, advanced technologies would be intended for use in developed economies, while older, less advanced, and less environmentally sustainable technologies would be appropriate for developing economies. In addition, such a perspective could impede catching up or "leapfrogging" by developing economies. A geographic mapping of TOT along technological life cycles has been challenged with the increasing number of R & D facilities located in developing economies.

The *cost of technology transfer* extends beyond the mere purchasing cost of technology for the recipient. The costs of technology search, evaluation, design and engineering skills, training, communication, installation, adaptation, problem diagnosing, integration, and learning incur in TOT. The degree of absorptive capacity and prior experience in TOT of the recipient are important factors of cost. Resources are needed for adaptation of the transferred technology to fit with the existing physical and knowledge systems. The technologies at emerging and progressing stages are at a flux, and frequent alterations cause high technical risks and more costs than the mature technologies with established design, functionality, safety conditions, and codified technical information available.

From a process perspective, the strategic, functional, and behavioral forms of *technology transfer barriers* hinder the transfer's effectiveness. While smaller institutions lack the resources and capability acquisitions of new technologies, larger firms are hindered by complex bureaucracies, which reduce the flexibility for new technology adoptions and implementations. The lack of sufficient functional capabilities in operational, engineering, design, and development inhibit the effective absorption of the transferred technology. Cultural dissonance, lack of communication, and the consequent information gap among interacting parties hinder effective integration.

Attitudinal barriers, such as the not-invented-here syndrome, result in behaviors that impede information flows critical for effective TOT into the organization. This syndrome is based on theory of social identity and has similarities with the *groupthink* phenomenon. Recent research identified preferences for external knowledge.

The elements of market, trade policy, legal and regulatory forms, and the national and regional innovation systems are the dimension of country context for organizational TOT. In the international context, a strong system of intellectual property protection accelerates TOT between countries and induces more innovations. The presence of strong national and sectoral innovation systems enhances the absorptive capacity of the recipient and the potential for realization of technology spillover benefits by domestic industries of the recipient economy. A moderate technology gap between the interacting economies is also favorable for a transfer's effectiveness.

The development of technological capabilities through technology acquisition relates to the assimilation theory of development that differentiates accumulation through the investment of physical capital and human resources from the assimilation such as entrepreneurship, innovation, and learning. The accumulation is a necessity but far from sufficient for the assimilation process in technological development of the recipient. Technological capability development involves acquiring, assimilating, improving, and generating technologies and capitalizes on both potential and realized absorptive capacities by the strategic use of advanced skills and knowledge and the investment in learning through research and development for generating competitiveness.

Concept Evolution

Traditionally, TOT theories focused on deliberate and contractual arrangements between institutions such as universities or government R & D laboratories with industry. In the international context, TOT was typically "north to south" or "west to east," mainly from headquarters to subsidiaries or from foreign multinationals to domestic small- and medium-size enterprises. Theoretically, they were part of developmental economics and international business management and of diffusion of innovation. Recently, with the increased pluralism of technology sources and globalizations and deeper understanding of the technology construct, the context has expanded and constructs were elaborated. In parallel, the types of mechanisms and participants in the transfer process have been expanded to address new concepts such as open innovation, social media, integration of technologies based on natural and life sciences, and Internet-based innovations.

Importance

As a practice-based, midrange theory and collection of empirical observations, the TOT framework has spurred a rich interplay between applied research and its application. The constructs and their interactions have been tested in a variety of contexts and fine-tuned conceptually and in terms of constructs measurements. The framework influenced *scholarly research* in the management of innovation, management of R & D, international management, and policy of science, technology, and innovation. Elements of the framework found its way into research of legal and management aspects of *intellectual property rights* and studies of university research and its commercialization. Another important aspect that is getting recent attention is the context of global outsourcing of knowledge.

The TOT framework has been driving relevant academic management curricula and training, from specific subjects in bachelor and master of business administration (MBA) degrees to certificates of proficiency and professional expertise. Its incorporation in technical and engineering curricula bring in "softer" skills, beyond technical understanding or operational expertise, to include managerial and organizational mechanisms and approaches, the role of culture, and the principles of absorptive capacity and organizational capabilities.

The penetration of the framework as embodying unique expertise into practice is global and associated with activities critical for the success of both modern enterprise and national innovation systems. The United Nations Industrial Development Organization (UNIDO), United Nations Children's Fund (UNICEF), Organisation for Economic

Co-operation and Development (OECD), and the World Bank have published guiding manuals and reports. National policy is designed on the basis of expectations beyond the basic framework, to include spillovers, and revised when these do not materialize. Consulting firms advertise TOT as a practice for both clients and potential employees. There are offices of technology transfer and commercialization in universities, government laboratories, and government agencies around the world, with positional a title, such as officer, manager, or director of technology transfer. There are numerous national and international associations, and TOT is bundled with best practice principles of the International Organization for Standardization (ISO).

Oscar Hauptman and
Dilupa Jeewanie Nakandala

See also Innovation Diffusion; Patterns of Innovation; Stages of Innovation; Tacit Knowledge; Technological Discontinuities; Technology S-Curve

Further Readings

Bennett, D. (2002). *Innovative technology transfer framework linked to trade for UNIDO action.* Vienna, Austria: UNIDO.

Bessant, J., & Rush, H. (1995). Building bridges for innovation: The role of consultants in technology transfer. *Research Policy, 24,* 97–114.

Bozeman, B. (2000). Technology transfer and public policy: A review of research and theory. *Research Policy, 29,* 627–655.

Kedia, B. L., & Bhagat, R. S. (1988). Cultural constraints on technology transfer across nations: Implications for research in international and comparative management. *Academy of Management Review, 13,* 558–571.

Mansfield, E., & Romeo, A. (1980). Technology transfer to overseas subsidiaries by U.S.-based firms. *Quarterly Journal of Economics, 95,* 737–750.

Menon, T., & Pfeffer, J. (2003). Valuing internal vs. external knowledge: Explaining the preference for outsiders. *Management Science, 49,* 497–513.

Lichtenthaler, U. H. E. (2006). Attitude to externally organizing knowledge management tasks: A review, reconsideration and extension of the NIH syndrome. *R & D Management, 36,* 367–386.

Reddy, N. M., & Zhao, L. (1990). International technology transfer: A review. *Research Policy, 19,* 285–305.

Schumacher, E. F. (2000). *Small is beautiful, 25th anniversary edition: Economics as if people mattered, 25 years later . . . with commentaries.* Vancouver, British Columbia, Canada: Hartley and Marks.

Szulanski, G. (1996). Exploring internal stickiness: Impediments to the transfer of best practices with the firm. *Strategic Management Journal, 17,* 27–43.

TRANSFORMATIONAL THEORY OF LEADERSHIP

Transformational leadership is about inspiring employees to perform beyond expectations. It consists of two major elements: transactional and transformational. Transactional leaders focus on using rewards and punishment to induce certain behaviors in followers. The transformational component focuses on inspiring followers to go beyond mere transactional exchanges and consists of four roles: idealized influence, inspirational motivation, intellectual stimulation, and individualized consideration. Research has shown these constructs to have good validity and reliability and has been positively related to organizational effectiveness and follower satisfaction. The following sections briefly discuss the heritage of the construct, describe the roles in more detail, present some of the relevant research, indicate where the research should go next, and trace important implications for management practice.

Fundamentals

In 1978, James McGregor Burns introduced the concept of *transforming leadership* in the arena of political science. He defined it as persuading others to act to achieve definite goals that were about the values and the motivations, the wants and needs of followers as well as their leaders. The alignment of leaders' and followers' values and motivations is an essential part of transforming leadership, because it is only when this condition is present that leaders can induce followers to rise above their own self-interest and work for the greater good. In other words, it is then that transforming leadership can take place.

In addition to the concept of transforming leadership, Burns also used the concept of transactional leadership that was based on exchanging valued items, which could be political, economic, or emotional. Unlike what has been posited in the later work of Bernard Bass and his colleagues, Burns believed that leaders were either transforming or transactional rather than both.

Burns's work attracted the attention not only of political science scholars but also those from the fields of management and leadership. The introduction of transforming leadership led to a rejuvenation of leadership research in management studies. One of the first management and leadership scholars to apply the idea of transformational leadership was Bass in his 1985 book *Leadership and Performance Beyond Expectations.*

Bass and his colleagues built a significant body of work around the identification of the key competencies that allow leaders to transform their followers and their business; they referred to this as the *full range leadership theory* (FRLT). The FRLT has two main components, namely, transactional and transformational leadership. Transactional leadership is about outlining what actions leaders expect their followers to take to achieve their goals. Here the leaders clarify the subordinates' roles and the tasks required for them to meet expectations; they are aware of what their followers need or want to be happy and ensure they know how they will be rewarded if goals are achieved. One can summarize this style as, "If you achieve X, I will give you Y."

There are three behaviors that fall into the transactional leadership style. The first is laissez-faire, which is basically about avoiding leadership. The second is *management by exception,* which can be split into active and passive. *Passive management by exception* is when leaders wait for their subordinates to do something wrong and then tell them what has been done incorrectly. *Active management by exception* is when leaders actively monitor subordinates' results and, in a timely manner, communicate and/or punish those failures with actions, such as fines, suspension, loss of the boss's political support, or even loss of employment. The third transactional leadership behavior is *contingent reward.* This is when leaders communicate their expectations and then praise and reward subordinates for their successes.

Transformational leadership is about inspiring followers to achieve results and go beyond what is expected. This power comes from the "four Is." The first I relates to *idealized influence,* which is when leaders behave as role models for their followers; induce admiration, trust, and respect; demonstrate high ethical standards; consider the needs of others above their own; share risks; and delegate

tasks. The second I refers to *inspirational motivation,* where leaders provide meaning and challenge to their followers thereby motivating and inspiring them, stimulate team spirit, are enthusiastic and optimistic, and engage their followers when thinking about the future. The third I is for *intellectual stimulation,* which is when leaders stimulate innovation and creativity by questioning assumptions and looking at problems from different perspectives, encourage creativity, discuss mistakes privately rather than publicly, engage team members in finding creative solutions to problems, and encourage risk taking. The fourth I pertains to *individualized consideration,* whereby leaders coach and mentor their subordinates to help them meet their personal and organizational needs to achieve and grow. This is characterized by delegating tasks; creating new, challenging learning opportunities in a supportive climate; accepting individual and different needs for attention, encouragement, autonomy, and structure; and listening.

Laissez-faire management has been shown not to be effective. Bass and his colleagues have shown that contingent reward has been positively related to outcomes, while both types of management by exception were not. Transformational leadership behaviors were much more effective in achieving goals. The FRLT holds that at some point leaders will use all the behaviors described above, while effective leaders will use more contingent reward and transformational behaviors rather than the less effective ones (management by exception and laissez faire).

Importance

Overall, transformational leadership is measured using the Multifactor Leadership Questionnaire (MLQ). All the roles have been studied extensively and found to be valid and reliable. The research further shows that transformational, contingent reward, and active management leadership behaviors are positively correlated to leader outcomes, such as organizational effectiveness and follower satisfaction, whereas passive management by exception and laissez-faire behaviors are not.

The leadership role that has received the most attention is that of idealized influence or, as it was referred to by most researchers, charisma. While Max Weber was one of the first to mention the concept, it was Robert House who stimulated the empirical research in this area. His theory examined how charismatic leaders influence their followers and the leaders' traits. He stated that charisma had measurable components. Specifically, he proposed that charismatic leaders are able to make an emotional connection with their followers and thus persuade them to achieve their goals. Key in doing this is that leaders show confidence in their own abilities and those of their teams. They also set high expectations for everyone—themselves and their team—and project a belief that those expectations can be met.

Jay Conger and his colleagues proposed a three-step attributional model for charismatic leaders, in which they must evaluate what the followers' needs are and assess the available resources to get their followers interested in what they have to say. They also have to provide an inspiring vision for their followers and goals that will help them all meet those objectives. Lastly, they must show they are confident that their vision is achievable in order to inspire followers to feel confident as well.

Researchers have found that charismatic leaders use verbal devices, such as metaphors, stories, or anecdotes, demonstrating moral conviction, showing they share the sentiments of the collective, setting high expectations for both themselves and their followers, and communicating confidence that their expectations can be met. Nonverbally, they clearly convey their emotional states, demonstrate passion, and use body and facial gestures and animated voices. These strategies help make the messages of charismatic leaders more memorable. Recently, John Antonakis and his colleagues showed that charismatic leadership can indeed be taught. The managers they studied were perceived as more effective after having followed active training in charismatic leadership behaviors. Based on the above research, scholars suggest that the research on transformational leadership should both refine the FRLT to reflect those elements that work and to add two elements that are missing.

First, in terms of refining the FRLT to reflect the elements that work, the Podsakoff transformational-transactional leadership model includes many of the same ideas as Bass's but not active or passive management by exception and laissez-faire leadership styles. In other words, the elements proven not to be related to improving effectiveness have been left out.

Second, Antonakis identifies two important elements that are missing: an instrumental leadership factor and relevant dependent variables.

Instrumental leadership. For transformation to occur in business it is not enough to have emotional connections with people and to stimulate them intellectually. Leaders must also relate the strategic vision to organizational decisions that will help achieve their vision. For example, leaders must decide how to allocate budgets and human resources to conform to the strategy, what parts of the business may need to be divested, what acquisitions may need to be made, how to manage stakeholders, whether to pay out dividends or reinvest them into the business, how to convince shareholders, and so on. This is consistent with Marshall Sashkin's visionary leadership theory, which overlaps substantially with the FRLT. Sashkin added the strategic functions leaders must also undertake, namely, those that enable them to translate their vision into goals and actions at all organizational levels in ways that will contribute to reaching the vision.

Dependent variable. While some research links transformational leadership positively to such outcomes as improved organizational effectiveness and follower satisfaction, this does not necessarily mean that a transformation at either the organizational and/or individual level has taken place. In that sense, at the organizational level, researchers should explore to what extent the transformational roles can help organizations move from being national to global players, shift from being product companies to becoming service providers, move from selling rubber boots to selling mobile phones (à la Nokia), move from mining coal to producing commodity chemicals to specializing in life sciences and performance materials (à la the Dutch company DSM), and so on. At the team level, one should explore how the transformational roles help a group of individuals become a coherent team, how a coherent team becomes a highly performing team, and how a highly performing team can maintain its performance even when its members are not physically co-located. And at the individual level, one should explore how the transformational roles help functional experts become general managers, and how general managers can acquire a global mind-set. In other words, it is time to test the theory on real transformations.

The implications of this theory are threefold. First, if leaders want their direct reports (or subordinates) to go beyond the call of duty, they need to inspire them. Second, in order to inspire direct reports, leaders need to use charisma, intellectual stimulation, and individual motivation and consideration. The good news is that while many people have been trained in motivational techniques, research now shows that leaders can also learn how to be more charismatic. Third, while these tools can help transform individuals, they are not sufficient for organizational transformations. In order for leaders to transform organizations, they will also need to exercise instrumental leadership. That is, they will need to use organizational resources, such as budget allocations, human resources deployment, and investment decisions, to create the organization necessary to attain the vision.

Robert Hooijberg and Nancy Lane

See also Behavioral Perspective of Strategic Human Resource Management; Charismatic Theory of Leadership; Organizational Structure and Design; Path-Goal Theory of Leadership; Strategy and Structure

Further Readings

Antonakis, J. (2011). Transformational and charismatic leadership. In D. Day & J. Antonakis (Eds.), *The nature of leadership* (pp. 256–288). Thousand Oaks, CA: Sage.

Antonakis, J., Fenley, M., & Liechti, S. (2011). Can charisma be taught? Tests of two interventions. *Academy of management learning & education, 10,* 374–396.

Antonakis, J., & Hooijberg, R. (2007). Cascading vision for real commitment. In R. Hooijberg, J. G. Hunt, J. Antonakis, K. B. Boal, & N. Lane (Eds.), *Being there even when you are not: Leading through strategy, structures and systems* (pp. 231–244). Oxford, England: Elsevier JAI.

Avolio, B. J., Bass, B. M., & Jung, D. I. (1996). *Construct validation of the multifactor leadership questionnaire MLQ-Form 5x.* Binghamton: Center for Leadership Studies, State University of New York.

Bass, B. M. (1985). *Leadership and performance beyond expectations.* New York, NY: Free Press.

Bass, B. M., & Avolio, B. J. (1997). *Full range leadership development: Manual for the multifactor leadership questionnaire.* Palo Alto, USA: Mind Garden.

Burns, J. M. (1978). *Leadership.* New York, NY: Harper & Row.

Hooijberg, R., Hunt, J. G., Antonakis, J., Boal, K., & Lane, N. (Eds.). (2007). *Being there even when you are not: Leading through strategy, structures, and systems.* Oxford, England: Elsevier JAI.

House, R. J. (1977). A 1976 theory of charismatic leadership. In J. G. Hunt & L. L. Larson (Eds.), *Leadership: The cutting edge* (pp. 189–207). Carbondale: Southern Illinois University Press.

Judge, T. A., & Piccolo, R. F. (2004). Transformational and transactional leadership: A meta-analytic test of their relative validity. *Journal of Applied Psychology, 89,* 755–768.

Transnational Management

Christopher Bartlett and Sumantra Ghoshal described the emergence of a new corporate form—the transnational—in their widely acclaimed 1989 book, *Managing Across Borders.* Since then it has become one of the most prescribed configurations for multinational corporations (MNCs). The transnational corporation was offered as a new type of MNC that was simultaneously locally responsive, globally efficient, and innovative. Bartlett and Ghoshal suggested that MNCs needed to evolve beyond multinational, global, or international to transnational in order to address complex strategic and organizational challenges of the global marketplace. Their depiction of a transnational corporation illustrated that success in global strategy, in addition to creating and implementing an innovative strategy, is also a function of an organization's ability to organize and manage, thereby, laying the foundation of *transnational management* as a concept. Hence, transnational management emphasized the ability to develop a common global approach to coordination and control across subsidiaries in order to link them with each other and the headquarters, for the seamless flow and transfer of people and knowledge across borders, cross-national learning, effective use of corporate philosophy, appropriate cultural values, and informal socialization.

Described "as a new management reality," transnational management emerged as an important concept in international business because it extended the unidimensional space within which management of MNCs were often described, either as focusing upon cultural differences or being globally efficient, for example. Transnational management recognized the increased complexity of the global environment within which managers operate and sought to make sense of the conflicting demands that they are faced with. It also expanded the scope of traditional management theory by exposing the simultaneity and multiplicity of global management activities, including capturing global scale efficiency, being aware of and responding to local differences, and cultivating a global learning capability for driving continuous innovation. Finally, the concept linked the success of global strategy to building organizational capability via effective management systems and processes.

In the remainder of this entry, a detailed discussion of transnational management is organized as follows. First, fundamentals of transnational management are presented, including a typology of various MNCs forms and their descriptions. Next an assessment of validity and impact of transnational management is offered. The degree to which it is supported by research and helps explain management theory and practice is also evaluated. Finally, implications for future research are outlined.

Fundamentals

Bartlett and Ghoshal conducted an in-depth study of nine MNCs from three countries operating in three industries. Using personal interviews and survey questionnaires, they formulated a typology of organizations operating in the global marketplace. Labeled as *multinational, global, international,* and *transnational corporations,* they laid out specific characteristics associated with each type that differentiated their management practices from one another. In explaining each structural type, Bartlett and Ghoshal relied upon two key determinants, including the need for firms to match their capabilities to the strategic demands of their businesses and existing organizational systems and processes. They argued that multinational companies build a strong local presence through sensitivity and responsiveness to national differences and are decentralized with distributed resources and delegated responsibilities. A global company, on the other hand, builds cost advantages through centralized global operations, and it is often structured as a centralized hub based upon group-oriented behavior, intense communication, and a complex system of personal interdependencies. They described an international company

as a coordinated group of professional companies with sophisticated and control-driven management systems that exploit parent company knowledge and capabilities through worldwide diffusion and adaptation. These three types were presented as traditional organizations that varied on the basis of (a) configuration of assets and capabilities, (b) role of overseas operations, and (c) development and diffusion of knowledge. Specifically, a multinational was described as decentralized and nationally self-sufficient that allowed overseas operations the autonomy to adapt and exploit local opportunities, thus, develop and retain knowledge within each individual subsidiary. In contrast, a global company is globally scaled and centralized. Its overseas subsidiaries follow parent company practices and strategies and develop and retain knowledge at the headquarters level. International companies are both decentralized and centralized, adapt and leverage parent company competencies, and develop knowledge at the headquarter level with an emphasis on transferring it to subsidiaries.

Further, in 2004 Bartlett, Ghoshal, and Julian Birkinshaw argued that diverse, and often contradictory, forces were reshaping organizations and the managerial mind-set; they stated that the environmental forces "have collectively led to a new and complex set of challenges that require managers of MNCs to respond to three simultaneous yet often conflicting sets of external demands—the need for cross market integration, national responsiveness and worldwide learning" (p. 91). They concluded that organizations *with a transnational structure* and mind-set are most effective and efficient. As the fourth type of MNC in Bartlett and Ghoshal's typology, the transnational seeks global competiveness through multinational flexibility and worldwide learning capability. Its organizational characteristics include being dispersed, interdependent, and specialized, having differentiated contributions by national units to integrate worldwide operations and in developing knowledge jointly and sharing it worldwide.

Transnational management emphasizes a decentralized, bottom-up approach and shows strong commitment to genuine empowerment of employees. It eliminates traditional hierarchical authority and requires transformation of managerial roles at three critical levels, including operating managers, senior managers, and top executive managers. However, a close interplay among these roles is critical to integration of knowledge and processes across the entire organization, including headquarters and subsidiaries. Three core processes characterize effective transnational management: (a) entrepreneurial process drives the externally focused ability of the organization to tap new markets, (b) integration process allows linking and leveraging of dispersed resources and capabilities, and (c) renewal process enhances the ability to challenge organizational beliefs and practices in order to revitalize its processes and systems. Entrepreneurial process requires operating managers to become aggressive entrepreneurs in order to create and pursue new opportunities and senior managers to serve as inspiring coaches in order to develop and support initiatives. In particular, top management executives need to become institutional leaders who can establish strategic mission and performance standards. They need to create the infrastructure and the contexts necessary for others to play the new roles demanded of them. In terms of integration process, operations managers manage operational interdependencies; senior managers link skills, knowledge, and resources; and top executives develop and embed values. Management tasks and roles for the renewal process include frontline managers sustaining bottom-up energy and commitment, senior managers building and maintaining organizational flexibility, and top management managing the tension between short-term performance and long-term ambitions. Given a diversity of the roles that each type of manager serves, they each possess distinct knowledge and skills. For example, operating managers ought to possess detailed operating knowledge and focus their energy on capitalizing on opportunities through motivation and clear objectives; senior managers have broad organizational experience who focus on developing people and relationships and teams. Finally, top-level leaders understand a company in its context, inspire confidence, and create an exciting, demanding work environment. In essence, well-coordinated processes, systems, communication, capabilities, and competencies are therefore necessary for effective transnational management.

Importance

Transnational management has served as an important practical concept in the field of international business and management. Scholars argue that it is both influential and extensive. Although founded upon recognition of complexity of the business environment, it has been able to reduce the complexity of MNCs into a manageable number of characteristics, thus, making it easier to understand the management of MNCs. The concept provided propositions for empirical testing necessary for theory building and extension. Subsequently, researchers have used it in predictive ways to classify and evaluate management practices of a variety of organizations in diverse contexts. However, studies have not found clear-cut support for transnational management (and the typology). Based upon a British and French sample, Mehdi Bousseba and G. Morgan argued that there are concrete problems in developing global managerial groups, which are at the heart of competitive advantage of transnational firms. Similarly, other studies have found that, despite a recognized strategic importance of transfer of organizational practices within MNCs in transnational management, these transfers are not always successful.

Many other limitations of transnational management have also been discussed. First, since it is based upon only nine case studies from three countries, its generalizability is highly questionable. Insights for adopting transnational management approach are nonsystematic and appear to be prescriptive in nature. Some scholars have even called it "impressionistic" and lacking in empirical grounding. Empirical testing of the concept in the past two decades has also suggested that there are many ways of becoming transnational, not all of which are adequately captured in the original concept, which appears to be universalistic in nature.

Following a fast-paced and persistent flow of globalization, the field of international business has grown significantly in the past two decades, leading to conceptualization of many new concepts and discussion of more complex issues. Although Bartlett and Ghoshal's concept of transnational management has neither received much support nor refinement by other scholars, it has influenced research relating to the managerial and leadership mind-set. Hence, it still remains a much-cited concept.

Contemporary managers are increasingly faced with a complex and dynamic global environment. Bartlett and Ghoshal's transnational model provides useful insights and proposes a shift in the thinking required to lead successfully by focusing upon learning and flexibility. Some scholars have used this as the foundation for the concept of global mind-set. Managers can employ the roadmap of the three core processes (including entrepreneurial, integration, and renewal) in order to revitalize their organizations. This is likely to address the many challenges that they face and help them tap existing opportunities more by designing effective structures and strategies.

Shaista E. Khilji

See also Cultural Attitudes in Multinational Corporations; GLOBE Model; Leadership Practices; Management (Education) as Practice; Organizational Structure and Design; Strategy and Structure

Further Readings

Bartlett, C., & Ghoshal, S. (1989). *Managing across borders*. London, England: Hutchinson.

Bartlett, C., & Ghoshal, S. (1998). *Managing across borders: The transnational solution*. Boston, MA: Harvard Business School Press.

Bartlett, C., Ghoshal, S., & Birkinshaw, J. (2004). *Transnational management: Text, cases and readings in cross-border management* (4th ed.). Boston, MA: Irwin.

Bousseba, M., & Morgan, G. (2008). Managing talent across national borders: The challenges faced by an international retail group. *Critical Perspectives on International Business, 4*(1), 25–41.

Dickmann, M., Muller-Camen, M., & Kelliher, C. (2009). Exploring standardization and knowledge networking processes in transnational human resource management. *Personnel Review, 38*(1), 5–25.

Harzing, A. W. (2000). An empirical analysis and extension of Bartlett and Ghoshal's typology of multinational companies. *Journal of International Business Studies, 31*(1), 101–120.

Hedlund, G., & Ridderstrale, J. (1997). Towards a theory of self-renewing MNC. In B. Toyne & D. Nigh (Eds.), *International business: An emerging vision* (pp. 329–354). Columbia: University of Southern California Press.

Kostova, T. (1999). Transnational transfer of strategic organizational practices: A contextual perspective. *Academy of Management Review, 24*(2), 308–324.

Leong, S. M., & Tan, C. T. (1993). Managing across borders: An empirical test of the Bartlett and Ghoshal [1989] organizational typology. *Journal of International Business Studies, 24*(3), 449–464.

Triple Bottom Line

Given the nature and focus of modern accounting, the financial bottom line is generally an inadequate (and often actively misleading) expression of the total value equation. The term was coined in 1994 by John Elkington, as a means of countering the narrower focus on the then-fashionable term *eco-efficiency*, which focused on the financial and environmental dimensions of performance. Triple bottom line (TBL) thinking, by contrast, extended both to social impacts and to the wider economic impact issues that are rarely captured in the traditional financial bottom line. In this entry, a brief overview is provided of both the initial theory and its subsequent evolution.

Fundamentals

The TBL approach was introduced in detail in Elkington's *Cannibals with Forks* and has been further elaborated both in hundreds of company reports aligned with the Global Reporting Initiative (GRI) and in a growing number of books. It has been widely adopted in countries such as Australia in shaping policy in all levels of government. A linked phrase, "people, planet, profit," alternatively "people, planet, prosperity" (3Ps), was also coined by Elkington in 1995—and subsequently adopted by Shell as the title of its first sustainability report in 1997.

In the early 1990s, the leading edge of management thinking in this space focused on *eco-efficiency*, a term advanced by the World Business Council on Sustainable Development. This focused on the money to be made or saved in the more efficient use of natural resources and in pollution reduction. The TBL approach both widened the financial dimension to consider a range of economic externalities and introduced the social dimension—which at the time was much less acceptable to business leaders, particularly in the United States.

In headlines, the TBL framework was designed to encourage business leaders to identify, value, invest in, account for, and manage three increasingly interlinked dimensions of value creation—and destruction. To take the 3P formulation, these were the following:

- People: Business is increasingly used to treating employees well (think human resources) and customers and consumers well (think customer relationship management or total quality management), but the human and social dimensions of wealth creation increasingly call for attention to human rights and intragenerational and intergenerational equity. A central insight is that to be sustainable, a business model, technology, or product would need to be viable in a world of 9 billion people by 2050.

- Planet: Issues such as stratospheric ozone depletion, climate change, and large-scale species loss signal the downsides of the dawn of the Anthropocene era, in which human activities shape the planet, for good and ill. Business is increasingly being held to account for such externalities.
- Profit/prosperity: The rules of capitalism, markets, and business require shareholder-owned companies to make a profit and build value. Here the central idea is that by protecting other forms of capital (e.g., human, social, cultural, natural) companies can, among other things, secure their license to operate and to innovate, reduce future liabilities, build brand value, and drive down costs.

As the 3Ps, this second phrase then became central to the sustainable development debate in countries like The Netherlands. It sparked debates about the double bottom line (combining social and financial performance, as in social enterprise) and, variously, quadruple and quintuple bottom lines, in which issues like ethics and governance were added in. More recently, it has inspired the work of companies like Puma, which aims to develop profit and loss accounting processes and statements for its environmental, social, and economic value added—or destroyed.

The TBL concept aims to help business people think through the question of how to make corporations more sustainable in the context of major emerging economic, social, and environmental challenges, among them corruption, human rights, and climate change. To date, sustainability factors have only very rarely affected capital availability, but understanding of the relevant linkages is likely to grow fairly rapidly. Among the institutions founded on TBL lines have been the Dow Jones Sustainability Indexes (DJSI), the Global Reporting Initiative (GRI), and Triple Bottom Line Investing (TBLI), which organizes major events on sustainable finance and investment.

Corporate sustainability is probably better understood not so much as the discipline by which companies ensure their own long-term survival—though that is clearly part of the equation—but as the field of thinking and practice by means of which companies and other business organizations work to extend the life expectancy of ecosystems (and the natural resources they provide), societies (and the cultures and communities that underpin commercial activity), and economies (that provide the governance, financial, and other market context for corporate competition and survival). By paying attention to such wider issues, it is often argued, companies are better placed to ensure that their own business models remain valid and adaptable.

Importance

As for the corporate sustainability agenda, recent decades have seen sustainability issues gradually being forced up through corporate hierarchies. They started very much on the fringes, being handled (if at all) by professionals in such areas as site security, public relations and legal affairs. Through the 1970s, as new techniques such as environmental impact assessment evolved, new groups of people became involved, among them project planners, process engineers, and site managers. Then, during the late 1980s, the spotlight opened out to illuminate new product development, design, marketing, and life cycle management. As the triple bottom line agenda of sustainable development spread through the 1990s, with an inevitable growth in the complexity and political impact of key issues, the agenda was driven up to top management and boards. In the next round, in addition to all those already involved, expect to see new ventures people, chief financial officers, investment bankers, and venture capitalists getting involved.

Over time, the agenda has opened out profoundly, increasingly embracing challenging issues such as transparency, corporate and global governance, human rights, bribery and corruption, and global poverty. The key text in this area has been 1987's Brundtland Commission report, *Our Common Future*. Its definition of sustainable development is now widely accepted. It was brought into greater focus in 1994 with the introduction of the TBL concept, which has subsequently been widely adopted—for example, by the Global Reporting Initiative (GRI). The concept has also been adopted by leading companies, most strikingly perhaps by Denmark's Novo Nordisk, which used the TBL framework in its rechartering.

Work on implementing the TBL agenda has shown that there are many points at which it potentially engages with and influences business thinking, strategy, investment, and operations. For a closer insight into current practice, take a look at the websites of TBL-oriented organizations, such as the Global Reporting Initiative and the Dow Jones Sustainability Indexes. Meanwhile, the corporate work of organizations like SustainAbility and Volans have suggested that a potentially powerful way of approaching TBL-focused corporate change is to think in terms of brands, balance sheets, boards, and business models, or 4Bs.

This often starts with external challenges targeting *brands*, often led by activists, nongovernmental organizations (NGOs), and the media. Few things stimulate corporate action faster than threats to brand value, with the result that the TBL agenda crosscuts the world of brand management. Over time, corporate leaders are then encouraged to adapt their management, accounting, disclosure, communication, and external engagement strategies (*balance sheets*). Some companies can hold the challenge at this level, but increasingly, often the issues have a sufficiently intense political spin that they are forced up to *boards*, cross connecting with the world of corporate governance. If the pressures are sustained, presenting new forms of risk and opportunity, then we may see companies adapting their *business models*, as General Electric (already mentioned above as a long-term corporate survivor) has begun to do with its "ecomagination" strategy. This turn of the wheel brings us back to branding, a point underscored by the success of GE's initiative (http://www.ecomagination.com).

The TBL agenda has spawned a broad range of management tools, ranging from auditing and reporting processes through to new thinking about how to blend the different dimensions of value creation. See, for example, the triple top line thinking of William McDonough or the blended thinking of Jed Emerson and others (at http://www.blended-value.org). In the end, however, there are few "drop-in" TBL solutions. And work is still in progress on development of new assessment methods, for example, by Puma, with its environmental profit and loss accounting method, designed as a stepping stone toward a full triple bottom line accounting.

At the same time, we see growing interest in integrated accounting and reporting across the TBL agenda, as advanced by the International Integrated Reporting Committee. Integration was always the ultimate goal of the TBL movement, but the challenge will be to ensure that the next generation of integrated accounting, reporting, and assurance techniques fully capture the material dimensions of multicapital, long-term wealth creation.

John Elkington

See also Corporate Social Responsibility; Cultural Intelligence; Leadership Practices; Organizational Learning; Participative Model of Decision Making; Stakeholder Theory; Strategies for Change; Transnational Management; Trust; Value Chain

Further Readings

Eccles, R. G., & Krzus, M. P. (2010). *One report: Integrated reporting for a sustainable strategy.* New York, NY: Wiley & Sons.

Elkington, J. (1997). *Cannibals with forks: The triple bottom line of 21st century business.* Oxford, England: Capstone/Wiley & Sons.

Elkington, J. (2012). *The zeronauts: Breaking the sustainability barrier.* Oxford, England: Earthscan/Taylor & Francis.

Henriques, A., & Richardson, J. (2004). *The triple bottom line: Does it all add up?* London, England: Earthscan.

Savitz, A. (with Weber, K.). (2006). *The triple bottom line: How today's best-run companies are achieving economic, social, and environmental success—and how you can too.* San Francisco, CA: Jossey-Bass.

TRUST

All organizations comprise people who work together to accomplish objectives. Since the mid-1990s, trust has become recognized as a fundamental building block of such working relationships both within organizations and between people, groups, and organizations themselves. Scholars in a variety of disciplines have considered the concept of trust as it relates to their respective fields. The history of trust within management research dates back arguably to the work of Morton Deutsch in the 1950s. This work was highly insightful and began to provide a foundation for thinking about the topic.

Subsequent work in management for many years was sporadic, with little in mainstream journals. By the 1980s, trust was frequently mentioned as being important to other issues, but then, attention would be turned to issues that were more tangible and easier to define. In 1995, Roger C. Mayer, James H. Davis, and F. David Schoorman defined trust as "the willingness of a party to be vulnerable to the actions of another party based on the expectation that the other will perform a particular action important to the trustor, irrespective of the ability to monitor or control that other party." (p. 712). They went on to clarify that the definition applied to a relationship with a definable other party. The other party must be perceived to behave in ways that demonstrate conscious choices. Trust is not dichotomous, in that one either trusts or does not trust another party, but is a continuum from not being willing to be vulnerable to the focal party to being highly willing to be vulnerable to that party. This entry will next consider the antecedents of trust, its relationship with risk and risk taking, how it is different from cooperation, its multilevel nature as defined here, the evolution of the field's view of trust, and finally applications of this approach to trust for practicing managers.

Fundamentals

There are several major factors that cause a party to trust another. They can be broadly categorized into three areas: factors about the trusting party (trustor), factors about the to-be-trusted party (trustee), and factors about the context or situation in which the relationship takes place. Julian B. Rotter is recognized as being among the first to carefully consider the general willingness to trust others as being an important issue. He published a 25-item scale of interpersonal trust in the late 1960s, which for years dominated how the field thought about trust. More recently, this has come to be commonly referred to in the management literature as the propensity to trust.

Three factors about the trustee have been found to determine a great deal of variance of how much a trustor will trust a given trustee or antecedents of trust: (a) ability, (b) benevolence, and (c) integrity. These collectively determine the perception of the trustee's trustworthiness.

Ability is the capacity of the trustee to do things important to the trustor. It is task specific and situation specific, meaning that a given party could be perceived to have strong ability in one domain but in a somewhat different domain have somewhat weaker skills. The second factor that makes one perceived as trustworthy is benevolence, which is the perception that the trustee wants to do positive things for the trustor. It is more individualistic than a notion of being "benevolent toward all"; it is the perception that the trustee has the trustor's interests at heart because of the relationship. The third factor that makes a trustee seem trustworthy is integrity. Integrity is the perception that the trustee follows a set of values the trustor finds acceptable. This does not mean that the trustee has the same set of values, as the value sets people have can vary in many dimensions. Rather, it means that the important values that matter to the issue at hand are sufficiently matched. In addition, a perception that the trustee has integrity requires the trustee to adhere to the professed values. It is not enough that the trustee merely claims to have a set of values, as a discrepancy between the party's professed values and observed actions would decrease the perception that the trustee has integrity.

While propensity is relatively stable and resides within the trustor, akin to a personality trait, the factors of trustworthiness (i.e., ability, benevolence, and integrity) and trust itself exist within a context. As the context changes, so can the evaluations of these. For example, a person's supervisor may be very effective at garnering resources for an employee's projects and raises for the employee. A change in management above the supervisor's level may bring a marked change in the organization's politics and severely undercut the supervisor's effectiveness at getting resources. While the supervisor's inherent competencies do not change, the realities of the new political situation change the context such that the supervisor's ability in the new situation is reduced. Thus, ability is context specific. Similar arguments can be made for the contextual specificity of benevolence and integrity.

Trust increases the likelihood that a party will take a risk in the relationship with the trustee. The nature of risk is that there is uncertainty about outcomes that will occur in a situation. The outcome may involve a loss of resources or not achieving a potential gain in resources that is being sought by the trusting party. Trust allows the trusting party to accept risk and engage in an action (e.g., sharing sensitive information) that allows a trustee's influence to effect either loss or gain for the trusting party.

Trust is different from cooperation, because one can cooperate with a party who one does not trust. Cooperation could be motivated by a power differential or by a lack of perceived options other than cooperating. For example, an employee may comply with his or her supervisor's request for working overtime despite having made plans for after work that must be canceled. While the behavior is cooperative, it does not necessarily mean the employee trusts the supervisor. The cooperative act of staying late may be due to fear of reprisal from the supervisor.

Trust as described here is isomorphic, meaning that it is applicable across multiple levels of analysis: interpersonal, intergroup, and interorganizational. Two persons can trust one another; such is the foundation of a good interpersonal relationship. Likewise, two groups can trust one another, as can be seen in relationships between two departments that are in a position to compete for resources but opt to act in ways that protect one another's interests. Organizations can trust one another; indeed some research has found this to be a key ingredient to the formation of a joint venture. In addition to these three examples that each involve a single level, cross-level trust involves mixes of these such as a top management team (i.e., a group) trusting a given employee to negotiate a relationship with another company or with a union.

Importance

Throughout this time period a variety of definitions of trust evolved. Each had strengths and weaknesses from a conceptual perspective. 1995 seemed to be a pivotal year for this topic, as three papers on trust were published in Academy of Management journals. Attention to trust as a topic of management research spiked sharply after that point, and has remained high to the writing of this entry. The same year this entry was written, a new journal was launched named for trust and focused specifically on publishing research in this rapidly growing area.

Several concerns with extant approaches were listed by Mayer, Davis, and Schoorman in the 1990s. Drawing on the insights of several authors over the previous decades, they pointed out a list of problems with prior approaches to trust. They noted that there were problems with the definition of trust. They showed that there was confusion in the literature between trust and its antecedents and outcomes. They demonstrated a lack of clarity in the

relationship between trust and risk. They explained that a lack of specificity of trust referents was leading to ambiguities in levels of analysis. They also showed that most extant work did not consider both the trusting party and the party to be trusted. Accordingly, they developed a model that differentiated the antecedents and outcomes of trust from trust itself.

Viewing trust as a willingness to be vulnerable to another party has become the dominant approach in the field (based on citation counts in the major databases). This approach lays out important boundary conditions of the construct of trust. Trust has been described as an approach to dealing with risk in a relationship with other parties. Trust is more important in situations where the trusting party is at a greater level of risk. There is a well-established literature on judgment and decision making (JDM), which has for years studied how people make decisions about a variety of topics such as investments, health, and selling a business. Many conditions have been found to affect how people appraise risk in a situation and how they respond to it. An important boundary condition that delimits trust from the broader JDM literature is that it is defined to be within a relationship. Thus, while such expressions turn up repeatedly in common language, one does not "trust" the weather to be favorable on a given day, nor does one "trust" a machine to operate properly. Such use of the term trust would imply that the weather or a given machine in question makes conscious, intentional decisions about whether to honor the party's trust or to defect on it. Since such intentional decisions are beyond the ability of the weather or a machine, these are more appropriately considered under the broader realm of judgment and decision making.

This model provides a useful tool for practicing managers to understand the major factors that lead to trust. This enables them to focus their efforts on practical means of garnering greater levels of trust from employees, peers, and their own managers. It is important for them to note that depending on the role the other person is in, how they evaluate the importance of ability, benevolence, and integrity is likely to vary. It is important to take the perspective of the other party and view one's own trustworthiness factors through the eyes of the other person.

Roger C. Mayer

See also Causal Attribution Theory; Multilevel Research; Personal Engagement (at Work) Model; Positive Organizational Scholarship; Principled Negotiation; Social Power, Bases of; Theory of Cooperation and Competition; Transformational Theory of Leadership

Further Readings

Colquitt, J. A., Scott, B. A., & LePine, J. A. (2007). Trust, trustworthiness, and trust propensity: A meta-analytic test of their unique relationships with risk taking and job performance. *Journal of Applied Psychology, 92,* 909–927.

Deutsch, M. (1958). Trust and suspicion. *Journal of Conflict Resolution, 2,* 265–279.

Dirks, K. T., & Ferrin, D. L. (2002). Trust in leadership: Meta-analytic findings and implications for research and practice. *Journal of Applied Psychology, 87,* 611–628.

Mayer, R. C., Davis, J. H., & Schoorman, F. D. (1995). An integrative model of organizational trust. *Academy of Management Review, 20,* 709–734.

Rotter, J. B. (1967). A new scale for the measurement of interpersonal trust. *Journal of Personality, 35,* 651–665.

Schoorman, F. D., Mayer, R. C., & Davis, J. H. (2007). An integrative model of organizational trust: Past, present, and future. *Academy of Management Review, 32,* 344–354.

Tomlinson, E. C., & Mayer, R. C. (2009). The role of causal attribution dimensions in trust repair. *Academy of Management Review, 34,* 85–104.

Williams, M. (2001). In whom we trust: Group membership as an affective context for trust development. *Academy of Management Review, 26,* 377–396.

Zand, D. E. (1972). Trust and managerial problem solving. *Administrative Science Quarterly, 17,* 229–239.

TWO-FACTOR THEORY (AND JOB ENRICHMENT)

Few theories within the domain of management discourse have provoked more debate than *The Motivation to Work,* by Frederick Herzberg, Bernard Mausner, and Barbara Bloch Snyderman, published in 1959. The book created a furor that continues to this day. Its relevance to this encyclopedia lies in the fact that it challenges a popular conception that money motivates. This entry explains why the work remains contentious. As a first step, it explores the background context and offers an explanation of the theory itself and how its findings broke with the past. Next, the research method and its limitations are explored, followed by an assessment of the impact of the findings on other research and upon management thought. The conclusion assesses the implications for managers facing contemporary challenges in the modern context.

Fundamentals

Two-factor theory challenged a well-established motivational paradigm. It was predicated on the idea that a range of different stimuli contribute to employee job satisfaction and dissatisfaction. Stimuli could be arranged along a continuum. Typical factors included the working conditions, holidays, training and development opportunities, prospects for promotion, quality of the relationship with a supervisor or manager, recognition of achievement, the wage rate, and the correlation between effort and reward. The assumption was that the importance an individual assigned to each of the factors would have a different weighting, duration, and impact. Thus, at any given moment, the overall balance would tip in favor of the employee being either satisfied or dissatisfied. It was also theoretically possible for an individual to experience a neutral state in which positives cancelled out negatives. Herzberg's results challenged the dominant assumptions of behaviorism and of rational economic man.

When *The Motivation to Work* was published, the ideas of Frederick.W. Taylor, enshrined as "scientific management," predominated. Taylorism emphasized the importance of scientifically analyzing the design and content of work, the measurement of performance, and the linking of reward to performance through piece rate systems. Clearly, any suggestion that the link between motivation and reward could be more tenuous than was previously believed challenged a wide range of vested academic and managerial interests.

The Two Factors

Herzberg's two-factor theory was developed as a result of an experiment that explored the impact in terms of both frequency and duration of 14 factors on job satisfaction and dissatisfaction. The method of data collection was based on interviews and the use of critical incident analysis. Respondents were required to recall incidents that were linked to each of the 14 factors and to recall what impact each factor had on the motivation to work.

The results clustered within two distinct categories, depending on whether job satisfaction or dissatisfaction was the focus of concern. First, sources of satisfaction included the nature of the work itself, a sense of achievement, recognition by a supervisor and colleagues, prospects of promotion, and the opportunity to assume more responsibility. These were defined as *motivators*. Second, respondents reported feelings of dissatisfaction when extrinsic factors, such as company policies or administration, were perceived to be lacking, technical or interpersonal supervision was poor, working conditions were inadequate, or the financial reward inappropriate. These were defined as *hygiene factors*. Thus, external rewards, if they were wrongly conceived, appeared to demotivate, and even if well conceived, their motivational value was limited.

Herzberg and his team went on to categorize the sources of satisfaction as motivators and those of dissatisfaction as hygiene factors. What distinguished the two was that the former generated energy from within, while the latter were external stimuli that induced either compliance or movement in a direction desired by management.

The ensuing article caused consternation. During the years that followed, a series of replication studies were undertaken. Those that deployed Herzberg's methodology generated findings that showed consistency with the original results. Unfortunately, those who adopted alternative methods delivered less consistent findings. This raised doubts about both the reliability and the validity of the original work. Victor Vroom offered one of the most potent critiques. He suggested that any methodology involving recall could invoke ego defense mechanisms. This would prompt alignment of motivators with a respondent's personal standing and achievement, while dissatisfaction would be assigned to factors beyond the respondent's control. Einar Hardin argued that Herzberg's results were flawed by poor respondent recall. Robert Opsahl and Marvin Dunnette claimed to be mystified by the assertion that money was more likely to act as a dissatisfier (hygiene factor).

Conclusions and Implications

Having formulated the two-factor theory, Herzberg and his team used the evidence of the existence of motivators to challenge the less humane aspects of the dominant ideologies of Taylorism and Fordism. Taylor had argued for work specialization and simplification as a means of improving productivity and rewarding fairly, but Henry Ford had gone a stage further. His aim was to produce a productive worker within a few hours of entering his factory. To achieve this, he used machines to de-skill work. By organizing machines in lines and eventually mechanizing the processes that linked the different activities, he developed assembly-line production, a push system that proved to be the key to 20th-century mass production and prosperity.

Between 1913 and 1955, productivity levels climbed exponentially. The standard of living in the United States and across the developed world mirrored the rise in productivity. Workers became consumers. They created levels of demand that only mass production could satisfy.

Unfortunately, the rise in wealth and productivity came at a price. That price was unrelenting, grinding, repetitive work, involving simple boring tasks repeated endlessly for shifts of 8 hours or more, 6 days a week. Workers rotated through shifts involving several weeks when work commenced in the morning then the early evening and then to nights for up to 50 weeks a year. In short, there was little dignity or mental stimulation to be found in work. High absenteeism, low productivity, and sabotage were some of the by-products of the Taylor and Fordist approaches.

Recognizing the appalling cost as well as the enormous benefits of mass production, Herzberg began to formulate the case for job enrichment. He concluded that rather than seeking to motivate employees through reward, organizations should aim to create intrinsic satisfaction in the work itself by designing in more task variety, more autonomy, and greater capacity to exercise judgment and responsibility. This involved adding some of the planning and evaluating duties normally undertaken by managers. The approach came to be known as orthodox job enrichment.

Herzberg also made a series of observations in relation to hygiene factors, three of which are of special note. First, people are made dissatisfied by a bad environment, but they are seldom made satisfied by a good one. Second, the prevention of dissatisfaction is just as important as delivering motivation through job satisfaction, and, finally, hygiene factors operate independently of motivation factors. Employees may be highly motivated in their work while being dissatisfied with their work environment.

Persistent challenges to his work and findings over a period of a decade prompted Herzberg to make one last attempt to quell his critics. In 1968, he published "One More Time: How Do You Motivate Employees?" The article sold more than 1.2 million reprints, the largest volume of offprints ever achieved by the *Harvard Business Review*. Thereafter, he and his collaborators developed their ideas on job enrichment in a series of publications that included *Job Enrichment Pays Off; Orthodox Job Enrichment: Measuring True Quality in Job Satisfaction; The Managerial Choice: To Be Efficient and to Be Human;* and *New Perspectives in the Will to Work.*

Importance

Each of the above contributions provided impetus for the human relations and sociotechnical movements. It placed Herzberg in the human relations pantheon along with Elton Mayo, Kurt Lewin, Douglas McGregor, and others.

Herzberg's later work provided the foundations for the *job characteristics model* developed by J. Richard Hackman and colleagues. The model posits that three critical psychological states must be fulfilled to deliver intrinsic work motivation. These are experienced meaningfulness, experienced responsibility, and knowledge of the results achieved. Creating these mind states demands that five core job characteristics be isolated. These are defined as the following:

Identity: the extent to which a job demands the completion of a "whole" or identifiable piece of work

Significance: the degree to which a job has a substantial impact on the lives of others

Variety: the degree of challenge the different elements of the job demand

Autonomy: the amount of discretion in scheduling work and determining how it should be done

Feedback: the extent to which the job holders can judge the effectiveness of their personal effort

The impact of this thinking prompted various sociotechnical initiatives. The most famous were the Saab and Volvo experiments in job enrichment and autonomous team working. Significant improvement in productivity and performance were reported. Other Danish research was less convincing. It highlighted the need for particular contingencies to be present, including company stability, employment continuity, and financial health as preconditions for success. The sociotechnical approach was further damaged when Volvo elected in 1992 to close its assembly plant in Kalmar. Despite the setbacks, these studies prompted research into goal setting, alternative methods of work scheduling, flexible working, and job sharing.

Total quality management (TQM) and just-in-time production (JIT) posed a serious challenge to complex sociotechnical system designs. The latter were increasingly seen as challenging and risky at a time when Japanese discipline and methods promised significant cost reduction with less risk. At the same time, the removal of overhead roles associated with maintenance, control, and programming activity enabled TQM and JIT advocates to assert that the remaining jobs were both enlarged and enriched. Eventually, the two views merged once it was seen that ideal TQM and JIT conditions were dependent upon good sociotechnical design. A view that was further bolstered by W. Edwards Deming's "red bead" experiment pointed to the difficulties in setting bonuses that are tied to performance.

Many organizations across the world continue to reject Herzberg's thesis. They adhere to a conviction that extrinsic reward needs to be linked to individual short-term performance. A joint study conducted in 2007 by the *Wall Street Journal* and Hay Consulting found that in 1965, the average American CEO was paid 24 times the average employee. By 2007, this had risen to 275 times. Research undertaken by Mike Mayo following the financial crash of 2007 found pay for the CEOs of Europe and America's biggest banks rose by 36% in a year, an average of $10 million per head, despite the fact that revenues across the board rose by less than 3%. These studies are consistent with earlier findings conducted at the time of the Great Depression thereby establishing consistency over time.

To conclude, Herzberg's theory raises important questions for the contemporary management context. Knowledge-intensive companies rely upon human and social capital to create core competence and distinctive capability. Staff turnover is costly. Skill dilution and loss of tacit knowledge impedes performance, erodes customer service, and can damage brands. Staff turnover is a product of push and pull factors. Herzberg's results suggest that getting the motivators right makes an organization "sticky." Push factors associated with hygiene considerations, in contrast, stimulate an employee to look for new opportunity. Extrinsic considerations, like salary and working conditions, then move to the fore. Careful monitoring of employee perceptions and attitudes toward motivating factors is called for if employee retention is to be sustained. Organizations that are committed to high-performance work systems can use headline pay and reward to attract, but it will not necessarily retain. Motivation is often associated with commitment; however, commitment takes three forms: continuity, or willingness to remain; normative, or identification with the organization's values; and affective, or identification with the work itself and a sense of responsibility to colleagues. High affective and normative commitment correlates more closely with motivators, while continuity is associated with both. Although high pay can stimulate high continuity, it does not deliver commitment to colleagues or to organizational values. If these factors are important considerations, managers must ask searching questions regarding organizational priorities and align human resource policy and practice accordingly. As David McLelland observed, whereas managers have a high need for power and achievement, others have a need for achievement and affiliation. These insights point to the importance of harnessing intrinsic motivation when managing people.

Nigel Bassett-Jones

See also Achievement Motivation Theory; Competing Values Framework; Contingency Theory; Goal-Setting Theory; Human Resource Management Strategies; Human Capital Theory; Job Characteristics Theory; Organizational Commitment Theory; Total Quality Management

Further Readings

Hackman, J. R., & Oldham, G. R. (1976, August). Motivation through the design of work: Test of a theory. *Organizational Behavior and Human Performance, 16*(2), 250–279.

Herzberg, F. (1982). *The managerial choice: To be efficient and to be human* (2nd Rev. ed.). Salt Lake City, UT: Olympus. (Original work published 1976)

Herzberg, F. (1987). One more time: How do you motivate employees? [With retrospective commentary]. *Harvard Business Review, 65*(5), 109–120. (Original work published 1968)

Herzberg, F., & Zautra, A. (1976, September/October). Orthodox job enrichment: Measuring true quality in job satisfaction. *Personnel, 53*(5), 54–68.

Lawler, E. E. (1994). Total quality management and employee involvement: Are they compatible? *Academy of Management Executive, 8*(1), 68–76.

Opshal, R. L., & Dunnette, M. D. (1966). The role of financial incentives in industrial motivation. *Psychological Bulletin, 66,* 95–116.

Vroom, V. H. (1964). *Work and motivation.* Oxford, England: Wiley.

TYPE A PERSONALITY THEORY

Type A personality theory holds that the incidence of heart disease in those classified as high-achievement workaholics—those who push themselves, dislike ambivalence, multitask, are controlling, feel the pressure of deadlines, and respond negatively to even minor time delays—is nearly twice as high as those not diagnosed with these symptoms. The theory was first developed in the 1950s by two San Francisco cardiologists, Drs. Meyer Friedman and Ray H. Rosenman, who began a series of studies using data from their clinical practice. They concluded that the accepted risk factors for heart disease (hypertension from smoking and high cholesterol) did not sufficiently account for its increase in the general population. Their findings have received mixed support from some researchers, but the theory continues to exert a strong influence on diagnosis and treatment. The implication for management practice is that left unaddressed, Type A individuals are at risk to place themselves *and* those around them under unnecessary stress and an increased risk of heart disease. This entry reviews the main findings and management implications of the theory.

Fundamentals

Type A personality traits include impatience, aggressiveness, chronic anger and hostility, a chronic sense of urgency, a preoccupation with deadlines, ambitiousness, an excessive desire to achieve recognition and advancement, an excessively high need for control, high competitiveness, and a preoccupation with status. Friedman and Rosenman hypothesized a converse syndrome, Type B personality, which was not linked to heart disease, and simply consisted of opposite tendencies. They considered Type B personalities to lack an acute sense of urgency and to be more relaxed, patient, and easygoing. Their treatment regimens, aside from medication, revolved around lifestyle changes and included diet, exercise, relaxation techniques, and support groups for changing habitual stressful behaviors.

While their own research tended to confirm their hypothesized link between Type A personality and heart disease, the results of other researchers provided mixed results, and many studies did not support their findings or theory at all. Critique of their work appeared soon after their theory was first made and centered around methodology—biased samples, statistical inference of causality from correlational data, lack of adequate sample and control groups, and the weakness of psychological "Type" research in general. The fundamental objection to their findings is the difficulty in testing whether an emotional disorder predisposes an individual to mechanical blockage of blood supply to the heart, because such a study would have to be initiated *before* the onset of the disease in order to separate the degree to which the emotional disorder is a contributing *cause* or an ancillary *effect* of that disease. Researchers also believe that the discrepancies in the studies are due to the lack of standard criteria for defining Type A behavior. In addition, some researchers believe that the sweeping breadth of the concept is too general to be easily measured, making the research results too difficult to replicate. Consequently, recent research focuses on exploring more narrowly defined factors. Despite the mixed support for the hypothesis that personality type is associated with coronary heart disease, medical practitioners and the public have continued to use the terms Type A and Type B personalities. The resilience of the theory suggests that Friedman and Rosenman may have been on to something after all.

Their initial clinical intuition may have pointed to an underlying factor or trait that first appeared in the speculations of ancient Greek philosophical and medical thought. Empedocles (circa 450 BCE) propounded an early theory that the "cosmos" consisted of four primary elements. But it was Hippocrates (circa 400 BCE) who, observing individual behavior, noticed marked differences in temperament, and reasoned that Empedocles's four "macrocosmic" elements—air, earth, fire, and water—were naturally expressed in four "microcosmic" individual temperaments—sanguine (hopeful), melancholic (sad), choleric (angry), and phlegmatic (slow moving). These ancient temperaments resemble recognizable clinical personality traits even today.

Some recent research supports the contention that at least one trait commonly attributed to the Type A personality—anger and hostility—can be a significant factor in coronary disease and increased workplace and life stress. Friedman and Rosenman may have intuitively initiated a line of contemporary research that lends support to the central importance of at least one of the four fundamental temperaments—the choleric temperament. Put into the more contemporary idiom of Type A personality theory, the individuals who are chronically angry or hostile engender an atmosphere of fear and stress around themselves.

The organizational and management implication of these findings are clear. Motivation by anger, hostility, and fear has its limitations. Frustration, aggression, anger, and hostility have their place to play in human life—but it all depends on the origins, the expression, and the context of these emotions. Anger and hostility can help mobilize others in support of a benevolent collective vision or mobilize them in the service of a malevolent collective digression. History is replete with examples of both. The significance is not that anger or hostility per se is helpful or unhelpful, it is the clinical "authenticity" and relevance of the emotions within a particular context. If the source of the anger is "real," that is, directed at a realistic external target, it is authentic; but to the extent that the anger is the expression of an individual or collective pathology, it is disconnected from reality, and the individual, group, or organization risks being guided in a tangential, potentially disastrous direction. Those hard-driving executives with Type A personality traits who chronically inject their own anger and hostility into the immediate environment of their family, work groups, or organizations might increase short-term employee motivation and performance. But enhanced performance by this kind of "extrinsic motivation" is often short term. Dominance is not always the appropriate leadership style, and a subordinate's compliance does not guarantee his commitment. Furthermore, research suggests that long-term job satisfaction, employee well-being, individual life span, and ultimately individual and organizational health may be unintended casualties of unexamined or unmitigated Type A behavior.

Type A personality theory in its present form has been around for well over a half a century—and in its previous incarnation for well over two millennia. The robustness of the underlying constructs serves as a warning and a challenge for modern management. Thoughtful and self-aware managers can use the insights of Type A personality theory to pursue their goals while creating healthier conditions for themselves and others.

Jack Denfeld Wood

See also Authentic Leadership; Big-Five Personality Dimensions; Causal Attribution Theory; Compliance Theory; Groupthink; Locus of Control; Reinforcement Theory; Theory X and Theory Y

Further Readings

Frei, R., Racicot, B., & Travagline, A. (1999). The impact of monochronic and Type A behavior patterns on research productivity and stress. *Journal of Managerial Psychology, 14*(5), 374–387.

Friedman, H. S., & Booth-Kewley, S. (1987, October). Personality, Type A behavior, and coronary heart disease: The role of emotional expression. *Journal of Personality and Social Psychology, 53*(4), 783–792.

Friedman, M. (1996). *Type A behavior: Its diagnosis and treatment.* New York, NY: Plenum (Kluwer Academic Press).

George, J. (1992). The role of personality in organizational life: Issues and evidence. *Journal of Management, 18*(2), 185–213.

Haynes, S. G., Feinleib, M., & Kannel, W. B. (1980). The relationship of psychosocial factors to coronary heart disease in the Framingham study: Eight year incidence of coronary heart disease. *American Journal of Epidemiology, 111,* 37–58.

Ivancevich, J. M., & Matteson, M. T. (1988). Type A behavior and the healthy individual. *British Journal of Medical Psychology, 61,* 37–56.

Rosenman, R. H., Brand, J. H., Jenkins, C. D., Friedman M., Straus R., & Wurm, M. (1975). Coronary heart disease in the Western Collaborative Group Study: Final follow-up experience of 8.5 years. *Journal of American Medical Association, 233*(8), 872–877.

Rosenman, R. H., Friedman, M., Straus R., Wurm, M, Kositchek, R., Han, W., & Werthessen, N. T. (1964). A predictive study of coronary heart disease: The Western Collaborative Group Study. *Journal of the American Medical Association, 189*(1), 15–22.

Williams, R. B. (2001). Hostility: Effects on health and the potential for successful behavioral approaches to prevention and treatment. In A. Baum, T. A. Revenson, & J. E. Singer (Eds.), *Handbook of health psychology* (pp. 661–668). Mahwah, NJ: Erlbaum.

TYPOLOGY OF ORGANIZATIONAL CULTURE

Organizational culture is defined as the values, beliefs, norms, and systems of meaning or symbolism that are learned and come to be taken for granted among organizational members about how things are done and what are the right things to do. This entry describes the development of interest in the concept of organizational culture, the key dimensions of typologies of organizational culture, some of the issues that have been raised about how to study organizational culture, and some of the main concerns about research on the topic.

Fundamentals

Interest in the culture of organizations has gone through stages. A number of classic works were published in the 1950s and 1960s in fields like sociology and political science that described topics such as life on the factory floor or how cohesiveness in work groups is shaped by the nature of work and the characteristics of the organization. Interest in such ethnographic work subsided as attention turned to more systematic studies across organizations that used quantitative measures of concepts and statistical analysis to describe patterns and relationships that held across context. Interest in the study of organizational culture gained renewed attention in the early 1980s, however, when a number of books on management written first by consultants and later by academics reached best seller status and captured the attention of managers and a general readership, as well as professors. Such studies purported to offer explanations for why U.S. industries were struggling at the time when Japanese industries were growing and prospering. Across these publications, there were wide variations in the definitions offered of organizational culture and disagreements on how and why understanding culture is important to business outcomes. Most studies of organizational culture endeavored to compare organizations with cultures that differed from each other (e.g., American firms to Japanese firms or successful American firms to less successful ones), and hence, they developed typologies or organizational profiles to distinguish organizations. In this body of literature, claims were often made that some kinds of organizational cultures were more productive or successful than others or that organizational culture had to be aligned with or consistent with the company environment and goals in order to be successful.

Through the development of this literature, many different typologies of organizational culture have been offered, with different names given to similar concepts by different authors. There are, though, some common themes about how organizations differ from each other that cut across this research. Perhaps of most interest in the literature is whether an organization's culture can be said to be strong or weak. A strong culture is assumed to be one that pervades the organization and where most organizational members understand and buy into the organization's values. In initial formulations, it was argued that having a strong culture was an essential element of organizational success. Later discussions, however, called attention to the difficulty organizations with strong cultures had adapting to and being willing to change as needed, leading to an effort to distinguish what about strong cultures was positive and what might have a dark side. Another major theme within the organizational culture literature is whether the culture of the organization gives preference to "hard" versus "soft" issues. Hard issues are defined as attention to the numbers, to the bottom line, and primarily to tasks. Soft issues are defined as concern for people, for hiring the right people, and fostering commitment and enthusiasm among organizational participants. William Ouchi's book *Theory Z* provides a good example of this argument.

Early proponents of the focus on organizational culture argued that U.S. firms were differentiated more in their attention to people than they were in their attention to the bottom line. Other researchers argued that the ability to innovate and adapt to change was the most important characteristic of successful organizations, so organizations were differentiated in terms of their adaptability versus stability. Along the same lines, within this same context, a lot of attention has been given to what has been called "learning organizations," or those that are able to get better over time, and both use existing knowledge among organizational members and build upon it. In some ways, a parallel literature on the characteristics of high-performance organizations is consistent with the research on organizational culture and especially with the effort to differentiate the characteristics of successful organizations from less successful ones.

One of the main critiques of the organizational culture literature, and especially of the attempts to develop typologies that presumed to characterize organizations and distinguish one from another, was that doing so did not sufficiently recognize that organizational cultures are complex; often differentiated across units, levels, and occupational groups; and that it may be a mischaracterization to assume that there is a unified culture in large, complex, and often global firms. Further, some argued that organizational culture, to the extent that it exists, may change as external circumstances change or as the skills, competencies, and internal composition of the firms change. In addition, some have argued that assumptions about the effects of organizational culture on organizational success were, on the one hand, manipulative and, on the other hand, naive to think that culture could so easily be managed or changed. Thus, the research literature on organizational culture has faced many of the same difficult conceptual and methodological issues that have been faced otherwise in fields that have tried to study culture, whether at the societal level, the organizational level, or the level of the group or team. Culture is an elusive concept because it is intended to describe something that is collective in concept but accessible only by studying what individuals do and what they understand. It is reflected in how people live their lives, but it is hidden from view even from the participants themselves. Culture, therefore, has to be interpreted as well as characterized or typified, and its meaning often depends on the standpoint and the purpose.

The major lesson managers should learn about typologies of organizational culture is that success depends on creating an environment that shapes the norms and behavior of organizational participants in ways that will serve the organization well as circumstances and competition change.

Nancy DiTomaso and Julia R. Eisenberg

See also High-Performance Work Systems; Meaning and Functions of Organizational Culture; Organizational Culture and Effectiveness; Organizational Culture Model; Organizational Culture Theory

Further Readings

Alvesson, M. (2002). *Understanding organizational culture.* London, England: Sage.

Arshanasy, N., Wilderom, C., & Peterson, M. (Eds.). (2000). *Handbook of organizational culture and climate.* Thousand Oaks, CA: Sage.

Cameron, K. S., & Quinn, R. E. (2006). *Diagnosing and changing organizational culture: Based on the competing values framework.* San Francisco, CA: Jossey-Bass.

Denison, D. R. (1990). *Corporate culture and organizational effectiveness.* New York, NY: Wiley.

Frost, P. J., Moore, L. F., Louis, M. R., Lundberg, C. C., & Martin, J. (1991). *Reframing organizational culture.* Thousand Oaks, CA: Sage.

Kilmann, R. H., Saxton, M. J., Serpa, R., & associates. (1985). *Gaining control of the corporate culture.* San Francisco, CA: Jossey-Bass.

Martin, J. (2002). *Organizational culture: Mapping the terrain.* Thousand Oaks, CA: Sage.

Ouchi, W. G. (1981). *Theory Z.* Reading, MA: Addison-Wesley.

Schein, E. H. (1985). *Organizational culture and leadership.* San Francisco, CA: Jossey-Bass.

Trice, H., & Beyer, J. (1993). *The cultures of work organizations.* New York, NY: Prentice Hall.

"Unstructured" Decision Making

For the better part of the past century, an increasing amount of attention has been paid to understanding how managers make decisions. Yet much of the available knowledge has settled on decisions that are rather common and repeatable, even if they are not easy to tackle. Far less attention has been given to the decision making that is required when conditions are the exception and not the norm. These conditions are considered to be "unstructured" and demand decision-making processes of their own. At present, managers have access to an abundance of studies and analyses about methods and processes for making decisions in every facet of the organization—operations, finances, marketing, sales, research and development, production, human resources, and so on. Many of the decisions made in these areas on a day-to-day or even hour-to-hour basis are rather routine, including those for the most complicated tasks and at the highest levels. Decisions of this sort are, essentially, tactical; that is, the conditions are largely prescribed, and the requirements are largely understood. The real challenge, therefore, is to organize the most efficient and effective way to accomplish the task. So, when it comes to the actual decision making, managers can often rely on experience and known patterns of what works because the solutions already exist. But there are conditions in which the standard decision-making process and prevailing solutions

are unsuitable. In these conditions, managers must go about developing a process for decision making that involves learning more about the situation, its elements and requirements, what objectives are relevant, and the results they hope to achieve. This entry provides an overview of research based on empirical observations of decision making in organizations and interviews with managers that was developed into a comprehensive model for "unstructured" decision making.

Fundamentals

Decisions are a primary responsibility of management. And the higher up managers are in the organizational hierarchy, the weightier, strategic, and far reaching are their decisions. One of the earliest dissections of decision making applied specifically to management was offered by Peter Drucker in the 1950s. He submitted that managerial decision making generally involves five general phases: definition of the problem, analysis of the problem, development of possible solutions, selection of a perceived best solution, and translation of the decision into action. But, Drucker cautioned, the entire process and its results can be thrown off because what is often identified as the problem is actually a symptom rather than the underlying issue. He also advised that, among other things, even the most prepared managers are likely to face realities in which making the right decisions is less dependent on accumulated experience than on systematic analysis. Taken to an extension, this suggests that strategic decisions are, by and large, unstructured.

Within the next 20 years, an increasing amount of research focused on managerial decision making, including a portion dedicated to the concept that strategic decisions are, by nature, generally unstructured. In a study led by Henry Mintzberg, researchers analyzed 25 strategic decision-making processes in organizations and proposed that a framework does exist for unstructured decision making. Unlike in structured decision environments, in which an alternative is given, but its consequences are not definitive, unstructured decision environments involve conditions in which neither an alternative nor its consequences are easily established. Put another way, there is a distinction between uncertainty and ambiguity, with unstructured decisions falling into the latter category, distinguished by their unconventional and changing conditions, intricate steps, indeterminable boundaries for factors such as time, pressures both internal and external, and how little is understood at the outset about the situation and its possible solutions.

But the Mintzberg study is even more significant because it offers a model for categorizing decisions according to the specific stimulus for decision making, the solutions, and the decision-making process used to arrive at those decisions. According to the study, decision making is stimulated not only by some event but also by its perceived magnitude across a continuum. On one end of the continuum is the opportunity decision, which is initiated as a means to improving an already stable condition or comfortable position. On the other end is the crisis decision, which is initiated in response to conditions that have amounted to and reached a tipping point. In between these extremes lies the problem decision. Further, depending on the timing of managerial action and resources devoted to the condition, there may also be opportunity-problem decisions and problem-crisis decisions. Yet in whichever category the decision is placed, the researchers propose that a solution can then be classified in one of four ways: "given" (fully developed at the start of the process), "ready-made" (developed organically during the process), "custom-made" (developed specifically for the decision), or a combination of "ready-made" and "custom-made," in which a ready-made solution is modified and adapted for the situation. For all of this, however, it may be that the decision-making process itself has the most to recommend about strategic, unstructured decisions.

Mintzberg and his colleagues suggest that the decision-making process comprises an identification phase, developmental phase, and selection phase:

Identification. The identification phase includes two routines: recognition of an opportunity, problem, or crisis that requires a decision be made; and diagnosis of the stimuli and relationships associated with the situation. It is typical that both opportunity and crisis decisions are set off by a single stimulus, whereas problem decisions are evoked by multiple stimuli. Any stimulus originates either inside the organization or outside of it, but it must individually or in concert with other stimuli reach a threshold level before decision makers recognize that they face an unfamiliar situation. Once they accept this reality, they can then diagnose the situation by drawing on existing information and collecting new information. The information gathering may be accomplished through formal or informal means and, in either case, is the beginning of the decision-making process.

Development. The developmental phase entails using a search routine, in which different types of methodologies may be used to identify ready-made solutions to the situation, and a design routine, in which a solution is developed through innovation. This phase also often requires a decision be rendered in light of associated decisions at several points along the way. In the search routine, solutions may come from institutional memory within the organization, unsolicited outside sources, specifically informed outside sources, and direct attention to finding a solution by conducting an environmental scan. In the design routine, custom-made and modified solutions are developed, though often in small amounts; both types of solutions can be expensive and in terms of time, money, and labor. Decision makers often choose the search routine over the design routine because the trade-off in costs is smaller.

Selection. Development of solutions is tightly bound to the selection phase, the stage in the decision-making process where an ultimate decision is achieved. But because so many factors may need to be considered at this point, the selection phase may inevitably include several steps of investigation of solution alternatives, any of which may be based on a combination of judgment, bargaining, and analysis. Throughout all of this, there can be natural and human factors—expected or not—that interrupt or constrain the process and cause the decision makers to return to the developmental phase. At a point, however, an appropriate solution is certain to emerge and become available for authorization by the respective level of management. To arrive at a solution, decision makers employ a pattern in which they generally filter the range of available alternatives so that they have a manageable amount and reasonable options to work from ("screening"), mine these options and select a plan of action ("evaluation-choice"), and, finally, gain endorsement from higher levels within the organizational hierarchy (authorization).

The above general model, Mintzberg and his colleagues determined, could serve seven types of path configuration, each dependent on the solutions and factors developed earlier on in the decision-making process. The different types of path configurations range from a "simple impasse," such as when a policy proposal is considered several times over and rejected on each occasion, to a complex matter that stems from changing dimensions in virtually every facet of the organization, situation, and environment.

Importance

While the Mintzberg-led study was not alone at the time in an aim to sketch a framework for "unstructured" decision making, it is generally considered to be high among the most comprehensive and classic analyses of the subject. The researchers make a decided and important reference to other studies that suggest the human element must be accounted for as underlying the stresses and strains of the decision-making process. In the interim, and despite all manner of studies concentrated on decision-making frameworks and matrices, a considerable amount of research from various areas of psychology and, increasingly, behavioral economics indicates that people generally have a deficient understanding of the policies and procedures they use in accomplishing decisions. Moreover, the research often demonstrates that people's thoughts and actions are usually more irrational than conventional wisdom would lead anyone to believe.

Whether at the individual, group, or organizational level, people have a natural tendency to frame and describe decision problems and alternative solutions in ways that are personally beneficial and that engage selective memory. They basically employ cognitive biases—mental actions based on knowledge and experience—as a means to managing the typical overflows of information they encounter. From a behavioral perspective, this might be expressed in a range of actions such as automatically rejecting new information in favor of maintaining the status quo (the so-called Semmelweis reflex) or complacently accepting information that supports a prior assertion. It may be expected that these and similar biases will arise with greater intensity in unstructured decision-making situations than in structured ones.

Another aspect to consider is to what extent cultural perspectives about decision making play a role. For example, the Japanese style of decision making bears little resemblance to the Western style. The Japanese decision-making process involves several cycles of understanding, review, and comment by managers at various levels; also, unlike throughout much of the Western world, the Japanese regard management as an organ of the enterprise and not master of it. It is a time-consuming approach, especially from the Western perspective. But it is an approach that inevitably concentrates decision making on the larger, strategic issues rather than the smaller, tactical ones.

Ultimately, a decision is a judgment of alternatives. This is a risk-taking venture and, thus, requires that hypotheses about a situation be developed and tested, with facts then determined by relevant criteria. It also then requires feedback mechanisms, which are built from available information as well as exposure to the realities of the situation. This is all the more imperative considering that managements are responsible for putting knowledge to work throughout an organization—and that includes how to put people with different skills and knowledge together to achieve common goals. All of this may be amplified in situations that are perceived to be extraordinary and without existing stepwise procedures. But, as in any decision-making process, what is of central importance is an understanding of the basic problem and management's orientation toward action around it.

Lee H. Igel

See also Decision-Making Styles; Intuitive Decision Making; Managerial Decision Biases; Needs Hierarchy; Strategic Decision Making

Further Readings

Argyris, C. (1991). Teaching smart people how to learn. *Harvard Business Review, 69*(3), 99–109.

Ariely, D. (2008). *Predictably irrational: The hidden forces that shape our decisions.* New York, NY: HarperCollins.

Drucker, P. F. (1954). *The practice of management.* New York, NY: Harper & Row.

Drucker, P. F. (1974). *Management: Tasks, responsibilities, practices.* New York, NY: Harper & Row.

Kahneman, D., Slovic, P., & Tversky, A. (1982). *Judgment under uncertainty: Heuristics and biases.* Cambridge, England: Cambridge University Press.

Mintzberg, H., Raisinghani, D., & Théorêt, A. The structure of "unstructured" decision processes. *Administrative Science Quarterly, 21*(2), 246–275.

Bar-Zohar, M. (2007). *Shimon Peres: A biography.* New York, NY: Random House.

Ross, L., & Nisbett, R. E. (1991). *The person and the situation: Perspectives of social psychology.* New York, NY: McGraw-Hill.

UPPER-ECHELONS THEORY

The upper-echelons theory (also referred to as "top management team" theory) focuses on a firm's top executives. They include chairman, chief executive officer, heads of business divisions, and other general managers. Upper-echelon members collectively represent the most vital human capital of the firm. The top management team can be a source of competitive advantage of the firm and a key determinant of the firm's financial and nonfinancial performance. Firms such as General Electric (GE), Federal Express (FedEx), and Walt Disney are admired in the business press because their top management teams are judged to be superior in quality. Along the same lines, when firms fail, as Enron did in 2001, the top management team is held responsible. The theory focuses on two interrelated questions: Why do the top management teams do what they do—in terms of actions, decisions, and choices? What are the consequences of what the team does to the organization as a whole? The theory looks at the top management team as a whole rather than at individuals within the team. A general argument for treating the whole team as a unit of analysis is that it would be more productive in explaining what firms do and their performance. The following sections elaborate upon the theory, its validity, and its limitations.

Fundamentals

Chester Barnard wrote the seminal book on the functions of the executive in 1938 and pushed top executives to the front and center of management theory. Even though the environment in which the firm resides constrains its top executives from doing certain things, powerful top executives can overcome these constraints and assert their choices. The Harvard Business School, pursuing an emphasis on top executives, has shown that top executives' values, beliefs, and personal preferences play a role in what they do. When presented with the same situation, different executives may notice different aspects of the situation and act accordingly. The interpretation of the situation by the executive is shaped by several characteristics such as functional background, ethnic background, and nationality. As Donald Hambrick and Phyllis Mason put it in a seminal paper that crystallized the upper-echelons theory, an organization is a reflection of its top managers. And what the organization does and performance of the organization may be attributed to the upper echelons. The theory also has intellectual roots in the Carnegie school: It argues that executives, as human beings, have limitations—they engage in a rather limited search for solutions, cope with information overload, and deal with organizational politics—and, therefore, executives' behaviors may not be that rational. This is in sharp contrast to the neoclassic approach that assumes that organizations act like machines, act rationally, and make decisions to optimize or maximize.

Identifying Top Management Team Members

Members of the upper echelon are the most powerful individuals in the firm, have vast networks of relationships within and outside the firm, and often have celebrity status. They perform the boundary-spanning tasks for the firm by connecting the firm to its environment.

There are two approaches to identifying the top management team members. A more inclusive approach, based on the titles and formal positions, considers the chairman of the board of directors, chief executive officer, president, chief financial officer, and other senior executives as top management team members. An alternative approach starts with the specific decision that is under consideration, such as going global, and includes the top executives that are directly involved in the decision (e.g., the chief executive officer, senior marketing executive, senior operations executive) and excludes the others. This approach suggests that subteams exist within a top management team and the particular executives involved and the number of executives engaged will differ depending on the decision to be made. For this reason, the former approach is relatively more convenient.

Top Management Team Characteristics

An executive's construction of reality may not correspond to the reality as construed by other executives or to an "objective" reality. What the executive sees or does not see is determined by a variety of attributes:

Background characteristics. The demographic characteristics (e.g., average age of the top management team) affect its actions (e.g., a decision to diversify into a risky business) and firm outcomes (e.g., growth of the firm). The background characteristics are simple to work with, but it is difficult to identify and interpret the mechanisms through which these characteristics move the top management teams to act in certain ways and not others. Therefore, the relationship between top management team's background characteristics and its actions and outcomes of these actions is not obvious and remains a black box. Notwithstanding the above noted challenge, several background characteristics of top management teams (e.g., educational and functional background of the executives and the duration for which executives have been employed with a firm and within an industry) are found to be reliable predictors of how the team will act and what the outcomes of these actions will be.

Process-related characteristics. In contrast to the top management team's background characteristics, a number of team process-related characteristics attempt to describe the way the team members relate to one another (e.g., collaborate or compete), the way the team members share information in arriving at a decision, the frequency with which they communicate with one another, and conflicts between members at either a personal level or on account of political tensions between different parts of the firm. These process-related characteristics collectively capture how the team functions. The assumption here is that certain background characteristics determine the way the team functions, and this, in turn, explains the team's actions, the speed with which the team acts, and the consequences of these actions.

Roles of Other Variables

Upper-echelons theory rests on two key assumptions: The theory assumes that the top executives of a firm all act as a team. In order for the assumption to hold, team members must be behaviorally integrated—that is, all members are engaged and collectively work toward the common good of the firm. In the absence of such behavioral integration, team members' characteristics may not explain what the team does, why it does what it does, and also consequences of its actions for the firm as a whole.

The second assumption is that the top management team has alternatives to work with and choose from within this array of alternatives. However, not all situations present top executives with alternatives to choose from—some situations may present more choices than others. Accordingly, top executives may not have much discretion in all situations. Recent writings on the theory of upper echelons suggest that managerial discretion may be relatively high:

- In the case of activities that are complex and activities where there is a high degree of uncertainty or opaqueness with respect to execution and outcomes
- In firms that are entrepreneurial (vs. bureaucratic), have a ready disposition to change and adapt (vs. maintain status quo), or have abundant resources (vs. meager resources); likewise, demands placed by various stakeholders (e.g., owners and the society at large) in the firm to meet their expectation may impact the managerial discretion of the top management team.

- In industries that are dynamic, growing, and subject to rapid changes and innovations (vs. industries that are stable, stagnant, and subject to minimal innovation) and in which there is room for differentiation (vs. commoditization)

In the final analysis, how much managerial discretion there is and how many alternatives top executives have to choose from in a given situation is up to the individual's entrepreneurial orientation. An executive who thinks and acts like an entrepreneur is opportunity-driven (seeks out opportunities) rather than resource-driven (feels constrained by the resource situation), and tends to "discover" alternatives even when none seem present.

In sum, managerial discretion acts as a third variable in that it tends to enhance or diminish the relationship between top management team characteristics and what actions they take and the consequences of their actions for the firm.

Importance

The seminal work by Hambrick and Mason in 1984 offered a big impetus to the study of the role played by a firm's top executives. Their work has spawned a significant spurt of research on top management teams not only in the field of management but also in adjacent fields, such as psychology and sociology. According to Web of Science index, there were over one thousand citations of their work at the time this entry was written. This high and growing citation figure demonstrates the continuing interest in upper echelons—the theory and its significance to practice. Chief executive officers, such as Henry Ford, Sam Walton, Bill Gates, and Steve Jobs are recognized for their leadership and contributions to their industries, the global economy, and the society at large. They receive much attention in management research and in the business press. Their decisions and actions have the power to change the world.

Upper-echelons theory has been tested in a wide range of situations in which top management teams play vital roles. The catalog of studies is thick: Studies have tested the theory with respect to growth strategies and growth rates of firms, adaptation of firms to major threats (such as the threats posed to the tobacco companies by the Surgeon General's warning about smoking and cancer), changes in corporate strategy, strategic process, propensity to take risks, decisions to go global, and the adoption of technological and administrative innovations, to mention only a few. The upper-echelons theory also has been tested in both large and small corporations and in both established businesses and new ventures. The relatively consistent results speak to the overall robustness of the theory and its relevance in a wide range of situations.

One limitation, however, is that the theory has been tested mostly in the context of U.S. firms or on executives within just one country such as the United Kingdom. Top executives are products of their environment; they are groomed by the society at large, culture, and national systems, such as the educational system. Some national systems produce a relatively homogeneous pool of top executives, whereas other systems may produce a relatively heterogeneous pool. The upper-echelons theory relies on having a relatively diverse pool of executives within the top management team. Absent a supply of a diverse pool of executives, the impact of top management teams on their respective firms' actions and performance may be weak.

From the standpoint of management practice, upper-echelons theory and its findings offer modern managers several useful guidelines. Managers must *match* top management teams and organization strategies: Different teams may be effective in formulating and executing different types of strategies. For example, top management teams that are dominated by executives with experience in marketing and in research and development may very aptly pursue an innovation-based strategy. In contrast to that, teams that are dominated by executives with engineering and finance background may be appropriate to pursue a defensive strategy. When initiating major strategic changes, executives must include appropriate changes in the executive suite among the portfolio of changes. Since different executives may be effective in different contexts—industry and organization contexts—hiring top executives from a different context, specifically a different industry, could cut both ways. It all depends on whether the new hire "fits" in the new situation.

Rajeswararao Chaganti

See also Core Competence; Organizational Demography; Organizational Structure and Design; Strategy and Structure

Further Readings

Carpenter, M. A. (Ed.). (2011). *The handbook of research on top management teams*. Northhampton, MA: Edward Elgar.

Carpenter, M. A., Geletkancyz, M. A., & Sanders, G. W. (2004). Upper echelons research revisited: Antecedents, elements, and consequences of top management team composition. *Journal of Management, 30*(6), 749–778.

Dansereau, F., & Yammarino, F. J. (Ed.). (2004). *Research in multi-level issues* (Vol. 4, Especially Part III: Upper echelons). New York, NY: Elsevier.

Finkelstein, S., Hambrick, D. C., & Cannella, A. A., Jr. (2008). *Strategic leadership: Theory and research on executives, top management teams, and boards*. New York, NY: Oxford University Press.

Hambrick, D. C. (2007). Upper echelons theory: An update. *Academy of Management Review, 33*(2), 334–343.

Hambrick, D. C., & Mason, P. A. (1984). Upper echelons: The organization as a reflection of its top managers. *Academy of Management Review, 9*(2), 193–206.

Mayo, A. J., & Nohria, N. (2005). *In their time: The greatest business leaders of the twentieth century*. Boston, MA: Harvard Business School Press.

VALUE CHAIN

The value chain is a theory of the firm: a description and explanation of how business firms make profits by producing and trading goods and services. It also serves as an analytical tool managers can use to choose and organize their firms' activities in order to gain and sustain advantage over competitors—to maximize profits. The central idea of the value chain is that by processing inputs, such as raw materials, into end products that they sell, business firms create value for their customers either in the form of low prices (like Tata Cars of India) or some other feature such as high-product quality for which customers are willing to pay a premium (such as Mercedes-Benz). If the customers' willingness to pay for the firm's goods or services exceeds its cost of providing them, the firm makes a profit. The value chain consists of a sequence of primary activities involved in converting inputs into outputs as well as support activities such as research and development and human resource management. By optimizing each activity either by lowering its costs or by enhancing its contribution to other qualities valued by customers—so that each activity adds value to the final product—managers strive to outperform their firms' competitors and thus to maximize profits. This entry starts with a brief description of the concepts of economic value and value creation. It then explains the idea of a firm (and an industry) as a value chain and identifies the activities of which the chain consists, illustrated with examples. The theory's contribution to the theory of the firm is also explained, as is its managerial application in creating and sustaining competitive advantage for firms. The limitations of value chain are discussed next, followed by a description of further developments and offshoots of the theory. The theory's importance and relevance to managerial practice is then assessed. Finally, further reading on the value chain is suggested.

Fundamentals

The purpose of business firms is to create maximum economic value (profit) for their owners through producing and trading goods and services. But in order to create value for shareholders, firms must first create value for their customers. This happens when customers perceive the product or service they purchase more valuable than the price they pay for it—such as when they walk out of the store with their purchase, thinking "this was a good deal." But having customers willing to pay for a company's products is not enough by itself to create value for shareholders. The cost of producing and trading goods and services must also be lower than the price customers are willing to pay. So the fundamental task of a firm's managers is to make the gap between what customers are willing to pay (price) and cost of providing products as wide as possible.

Widening the gap between customers' willingness to pay and the firm's costs can be achieved in two basic ways: lowering costs and increasing customers' willingness to pay by enhancing the quality of products and services or some other factor (such as customer service) so that a higher price can be obtained. Examples of both of these can be found in the airline industry. This is how the value chain theory can be applied: It shows managers how to tailor all of the firm's activities systematically to either lower costs or to enhance customers' willingness to pay. Southwest Airlines and Ryanair are good examples of lowering costs in all of their activities from ticket purchase to baggage handling to onboard service and thus creating value for their customers in the form of low prices. A regional Canadian carrier, Toronto-based Porter Airlines, is an example of increasing the customers' willingness to pay through its activities. Porter has done it by offering convenience (operating an airport next to downtown) and added services (a comfortable lounge for all passengers, complimentary alcoholic beverages on board, etc.).

Primary Activities

The value creation chain of a firm consists of the following primary activities:

- Inbound logistics
- Operations
- Outbound logistics
- Marketing and sales
- After-sales service

The personal computer manufacturer Dell is an example of how a company is able to successfully lower costs or enhance customer willingness to pay, or both, in each of these activities. Based on the Harvard Business School case "Matching Dell," the following discussion describes Dell's value creation activities when it was the unrivaled leader in the personal computer (PC) industry in the mid-to-late 1990s. The fundamental characteristic of Dell's business model was direct distribution. In contrast to competitors, it did not use any retailers as middlemen; all PCs were manufactured to order and shipped directly to customers.

In its *inbound logistics,* Dell closely coordinated with their component suppliers by sharing information to help suppliers to become more efficient and by encouraging suppliers to locate near Dell's manufacturing plants, in order to reduce shipping costs. More importantly, the co-location shortened the time to deliver parts. Dell had its parts delivered just-in-time (JIT)—within 90 minutes of order.

Dell increased the efficiency of its *operations* by assembling PCs only to order: No assembly took place until an order was received. This meant that Dell held no finished goods inventory—a significant cost reduction. Building PCs to order and using a JIT component delivery required only very limited raw materials or work-in-progress inventories as well, which was particularly important in reducing costs as PC component prices were decreasing rapidly. Dell increased customers' willingness to pay by allowing them to "customize" their PCs from a wide range of choices and by installing customers' proprietary software upon request. (Knowledgeable customers who appreciated this were targeted explicitly).

The costs of *outbound logistics* at Dell were reduced by shipping directly to customers—no warehousing was needed. Components, such as monitors, that were sourced from outside suppliers never passed through Dell's facilities but were shipped directly to customers. This approach worked well with Dell's knowledgeable customers who did not need to go to a retail store to see PCs and to get information from a sales clerk—and it saved time and money for them and for Dell.

Marketing and sales—the starting point of the value chain for Dell—also differed from what was typical in the industry. Instead of selling PCs to distributors and retailers, Dell took orders directly from the end customers (mostly businesses and government departments but also home users and educational institutions). Not having an outside sales and distribution channel—which Dell's knowledgeable customers did not need—reduced Dell's costs significantly. Dell employed a large outside sales force that worked in the field, obtaining valuable information about customers' needs and thus helping forecast and find ways of enhancing customers' willingness to pay. Inside sales people at call centers helped customers place orders, but increasingly, ordering was done online, further reducing costs.

Dell offered *after-sales service* in many ways. Technical support was available through a 24-hour hotline and through tens of thousands of pages of online information. Most problems were solved over the phone and by using diagnostic software installed in all Dell PCs. For problems requiring a site visit, Dell contracted the services of outside companies. In essence, Dell was offering after-sale service comparable to retailers but at lower cost and typically much faster.

Support Activities

The above primary value chain activities are facilitated by support activities that enable further reduction of costs or help enhance customers' willingness to pay. Michael Porter identified four such activities:

- Firm infrastructure
- Human resource management
- Technological development
- Procurement

Firm infrastructure refers to things such as organizational structure (e.g., few management layers to reduce costs or to enhance customer responsiveness) and various management systems (e.g., planning, accounting, information systems) for lowering costs and/or increasing customer willingness to pay. Dell's infrastructure included hiring experienced managers from other companies to help the transition from a small business Michael Dell started in his college dorm room to the industry leader Dell had become by the mid-1990s. These managers introduced formal control systems and monitored Dell's costs and performance systematically. The finance function, also part of firm infrastructure, was an important aspect of lowering costs for Dell. Dell did not pay its suppliers until it received money from its customers; therefore, the company did not have to bear the normal costs of financing. In essence, customers were financing Dell.

There is no specific information available about human resource management practices or technological development at Dell. However, companies use the *human resource management function* to lower costs and/or enhance customer willingness to pay by devising effective hiring, training, motivation, and compensation practices. Consider Google's practices of using small teams to enhance speed and creativity and providing "80–20" work-fun time—designed to boost innovation for products that attract more end users and, thus, customers. Similarly, *technological development* can facilitate lowering costs or introducing new products with attractive new features that garner premium prices. An example of the former is Laitram limited liability company, a New Orleans-based global manufacturer of industrial equipment that was founded in the 1940s on the invention of a shrimp-peeling machine that revolutionized the shrimp processing industry. An example

of the latter is Apple, Incorporated, which has successfully introduced several new products, from MacBooks to iPads, for which customers are willing to pay a premium.

The last support activity, *procurement,* can pay a significant role in lowering a company's costs or enhancing the quality of its products. This involves sourcing lowest cost raw materials or suppliers that offer the highest quality and monitoring suppliers' performance. Dell achieved cost savings in its procurement function by reducing its number of suppliers from 250 to 50 and working closely with them to help lower their costs.

While the focus here has been on the value chain within firms, it should be noted that entire industries can be conceptualized as value chains. Consider, for example, the furniture industry. The industry value chain starts with the production of raw materials, such as wood. Manufacturers design furniture, source the raw materials, and construct the furniture. Some manufacturers may be involved in distributing and selling their products, whereas others are not. By analyzing the industry value chain, furniture companies can determine in which activities they can lower costs or enhance customer willingness to pay more than their competitors do and focus on those activities. For example, the global furniture retailer IKEA does not manufacture any furniture but maximizes its margins by designing, distributing, and selling it.

Evolution

The value chain is a relatively young theory: It was introduced by Michael Porter of Harvard Business School in his book *Competitive Advantage* in 1985. Porter first developed a theory of competitive strategy, wanting to contribute to the fledgling field of strategic management. Drawing from industrial organization economics (which analyzes structures of industries and predicts their evolution), Porter argued that firms can gain advantage over their competitors by finding positions (either through lower costs or other differentiation from competitors) in the industry that are sheltered from the competitive forces: the threat of new entrants, the bargaining power of suppliers and buyers, competitive rivalry, and the threat of substitute products. For example, a firm such as Nike has positional advantage through its strong brand name. The brand name protects

Nike not only against the threat of new entrants in the athletic shoe and apparel industry but also against the bargaining power of its customers and suppliers and against its existing competitors. (There are no real substitutes for athletic shoes.)

This theory of competitive advantage being based on position was criticized as too static and not accounting for the dynamic nature of competition among firms. In other words, it did not explain *how* firms gain and sustain their position amid the competitive forces that are trying to counteract the firms' efforts. In response to the criticism, Porter developed the value chain as a more dynamic framework and a tool for analyzing how firms can identify, develop, and perform activities in each stage of the chain in order to gain a sustainable competitive position, based on either lower costs than competitors or on some way of differentiating from them.

The value chain theory has remained unchanged in its fundamentals, but extensions, such as value shops and customer participation in value creation, as discussed below, have been added.

Importance

The value chain theory has generated substantial empirical research, particularly company-specific case studies. The breadth of the theory and its complex variables has delimited its statistical validation and therefore its ability to predict firms' behavior. However, case study researchers describe and explain behavior of firms thus helping scholars understand why Dell, IKEA, Nike, and others make the choices they do regarding value creation activities. A number of teaching cases, such as "Matching Dell" and "Zara—Fast Fashion," based on the value chain framework have been developed and are some of the most widely used in business school courses on competitive strategy. The value chain is also invariably included in strategy textbooks as a tool of competitive strategy for analyzing industry and firm-level value creation.

The impact of the value chain theory is not limited to business schools and the academia alone. It is used widely by management consultants, and there are professional and industry associations dedicated to helping their members manage and optimize their value chains. The value chain is a theory that has proven its applicability and is being used widely in managerial practice.

Where Does the Value Chain Theory Apply?

The value chain theory conceptualizes the firm, and the industry, as a value creation chain in which raw materials or components are converted into more or less standardized end products and sold and distributed to customers in a routinized sequence of stages (as discussed above). Therefore, the value chain is best applied to companies and industries that create value in a predictable sequence of routines, mostly in manufacturing, distribution, and retail. Good examples of companies that can be conceptualized as value chains are chemical and car manufacturers, or supermarket and restaurant chains. However, when firms create value in non-routine ways that do not involve a sequential chain of predictable activities, such as professional service companies, value chain is less applicable as a description and prediction of a firm's activities.

Professional service firms—for example, in architecture, engineering, health care, law, and management consulting, or research and development units within companies—create value by solving client problems that are often unique. Such problem solving does not consist of sequential, routine activities but rather nonroutine, iterative processes that depend on any given client's unique context and needs. Therefore, such firms or units are best characterized as "value shops" (labeled after a mechanic's shop). In value shops, the central issue is not lowering costs (although they cannot be ignored) but finding a solution to a client's problem, whether it has to do with health or productivity of his business. In order to find effective solutions to clients' problems at acceptable cost, value shops need to have a right combination of resources given the type of problems they are solving. Cancer clinics need different resources than do cardiac wards at hospitals. Similarly, management consultants specializing in productivity problems need a different set of resources than consultants focusing on mergers and acquisitions. The value shops, but also many other firms, require their clients' active participation in order to optimize the value creation process. For example, Dell's customers "design" their own PCs from a broad menu of choices, IKEA's customers transport and assemble their own furniture, and at the Mayo Clinic, the outpatients improve their own care with online guidance.

The Value Chain as a Theory of the Firm and a Tool of Competitive Strategy

All theories of the firm aim to explain how firms maximize profits. Many focus on questions such as how firms should be governed (the agency theory), or whether firms should produce their own components and products, or whether they should source them from outside (the transaction cost theory). The value chain theory is broader than these theories in that it covers the entire value creation process by explaining in which activities a firm optimally engages, including governance. The breadth delimits the theory's exactness, however: It does not explain *how* to perform each activity better than competitors. The value chain is complemented by other theories, such as the resource-based view of the firm, which identifies resources and capabilities for performing value activities.

It should be noted that the value chain is intended for the analysis of profit maximization at the level of a business unit (such as a division of a corporation or a company operating in a single industry), although it can help identify how business units of a corporation can share value activities, such as a shared sales force for the household goods and the personal products divisions at Procter & Gamble Company.

The systematic and integrated nature of the value chain theory also makes it helpful as a tool of competitive strategy. Managers can analyze the industry value chain to determine in which stages their companies should participate to maximize profits. Once the firm's value creation stages have been chosen, the managers can use the value chain to identify the optimal activities in each stage in order to lower costs or to increase customer willingness to pay.

Jaana Woiceshyn

See also Business Policy and Corporate Strategy; Competitive Advantage; Core Competence; Dynamic Capabilities

Further Readings

Normann, R., & Ramirez, R. (1993, July/August). From value chain to value constellation: Designing interactive strategy. *Harvard Business Review*, 65–77.

Porter, M. E. (1980). *Competitive strategy.* New York, NY: Free Press.

Porter, M. E. (1985). *Competitive advantage.* New York, NY: Free Press.

Porter, M. E. (1999, November/December). What is strategy? *Harvard Business Review*, 61–78.

Ramirez, R. (1999). Value co-production: Intellectual origins and implications for practice and research. *Strategic Management Journal, 20*(1), 49–65.

Rivkin, J. W., & Porter, M. E. (1999). *Matching Dell.* Boston, MA: Harvard Business School.

Sheehan, N. T., & Foss, N. J. (2009). Exploring the roots of Porter's activity-based view. *Journal of Strategy and Management, 2*(3), 240–260.

Stabell, C. B., & Fjeldstad, Ø. D. (1998). Configuring value for competitive advantage: On chains, shops and networks. *Strategic Management Journal, 19,* 414–437.

Woiceshyn, J., & Falkenberg, L. (2008). Value creation in knowledge-based firms: Aligning problems and resources. *Academy of Management Perspectives, 22*(2), 85–99.

VIRTUAL TEAMS

Virtual teams are gaining in popularity in today's global, technologically advanced business environment. They help companies leverage their global expertise and knowledge, promote broader participation in decision making, take advantage of time differences to get more work done (e.g., following the sun), and lower travel costs. However, reaping these benefits presents unique challenges. This entry describes these challenges and addresses factors and the life cycle that must be managed to overcome the challenges and make virtual teams effective. It concludes with research insights. *Virtual teams* may be defined as two or more people who (a) work together interdependently with mutual accountability for achieving common goals, (b) do not work in either the same place and/or at the same time, and (c) must use electronic communication technology to communicate, coordinate their activities, and complete their team's tasks. Initially, virtual teams were seen as the opposite of conventional, proximate teams who meet face-to-face. However, this binary view of a team as either virtual or not is rather simplistic, and researchers are now struggling to assess the degree of virtuality of teams, which typically includes some combination of points b and c above.

Fundamentals

Virtual teams, which are alternatively called distributed and geographically dispersed teams, frequently face three major challenges to a greater extent than proximate teams: communication, technology, and team diversity challenges. Communication challenges stem from the use of lean media that make it difficult for members to convey nuances and ambiguity in their messages. Virtual members need to learn to work with new technologies, and organizations must ensure adequate technological support for virtual teams. Finally, many virtual teams are composed of members who come from different national, societal, and organizational cultures. A challenge for members and leaders in diverse virtual teams is to deal effectively with different languages and cultures.

The virtual team literature draws from a wide range of disciplines including organizational behavior, human resources, communication, psychology, and information systems. Early virtual team studies relied heavily on findings from prior research on teams, small groups, group support systems, and computer-mediated communications. Defining a team as a single, identifiable phenomenon (i.e., virtual or not) meant that much early research used lab experiments with student subjects to compare proximate teams with virtual teams. While early studies surfaced challenges faced by virtual teams, they provided only limited insights about how to deal with these challenges. Further, several thorough reviews of the literature noted the contradictory findings of these early studies. The remainder of the early research tended to be anecdotal and descriptive of team characteristics, costs, benefits, and challenges.

Inputs-Processes-Outputs (IPO) Models

Broadly defined, inputs-processes-outputs (IPO) models often focus on combinations of factors of virtual team inputs, processes, and outputs. Inputs include team composition, culture, task, and training; processes include a heavy focus on communicating, collaborating, building trust, resolving conflicts, building relationships, leading, and more recently on knowledge sharing; outputs include performance, team member satisfaction, and team well-being. Virtual team research to date has combined two or three of these factors at a time. Typical studies might look at how various types of conflict reduce team member satisfaction or how various collaboration strategies enhance knowledge sharing and decision quality. In total, research based on IPO models suggests that all of the inputs and processes mentioned above are important factors in improving virtual team outputs.

Life Cycle Model

In contrast to the IPO models is one which describes stages in a virtual team's life cycle (i.e., preparation, launch, performance management, team development, and disbanding). In life cycle models, teams are formed, their work is completed, and the team is disbanded. But in this cycle, team members learn to work not only with specific individuals but also as virtual teams. So the concept of disbanding and then forming new teams with the same people or new ones makes the concept of team development very important.

Insights

No single model is widely used by virtual team researchers. Virtual team research covers a gamut of issues and has yielded a number of insights that are beneficial to practitioners (e.g., schedule synchronous meetings regularly, establish technology and communication norms early, match technology tools with the task and team members, build trust early and sustain it throughout the life cycle, employ leadership strategies to motivate remote workers, and measure performance using clearly defined deliverables). It clearly shows that virtual teams cannot be managed just like proximate teams.

Virtual team research is likely to thrive as long as virtual teams remain important to today's businesses and their management remains an enigma. Researchers and practitioners alike will continue striving to understand what processes and team characteristics can overcome virtual team challenges and make teams effective over their life cycle.

Carol Saunders

See also Cultural Values; Group Punctuated Equilibrium Model; High- and Low-Context Cultures; High-Performing Teams; Knowledge Workers; Leadership Practices; Multicultural Work Teams; Trust

Further Readings

Cohen, C. B., & Gibson, S. G. (2003). *Virtual teams that work: Creating conditions for virtual team effectiveness.* San Francisco, CA: Jossey-Bass.

Duarte, D. L., & Snyder, N. T. (1999). *Mastering virtual teams.* San Francisco, CA: Jossey-Bass.

Hertel, G., Geister, S., & Konradt, U. (2005). Managing virtual teams: A review of current empirical research. *Human Resource Management Review, 15,* 69–95.

Lipnack, J., & Stamps, J. (1997). *Virtual teams.* New York, NY: Wiley.

Martin, L. L, Gilson, L. L., & Maynard, M. T. (2004). Virtual teams: What do we know and where do we go from here? *Journal of Management, 30,* 805–835.

Powell, A., Piccoli, G., & Ives, B. (2004). Virtual teams: A review of current literature and directions for future research. *Data Base for Advances in Information Systems, 35,* 6–36.

Schweitzer, L., & Duxbury, L. (2010). Conceptualizing and measuring the virtuality of teams. *Information Systems Journal, 20,* 267–295.

WORK TEAM EFFECTIVENESS

Work teams are defined as interdependent collections of individuals who share responsibility for specific outcomes in their organizations. Two elements of this definition are worth emphasizing. First, *interdependence* indicates that team members depend on each other to do their work. Consider a basketball or softball team where each person depends on the others when trying to produce a win. Second, team members share responsibility for delivering a certain product or result to the organization or larger *social system* within which they operate. These two elements of how teams function are important to keep in mind when considering theories of team effectiveness. Theories of team effectiveness address the definition of effectiveness, seek to identify factors that predict it, and explain how those factors operate. Examples include early models of team performance offered by Joseph E. McGrath as well as later ones focused on effectiveness, such as those offered by Susan G. Cohen and Diane E. Bailey, Steve W. J. Kozlowski, John E. Mathieu, Eric D. Sundstrom, and others. Team effectiveness should be conceptualized as part of a multilevel system with individual-, team-, and organizational-level factors and that requires special attention to the context within which teams perform their tasks. Team contexts are multifaceted and this, among other challenges, has prevented research on teams from being readily and consistently applied to real organizational situations. In the following section, a history of team effectiveness is briefly considered. Next, different approaches to team effectiveness are discussed and suggestions are made regarding which approaches are most relevant. Finally, a discussion of the validity and impact of the most relevant approaches to team effectiveness is provided.

Fundamentals

The application of work teams is centuries old. However, the documentation of their application in book chapters and research articles often begins with the Hawthorne studies conducted in the 1920s and 1930s, which included a series of empirical investigations of factors related to group outcomes. During this time period, however, the vast majority of organizational work was still performed by individual employees. The exceptions were primarily from military and manufacturing environments (i.e., cockpit and tank crews and informal automobile assembly teams). After the Hawthorne studies, the majority of interest in work teams was expressed by researchers rather than managers. In other words, the rate of research increased, whereas the application of work teams did not. Much of the early research involving work teams was performed by psychologists. Industrial/organizational psychologists followed their colleagues in social psychology by studying teams in organizational settings as opposed to the laboratory. While there was a significant amount of research being conducted through the 1950s, the application of teams did not become popular until the 1980s.

The increased interest from organizations for implementing work teams can be linked to the advent of total quality management (TQM). Organizations such as Ford Motor Company, Lockheed-Martin, and Motorola began experimenting with multiple types of teams. First, quality circles were attempted, and then some companies started performing production, project, and service work with teams. Many organizations realized the benefits of team-based approaches by achieving increases in productivity, efficiency, and quality. For other organizations that failed to implement appropriate support mechanisms, the benefit of teams fell far short of their promise. This, however, did not deter a number of companies from experimenting with team-based structures. The implementation of teams to perform a variety of tasks became commonplace in the 1990s. Kodak (customer service teams), Chevron (interfunctional teams), Dow Corning (self-managed teams within a unionized context), Motorola (self-managed teams within a nonunionized context), and Miller Brewing Company (cross-functional teams) are just a few examples of the application of teams within organizations. Today, the pursuit of effective teams is ubiquitous across continents, industries, and organizations.

Types of Teams

It is important to categorize teams to gain a better understanding of what they do and how they are different. Most typologies focus on the following types of teams: (1) action and performing teams (e.g., surgery and SWAT teams), (2) advisory teams (e.g., task force), (3) management teams (e.g., top management teams, regional leadership teams), (4) production teams (e.g., paper mill work crews), (5) project teams (e.g., new product development teams), and (6) service teams (e.g., consulting teams).

Team Effectiveness

McGrath pioneered the most widely used "input-process-output" (IPO) model of group performance that is still relied on today to some extent. McGrath suggested that inputs are the key cause of processes that then mediate the effect of inputs on outcomes. Inputs can be defined as things people bring to the group (expertise, status, personality, and experience); processes can be defined as the interaction among group members (social exchange of information, influence attempts, and leadership); and outputs can be defined as products yielded by the group (performances, reports, and services). Of these, process variables have been the most difficult to accurately measure and understand because they are highly context dependent and dynamic. The dynamic nature of these processes contradicts their static operationalization in most research on teams.

In works that followed, several potential factors influencing effectiveness were considered. Jonathon Cummings offered a model based on sociotechnical theory that focused on control over social and task-related processes and group self-regulation. Another model in the early 1980s was based on the IPO sequence that suggested organizational context, interpersonal processes, design features (group task, composition, and norms), technology, and intermediate criteria of effectiveness (application of effort, knowledge and skill, and strategies) as key factors. This resulted in a new, comprehensive model containing six team effectiveness factors: group structure, resources, group process, task, organizational structure, and group composition. Others added group design, synergy, autonomy, physical environment, and a factor for group boundaries as additional variables important in a model of group effectiveness. Additional models were suggested in subsequent work and added emphasis to the utility of using five categories of factors related to work group effectiveness. These categories generally include (1) organizational context (e.g., training, reward, measurement, and information systems), (2) group composition (e.g., number of members and the mixture of individual traits such as personality and ability), (3) group work design (e.g., task interdependence, task predictability, task complexity, task significance, level of group autonomy, and degree of self-management), (4) intragroup processes (e.g., conflict, communication, collaboration, cohesion, and team norms), and (5) external group processes (e.g., external member interactions with peers, managers, suppliers, and customers). All together, these models suggest a number of factors contribute to team effectiveness.

These more recent depictions have explicitly attempted to incorporate time as a critical factor in accurately modeling team effectiveness. Time can be modeled in a number of ways, but there have been two primary approaches: (1) developmental models that illustrate how teams change and are differentially influenced by various factors as they mature and (2) episodic models that suggest teams must execute different processes at different times based on the demands of their tasks and that these recur cyclically. The emergence of a large number of models has resulted in a far more understanding of what constitutes "team effectiveness."

Importance

Research on team effectiveness has a robust history and has received considerable recent attention. However, several critical areas would improve the accuracy and potential benefit of research. These areas include but are not limited to (1) the explicit consideration of time, (2) adequately capturing the complexity of organizational teams, and (3) the development of research frameworks that move beyond IPO and IMOI (input-mediator-output-input) conceptualizations to more accurately model the numerous ways teams are organized today.

Prominent researchers who focused on teams, such as Kozlowski, Mathieu, Dan Ilgen, Sundstrom, and others, have long called for the need to more explicitly consider time and the overall complexity of groups when attempting to assess group effectiveness. Developmental and episodic approaches to time have contributed greatly to the field, but there is a need to consider time as a more substantive variable when examining teams. For example, how do teams manage the ever-changing dynamic context within which most of them operate? The reality is that team membership changes (i.e., team members leave, new ones are hired) and contextual issues shift constantly because of an evolving business environment (i.e., global economic environment, competitive presses) to mention just two. How do teams manage these dynamic issues over time? An additional related issue regarding time involves how much time team members have allocated to the team in question? Most team members are members of multiple organizational teams that compete for their attention and are typically not well coordinated. The issue of resource allocation regarding how much time team members are able to put toward specific team functions is an important one, as is the overlapping issue of multiple team memberships. The issues of time are related to the next challenge, accurately capturing the true complexity of teamwork.

Most work on teams collects data at one or two points in time and then attempts to identify key predictors of group effectiveness. While this is a very legitimate method, it does not permit researchers to consider enough of the context to accurately understand what truly impacts group effectiveness. For example, teams *and* their members have varied histories leading up to the point where they are examined in a research study. These histories undoubtedly have a significant impact on what drives their effectiveness, but this history is rarely assessed beyond team and organizational tenure. It is also likely that there are significant differences involving maturation, history, and developmental stage, among other differences, that are not measured and threaten the validity of subsequent findings. The research designs necessary to adequately capture at least some of this complexity will be very complex, time-consuming, and resource intensive. However, these types of approaches will be necessary to more fully and accurately understand what drives team effectiveness. Unfortunately, team arrangements in today's business environment that fit within the IPO-style frameworks are very rare.

Developing frameworks that more accurately represent the manner in which teams are organized today is another area that will contribute to better understanding team effectiveness. New frameworks are emerging, especially in work focused on top management teams. In fact, this likely represents the next paradigm in work on team effectiveness. That is, researchers will likely employ frameworks that accurately model the teams being studied and move away from the restrictions enforced by IPO-like frameworks.

In conclusion, evaluating team effectiveness calls for recognizing their expanding role in today's organizations, which has grown more ambiguous and less formal, because employees may have multiple team assignments and teams may have fluid memberships and timelines. Recent reviews have noted that organizations hold teams accountable for outcomes beyond those included in now-traditional definitions of effectiveness. Research on team effectiveness has adopted criteria at multiple levels of analysis, including beneficial individual-level impacts for members and organization-level outcomes. As Ilgen has indicated, research on teams has primarily focused on *who* is a member of the team, *how* they work together, and *what* they do to perform their work, but researchers have spent relatively less time considering the many elements that comprise team's "effectiveness." Therefore, managers today can use these insights to more fully appreciate the challenges and success factors associated with team-based work. The dynamic nature of teamwork and the necessity of managing multiple perspectives make team effectiveness a challenging goal. However, four important success factors stand out. First, all team members must feel part of a team that is easily identifiable and distinct from others. Second, compelling team goals should be effectively aligned with individual roles. Third, effective training and technology systems should be established that facilitate the effective functioning of virtual teams. Finally, there should be organization-level systems (e.g., leadership, reward structures, measurement and feedback, training, etc.) designed to explicitly support the complex, dynamic nature of the work carried out by teams.

Tjai M. Nielsen

See also Complexity Theory and Organizations; Dynamic Capabilities; Group Development; Group Punctuated Equilibrium Model; Groupthink; High-Performing Teams; Multilevel Research; Virtual Teams

Further Readings

Cohen, S. G., & Bailey, D. (1997). What makes teams work: Group effectiveness research from the shop floor to the executive suite. *Journal of Management, 23,* 239–290.

Hackman, J. R. (1987). The design of work teams. In J. Lorsch (Ed.), *Handbook of organizational behavior* (pp. 315–342), New York, NY: Prentice-Hall.

Hackman, J. R. (1990). *Groups that work (and those that don't)*. San Francisco, CA: Jossey-Bass.

Klein, K. J., & Kozlowski, S. W. J. (2000). *Multilevel theory, research, and methods in organizations: Foundations, extensions, and new directions*. San Francisco, CA: Jossey-Bass.

Kozlowsk, S. W. J., & Ilgen, D. (2006). Enhancing the effectiveness of work groups and teams. *Psychological Science in the Public Interest, 7,* 77–124.

Mathieu, J., Maynard, M. T., Rapp, T., & Gilson, L. (2008). Team effectiveness 1997–2007: A review of recent advancements and a glimpse into the future. *Journal of Management, 34,* 410–476.

Nielsen, T. M., Edmondson, A. C., & Sundstrom, E. (2007). Group wisdom: Definition, dynamics, and applications. In E. Kessler & J. Bailey (Eds.), *Handbook of organizational and managerial wisdom* (pp. 21–42). Thousand Oaks, CA: Sage.

Sundstrom, E., & Associates (1999). *Supporting work team effectiveness: Best management practices for fostering high performance*. San Francisco, CA: Jossey-Bass.

Sundstrom, E., De Meuse, K., & Futrell, D. (1990). Work teams: Applications and effectiveness. *American Psychologist, 45,* 120–133.

Sundstrom, E., McIntyre, M., Halfhill, T., & Richards, H. (2000). Work groups: From the Hawthorne Studies to the work teams of the 1990s. *Group Dynamics, 4,* 44–67.

Encyclopedia of Management Theory: Appendix A

CHRONOLOGY OF MANAGEMENT THEORY*

Nicholas J. Beutell

1905: Max Weber's *The Protestant Ethic and the Spirit of Capitalism*—published in English in 1930; 1922: *The Theory of Social and Economic Organization* Weber is known for numerous contributions to management, including the theory of "bureaucracy," a formalized and idealized view of organizations administered on the basis of knowledge and known for efficiency, impersonal relationships, task competence, and rules and procedures.

1910–1915: Henry L. Gantt designs a project-scheduling model for increasing the efficiency of project completion (Gantt Chart); protégé and associate of Frederic Taylor.

1911: Frederick W. Taylor's *Principles of Scientific Management*—proposes an objective, systematic method rather than "rules of thumb" to indentify the "one best way" to perform a job; advocated scientific selection and training methods; cooperation between workers and managers with each doing what they are best suited to do; and pay tied to work performance.

1912: Frank Gilbreth becomes a disciple of Taylor's—develops, along with his wife Lillian, a scheme for labeling hand movements; identified "therbligs" (Gilbreth spelled backward with the "t" and "h" transposed) as the basic unit of motion studies.

1913: Hugo Münsterberg's *Psychology and Industrial Efficiency*—presents a scientific study of human behavior in the work environment; analysis of individual differences.

1916: Henri Fayol, an engineer and managing director, publishes *Administration Industrielle et Générale* (General and Industrial Administration); identifies 14 principles of management such as authority and responsibility, unity of command, scalar principle, remuneration, esprit de corps, etc.; believed that management could be taught.

1924: Lillian Gilbreth takes over management consulting company after her husband, Frank Gilbreth, dies. Lillian was the first woman to obtain a PhD in management; she made numerous contributions to industrial psychology.

1933, 1939: Elton Mayo, *The Human Problems of an Industrial Civilization* (1933) and 1939: Fritz Roethlisberger and William Dixon, *Management and the Worker* (1939), Hawthorne Studies conducted at Hawthorne Plant of Western Electric Corporation—examines various changes (e.g., lighting) to gauge the effect on employee productivity in a factory environment; studies are widely criticized for experimental errors yet have a wide-ranging impact and provide the genesis of the *human relations* school; the "Hawthorne effect" refers to changes in behavior resulting from being studied rather than effects associated with experimental manipulations (although this interpretation has been questioned).

Note: *Chronology covers a time period beginning at the onset of the 20th century and ending 5 years prior to the writing of this appendix.

1925: Mary Parker Follett, *The Psychological Foundations of Business Administration*—suggests that organizations are communities involving networks of groups; manager's job is to coordinate group effort; anticipated many contemporary concepts like motivation, leadership, and empowerment.

1938: Chester Barnard, business executive, publishes *The Functions of the Executive*—argues that managers should communicate and encourage workers to high levels of success; proposes the acceptance theory of authority—that success depends on cooperation of employees.

1944–1951: Kurt Lewin's action research model, including in *Action Research and Minority Problem*—presents a model of social research leading to action along with feedback on the effects of that action; noted for work on group dynamics and behavioral commitment; identifies a model of planned change (unfreezing, change, refreezing); and force field analysis. Also credited for beginning t-groups.

1947: Herbert A. Simon, *Administrative Behavior: A Study of Decision-Making Processes in Administrative Organizations*, based on his doctoral dissertation—coins the terms *bounded rationality* (people have limits or boundaries on the amount of information they can process to make a decision) and *satisficing* (selecting the first solution that satisfies decision criteria even though better solutions might exist) related to decision making.

1950: George Homans, *The Human Group*—advances small-group theory and research; attempts to extrapolate from a single group to understanding the social system.

1952: Solomon Asch studies of social influence (Asch Effect)—proposes that social pressure can induce people to select choices that are objectively incorrect.

1954: Peter F. Drucker, *The Practice of Management*—examines management and the managerial role as a distinct business function bridging theory and practice.

1954: Abraham Maslow, *Motivation and Personality*—develops a theory of human motivation by proposing a universal, prepotent hierarchy of needs.

1957: Chris Argyris, *Personality and Organization*—identifies fundamental conflicts between individual and organizational needs.

1958: James March and Herbert Simon, *Organizations*—presents a comprehensive review of organizational theory revealing a number of limitations and gaps, highlighting themes relating to cognition and decision making, and presenting directions for subsequent research.

1959: Frederick Herzberg et al., *The Motivation to Work*—proposes a two-factor theory (motivator-hygiene) suggesting that motivator factors (e.g., recognition, the work itself) can lead to job satisfaction and motivation, while a separate set of factors (hygiene factors—e.g., work environment, pay) can lead to job dissatisfaction.

1959: John R. P. French and Bertram Raven, *The Bases of Social Power*—argues that five types, or bases, of power (coercive, reward, legitimate, referent, and expert) are linked with leadership.

1959: John Thibaut and Harold Kelley, *The Social Psychology of Group*—argues that social behavior is an exchange process based on rewards and costs with the goal of maximizing rewards and minimizing costs.

1959: Ford Foundation and Carnegie Foundation reports that blasted business schools for lack of intellectual content and fostered the hiring of people from "the disciplines" into business schools thereby fostering business school research.

1960: Fred E. Emery and Eric L Trist discuss "sociotechnical systems"—suggests that any production system consists of two elements: a technological organization (i.e., equipment, process) and a work organization (those who do the work having social and psychological needs).

1960: Douglas McGregor, *Human Side of Enterprise*—propounds an overall approach to organizations and organizational change; a model for improving relationships with employees to the extent to which managers can model the hypothetical "Manager Y," a supportive and understanding manager who trusts employees to work hard (Theory Y vs. Theory X).

1960–1970: Development of SWOT (strengths, weaknesses, opportunities, and threats) analysis at

Stanford Research Institute, often credited to Albert Humphrey; this concept emerged for a number of theories and corporate planning approaches.

1961: David McClelland's *The Achieving Society*—discusses the need for achievement (first identified by Henry A. Murray), need to excel, to perform against standards, and to win; McClelland extended his theory to other acquired needs such as need for power and need for affiliation.

1961: T. Burns and G. M. Stalker, *The Management of Innovation*—examines mechanistic and organic organizational designs and the environments conducive for each.

1961: Harold Koontz, "*Management Theory Jungle*" (*Academy of Management Journal*, Vol. 4, No. 3)—identifies schools of management thought such as empirical, human behavior, mathematical, social system, decision theory, and management process; convergence of approaches seems unlikely.

1961: Rensis Likert, *New patterns of management* and 1967: *The Human Organization*—proposes a "linking-pin" (organizations consist of "families" that are linked together) model to bridge human relations and organization structure.

1961: Warren Bennis, Kenneth Benne and Robert Chin, *The Planning of Change*—lays out a foundation for planned organizational change such as organization development.

1962: Kaoru Ishikawa develops the *quality circle* concept with the Japanese Union of Scientist and Engineers quality research group; begun as an experiment to test the influence of the "leading hand" (*Gemba-cho*) on quality; W. Edwards Deming is also associated with this concept, where small groups of employees and supervisors meet regularly to solve quality issues and operational improvements.

1962: Peter M. Blau and W. Richard Scott, *Formal Organizations: A Comparative Approach,* one of the founding texts of organizational sociology—analyzes formal organization in a way that goes beyond individuals and groups to explore organizations as collective actors.

1962: Everett Rogers, *Diffusion of Innovations*—attempts to explain how, why, and the rate of adoption of new ideas and technologies in a culture.

1962: Alfred Chandler, *Strategy and structure*—analyzes large corporations and the way executives plan, coordinate, and appraise in such structures; proposes that strategy determines long-term organizational goals, tactics, and resources; structure is the design for administering organization activities; structure follows strategy.

1963: Warren T. Norman, *Toward an Adequate Taxonomy of Personality Attributes: Replicated Factor Structure in Peer Nomination Personality Ratings*—finds five essentially orthogonal personality factors (empirically derived) that were the basis for Big Five personality traits (openness to experience, conscientiousness, extraversion, agreeableness, and neuroticism).

1963: Richard Cyert and James March, *Behavioral Theory of the Firm*—explains decision making within the firm suggesting, based on Simon's work, that individuals and groups "satisfice" as they pursue goals rather than attempting to maximize the utility or profitability of a decision.

1964: Victor Vroom, *Work and Motivation*—uses expectancy theory to integrate various scholarly approaches to work motivation by examining how valence, instrumentality, and expectancy can be managed to align individual and organizational objectives.

1964: Robert Kahn, Donald Wolfe, Robert Quinn, J. Diedrick Snoek, and Robert Rosenthal, *Organizational Stress: Studies in Role Conflict and Ambiguity*—examines role expectations in the organizational environment leading to conflict and ambiguity such that maintained stress leads to health issues and diminished sense of well-being.

1965: J. Stacy Adams, *Inequity in Social Exchanges*—uses equity theory to argue that employees compare their ratio of inputs to outputs from the job with others; an imbalance leads to actions to reduce the perceived inequity.

1965: Joan Woodward, *Industrial Organization: Theory and Practice*—argues that technology and production systems were critical aspects of organizational design; advanced a contingency approach to organizing.

1966: Daniel Katz and Robert L. Kahn, *The Social Psychology of Organizations*—presents a unified, open systems approach extending organizational theory beyond the boundaries of a single organization.

1966: Peter Berger and Thomas Luckmann, *The Social Construction of Reality: A Treatise in the Sociology of Knowledge*—identifies the ways in which individuals and groups actively participate in constructing their notions of reality as an ongoing and dynamic process.

1967: Paul Lawrence and J. W. Lorsch, *Organization and Environment: Managing Differentiation and Integration*—studies organizational differentiation and integration, suggesting that successful organizations match their structure to the nature of the environment.

1967: Fred Fiedler publishes *A Theory of Leadership Effectiveness*—argues that leader effectiveness is contingent upon two interacting factors, leadership style, and situational favorableness.

1967: James Thompson, *Organizations in Action: Social Science Bases of Administrative Theory*—analyzes organizations and their functioning based on uncertainty, technology, and interdependencies.

1968: Bruce Henderson creates Boston Consulting Group Matrix to help companies analyze their product lines or business units; uses market share and growth rate to classify business units as cash cows, dogs, question marks, or stars.

1968: Edwin A. Locke, *Toward a Theory of Task Motivation and Incentives* (and later 1984: E. A. Locke and J. P. Latham, *Goal Setting: A Motivational Technique That Works*)—argues that specific and difficult goals result in higher task performance.

1969: B. F. Skinner, *Contingencies of Reinforcement: A Theoretical Analysis*—argues that operant conditioning can shape behavior; identifies a reinforcer as any contingent stimulus that increases the target behavior.

1969: Karl Weick, *The Social Psychology of Organizing* (second edition published in 1979)—defines organizing as "the consensually validated grammar for reducing equivocality by means of sensible interlocked behaviors"; his notable works have made many theoretical contributions, including concepts such as enactment, mindfulness, sensemaking, and loose coupling.

1972: Michael Hunt, *Competition in the Major Home Appliance Industry*—coins the term *strategic group* based on an analysis of the appliance industry; an analytic tool for grouping companies using similar business models or strategies into direct and indirect competitors.

1973: Henry Mintzberg, *The Nature of Managerial Work*—expands the view of managerial work by observing and categorizing what managers actually do.

1974: Ken Thomas and Ralph Kilmann, The Thomas-Kilmann Conflict Mode Instrument—measures conflict situations along two dimensions (assertiveness and cooperativeness) along with five options for resolving conflict including competing, accommodating, avoiding, compromising, and collaborating.

1974: Robert House and Terence Mitchell, *Path Goal Theory of Leadership*—examines how leader behavior can clarify paths to goals that subordinates value, and, in so doing gains increased acceptance from subordinates.

1974: Ralph Stogdill, *Handbook of Leadership: A Survey of the Literature*—identifies the major traits (e.g., decisive, dependable) and skills (e.g., intelligent, creative) of managers based on previous research studies.

1974: Chris Argyris and Donald Schön, *Theory in Practice: Increasing Professional Effectiveness*—examines "organizational learning" practices from a perspective other than Carnegie Mellon.

1975, 1981: Oliver E. Williamson, *Markets and Hierarchies: Analysis and Antitrust Implications* (1975) and *The Economics of Organization: The Transaction Cost Approach* (1981)—shows that "transactions" go beyond buying and selling to include a variety of behaviors such as emotional interactions and informal gift giving; transaction costs are influenced by factors including frequency, specificity, uncertainty, bounded rationality, and opportunistic behavior; formulate the basis of the "make vs. buy" decision.

1976: J. Richard Hackman and Greg R. Oldham, "Motivation Through the Design of Work: Test of a Theory" (*Organizational Behavior and Human Performance*, Vol. 17, No. 2)—presents a job characteristics model that includes employee psychological states, task characteristics that arouse these psychological states, feedback, and employee growth need strength (based on higher order needs from A. Maslow).

1976: Derek S. Pugh and David J. Hickson, *Organizational Structure in Its Context: The Aston Programme I* (and subsequent series of empirical findings from the Aston Program)—systematically analyzes dimensions of organizational structure applicable to all organizations.

1977: Rosabeth Moss Kanter, *Men and Women of the Corporation*—reveals a workplace dominated by men with women caught in a cycle of powerlessness largely determined by corporate structure.

1977: Albert Bandura, *Social Learning Theory*—shows that learning derives from observation and modeling; that mental processes are a critical component (in contrast to purely behavioral approaches) and that learning can occur even though the learned behaviors are not immediately exhibited. Also "Self-Efficacy: Toward a Unifying Theory of Behavioral Change" (*Psychological Review*, Vol. 84, No. 2)—identifies self-efficacy, a person's belief that he or she can be successful in a particular situation, as a major factor in changing behavior.

1977: B. J. Calder, "An Attribution Theory of Leadership" (in *New Directions in Organizational Behavior*, edited by Staw and Salancik)—posits that leadership is an attribution that people make rather than a set of traits or behaviors.

1977: Michael Hannan and John Freeman, "The Population Ecology of Organizations" (*American Journal of Sociology*, Vol. 82, No. 5)—examines dynamic changes within a set of organizations, statistically investigating organizational birth and mortality as well as emerging organizational forms in a longitudinal fashion.

1977: John Meyer and Brian Rowan, "Institutional Organizations: Formal Structure as Myth and Ceremony" (*American Journal of Sociology*, Vol. 83, No. 2)—perhaps the first article in making institutional theory salient, focuses on social pressures rather than "rational-economic" behavior in determining organizational practices.

1978: Chris Argyris and Don Schön *Organizational Learning: A Theory of Action Perspective*—distinguishes between single-loop and double-loop learning—the former refers to corrective actions required to maintain homeostasis, whereas double-loop learning examines the assumptions and values of the actions taken.

1978: Jeffrey Pfeffer and Jerry Salancik, *The External Control of Organizations: A Resource Dependence Perspective*—advances the idea that resource exchange is necessary for organizational survival, and acquiring resources can result in organizational competition and unequal, dynamic interdependencies since the supply of resources is finite.

1979: Gibson Burrell and Gareth Morgan, *Sociological Paradigms and Organizational Analysis*—examines fundamental sociological approaches that underlie ways of thinking about organizations; proposes four major paradigms: radical humanist, functionalist, radical structuralist, and interpretive.

1979: Daniel Kahneman and Amos Tversky publish "Prospect Theory: An Analysis of Decisions Under Risk" (*Econometrica*, Vol. 47, No. 2)—argues that decision makers examine potential losses and gains rather than the overall decision outcome; also examines the heuristics used to evaluate potential losses and gains.

1979: Anthony Giddens, *Central Problems in Social Theory: Action, Structure, and Contradiction in Social Analysis*—considers the concept of action in the context of structural components of social institutions; attempts to resolve the long-standing agency-structure quandary in social analysis.

1980: Michael Porter, *Competitive Strategy*—develops Hunt's (1972) concept of strategic groups arguing that such groups create mobility barriers that function like entry barriers except they are created within industry groups; seminal work on strategy considers generic strategies and competitive forces (rivalry among existing competitors, new entrants, buyers, suppliers, and substitute products or services) that contribute to the profitability on an industry.

1980: R. Revans, *Action Learning: New Techniques for Management*—allows learners to reflect and review their own experiences and behaviors as a basis for making improvements.

1980: Geert Hofstede, *Culture's Consequences: International Differences in Work-Related Values*—summarizes the results of a major survey of IBM employees' cultural values conducted between 1967 and 1973; the primary dimensions of national cultural values include power distance, individualism, uncertainty avoidance, and masculinity/femininity; widely used in international human resource management.

1981: Lawrence Kohlberg, *The Philosophy of Moral Development: Moral Stages and the Idea of Justice* (*Essays on Moral Development*, Vol. 1)—examines preconventional, conventional, and postconventional levels of moral development, each having distinct stages. Justice is a central characteristic of moral reasoning.

1981: William G. Ouchi, *Theory Z: How American Management Can Meet the Japanese Challenge*—argues that American companies should employee Japanese-style management techniques, the essence of which is a unique way of managing people (e.g., staff development, consensual decision making); based on McGregor's Theory X and Theory Y as well as Abraham Maslow's Theory Z.

1981: Roger Fisher and William Ury, *Getting to Yes: Negotiating Agreement Without Giving In*—espouses principled negotiation, a method that seeks win-win agreements between negotiators.

1982: W. Edwards Deming, *Out of the Crisis*—presents an approach to a total quality management system for improving quality, productivity, and competitiveness.

1983: Robert E. Quinn and J. A. Rohrbaugh, "A Spatial Model of Effectiveness Criteria: Towards a Competing Values Approach to Organizational Analysis" (*Management Science*, Vol. 29, No. 3)—develops the competing values framework in relation to organizational effectiveness consisting of two dimensions: organizational focus (internal vs. external) and stability/control versus flexibility/change.

1983: Teresa Amabile, *The Social Psychology of Creativity: A Componential Conceptualization*—identifies three necessary and sufficient conditions for creativity: domain-relevant skills, creativity-relevant skills, and task motivation; examines the impact of personality, cognitive ability, and social factors.

1984: Eliyahu Goldratt and Jeff Cox, *The Goal*—advances a theory of constraints ("a chain is no stronger than its weakest link") through a fictional account of UniCo Manufacturing.

1984: Anthony Giddens, *The Constitution of Society: Outline of the Theory of Structuration*—explores the extent to which individual or social forces shape our reality; all human action occurs against the backdrop of a social structure that shapes and is shaped by such action.

1984: R. Edward Freeman, *Strategic Management: A Stakeholder Approach*—argues, in contrast to the traditional shareholder view of the firm, that stakeholders ("those groups without whose support the organization would cease to exist") need to be considered as well.

1985: Chris Argyris, Robert Putnam, and Diana McLain Smith, *Action Science: Concepts, Methods and Skills for Research and Intervention*—argues that research should be useful in solving practical problems.

1985: Michael Tushman and Elaine Romanelli, "Organizational Evolution: A Metamorphosis Model of Convergence and Reorientation" (*Research in Organizational Behavior*, Vol. 7)—presents a model of organizational evolution that examines forces for stability, forces for change, and the role that executive leadership plays in these processes.

1985: Edward Deci and Richard Ryan publish *Intrinsic Motivation and Self-Determination in Human Behavior*, the first comprehensive statement of self-determination theory—proposes that humans have an intrinsic tendency to behave in effective and healthy ways.

1985: Mark Granovetter, "Economic Action and Social Structure: The Problem of Embeddedness" (*American Journal of Sociology*, Vol. 91, No. 3)—examines the embeddedness of economic actions in structures of social relations in industrial society.

1985: Michael Porter publishes *Competitive Advantage: Creating and Sustaining Superior Performance*—shows how firms leverage a combination of attributes and resources across a "value-chain" enabling the firm to outperform other firms in the industry.

1985: Stuart Albert and David Whetten, *Organizational Identity* (in *Research in Organizational Behavior*, Vol. 7, edited by Cummings and Staw)—introduces thinking about elements of an organization that are believed to be central, enduring, and distinctive.

1986: Bill Smith, Motorola Corporation—develops the Six Sigma methodology as a way to count quality defects in manufacturing based on conceptual developments at Motorola begun in the 1970s; six sigma quality standard is fewer than 3.4 defects per million parts or opportunities; widely used as a tool for quality improvement as well as reducing costs.

1986: Michael Tushman and P. Anderson, "Technological Discontinuities and Organizational Environments" (*Administrative Science Quarterly*, Vol. 31, No. 3)—examines the impact of technological discontinuities on different industries; technological evolution has long periods of incremental change followed by competency-destroying or competency-enhancing discontinuities.

1986: J. M. Juran, "The Quality Trilogy: A Universal Approach to Managing for Quality" (*Quality Progress*, Vol. 19, No. 8)—argues that "quality does not happen by accident"; gave rise to the quality trilogy: Quality planning, quality control, and quality improvement.

1987: Randall Schuler and Susan Jackson, "Linking Competitive Strategies With Human Resource Management Practices" (*Academy of Management Executive*, Vol. 1, No. 3)—argues that employee role behaviors mediate the relationship between a firm's strategy and performance.

1987: Marvin R. Weisbord, *Productive Workplaces: Organizing and Managing for Dignity, Meaning, and Community*—provides a foundation for large-group interventions, an important form of organizational change.

1987: David L. Cooperrider and Suresh Srivastva, "Appreciative Inquiry in Organizational Life" (in *Research in Organizational Change and Development*, Vol. 1, edited by W. Pasmore and R. Woodman)—first introduces appreciative inquiry and its underlying philosophy as a new approach to intervention.

1989: Blake Ashforth and Fred Mael, "Social Identity and the Organization" (*Academy of Management Review*, Vol. 14, No. 1)—argues that people categorize themselves and others into categories (e.g., organizational membership, age, gender) and that social classification permits people to locate themselves in a social environment.

1989: Warren Bennis, *On Becoming a Leader*—offers a unique view of leadership as self-development coupled with passion and building trust among followers.

1989: Andrew Van de Ven, Harold Angle, and Marshall Scott Poole, *Research on the Management of Innovation*—reveals that the stages of innovation from invention to implementation do not follow a straightforward set of stages, suggesting a higher level of complexity to this process than previously believed.

1989: David Whetten, "What Constitutes a Theoretical Contribution?" (*Academy of Management Review*, Vol. 14, No. 4)—offers a look into the building blocks of theory, assessing the value added by theoretical constructs and judging theoretical papers in the organizational sciences.

1990: C. K. Prahalad and Gary Hamel, "The Core Competence of the Corporation" (*Harvard Business Review*, Vol. 68, No. 3)—coins the term *core competence* and showed this concept as the basis for corporate competitiveness.

1990: Edgar H. Schein, *Career Anchors*—identifies eight major career themes (e.g., autonomy/independence, general managerial competence) that tend to keep employees anchored to their primary theme that emerges from life and occupational experience.

1990: Peter Senge, *The Fifth Discipline*—popularizes the concept of the learning organization based on five disciplines: systems thinking, personal mastery, mental models, shared vision, and team learning.

1990: Michael Porter, *Competitive Advantage of Nations*—examines the role played by a country's economic environment in relation to success of firms in different industries; his diamond model includes firm strategy, structure, and rivalry; demand conditions (expectations of customers); related and supporting industries; and factor conditions (key production factors are created not inherited).

1991: Walter W. Powell and Paul J. DiMaggio, eds., *The New Institutionalism in Organizational Analysis*—examines the institutional approach to organizational analysis from a sociological perspective; going beyond economic approaches the institutional model shows how institutions interact and how these interactions affect society.

1992: Robert Kaplan and David Norton, *The Balanced Scorecard*—builds on the work of consultant Arthur Schneiderman of Analog Devices to present a comprehensive management control and performance measurement system that examines strategic success factors in addition to traditional financial measures affecting a firm's performance.

1992: Ronald S. Burt, *Structural Holes: The Social Structure of Competition*—introduces and applies social network analysis to the understanding patterns of relationships among individuals and organizations.

1993: Michael Hammer and James Champy, *Reengineering the Corporation: A Manifesto for Business Revolution*—advances the idea that business processes should be reengineered to eliminate activities that do not add value and redesign core processes that support the organization's mission.

1993: Jeffrey Pfeffer, "Barriers to the Advancement of Organizational Science: Paradigm Development as a Dependent Variable" (*Academy of Management Review*, Vol. 18, No. 4)—argues that organizational science is not well developed paradigmatically; examines how certain values (e.g., theoretical and methodological diversity) have slowed scientific progress.

1995: Mark Huselid, "The Impact of Human Resource Management Practices on Turnover, Productivity, and Corporate Financial Performance" (*Academy of Management Journal*, Vol. 38, No. 3)—demonstrates the impact of high performance work systems on employee behavior and corporate financial performance.

1995: Denise Rousseau, *Promises in Action: Psychological Contracts in Organizations*—conceptualizes the psychological contract (originally used by Argyris in 1960) as the beliefs that employees hold about their employment relationship that becomes relatively stable over time.

1995: Daniel Goleman, *Emotional Intelligence: Why Can It Matter More Than IQ*—suggests that emotions should be given a greater role in human behavior, decision making, and individual success.

1996: Gary Hamel and C. K. Prahalad, *Competing for the Future*—redefines corporate strategy, indicating that companies need to develop a view of the future based on industry foresight to create a new competitive space.

1996: John Kotter, *Leading Change*—develops an eight-step model of planned change that has guided change efforts for years; examines the profound significance of leaders in the change process.

1997: Clayton Christensen, *The Innovator's Dilemma: When New Technologies Causes Existing Firms to Fail*—shows how a company's successes and competencies can create barriers to coping with changing technologies and markets.

2000: Anne Huff, "Changes in Organizational Knowledge Production" (*Academy of Management Review*, Vol. 25, No. 2)—reveals how the knowledge explosion has challenged business school teaching and research.

2001: Sara Rynes, Jean Bartunek, and Richard Daft, "Across the Great Divide" (*Academy of Management Journal*, Vol. 44, No. 2)—lays out boundaries differentiating academic and practitioner approaches to knowledge as well as strategies for overcoming them.

2001: James Collins, *Good to Great*—describes the reasons that some companies excel while others do not; "Level 5 Leadership" (*Harvard Business Review*, Product 5831)—contributes to enduring greatness by blending humility and resolve to do what is best for the company.

2002: Michael Hitt, R. Duane Ireland, Michael Camp, and Donald Sexton, *Strategic Entrepreneurship: Creating a New Mindset*—identifies how firms can identify entrepreneurial opportunities by focusing on the most promising prospects and exploiting them using a strategic business plan.

2003: Kim Cameron, Jane Dutton, and Robert E. Quinn, "Positive Organizational Scholarship" (*Journal of Management Inquiry*, V01.17, No. 1)—provides a framework for and highlights the effects of positive, enriching organizational dynamics that give rise to extraordinary outcomes.

2004: C. K. Prahalad, *The Fortune at the Bottom of the Pyramid*—shows how the billions of poor people in the world represent a great, untapped market; serving this population helps companies and helps the economic aspirations of those being served.

2004: Henry Mintzberg, *Managers Not MBAs: A Hard Look at the Soft Practice of Management and Management Development*—offers a critique of management education revealing how MBA programs are ineffectual in training practicing managers; suggests a new paradigm to increase managerial effectiveness.

2005: Sumantra Ghoshal, "Bad Management Theories Are Destroying Good Management" (*Academy of Management Learning and Education*, Vol. 4, No. 1)—shows how academic business and management research have had a negative impact on practice stemming from the ideas and assumptions that have guided research.

2006: Jeffrey Pfeffer and Robert Sutton, *Hard Facts, Half-Truths, and Total Nonsense: Profiting From Evidence-Based Management*—shows how many accepted management truisms are not only incorrect but, when used by managers, may actually harm the organization; argues for a new model based on evidence.

2007: Eric Kessler and James Bailey, *Handbook of Organizational and Managerial Wisdom*—proposes a framework for reconciling management theory with fundamental philosophical principles.

2007: Andrew Van de Ven, *Engaged Scholarship*—proposes a participative and collective form of scholarship that transcends the capability of individual researchers.

Encyclopedia of Management Theory: Appendix B

CENTRAL MANAGEMENT INSIGHTS

Entry	Central Management Insight
Academic-Practitioner Collaboration and Knowledge Sharing	It is possible to create more insightful knowledge for theory and practice if academics and practitioners collaborate.
Acculturation Theory	People's cultural beliefs and behaviors need to be understood and incorporated into organizational policies and practices in order to achieve effective operations.
Achievement Motivation Theory	Acquired motives—achievement, affiliation, and power—are important for managerial performance and should be used for global selection and assessment of managers.
Action Learning	It is possible to develop organizational members' competencies in the process of solving real, difficult management issues.
Action Research	Actionable knowledge is most effectively produced through deep inquiry into a group's practices via systematic, iterative processes of data gathering, reflection, and action.
Actor-Network Theory	Human and nonhuman organizational actors are generated and "held together" by interactive, continuous, and heterogeneous network forces and strategies.
Adaptive Structuration Theory	Information technologies do not automatically change behavior or improve effectiveness; this depends on how effectively managers facilitate the appropriation of information technology (IT) by users.
Affect Theory	If jobs are structured as joint tasks in which responsibility for results is shared, then employees develop stronger affective commitments to the organization.
Affective Events Theory	Work and life experiences are proximal influences on people's subjective mood and emotional episodes, which in turn are related to work performance and job attitudes.
Agency Theory	The interests of shareholders and managers tend to differ but can be aligned to achieve the maximization of shareholder value.
Analytic Hierarchy Process Model	Managers can utilize a relatively easy and robust process for establishing priorities in multicriteria decision settings.
Analytical and Sociological Paradigms	The study of organizations, and the body of knowledge about them, is shaped by researchers' implicit assumptions and training, which reflect a range of orthodox and heterodox "paradigms."
Appreciative Inquiry Model	Teams, organizations, and society evolve in whatever direction people collectively, passionately, and persistently ask questions about.

Architectural Innovation	Significant competitive advantage can be gained from innovations that change the linkages between product components.
Asch Effect	Social pressure can convince group members to falsify their beliefs in order to achieve group consensus.
Attraction-Selection-Attrition Model	People make organizations through a process of attracting and selecting matching employees and attritioning out nonmatching employees.
Attribution Model of Leadership	Leaders' and employees' causal explanations for employee performance uniquely and interactively influence performance responses including future expectations and behaviors.
Authentic Leadership	Leaders who remain true to their personal values and convictions and display consistency between their words and deeds will foster elevated levels of follower trust and performance.
Bad Theories	Academia perpetuates a number of bad management theories that promote detrimental business practices, and those theories must be carefully reexamined.
Balanced Scorecard	Strategy development and execution can be enabled by a balanced set of performance measures focusing on organizational goals—financial, customer, processes, and learning and growth.
BCG Growth-Share Matrix	The basis of competitive advantage and growth is derived by managing the relationship of the company's portfolio of product lines or business units.
Behavioral Perspective of Strategic Human Resource Management	Human resource (HR) management systems are most effective when they are designed to support strategic business objectives.
Behavioral Theory of the Firm	Managers will behave differently from what is assumed in rational actor views of the organization both with respect to internal processes and relations to the environment.
Big Five Personality Dimensions	Individual differences along five personality traits (extraversion, agreeableness, conscientiousness, emotional stability, openness to experience) affect many management issues.
Bounded Rationality and Satisficing (Behavioral Decision-Making Model)	The concept of rational economic man must be reconciled with the many cognitive, perceptual, situational, and other limits on rationality that influence decision makers to make satisfactory rather than optimal choices.
Brainstorming	Efforts at creative idea generation deserve focused attention and can benefit from adopting a formalized structure.
Bureaucratic Theory	Bureaucracy remains the dominant, albeit an imperfect and double-edged, system of administration for shaping intendedly rational, goal-oriented human interactions through objective knowledge and scientific analysis.
Business Groups	Firms in many parts of the world are part of business groups and derive unique advantages as well as disadvantages from their affiliation.
Business Policy and Corporate Strategy	Companies can create value through the configuration and coordination of their multibusiness activities by aligning vision, resources, businesses, and role of the headquarters.
Business Process Reengineering	Dramatic business improvement can be accomplished with radical process redesign that is supported by information technology.
BVSR Theory of Human Creativity	Human creativity requires individuals to generate and test low-probability ideas whose utilities are unknown in advance.

Career Stages and Anchors	Career choice should be seen as an ongoing journey of exploration and self-construction driven by patterns of self-perceived competence, motivators, and values that guide and constrain development.
Causal Attribution Theory	The behaviors and emotions of leaders and followers are driven by their beliefs about the causes of their own as well as others' successes and failures.
Charismatic Theory of Leadership	Charismatic leadership is an attribution based on followers' interpretations of their leader's behavior; a set of distinct behaviors leads to this attribution.
Circuits of Power and Control	Power is not a thing that people have but a social relation that is dynamic, potentially unstable, and resisted.
Cognitive Dissonance Theory	Individuals' deep-seated desire for consistency can have profound consequences, including shifts in attitudes, behavioral changes, and self-justification of decisions.
Cognitive Resource Theory	Leaders tend to use their raw intelligence to make decisions; however, in some situations, leaders' relevant experience strongly contributes to effectiveness.
Competing Values Framework	In every organization, competing and contradictory values exist; the most effective organizations, as well as the most effective leaders, are paradoxical—they simultaneously represent and display competing values.
Competitive Advantage	The primary objective of a firm's strategy is to identify, create, and sustain a competitive advantage over its industry rivals by identifying a unique position so as to reduce or counter the profit-reducing effect of the forces in that industry.
Complexity Theory and Organizations	Managers need to understand how individuals and firms interact and not only how they perform individually; organizational performance depends on interdependent interactions within the system as a whole.
Compliance Theory	Management "styles"—good practices, patterns of achievement—cannot be transferred; each kind of organization needs a form of management tailored to its special kind of hierarchy, rewards, incentives, and possible sanctions.
Componential Theory of Creativity	The work environment can be as important for creativity as employee talent; creativity should be highest when intrinsically motivated, expert, creative thinkers work in a social environment that supports creativity.
Conflict Handling Styles	Managers can choose from a variety of conflict styles, varying in concern for self and for others, which will be most effective in different situations.
Contingency Theory	There is no one best way to manage people or to design an organization; rather, the choices which are made must fit the situation faced.
Contingency Theory of Leadership	Leadership behaviors will not necessarily yield the same results in all situations; a fit between leadership style and contingency variables is positively related to leadership effectiveness.
Continuous and Routinized Change	Revolutions are not necessary for organizational development; continuous, routinized change shifts the focus from "change" to "changing" through an ongoing mixture of reactive and proactive modifications guided by purposes at hand.
Cooptation	Organizations reflect not only the aim of its principals but also to some degree other stakeholders' aims, such as external collaborators, professional groups, and senior management.
Core Competence	Core competence—firm-specific bundles of skills, insights, and capabilities gained from accumulated knowledge, learning, and investment—enable organizations to create, innovate, and deliver value to its stakeholders.

Corporate Social Responsibility	Business is embedded in society; therefore, every business decision must consider the resulting direct or indirect social impacts.
Critical Management Studies	Management and organization need to be assessed broadly; in their operations and in outcomes, there are dark aspects calling for careful scrutiny and exploration.
Critical Theory of Communication	Organizations and the various forms of knowledge and the human identities of members are products of complex interaction processes conducted under conditions of inequality.
CSR Pyramid	Corporate social responsibility (CSR) embraces four distinct but overlapping responsibilities: economic, legal, ethical, and philanthropic.
Cultural Attitudes in Multinational Corporations	The seemingly limitless ways that firms seek to internationalize can be compared and meaningfully understood by examining the cultural mind-sets of senior organizational decision makers.
Cultural Intelligence	Managers' adjustments in new cultural contexts can be explained by a faceted model of cultural intelligence (CQ) that considers cognitive/ metacognitive, motivational, and behavioral elements.
Cultural Values	To fit in with emerging globalization challenges, managers should try to understand the meaning of value systems and how they may affect the business environment.
Decision Support Systems	People can make better decisions with computer support that uses data access and models to aid learning about decision environments.
Decision-Making Styles	Managers should be mindful of differences in individuals' preferred ways of perceiving and responding to problem-solving situations and understand their impact on decisions made.
Dialectical Theory of Organizations	Organizational structures and practices are shaped by complex and contradictory social forces only partially controlled by rational decisions.
Diamond Model of National Competitive Advantage	A number of structural factors work together to create the conditions for the competitiveness of industries and firms within particular nations which can derive benefits from their "home base."
Differentiation and the Division of Labor	The distribution of work into specialized tasks, roles, and functions are key characteristics of modern management; however, this must be balanced with integration, control, and organizational flexibility needs.
Discovery Theory of Entrepreneurship	There are reasons—such as position, cognition, and deliberation—why some people may be more likely to discover entrepreneurial opportunities than others.
Diversification Strategy	Expanding the scope of the business segments where the firm competes can be a value-enhancing strategy.
Double Loop Learning	Entrenched assumptions and governing values inform peoples' theory-in-use which influences their action strategies; deep reflection on this underlying reasoning process questions the status quo and enables productive change.
Dramaturgical Theory of Organizations	The organization can be seen through metaphor as an acting unit that presents strategies and tactics designed to enhance the power and authority of the organization.
Dual-Concern Theory	Managers can often achieve good outcomes if they care not only about their own interests but also other's interests and seek outcomes of negotiation that maximize collective welfare.

Dual-Core Model of Organizational Innovation	Organizations implement administrative and technical innovations via different organizational groups and management processes.
Dynamic Capabilities	Top management needs to add and shed organizational resources as it detects opportunities, threats, and changes in the business environment.
Emotional and Social Intelligence	Emotional and social capabilities are direct characteristics of an individual that lead to or cause effectiveness in management, leadership, and other occupations.
Empowerment	When individuals feel psychologically empowered—through meaning, competence, self-determination, and impact—their intrinsic motivation and personal efficacy expectations are strengthened.
Engaged Scholarship Model	Collaborative inquiries between universities, practitioners, and other relevant community partners help bridge the theory-practice gap and yield more relevant solutions to societal issues.
Entrepreneurial Cognition	Entrepreneurs use mental models to connect seemingly dissimilar pieces of information in thinking through new opportunities and making decisions.
Entrepreneurial Effectuation	Effectual action inverts predictive strategies to offer entrepreneurs a learnable method for shaping their environment and better controlling situations.
Entrepreneurial Opportunities	Entrepreneurs should match the type of opportunity they are trying to exploit with the appropriate processes to increase their chances for successful exploitation and wealth creation.
Entrepreneurial Orientation	An organization can be considered more (or less) entrepreneurial as a collective entity; it may develop a strategic orientation toward entrepreneurial activity and behavior.
Environmental Uncertainty	Managers should adjust their attitudes toward environmental uncertainty, analyze its multidimensional sources and attributes, and then manage direct and moderating effects accordingly.
Equity Theory	Employees feel fairly compensated based on perceptions of rewards relative to contributions as compared with a benchmark rewards/contributions ratio.
ERG Theory	Three types of human needs—existence, relatedness, and growth—influence behavior and highlight the necessity of both extrinsic and intrinsic motivational options.
Escalation of Commitment	Decision makers should understand and reduce the danger of becoming increasingly committed to courses of action that have become unprofitable.
Ethical Decision Making, Interactionist Model of	Ethical decision making in organizations is driven largely by the individual's cognitive moral development but also results from its interaction with other individual differences and contextual features.
European Model of Human Resource Management	Managing people, more than most other areas of management, is contextual; HR managers should consider factors such as culture, stakeholders, decision processes, markets, organization, and the state.
Evidence-Based Management	To the extent that research findings are incorporated into practice, managers at all levels will decrease inefficiencies; currently, many optimal solutions are being neglected.
Excellence Characteristics	Excellence is not a static destination; rather, it is an attitude and a pursuit where there are many ways individual or organizational actors can realize their potential and grow continuously.

Expectancy Theory	Aligning individual goals with organizational objectives is critical to effective management; there are several components of successful alignment: expectancy, instrumentality, and valence.
Experiential Learning Theory and Learning Styles	The management process involves creative tension among four learning modes—based on dual dialectics of grasping and transforming experience—within a dynamic learning cycle that is responsive to contextual demands.
Fairness Theory	Actions seem unfair when people feel that those actions *would* have been better if the relevant person *could* have and *should* have acted differently.
Firm Growth	The administrative and management structures of a firm play vital roles in configuring and utilizing its resources, which in turn enables and constrains its growth trajectory.
First-Mover Advantages and Disadvantages	Being first to market carries a host of threats and opportunities; understanding the underlying mechanisms is essential for positive economic performance in new or substantially reorganized markets and industries.
Force Field Analysis and Model of Planned Change	The composition of a dynamic "field" with driving and resisting forces influences intended, rational change on multiple levels and across different stages—unfreezing, movement, and refreezing.
Functions of the Executive	Individuals cannot achieve their aspirations independently; organizations are formed for cooperative purposes through inducements and contributions, communication and interaction, and accepted or legitimated authority relationships.
Game Theory	Managers need to behave strategically when their own rewards depend on decisions made by competitors or partners.
Gantt Chart and PERT	Various forms of critical path analyses can assist in effectively scheduling, organizing, and coordinating activities in time-constrained projects.
Garbage Can Model of Decision Making	Decisions that might appear arbitrary and chaotic should be understood in the context of disconnected problems, solutions, opportunities, and decision makers.
Genderlect and Linguistic Styles	Understanding how communication patterns are shaped by gender-related characteristics, and how they influence performance, is important for managers when interacting with internal and external stakeholders.
GLOBE Model	In each society, leaders are expected to act in ways that are compatible with the society's cultural values.
Goal-Setting Theory	A powerful way to motivate employees is to give them specific, challenging goals.
Group Development	To be most effective, small groups must progress through a series of developmental stages each with their own tasks and challenges.
Group Polarization and the Risky Shift	Group interactions will often enhance, rather than moderate, the average preexisting tendency of individual members, yielding more extreme decisions and actions.
Group Punctuated Equilibrium Model	Timing is important when introducing changes to a team; habitual behavioral patterns are established in the first meeting, and groups are not susceptible to change until temporal milestones come up for review.
Groupthink	There are potential sources of dysfunctions in cohesive groups facing stressful decision situations as well as potential remedies for these dysfunctions.

High- and Low-Context Cultures	There are cross-cultural differences in the way people communicate meaning, which is a combination of information and inextricably bound up context.
High-Performance Work Systems	Human resource practices can be configured in a specific way to attain horizontal and vertical alignments and improve individual and organizational effectiveness.
High-Performing Teams	Applying a clinical approach to the study of teams allows us to develop a more in-depth understanding of potentially counterproductive interpersonal, intrapersonal, and organizational dynamics.
High-Reliability Organizations	A more mindful approach to managing structures, practices, and processes is advisable for an increasing number of organizations that must perform in complex, dynamic, and error-intolerant environments.
Human Capital Theory	People are as important as other types of resources; proper investments in human capital can result in improved performance at the individual, group, organization, and country levels.
Human Resource Management Strategies	Human resource management strategies will have greater positive impact when they elicit the workforce characteristics required to support the strategy of the organization.
Human Resources Roles Model	There are five roles that define expectations of what HR professionals should be, know, and do to deliver value: employee advocate, human capital developer, functional expert, strategic partners, and leader.
Humanistic Management	Managers need to treat workers and other stakeholders with dignity and sensitivity, attending to their psychological needs and "informal" social dynamics, to achieve ethical and sustainable success.
Hypercompetition	Competitive moves and responses can escalate to the point where traditional advantages, such as positioning and resource superiority, are no longer effective.
Image Theory	Professional managers create an image of what they want their organization's future to be, and decisions and subsequent actions are directed toward ensuring that the image becomes reality.
Individual Values	Individuals' value priorities relate to their attitudes, behaviors, and roles; by developing greater awareness of one's own and others' values, it is possible to influence people in desirable directions.
Influence Tactics	Organizational participants employ a finite and identifiable set of behaviors which are more successful at gaining compliance from others when appropriately matched to their circumstances.
Informal Communication and the Grapevine	Emergent, unofficial, and unsanctioned information flows, notably gossip, occur in predictable ways to serve different functions which have the potential to be managed.
Information Richness Theory	Information channels differ in information carrying capacity; effective managers select channels to fit the messages that they want to convey.
Innovation Diffusion	Forces within organizational or individual collectivities cause management ideas, practices, or techniques to be perceived as innovations and to spread more or less quickly, extensively, and effectively among collectivity members.
Innovation Speed	Managers should embrace time orientation and, when appropriate, align their innovation strategy, process, staff, and structure to prudently speed up.

Institutional Theory	The adoption and retention of many organizational practices is often more dependent on powerful social pressures for conformity and legitimacy than technical pressures for economic performance.
Institutional Theory of Multinational Corporations	Organizations' success in the management of cross-border operations is often determined by their ability to adapt to the institutional environments in which they operate.
Integrative Social Contracts Theory	Confronting ethical problems in business demands the integration of universally applicable norms with specific standards that are voluntarily accepted in economic communities.
Interactional Model of Cultural Diversity	The existence of cultural diversity presents specific challenges and opportunities which, depending on several climate factors, can produce either positive or negative effects on organizational performance and societal well-being.
Interactionist Model of Organizational Creativity	Managers can have the most positive impact on organizational creativity by designing the work setting in such a way as to enhance individual and team creative behavior.
Interorganizational Networks	Favorable structural positions within a group of organizations connected by common affiliations or exchange relations bring advantages, including greater social capital, over others of similar ability.
Intuitive Decision Making	Under the right conditions, intuition—or "trusting your gut"—can result in both fast and effective judgments.
Investment Theory of Creativity	Creativity is itself an investment activity in which personal and environmental resources are deployed to achieve novel, appropriate valued outputs.
Job Characteristics Theory	Employees' psychological states and work effectiveness can be enhanced by designing jobs high in five key characteristics and ensuring that employees with appropriate personal qualities are assigned to these jobs.
Job Demands–Resources Model	Job resources can buffer the impact of job demands on strain, stress, and burnout and may foster employee engagement and performance.
Kaizen and Continuous Improvement	Organizations should engage in a continuous, meticulous drive for excellence across the enterprise to achieve lowest cost, highest quality, and best service to the customer.
Knowledge Workers	Knowledge workers play a central role in modern, technology-driven organizations; these highly trained, specialized, and connected employees must be managed appropriately.
Knowledge-Based View of the Firm	Firm-wide tacit capabilities form a firm's core; cultivation and refinement of these capabilities determine current and future firm vitality.
Large Group Interventions	Changing complex systems is more effective when system stakeholders, internal and external, are engaged in all aspects of the change process.
Lead Users	It pays to carefully identify, through a defined methodology, those cutting-edge users who really can foster a firm's ideation and new product development efforts.
Leader–Member Exchange Theory	A leader develops different exchange relationships with his or her subordinates which vary in quality and impact important outcomes.

Leadership Continuum Theory	The range of managerial choices during decision-making efforts can be conceptualized along a continuum, from autocratic to democratic approaches, and are more or less appropriate under different conditions.
Leadership Practices	Leadership is a set of identifiable skills and abilities that are available to anyone; leadership is not about who you are; it's about what you do.
Lean Enterprise	The application of seven core "lean" principles to complex enterprises requires a focus on the enterprise value proposition across all key stakeholders.
Learning Organization	Learning involves more than transferring information; it is embedded in ongoing social interactions and cyclical, multilevel practices and routines by which organizations notice, interpret, and manage their experience.
Level 5 Leadership	The pinnacle of executive leadership styles is that of a "Level 5" leader who embodies personal humility and strong and willful persistence in pursuing common goals and objectives.
Locus of Control	Managers can use their understanding of an individual's source of perceived power to effect an outcome to influence the individual's behavior, especially toward empowerment and planned change.
Logical Incrementalism	Strategic decisions are rarely brought about deliberately; they often emerge from an iterative yet logical process of proactively developing a course of action and reactively adapting to unfolding circumstances.
Management (Education) as Practice	Learning how to manage is best done by reflecting on current experience, informed by concepts, and usually in conversation with other managers.
Management by Objectives	All employees, in all levels of an organization, should know explicitly what they need to do to accelerate the implementation of their organization's strategic plan.
Management Control Systems	Organizational structure, procedures, practices, and norms—that is, controls—are integral to organizational functioning, effectiveness, and goal achievement.
Management Roles	How managers behave at work is influenced by predictable, multidimensional roles related to the context, content, and forms of managerial jobs that specify rights, duties, expectations, and norms.
Management Symbolism and Symbolic Action	Focusing on symbolic action reveals the importance of meaning making within processes of organizing and the related understanding of management as cocreating meaning.
Managerial Decision Biases	Systematic and predictable biases can lead to irrational decisions that are oftentimes outside of the individual's own awareness.
Managerial Grid	There are two primary dimensions or orientations in leaders' behavior—concern for production and concern for people—and this resultant leadership style impacts organizational effectiveness.
Managerialism	Managers wield great power and control over firms to the potential detriment of both narrow shareholder and broader societal interests.
Managing Diversity	Effective management of a demographically diverse workforce requires an integrated strategic approach incorporating recruitment, development, and retention initiatives.

Matrix Structure	Complex organizational structures can be designed to achieve goals of both specialization and scale economies along with coordination and product focus.
Meaning and Functions of Organizational Culture	People's behavior in organizations is guided by relatively shared meaning structures that influence how they make and give sense of themselves, their organization, and their workplace reality.
Modes of Strategy: Planned and Emergent	Strategic execution contains uncertainty that necessitates the balanced use of both proactive, explicitly planned strategy and flexible, reactive emergent strategies.
Moral Reasoning Maturity	Individual cognitive dynamics determine how people—including managers—understand, and make judgments and decisions in, ethical problems and issues involving moral dilemmas.
Multicultural Work Teams	Potential coordination difficulties between team members separated by culture, distance, and time zones need to be addressed and actively managed for optimal multicultural work team performance.
Multifirm Network Structure	A great deal of activity in the global economy is performed by groups of firms working together in well-defined network structures.
Multilevel Research	Organizational outcomes are the result of a confluence of effects emanating from different levels of analysis; managers must consider factors at multiple levels to improve understanding and influence.
Narrative (Story) Theory	Linear narratives are in interplay with other forms of storytelling, such as living stories and antenarratives, as one of the preferred sensemaking currencies of management and organizations.
Needs Hierarchy	Humans are motivated by unmet needs; these needs vary along a universal, prepotent hierarchy according to different stages in their lives and careers.
Neo-Institutional Theory	Managers need to be conscious of social pressures to follow other organizations in adopting new structural arrangements and assess their conditions and impact before making their own decisions.
Norms Theory	An individual's attitudes and behaviors are fundamentally shaped and guided by the attitudes and behaviors of other actors in that individual's social world.
Occupational Types, Model of	Analyzing fit between attributes of individuals and attributes of jobs and careers provides a system to parse a complex entity into categorized, manageable attributes to improve occupational congruence.
Open Innovation	Companies must open their innovation process to inflows and outflows of knowledge in order to leverage their research and development (R & D) competencies and speed up their product, process, and technology development.
Organic and Mechanistic Forms	Mechanistic management systems, which facilitate decision making bureaucratically, are better suited for stable environments whereas organic management systems, applying more decentralized and fluid practices, are more appropriate for dynamic environments.
Organizational and Managerial Wisdom	A wisdom-based management paradigm goes beyond traditional information- and knowledge-based perspectives by applying philosophic insights across organizational levels to facilitate personal and professional success and enable it for others.

Organizational Assimilation Theory	The processes by which newcomers become integrated into an organization is neither simple nor guaranteed and therefore should be properly facilitated to better anticipate and facilitate successful assimilation.
Organizational Commitment Theory	Employees with greater organizational commitment (i.e., attachment to the work organization) are more effective, more motivated, and more likely to remain with the organization.
Organizational Culture and Effectiveness	The cultural systems that evolve over time within organizations have important consequences for an organization's survival and effectiveness.
Organizational Culture Model	Organizational culture is a powerful, yet largely invisible, multilayered (deep assumptions, intermediate values and principles, visible artifacts) social force that is not easily understood or changed.
Organizational Culture Theory	To understand how and why organizations function and the nature of employees' work experiences, researchers have to go beyond structure, size, technology, job descriptions, reporting relationships, and so on to also study culture.
Organizational Demography	Demographic composition—for example, the gender, tenure, and functional backgrounds—of organizational units matter for understanding organizational dynamics.
Organizational Development	Organizational change can occur successfully provided it is planned, supported by organizational leaders, and involves organizational members and intensive effort to sustain the transition.
Organizational Ecology	Organizational dynamics can be fully understood only when all like organizations in a market are examined over time; evolving interdependence among organizations shapes and is shaped by social structure.
Organizational Effectiveness	There is no one single theory of effectiveness; rather, there are multiple models, each of which has a legitimate claim to being the key approach for defining and determining the effectiveness of an organization.
Organizational Identification	The sense of "us-ness" associated with self-definition in terms of shared organizational or subunit identity provides a strong and distinct basis for key forms of organizational behavior.
Organizational Identity	A shared understanding of "who we are" as an organization—what is central, enduring, and distinctive—is essential for effective organizational self-management, over time and across situations.
Organizational Learning	Managers need to recognize the many complications brought by the experiential nature of organizational learning and their implications for risk taking, feedback, interpersonal networks, and learning curves.
Organizational Socialization	Socialization processes that are strategically aligned and properly executed to integrate new members and influence existing members can benefit both employee well-being and organizational effectiveness.
Organizational Structure and Design	To attain its goals, an organization has to have an organizational structure to provide coordination and control; core structural dimensions must be designed to fit multiple contingency factors.
Organizationally Based Self-Esteem	An individual's self-esteem can be shaped by the work setting, affecting the individual's view of how capable and valuable he or she is as a member of the organization.

Participative Model of Decision Making	The degree of participation in decision making can be determined by applying multidimensional criteria that, when assessed, result in different approaches for soliciting and using employees' input.
Path-Goal Theory of Leadership	Situational factors determine the choice of optimal leader behaviors designed to help remove obstacles and motivate employees as they strive to achieve work-related goals.
Patterns of Innovation	Firms shift from product to process innovation as their industries evolve and their productive processes become increasingly specialized.
Patterns of Political Behavior	Recognizing the patterns of political behavior in organizations, frequently undervalued by management theories, helps managers understand and influence a wide range of organizational phenomena.
Personal Engagement (at Work) Model	Workers invest degrees of themselves into role performances based on the extent to which certain psychological conditions are met.
Positive Organizational Scholarship	Human, organizational, and societal well-being is facilitated by focusing on the generative organizational dynamics that lead to developing human strength, producing resilience and restoration, fostering vitality, and cultivating extraordinary individuals.
Practice of Management, The	The practice of management is a polycentric configuration of related elements that should be viewed as a whole so that it can be taught, learned, institutionalized, and executed systematically.
Principled Negotiation	Parties in a negotiation can follow a specified integrative process manifest in five major components—such as focusing on interests, not positions—to achieve an agreement that maximizes joint gain.
Principles of Administration and Management Functions	Management consists of the same fundamental functions and activities—planning, organizing, commanding, coordinating, controlling—in all kinds of organizations irrespective of their production or formal affiliation.
Process Consultation	Building a collaborative relationship between consultant and client helps the client perceive, understand, and act on process events to think out and work through problems.
Process Theories of Change	Managers need to understand how and why organizational change unfolds over time and the different motors or mechanisms that drive the process.
Product Champions	The product champion role of identifying with an innovation and pushing it through despite personal risks is important to mediate the political process of change in complex organizations.
Product-Market Differentiation Model	Managers need to relate a firm's product-market engagements with its general strategic direction; growth strategies include expanding or developing markets and diversifying or developing new products.
Profiting From Innovation	An innovator must develop a commercialization strategy that avoids the sharing of undue value with the owners of key complementary assets.
Programmability of Decision Making	Some decision situations faced by managers can be programmed (routinized and modeled) whereas others involve some fundamental uncertainties and are not amenable to processing by computer systems.
Prospect Theory	People evaluate the potential outcomes of risky choices as changes from their current situation and take more risk when facing potential losses than when facing potential gains.

Protean and Boundaryless Careers	The changing workplace and nature of work necessitates new ways for individuals to manage their careers and new ways for organizations to offer career management options.
Psychological Contract Theory	Understanding of employees' beliefs about their exchange relationship with the employer is important in fostering positive employee attitudes and behaviors.
Psychological Type and Problem-Solving Styles	People with different personality preferences may have complementary strengths (and weaknesses) that lead to distinctive, potentially valuable approaches to problem solving.
Punctuated Equilibrium Model	The process of organizational change is marked by long periods of incremental or evolutionary change "punctuated" by sudden bursts of radical or revolutionary change; each needs to be managed differently.
Quality Circles	Voluntary improvement activities in groups are powerful tools for quality management in an integrated system oriented toward the development of the enterprise.
Quality Trilogy	Managers need to plan for quality, control performance variations, and enhance systems' capability to excel on all dimensions of quality all the time.
Quantum Change	Large-scale change should be carried out rapidly across an organization's structures, systems, and values when initiating or responding to a transformative event.
Reinforcement Theory	Employee behavior is a function of both antecedents (e.g., training, job redesign) and contingent consequences (e.g., rewards, punishment); behavior increases in strength and/or probability when positively reinforced.
Resource Dependence Theory	To understand organizational choices and actions, consider its environment and particularly the constraints emanating from transaction partners.
Resource Orchestration Management	Managerial actions of structuring, bundling, and leveraging resources, along with the synchronization of these actions, affect competitive advantage.
Resource-Based View of Firm	Managers can attain competitive advantages by exploiting the unique resources and capabilities to which their firms have access.
Role Theory	Roles, created at the intersection of social structure and individual behavior, enable consistent performances across individuals and situations.
Schemas Theory	Individuals interpret, evaluate, and apply information and knowledge by organizing them into cognitive structures which can be managed to facilitate understanding and shape behavior.
Scientific Management	Conflicts between managers and/or employers and employees need to be economically resolved through proper incentives and precisely designed job structures, content, processes, and targets.
Self-Concept and the Theory of Self	Construals and understandings of self play important functions in individual and organizational behavior.
Self-Determination Theory	Two different motivation types—autonomous and controlled—have very different consequences and are prompted by different managerial behaviors.
Self-Fulfilling Prophecy	Managers get the employees they expect; managers can boost effectiveness by expecting more of their subordinates.
Sensemaking	Developing retrospective images and words that rationalize what people are doing makes meaningful the social action taking place in an organization and illuminates how organizations work, change, and grow.

Servant Leadership	Leaders must make their top priority that of providing followers with the tools and support they need to develop mutual trust and reach their full potential.
Seven-S Framework	Conceptualizing organizations' main elements in terms of interdependent, mutually reinforcing soft- and hard factors provides a powerful tool for diagnosing and analyzing organizational performance.
Situational Theory of Leadership	Managers can best lead and develop subordinates by using specified leadership styles to match a subordinate's level of ability and commitment.
Six Sigma	Through a specified process of variation and defect reduction, organizations can simultaneously improve the quality of process outputs, increase customer satisfaction, and reduce waste, time, and costs.
Social Cognitive Theory	Human agency operates in concert with social and structural factors in determining organizational well-being and productivity.
Social Construction Theory	Social interaction influences the creating and institutionalizing of taken-for-granted knowledge, practices, and structures that can both enable and constrain activities.
Social Entrepreneurship	Entrepreneurship principles are applicable to multiple forms of (social) value creation which are not necessarily independent of or contrary to but instead can complement economic value creation.
Social Exchange Theory	Social systems can be understood as sets of interdependent economic and noneconomic transactions and relationships; managers can facilitate positive, cooperative exchange relations to produce benefits and limit costs.
Social Facilitation Management	The social context created by managers and coworkers can augment or reduce employee performance.
Social Identity Theory	Individuals' identities are influenced by their perceived social group memberships; classifications and comparative perspectives of in- and out-groups generate meaning and shape members' self-concept, attitudes, values, and behavior.
Social Impact Theory and Social Loafing	The magnitude of social impact is based on the strength, immediacy, and number of sources of social influence; managers need to particularly understand and reduce factors for social "loafing."
Social Information Processing Model	People's attitudes and behavior at work are affected both by what others do and say as well as by the need to rationalize their own past behavior.
Social Movements	Challenger groups are often sources of innovation in organizations, influencing managers to overcome the status quo and developing the energy and resources needed for transformative change.
Social Network Theory	Organizations generally exist for the purpose of establishing interaction and exchange with other entities, and they do so by bounding and coordinating the interactions of multiple individuals to achieve ends not achievable separately.
Social Power, Bases of	Managers must appropriately acquire and use bases of power—referent, expert, legitimate, reward, and coercive—if they are to exercise effective leadership.
Sociotechnical Theory	People and technology interact in complex ways such that their implications must be considered together to optimize performance.

Stages of Creativity	Creativity results from a process, each stage of which can be facilitated or frustrated by managers.
Stages of Innovation	The process of developing and implementing new ideas cannot be controlled, but managers can learn to maneuver the process.
Stakeholder Theory	Effectively managing relationships with internal and external parties who impact and are impacted by an organization is a primary responsibility of managers and is central to value creation.
Stewardship Theory	By pursuing cooperative, pro-organizational outcomes, stewards maximize their own utility as well as the performance of the organization.
Strategic Alliances	Strategic alliances can facilitate effective cooperation between firms by combining needed resources to achieve mutually compatible objectives.
Strategic Contingencies Theory	Intraorganizational power is derived from a subunit's ability to support the critical tasks of other subunits in a way that no others can.
Strategic Decision Making	Managers can improve the chances of making successful strategic decisions by choosing the right decision-making processes across various levels of the organization.
Strategic Entrepreneurship	Strategy and entrepreneurship go together—successful entrepreneurship requires attention to strategy, and strategy is inherently entrepreneurial; opportunity-seeking and advantage-seeking are processes that should be considered jointly.
Strategic Flexibility	In a rapidly changing business environment, an organization's capability for attention, assessment, and action in balancing commitment and timely change contributes to sustainable, positive performance.
Strategic Frames	Strategic frames—distinct cognitive constructs anchored in social schema and sensemaking—organize collective interpretations and support prospective guides to action.
Strategic Groups	By identifying the emergence and persistence of competitive structure within an industry, members of a strategic group can formulate their own strategies to remain competitive.
Strategic Information Systems	The strategic application of information systems to align investments and support an organization's business model can provide a source of competitive differentiation.
Strategic International Human Resources Management	An integrative framework of five major factors explains how human resource management issues affect the success of a firm that is operating in an international environment.
Strategic Profiles	An accurate, comprehensive profile of a firm's configuration, competitive strategy, and its industrial environment is useful in making strategic decisions.
Strategies for Change	Gaining organizational alignment with an external environment where change seems the only constant requires managers and leaders to implement systematic strategies for change.
Strategy and Structure	The relationship between strategy and structure is a reciprocal one where each should fit and complement one another optimally.
Strategy-as-Practice	Strategy is a kind of work; it is something that people do, rather than something that organizations have.

Structuration Theory	While structural properties of societies are real, they depend upon regularities of social reproduction; structure exists only in and through the activities of human agents.
Substitutes for Leadership	There are multiple contextual factors that enhance, neutralize, or substitute for relationship-oriented versus task-oriented leadership across three categories: subordinate, task, and organizational characteristics.
SWOT Analysis Framework	Assessing internal and external strategic issues enables managers to understand how current and future strengths can be leveraged to realize opportunities and how weaknesses can slow progress or magnify organizational threats.
Systems Theory of Organizations	Interventions to one part of an organizational system can affect other interrelated, interacting parts in intended as well as unintended ways, possibly undoing or otherwise altering the original interventions.
Tacit Knowledge	All knowledge used (in organizations) has a tacit dimension that carries implications for creating, storing, transferring, coordinating, and applying knowledge.
Technological Discontinuities	Nonparadigmatic changes in value creation and capturing pose fundamental challenges to incumbent organizations and can radically reshape industry structures.
Technology Acceptance Model	The use of a technology is significantly and primarily influenced by the user perceptions of its ease-of-use and usefulness.
Technology Affordances and Constraints Theory (of MIS)	The uses and outcomes of information systems are best understood in terms of dynamic relationships between the individual or organizational users and the technology features.
Technology and Complexity	Effective organizational responses to complex challenges are achieved through dynamic and holistic technologies cocreated by designers, implementers and users, which in turn influence organizational structure and social processes.
Technology and Interdependence/Uncertainty	Managers need to protect an organization's technical core from environmental uncertainty and optimize coordination by matching its structure to technological and inter-unit interdependencies.
Technology and Programmability	The nature of technology used by a firm—the degree to which the production system is controllable and predictable—has important ramifications for how it should be structured.
Technology S-Curve	The management of, and transition from, a technology is influenced by multiple actors over time that affect technology performance through slow initial improvement, rapid increase, and eventual maturity.
Theory Development	Strong theories offer better causal explanations of important outcomes; for the majority of management theorizing, the objective is to answer, within specified contextual conditions, What causes what and why?
Theory of Constraints	Managers can structure their thinking about how to improve system performance by examining its component processes and sequentially addressing the most significant constraints.
Theory of Cooperation and Competition	Management involves creating and facilitating cooperation among the organization's members while minimizing competitive and individualistic efforts.

Theory of Emotions	Emotion is a diverse multistage process, not a unitary experience, with each stage having important implications for organizational life.
Theory of Organizational Attractiveness	An individual's perception of and desire to work for an organization is influenced by organizational, individual, and job or task characteristics; organizations can manage these to increase their attractiveness to potential applicants.
Theory of Reasoned Action	Behavioral intentions, influenced by subjective norms and attitude toward the act, are the most proximal and reliable predictors of whether a person will engage in a specific volitional act.
Theory of Self-Esteem	Self-esteem is a complex construct that is potentially developable and may be related to a number of important work-relevant variables.
Theory of the Interesting	It is more important for a theory to be interesting than true; challenging some assumptions can help achieve this.
Theory of Transfer of Training	To achieve transfer of training, designers and trainees must actively pursue those training elements and activities known to foster generalization, maintenance, and adaptation of learned skills and knowledge.
Theory X and Theory Y	Manager's assumptions about human behavior, whether pessimistic (theory x) or optimistic (theory y), tend to result in corresponding patterns of behaviors; managers should assist employees in reaching their full potential.
Total Quality Management	Organizations can apply the philosophy and specified principles of total quality management to reduce costs, improve reliability, and enhance customers' and other stakeholders' satisfaction.
Trait Theory of Leadership	Leadership emergence and effectiveness is a function of the exceptional qualities, abilities, or traits—such as personality and intelligence—which one possesses.
Transaction Cost Theory	Firms organize their relationships with customers, suppliers, employees, and partners to economize on the costs of transacting business; these relate to search, communication, bargaining and contracting, and enforcing activities.
Transfer of Technology	Effective transfer of technical, organizational, and operational knowledge between providers and recipients is a function of the engaged entities' characteristics, their interactions and context, and technology and transfer mechanisms.
Transformational Theory of Leadership	Inspiring employees is a better way to achieve your goals than motivating them with rewards and punishments; this power comes from idealized influence, inspirational motivation, intellectual stimulation, and individualized consideration.
Transnational Management	Managers must recognize the increased complexity and conflicting demands of the global environment to simultaneously cultivate multinational flexibility, global scale efficiency, and worldwide learning capability.
Triple Bottom Line	Value creation is multidimensional—comprising "people, planet, and profit" considerations—with money alone being a poor measure of both positive and negative externalities.
Trust	Trust can be defined and measured, has several key antecedents that apply to multiple organizational levels, and can be managed based on attention to several factors.

Two-Factor Theory (and Job Enrichment)	There are two clusters of variables that influence humans' motivation to work; the first motivates, the second can potentially demotivate.
Type A Personality Theory	Managers who manifest unmitigated "Type-A" behavior of high-achievement workaholics, especially anger and hostility, can have a negative long-term impact on themselves as well as their subordinates, groups, and organizations.
Typology of Organizational Culture	Organizational success depends on creating an environment that shapes the norms and behavior of participants in ways that will serve the organization well as circumstances and competition change.
"Unstructured" Decision Making	Processes and models for decision making can be developed for unfamiliar or unprecedented conditions in which accepted decision-making methods and solutions are unsuitable.
Upper-Echelons Theory	Organizations are reflections of their most senior level managers; top management team characteristics and actions explain strategic and performance consequences of the organization as a whole.
Value Chain	A firm's primary and support activities, from purchasing raw materials to distributing products, must be systematically analyzed, organized, selected, and optimized for customer value creation and competitive advantage.
Virtual Teams	Virtual teams, whose members are separated by distance and time and who use technology to communicate, face unique challenges and should not be managed just like proximate teams.
Work Team Effectiveness	Teams are multifaceted, complex, and dynamic entities that create unique management challenges but offer the potential for superlative performance.

Index

Entry titles and their page numbers are in **bold**. Page numbers preceded by 1: are in volume 1, and page numbers preceded by 2: are in volume 2.